JOSHUA COFFIN.

A
Sketch of the History
of
Newbury, Newburyport and West Newbury

by
Joshua Coffin

Published by

Peter E. Randall, Publisher

for the

Sons and Daughters of the First Settlers

of Newbury, Massachusetts, Inc.

ANNE COLMAN MOODY, Founder

This facsimile reprint of Joshua Coffin's *A Sketch of the History of Newbury, Newburyport, and West Newbury* is reproduced from the original 1845 edition. To it has been added photographs of Coffin and his home, a new introduction, and a new index. The first edition of the reprint was published in 1977, the 50th anniversary of the founding of the Sons and Daughters of the First Settlers of Newbury, Massachusetts, Inc. A second reprint edition was published in 1980.

August 2001

Additional copies available from
Sons and Daughters of the First Settlers of Newbury,
Massachusetts, Inc.
P.O. Box 444, Newburyport, MA 01950

Produced by
Peter E. Randall Publisher
Box 4726
Portsmouth, NH 03802

Library of Congress Cataloging in Publication Data

Coffin., Joshua, 1792-1864.
    A sketch of the history of Newbury, Newburyport, and West Newbury.

    Reprint of the 1845 ed. published by S. G. Drake, Boston, under title: A sketch of the history of Newbury, Newburyport, and West Newbury, from 1635 to 1845.
    Narrative of the captivity of Joseph Bartlett among the Indians: p.
    Includes index.
    1. Newbury, Mass.--History. 2. Newburyport, Mass.-History. 3. West Newbury, Mass.--History.

I. Bartlett, Joseph, 1686-1754. II. Title.
F74.N53C63 1977   977.44'5   77-22368

Introduction to the Reprint Edition

The reprinting of Joshua Coffin's *History of Newbury, Newbury-port, and West Newbury* is a fulfillment of John Greenleaf Whittier's prophecy when, after calling it "the best and most complete Town History which has yet been given to the public" he said that Coffin's work would be "better appreciated hereafter:"

Joshua Coffin (1792-1864) was born in the Coffin House in Newbury. At the age of seventeen he was qualified to teach a district school. He entered Dartmouth College but was forced to leave when his sight was affected by a cataract. After his recovery he did not return to Dartmouth but because of his scholarly attainments was given the degree of Bachelor of Arts with the class of 1817.

For over a quarter of a century he taught in various schools including Bradford Academy and Hampton Academy and public and private schools in Newbury, Haverhill, and Ipswich and in Vermont and Philadelphia. Among his pupils were Cornelius Conway Felton, Professor of Greek and President of Harvard, who said of him, "I have never forgotten his kind and genial manners and his unwearied labors in helping his classes forward in their studies," and John Greenleaf Whittier, who described him in "To My Old Schoolmaster" as

> Luring us by stories old,
> With a comic unction told,
> More than by the eloquence
> Of terse birchen arguments
> (Doubtful gain, I fear) to look
> With conplacence on a book!

In Philadelphia he was employed in the Post Office until he lost his position because of his Anti-Slavery activities. He was one of the founders of the New England Anti-Slavery Society, and for a time in Philadelphia taught a school for black children. He was especially helpful in Anti-Slavery activities in Philadelphia by keeping potentially hostile crowds in good humor. In 1838 he was sent to the South on a dangerous mission to rescue two black men who had been kidnapped and illegally sold into slavery.

Coffin returned to Newbury about 1843 and began work on his History. He corresponded with other historians and antiquarians, generously helping them in their work. He was thorough and accurate, as anyone will testify who has compared his History with the original records, and he made a careful distinction between fact and tradition. Neither his History nor his other antiquarian writings brought him adequate remuneration, and fear of poverty contributed to the depression and mental illness of his later years.

The reprinted History will fill a real need. More people than ever before are interested in local history, and the remaining copies of the original edition are too worn and fragile for extensive use.

Roland H. Woodwell

Tristram Coffin house, Newbury. The oldest portion of the house is at left, c. 1652. The section at right was built in 1751. The house was the home of the author and remained in the same family from the day it was built until this century. It is now owned by the Society for the Preservation of New England Antiquities. Photograph by Lewis Rubinstein, courtesy Historical Society of Old Newbury.

DR. JOHN CLARKE,
Physician in Newbury, Mass. from 1637 to 1651.
Died in Boston 1664 Aged 66.

Lith.ᵈ from a picture in the Mass. Historical Society, by E. W. Bouvé
for Coffin's History of Newbury.

A SKETCH

OF

THE HISTORY

OF

NEWBURY, NEWBURYPORT, AND WEST NEWBURY,

FROM 1635 TO 1845.

By JOSHUA COFFIN, A. B. S. H. S.

'For out of the old fieldes, as men saithe,
Cometh the new corne from yere to yere,
And out of old bookes in good faithe
Cometh this new science that men lere.'

Chaucer.

'Lives there a man with soul so dead,
Who never to himself hath said,
This is my own, my native land?'

Scott.

BOSTON:

PUBLISHED BY SAMUEL G. DRAKE,

No. 56 CORNHILL.

PRINTED BY GEORGE COOLIDGE, NO. 57 WASHINGTON STREET.

1845.

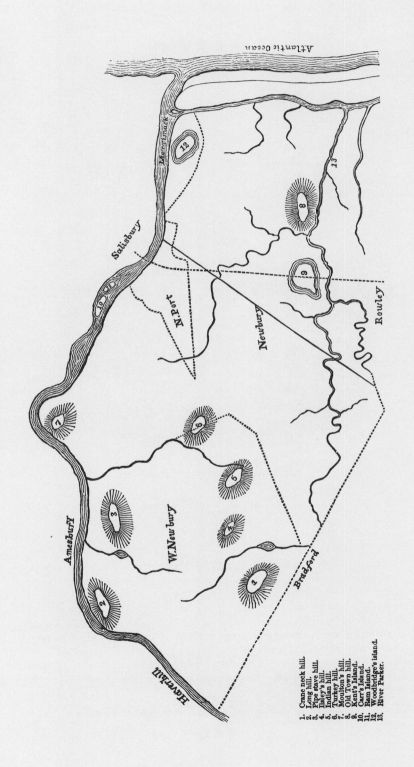

1. Crane neck hill.
2. Long hill.
3. Pipe stave hill.
4. Daley's hill.
5. Indian hill.
6. Turkey hill.
7. Moulton's hill.
8. Old Town hill.
9. Kent's Island.
10. Carr's Island.
11. Ram Island.
12. Woodbridge's Island.
13. River Parker.

OLD-TOWN MEETING-HOUSE, 1700–1806.

PREFACE.

THOSE who are familiar with ancient mythology, will recollect the story of the 'good Isis who went forth wandering and weeping to gather up the parts and fragments of her murdered and scattered Osiris, fondly yet vainly hoping that she might recover and recombine all the separate parts, and once more view her husband in all his former proportions and beauty.'* With equal assiduity, but with far less lamentation, has the compiler of the following pages been for many years engaged at intervals, in collecting the scattered fragments of ' Ould Newberry,' and has arranged his imperfect materials in the form which they now exhibit to the reader. No one can be more sensible than himself, of its deficiences, its want of symmetry and proportion, which the reader may, if he chooses, attribute as much to the want of skill in the artist, as to the lack of

* Quarterly Register.

the requisite materials. Throughout the whole of this compilation he has endeavored to make a broad distinction between fact and tradition, and to relate nothing as fact, which he does not believe to be true. Strype in his annals says, ' I have chosen to set down things in the very words of the records and originals, and of the authors themselves, (rather than in my own, without framing and dressing them in more modern language,) whereby the sense is sure to remain entire as the writers meant it, whereas by affecting too curiously to change and model words and sentences, I have observed the sense itself to be often marred and disguised.' This is the course that the compiler has taken. He has endeavored to give as accurate a representation as possible, of the character of the inhabitants of Newbury and their transactions, for over two hundred years, and has been desirous, in the language of Tacitus, 'sine ira, sine studio,' without fear, favor, or affection, neither 'to extenuate, nor aught set down in malice.' He is well aware that his statements in many places do not agree either with the tradition, or the belief, of many of the inhabitants of the town, or with history. Where he has been obliged to differ from common opinion, he has done so for reasons, which to him appeared entirely satisfactory, and has been pleased to find that the instances have been very few where fact and tradition do not substantially agree. It is however much to be lamented, that so small a number of the first settlers were in the habit of recording the transactions of the day, and that the journals or diaries of those who made a record, should have been in so many instances lost or destroyed. Mr. Anthony Somerby, the first school-master of Newbury, the ancestor of all of that name in this country, and one of our best and most useful citizens, kept a diary of passing events, as I have been informed by those who have seen it, but of which no trace can now be found. An aged lady, one of his descendants, informed me that he versified the whole book of Job. Numerous instances might be given where valuable papers in large quantities, have been destroyed, because they were 'so old that nobody could read them.' ' All are not such,' and among the many persons, who have in various ways rendered valuable assistance in the compilation of this work, the author cannot forbear mentioning the names of Messrs. Robert Adams, reverend William S. Bartlet, Daniel Dole, Moses Davenport, George Danforth, doctor Ebenezer Hale, doctor E. G. Kelley, Tristram Little, Josiah Little, Moses Pettingill, esquire, Horatio G. Somerby, of Boston, and Charles Toppan, of Philadelphia, to whom he tenders his warmest acknowledgments for the interest they have manifested in the work, and the aid they have afforded toward its completion, and to all others not mentioned by name, who have rendered any assistance. If, as is undoubtedly the case, he has made any mistakes, or omitted any necessary or valuable information, he will be greatly obliged to any person or persons, who will correct those mistakes, or supply those omissions, as it is his intention still to continue to collect information, in order that some future historian may be able to supply his deficiences, and at some future day may prepare a work, which will do justice to the reputation of 'Ould Newberry.' The sources whence the compiler of the present history has derived his materials, are almost innumerable, and to specify them all, would require a small volume. The principal are the colonial, province, state, county, town, church, and parish records. The town records have been well kept, and with the exception of a few missing leaves of the first book, are full and accurate. The records of the first church commence in 1674, the preceding transactions of the church, having been to all appearance intentionally destroyed; a loss very much to be regretted, but which has in part been supplied by copious quotations from the county records. Some persons may suppose, that too many pages are occupied with the ecclesiastical affairs of the town. It should be remembered that in no other way could the peculiar traits in the character of our ancestors be fully developed. It was the religious doctrines that they had embraced, and the consequent principles of religious and civil liberty, which they could not enjoy in their own land, that induced such a company of gentlemen, merchants, and mechanics, to emigrate from the populous and cultivated towns of their father land, to this then wilderness, and exchange, as many of them did, the sword, the awl, the needle, and the yard-stick, for the hoe, the axe, the anvil, and the plough; and to omit a sufficient allusion to their religious principles and their actual development in practice, would be to narrate effects, and not notice the causes which produced them. No one can justly appreciate the character of our forefathers, and the sacrifices they made for their posterity, without a knowledge of those principles, which, like a main-spring, set every thing in motion. But enough has been said on this subject. Our attention for a few pages will be given to affairs more secular.

The town of Newbury was originally one of the largest towns in the county. It was about thirteen miles long, and about six miles broad in the widest place, and contained about thirty thousand acres, of which nearly two thousand are covered with water.

In 1764, it was divided into two towns, Newbury and Newburyport. In 1771, a province valuation was taken, and in 1781, a valuation was taken by the state, in which Newbury and Newburyport stood thus.

Newbury.	Newburyport.	
750	875	Polls ratable.
10	7	" supported by the town.
75	51	" not supported by the town.
437	430	Dwelling houses.
36	60	Shops separate or adjoining other buildings.
26	38	Tan houses, slaughter houses, &c.
393	210	Barns.
14	45	All other buildings of £5 value and upward.
1450	113 1-2	Acres of tillage land.
2380	86 3-4	" of English and upland mowing.
10,802	113 1-2	" of pasturage.
192	7176	Tons of vessels, of 5 tons burthen and upward.
592	£ 74,131	Stock in trade.
341	146	Horses and mares, 3 years old and upward.
562	30	Oxen, 4 years old and upward.
1468	1741	Cows, 4 years old and upward.
645	160	Swine, 6 months old and upward.
318	5149	Ounces of silver plate.
£ 57,726	£ 24,668	Debts due to any persons.
———	£ 2825	Monies on hand.

Newburyport also in 1781, had ten distil and sugar houses, three rope walks, thirty-nine ware-houses, and eighty-seven thousand nine hundred superficial feet of wharf. Newbury also had in 1781, sixteen grist, saw, fulling, and slitting mills, one thousand one hundred and six acres of fresh meadow, three thousand one hundred and sixty-seven acres of salt marsh, made one thousand four hundred and thirteen barrels of cider, had eight hundred and fifty-two acres of wood land, three hundred and three acres of unimproved land, and thirty-five acres of land unimprovable, had ten colts, two years old, fourteen colts one year old, three hundred and one neat cattle three years old, three hundred and ninety, two years old, three hundred and fifty-five, one year old, and two thousand three hundred and seventy-six sheep and goats. In 1819, West Newbury was set off and incorporated as a separate town. The state valuation for 1840, is as follows :

Newbury.	Newburyport.	West Newbury.	
859	1249	404	Ratable Polls 16 years old and upward.
182	304	32	Male polls not taxed nor supported by the town.
18	56	4	" " " supported by the town.
401	832	301 1-2	Dwelling houses.
6	1	—	Rope walks.
3	—	1	Grist mills.
9	53	4	Shops within, or adjoining to dwelling houses.
74	103	79	other shops.
4	—	1	Tan houses.
—	238	4	Ware houses and stores.
6	1	—	Rope walks.
—	4	—	Cotton factories, 11,046 spindles, and 280 looms in the same.
2	1	—	Woolen factories.
240	800	—	Spindles.
376	318	219 5-12	Barns.
80 1-8	161	141	All other buildings and edifices of the value of $20 and upward.
—	453,812	—	Superficial feet of wharf.
2,397 1-2	13,456	—	Tons of vessels and small craft of 5 tons burthen and upward.
2,011 1-2	41	2496 1-2	Acres of English and upland mowing.
346	—	1084 1-2	Acres of fresh meadow.
6,947 3-4	88 1-2	4,084 1-2	Acres of pasturage.
888 1-4	—	279	Acres of woodland.
201 1-2	—	190	Acres of unimproved land.

The three towns also raised in 1840, eight hundred and eleven bushels of wheat, one thousand two hundred and forty bushels of rye, six thousand and seventy-three bushels of oats, fifteen thousand six hundred and thirty-five bushels of Indian corn, and three thousand one hundred and sixty-six bushels of barley. There were also in Newbury, three thousand eight hundred and twenty-five and one half acres of salt marsh, and two thousand eight hundred and sixty-five and one half tons of salt hay cut on the same. Newbury also had two carding machines, two fulling mills, and one and a half saw mills.

Since the first settlement of the town, that part of it now called Newburyport, has witnessed great changes, not only in its business, but in its external appearance. In the printed programme of the procession, which honored general Washington with an escort in 1789, a conspicuous place was assigned to the 'distillers,' who were then a numerous body of men. At that time there were ten or twelve distilleries in the town, and six rope walks. Now there are but one of each, and manufacturing, a new and rapidly increasing business, is taking the place of the West India trade, by which it once rose to great wealth.

In 1796, doctor Dwight thus writes :

' Newburyport is probably the smallest township in the state, including only six hundred and forty acres. It lies on the southern shore of the Merrimac. The town is built on a declivity of unrivalled beauty. The slope is easy and elegant ; the soil rich, the streets, except one near the water, clean and sweet ; and the verdure, wherever it is visible, exquisite. The streets are either parallel, or right angled, to the river ; the southern shore of which bends, here, towards the south east. None of them are regularly formed. Still there is so near an approximation to regularity as to awaken in the mind of a traveler, with peculiar strength a wish that the regularity had been perfect. For myself I was not a little mortified to see so fair an opportunity of compassing this beauty on so exquisite a spot finally lost. As it is, however, there are few towns of equal beauty in this country. . . . The houses taken collectively, make a better appearance than those of any other town in New England. Many of them are particularly handsome. Their appendages also unusually neat. Indeed, an air of wealth, taste and elegance, is spread over this beautiful spot, to which I know no rival. . . . From the tower of the church belonging to the fifth Congregation, a noble prospect is presented to the spectator. On the west and south, spreads an extensive champaign country, ornamented with good farmers' houses, orchards, and cultivated fields, and varied by a number of beautiful hills. Behind them rise, remotely, two mountains, finely connecting the landscape with the sky. On the north flows the Merrimac, visible about four miles ; exhibiting two islands in its bosom, near the point, where it first appears ; and joining the ocean between two sand banks, on which are erected two movable Light houses. On the North shore stand the towns of Salisbury and Amesbury. Behind this the country rises gradually, parted into a variety of eminences ; one of them, which from its appropriation by the savages, is called Powow hill, particularly handsome. Over all these ascends at the distance of twenty-five miles, the round summit of Agamenticus. North eastward, the Isles of Shoals appear at the distance of eight leagues, like a cloud in the horizon. Eastward the ocean spreads illimitably. At a small distance from the shore, Plum Island, a wild and fantastical sand beach, is thrown up by the joint power of winds and waves into the thousand wanton figures of a snow drift. Immediately beneath is the town itself, which with its churches and beautiful houses, its harbor and shipping, appears as the proper centre of this circle of scenery, and leaves on the mind a cheerfulness and brilliancy, strongly resembling that, which accompanies a delightful morning in May.

' Newbury contains five parishes, in which are five congregations and a society of Friends. It is all settled in plantations, formed especially along the Merrimac of excellent land under good cultivation. The surface is generally pleasant, and remarkably so on the borders of the river from some of the eminences.' These eminences, of which the doctor speaks, are principally in

West Newbury, and are called Pipe-stave, Crane-neck, Archelaus, Old-town, and Indian hills. With the exception of the summit of Old-town hill, the land on all the. swells in Newbury, is of the first quality. The Indian-hill farm, owned by colonel Benjamin Poore, is in a high state of cultivation, and received in 1843, the premium of two hundred dollars, from the committee of the agricultural society, who deemed it the best managed farm in the county. Newbury has also the honor of having the first incorporated academy in the state, the first toll-bridge, the first chain bridge, the first incorporated woolen factory; and the first vessel that displayed the American flag in the river Thames, was the Count De Grasse, commanded by captain Nicholas Johnson, of Newburyport. Many other interesting facts might be mentioned, for which I have no room. I will only add, for the information of the reader, that a brief sketch of the life of doctor John Clark, whose portrait is prefixed to this work, may be found in Thacher's Medical Biography. See also page 391. The wood cut of the first parish meeting-house, built in 1700, and demolished in 1806, is not an exact representation. It was drawn from the recollection of one person, by another, who never saw it. ' The roof was originally constructed with four gable ends or projections, one on each side, each containing a large window, which gave light to the upper galleries, where the young people sat. The children sat on a seat in the alley, fixed to the outside of the pews. Before the pulpit and deacon's seat, was a large pew containing a table, where sat the chiefs of the fathers. The turret was in the centre, and the bell was rung and tolled in the centre of the broad aisle. Originally, the space within was open to the roof, where were many ornaments of an antique sculpture and wainscot, and was, in the day of it, a stately building, but long before it was torn down, a steeple was substituted for the turret, the dormar windows were removed, and the roof thus made plain,' * as it appears on the third page. The reader of the following pages, will make the following corrections. Page 244, ' June seventeenth, 1774,' should be placed in 1775. On page 270, for ' captain Michael Smith,' read ' captain Samuel E. Bailey.' On page 363, for ' tattle,' read ' cattle.' On page 285, add ' reverend Daniel P. Pike, pastor.' Other errors the intelligent reader will undoubtedly notice, in the following sketch of Ould Newberry.

* Reverend doctor Popkin.

HISTORY OF NEWBURY.

1635.

'OULD NEWBERRY,' as it was anciently called, was settled, incorporated, and paid its first tax, in the spring of 1635. It derives its name from Newbury, a town in Berkshire, England, situated in the south part of the county, on the river Kennet, fifty-six miles west from London. It was so named in honor of the reverend Thomas Parker, who had for some time preached in Newbury, England, before his arrival in America. Till its incorporation in 1635 it was called by its Indian name, Quascacunquen, a name, which the natives gave, not to the whole territory, (as the word signifies a 'waterfall,') but to 'the falls,' on what is now called the river Parker, on whose banks the first settlers fixed their habitations. As different dates have been assigned by different persons for the first settlement of the town, some placing it in 1633, others in 1634, and others in 1635, I will here mention all the facts and assertions I have been able to find on the subject, and the reasons which induce me to suppose, that, if any, no permanent settlement was here made till early in the spring of 1635. In the Newbury records, under the year 1752, I find the following entry, which, as far as I can learn, is the origin of all the assertions, any where to be found, that Newbury was settled in 1633.

'For religion's sake, as I trust, our forefathers left their native shore; they bid adieu to their stately buildings and goodly seats, and many of them took a final farewell of their friends, and shipped themselves and families on board the ship Hector for New England, and by the grace of God, they arrived in this wilderness in the year 1633, and this place was then called by the natives Quascacunquen. Our fathers began with courage to clear, manure, and till the land; the Lord was pleased to bless their industry, and the earth brought forth increase, and also the Lord added to their families and increased their number; and in the year 1635, on the third month, called May, the great and general assembly was pleased to incorporate them into a town, and invested them with town privileges, and called the name thereof Newbury; and our fathers began the year of births and deaths, as by record do appear, on the first

2

of March, and it hath been so continued, from time to time, until this day, and now, by an act of Parliament, we are ordered to begin the year on the first of January, and in humble obedience to the crown and dignity, I shall proceed accordingly; viz. January ye first, 1752.

JOSEPH COFFIN, *Town Clerk.*'

From the preceding statement, any person, without examination, would be induced to believe that 'our fathers,' the first settlers of Newbury, all came here in the year 1633, in the ship Hector. That this was not the case, we have abundant proof. In the first place, the word, Hector, the name of the ship in which it is said they came, is not in the original record, but was inserted there by some subsequent hand, and cannot be true, as we have abundant evidence that a large majority of the first settlers of Newbury, came to New England at different times and in different ships, between the last of April, 1634, and July, 1635, as we shall hereafter see. In the next place, we have no proof that the Hector came to New England till 1636, when Mr. Thomas Milward, who afterward settled in Newbury, came over as mate of that ship, as will be seen under that year. It is, however, possible, that the Hector came to New England in 1633, as, out of eight ships that arrived in 'this wilderness' in that year, the name of one only is not known. In the year 1634, twenty-two ships arrived in New England. Of these, we know the names of nearly all, but the name of the Hector is not among them. Those, therefore, who have supposed that their ancestors came to Newbury in 1633, in the Hector, must, in the absence of all proof, place no dependence on the apocryphal tradition, part of which has been interpolated by some anonymous writer.

I now proceed to give my reasons for believing, that the territory which was afterward incorporated by the name of Newbury, was not settled till the spring of 1635. Possibly, there might have been a few interloping fishermen, who occupied a part of the coast, and the banks of the Merrimac and Quascacunquen during the fishing season, but who were not among the permanent settlers of Newbury.

Governor Winthrop, in his invaluable History of New England, vol. 1, pp. 98, 99, thus writes, under date of seventeenth of January, 1632-3.

'The governor, having intelligence from the east, that the French had bought the Scottish plantation near cape Sable, and that the fort and all the ammunition were delivered to them, and that the cardinal, having the managing thereof, had sent some companies already, and preparation was made to send many more the next year, and divers priests and jesuits among them — called the assistants to Boston, and the ministers and captains, and some other chief men, to advise what was fit to be done for our safety, in regard the French were like to prove ill neighbours, (being papists;) at which meeting it was agreed that a plantation and a fort should forthwith be begun at Natascott, partly to be some block in an enemy's way, (though it would not bar his entrance,) and especially to prevent an enemy from taking that passage from us; and also, that a plantation should be begun at Agawam, (being the best place in the land for tillage and cattle,) least an enemy, finding it void, should possess and take it from us. The governor's son, (being one of the assistants,) was to undertake this, and to take no more out of the bay than twelve men; the rest to be supplied at the coming of the next ships.'

Referring to this subject, governor Hutchinson remarks:

' It appears that the Massachusetts people took possession of the country at a very critical time. Richlieu, in all probability, would have planted his colony nearer the sun, if he could have found any place vacant. De Monts and company had acquired a thorough knowledge of the coast from cape Sables beyond cape Cod in 1604; indeed, it does not appear that they went round or to the bottom of Massachusetts bay. Had they once gained footing there, they would have prevented the English.'*

From these quotations it is evident, that it was the determination of the Massachusetts colony, to extend their settlements eastward as fast as possible, and, as it was of great importance that the first settlers especially should be men of the right stamp, in 1630, September seventh, 'all persons were forbidden,' by the court, ' to plant within the limits of their patent without leave.' ' A warrant shall forthwith be sent to Agawam, to command those who are planted there, forthwith to come away.'† Again, the court, April, 1633, ' ordered that no person whatsoever shall go to plant or inhabit at Agawam, [now Ipswich,] without leave from the court, except those that are already gone with Mr. John Winthrop, junior, namely, Mr. [William] Clerk, Robert Coles, Thomas Howlett, John Biggs, John Gage, Thomas Hardy, Mr. [John] Thorndike,' and three others, names not given, all of whom had removed to Agawam the preceding month.

In the course of the year 1633, eight ships with passengers, arrived in New England. In 1634 twenty-two ships arrived, of which six arrived in May, fifteen in June, and one in November. These ships brought a large number of passengers, who soon found places to settle. In one of the ships, that arrived in May, came ' Mr. [Thomas] Parker, a minister, and a company with him, being about one hundred, [and] went to sit down at Agawam, and divers others of the new comers.'‡

So great, in fact, was the influx of emigrants to New England, that in many places they could not be accommodated. ' Those of Newtown, [now Cambridge,] complained of straitness for want of land, especially meadow, and desired leave of the court, May, 1634, to look out either for enlargement or removal, which was granted; whereupon they sent men to see Agawam and Merrimack, and gave out they would remove.'§ They, however, went the next year, (October, 1635,) to Connecticut.

Hubbard, in his history of New England, page 192, states, that ' the plantation at Agawam, was from the first year of its being raised to a township, [August, 1634,] so filled with inhabitants, that some of them presently swarmed out into another place a little farther eastward. Mr. Parker was at first called to Ipswich to join with Mr. Ward; but he choosing rather to accompany some of his countrymen (who came out of Wiltshire in England,) to that new

---

* Hutchinson, vol. 1, page 30.   † General court record.
‡ Winthrop, vol. 1, page 133.   § Winthrop, vol. 1, page 132.

place, than to be engaged with such as he had not been acquainted withal before, removed *with them* and settled at Newbury, which recess of theirs made room for others, that soon after supplied their places.'

Now, as it is well known that Messrs. Parker, Noyes, Woodbridge, and company, did not remove to Quascacunquen till May, 1635, the inquiry naturally arises why they did not remove to that place before, especially as Agawam was 'filled with inhabitants,' the situation of Quascacunquen being one of the best in the country, and the general court extremely anxious to extend their settlements as fast as possible. The answer to these questions may be found in Edward Winslow's 'Hypocrisie Unmasked; whereunto is added a Brief Narration, (occasioned by certain aspersions,) of the true grounds or cause of the first planting of New England,' and so forth; lately reprinted in the 'Chronicles of the Pilgrim Fathers of the Colony of Plymouth,' by reverend Alexander Young, Boston. As no copy of the original work, which was printed in small quarto in 1646, was to be found in America, Mr. Young procured a transcript of the work from one in the British Museum. On pages 402, 3, and 4, of that extremely valuable and ably edited collection, I find the following:

'The next aspersion cast upon us, is, that we will not suffer any that differ from us never so little, to reside or cohabit with us; no, not the presbyterian government, which differeth so little from us. To which I answer, our practice witnesseth the contrary. For 't is well known that Mr. Parker and Mr. Noyce, who are ministers of Jesus Christ at Newberry, are in that way and so known, so far as as a single congregation can be exercised in it; yet never had the least molestation or disturbance, and have and find as good respect from magistrates and people, as other elders in the congregational or primitive way.'
'So also 't is well known that before these unhappy troubles arose in England and Scotland, there were divers gentlemen of Scotland that groaned under the heavy pressures of those times, wrote to know whether they might be freely suffered to exercise their presbyterial government amongst us; and it was answered affirmatively that they might. And they sending over a gentleman to take a view of some fit place, *a river called Meromeck, near Ipswich and Newberry aforesaid, was showed their agent, which he well liked,* and where we have since four towns settled, and more may be for aught I know; so that there they might have had a complete presbytery, *and whither* they intended to *have come. But meeting with manifold crosses, being half seas through, they gave over their intendments;* and as I have heard, these were many of the gentlemen that first fell upon the late covenant in Scotland.'

Cotton Mather, in his Magnalia, vol. 1, page 73, makes a similar statement, but neither he nor Winslow gives the date of the letter, or the time when the agent arrived. This deficiency is supplied, not only by Winthrop, but by the court records. The former, vol. 1, page 135, says, 'we received letters from a godly preacher, Mr. Levinston, a Scotchman in the north of Ireland, whereby he signified that there were many good christians in those parts resolved to come hither, if they might receive satisfaction concerning some questions and propositions, which they sent over.' This was in July, 1634. The court records for September state, vol. 1, p. 128, 'it is ordered, that the Scottishe and Irish gentlemen, who intends to come hither, shall have liberty to sett doun upon any place upp Merrimack river, not possessed by any.' From all these quotations it is evident, that the general court, in September, 1634, had granted to this expected company, through their agent, a township of land at the mouth of Merrimack river, and 'whither they intended to have come;' that, after receiving satisfactory answers to their 'questions and propositions,' they embarked for New England, and, after performing about one half their voyage, 'they gave over their intendments,' in consequence of the 'manifold crosses' they met, and returned home. Now, when it is recollected, that 'the court had forbidden all persons to plant within the limits of their patent without leave,' and that the territory now called Newbury had actually been granted to a company of 'good christians' who had 'resolved to come hither,' and that the settlers at Agawam, [Ipswich,] must have known these facts, the reason is obvious why they neither took possession of the territory, nor asked permission so to do. Neither is it at all probable that they had heard of the failure of the intended expedition till the next spring. The reasons for this opinion are these. Of the twenty-two ships, which arrived in New England during the year 1634, one only arrived after June, and that was the 'Regard,' which came in November. This opinion is corroborated by the following extract from the Ipswich records, namely:

'December 29th, 1634. It is consented unto that John Perkins, junior, shall build a ware, [fish trap,] upon the river of Quasycung, [now river Parker,] and enjoy the profitts of it, but in case a plantation shall there settle, then he is to submit himself unto such conditions, as shall by them be imposed.'

This conditional grant certainly implies, that no settlement had then been commenced, and the probability, that a plantation in that place would soon be established, when their jurisdiction would of course cease. There are also other proofs. On the tombstone of Henry Sewall, now standing in the burying yard of the first parish in Newbury, is the following inscription.

'Henry Sewall, sent by his father, Henry Sewall, in the ship Elizabeth and Dorcas, arrived at Boston 1634, wintered at Ipswich, helped begin this plantation 1635, furnishing English servants, neat cattle, and provisions. Married Mrs. Jane Dummer March 25, 1646, and died May 16, 1700. His fruitful vine, being thus disjoined, fell to the ground January following. Ps. 27: 10.'

This inscription was undoubtedly written by his son, judge Samuel Sewall, in whose diary I find the following. 'Newbury was planted in 1634. My father has told me so, who was one of the first inhabitants.' The reverend Samuel Danforth, 'a great antiquary,' in his almanac for 1647, states that 'Newbury was begun in 1634.' Captain Edward Johnson, in his 'Wonder-working Providence,' written in 1651, states, that 'Messrs. Parker and Noyes began to build the tenth church at a place called Newberry in the latter end of the year 1634.' These apparent contradictions can be easily reconciled, if we bear in mind the fact, that the year, with our puritan forefathers, began on the twenty-fifth of March, and not on the first of January, as the custom now is. Not satisfied with renouncing all rites and ceremonies, not, in their opinion, clearly warranted by the bible, they attempted a reformation in the calendar by repudiating the names of the months, and of the days of the week, as of heathenish origin, and altogether unsuitable to be used by christians, for, in the language of Johnson, in his 'Wonder-working Providence,' 'the practice was designed of purpose to prevent the heathenish and popish observation of days, months, and years, that they may be forgotten among the people of the Lord.' They also commenced their year in March, the twenty-fifth of that month being new year's day. In order, however, to accomdate all those who did not desire this reformation, a double date was used between January first and March twenty-fifth. Thus twelfth mo. 1634–5, meant either February the twelfth month, 1634, or February the second month, 1635, according to the different opinions of the reader. 'The latter end' of 1634 might mean, and probably did mean, the time between January first, and March twenty-fifth, which would then be considered as the beginning of 1635. From all these considerations, the probability, therefore, is, that no settlement was made in Quascacunquen, before the year 1635, as it is not probable that the first settlers removed in the depth of winter, as the land was then, according to all accounts, covered with a thick and heavy growth of timber. Horses and carts, as a means of conveyance, could not then be used, as nothing but a narrow and winding footpath led from Agawam to Quascacunquen. The most rational supposition, and one which accords with all the information we have on the subject, either traditional or recorded, is, that they, with Henry Sewall, 'wintered at Ipswich,' and made preparations for a removal in the spring. The first notice we have of their determination, is given by Winthrop, volume 1, page 160, in these words: 'at this general court, [May, 1635,] some of the *chief* of Ipswich desired leave to remove to Quascacunquen, to *begin* a town there, which was granted them, and it was named Newberry.' In the colonial records, it is thus noticed.

'*May* 6th, 1635. Quascacunquen is allowed by the court to be a plantation, and it is referred to Mr. [John] Humphrey, Mr. [John] Endicott, captain [Nathaniel] Turner, and captain [William] Trask, or any three of them, to set out the bounds of Ipswich and Quascacunquen, or so much thereof as they can, and the name of the said plantation shall be changed, and shall hereafter be called Newberry.

'Further it is ordered, that it shall be in the power of the court to take order that the said plantation *shall* receive a sufficient company to make a competent towne.'

From the preceding quotations, it is apparent, that the first inhabitants of 'Newberry' obtained 'leave of the general court' to remove to Quascacunquen, settled there, and were incorporated as a township in the spring of 1635. If any persons, prior to that

period, had commenced a settlement within the territorial limits of
' ould Newberry,' of which we have no positive proof, they must
have been considered as intruders, or ' squatters,' or they supposed,
as in the case of John Perkins, that the northern limit of Agawam
was the river Merrimack.   Indeed, we are told that when Agawam
was settled, in 1633, it was bounded on the north by the Merrimack,
and on the West by Cochichawick, [now Andover.]   The jurisdiction of Masconomo, the sagamore of Agawam, extended from
Naumkeag river to the Merrimack.   William Wood, in his ' New
England Prospect,' thus speaks :   ' Agawam is the best place but one,
which is Merrimack, where is a river twenty leagues navigable.
All along the river side is fresh marshes, in some places three
leagues broad.'   ' These two places may contain twice as many
people as are yet in New England, there being *as yet scarce any*
inhabitants in these two spacious places.'   He was in America in
1633, and set sail for England on the fifteenth of August of that
year.   At that time we know of thirteen persons only, who were in
Agawam, besides John Winthrop, junior, namely, the twelve who
came with him, and ' Thomas Sellan,' who on ' June eleventh was
admitted as an inhabitant.'   There were probably fishermen in
various places on the banks of the Quascacunquen and the Merrimac, ' where,' says Wood, ' much [sturgeon] is taken, pickled, and
sent to England, twelve, fourteen, eighteen feet long.'   He, as it will
be seen, is not remarkable for his accuracy, either respecting the navigation of the Merrimack, the width of the fresh marshes on its banks,
or the length of the fish in its stream.   We will therefore leave him and
return to the first settlers of Newbury.   Uniform tradition asserts
that they came by water from Ipswich, through Plum island sound,
and up the river Quascacunquen, [now river Parker,] to the place
they had selected as their future habitation.   Tradition asserts that
they landed on the north bank of the river, about one hundred rods
below the spot where the bridge now stands, and that Nicholas
Noyes was the first person who leaped ashore.   This company
was few in number, and probably consisted of Mr. Henry Sewall
and servants, William Moody, his wife and four sons, Anthony
Short, Henry Short and wife, Mr. John Spencer, Mr. Nicholas
Easton, his wife and son John, Richard Kent, senior, and Stephen
Kent, brothers, with their wives, Richard Kent, junior, and James
Kent, brothers, Mr. Thomas Parker, Mr. John Woodbridge, Mr.
James Noyes, his wife, and brother Nicholas Noyes, Thomas
Brown, Richard Brown, George Brown, Mr. James Browne and
wife, Thomas Coleman, Francis Plumer and wife, with his two
sons Joseph and Samuel, with a few others, whose names are not
known with certainty.   For a short time the business of the town
was transacted in committee of the whole, but the population
increasing rapidly, fifteen ships with passengers, having arrived in
June, one in August, one in November, and one in December,
bringing with them many families, who immediately settled in
Newbury, ' the plantation ' soon received ' a sufficient company to

make a competent toune,' according to the order of the general
court, which in the same month, May, 1635, ordered the same men,
namely, Humphrey, Endicott, Turner, and Trask, to set out a farm
for Mr. Dummer, about the falls of Newberry, not exceeding the
quantity of five hundred acres, provided it be not prejudicial to
Newberry.' At the same time 'liberty was granted to Mr. [Richard]
Dummer and Mr. [John] Spencer, to build a mill and weire at the
falls of Newberry, to enjoy the said mill and weire with such privileges of ground and timber as is expressed between them and the
toune, to enjoy to them and their heires forever.'* The court also
ordered that 'no dwelling house shall be built above a half mile
from the meeting house in any new plantation, without leave from
the court, except mills and farm houses of such as have their
dwellings in toun.' 'John Humphrey, esquire, and captain Turner,
were ordered to set out the bounds between Salem and Ipswich, and
Ipswich and Newbury, before midsummer next, and also to view,
and inform the next general court if there may not be another
toune settled conveniently betwixt them, and it is agreed that the
bounds of said tounes shall be six miles apiece into the country.'
At the same court, [May, 1635,] 'it was ordered, that Mr. [Richard]
Dummer, and Mr. Bartholomew, shall set out a convenient quantity of land within the bounds of Newberry, for the keeping of the
sheep and cattle that came over in the Dutch shipps this yeare, and
to belong to the owners of said cattle.' These 'owners' were
Richard Saltonstall, Richard Dummer, Henry Sewall, and 'divers
other 'gentlemen in England.' With the exception of the lands
above mentioned, the first settlers of 'ould Newberry,' granted,
surveyed, and settled the lands according to their own judgment.
For a short time, a year or more, the business of the township was
transacted in committee of the whole. Mr. John Woodbridge was
chosen their first town clerk, and Richard Kent and Henry Short,
lot layers. All their records pertaining to grants of land, are full
and complete, having been very accurately copied into a new set of
books, now called the 'Proprietors' Books,' which for many years
have been kept separate from the town records. As there are a few
leaves wanting in the first volume of the transactions of the town,
the deficiency in that respect, must be supplied from other sources.
In the records of the court at Salem, I find the following.

'I John Pike do testifie that I was present at the gathering of the church at
Newbury, and I did hear our reverend pastor preach a sermon on the eighteenth
of Matthew, seventeenth verse; 'And if he shall neglect to hear them, tell it
unto the church: but if he neglect to hear the church, let him be unto thee as
an heathen man and a publican,' wherein he did hould forth that the power of
discipline belonged to the whole church, yt the matter of the church ought to be
visible saints joyned or gathered together, that the manner of their joyning
together ought to be by covenant, yt the end of it is for the exercisinge and
enjoyinge of the ordinances of Christ togeather. He strongly proved his doctrine by many places of the scripture, both in the old and new testament. The

* Court records, page 152.

which sermon togeather with the scriptures did much instruct and confirme us in that waye of church discipline which as I understood he then preached for, namely, the congregational waye, some noates of the said sermon, which I then took from his mouth I have here ready to shew if you please. The sermon being ended the brethren joyned together by express covenant, and being joyned they chose their pastor, Mr. Parker, who accepted the call, and joyned with them according to the covenant aforesaid; and those that afterward joyned to the church, consented to the said covenant explicit. The brethren of the church acted in these admissions of ye members, expressinge their voats therein by lifting up the hande, and soe continued together lovingly a considerable number of yeares untill other doctrine began to be preached amongst us.'

'Per me JOHN PIKE.

'Sworne in court, 30 March, 1669.

'Robert Pike also testifies that the meeting was on the sabbath and in the open air under a tree.'

'At the same time that Mr. Parker was chosen pastor, Mr. James Noyes was chosen teacher.'

Similar testimonies were given by John Emery and Thomas Browne. The cause of these testimonies' being given, was a contention in the church, which was carried to the court at Ipswich, as will be seen under the years 1669, 1671, and 1672. They give us the place and the manner in which the church was formed, but not the time. It could not have been earlier than the month of June, as John Pike, Robert Pike, and John Emery, did not arrive in New England till that month. Tradition states that Mr. Parker preached his first sermon under the branches of a majestic oak, which stood on the north bank of the river, about one hundred yards below where the bridge now stands, and which, like the auditory it once shaded, has long since crumbled into dust. Under the same tree, probably, the church was gathered, and their spiritual guides set apart by them for their appropriate work. A meeting-house was also built. That, tradition informs us, stood on the lower green, a few rods northwest from the spot where captain Enoch Plumer's house now stands. The first grave yard was near it, as appears by a petition to the general court in or about the year 1647.

A house for the ministers was built, a large number of house lots, planting lots, and meadow lots were granted. How many houses were erected and how many families were in Newbury during the first year, there is no record to inform us. Houses were erected on both sides of the river Parker, and on Kent's island, and as then meadow land was very valuable, and in fact almost essential to their very existence as a support for their cattle, many were built on the margin of the meadows, not only on the banks of the river Parker, then called 'the Great river,' but also on the banks of the 'Little river,' as far as Trotter's bridge, and in various other places, so that in a very short time the law prohibiting any person from erecting 'a dwelling house above half a mile from the meeting-house without leave of the court,' was entirely disregarded. The principal settlement was around the meeting-house on the lower green, and there was to be, as the first settlers supposed, the future commercial metropolis of Newberry. During this year sir Henry Vane and

3

reverend Hugh Peter arrived in Massachusetts, grand juries were established by law, the circulation of brass farthings was prohibited, and musket bullets were to be used instead.   This year, August fifteenth, 'about midnight the wind came up at northeast, having blown hard at south and southwest the week before, and blew with such violence with abundance of rain that it blew down many hundreds of trees, overthrew some houses, drave ships from their anchors. In the same tempest a bark of Mr. Allerton's was cast away upon cape Ann, and twenty-one persons drowned.   Among the rest, a Mr. Avery, a minister in Wiltshire, with his wife and six small children, was drowned.'   'This Mr. Avery,' says Cotton Mather, 'went to *Newberry*, intending there to settle, but being urged by magistrates and ministers to settle in Marblehead, he embarked with his own family, and his cousin Mr. Anthony Thacher's, all of whom were lost except Mr. Thacher and his wife.'

The ship angel 'Gabriel,' in which came passengers John Bailey, senior, and John Bailey, junior, who afterward settled in Newbury, was 'lost at Pemaquid,' now Bristol, in Maine, and 'the Dartmouth ships cut all their masts at St. George.'   'The tide rose at Narraganset fourteen feet higher than ordinary and drowned eight Indians flying from their wigwams.' *   'The effects of this tempest, one of the most violent and destructive probably that the country has ever experienced, were visible,' says Morton in his Memorial, 'many years.'

In September of this year the court assessed £200 on the towns in the colony.   Of this rate Newberry paid £7 10s., Ipswich £14, Salem £16, Charlestown £15, Boston £25 10s., and so forth.

In the court records, under date of November, 1635, is the following, namely:

'Whereas Thomas Coleman hath covenanted with Richard Saltonstall and divers other gentleman in England and here for the keeping of certain horses, bulls and sheepe in a general stock for the space of three years, and now since his coming hither hath been exceedingly negligent in discharging the trust committed to him, absenting himselfe for a long time from the said cattle and neglecting to provide something for them, by reason whereof many of the said cattle are dead already and more damage likely to accrue to the said gentlemen : it is therefore ordered that it shall be lawful for the said gentlemen to divide the oates and hay provided for said cattell among themselves, and soe every one take care of their own during the winter.'

The tract of land, which was set apart as the place for pasturing these cattle, was near the falls of Newbury.   Of this land, Mr. John Spencer had a mill lot of fifty acres, Mr. Richard Dummer three hundred acres, Mr. Henry Sewall five hundred acres, Mr. John Clark four hundred acres, 'beginning at the mouth of cart creek.' Of Mr. Henry Sewall we are told in the life † of his son, judge Samuel Sewall, 'Mr. Cotton would have him settle in Boston, but he preferring an inland situation *on account of his cattle*, he removed to Newberry.' How large the number was who owned stock in the cattle community, and which was so soon dissolved by the negligence of shepherd Coleman, we have no means of knowing. All we know is that there were 'divers gentlemen,' not only here, but 'in England,' each of whom soon found that he could best take care of 'his owne cattle.' In the division of the land throughout the town, the first settlers recognized the scripture rule, 'to him that hath shall be given,' and the wealth of each of the grantees, as well as others of the first settlers, can be very nearly estimated, by the number of acres of land, which were granted them.* This was according to the rule agreed upon in London, in 1629, by 'the assistants of the company,' who settled Massachusetts. They gave to each adventurer two hundred acres for every £50 he put into the common stock, and so in proportion. 'Such adventurers as send over any person, were to have fifty acres for each person, whom they send.' Every person, who transported himself and family to New England at his own expense, should have fifty acres.

This year, second of September, 'Francis Plumer was licensed to keep an ordinary,' † that is, a tavern.

Mary Brown, daughter of Thomas Brown, the first white child born in Newbury, was born this year. May thirteenth, 1656, she was married to Peter Godfrey, and, 'having had a good report as a maid, a wife and a widow,' she died April sixteenth, 1716, in her eighty-first year.

1 6 3 6 .

This year the general court enacted, that 'every particular township should have power over its own affairs, and to settle mulcts upon any offender, upon any public order not exceeding twenty shillings, and liberty to chuse prudential men, not exceeding seven, to order the affaires of the towne.'

The town of Newbury, availing itself of this privilege, chose, 'by papers,' the following men, namely: Mr. Edward Woodman, Mr. John Woodbridge, Henry Short, Mr. Christopher Hussey, Richard Kent, Richard Brown, and Richard Knight. They were at first called by the name of 'the seven men,' then 'towne's men,' then 'towne's men select,' and finally 'select men,' as they are still called. They 'were chosen,' says the reverend Richard Brown, in his diary, 'from quarter to quarter by papers to discharge the business of the town, in taking in, or refusing any to come, into town, as also to dispose of lands and lots, to make lawful orders, to impose fines on the breakers of orders, and also to levy and distrain them, and were fully impowered of themselves to do what the town had power for to do. The reason whereof was, the town judged it inconvenient and burdensome to be all called together on every occasion.'

About this time it is probable the town made some regulations

---

* See appendix, A.   † Colonial records.

concerning the manner, in which their town meetings or meetings of the 'freemen' should be held. As the town records are lost prior to the tenth of June, 1637, and as the manner of proceeding in the neighboring towns was essentially the same, the following from the Salisbury records will supply the deficiency :

In the year 1640 the town ' ordered that in the first of every meeting there shall be a moderator chosen by the companie. He shall have power to interrupt and call to accompt any that shall exceed in speaking and in case of fayling herein he shall be fyned at the discretion of the companie, and in case the moderator shall refuse so to doe he shall for such offence pay two shillings and sixpence. Also that every freeman shall speak by turne, and not otherwise, and shall signifie when he is to speak by rising or putting off his hatt, and his speech being ended, shall signifie it by putting on his hatt or sitting downe, and in case he be interrupted by the moderator and shall refuse to cease shall forfeit for every such offence one shilling. Also that no person shall depart from meeting without leave on the like penalty.'

In Hampton, New Hampshire, the regulations adopted in 1641 were somewhat different.

' 1. The moderator was to be chosen at the *end* of every meeting for the next succeeding one. 2. The moderator, if the elders were not present, was to open the meeting with prayer. 3. He was then to state some proposition or call on some one to do it. 4. When any person addressed the moderator he was to stand up or put off his hat, and no other person was to speak at the same time, or be talking of any other thing (when a matter is in agitation) within the meeting roome. The clerk was to call over the ' freemen ' and note the absent.'

Such substantially were the rules and regulations, adopted by the first settlers of Newbury in their town meetings, as will in part appear hereafter.

This year ' another windmill was erected at Boston, and one at Charlestown ; and a watermill at Salem, and another at Ipswich, and another at Newbury.' *

This mill, the first erected in Newbury, was built at ' the falls,' on the river Parker, by Messrs. Dummer and Spencer, in accordance with the grant from the general court, and an agreement with the town in 1635.

February eleventh, Newbury neck was leased to Richard Dummer for two years.

This year, the general court passed the following sumptuary law, to which, and other similar laws, allusion will be frequently made.

' No person after one month shall make or sell any bone lace or other lace to be worne on any garment upon pain of five shillings the yard for every yard so made or sold, or set on, provided that binding or small edging laces may be used on garments or linen.'

Joshua Woodman, son of Mr. Edward Woodman, was the first white male child born in Newbury. He died the thirtieth of May, 1703, in his sixty-seventh year.

This year, the third of March, the general court laid a tax of £300 on Massachusetts, of which Newbury was to pay £11 5s., Salem £24, and Boston £37 10s., and 'ordered that courts in Essex county should be held quarterly, two in Salem, one in Ipswich to which Newbury shall belong.'

May twenty-fifth, 'Newbury men were fined sixpence apiece for choosing and sending a deputy to the court, who is no freeman.' ✳ Military men were to be ranked in three regiments, of which one is to consist of Saugus, Salem, Ipswich, and Newbury. Mr. John Spencer was chosen captain for Newbury. Mr. Richard Dummer and Mr. John Spencer were chosen magistrates.

In the month of March, 1634, ' Mr. [John] Endicott of Salem was called' before the court 'to answer for defacing the cross in the ensign; but, because the court could not agree about the thing, whether the ensigns should be laid by, in regard that many refused to follow them, the whole cause was deferred till the next general court; and the commissioners for military affairs, gave order in the mean time, *that all the ensigns should be laid aside.*' †

At the next court, Mr. Endicott was ordered to be 'sadly admonished' for cutting the cross out of the king's colors, 'and to be disabled for one year from bearing any publick office.' He was instigated to do this by Roger Williams, who considered it as 'a relique of antichristian superstition.' In 1635, each military company was to have colors, *the cross to be left out.* The objection to the cross in the ensign, was, that it was idolatrous and sinful. It was deemed of so much consequence, that 'the ministers promised to take pains about it, and to write into England to have the judgments of the most wise and godly there.' In this state of feeling, Mr. 'Thomas Milward, mate of the ship Hector,' and who was afterward one of the proprietors of Newbury, 'spake to some of our people aboard his ship, [June, 1636,] that we had not the king's colours at our fort, we were all traitors and rebels,' and so forth.‡ Such language could not, in the opinion of our fathers, be tolerated. He was accordingly sent for, the words proved against him, and he committed. He was discharged on signing the following submission, which may be found in the colonial records, 1, 179.

'Whereas I, Thomas Millerd have given out most false and reproachful speeches against his majesty's loyal and faithful subjects dwelling in the Massachusetts Bay in America, saying that they were all traitors and rebels and that I would affirm so much before the governor himselfe, which expressions I do confess (and so desire may be conceived) did proceed from the rashness and distemper of my own brain, without any just ground or cause, so to think or speak, for which my unworthy and sinful carriage being called in question, I do justly stand committed. My humble request therefore is, that upon this my full and ingenuous recantation of this my gross failing, it would please the governor

✳ See appendix.   † Winthrop, vol. 1, p. 156.   ‡ Winthrop, vol. 1, pp. 187, 188.

and the rest of the assistants to accept of this my humble submission to pass by my fault, and to dismiss me from farther trouble and this my free and voluntary confession I subscribe with my hand this ninth June 1636.

'THOMAS MILLERD.'

Shortly after this, Mr. Millerd moved to Newbury, and became one of the proprietors of the town. He is called in our records 'Mr. Thomas Milward, mariner.' This scruple concerning the use of the cross in the colors, continued many years, as we shall hereafter show. The whole country was agitated by the controversy, and in addition to this, the theological difficulties, and prosecutions growing out of the 'revelations' of Mrs. Hutchinson, 'that master-piece of woman's wit,' as Johnson calls her, began to create a great excitement.

The Pequods, about this time, were beginning to be troublesome, and 'cattle,' says Winthrop, 'were grown to high rates; a good cow cost £25 or £30; a pair of bulls or oxen, £40. About thirty ploughs were used in Massachusetts this year, and much rye was sown.'

In November, the town ordered, that 'John Woodbridge should have £5 a year and be free from all rates and payments, while he is the towne register.' 'The general court empowered Richard Dummer and John Spencer to build a house at Winnicowett at the expence of the colony. The architect was Nicholas Easton who soon after removed to Newport and built the first English house there. The house at Winnicowett was called the Bound-House,' and was situated in what is now called Seabrook.*

1637.

In April, one hundred and sixty men, under the command of captain Stoughton, were raised to go against the Pequods. Of this number Newbury raised eight, Ipswich seventeen, Salem eighteen, Lynn sixteen, and Boston twenty-six. It will serve to give the reader some idea of the all-pervading influence of the theological discussions, which were then agitating the whole community, to inform him, on the authority of Neal, that these very troops deemed it necessary to halt on their march to Connecticut, in order to decide the question, whether they were under a covenant of grace or a covenant of works, deeming it improper to advance till that momentous question was settled. These soldiers were to have twenty shillings per month, lieutenants £4, and captains £6. In May Mr. John Spencer was discharged from being captain. This was probably owing to his religious tenets, he being an adherent of Mrs. Hutchinson. 'Mr. Edward Woodman was chosen lieutenant, and Mr. John Woodbridge, surveyor of the armes at Newbury.' In the same month the election was held at Newtown, (now Cambridge,) in the open air. Then the law required all the 'freemen' from all the towns in the province, to meet at the general

* Belknap, vol. 1, p. 38.

court of elections, and choose the magistrates, including the governor and lieutenant governor. This practice continued till 1663. In order to prevent the re-election of sir Henry Vane as governor, and to strengthen the friends of governor Winthrop, Henry Sewall, junior, Nicholas Noyes, Robert Pike, Archelaus Woodman, Thomas Coleman, Thomas Smith, James Browne, John Cheney, Nicholas Holt, and John Bartlett, went from Newbury to Cambridge on foot, (forty miles,) qualified themselves to vote by taking the freeman's oath, seventeenth of May, 1637, or, in other words, 'were made freemen.'* Winthrop was chosen governor, and sir Henry Vane and the friends of Mrs. Hutchinson were in a minority.

On the morning of May twenty-sixth, the fort of the Pequods was attacked with fire and sword, and their whole tribe, four or five hundred in number, extinguished, in that and the subsequent attack by captain Stoughton the latter end of June.

In August, a synod of ministers, messengers of churches, and magistrates, was held in Newtown, (Cambridge,) and condemned above eighty erroneous opinions. The general court then took up the business, and proceeded to disfranchise, or banish, or disarm, many of those who held these erroneous opinions. 'A great number,' says Hutchinson, 'removed out of the jurisdiction.' The court ordered about sixty of the inhabitants of Boston to be disarmed, and several of other towns; among them were three belonging to Newbury, Mr. Richard Dummer, Mr. John Spencer, and Mr. Nicholas Easton. Spencer returned to England, Easton went to Rhode Island, but Dummer remained in Newbury. In June, two ships arrived with passengers. With them came Mr. Hopkins, Mr. Eaton, and Mr. Davenport, and many others of good note. Great pains were taken to induce them to settle in Massachusetts. 'The court offered them any place they would pitch upon.' 'The town of Newbury offered to give up their settlement to them,' but they chose to remove to Connecticut, where they built New Haven, and so forth.

'It was ordained in a lawful meeting, November fifth, that whosoever is admitted into the towne of Newbury as an inhabitant thereof, shall have the consent and approbation of the body of freemen of sayd towne.' †

'The seven men, mentioned in 1636, were again chosen by papers,' were desired to serve 'for one quarter longer and shall labor in the case according to what the Lord shall direct to doe according to what is prescribed.' ‡

The preceding directions to the selectmen, remind me of the following extract, which may be found in Friend's records, in Rockingham county, New Hampshire.

'*Hampton*, 1707. This meeting not having unity with John Collins' testimony desires him to be silent *till the Lord speak by him to the satisfaction of the meeting.*'

* Judge Sewall's diary.   † Town record.   ‡ Town record.

In October, Richard Singleterry, William Palmer, John Moulton, Thomas Moulton, Nicholas Busbee, and Abraham Toppan, were admitted as inhabitants of Newbury. The following is a specimen of the form of admission.

'Abraham Toppan being licensed by John Endicott esqr. to live in this jurisdiction was received into the towne of Newberry as an inhabitant thereof and hath heere promised under his hand to be subject to any lawful order, that shall be made by the towne.' *

ABRAHAM TOPPAN.

In the same month, fourteen individuals were fined £4 15s. 'for defect of fences whenever they shall be called on.' *

'In September, William Schooler, a vintner from London, was hanged in Boston for an alleged murder. He lived with another fellow at Merrimack, and there being a poor maid at Newbury, one Mary Sholy, who had desired a guide to go with her to her master, who dwelt at Pascataquack, he enquired her out and agreed for fifteen shillings to conduct her thither. But, two days after, he returned, and being asked why he returned so soon, he answered that he had carried her within two or three miles of the place, and then she would go no further. Being examined by the magistrates at Ipswich, and no proof found against him, he was let go. About half a year after, the body was found by an Indian ten miles short of the place he said he left her in. About a year after, he was again apprehended, examined, arraigned, and condemned,' † on circumstantial evidence.

In November, the church petitioned the general court for relief, who passed the following order, namely:

'November 2d, 1637. Whereas it appeareth unto this court that the inhabitants of the towne of Newbury owe divers persons neare the sum of £60, which hath been expended upon publick and needful occasions for the benefit of all such as do, or shall, inhabit there, as building of houses for their ministers &c. whereas such as are of the church there are not able to bear the whole charge and the rest of the inhabitants there do or may enjoy equal benefit thereof with them, yet they do refuse against all right and justice to contribute with them. It is therefore ordered that the freemen of the said towne or such of them as shall assemble for that end, or the greater number of them, shall raise the said sum of £60 by an equal or proportionable rate of every inhabitant there, having respect both to land or other personal estate, as well of such as are absent, as of those dwelling there present, and for default of payment shall have power to levy the same by distress and sale thereof by such persons as they shall appoint, and the same being so collected shall satisfy their said debts, and if any remainder be, the same to be employed on other occasions by the towne.' ‡

November. 'The inhabitants of Newbury haveing been moved to leave their plantation, the court granted them Winnicowet, [now Hampton,] or any other plantation upon the Merrimack below the first falls, and to have six miles square, and those that are now inhabitants and shall remove within one yeare, shall have three yeares immunity, (as Concord hath,) the three yeares beginning the first of first month next, namely, March first, 1638.' ‡

* Town record.   † Winthrop.   ‡ Colonial records.

1638.

January 18*th.* ' The lease of the neck of land to Mr. Dummer for two years being expired, the towne doth take it into their own hands and intendeth to dispose of it at their pleasure.' *

' It was ordered that Richard Knight, James Brown and Richard Kent shall gather up the first payment of the meeting house rate and the towne rate within one fourteenight on the penalty of six shillings and eight pence apiece.' *

February 1*st.* ' John Emery shall make a sufficient pound for the use of the towne two rod and a halfe square by the last of the present month if he cann.' *

' It is agreed that Mr. Woodman shall have a house lott between Mr. Easton's and the river provided that if *there shall be a fort built by the water's side* hereafter that then his lott shall give way.' *

February 24*th.* ' It was voted, that Thomas Cromwell, Samuel Scullard, John Pike, Robert Pike, and Nicholas Holt, are fined two shillings and sixpence apiece for being absent from towne meeting at eight o' clock in the morning, having due and fitt warning.' *

' Having taken into serious consideration the weight of managing all publick affaires and being desirous that *those whom God hath fitted and who necessarily are called* forth unto such publick services, may not be overburdened with expense of time and other charges, which necessarily attend such publick busynesses, but rather should be encouraged to the end that they may bear that burden, and faithfully discharge that service to which they are called, and considering likewise the practice of other townes and places in this government in putting their shoulders to help bear up and sustain this common worke, either in person or estate, or both, wee have therefore thought fitt to settle some way and course in this behalfe to the end that such publick busynesses may be carried on without murmuring by any, who shall be appointed thereunto, and have for the present thought fitt that those, who are sent for deputyes and grand jurors shall be allowed two shillings and sixpence, for foure dayes, in which they goe and returne, and twelve pence a day for every other day, which they necessarily attend towne's service, if the county find the charges of diett, otherwise more as shall be thought fitt upon due consideration.' *

April 14*th.* ' It is ordered that Richard Brown, the constable, shall cause a sufficient pound to be made by the twenty-first of this moneth to impound swyne and other cattell, in the place, that shall be shewed him and of that largeness which shall be thought fitt.'

April 19*th.* Two constables and two ' surveyors of the high wayes' were chosen ' for one whole yeere.'

' This,' says Winthrop, ' was a very hard winter. The snow lay half a yard deep about the Massachusetts from November fourth to

* Town records.

4

March twenty-third, and a yard deep beyond Merrimack and so the more north, the deeper.'

April 21st. ' Henry Short, John Cheney, Francis Plumer, Nicholas Noyse, and Nicholas Holt are fined two shillings and sixpence apiece for being absent from the towne meeting, having lawful warning, and so forth.' *

It was ordered that ' Nicholas Batt shall keep the herd of cows ' eight months from the sixteenth of March till the sixteenth of November for eighteen pounds, ' nine pounds in money ' and forty bushels of corne, ' provided he is to keep them one Lord's day, and the towne, two.' *

May 5th. ' It is ordered that John Pike shall pay two shillings and sixpence for departing from the meeting without leave and contemptuously.' *

William Morse was the keeper of the ' towne's heard of goates,' and, ' as part of his wages,' he was to have three pence for every goate above a yeere old,' and Nicholas Batt was to have twenty-two pence for every cow or heifer either in money or corn at seven shillings the bushel.'

June 1st. ' Being this day assembled to treat or consult about the well ordering of the affairs of the towne, about one of the clocke in the afternoone, the sunn shining faire, it pleased God suddenly to raise a vehement earthquake coming with a shrill clap of thunder, issuing as is supposed out of the east, which shook the earth and the foundations of the house in a very violent manner to our great amazement and wonder, wherefore taking notice of so great and strange a hand of God's providence, we were desirous of leaving it on record to the view of after ages to the intent that all might take notice of Almighty God and feare his name.' †

June 19th. ' It is agreed that Richard Singleterry and William Allen shall have each of them four acres of planting ground on Deer island, provided the island be not [over?] twelve acres.'

' The court having left it to the liberty of particular townes to take order and provide according to their discretion for the bringing of armes to the meeting house, it is for the present thought fitt and ordered that the town being divided in four several equal parts, sayd part shall bring compleat armes according to the direction of those, whom the towne hath appointed to oversee the busynesse in order and manner as followeth, namely, John Pike, Nicholas Holt, John Baker, and Edmund Greenleafe being appointed as overseers of the busynesse, are ordered to follow this course, namely. They shall give notice to the party of persons under their severall divisions to bring their armes compleat one Sabbath day in a month and the lecture day following in order successively one after another and the

* Town records.
† Town records. ' It came,' says Winthrop, ' with a noise like continued thunder, or the rattling of coaches in London. The noise and shakings continued about four minutes.' ' The course of it,' says Hutchinson, ' was from west to east. It shook the ships, threw down the tops of chimnies, and rattled the pewter from the shelves.' 'This was a very great earthquake and shook the whole country.'

June the 15th 1638.

The Court having left it to the liberty of particular townes to take order & praise according to their discretion for the bringing of armes to the meeting house, it is for the present thought fit & ordered. That the townes being divided into 4 severall & equall parts, each part shall bring comp[l]eat armes according to the direction of these severall townes that are appointed to oversee the businesse, in order & manner as followeth.

for m̃ Pike, Ellis, Holt, John Bacon, & Edmund Greenleafe being appointed as overseers of the townshipp are ordered to follow this course viz. They shall give notice to the party of persons under their severall divisions to bring their armes comp[l]eat one sabbath day in a moneth & the persons aforesaid ing successively one after another & the persons aforesaid shall cause every person under their severall division, to stand sentinell at the doores all the time of publick meeting, in order accordingly every one after either himselfe in person, or by a sufficient substitute to be allowed by the overseer of the ward.

Edmund
woodman
Jo Woodbridge
Edward Rawson
William Moody
James Browne
Josh Knight
Abraham Toppan

persons afore mentioned shall cause every person under their severall divisions to stand sentinell at the doores all the time of the publick meeting every one after another either by himself in person or by a sufficient substitute to be allowed by the overseer of the ward. And further it is ordered that the sayd overseers shall diligently mark and observe any that shall be defective in this respect, having lawfull warning, and they together with the surveyour of the armes shall collect or distrain twelve pence for every default according as hath been thought fitt by order of the court in this case provided.' *

Trumbull, in his McFingal, thus alludes to this practice of the early settlers in Connecticut, as well as Massachusetts :

' So once, for fear of Indian beating,
Our grandsires bore their guns to meeting ;
Each man equipped on Sunday morn
With psalm book, shot, and powder horn,
And looked in form as all must grant,
Like th' ancient true church militant,
Or fierce like modern deep divines,
Who fight with quills like porcupines.'

July 6th. ' Whereas there hath bin notice taken of much disorder in publick towne meeting by reason of divers speaking at one and the same time, some walking up and downe, some absent, and divers other miscarriages, it is henceforth ordered that if any person shall offend against any order prescribed in this case, there shall be exact notice of such offence in this respect, and hee shall be censured accordingly.' *

' Mr. Woodman, Mr. Rawson, Abraham Toppan and John Knight were chosen [selectmen] for one whole quarter and till new be chosen.'

' There is granted to goodman Goffe *some* fresh marsh, *where Richard Kent mowed hay* on *this* side of Mr. Greenleaf's farme,' and so forth.

August 6th. ' Whereas it is agreed with Mr. Richard Dummer of Newbury by the persons, whose names are underwritten, hereunto subscribed that in case Mr. Dummer doe make his mill fitt to grynd corne and doe maintaine the same, as also doe keep a man to attend grynding of corne, then they for their part will send all the corne that they shall have ground and doe likewise promise that all the rest of the towne (if it lye in their power to promise the same) shall also bring their corne from tyme to tyme to be ground at the same mill. And it is further agreed that (the aforementioned conditions being observed by Mr. Dummer) there shall not any other mill be erected within the sayd towne.

EDWARD WOODMAN.
JOHN KNIGHT.
EDWARD RAWSON.
RICHARD BROWN.
HENRY SHORT.'

To this the town agreed and assented, at a public meeting, October sixth, 1638.

* Town records.

August 10*th*. ' Thomas Hale and John Baker are appointed hay wards till the town shall appoint new.' *

' The towne hath appointed that a rate of twenty-six pounds shall be made speedily and gathered within one fourteenight for the finishing of the meeting house.' †

' At a general towne meeting, twenty-eighth of September, 1638, it was granted that Mr. [doctor] Clarke in respect of his calling should be freed and exempted from all publick rates either for the county or the towne so long as he shall remayne with us and exercise his calling among us.' *

November 19*th*.   A rate of twenty-six pounds was ordered to be made ' for the officers,' [that is, ministers,] ' rating all lands as they are divided at ten pence or five pence the acre.' *

' It is ordered that Edward Rawson shall supply the place of Mr. Woodbridge and be the publick notary and register for the towne of Newbury and whilst he so remains, to be allowed by the towne after the rate of five pounds per annum for his paynes.' *

May 17*th*. ' Newbury was fined six shillings and eight pence for defects in the roads.' †

' Anthony Emery was fined twenty shilings for a pound breach and to give thirteen shillings and fourpence to Thomas Coleman for his charges.' †

' Newbury was fined five pounds for want of a pair of stocks, and time given till next court to make them.' †

' There came over this summer,' says Winthrop, ' twenty ships and at least three thousand persons, so as they were forced to look out new plantations.   One was begun at Merrimack, and another at Winicowett,' [now Hampton.]

Mr. Edward Rawson, Mr. John Woodbridge, and Mr. Edward Woodman, were chosen commissioners for small causes in Newbury.

In a book printed in London, 1638, and entitled, ' a true relation of a battell fought in New England between the English and Pequot salvages,' I find the following sentence :

' They that arrived out there this year [1638] out of divers parts of Old England, say they never saw such a field of four hundred acres of all sorts of English grain as they saw at Wintertown there, yet that ground is not comparable to other parts of New England, as Salem, Ipswich, Newbury, and so forth.'

1639.

March 13*th*. ' Plum Island is to remain in the court's power; only for the present, Ipswich, Newbury and the new plantation [Rowley] between them may make use of it, till the court shall see cause otherwise to dispose of it.' ‡

In the spring of this year, Mr. Ezekiel Rogers, who had arrived in New England in December, 1638, with about twenty families from Yorkshire, having received an addition to his company of

* Town records.   † Colonial records.   ‡ Colonial records, vol. 1, p. 205.

about forty families, settled down on that tract of land, which was incorporated by the name of Rowley in the following September. This tract belonged partly to Ipswich and partly to Newbury, ' and because some farms had been granted by Ipswich and Newbury, which would be prejudicial to their plantation, they bought out the owners, disbursing therein about eight hundred pounds.' *

The proprietors' records of Newbury give us the following account, the date not being recorded :

'The towne being assembled together and being desirous to manifest theyr earnest desires and willingness to give due incouredgment unto the worthy gentilmen, who desire to set down between us and Ipswich as to part with such a portion of land as cannot any way be expected from them, or they may without endangering their present necessityes afford. Hoping on good grounds it may fully answer their desires and expectations they have determined as followeth :

'By the common and general suffrages of the body of freemen, none excepted, there was granted to the said gentilmen all the upland and meadow and marish between us and Ipswich incompassed by the line heer underwritten, namely :

1. That their line shall begin from the head of the great creek between the great river and Mr. Dummer's, running due west as we come to the great creek being the bounds of John Osgood's farm, which issues into Mr. Easton's river and above that creek all the lands southward of Mr. Easton's river, and from that river from the pafh leading to the falls to run a due west line into the country a mile and afterwards to run on a north west line so as it come not within half a mile of the side line of Mr. Dummer's farm. Likewise it comes two miles distant of Merrimack. Provided that if after they have entered by buildings or otherwise on this part of land granted to them and leave off from going on with a plantation or a towne between us that then the grants abovesaid shall be void to all intents and purposes and to remaine the proprietyes and inheritances of the towne of Newbury in as ample a manner as before the grant hereof in all respects.' †

'Another plantation was begun upon the north side of the Merrimack called Salisbury, another at Winicowett, called Hampton.' ‡

The reverend Stephen Bachiler and his company, who had received permission from the general court, October, 1638, when united together by church covenant, commenced a settlement at Winicowett. He was at this time residing in Newbury. On Mr. Rawson's request, the place was called Hampton. The following persons, residents of Newbury, went with Mr. Bachiler. John Berry, Thomas Coleman, Thomas Cromwell, James Davis, William Easton, William Fifield, Maurice Hobbs, Mr. Christopher Hussey, Thomas Jones, Thomas Marston, William Marston, Robert Marston, John Moulton, Thomas Moulton, William Palmer, William Sargent, and Thomas Smith. Smith, however, soon returned to Newbury. A few went to Salisbury. Those who remained deemed it necessary to make some preparations for defence. They again contemplated building 'a fort by the water's side' just below where Parker river bridge now stands. It was probably never built. The records say, ' it is ordered and determined by the body of freemen

* Winthrop, vol. 1, 294.   † Proprietors' records.   ‡ Winthrop, vol. 1, p. 289.

that there shall be a walk of sixteen feet broad on the topp of the great hill from one end to the other, and a way of four feet broad through Stephen Kent his lott.' This 'walk' ran east and west, and the 'way' north and south from the green to the top of the 'hill.' Near the centre of this walk the place is still pointed out, where, tradition informs us, 'a sentry box, or watch house, was erected.' It is highly probable, from appearances, that the tradition is correct. The position is a commanding one, and a far better place to 'stand sentinell,' than 'at the doores' of the meeting house 'all the time of the publick meeting.'

June. 'There was at this time,' says Winthrop, 'a very great drouth all over the country, both east and west, there being little or no rain from the twenty-sixth of April to the tenth of June.'

In consequence of the complaints against excessive wearing of lace, and other superfluities, the general court, September, 1639, 'ordered that hereafter no garment shall be made with short sleeves, whereby the nakedness of the arme may be discovered in the wearing thereof, and such as have garments already made with short sleeves shall not wear the same unless they cover the armes to the wrist with linnen or otherwise. And that hereafter no person whatsoever shall make any garment for weomen or any of the sex with sleeves more than half an ell wide (twenty-two and a half inches!) in the widest place thereof and so proportionable for bigger or smaller persons.'

The court also forbade the wearing of 'immoderate great breeches, knots of rybands, shoulder bands, rayles, rases, double ruffs and cuffes.'

'Edmund Greenleaf was ordered to be ensign for Newbury and allowed to keep a house of entertainment.' *

'Mr. —— was fined ten shilings and sixpence for selling strong water without license.' *

'John Bayley,' senior, of Salisbury, afterward of Newbury, 'was fined five pounds for buying lands of the Indians without leave of the court, with condition if he yield up the land to be remitted.' *

'Richard Bartlett petitioned the general court and was granted twenty pounds according to his petition.' *

'Mr. Edward Rawson is allowed five hundred acres of land at Pecoit so as he go on with the business of powder, if the salt-petre come.' *

The people of Newbury having built a 'ministry house,' a meeting house, which was soon used as a school house, had their ferry established at 'Carr's island,' and become an orderly community, began not only to lay out new roads, but, as they were rapidly extending their settlement farther north, to take special care of the town's timber by prescribing a penalty of five shillings for every tree cut down on the town's land without permission. Nearly the whole of what is now called West Newbury, or that part above

* Colonial records.

Artichoke river, was called 'the upper woods.' The common land in the southerly part of the town was divided into the 'ox common,' the 'cow common,' the 'calf common,' and so forth. The sheep and the goats, of which the inhabitants had many, each had their prescribed limits, each flock were under the charge of a keeper, and were obliged to be folded at night to protect them from the wolves. The town also received a valuable addition to its population in the persons of Anthony Somerby, their first schoolmaster, Henry Somerby, Mr. John, Mr. Richard, and Mr. Percival Lowle, who had been merchants of Bristol, Mr. William Gerrish, and Richard Dole of Bristol, who had also been engaged in mercantile transactions before coming to Massachusetts. Not far from this time, though the date cannot be fixed with certainty, captain John Cutting, 'ship master,' and Mr. Thomas Milward, 'mariner,' who in 1640 owned a 'shallop' and was engaged in the fisheries at cape Ann, came to Newbury. Mr. Richard Dole commenced business as a merchant near the 'river Parker,' and was always called 'marchant Dole.' The town granted lots of land which were called the 'fishermen's lots.' John Knight had a lot of land granted him on condition that he 'follow fishing.' To encourage the fisheries the general court enacted that all estates, employed in catching, making, or transporting fish, should be free from all duties and taxes, and forbade 'all men after the twentieth of the next month to employ any basse or cod-fish for manuring of ground, and shall forfeit for every hundred weight of fish so employed in manuring of ground, twenty shillings.'* 'All ship-builders and fishermen during the season for business were excused from all trainings.' † At that time it does not appear that the inhabitants of Newbury had ever sent any vessel over Newbury bar. Their commerce centred in 'the river Parker,' and came up by the way of Ipswich. 'Merrimack,' says Hubbard, 'is another gallant river, the entrance into which, though a mile over in breadth, is barred with shoals of sand, having two passages, that lead thereinto, at either end, of a sandy island, that lieth over against the mouth of sayde river. Near the mouth of that are two other lesser ones, about which are seated two considerable townes, the one called Newberry, the other Ipswich, either of which have fayre channels, *wherein vessels of fifty or sixty tons may pass up safely to the doores of the inhabitants whose habitations are pitched neere the banks on either side.'* ‡

The first vessels built in Newbury were undoubtedly erected on the banks of the 'river Parker,' and were designed for the fishery, and for the 'coasting trade.' At that time the channel of the river was much deeper than it now is, or vessels of fifty or sixty tons 'could not pass safely up to the doors of the inhabitants.' The river Parker was once celebrated for the abundance of the fish in its stream. 'There was,' says Hubbard, 'a noted plantation of them' [Indians] at the falls of the river of Newberry, by reason of the plenty of fish,

* Colonial records.   † Hutchinson.   ‡ Hubbard, p. 17.

that ' at almost all seasons of the year used to be found both in winter
and summer.' *   In the will of Richard Kent, who died in 1654, I
find the following bequest.   ' Also I give the first salmon that is
caught in my weir yearly to Mr. Noyes, and the second to Mr.
Rogers till my son be nineteen years of age,' and so forth.   After
that, his son might do as he saw good.

This year Anthony Somerby came to Newbury, and was employed to teach school.   It is thus noticed on the town records:

' There was granted unto Anthony Somerby in the year 1639 for his encouragement to keepe schoole for one yeare foure akers of upland over the great river
in the necke, also sixe akers of salt marsh next to Abraham Toppan's twenty
akers.'

1640.

This year emigration to New England almost entirely ceased, in
consequence of the political change in the affairs of England.

' This sudden stop,' says Hutchinson, ' had a surprizing effect on
the price of cattle.'   Cows which had for some time sold for twenty-
five or thirty pounds, could now be bought for five or six pounds
each.   The whole number of neat cattle in New England was
estimated at twelve thousand, their sheep at three thousand.   The
number of passengers, who had arrived from the beginning of the
colony in two hundred and ninety-eight ships, were estimated at
twenty-one thousand and two hundred, about four thousand families,
and it is probable, in the language of Hutchinson, that, since 1640,
' more persons have removed out of New England to other parts of
the world than have come from other parts to it.'   The number of
new settlers in this and subsequent years was small.   Among them
may be mentioned Robert Adams, Henry Jaques, George Little.

The great influx of provisions, the cessation of emigration, with
various other causes, occasioned a scarcity of money, and of course
a great abatement of the price of all commodities.   As neither
' money nor beaver,' says Winthrop, ' were to be had,' the court
ordered that ' Indian corn at four shillings, rye at five shillings, and
wheat at six shillings should pass in payment of all new debts.'   ' Men
could not pay their debts though they had enough.'   ' And he that
three months before was worth one thousand pounds could not, if
he should sell his whole estate, raise two hundred pounds.'

Notwithstanding the distresses of the times, Winthrop informs us
that ' it was a common rule that most men walked by in all their
commerce to buy as cheap as they could and sell as dear,' and
complains of it as a ' notorious evil.'

' Most men ' at the present day are probably liable to the same
charge, ' notorious' as the ' evil' may be.

' Henry Sewall, senior, was bound over to his good behaviour in
sixty-six pounds, thirteen shillings, and fourpence, for contemptuous
speeche and carriage to Mr. Saltonstall.' *

* Colonial records.

'Mr. John Woodbridge, presented for releasing a servant, is discharged by paying two shillings and sixpence.' *

This summer Mr. John Ward and some inhabitants of Newbury petitioned for a place of settlement.

In the court records is the following, namely:

'At a general court held at Boston the thirteenth of the third month, 1640, [thirteenth of May, 1640,] the desires of Mr. Ward and Newbury men, is committed to the governor, deputy governor and Mr. Winthrop sen. to consider of Pentucket and Cochichawick, and to grant it to them, provided they return answer within three weeks from the twenty-first present and that they build there before the next courte.' The names of the 'Newbury men' who with Mr. Ward settled Pentucket, (now Haverhill,) are these. William White, Samuel Gile, James Davis, Henry Palmer, John Robinson, Christopher Hussey, John Williams, and Richard Littlehale, with four others.

The same month, in consequence of the great loss which governor Winthrop had suffered 'in his outward estate,' through the unfaithfulness of his bailiff, 'the elders' agreed, 'that supply should be sent in from the several towns by a voluntary contribution.' 'The whole came not to five hundred pounds whereof near half came from Boston, and one gentleman of Newbury, Mr. Richard Dummer, propounded for a supply in a more private way, and for example himself disbursed one hundred pounds.' †

'This unexampled liberality to Winthrop in his distress,' says Mr. Savage, in a note, 'is a more satisfactory proof of the high estimation in which he stood than could be afforded by the most elaborate eloquence of eulogy. But the generosity of Dummer is above all praise. His contribution is fifty per cent. above the whole tax of his town, and equal to half the benevolence of the whole metropolis; yet he had been a sufferer under the mistaken views of Winthrop and other triumphant sound religionists.'

The state tax this year was £1200, of which Boston paid £179, Ipswich £120, and Newbury £65.

May, 1640. 'Mr. Edward Woodman, Mr. Christopher Batt, and John Cross are appointed (when the way is settled) to settle the ferry, if they think meet.' *

July 3d, 1640. The town of Salisbury granted to George Carr, shipwright, the island, which still bears his name.

1 6 4 1 .

This general court desired 'the elders would make a catechism for the instruction of youth in the grounds of religion.' In compliance with this desire, Mr. James Noyes, of Newbury, composed 'a short catechism for the use of the children there.' For a copy of the work, which was reprinted in 1714, see appendix, B.

'Mr. John Woodbridge, Mr. Edward Woodman, and Mr. Edward

* Colonial records.   † Winthrop, vol. 2, p. 4.

Rawson, appointed commissioners for small causes in Newbury.' ∗
' Mr. Rawson instead of Mr. John Oliver.'

' At a court holden at Ipswich the twenty-eighth of —— month,
1641, George Carr is appointed to keep the ferry at Salisbury at the
island where he now dwelleth for the space of two years provided
that he find a sufficient horse boate and give diligent attendance.
The ferriages are as follows, namely. For a man present pay two-
pence, for a horse sixpence, great cattle pay sixpence, calves and
yearlings pay two-pence, goates one penny, hoggs two-pence. If
present pay be not made that hee must book any ferriage, then a
penny apiece more. If any be forced to swim over their horses for
want of a great boat, they shall pay nothing. Per curiam.' †

Johnson, in his ' Wonder-working Providence,' published in 1651,
thus speaks: ' over against this towne [that is, Salisbury,] lyeth the
towne of Newberry on the southern side of the river, a constant
ferry being kept between, for although the river be about half a mile
broad, yet by reason of an island, that lies in the midst thereof, it is
the better passed in troublesome weather. The people of this
towne have of late placed their dwellings so much distance the one
from the other that they are likely to divide into two churches.'

The difficulty, as will be seen, was settled without a division.

' This court,' (February second, 1641,) says Winthrop, ' having
found by experience that it would not avail by any law to redress
the excessive rates of labourers' and workmen's wages and so forth
(for being restrained, they would either remove to other places,
where they might have more, or else being able to live by planting
and other employments of their own, they would not be hired at
all) it was therefore *referred to the several towns* to set down rates
among themselves. This took better effect, so that in a voluntary
way, by the counsel and persuasion of the elders, and example of
some, who led the way, they were brought to more moderation than
they could be by compulsion. But this did not last long.' ‡

If the town of Newbury at this time passed any laws regulating
the wages of laborers, or the price of goods, the record is lost. To
supply the deficiency we shall again quote from the Salisbury
records.

' *April 5th*, 1641. At a general meeting of the freemen it was ordered that
the year shall be accompted thus : from the first of November to the last of the
first month [March] shall be winter months and the seven other, summer months,
and all labourers for the winter months shall have no more but sixteen pence
per day, and for the summer months twenty pence per day, and all carpenters
shall have two-pence per day more than labourers, that is eighteen pence per day
in winter, and twenty-two pence per day in summer.' ' Also that mowers shall
have no more but two shillings per day, and if they mow per the acre they shall
not exceed two shillings per acre.

'Also that no man shall sell clabords of five foot in length for more than three
shillings per hundred, and if shorter according to proportion, and if they cleave
by the hundred they shall not exceed sixpence per hundred for five foot in
length.

∗ Colonial records.   † Court records, [*i. e.* county court.]   ‡ Winthrop, vol, 2, p. 25.

'Also that noe man shall sell ani sawn bord for more that five shillings per hundred, and for the sawing no more than three shillings and sixpence per hundred, and for slitt work no more than four shillings and sixpence per hundred.

' Also that butter shall nott be sould for above sixpence per pound.

' Also that milk shall be sould for three half pence a quart, new milk, and one penny skimmed milk ale measure.'

From the above extracts it is evident, that what are now called clap-boards, were originally boards that were 'cloven,' and not 'sawn,' and were thence called ' clove-boards,' and in process of time cloboards, claboards, ' clap-boards.'

The Hampton records give us a similar tariff of prices with this addition. ' A cart, four oxen and a man five shillings for the winter months and six shillings and eight-pence for the summer months.'

Early this year, through the agency of Hugh Peter, 'a man of a very public spirit and singular activity on all occasions,' * a ship of three hundred tons was built at Salem, and soon after another at Boston of one hundred and sixty tons, called the Trial. All foreign commodities at this time ' grew scarce, and our own of no price.' ' Corn would buy nothing — and no man could pay his debts, and so forth. These straits set our people on work to provide fish, clapboards, plank, and to sow hemp and flax (which prospered very well) and to look out to the West Indies for a trade for cotton.' *

' This year about three hundred thousand dry fish were sent to the market.' * The town of Rowley made laudable efforts to raise hemp and to some extent succeeded.

' These straits,' the settlement of Hampton, Salisbury, and Haverhill, the establishment of a ferry at Carr's island, and the addition to the population of five or six wealthy men, who had been educated as merchants, all undoubtedly conspired to extend the limits of their settlement, and to make the centre of their village two or three miles farther north. This, however, was not effected without much difficulty, as we shall hereafter see.

The general court, determining that the whole of New Hampshire came under their jurisdiction, as a line to run east from three miles north of the head of Merrimack river would take in the whole of that state, passed a law accordingly, the ninth of October, 1641.

1642.

The winter of 1641-2 was unusually severe. ' All the bay was frozen over, so much and so long, as the like, by the Indians' relation, had not been for forty years. It continued from the eighteenth of November to the twenty-first of February so as horses and carts went over in many places where ships have sailed.' †

' February 23d, a generall towne meeting. By the generall consent of all the freemen the stinting of the commons was referred to Henry Short, Mr. [Edward] Woodman, Edward Rawson, Thomas

* Winthrop, vol. 2, p. 24, 31.   † Winthrop, vol. 2, p. 60.

Hale and Mr. [John] Woodbridge, according to their best judgments and discretions.'

Accordingly, twelfth of March, 1642, they determined, that the several numbers or rights ' shall perpetually belong to the several persons to whom they are allotted and to no other persons whatsoever, except he gett them by purchase or some other legal way,' and that 'all the commons within the limits of the towne shall be equally divided into three several parts and that the same number of cattle that are allowed in the stint of the cows and oxen shall be allowed in the heifer common and a third like quantity of young cattle above Mr. Rawson's farme.' The number of persons was ninety-one. One right was assigned to the 'towne house,' one 'to lye at the towne's appointment,' one to ' the ferry lott ' and three ' for them that shall be schoolmasters successively.' This ' stint' allowed five hundred and sixty-three cattle in each of the three pastures, namely : the cow common, the ox common, and the heifer common. The highest number of ' rights' was sixty-two and a quarter to R. Dummer, the lowest, Lewis and Mattox, one.

On March twenty-first ' the town also ordered that all commons and waste grounds above Mr. Rawson's farme and so to and above Mr. Dummer's farme to our line next Rowley line *shall lie perpetually common*, according to the former order for common, the meadows only excepted within the verge.' *

This tract of land, which was thus ' ordered to lie *perpetually common*,' comprehended not only a part of Newbury, but nearly the whole of what is now called West Newbury, now containing some of the best farms in the county, but then considered, with the exception of ' the meadows,' as ' waste grounds,' fit only for ' perpetual commons.' In 1686, six thousand acres, a tract more than nine times as large as the whole of the territory of Newburyport, situated above Artichoke river, in what was then called ' the upper woods,' was divided for the first time among the inhabitants. It was then called ' the upper commons.'

From the first settlement of the town till this year, the inhabitants had made the ' lower green,' on the banks of ' the great river,' as they called it, their central place of business. At this time, however, a majority of them had determined on a removal from the ' old town' to the ' new town.' Their reasons for this removal will be given from the records in their own words, though it is probable that some pages are lost. It thus commences :

' Whereas the towne of Newbury well weighing the streights they were in for want of plough ground, remoteness of the common, *scarcity of fencing stuffe*, and the like, did in the year 1642 grant a commission to Mr. Thomas Parker, Mr. James Noyes, Mr. John Woodbridge, Mr. Edward Rawson, Mr. John Cutting, Mr. John Lowle, Mr. Edward Woodman and Mr. John Clark, for removing, settleing and disposeing of the inhabitants to such place as might in their judgements best tend to theyr enlargements, exchanging theyr lands and making such orders as might bee in theyr judgments for the well ordering of

* Tristram Coffin's manuscript.

the towne's occasions and as in their commission more largely appeareth, the said deputed men did order and appoint John Merrill, Richard Knight, Anthony Short, and John Emery to go to all the inhabitants of the towne, taking a true list of all the stock of each inhabitant and make a true valuation of all their houses, improved land, and fences that thereby a just rule might be made to proportion each inhabitant his portion of land about the new towne, and removing of the inhabitants there.'

' It was ordered at a meeting of the eight deputed men abovementioned that each freeholder should have a house lott of foure akers.   It was further ordered that in respect of the time for the inhabitants removeing from the place they now inhabit to that, which is layd out and appointed for their new habitations, each inhabitant shall have their house lotts foure years from the day of the date of this commission.'

The day of the month is, however, not given.   However great might be the difficulties they found in remaining together, still greater ones in some respects awaited their removal.   As it has often been since, both here and elsewhere, the main object of their contention was their meeting-house.   The minority, that remained, were unwilling to have the house removed, and the majority were equally unwilling to go without it, and when it was removed, where to place it was the difficulty, and it was not until four years after, and then not without great opposition, that a decision was finally made.

The first intimation that we have of a new place to set the meeting-house upon, is contained in the following grant:

' There was granted unto Mr. James Noyes that four acres of land upon the hill by the little pine swamp, *which was marked to sett the meeting house* about the year 1642.' *

This year it appears that the fishing business commenced on the Merrimack.   On the twenty-sixth of March, 1642, the town of Salisbury ' granted to Robert Ring two acres of upland upon the island † over against Watts' sellar ‡ to be employed about fishing for two years.'

In the year 1671, ' Robert Ring testifies that he did build a cellar upon that land and a little house and did keep fishing there and did set up stages upon the salt marsh, being a little cove next the river and this was about twenty-nine years agoe.'   1671—29=1642.

The house of commons this year passed a resolve, exempting from custom, subsidy, or taxation, the exports and imports of New England.

In September the governor of Massachusetts received information from Connecticut, that ' the Indians all over the country had combined themselves to cut off the English.' §   It was therefore thought fitt to disarm all the Indians who were within our jurisdiction.   A warrant was accordingly sent to Ipswich, Rowley, and Newbury, ' to disarm Passaconaway, who lived by Merrimack.'   ' The next day, being Lord's day, forty armed men were sent for that purpose, but

* Proprietors' records, p. 12.					† Ring's island.
‡ ' Watt's cellar ' stood near where Newburyport market-house now stands.
§ Winthrop, vol. 2, pp. 78, 87.

as it rained all day, they could not go to his wigwam, but went to his son's and took him which they had warrant for, and a squaw and her child, which they had not warrant for,' * wherefore fearing the consequences 'an order was sent to lieutenant Greenleaf, or in his absence to Mr. Woodman for sending home the Indian woman and child from Newbury and to send to Passaconaway for satisfaction.' †

On the fifteenth of November, Passaquo and Saggahew, with the consent of the above-mentioned Passaconaway, sold for £3 10s. 'to the inhabitants of Pentucket,' now Haverhill, a tract of land fourteen miles long and six miles broad, 'with ye isleand and the river that ye isleand stands in,' and so forth.   Among the witnesses to this deed was Tristram Coffyn, who this year came to New England, and went from Salisbury to Haverhill.

In September, 'nine bachelors commenced at Cambridge, young men of good hope.' *   It was the first class that graduated at Harvard college.   The students then took their degrees, and are arranged in the catalogue, according to the rank of their parents.   The first graduate was Benjamin Woodbridge of Newbury. See appendix, C.

December 7th, 1642. 'The men deputed for the managing of those things that concerned the ordering of the new towne, declared and ordered according to the former intentions of the towne that the persons only abovementioned [ninety-one in all,] (see appendix, letter D,) are acknowledged to be freeholders by the towne and to have a proportionable right in all waste lands, commons and rivers undisposed and such as from, by or under them, or any of them or theyr heyrs, have bought, granted or purchased from them or any of them theyr right and title thereunto and none else, provided also that no freeholder shall bring in any cattle of other men's or townes, on the towne's commons above or beyond theyr proportions otherwise than the freemen shall permit.' ‡

1643.

This year, the fifth of March, 'at seven in the morning, being the Lord's day, there was a great earthquake. It came with a rumbling noise like the former but through the Lord's mercy it did no harm.' §

March 28th.   The town 'ordered that every house lott shall be foure acres' and 'that he that hath least land in the new towne shall have eight acres except John Swett, Thomas Silver and John Russe.' ‡

'For the confirmation of all men's proprietyes, and direction likewise for the exchanges in the new towne, itt is ordered that all the lands as they are entered into the towne's book shall be established and confirmed to the owners according as they are entered, unlesse that any man shall bring in just and right exception against any man's portion of land within fourteene days after this time to

* Winthrop, vol. 2, pp. 78, 87.   † Colonial records.
‡ Town records.   § Winthrop, vol. 2, p. 93.

Mr. Lowle, and if there come in none, then the owners thereof shall quietly and peaceably thenceforth enjoy the same and shall have liberty to buy or exchange the same or any part or parcels thereof as they please.' *

'Corn,' says Winthrop, 'was very scarce all over the country and many families in most towns had none to eat by the end of April, but were forced to live of clams, muscles, dry fish, and so forth, but the merchants had great success in the sale of their pipe-staves and fish.' The Trial, of Boston, 'made a good voyage, which 'encouraged the merchants and made wine, sugar and cotton very plentiful and cheap in the country.' † ' Our supplies from England failing much, men began to look about them, and fell to a manufacture of cotton, whereof we had store from Barbadoes, and of hemp and flax, wherein Rowley, to their great commendation, exceeded all other towns.' †

This year the thirty towns in the colony were divided into four counties, Essex, Middlesex, Norfolk, and Suffolk. Norfolk contained Salisbury, Haverhill, Exeter, Dover, and Portsmouth. Essex was as it now is with the exception of the first two towns.

This year also, May nineteenth, the colonies of Massachusetts, New-Plymouth, Connecticut, and New Haven, adopted articles of confederation for their mutual advantage.

July 5th. ' There arose a sudden gust at northwest so violent for an hour as it blew down multitudes of trees. It lifted up their meeting house at Newbury, the people being in it. It darkened the air with dust, yet through God's great mercy it did no hurt, but only killed one Indian with the fall of a tree. It was straight ‡ between Linne and Hampton.'§ This was a removal of their meeting-house which neither party anticipated. It was then standing on the lower green.

August 4th. ' There was an assembly at Cambridge of all the elders in the country (about fifty in all) such of the ruling elders, as would, were present also, none else. The principal occasion was because some of the elders went about to set up some things according to the presbytery as of Newbury and so forth. The assembly concluded against some parts of the presbyterial way and the Newbury ministers took time to consider the arguments,' and so forth.§ ' There was little rain this winter and no snow till the third of March, the wind continuing west and northwest near six weeks.' §

1644.

'*January* 10th. Remembering the severall inconveniencyes, multiplicity of suites and vexations arising from the insufficiency of fences, which to remedy in the *old* towne hath been so difficult, yett in our removal to the place appointed for the *new* towne *may*

---

* Town records.   † Winthrop, vol. 2, pp. 94, 95.
‡ ' Straight,' that is, ' narrow in extent between Lynn and Hampton.'
§ Winthrop, vol. 2, pp. 124, 136, 155.

easily *be prevented.* Itt is therefore ordered that all fences generall
and particular at the *first setting up shall be made* so sufficient as to
keepe out all manner of swyne and other cattle great or small and
at whose fence or part of fence any swyne or other cattle shall
break thorough, the party owning the fence shall not only beare and
suffer all the damages, but shall further pay for each rod so insufficient the somme of two shillings' and so forth. 'It is likewise
ordered that the owners of all such cattle as the towne shall declare
to be *unruly* and *excessively different* from all other cattle shall pay
all the damages their unruly cattle shall doe in breaking thorough
fences.' *

'In consideration of Mr. Rawson's keeping the towne book it is
ordered by us according to our power from the towne and courte
granted to us, that he shall be freed and exempted from all towne
rates for one whole yeare from the twenty-ninth of September last
to the twenty-ninth of September next 1644.' *

'*January* 11*th.* Itt is hereby ordered and determined by the
orderers of the towne affaires that the plan of the new towne is, and
shall be laid out by the lott layers as the house lotts were determined
by their choice, beginning from the farthermost house lott in the
South streete [now called West India lane] thence running through
the Pine swampe, thence up the High streete, numbering the lotts in
the East street to John Bartlett's lott the twenty-ninth then through
the west side of the High streete to Mr. Lowell's the twenty-eighth
and so to the end of that streete, then ***** the Field streete to
Mr. Woodman's the forty-first, thence to the end of that streete
to John Cheney's the fiftieth then turning to the first cross street
to John Emery's the fifty-first thence comming up from the river
side on the east side of the same streete to the other streete the west
side to Daniel Pierce's the fifty-seventh and so to the river side on
the side the streete to Mr. Clarke and others to Francis Plummer the
sixty-sixth as heereinunder by names and figures appeare.' * Here
follow, in the original record, the names of sixty-five men and three
women. There is also one lot called 'the ferry lott,' and one to
'John Indian.' This is the first intimation we have on the records,
that there were any of the aboriginal inhabitants residing in Newbury. His lot is numbered sixty-one. The numbers of the lots
which they chose, are affixed to the names, except seventeen. The
highest number given is sixty-six. The tract of land which was
laid out as the 'new towne,' contained, probably, about seven
hundred acres. The exact limits of the 'new towne' cannot be
accurately ascertained, as the original plan is lost. It, however,
extended farther north and south than the town of Newburyport
now does, but not so far west, and east by the waters of the
Merrimac.

On the same day they determined, that 'their lands shall be liable
to maintaine all publick towne charges, as ministry and such like,

* Town records.

and that thereby they acknowledge their lands.' * They also annexed a penalty of two shillings and sixpence for every tree ' fit for timber or fence' within certain prescribed limits, and ' that all trees already felled shall be under the like penalty,' and ' the trees shall lye and remayne on the ground, till the party be knowne to whom the land belongs that so paying for the labour he may have them to serve his occasions.' *

March. ' Upon the motion of the deputies' to the general court, ' it was ordered that the court should be divided in their consultations, the magistrates by themselves, and the deputies by themselves, what the one agreed upon they should send to the other, and if both agreed, then to pass and so forth. This order determined the great contention about the negative voice.' † From this division originated the phraseology, upper and lower house, in consequence of the deputies holding their sessions in the lower story, and the magistrates occupying the room over their heads. We still hear the phrases ' sent up' or ' sent down, for concurrence,' when in fact both houses are on the same floor.

June 5th. ' Two of our ministers' sons,' says Winthrop, ' being students in the college, robbed two dwelling houses in the night of some fifteen pounds. Being found out they were ordered by the governors of the college to be there whipped, which was performed by the president himself.' This was probably the first instance of the infliction of such a punishment within the walls of old Harvard. ' The names of these offenders' has escaped the notice of Mr. Savage, whose information concerning the early history of New England, is as remarkable for its variety and extent as its accuracy. Their names were James Ward, son of Nathaniel Ward of Ipswich, and **** Welde of Roxbury, son of reverend Thomas Welde. They robbed the houses of Joshua Hewes, and Joseph Welde, the one in March, the other in April, of eleven pounds in money, and thirty shillings worth of gunpowder.

April 10th. ' There was laid out unto John Emery junior, fourscore akers of upland, bee it more or lesse joyneing unto Merrimacke river on the north and running from the mouth of Artichoke river unto a marked tree by a swampe on the northwest corner being about one hundred and thirty-two rods long at the head of the cove thence about an hundred rods to the southwest corner, thence running on a strait lyne about an hundred and fifty-six rods to Artichoke river on the east about eighty rods broad.' *

In this month, June, William Franklin, one of the first settlers of Newbury, and one of the ninety-one grantees in 1642, was hung in Boston, for murder. ' He had been found at the last court of assistants, guilty of murder, but some of the magistrates, doubting of the justice of the case, he was preserved till the next [this] court of assistants. The case was this. He had taken to apprentice one

* Town records.   † Winthrop, vol. 2, p. 160.
6

Nathaniel Sewell, one of those children sent over the last year'
from England. 'He used him with continual rigor and unmerciful
correction, and exposed him many times to much cold and wet in
the winter season, and used divers acts of rigor towards him, as
hanging him in the chimney and so forth and the boy being very
poor and weak he tied him upon an horse and so brought him
(sometimes sitting and sometimes hanging down) to Boston, being
five miles off, to a magistrates, and by the way the boy calling much
for water, would give him none, though he came close by it, so as
the boy was near dead when he came to Boston, and died in a few
hours after.' *   The governor, magistrates, and elders, having met at
Salem, May thirtieth, to consider this and several other cases, 'the
magistrates seeming to be satisfied, warrant was signed by the
governor a week after, which was not approved by some in regard of
his reprieval to the next court of assistants.' *   'He had been
admitted into the church at Roxbury about a month before.' *

The following order is transcribed from the Ipswich records :

May 11th. 'It is ordered that all doggs for the space of three weeks after the
publishing hereof shall have one legg tyed up, and if such a dogg shall break
loose, and be found doing any harm, the owner of the dogg shall pay damages;
if a man refuse to tye up his dogg's legg, and hee bee found scrapeing up fish
in a corne fielde the owner thereof shall pay twelve pence damages, beside
whatever damage the dogg doth. But if any fish their house lotts and receive
damage by doggs, the owners of those house lotts shall bear the damage
themselves.'

In the Exeter records, I find the following, namely :

'*May* 19*th*, 1644.   It is agreed that all dogs shall be clog'd and side lined in
ye day and tied up in the night and if any dogs shall be found trespassing in
the lots, they that shall find them shall showt them.'

As in these days 'doggs' were very numerous, and fish almost
everywhere were necessary as manure for the corn, similar regulations were undoubtedly made in Newbury and other places, though
the record of such penalties and the intimation of such a custom, if
any were made, are now lost.

At the same meeting it was ordered, that for every wolf killed
with hounds, ten shillings should be paid, 'and if with a trappe or
otherwise five shillings; provided they bring the heads to the meeting house and there nayle them up and give notis thereof to the
constable, whom wee appoynt to write in his books due remembrance
thereof for the clearing of his account to the towne.' †

In the Hampton records of the same year we find a declaration
somewhat similar. 'It is hereby declared that every townsman,
which shall kill a wolf and bring the head thereof and nayle the same
to a little red oake tree at the northeast end of the meeting house,
shall have ten shillings a wolfe for their paynes.'

As early as this year Water street was laid out. This street at

* Winthrop, vol. 2. pp. 184, 185.   † Ipswich records.

that time was between Thomas Milward's fish house, and dwelling-house, which stood near the foot of what is now called Federal street.

' Tristram Coffyn is allowed to keep an ordinary, sell wine, and keep a ferry on Newbury side and George Carr on Salisbury side ' of Carr's island.

' The winter of 1644-5 was very mild, and no snow lay, so as ploughs might go most part of the winter, but on February sixteenth there fell so great a snow in several days as the ways were unpas-sable for three weeks, so as the court of assistants held not ' * their usual session.

1645.

March 4th, 1645. ' There was granted by the towne of Newbury to Daniel Pierce twelve akers of upland which was formerly Mr. Woodman's, which the said Daniel Pierce requested, promising he would remaine with us in Newbury as long as hee liveth unlesse hee should returne to Old England.' †

' By an agreement each family in each colony gave one peck of corn or one shilling to Cambridge college.' ‡

March 5th. This day ' the elders of the churches throughout the united colonies met at Cambridge' to agree upon some answers 'to books written in defence of anabaptism and other errours and for liberty of conscience as a shelter for their toleration and so forth, others in maintenance of the Presbyterial government.' §

September 12th. ' There was granted to William Ballard seven akers and a halfe of land and five rod in the great field beyond the new towne called by the name of dividaut land to enjoy to him and his heirs forever.' †

December 18th, 1645. GRIST MILL NUMBER TWO. A committee of seven men were appointed ' at a publique meeting for to procure a water-mill ‖ for to be built and set up in said towne [of Newbury] to grind theyr corne.' And they agreed to give John Emery and Sam-uel Scullard £20 in merchantable pay, to ' give them ten acres of upland and six acres of meadow' and that the said mill is to be free from all rates for the first seven years and to be a freehold to them and their heirs forever, they on their part agreeing to sett up said mill between Nicholas Holt's point and Edward Woodman's bridge ready for the towne's use to grind the town's grists at or before the twenty-ninth of September, 1646. ‖

December 22d. ' Thomas Colman having taken a farme so that he cannot attend to lay out lotts, John Pemberton was appointed lott layer in his roome and to joyne with Richard Knight and to have fourpence per acre and what they are not paid for the towne is to see them satisfyed for, the legall means being first used to ob-tayne it.' †

* Winthrop, vol. 2, p. 210.   † Town records.   ‡ Winthrop, vol. 2, p. 216.
§ Winthrop, vol. 2, p. 248.   ‖ Proprietors' records, vol. 1, p. 6.

During this year the difficulty commenced between Mr. Parker and the church, concerning church government, and was not finally settled till 1672.

1646.

'At a towne meeting of the eight men, January second, 1646.'

'Wee, whose names are in the margent expressed,* for the settleing the disturbances that yett remayne about the planting and setling the meeting house that all men may cheerfully goe on to improve their lands at the new towne, doe determine that the meeting house shall be placed and sett up at or before, the twentieth of October next in, or upon, a knowle of upland by Abrahams Toppan's barne within a sixe or sixteen rodd of this side of the gate posts, that are sett up in the high way by the said Abraham Toppan's barne.' †

'Edward Rawson contradicente this order.'

This 'knowle of upland,' where the meeting-house stood after its removal, was on the northwest corner of the present burying ground in the first parish. The following petition to the general court, very clearly presents the views of those who were opposed to the removing of the meeting-house, and shows that 'Edward Rawson' was not the only one who 'contradicented this order.'

'To the right worshipfull, the ever honored court, the governor, deputy governor, with the rest of the assistants and deputies now assembled in Boston.'

'The humble petition of us the inhabitants of Newbury.'

'The true sense and feeling of the great distractions and sad grievances among us, which as far as we see) are likely dayly to increase upon to our farther smart, if not utter confusion rather than to amend, have caused us right worshipful with truly mournful hearts, after encountering with many difficulties and using the utmost of means yt we know, to bring our sad complaints to your ears, intreating you that while yet there is a little hope, which may possibly decrease dayly, and so the advantage be lost, you would shew a fatherly affection to us and strike in to save us, if it may be from utter breaking. If you knew our hearts they would speak far more affectionately than our papers, and the sad sighs that are on us (when we consider with ourselves how many thousand miles we are come to enjoy ordinances, and the shadow of a godly government, and to bequeath so much, if we could to our little ones after us, that have adventured their lives with us, yet as things now stand we are likely to miscarry both of our aims) were you sensible of them, could not but move you to the very heart. It is very griefe to us to lay open our case in such manner as it is, lest we too much discover the shame that is amongst us, yet as there hath formerly been some smoke of this fire in some small occasions presented to this court, which hath vanished because the depth hath been not considered, the truth soundly evidenced, nor the just cause of our grief discovered, therefore we are inforced to set down things as they are, and though in some particulars some persons only have been active, yet it hath bin with the well wishes of many, whose eyes have been on them expecting and desiring their good issue. And we alone at this time appear in this complaint, yet the proceedings and carriage of some of their chief affaires are very distasteful to most of the town, though it may be on some other grounds, yet we doubt not but to say that more of us appear in this complaint than can be produced on the other side, a great many expecting what the issue will be, not able any way to help, and so not willing to displease, standing neuter. The foundation of all our troubles is a pretended commission, illegal in itselfe, and

* These names are James Noyes, Edward Woodman, John Cutting, John Lowle, Richard Knight, Henry Short.

† Town records.

as illegally presented, faire pretences to draw men's consent (nothing in the issue answered) at first urged some men in particular, privately drawn by over persuasions of fair speeches, and when all was done, so many never subscribed, whose estates were as much, if not more, than half the towne, without which we doubt not to affirme they had no commission to do any thing as they did. Professions and protestations were made against their proceedings in the beginning, the illegality and hurt of it often urged, other and far better waies of helping the towne's necessity, proposed. Yet they proceed and secretly winding in and intangling most men by some unadvised act or other of their owne seemed at last to be masters of their purpose. The main and very end of the said commission [is] in their own confession utterly impossible to be performed (whereupon we should think the commission voide) the promises and ingagements in the same, impossible to be made good and the very principles which themselves insisted on, without which they pretend no face or colour to do any thing by them in the execution, utterly subverted to the unjust oppression of many. Besides private oppositions (not to speake of all the publicke) one notorious was this. An action was brought to ye court by some of us, and eleven of the jury (as was evident by the frequent verdicts not accepted brought in by them) were for us, and as far as we could discerne half the bench, though all were not present when sentence was given, so a special verdict being accepted the case went against us, though from different grounds in the judges. Appeale was made from the sentence, and sufficient bond put in at the request of those, that managed these affaires, with faithful promise of referring it, and standing to the arbitration of those, that were chosen by us, we surceased to prosecute appeal, yet have often called upon them, also we found ourselves deluded with such a carriage, as our simplicity was not able to reach unto. It were too long and tedious to mention all the particulars, wherein their policy (their whole carriage has been full of it) hath wrought on our simplicity and so left us all at last in misery. To come to the last passages, which stir and set on the great [burden] of our sorrows. Discourse at last was had of taking down ye meeting-house. Those (as well as we can guesse) that paid two parts of three to the building of it, consented not, many strongly opposed it, yet the voices of many, that were then servants, and never paid penny to it, prevailed, down it is taken without any satisfaction given us, and besides what we are forced to pay toward it. The high way in part, that served both town and country and the very places assigned to bury the dead, and where many dead bodys lye are sold away (as wee are informed, though all things are secretly carried) to sett up againe, where both old and new towne judge it unmeete for both, but especially for us of the ould. The present and already seen inconveniences in respect of enjoying the ordinances, which we came so many miles to be partakers of, hath caused us oft to sigh in secret, and forcibly put us on thought to provide for ourselves, and not to betray the blood of our poor innocents, which cannot (or exceeding rarely) be partakers of the ordinary means of salvation, nor we ourselves, but uncomfortably, and with great distractions, which they of the new towne can experience to us by that little they have already felt. Divers propositions wee have made. Att the beginning of these motions we promised the elders both of ym their maintenance (which must needs be to our great charge) if they would engage themselves to abide with us. We were rejected in this. Since we have made several propositions. The towne being continued and stretched out neare five miles, if not upwards, besides the inconveniences of a great river at the old towne, whereby it cannot be imagined that we, ould, feeble men, women and children of all sorts, can possibly many of ym goe above three miles to meeting, besides the necessary occasions in the winter time of attendance of cattell, which will require divers to be neerer, most men having small help but by themselves and ye two ends of ye towne being most populous, wee have therefore desired either first, that one of the elders might be resident with us, though the other be there, the church and maintenance still continuing one, and the same, or secondly that there might be two churches and one elder might be ours, or thirdly, if neither of the former might be obtained, then to let us be a church of ourselves, and let us have their helpe and furtherance to provide an elder for ourselves, all which they know with dutyful expressions and sufficient reasons we have rendered to the church in writing, and wee know not what farther to think to propose, yett we can receive no answer of our desires, and wee suppose they cannot answer otherwise if they deny us these but that wee must live at home and turn ignorant atheists wee and ours, or attend on the ordinances bee our conditions what [they] will with such extraordinary inconveniences, as are not to be borne which wee hope that godly magistrates will not suffer, whose authority is for our good to see the townes and churches builded and not destroyed. Having thus showed our complaints, every particular charge whereof we stand to defend and maintaine, and least wee be overtedious we shall now in a word humbly tender to you the sum of our requests.' [Here the remainder of the sheet on which the petition was written is torn off, and all the names of the signers on the other side of the paper except four, lost with it. It concludes thus :] ' And wee profess and hereby engage ourselves to this honored court that if there should be thought any just cause of complaint against us that wee should have ye better in case these things are granted that wee shall bee ready at any time to be directed and take ye advice of others (in case wee cannot agree ourselves) to come to equal agreement and composition for the promoting of their prosperous estate suitable to our towne, whose good we desire, as well as our owne, whose prosperity we heartily wish, though (as we hope yourselves easily conceive) necessity forces us to seek your favour in our just petition. And wee the rather desire your speciall help in this case because where our whole hope was that in case of extremity ye court might and would help us. Two or three, if not more of their chiefe stike not to say and speake more than by intimation that the court generall hath nothing to do with it nor cannot help us, which, if it were so our sorrows would be multiplied.

> EDMUND GREENLEAFE.
> DANIEL THURSTON.
> STEPHEN KENT.
> JOHN POORE.'

Shortly after this petition was presented, three of the petitioners removed from Newbury. Mr. Greenleaf went to Boston. Stephen Kent moved to Haverhill, Mr. Henry Sewall, senior, moved to Rowley, that he might be near the meeting-house there.

April 8th. ' Mr. Henry Sewall, Mr. Woodman, Henry Lunt, and Archelaus Woodman, were fyned twelve pence apiece, and Steven Kent for their absence from the generall towne meeting, to be gathered within ten dayes. In case the constable bring it not by that time, Anthony Morse is appointed to distreyne on him for all the fynes.' *

At a town meeting of the eight men, ' the time being too short to finish and perfectly record all the grants, which have bin made by the eight men, it is ordered that whatever Mr. Rawson shall record that himself or Richard Knight doth perfectly remember was granted to any inhabitant shall be by all, and is by all, hereby acknowledged to be authentick and legall as any other grant allready recorded, so it be done within these six months.' *

' In the end of June we had a strong hand of God upon us. Upon a suddaine innumerable armies of caterpillars filled the country all over the English plantations, which devoured whole meadows of grasse, Indian corn, and barley. Wheat and rye not much. Much prayer was made about it and fasting and the Lord

---

* Town records.

heard and took them away againe suddenly in all parts of the country to the wonderment of all men.'*

At a general town meeting, the tenth of December, 1646, the town being informed that Mr. Thomas Parker was unwilling to act any longer in any matters concerning the new town and that Mr. Cutting was going to sea, ' did make choyse of Nicholas Noyes and William Titcomb to be added to the rest of the new towne men for six weeks,' † and so forth.

December 16*th*, 1646. ' At a meeting of the eight men, it is ordered that all those that do accept of any lands between the great river and Stephen Dummer's farme shall have it *on this condition that they goe not to divide the church*, or oppose the first order or agreement about the removeing of the towne.' †

' Granted to Aquilla Chase, anno 1646, four acres of land at the new towne for a house lott and six acres of upland for a planting lott where it is to be had, and six acres of marsh where it is to be had, also *on condition that he do go to sea, and do service in the towne with a boat* for foure years.' †

' The six acres of upland ' above granted were laid out to Aquilla Chase ' beyond the new towne.'

In what month of this year these conditional grants were made to Aquilla Chase, or what was the precise service, which he was obligated to perform, the records do not inform us. He, however, removed from Hampton to Newbury this year, and sometime prior to September, as we find in the county records the following presentment:

' *September*, 1646. We present Aquilla Chase and wife, and David Wheeler for gathering pease on the Sabbath day.' For this offence the court orders them to be admonished and their fines remitted. For a more particular account of Aquilla Chase see appendix, E.

September 1*st*. The assembly or synod met at Cambridge, and, having continued but about fourteen days, broke up, and was adjourned to the eighth of June, 1647.‡

' This winter [1646] was one of our mildest. No snow all winter long, nor sharp weather. We never had a bad day to go to the Indians.' §

1 6 4 7 .

' KENT's ISLAND.' This year, February seventh, ' the men deputed to order the affaires and exchanges of the new towne,' granted to Richard Kent, junior, the island, which is still called Kent's island, and is still owned by his descendants. It is thus mentioned in the

---

* Roxbury church records.
† Town records. There is a tradition in the Chase family, that he was the first person, who ever brought a vessel over Newbury bar. He was probably a pilot, and fisherman.
‡ Winthrop, vol. 2, pp. 270, 271.
§ Roxbury church records, written by the reverend John Elliot.

records.   After noticing ' the tenn acres of upland, which the towne
granted him on the island over the little river, and sixty four acres
of marish,' it grants him ' all the rest of the upland and marish on
the island over the little river being one hundred and seventy acres
or thereabouts, being formerly granted to particular persons.'   The
remainder of the island the said Richard Kent, junior, obtained
either by purchase or exchange, either with the town or individuals,
' all which land in the island above mentioned being two hundred
and fifty-eight acres or thereabouts to enjoy to him and his heires
forever,' and so forth. *

April 1st.   ' It was ordered that Mr. [Edward] Woodman should
be moderator of this assembly and appointed to execute the former
order, that so confusion be prevented.' *

This is the first time that mention is made in the records, of a
' moderator,' though such an officer had undoubtedly been chosen
annually from the first settlement of the town.   At the same meeting, the ' selectmen,' ' one grand jury man,' a ' constable,' three ' way-
wardens,' and a ' deputy ' to the general court, were chosen.   This
deputy was Mr. Edward Rawson, who this year was chosen
secretary of state, in room of Mr. Increase Nowell.   The next
town clerk was Mr. John Lowle, who dying June twenty-ninth,
'₂Anthony Somerby was chosen clerk of the writs at Newbury, and
to record births, deaths and marriages in the place of John Lowle
deceased.' †

In May, the following law was passed, namely: ' it is ordered that
when any towne shall increase to the number of one hundred families or householders they shall set up a grammar school and so forth.
And if any town neglect the performance hereof above one year, it
shall pay £5 per annum to the next such school till they shall perform
such order.' †   In May 1671 the fine was increased to £10, and in
1683 to £20.

May 18th.   The town for £3 'granted to John Emery that parcell
of land called the greene, about three akers, being more or lesse,
bounded by the half acre lotts on the west, the hye way on the south
east and his own land on the north, being in a triangle, only the
twenty rods [is] reserved in said land for a burying place as it is
bounded with stakes with a way to it from the east.' *

This ' burying place ' still remains, and is situated east of old town
hill, in land now owned by Mr. Paul Ilsley, and is still called the
' Emery lot.'

This year, in the month of January or February, Mary Johnson
was executed as a witch in Hartford, Connecticut.   This was the
first instance in New England.

May 10th.   ' Upon examination it appeared that there was not
enough corn in the whole country to last two months.' †

June 8th.   The synod again assembled at Cambridge.   In consequence, however, of an epidemical sickness, ' which went through
the country among the Indians and English, French, and Dutch,

---

* Town records.   † Colonial records.

the synod were forced to break up of a sudden,' as 'divers of the members were taken with it.' 'Not a family, nor but few persons, escaped.' *

It was about this time, according to Winthrop, that 'a trade was opened with Barbadoes, and other West India islands,' by which our cattle, provisions, staves, and so forth, were exchanged for 'sugar, cotton, tobacco and indigo,' which 'were a good help to discharge our engagements with England.' *

Of this trade the inhabitants of Newbury soon began to avail themselves, as we shall hereafter see, so that, in the language of Samuel Danforth, in his almanac for 1648,

> 'Heaps of wheat, pork, bisket, beef and beer,
> Masts, pipe-staves, fish should store both far and near,
> Which fetch in wines, cloth, sweets and good tobac-
> O be contented then, ye cannot lack.'

December 26th, 1647. 'Tristram Coffin [senior] is allowed to keep an ordinary, and retayle wine, paying according to order, and also granted liberty to keep a ferry at Newbury side.' † This ferry crossed the Merrimac at Carr's island, George Carr keeping the Salisbury side, and Tristram Coffin, senior, the 'Newbury side.'

1648.

April 27th. 'At a general meeting of the freemen of the towne it was ordered that from henceforth from yeare to yeare the meeting for the choyse of towne officers shall be upon the first Monday in March upon publick warneing.' ‡

'There was granted to Thomas Marvyn two akers of land lying near to the new pond on the back side of Mr. Nicholas Noyes his house lott at the new towne for encouragement to kill wolves, and that he shall endeavor to his utmost to catch them.' ‡

June. 'At this court Margaret Jones of Charlestown was indicted and found guilty of witchcraft and hanged for it.' § This was the first case of that lamentable delusion in Massachusetts, which required the services of an executioner. In Danforth's almanac for this year is the following note set against the fifteenth of June. '*Alice* Jones executed for witchcraft.' Alice should be Margaret.

July 15th. 'The synod met at Cambridge by adjournment.' § 'This synod,' says Mr. Savage, in a note, 'erected the famous Cambridge platform,' which continued so many years, and which was in a great degree occasioned by the change of sentiment respecting church discipline, entertained by the ministers of Newbury, Mr. Parker and Mr. Noyes.

'John Bartlett, constable, was fined forty shillings for not providing measures, and Newbury, presented for want of a sufficient

---

* Winthrop, vol. 2, pp. 308, 309, 310.   † Colonial records.
‡ Town records.   § Winthrop, vol. 2, p. 330.

pound,' and also presented ' for want of a convenient safe way for the new towne to the ferry side.'

' Lieutenant Edmund Greenleaf is allowed to keep an ordinary in Newbury.' †

' It was ordered that Isaac Buswell and George Carr shall have power to call upon Newbury to lay out the country way as far as belongs unto them from the island to Mr. Clark's farme.' *

Clark's farm was near Thurlow's bridge, so called.

This year the 'court desired Mr. Edward Rawson and Mr. [Joseph] Hills to compose the amendments of the book of laws passed and make them as one; one copy to remain in the hands of the committee for the speedy committing them to the press, and the other to remain in the hands of the secretary sealed up till the next court.'

December. Thomas Smith, aged twelve years, fell into a pit on his way to school, and was drowned.'

1649.

' At a generall towne meeting March sixth, 1649, Mr. Edward Rawson was appointed to serve deputy at the next courte of election for this towne and to stay and consumate the affayres of the country according to order for the year following.'

' At a meeting generall of the freemen the sixth of March 1649. ' There was chosen Mr. William Gerrish, John Saunders, Daniel Pierce, Henry Shorte, Richard Knight, Robert Coker, William Titcomb, Archelaus Woodman, and John Merrill, to bee a committee for the towne to view the passages into Plum island and to informe the courte by way of petition concerning the righte the towne hath to the sayd island and to have full power with Mr. Edward Rawson to draw forth a petition and present it to the next general courte.'

' Mr. Edward Rawson, Mr. John Spenser and Mr. Woodman was chosen by the towne to joyne with those men of Ipswich and Rowley, that was appointed to bee a committee about Plum island.' ‡

May 15*th*, 1649. The town of Newbury petition the general court to grant them the whole of Plum island. After declaring their confidence in the ' christian readiness of the court to uphold the meanest member of this jurisdiction from sinking under any pressure,' and so forth, and so forth, they go on to say:

' The substance of our desires is that, if after you have heard and perused what we say, that in right Plum island belongs not to us, yet out of your just favour, it may be granted to us to *relieve our pinching necessities, without which we see no way to continue or subsist.* Our feares were occasioned by a petition which was preferred to the last general court for it. Our apprehensions of our right to it are, first, because for three or four miles together there is no channel betwixt us and it. Second, because at low water we can go dry to it over many places, in most with carts and horses, which we usually doe, being

---

* Salisbury records.   † Colonial records.   ‡ Town records.

necessitated so to doe since our guift to Rowley on the court's request and promise that we should have any thing in the court's power to grant. Thirdly, because the court's order gives all lands to dead low water marke not exceeding one hundred rods, to towns, or persons, where any lands do so border. In many places Plum island is not ten rods, at no place one hundred rods from low water marke.

' Fourth, because we only can improve it without damage to our neigbouring plantations, which none can doe without much damage to your petitioners, *if not to the ruining of both the meadow and corne of your petitioners*, and so forth. The premises considered we hope (and doubt not) this honorable court will see just grounds to answer our request and confirme the island to our towne and we shall always as in duty we are bound pray, and so forth.

THOMAS PARKER.   JAMES NOYES.

PERCIVAL LOWLE.   WILLIAM GERRISH.

JOHN SPENCER.   EDWARD WOODMAN.

JOHN SAUNDERS.   HENRY SHORT.

RICHARD KENT in ye name of ye rest.'

In answer to this petition, the court, October seventeenth, 1649, granted two fifths of the island to Newbury, two fifths to Ipswich, and one fifth to Rowley.

March. ' Anthony Morse was presented for digging a pit and not filling it up seasonably.' In this pit Thomas Smith was drowned.

This year, Pentucket, [now Bradford,] ' ordered that the fence between us and Newbury shall be made sufficient with three rails on penalty of sixpence a rod fine for defect.'

On the tenth of May, 1649, governor Endicott, deputy governor Dudley, with seven of the assistants, bore the following testimony against the wearing of long hair. It is inserted as a curiosity.

' Forasmuch as the wearing of long hair after the manner of ruffians and barbarous Indians, has begun to invade New England, contrary to the rule of God's word, which says it is a shame for a man to wear long hair, as also the commendable custom generally of all the godly of our nation, until within these few years.

' We the magistrates, who have subscribed this paper (for the shewing of our own innocency in this behalf) do declare and manifest our dislike and detestation against the wearing of such long hair, as against a thing uncivil and unmanly, whereby men doe deforme themselves and offend sober and modest men, and doe corrupt good manners. We doe therefore earnestly entreat all the elders of this jurisdiction (as often as they shall see cause to manifest their zeal against it in their publike administrations) to take care that the members of their respective churches be not defiled therewith ; that so such as shall prove obstinate and will not reforme themselves, may have God and man to witness against them.'

In the Roxbury church records, and in the hand writing of the venerable John Elliott, I find the following. It is the seventh ' proposition about apparel and fashions.'

' 7. Locks and long haire (now in England called rattle heads and opposite to christians, who wear short haire all of a lengthe and therefore called round heads) is an offence to many godly christians, and therefore be it known to such, they walk offensively.'

The first tanner in Newbury, of whom we have any account, was Mr. Nicholas Easton, who was afterward governor of Rhode Island. He is called by Winthrop, 'one Easton, a tanner.' The remains of an old tan-yard are still visible, on land once owned by him, and which some years after came into possession of Mr. Richard Dole, who, as we learn from his will, carried on, among his other occupations, the business of tanning. The site of the yard, which is still owned by his descendants, is a few rods north from Parker river bridge, and a few rods east from the main road leading to the bridge. John Bartlett was also a tanner. His place of business was a short distance from the banks of the Merrimac, near the road leading to Amesbury ferry. In what year he commenced the business, it is impossible to say. Descendants of the same name are still engaged in the same business, on the same spot.

On the nineteenth of April, this year, the 'freemen' granted to Job Clements, from Haverhill, a freehold 'conditionally yt he live with us heere in Newbury exercising his trade four years or as long as he shall live within that tearme and also let the shoemakers of this towne have the first proffer or the forsaking of his leather, making him as good pay as others.' *

This attempt to secure the services of Job Clement, as tanner, failed, he 'not performing the conditions above specifyed.'

September. Newbury was presented for want of a pound, and their constable presented for not providing weights and measures according to order of court, but afterward the fine was remitted. †

' Newbury was presented for want of a sufficient pound and is to pay forty shillings, unless it is completed by the first of May next.' †

The following curious sentence of the court, on a citizen of Ipswich, is found on the county records.

' Thomas Scott upon his presentment is fyned ten shillings unless he learn Mr. Norton's chatachise by next court.'

The records of the court do not state the nature of the offence, which induced the court to inflict the 'chatachise' on the offending brother, or its value in money. It appears, however, that he chose rather to lose the money than to take the 'chatachise,' as the records of the 'next court' inform us, that ' Thomas Scott not appearing to make known that he hath learned Mr. Norton's chatachise his fyne is to be taken.'

In September, ' there was a general visitation by the small-pox.' ‡

1650.

The first notice we have, on the town records, of any Indians living in Newbury, is in January, 1644, where lot sixty-one in the new town is granted to ' John, Indian.' The next is in April sixteenth of this year, where the town, through their selectmen, William Ger-

---

* Town records.   † County records.   ‡ Roxbury church records.

rish, Abraham Toppan, and Anthony Somerby, purchase a tract of land of ' Great Tom, Indian.' It commences thus :

' Witness by these presents that I, Great Tom, Indian, for and in consideration of three pounds in hand paid by, and received of, the townsmen of Newbury, have given, granted, covenanted and fully bargained, and for and by these presents do give, grant, convey, confirme, bargain and sell all that my th*** acres of planting land as it is fenced in one entire fence in Newbury *lying neere Indian hill* with all my right, title and interest in all the woods, commons and lands that I have in the township of Newbury to have and to hold, and so forth, and so forth. In witness whereof I, the said Great Tom, Indian, have set to my hand and seale April sixteenth, 1650.

The mark ⋈ of
GREAT TOM, INDIAN.'

November 20*th.* The town ' granted to John Poore twenty-two acres of upland,' in consequence of 'his being so remote from meeting and difficulty in coming over the ferry and for his satisfaction.'

September 7*th.* Mr. John Spencer, nephew of Mr. John Spencer, deceased, sold to Henry Sewall, the mill lot, being fifty acres of upland and ten acres of meadow, for sixteen pounds sterling.

In this year, December nineteenth, ' the townsmen at a meeting ' voted to pay out of the ' towne rate one shilling for every dozen of black birds, two shillings for every dozen of wood-peckers' and jays' heads, and three shillings for every dozen of crowes, and so proportionable for any lesser number.'

' John Tillotson was presented for scandalous and reproachful speeches cast on the elders and others in a publick church meeting on a Lord's day.' *

' Henry Somerby was licensed to keep an ordinary instead of Mr. Greenleaf.' *

' John Perry of Newbury is ordered to sit in the stocks one house enxt lecture day for abusive carriage to his wife and child.' *

' John Tillotson on his many offences is fined twenty pounds, bound to his good behaviour, and fined twenty-seven pounds for killing a mare belonging to Mr. James Noyes.' *

In an old manuscript, once owned by the reverend James Noyes, and now by one of his descendants, Mr. Silas Noyes, is an account of the testimony taken in the case of John Tillotson, and some of ' his many offences,' which induced the court to lay so heavy a fine on him. The evidence concludes by saying: ' at last he killed our elder's mare, great with foal, and a special good beast she was, provoked with her at ye instant, he killed her with a long pike, thrust through both her sides,' and so forth, and so forth, and ' the morning after this transaction he made a deed to convay all his estate away from himselfe offering it to goodman ***** whereby our elder would have been wholly defrauded of his mare.'

* County records.

1651.

From Johnson's Wonder-working Providence, published this year, I make the following extract:

'This town [Newbury] is situated about twelve miles from Ipswitch, neere upon the wide venting streams of Merrimack river, whose strong current is such that it hath forced its passage through the mighty rocks, which causeth some sudden falls and hinders shipping from having any accesse far into the land. This towne is stored with meadows and upland. Their houses are built very scattering, which hath caused some contention about removal of their place for sabbath assemblies. It consists of about seventy families. The soules in church fellowship are about an hundred. The teaching elders in this place have carried it very lovingly toward their people, *permitting them to assist in admitting of persons into church society, and in church censures, so long as they act regularly, but in case of maladministration they assume the power wholly to themselves.*'

The preceding lines of Johnson very well express the principles of church discipline, held by Messrs. Parker and Noyes, and which occasioned the long and bitter controversy, which was not finally settled till a short time before the death of Mr. Parker in 1677. A majority of the church demanded as a right, what Messrs. Parker and Noyes, in the language of Johnson, 'lovingly permitted' as a favor, and believing that the church in its corporate capacity had a right, and were therefore under a sacred obligation, to manage its own affairs, they contended most strenuously, and with untiring pertinacity, against their 'elders' assuming,' under any pretext, 'the power wholly to themselves.' Full proof of this will be hereafter exhibited.

In consequence of 'divers complaints, having been made from time to time of disorder in the meeting house,' and believing that 'the abuses in the youth cannot be so easily reformed, unlesse every house-holder knows his seat in the meeting-house,' the selectmen, the twenty-fourth of January, 1651, 'hereby order that every house-holder both men and women shall sit in those seats, that are appointed for them during their lives, and not to presse into seats where they are full already.' They also declare that they 'have drawne a list of the names of the inhabitants and appointed them their places in the meeting-house and have set their names in each particular seat where they shall sit and the young men are appointed to sit in the four backer seats in the gallery and in the two lower seats at the west door.'

This was called 'seating the meeting-house,' and occasioned, as will be hereafter seen, much difficulty. At this time pews were not known. The foregoing extract was taken from the quarterly court files in Salem. It was a copy from the 'towne booke,' which cannot now be found.

As a specimen of some of the cases tried at Salem court, I give the following testimony. 'T—— —— junior of Newbury came to goodman Sanders' barne and with a great swingell did strike William Richerson athurt the bake and so run away.' *

The town granted to Richard Pettingell, fourteen acres of marsh, in consideration of his 'yielding up into the towne's hands a way 'four rods wide through his land.' † That way is now Green street, formerly called Rolfe's lane.

March 5th. Henry Short, agent for Mr. Stephen Dummer, sold to Thomas Brown and George Little, his 'farm at the Birchen meadows containing three hundred acres for twenty-one pounds.'

October 14th. The court made another abortive attempt to regulate the fashions of the people, to prescribe what certain classes of persons should not wear, and what exceptions ought to be made to the general rule. They declare that 'intolerable excesse and bravery hath crept in upon us and especially among people of mean condition and their utter detestation and dislike that men of mean conditions and callings should take upon them the garb of gentlemen by wearing gold or silver lace, or buttons, or points at their knees, to walk in great boots, or women of the same ranke, to wear silk or tiffany hoods or scarfs, which though allowable to persons of greater estates, or more liberal education, they judge it intolerable in persons of such like condition.'

They then order, that, with the exception of 'magistrates or any publick officer of this jurisdiction, *their* wives and children, military officers or soldiers, or any other, whose education or employment have been above the ordinary degree, or whose estates have been considerable, though now decayed, or who were not worth two hundred pounds, no person should trangress this law under penalty of ten shillings.'

1652.

On the court records at Salem, I find the following:

'This is to certify whom it may concern that we the subscribers being called upon to testify against [doctor] William Snelling for words by him uttered, affirm that being in way of merry discourse, a health being drank to all friends, he answered

> I'll pledge my friends,
> And for my foes,
> A plague for their heels,
> And a poxe for their toes.'

'Since when he hath affirmed that he only intended the proverb used in the west country, nor do we believe he intended otherwise.'

WILLIAM THOMAS,
THOMAS MILWARD.

'*March* 12, 1651-2. All which I acknowledge, and I am sorry I did not expresse my intent, or that I was so weak as to use so foolish a proverb.' *

GULIELMUS SNELLING.

So great, however, was the enormity of the doctor's offence, that neither explanation, nor apology, was of any avail, as the record

---

* County records. † Town records.

informs us that ' William Snelling in his presentment for *cursing* is fined ten shillings and the fees of court.' *

After this specimen of their abhorrence of profanity, we have a right to presume that doctor Snelling was especially careful of what he said concerning his neighbors' heels or toes.

This year a mint was established at Boston, for coining shillings, sixpences, and threepences. The pieces at first, had N. E. on one side, and XII. VI. or III. on the other. It was afterward ordered, that all pieces should have a double ring, with the word MASSA-CHUSETTS, and a tree in the centre, on one side, and NEW ENGLAND and 1652 on the other. The same date was continued for thirty years after. ' The mint master was John Hull, who raised a large fortune from it,' his perquisites being fifteen pence for every twenty shillings coined. Judge Samuel Sewall married his only daughter, and, it is said, received with her thirty thousand pounds in New England shillings.

This year, Hugh Parsons, of Springfield, was tried for witchcraft, but the jury and the magistrates not agreeing, the general court acquitted him.†

This year a prison was built in Ipswich, being the second in the Massachusetts colony.

' Stephen Kent formerly of Newbury was fined ten pounds for suffering five Indians to be drunk in his house in Haverhill and one wounded, shall pay the fine and satisfy for the cure of the wounded Indian.'

We present ' Elizabeth Randall of Nuberrie for useing reproachful language unto goody Silver base lieing divell, base lieing tode, base lying sow, base lying iade.' *

In December, ' there appeared a comet in Orion, which continued its course toward the zenith for the space of a fortnight *till* [*the reverend*] *Mr. Cotton died.*' ‡

It is thus mentioned in the records of the first church in Boston : ' December ninth, a large star with a long blaze appeared. It grew less and less till the twenty-second, when it disappeared.' The reverend John Cotton died the twenty-third of December.

November 29th, 1652. ' There was voted by the major part of the towne that there should be a convenient house built for a schoole.'

' There was also voted that there should be twenty pounds a yeare allowed for to maintaine a school master out of the towne rate.

' There was also voted that Mr. Woodman, Richard Kent, junior, lieutenant Pike and Nicholas Noyes should be a committee for the managing the business of the schoole.' §

These votes, with the exception of the grant of ten acres of land to Anthony Somerby in 1639, ' for his encouragement to keep

* County records.
‡ Roxbury church records.
† Hutchinson.
§ Town records.

schoole for one year,' contain the first notice on record of the town's intention to build a school-house and to support a master at their expense. This was, doubtless, in obedience to the law passed by the state in May, 1647, as may be seen in Ancient Charters, page 186, though a school had for many years been taught in the meeting house.

The following extract from the first section of the act of May, 1647, is worthy of perpetual remembrance, and is therefore here inserted.

'It being one chief project of Satan to keep men from the knowledge of the scripture, as in former times keeping them in unknown tongues, so in these latter times persuading from the use of tongues, so that at least the true sense and meaning of the original might be clouded and corrupted with false glosses of deceivers ; to the end that learning may not be buried in the graves of our forefathers, in church and commonwealth the Lord assisting our endeavours, it is therefore ordered,' and so forth.

1653.

'At a general meeting of the towne, the fourteenth of May, 1653, there was ordered that the towne should by an equal proportion according to men's estate by way of rate pay twenty-four pounds by the yeare to maintaine a free schoole to be kept at the meeting house, and the master is to teach all such inhabitants' children, as shall be sent to him so soon as they know their letters and begin to read.' *

Against the establishment of such a school, seventeen persons 'desired to have their dissents recorded,' all of whom, it appears, resided so far from the meeting-house that their children could not conveniently attend the school. They were therefore unwilling to be taxed to support an institution, which, however advantageous to the whole town, was not directly beneficial to them.

September. 'Tristram Coffyn's wife Dionis was presented for selling beer,' at his ordinary in Newbury, 'for three pence a quart.' Having proved 'upon the testimony of Samuel Moores, that she put six bushels of malt into the hogshead she was discharged.' †

The law, which she was supposed to have violated, was passed in 1645, and is as follows, namely :

'Every person licensed to keep an ordinary, shall always be provided with good wholesome beer of four bushels of malt to the hogshead, which he shall not sell *above* two pence the ale quart on penalty of forty shillings the first offence and for the second offence shall lose his license.'

Goodwife Coffyn probably reasoned thus :

'As four is to two, so is six to three. I'll have better beer than my neighbours and be paid for it. A fig for the law.'

Other presentments for violations of the law of more consequence

* Town records.   † County records.

8

than selling beer were multiplied. Many of these were for not regarding the sumptuary law of 1651.

For instance, ' Nicholas Noyes' wife, Hugh March's wife, and William Chandler's wife were each presented for wearing a silk hood and scarfe,' but were discharged on proof that their husbands were worth two hundred pounds each. John Hutchins' wife was also discharged ' upon testimony of her being brought up above the ordinary ranke.'

Joseph Swett's wife for the same offence was fined ten shillings. Agnes, the wife of deacon Richard Knight, was also presented. This troubled the good deacon exceedingly, and induced him to solicit Mr. Rawson to send the following letter to one of the magistrates at Salem.

'HONORABLE SIR,
         An honest godly man, a friend of mine in Newbury, whose name is Richard Knight, whether of ignorance or wilfulness by some neighbour is presented for his wife's wearing of a silk hood, supposing he has not been worth two hundred pounds. It being a grievance to him, who is advanced [in years] to be summoned to a court, that never useth to trouble any, at his request I thought fit to inform you on my owne knowledge his estate is better worth than three hundred, and therefore I desire you would, as you may, forbeare, in your warrant to insert his name in it, it may be ; if not, at least that you would take private satisfaction of him in your chamber, which he can easily give you, or any, in a moment. Not else at present but my service to you and Mr. Symon Bradstreet.

                   Your friend and servant,

                                      EDWARD RAWSON.
Now at Newbury, the fourteenth of August, 1653.'

' This letter, as it will be seen, was of no avail, though the woman was acquitted.'

This year, the road was laid out from Andover to Newbury, 'leaving Rowley way at the beginning of a plain by a little swamp called Barberry swamp, thence the old way to Falls river, thence over the head of Cart creek, thence to Hull's bridge over Hull's plain to the mill bridge,' and so forth.

This year Newbury gave fifteen pounds to Harvard college.

September 7th. ' The court, on hearing that lieutenant Robert Pike declared that ' such persons as did act in making that law restraining unfit persons from constant preaching did break their oath to the country, for, said he, it is against the liberty of the country, both civil and ecclesiastical,' declared that he had been guilty of defaming the general court, and order that he shall be disfranchised, disabled from holding any publick office, bound to his good behaviour, and fined twenty marks,' equal to thirteen pounds, six shillings, and eight-pence.

The law alluded to above was made to restrain Joseph Peasley and Thomas Macy, formerly of Newbury, then of Salisbury, new town, from exhorting the people on the sabbath in the absence of a minister. This order had no effect on Joseph Peasley, who still continued his preaching in defiance of the law, as we find, in the year 1659.

The punishment inflicted on lieutenant Pike caused a great sensation in the neighboring towns. Petitions were presented to the general court, containing the names of nearly all the citizens of Newbury, Andover, Hampton, Salisbury, and so forth, earnestly entreating the magistrates to remit the punishment and the fine imposed on lieutenant Pike. The whole case is a very instructive one. It exhibits, on the one hand, the watchful jealousy of the people, in consequence of any supposed or real incroachments on their civil or ecclesiastical rights, and on the other hand the determination of the magistrates not to have their authority lightly called in question.

They immediately chose a committee to call the petitioners of the several towns together, ascertain their reasons for signing the petition, and make return. This was done in 1654, and eight Newbury men were bound to their good behavior in a bond of ten pounds each for signing the petition, the remainder having acknowledged their offence.

October 29*th.* There was a small shock of an earthquake.

1654.

Kent's island, with sixteen cows and four oxen on it, was let this year, for seven years, by Richard Kent, to Launcelot Granger, for forty-six pounds a year.

' On the ninth of June this year there was a storme of thunder and haile, such as hath not been heard of in New England since the first planting thereof, which haile fell in the bounds of Hampton, the haile being to admiration for the multitude thereof, so that in some places it remained after the storm was over twelve inches in thickness and was not all dissolved in two days, many of which haile were said to be three or four inches in length.'*

September 21*st.* ' Liberty was granted to the inhabitants of the ' old towne' to make a fence and hang a gate acrosse the way about Anthony Short's or John Knight's provided they hinder not the cattell from going into the commons there.' †

Many such fences and gates were erected in various parts of the town. There were two on the south side of ' the river Parker,' one, a few rods north of the present first parish meeting-house, another, on the ' four rod way' south of Turkey hill, and in many other places. At this time, and for many years after, travelers, who usually went on horseback, were obliged every few miles to dismount and open a gate, which the town ordered to be made to open and shut ' flippantly.'

' John Emery was chosen to answer at the next court at Ipswich concerning the presentment about the way to Andover.' †

The selectmen were ordered to examine and require ' an account of the money or goods, that hath been gathered to purchase a bell, in whose hands it is, and to make report to the towne.' †

* Hampton records. † Town records.

The bell, we have reason to suppose, was obtained about this time, as we find in December, 1665, that Anthony Morse was chosen ' to keep the meeting-house and *ring the bell.*'

This year the general court declare that ' Richard Thorlay having built a bridge over Newbury river, at his owne cost hath liberty to take toll for cattle, sheep, and so forth, so long as he shall maintain and repair the same, passengers free.'

1655.

April 25th. ' The towne granted to captain Paul White a parcell of land, not exceeding half an acre, about Watts his cellar * for to make a dock, a wharf, and a warehouse, provided he do build a dock, and warehouse as aforesaid; but the town granteth no liberty of freehold or commonage hereby and if he shall hereafter sell it, when he hath built upon it, the town shall have the forsaking of it.' †

This is the first record of a grant to any person, for permission to build a wharf, and so forth, on the Merrimack. The grantee, captain Paul White, was a merchant, who had been engaged in trade for some years at Pemaquid, now Bristol, Maine, and had been in Newbury about two years.

May 25th, 1655. Joseph Swett petitions the honorable court to confirm to him the grant of ' Deer island, which the selectmen of Newbury have granted him, which is not above six acres of land, and is not above six or eight rods from Newbury shore,' and so forth.

This year, in July, an epidemical disease, like that in 1647, pervaded New England, ' whereof many died.'

June. George Carr made ' a floating bridge five feet wide with rails on each side,' from his island to Salisbury shore. ' The floate bridge,' says George Carr, ' is above two hundred and seventy feet long with ye faule.'

The people of Hampton, New Hampshire, proposed to join with Rowley, in petitioning the general court for a country way, from Carr's ferry to [doctor] Clark's farm, [near Thurrill's bridge,] and so ' as direct from thence as may be to Rowley line.' ‡

1656.

May 7th. On this day, ' the half acre of land,' granted last year to captain Paul White, was laid out ' at the end of Fish street [now State street] joyneing to Merrimack river on the northwest, and from the river by the great rocks upon a strait lyne to a stake by the way,

---

* ' Watts his cellar,' which is frequently mentioned in the town records, and in deeds of land, was on, or just below, the spot where the market-house in Newburyport now stands. This Watts was, undoubtedly, the first person who dug a cellar within the limits of ' ould Newberry.' He was probably engaged in fishing and trading with the Indians.

† Town records.   ‡ Hampton records.

and from that stake to another stake westerly by another great rocke,* and from a stake running over part of the rock upon a straight lyne westward to another stake by the dock.' †

With the conditions of the grant he complied, and built a wharf, warehouse, and 'stillhouse,' and made a dock. He was extensively engaged in business till his death, July twentieth, 1679.

In June, of this year, Mrs. Ann Hibbens was executed in Boston, for the supposed crime of witchcraft. 'This,' says Hutchinson, 'was the second instance on record of any person's being executed for witchcraft in New England. Her husband, who died 1654, had been a magistrate, and a merchant of note.'

'Mr. Noise, the blessed light at Newbury died.' ‡ This was the reverend James Noyes, who died October twenty-second, 1656. He had been teacher of the church in Newbury from its first formation.

1 6 5 7.

In the month of March, died, in Rowley, Mr. Henry Sewall, whose only son Henry, was one of the first settlers of Newbury. He came to Newbury soon after his father, and after the removal of the meeting-house from the lower green, to the place where it now stands, in 1646, he crossed the river to Rowley, and there resided through the remainder of his earthly pilgrimage. During the latter part of his life, he is said to have been occasionally a little deranged. This was probably the cause of his being two or three times presented by the grand jury for various offences. The first instance was in December, 1650. The testimony was as follows, namely:

'Mr. Showell was walking in the foremost seat in the meeting-house neare the pulpit and Mr. Rogers being present and ready to step into the place to begin prayer, said, Mr. Showell, cease your walking. Mr. S. answered, you should have come sooner, with more words to that purpose, but he not ceasing his walking, presently our pastour added these words, remember where you are, this is the house of God, to which Mr. S. answered with a lowd voyce I know how to behave in the house of God as well as you. Then our pastour said rather than that he disturb the congregation, putt him out, to which Mr. S. replyed, lett us see who dare. After this a brother spake unto Mr. Showell in a friendly way, but Mr. S. with a stearne countenance and threatning manner saide he would take a course with some of us and in many other wordes we doe not now remember. Upon another Lord's day Mr. S. was walking, a part of the congregation being assembled, Mr. S. did exclaim thus with an audible voyce, looking up, good Lord, this day is spent I know not how, and nothing is yet done, expressing some trouble in other words.'

October. General court ordered, that 'the penalty for entertaining quakers should be forty shillings.'

---

* 'The great rocke,' mentioned in the grant, stood where Mr. George Granger's store now stands, and was at least twenty feet high.
† Town records.
‡ Roxbury church records.

1658.

This year, it appears, incidentally, that the town contemplated building a new meeting-house, as a committee were appointed to sell Edward Woodman twelve acres of marsh, for which he 'engages to pay either in boards or nayles or both for the meeting-house.' *

At what time, precisely, the 'new meeting-house' was built, no record informs us. It was, however, erected prior to 1661, as will be seen under that year.

'Newbury upon their presentment for want of a lattin scoole is to pay five pounds to Ipswich lattin scool, unles they by the next court provyde a lattin scoole master according to law.' †

This year, in May and October, there was great difficulty among the military companies of Newbury, which was finally settled by the general court, who ordered four persons 'to be severally admonished and pay the several charges of their neighbours the last court, namely, four pounds, eight shillings.'

In this year, Salem paid fifty-three pounds, Ipswich seventy-two pounds, and Newbury thirty-four pounds, of the province rate.

1659.

'William Trotter for slanderous speeches, to make publick acknowledgement next lecture day.' †

October. Sixteen inhabitants of Newbury, and six of Dover, petition the general court to grant them 'a tract of twelve miles square,' in a 'place called Pennecooke,' and 'crave the liberty of three years to give in their resolution,' and, in case they determine to settle 'a plantation soe far remote,' 'to have ye grant of their freedom from publique charge for ye space of seven years,' and so forth. The court granted them eight miles square, on certain conditions, with which they did not comply. 'Pennecooke,' now Concord, was not settled till 1730, though the first white family moved there in 1727.

'April thirtieth, old style, there was a great storme of snowe, which lay three or four inches thick upon May-day in the morning.'‡

This year several persons were prosecuted and fined for violating the law of 1657, which prohibited 'entertaining quakers.' Among them was Thomas Macy, one of the first settlers of Newbury, but at this time a resident in Salisbury. Complaint having been made against him, he was summoned to appear before the general court, to answer the charges preferred against him. Instead of complying with the requisition, he sent a letter, of which the following is a copy.

---

* Proprietors' records.   † County records.   ‡ Hampton records.

' This is to entreat the honored court not to be offended because of my non-appearance. It is not from any slighting the authority of this honored court, nor from feare to answer the case, but I have bin for some weeks past very ill, and am so at present, and notwithstanding my illness, yet I, desirous to appear, have done my utmost endeavour to hire a horse, but cannot procure one at present. I being at present destitute have endeavoured to purchase, but at present cannot attaine it, but I shall relate the truth of the case as my answer should be to ye honored court, and more cannot be proved, nor so much. On a rainy morning there came to my house Edward Wharton and three men more; the said Wharton spoke to me saying that they were traveling eastward, and desired me to direct them in the way to Hampton, and asked me how far it was to Casco bay. I never saw any of ye men afore except Wharton, neither did I require their names, or who they were, but by their carriage I thought they might be quakers and told them so, and therefore desired them to passe on their way, saying to them I might possibly give offence in entertaining them, and as soone as the violence of the rain ceased (for it rained very hard) they went away, and I never saw them since. The time that they stayed in the house was about three quarters of an hour, but I can safely affirme it was not an houre. They spake not many words in the time, neither was I at leisure to talke with them for I came home wet to ye skin immediately afore they came to the house, and I found my wife sick in bed. If this satisfie not the honored court, I shall subject to their sentence : I have not willingly offended. I am ready to serve and obey you in the Lord.'

THO. MACY.*

Notwithstanding this explanation and apology, he was fined thirty shillings, and was ordered to be admonished by the governor, for ' entertaining quakers,' two of whom, William Robinson and Marmaduke Stephenson, were hung in Boston, December twenty-seventh, 1659.

Tradition informs us, that Thomas Macy, immediately after his sentence, took an open boat, and with his wife and children, went to Nantucket, was one of the first English settlers in that island, and there resided the remainder of his life. An amusing ballad, founded on the above-mentioned incidents, was written by the poet J. G. Whittier, and published some years ago in a Philadelphia annual. See appendix.

1660.

March 16th, old style. There was a very severe ' storm of driving snow, which drove up in drifts four feet deep.' †

The winter of 1659-60 was ' a very hard winter.' †

This year the county court ' order a road from Rowley to Newbury by Richard Thurrell's bridge.'

In September, a return was made of the road, which was laid out from the north end of Rowley to Thorla's bridge, and so on through the farms of Edmund Moore's and Robert Adams, then to Trotter's bridge, then to the meeting house of Newbury as Andover way is laid out.' ‡

This year the general court granted to several inhabitants of Newbury, on their petition, a tract of land on Saco river, ' provided they have twenty families and a minister settled within four years.'

---

* General court files.   † Hampton records.   ‡ County records.

1661.

January 28*th.* The selectmen agreed with Henry Jaques to 'build a gallery in the new meeting house at both ends and all along on the west side with three substantiall seats all along both sides and ends, the said Henry Jaques shall fell the timber and provide all the stuff both planks, boards, rayles, and juyces and nayles and to bring the stuff all in place and make for it three payre of stayres and whatever else is requisite to compleate the said gallery, for which he is to have 'thirty pounds in good current pay or provisions.' Also the said Henry Jaques shall have all the old stuffe of the old gallery in the old meeting house. The said Henry Jaques is also to lay a floore all over the meeting house from beame to beame and the towne doth engage to provide juyces, boards and nayles,' and so forth, and so forth.

From this it is evident that both houses were standing at the same time. The old house stood north of the new one.

June 22*d.* The selectmen discharged the lot layers, 'as there is no more land to be granted by the towne.'

The same month, ' the meeting house was seated,' as it was called. Every man and woman had his or her seat designated, the men and women in separate seats. The galleries were, as now, on the north, west, and south sides of the house, and were then considered as the most desirable parts of the house. In the foreseat of the west gallery, were thirteen men, ' which,' say the selectmen, 'are as many as can comfortably set in it, and no more may be imposed or intruded into it.'

September 23*d.* Plum island was divided, to 'every one his just right,' ' beginning at the upland neere Merrimack barre and so extending to Sandy beach.'

September 25*th.* Another division was made, ' beginning at Rowley bounds and reaching to Sandy beach.'

March 9*th.* General court repeal the laws against quakers.

Charles second proclaimed king, the eighth of August.

The following singular order is found in the Hampton records. It is a curious illustration of the state of society at that period.

May 16*th,* 1661. ' It is ordered yt if any person shall discharge a gunn in the meeting house, or any other house without leave of the owner or house holder, hee or they shall forfeit five shillings for every such offence nor shall any person ride or lead a horse into the meeting house under the like penalty.'

1662.

This year another physician, doctor Henry Greenland, with his wife Mary, came to Newbury. He appears to have to have been a man of good education, but passionate, unprincipled, and grossly immoral. He of course soon became involved in difficulties with his neighbors, and caused great excitement among the sober citizens of the town, who had not been accustomed to such specimens of immorality, as he had displayed before them.

'It pleased the Lord,' says the apostle Elliot, 'to exercise the country with a very severe drought, which some were so rash as to impute to the sitting of the synod, but the Lord was pleased to bear witness against their rashness, for no sooner was the synod met, June tenth, but they agreed to set the next day apart to seek his favorable presence, and to ask raine, and ye day following the Lord sent showers from heaven, and visited the land with seasonable showers of rain, week after week until the harvest.' *

March 3d. 'The marsh lands in the neck over the great river were divided as the lands were in Plum island, beginning at the west end.' †

This year the highway from Newbury to Haverhill was laid out.

'John Atkinson [hatter] had half an acre of land by the spring near Anthony Morse, junior's, house.' †

Newbury was fined ten pounds for not sending a deputy to general court. It was afterward remitted.

Captain Paul White was licensed by general court 'to still strong waters for a yeare and sell by the quart.' ‡

The county court ordered the road by Thorla's bridge, to be made passable by the twelfth of October, 1662, under penalty of ten pounds.

On the twenty-ninth of March, an event occurred in Ipswich, which caused great excitement in Essex county. On that day, one J. P. was incarcerated in Ipswich, and ' did that night break prison,' 'it being,' as the record informs us, ' the first offence of this nature committed in this country.'

The jailer, Theophilus Wilson, deposes, that, on that day, 'he, according to order of court, put him into prison, and lockt the dore fast, and *put the hasp on to the staple on the outsyde of the dore, which none within can unhasp,* and left no tooles or means of light in the prison.' ‡

It was afterward discovered that some of J. P.'s neighbors, not liking his confinement, went to Ipswich in the night, '*unhasped the dore on the outsyde,*' and so forth, and let him return home.

In the quarterly court, records, I find the following:

' We, James Ordway, John Woolcot, Peter Godfrey and Joshua Woodman, do acknowledge that we are justly to be blamed to come into the seats of other men contrary to the order of the selectmen and here by the presents we do engage ourselves that we will keep to our own seats and not disturb any man in their seats any more.' ' This engagement was unto the selectmen the sixth of June 1662.'

The cause of their offence was an apprehension that the selectmen had, without sufficient authority from the town, built some new seats in the gallery and assigned them to some individuals. They

---

* Roxbury church records.   † Town records.   ‡ General court records.

therefore took possession of these seats, to which the selectmen had not given them any right. Hence there was a contention in the meeting-house, a summons for them to appear at court, and a settlement by their promise to behave better in time to come.

'The winter was very moderate. No frost in the ground till the twentieth of December.' *

1663.

'*January* 26*th.* There was an earthquake, at the shutting in of the evening,' one of the greatest in New England, and on February fifth, another. The first shock continued above half an hour. On the same day, at evening, another, and did not cease till July following.

On the records of the court at Salem, I find the following, namely :

'*May* 5*th*, 1663. Lydia Wardwell on her presentment for coming naked into Newbury meeting house. The sentence of the court is, that she shall be severely whipt and pay the costs and fees to the marshall of Hampton for bringing her. Costs, ten shillings, fees two shillings and sixpence.

The maiden name of the person, who was induced to make such an exhibition in Newbury meeting-house, in the time of worship, was Lydia Perkins, but at this time the wife of Eliakim Wardwell of Hampton. The story is thus told by George Bishop, in his 'New England Judged.' It is proper to state, that, so far as I know, he is, with one exception, the only writer, who attempts to justify conduct so strange and fanatical.

'His wife Lydia, being a young and tender chaste woman, seeing the wickedness of your priests and rulers to her husband, was not at all offended with the truth, but as your wickedness abounded, so she withdrew and separated from your church at Newbury, of which she was sometimes a member, and *being given up to the leading of the Lord,* after she had been often sent for to come thither, to give a reason of such a separation, it being at length upon her in the consideration of their miserable condition, who were thus blinded with ignorance and persecution, to go to them, and as a sign to them she went in (though it was exceeding hard to her modest and shamefaced disposition,) naked amongst them, which put them into such a rage, instead of consideration, they soon laid hands on her, and to the next court at Ipswich had her, where without law they condemned her to be tyed to the fence-post of the tavern where they sat — and there sorely lashed her with twenty or thirty cruel stripes. And this is the discipline of the church of Newbury in New England, and this is their religion, and their usage of the handmaid of the Lord, who in a great cross to her natural temper, came thus among them, a sign indeed, significatory enough to them, and suitable to their state, who under the visor of religion, were thus blinded into cruel persecution.'

In the same year I find the following, namely :

'Elizabeth Webster for taking a faulse oath. The sentence of the court is that she shall stand at the meeting house dore at Newbury the next lecture day

* Hampton records.

from the ringing the first bell, until the minister be ready to begin prayer with a paper on her head, written in capitall letters, (FOR TAKING A FALSE OATH IN COURT,) the constable to see it done, or else to paye a fine of five pounds to the treasurer, and to be disabled from taking an oath, and to pay cost and fees.' ' She made choice to stand at the doore.' *

At the same court, ' John Emery was fined four pounds for enter-taining quakers.'

His offence consisted in granting food and lodging to two men and two women, who were traveling farther east. One of the witnesses ' testified that he [John Emery] took them by the hand and bid them welcome.' I shall make no comments on these extracts, nor any apology for inserting them. The duty of an historian is to *find* facts, and not to *make* them. An accurate picture of the sun should exhibit its spots as well as its brightness. To veil the one, or omit the other, would be a caricature, and not a likeness, and, should the features I have attempted to delineate, here or elsewhere, be deemed harsh and repulsive, the blame should be cast, not on the accuracy of the painter, but the inherent ugliness of the subject. The first settlers of New England were a noble race of men, and the wonder is, not that they had faults, but that they were so few in comparison with all other sects and people of the age in which they lived. In the language of Bancroft, ' they, of all contemporary sects, were the most free from credulity, and in their zeal for reform pushed their regulations to what some would consider a skeptical extreme. So many superstitions had been bundled up with every venerable institution of Europe, that ages have not yet dislodged them all. The puritans at once emancipated themselves from a crowd of observances. They established a worship purely spiritual. To them the elements remained but bread and wine; they invoked no saints; they raised no altar; they adored no crucifix; they kissed no book; they asked no absolution; they paid no tithes; they saw in the priest nothing more than a man. The church, as a place of worship was to them but a meeting house; they dug no graves in consecrated earth. Unlike their posterity, they married without a minister, and buried the dead without a prayer.'

On March thirty-first, doctor Henry Greenland was found guilty of the charge preferred against him by Mary Rolfe. The court sentenced him ' to be imprisoned till next sessions of the court, then to be whipt or pay a fine of thirty pounds and be bound to good behaviour.'

One of the witnesses in his behalf, testified, that ' he had been a soldier, and was a gentleman, and they must have their libertyes.' Another asserted, that, as he was a stranger, and a ' great man, it would be best not to make an uprore but to let him goe away privately.'

On the twenty-seventh of September, 1664, he was convicted, with captain Walter Barefoote, of an assault on William Thomas, and

* County records.

Richard Dole. He was again fined and bound to keep the peace. He appealed to the general court, who confirmed his sentence, and ordered him ' to depart the jurisdiction and not to practice physic or surgery.' From 1666 to 1672 he was living in Kittery, where, for the present, we will leave him.

June 18*th*. John and Rebecca Bishop sold to Peter Cheney ' all the mill and mill house lately erected in Newbury on the little river with the stone, wheel, and so forth, and so forth, for two hundred and fifty pounds sterling.'

July 26*th*. This day the reverend John Woodbridge returned from England, where he had resided about sixteen years.

He was immediately engaged to assist his uncle Parker in preaching. The town voted him thirty pounds for the first half year, beginning the twenty-fifth of September, ' for his encouragement in the ministry.'

November 10*th*. ' The country way according to order of court was laid out from Mill bridge to Rowley bounds,' notwithstanding the town's remonstrance.

As this ' country way' was laid out in a new place, causing the town much expense, the inhabitants had remonstrated in a petition sent to the general court the preceding June. Among other things, they state, ' wee have already for many yeares made and maintained an ancient country rode according to the order of the general court, according to which our towne hath been modelled and men have built and fenced, and also our ferry constituted, whereas our towne might otherwise have been modelled with great convenience, had it not been for the country high way. All which notwithstanding, the honorable county court is pleased to impose upon us this new country high way, and have enjoined us under a fine to make a way over a great marsh of about a hundred rod by the end of June, which the towne are in no wise comfortably capable to perform.' After speaking of 'the extreme charge, which the towne necessarily would be put to,' ' in purchasing land through men's proprietyes near three mile,' which must be fenced, and bridges built over several considerable swamps and small brooks, and so forth, ' beside the mirynesse of the said waye and unevenness of it by reason of the rocky and low lande, through which the way is to goe,' they then petition the general court, ' that so great a burthen may not be imposed upon us but that the country may be satisfied with the old antient country roade, which we have from the beginninge of our towne maintained,' or ' that their fine may be remitted, and that the said new waye may be purchased, made and maintained at the charge of the country or county, or by those that have occasion to make use thereof.' June second, 1663.

Jocelyn, who was in New England this year, thus writes:
' On the south side of Merrimack river, and near upon the wide venting streams thereof, is situated Newberrie. The houses are scattering, well stored with meadow, upland, and arable, and about four hundred head of cattle.'

1664.

March. On petition of lieutenant John Pike, an acre of 'land, eight rods broad and twenty-two long was laid out to his brother Thomas Turvill, beginning at a stake near the spring between Henry Jaques' and George Littles' for to set up tanning of leather, provided he follow his trade of tanning.' *

May 6th. 'All horses and dry cattle to be cleared out of Plum island, and all fences to be made up by the thirteenth of May.' *

July 6th. 'Giles Cromwell is to keep the boys in order in the meeting house, and to give notice to selectmen of such as are out of order, and to have six shillings for his paynes.' *

October 26th. 'Major part of the towne voted that Mr. Parker should have but sixty pounds per year.' *

Here we have indirectly the first intimation of any difficulty between the reverend Mr. Parker and a portion of the church. It had been of long standing, and originated, as we shall see hereafter, not from any difference in point of doctrine, or want of personal respect and esteem, but solely from his change of views respecting church government. Their first recorded manifestation of their disapproval of this change was the reduction of his salary, but the next June, their sense of justice induced them to raise it again to eighty pounds, per annum, which, notwithstanding all the subsequent difficulties, in which he was involved in consequence of his change of opinion respecting church government and discipline, was regularly paid to him through life.

June 26th. 'About this time began the blasting of the wheat to be perceived.' † This was construed by the quakers as a judgment from God, an evident token of his displeasure against the people of Massachusetts for the cruel persecutions, which had been inflicted on many of that persuasion in the state some years before. Similar opinions were at this time entertained by all denominations of christians. If any calamity should fall upon their opponents, it was a judgment; if on themselves, it was a trial.

1665.

'Town voted to pay forty shillings for every wolf that is killed within the towne.' *

June 3d. Town voted that Mr. Parker 'shall have eighty pounds a year, and Mr. Woodbridge sixty pounds.'

November 1st. 'It was voted whether Mr. Woodbridge should be chosen by papers to preach to the towne for one year. There were four votes in the affirmative and thirty-one blanks.' *

December 25th. Anthony Morse, senior, is to keep the meeting-house and ring the bell, 'see that the house be cleane swept, and the

* Town records.   † Roxbury church records.

glasse of the windows to be carefully look't unto, if any should happen to be loosed with the wind, to be *nailed close again.'* *

' The winter of 1664-65 was mild and moderate till the middle of the month. On the fourth of February a comet disappeared, which had been visible from the seventeenth of November 1664.'

' Winter and summer wheat again struck with mildew.' †

At the close of this summer, Philip Carteret, having been appointed governor of New Jersey, settled at Elizabethtown, which he made the seat of his government, and despatched agents into New England to publish the constitution and invite emigrants. In consequence of this invitation, several persons went from Newbury and settled in a township, which, in honor of the reverend John Woodbridge, of Newbury, was called Woodbridge, which name it still retains. Of these emigrants from Newbury some returned, while others remained, and became distinguished both in civil and military life. Among them may be mentioned the names of captain John Pike, the ancestor of general Zebulon Montgomery Pike, who was killed at the battle of Queenstown in 1812, Thomas Bloomfield, the ancestor of Joseph Bloomfield, for some years governor of New Jersey, John Bishop, senior and junior, Jonathan Haynes, Henry Jaques, George March, Stephen Kent, Abraham Toppan, junior, Elisha Ilsley, Hugh March, John Bloomfield, Samuel Moore, Nathaniel Webster, John Ilsley, and others.

Daniel Pierce bought a tract of land in New Jersey of Mr. Ogden Luke Watson, and sold it to Henry Jaques.

This year Thomas Thorlay killed seven wolves in Newbury.

1 6 6 6 .

' *March 8th.* Liberty was granted to such as would build a shelter for horses, by goodman [Abraham] Toppan's fence, provided they do not make it above twelve foot high.' *

March 13*th.* The town ordered that a small ' house shall be built for shelter of the herdsmen, and a large pen for the cattle, and two herdsmen shall attend the cattle all summer to keep them from coming to the lower commons [below Artichoke river] and pen them every night.' *

April 25th. ' Voted that Mr. Parker's eighty pounds by the yeare should be paid him yearly and Mr. Woodbridge to have sixty pounds a year till further order.' *

' An army of caterpillars came this season, and a severe drought.' ' Wheat mildewed again.' † ' The canker worm first appeared in New England this year.'

* Town records.   † Roxbury church records.

1667.

' At a general meeting of the town, March first, Mr. Woodbridge was voted (man by man called over,) to have sixty pounds a year for preaching.' *

' Winter very moderate, little snow or bad weather.'

1668.

In June the selectmen and other inhabitants of Newbury petitioned the court at Salem that ' captain Paul White be licensed to sell wine out of dores by retaile for the necessary relief of some sick or other indigent persons by whom the churches exigencies have sundry times been supplied, who also may the more conveniently accommodate the churches occasions from time to time, until some man be licensed to keep ordinary here.'

By this it appears, that, at this time, there was no ' ordinary,' or, in other words, no tavern in Newbury. From other documents in the general court records we learn that it was difficult, and for a time impossible, to induce any person to open a public house for the accommodation of travelers, and so forth. At last Hugh March consented to leave his farm and commence the tavern keeping on a large scale in the year 1670. His expenses, as he himself informs us, for fitting up his house, stables, and so forth, were more than five hundred pounds — a large sum for those days. His stand, which was, for many years, a noted place, was near the head of Marlborough street, on the spot where Messrs. John and Stephen Ilsley now reside. In 1673 he petitioned ' against Paul White's selling wine,' stating that ' so it is that captain White under colour of providing the sacrament wines, doth frequently retaile wines unto the inhabitants and others to the damage and disabling your petitioner.'

The quantity of wine used on sacramental occasions during the year, was, as we shall hereafter see, very great.

'*March 2d.* Town voted counting man by man, that Mr. Woodbridge shall have sixty pounds a yeare for his preaching.' * This was continued till May twenty-first, 1670, when the town voted that ' the order should be void.' *

In this year the meeting-house was again ' seated,' and a watchhouse built on the east side of the upper green.

March. ' The town ordered that no horses shall be tyed *within* side or *without* side the fence' by the meeting-house gate, ' under penalty ***** for each offence.' *

Tradition informs us that the meeting-house was surrounded with ' pales,' through which, by a gate or gates, the meeting-house was entered. Near these gates the horses were tied, and they would frequently get across the path, often to the great inconvenience of

---

* Town records.

those, who wished to go to ' meeting.' This induced the selectmen to prohibit all persons from tying their horses *outside* of the fence. To their great surprise, however, they found on the next public meeting, several horses ' tyed' *inside* the fence. This caused them to make the order above-mentioned, forbidding all persons hereafter to tie their horses any where, either *inside* the fence or *out*. Thus much tradition, which derives some confirmation from the order just mentioned, a great part of which on the origininal record, is entirely illegible.

December 3d. ' The selectmen granted liberty to five persons to build a pew for their wives at the east end of the south gallery to the pulpit.' * This was probably the first pew ever built in the ' meeting house.'

December 21st. A road was laid out ' from Goodwin's ferry to Amesbury mill,' and ' one from Newbury to Rowley village,' now Bradford.

April. Salisbury new town was called Amesbury, and a ferry established there.†

1669.

The ecclesiastical difficulties, with which, in a greater or less degree, the whole town had been agitated for the last twenty-four years, had at this time arisen to such a height, that an appeal to the civil authority was deemed necessary in order to adjust their differences and restore harmony among them. The primary cause of the disturbances, was a change of sentiment, which Messrs. Parker and Noyes manifested, respecting church government and discipline, as early as 1645, as may be seen in the former part of this book. In 1647 Mr. Noyes published in London a large quarto work of ninety-five pages, entitled the ' Temple measured or a brief survey of the Temple mystical, which is the instituted church of Christ.' Of the author, the preface, written by another hand, thus speaks: ' he is altogether free from a spirit of faction, seeking only truth and satisfaction; and therefore he hath ingeniously laid down his judgment, which is in some things coincident with the judgment of the reverend presbyters of New England; in some things consenting with our reverend assembly here 'in England and in some things distant from them both; being neither for Aristotle, nor for Plato, but for truth; neither for Paul nor for Apollos but for Christ.'

The sentiments of Mr. Noyes may be learned from the following extracts from the work above mentioned.

' The church is to be carried, not to carry; to obey, not to command; to be subject, not to govern.' In another place he thus writes: 'if all members, young and old, children and men, if thousands together must judge and govern upon conscience together with the presbytery, first, it must needs interrupt the work. Second,

---

* Town records.   † Colonial records.

it is work enough, a double labour for the elders to instruct the church how to judge. There is more time spent in informing the church, than in determining the case. Must elders hold the hands of the common members (as the master teacheth scholars to write) and act only by them? Third, pride is an epidemical disease in a democratical government. Who is sufficient to hold the reins of authority? Where there are no standing magistrates in the commonwealth, and in the church, no governors at all, the offspring is like to be an Ichabod. Fourth, confusion and disorder are inevitable. *Turba ruunt.* The church ought to be a pattern of punctual order. A democracie is called by Plato, nundines populares. Fifth, as a church must needs be too long a doing by so many, when it is easy, so it must needs be done too soon by such as are precipitant, when it is difficult. Some are conscientious and scrupulous, others unreasonable, ignorant, youthful. This is a paidocracy as well as a democracy. The seat of government is the seat of wisdom.'

Similar sentiments were embraced, we have reason to believe, by Messrs. Parker and Woodbridge. Of the former, the reverend Nicholas Noyes, in his letter in the Magnalia, expressly says: ' he no ways approved of a *governing vote* in the *fraternity,* but took their consent in a silential way.' Of his uncle, Mr. James Noyes, he thus writes: ' they who differed from him in smaller matters as to discipline, held a most amicable correspondence with him,' and that during the time of his ministry, which ended by his death in 1656, there was not ''any *considerable* trouble in the church.' That occasional difficulties had arisen between the ministers and the people, we have sufficient testimony. Differing as they did on the question into whose hands the power of church discipline was committed, occasions of disagreement must of necessity have arisen, especially among a people so tenacious of their supposed rights, and so exceedingly jealous of every real or apparent encroachment on their power. After the return of Mr. John Woodbridge from England, in 1663, he was employed by the town to assist his uncle Parker in preaching. We find no record of any difficulty between them and the people, till November first, 1665, when the record informs us, that thirty-five votes ' by papers,' were cast, of which four votes were for him, and thirty-five were blanks. Mr. Woodbridge continued to preach to the people, by an annual vote of the town, with a salary of sixty pounds a year, till November twenty-first, 1670, when the town agreed to employ him no longer. From 1665 to 1669, there is great reason to believe, that the whole church and town were in a very excited and unbrotherly state, not from any dislike to the doctrine, or objection to the character, of either Mr. Parker or Mr. Woodbridge, for they were both highly esteemed, and honored, but from a real or supposed infringement of their rights and privileges as men and christians. The church was divided into two nearly equal parties, the one was called Mr. Parker's party, and the other, Mr. Woodman's party, so called from Mr. Edward Woodman, a man of talents, influence, firmness, and decision. As our church records prior to 1674 have been lost or destroyed, we extract the following detailed account from the records of the quarterly court at Salem, where they may be found on file.

'To the honored court now sitting at Ipswich, March thirtieth, 1669.'
'We whose names are underwritten, for ourselves and others the inhabitants of Newbury, doe humbly present, though to our great grief, that Mr. Edward Woodman spake in a town assembly before strangers publiquely on March first, 1669, that Mr. John Woodbridge was an intruder, brought in by craft and subtilty, and so kept in, notwithstanding he was voated out twice, which we know to be untrue, and look upon as scandalous. Also he said to Mr. Parker that he was an apostate and backslider from the truth, that he would set up a prelacy, and have more power than the pope, for the pope had his council of cardinals, that his practice or actings did not tend to peace or salvation, that he was the cause of all our contention and misery. That you are an apostate and backslider.'
'Also he said to captain Gerrish that he was no lover of the truth, that his gray hairs would stand where captain Gerrish his bald pate would, all which we humbly conceive tends not only to the reproach of the parties concerned, but to the great disturbance of our peace both civil and ecclesiastical, and therefore leave it to the serious consideration of this honored court for some suitable redress as they shall think meet.

Witnesses.	RICHARD KENT.
NICHOLAS NOYES.	HENRY SHORT.
Ensign JOHN KNIGHT.	ANTHONY SOMERBY.
TRISTRAM COFFIN.	
THOMAS HALE, senior.	
JOSEPH MUZZEY.	
NATHANIEL CLARKE.'	

The following depositions were also taken and put on file :

'The deposition of James Ordway, Abraham Merrill, and John Bayley.'
'These deponents say that when Mr. Woodman saith that Mr. Parker was the occasion of these contentions by his apostacy and declension (he added) from the principles that you have preached and practised, and also proved by the word of God, that men's consciences were engaged in it that they cannot depart from it unto this day.'

'Sworn in court, the thirtieth of March, 1669.'

'Richard Bartlet, James Ordway, and John Emery.'
'We testify that Mr. Parker in a public meeting said that for the time to come I am resolved nothing shall be brought into the church, but it shall be brought first to me, and if I approve of it, it shall be brought in, if I do not approve it, it shall not be brought in.'

Sworn as above.

'The depositions of John Emery, senior, John Emery, junior, Abraham Merrill, and John Bayley.'
'These deponents say that as Mr. Woodman was speaking in the meeting, March first, 1669, captain Gerrish stood up and interrupted him, mentioning his gray hairs. Mr. Woodman said, captain Gerrish, my gray hairs will stand in any place where your bald head will stand.'

Sworn as above.

'The deposition of William Titcomb, John Emery, Robert Coker and Thomas Browne.'
'These deponents say that upon the Lord's day, the twenty-first of March, 1669, after the exercise was ended, Mr. Parker put this to the members.

That those that are for the discontinuance of my cousin Woodbridge in the way of preaching, as formerly he hath done until farther order be taken, let them speak.

'Afterwards Mr. Parker expressed thus, those that are for the continuance of my cousin Woodbridge in the way of preaching as formerly he hath done let them express themselves by their silence.'

Sworn, and so forth.

See also the testimony of Pike, Brown, Emery, and others, in the first part of this book, pages sixteen and seventeen.

To the complaint made against him to the court at Ipswich, Mr. Woodman replied. This occasioned the following answer from Mr. Parker's friends.

'Whereas Mr. Edward Woodman in his plea or answer to the charges exhibited against him hath laboured to prove Mr. Woodbridge to be voted from preaching by a town record dated March first, 1665, the honoured court may please to consider, first, it doth not appear that any notice was given to the inhabitants of that particular respecting Mr. Woodbridge's preaching and so the vote, if unanimous, had been invalid.

'Second, the vote as they call it consists of two parts. First, whether Mr. Woodbridge should be chosen to preach to the town for one year. Second, whether he should be chosen by papers. In which it may be observed that the vote was not understood for near half of the company stood off from both as not willing to have it questioned about silencing or calling Mr. Woodbridge from preaching, namely to the number of thirty-one persons, and of them that did vote by papers the record saith, and Mr. Woodbridge acknowledgeth, that four of them were for Mr. Woodbridge's preaching, which, if it be taken for a legal vote, the vote was for Mr. Woodbridge's preaching. These things considered we humbly conceive there will be no footing found for what Mr. Woodman and others labour to cloud the matter withal.'

After hearing the evidence on both sides, the court pronounced the following sentence:

'*March* 30*th*, 1669. Having heard the complaint presented to this court against Mr. Edward Woodman we do judge some passages relating to Mr. Parker and Mr. Woodman to be false and scandalous, and that concerning captain Gerrish reproachful and provoking, and the whole greatly offensive, and have therefore ordered that the said Mr. Woodman shall be seriously and solemnly admonished and enjoined to make a publique confession at the next publique town and church meeting at Newbury of his sinful expressions and just offence that he hath given, or else to pay five pounds costs and fees.

'I dissent from this sentence, Samuel Symonds.

'And I dissent, William Hathorne.

Mr. Woodman appealed from this judgment, to the next court of assizes at Boston.

From this it appears that the court were not unanimous in their sentence against Mr. Woodman. This is farther evident from the following communication.

'This court having heard the complaint made unto us by certayne members of the church of Newbury against Mr. Edward Woodman (a member of the same church) of several offensive words spoken by the said Woodman in a town meeting against the reverend Mr. Parker then pastor, and Mr. Woodbridge, who hath for divers years exercised his gifts amongst them, and having also heard the answer of the said Woodman unto the particulars expressed in the complaint, and weighing the testimonies on both sides sworn in the case, we apprehend and judge as followeth namely. That several words and passages in the writing or complaint presented to the court and owned by himself or proved by others, especially taken merely in themselves without his answer and the testimony of others then present, are highly offensive and scandalous. But considering his answers and the testimony together with the same, we find the matter to be much altered from what the naked words as they are expressed in the writing do hold forth. We perceive that a great part (if not a greater part) of that church doe stand for the congregational way of church government and discipline to be exercised amongst them (which is the way the churches here doe professe to the whole world to be the way and only way according to the gospel of Christ,) and that it is and hath been for a long time a very great burthen and grievance to them, that they have not freedom in that respect, (where there is occasion of actings) as by the word of God they ought to have, and other churches have in this country, and at the beginning their own church also quietly did enjoy for some space of time, and that the alteration hath occasioned much differences and unquietudes amongst them. The whole case thus considered and weighed together the court doth desire and require that all persons concerned on both sides, for the future doe their utmost endeavour to settle truth and peace amongst them and freely to blame themselves at a convenient church meeting for their errors and miscarriages and actings or unbecoming words in their publique agitations, and that Mr. Woodman in particular should soe doe.'

'This was presented to this court as a suitable determination of the whole case, heard in open court holden at Ipswich March thirtieth, 1669, to which we subscribe

SAMUEL SYMONDS,
WILLIAM HATHORNE.'

This 'determination of the whole case,' by Messrs. Symonds and Hathorne, did not, as will be readily supposed, give satisfaction to either party, especially to the friends of Mr. Parker. On the contrary, those who had complained to the court, against Mr. Woodman, soon after sent in the following paper.

'To the honored court now sitting at Ipswich this twenty-eighth of April 1669.

'Whereas upon searching the court records we find a paper in the court beginning [this court having heard the complaynt and so forth] subscribed Samuel Symonds, William Hathorne, wherein are several things charged, as we apprehend illegally, on sundry among us, to our just grief, we desire the favour of the court to accept this our paper, as a short vindication of ourselves, till the opportunity shall be offered for our farther clearing.

'First, we look not on the paper as the determination or sentence of the court, which, had it been, we durst not in any measure have replyed, or contradicted.

'Second, nor did we think it any legal evidence towards the issue of the case, in which Mr. Woodman was presented for his miscarriage.

'Third, nor can we think it any legal charge to answer whereunto any persons were summoned, or made any answer to; or if it were a censure we know not that ever it was first examined, and indeed we know not what to make of it, but think it very hard to be in such a matter taxed before we were examined.

'Whether the said gentlemen were the authors of it or no we cannot tell, neither dare we affirm, yet finding such a paper wherein there is so great reproof by false accusation insinuated against divers amongst us, we intreat the court to accept our complaint, that we suppose ourselves illegally dealt with, seeing that our law assures us of this liberty among other, that no man's name shall be blasted, but by virtue or equity of some law established among us.

'We acknowledge that no man is mentioned by name; yet when any man is so decyphered, that any man, who reads it, may easily ghesse [guess] who is intended there is lawful cognisance in law of such infamyes, unless the person shall publickly disown it, else how shall men be righted against infamous libels?

'These things being premised we desire the liberty of freemen to put in our plea against such a paper of accusation as we find, with all due submission to the court.

'First, we judge our case exceedingly prejudiced, that it is insinuated in the preamble, that the complaynt is betwixt some members of the church, as if the cause were merely ecclesiastical. We grant the persons interested on both sides to be such, yet the cause presented is civil and criminal, not arising from some difference of opinion about discipline, but a publick breach of the peace against the plain words, as well as the intention, of the laws, which breach of the peace and violation of the law, as freemen of this jurisdiction we present to the cognizance of authority, desiring the redress of so great an evil, which authority in other like cases hath taken notice of with just indignation.

'Second, we humbly conceive, that if the words taken in themselves are highly offensive and scandalous the defendants' answer hath not made them to be good, though he may pretend they may arise from difference of opinion, for as we must not lie, neither must we slander, for God and his cause. His putting of a fayr glosse will never make good by words, [that] which is evil by deeds, no more than a quaker pretending conscience for reviling.

'Third, we humbly present this to consideration that whereas the presenters of the said Mr. Woodman did out of duty to God, his ministers and the law, bring the case to the trial of justice, that for the time to come such irregularities, which tended to mutiny, and tumult might be prevented. We humbly conceive the sentence of the said paper is such as that it takes off the blame from the person presented, is a fact evident enough, else we know not the meaning of those words, 'we find the matter much altered,' and loads the plaintiffs and others of the church, ministers, and people with far greater crimes than either Mr. Woodbridge hath done or ever justly could doe, yet can we not find in any of the testimonies any one that proves in matter of fact any of the conclusions, on which such a censure should be grounded. Somewhat it may be there fell from Mr. Woodman in his speech, which among other falsehoods by him charged on us, might give a hint of such a thing, yet we suppose such a speech is far too weak to infer such conclusions, as the paper seems to brand us with. Such as these.

'First, it intimates that though a great or greater part of the church stand for the congregational way of church government and discipline, yet according as other churches doe enjoy it, as the way of God, they cannot, which in point of fact is utterly denied.

'Second, that they have not their freedom to vote, or act, according to the word of God, or according as other churches, or as themselves heretofore had, which, if it were true, as the paper seems to accept it for a truth, were such a scandal, as justly deserved reproof and censure, for that they who do it would be accounted sacrilegious robbers of the churches, yet we assure ourselves that none of the opposites dare affirm it, it being so notoriously and evidently false. Let any act within twenty years or upwards be produced of this nature, that hath been carried on without the churches' consent or the major part thereof. We can evidence that Mr. Parker hath been blamed for bringing things of too meane a nature to the churches examination, and strangers have taken notice of the over much liberty of some in church actings.

'Third, we hope we have not deserved to be noted as a singular people contrary to the professed persuasion and practice of all the churches which we know not what the intimation of such a charge should aim at, but to raise an odium on us in the country when we are innocent of any such thing.

'Fourth, then the alteration hath caused much difference and unquietness among those, which by the intimation lights on the plaintiffs, or ministers, who have made the alteration, which is as false as the rest, yet the difference in this case to be considered arises only from the manner of testifying the assent or dissent of the church, not from any substantial disagreement. Near thirty years since at a synod at Cambridge it was proposed, and it was consented unto by them, that if the ministers thought it most convenient to vote by speech and silence, rather than by lifting up the hand, they had nothing against it, seeing the one was a testimony of consent as well as the other, so this kind of voting began and continued in practice without difference or interruption for a good season. Afterwards when some difference arose at Newbury that there was need of a council, this among other things was put in, and in fine it was concluded and consented to by the people that things should be carried on in this manner without disturbance. A third time near six years since there being occasion of a council at Newbury (in all which transactions Mr. Woodman was the chief instrument to oppose the minister) this among other differences came into discourse. The same conclusion was as before that things should be carried on in this way with love and peace, yet several times since and more strongly now at last, Mr. Woodman by violence of opposition hath made open protestation and resistance against it; and no disturbance or alteration hath been made but by them against a thing so long used and approved, and so we leave it to any impartial judgment to determine who is the cause of that alteration, which hath occasioned so much difference and unquietness, which though it be imputed to the plaintiffs, yet we suppose it rather to be to the unquiet and turbulent spirits of the opposites, and let any man judge whether this course only (for there is no other) be a sufficient cause of complaining of so great a burthen.

WILLIAM GERRISH.   RICHARD KENT.
RICHARD DOLE.   HENRY SHORT.
TRISTRAM COFFIN.   ANTHONY SOMERBY.'

From subsequent events it is evident, that the action of the court on the complaint exhibited against Mr. Woodman by the friends of Mr. Parker, was not attended by any beneficial results. This, without doubt, was partly owing to the fact, that the magistrates who had cognizance of the case were divided in opinion. So far from resting satisfied with the decision, or decisions, of the court, as the case might be, each party returned home, confident of the rectitude and justice of their cause, and determined not to submit to the other. Each party claimed to be *the* church, as each claimed to have a majority of the members.

' So sit two kings of Brentford on one throne,
United, yet divided, twain in one.'

On the third of November, a council was called, who thus report:

' *November 5th*, 1669. We, the elders and messengers of our respective churches, (who in answer to your desires expressed in your letter to them have sent us hither where accordingly we have convened,) in the deep sense of your soul afflicted state, the difficulty and intricacy of the matters before us our own insufficiency to reach the narrows comprehended in your questions and case, as it is circumstanced in the momentousness both of the nature of your proposals and the issues of our answers in way of advice and determination therein, have earnestly sought the face of the great Counsellor of his people, and implored the mercy of the hearer of prayers in these so weighty concerns to his name, the order of his house, the peace and welfare both of this and of the rest of your churches. And in the awful apprehension of the all-seeing eye upon us, as in all our transactions about the case presented to us, and of the solemn account, which we must one day give thereof to the highest Lord and Judge of quick and dead, after solemn and serious considerations had, and disquisitions and searches made, of and into the particulars presented to us, we have been moved, and, as we trust by the Holy Ghost to accord and issue in this as the joint result of our minds, judgments and hearts therein as followeth, namely:

'First, that the particulars respecting their dissenting brethren, declared to us by the pastor of this church of Newberry and the brethren with him as grievances to them being proved before us as true, we judge they were matters of just offence to them, as being publique and deviations from the rules of the gospel order, presented in the holy scriptures, and the answerable principles of the churches here established and declared in the platform of discipline approved for the substance by our general court to be and accordingly practised by the congregational churches amongst us, namely, that in an organic church where the pastor stands in a state of right administration, any brother or brethren less or more in number should openly and frequently refuse to observe their pastor's counsels or charges, to attend order of speech or silence and peaceably demeaning themselves in any church assemblies and matters there acted, or that they should check, curb, oppose, contradict or molest him in the discharge of his pastoral office, work or duty or secondly, that Mr. Woodman with a great part of the members of the church instead of giving due satisfaction, oft times called for from him and sundry of them unto their pastor, and the brethren adhering to him, should publiquely without, yea against, the consent and prohibition of their pastor, meet in a church assembly, act as a church by themselves, voting these or those church orders of theirs, send messengers to call any other member before them to give satisfaction to the church for matters offensive to them, as if they were the church, which besides that it is cross to religion and reason that in an organic body, which is but one entire ecclesiastical whole, consisting of the officer and all the rest of the members of that church, that there should be any regular orderly church, consisting of the major part of the brethren, severed from others of their brethren, yea of their pastor, or persons without, and not within the church, and such a company so acting as a church being no regular church, all their actings as a church are to be accounted irregular. We judge that such practices are breaches of church order, unity and peace, reproachful to the way of our churches here, highly dishonorable to Christ and the gospel, and tend to confusion, undermining and destruction of gospel order and peace in congregational churches amongst us, and that all these former irregulars done by them as church acts are null, and it will be more offensive in the dissenting brethren to act in any such way for time to come.

'Secondly, that yet considering the time as an hour of churches' temptation, the envy and subtlety of the common enemy of the churches, and his too much influence upon the spirits even of godly minded ones also, together with the remnants of the powers and deceits of the old man in the best, and considering how most desirable, amiable, and every way most profitable it is for brethren to dwell together in unity, and most dearly to love and tender one another in the Lord, and therefore to study to be quiet, to follow after things, which make for peace and wherewith they may edify one another, we advise Mr. Parker and the brethren with him to use all gaining and winning means, that may be, that they with their dissenting brethren may become one in the Lord as in former times, meekly yet convincingly by arguments from scripture and reasons grounded thereupon, (whether spoken to them, if opportunity of peaceably doing thereof, or else by writing to them) to convince them of their irregularities and duly to acknowledge the same, improving also any other helps for that end and patiently waiting for a good issue of all means used and forbearing them in love meanwhile.

'Finally in hope and expectation of an amicable compliance we have suspended any further counsel, which, if necessitated thereto, we shall advise as God shall guide according to the rules of the gospel. And now reverend and dear brethren, we commend you to God and the word of his grace, which is able to build you up and give you an inheritance among them, which are sanctified.

And the Lord of peace himself give you peace always by all means. The
Lord be with you all.

Thomas Cobbet,

November fifth, 1669.
In the name, and with the consent, of the
rest of the members of the council.'

The above advice, so laboriously written, does not, as might be
supposed, appear to have done any good, or to have 'reached the
narrows comprehended in the questions.'   On the contrary the year
ended, leaving both parties less willing ' to love and tender one
another,' than they were at its commencement.   So completely were
not only the church, but the people absorbed in this subject, and so
important was the issue of the contest deemed in point of principle,
that it affected all other matters.   Even the military company was
in such a state as to require attention from the general court.   From
their records is copied the following :

'*May* 19*th*.   In consideration of the distractions of the military company in
Newbury, for the better composure and prevention of the increase thereof,
major general Leverett, and major Dennison are impowered to inquire into the
grounds thereof on the spot, and *settle it if possible.*'

As a curious illustration of the predominant influence, which, at
this time, and for many years before and after, ecclesiastical matters
in Massachusetts had in almost all transactions, the following letter
from the general court files is copied.   The signers, it will be recollected, were the two ministers of Rowley.

'Rowley, July 24th, 1689.

' May it please your honors,
        The occasion of these lines is to inform you that
whereas our military company have nominated Abel Platts for ensign, we conceive that it is our duty to declare that we cannot approve of their choice in that
he is corrupt in his judgment with reference to the Lord's supper, declaring
against Christ's words of justification, and hereupon hath withdrawn himself
from communion with the church in that holy ordinance some years, besides
some other things wherein he hath shown no little vanity in his conversation and
hath demeaned himself unbecomingly towards the word and towards the dis-
pensers of it.

' Having given you this intimation, we leave the matter with your honors to do
as you see meet.   Thus presenting our service to you and begging God's presence with you, rest your honors' servants for Jesus' sake.

Samuel Phillips.
Edward Paison.'

In the midst of these difficulties, ecclesiastical, military, and so
forth, Mr. Parker continued his labors, and the people of both parties regularly ' went to meeting.'   On the twenty-fifth of February,
the selectmen, in consequence of 'complaints of considerable
persons for want of seats in the meeting house,' ordered three new
seats to be built, and fifty or sixty persons placed in them by the
selectmen, on certain conditions.   For instance :
' In the second seat of the men's side below in the meeting house
is placed Daniel Lunt, James Smith and Joseph Coker, and if

Thomas Hale junior, refuse to pay his share to the new gallery seat as others do, then James Smith is placed in the new gallery seat; provided he pay his share, and Thomas Hale is to return to his own place again.   And if Stephen Greenleaf refuse also to pay his share accordingly, then he is to return to his own place againe,' and so forth, and so forth. ✻

From the Salem court record it appears, that some of the people were not satisfied with the seats assigned to them by the selectmen, but took the liberty of choosing for themselves.   Of two of them, the court records thus speak : ' John Woolcot and Peter Toppan for disorderly going and setting on a seat belonging to others are fined twenty-seven pounds and four shillings.'

On the seventeenth of November, there was a 'thanksgiving for relief from drought and lengthening out the harvest.' †

1670.

In the early part of this year, John Webster was presented to the court, ' for reading a paper libel against Thomas Parker on a Lord's day in February, a scandalous and reproachful libel.'   The following is a copy of the ' paper libel.'   It is entitled, ' the answer of Mr. Woodman and the brethren adhering to him and so forth.'

' Whereas Mr. Parker and the brethren adhering to him, as he saith, have lately read, or caused to be read, in the public congregation before the church and towne a writing wherein is contained divers charges (some implicit and some explicit) upon the brethren, which they say are opposed unto them, and that they say are justly offended with them for sundry scandalous practices by them committed, who by their disorderly carriage have demeaned themselves unsuitable to the order of the gospel, and irreverently towards their pastor in that they have not attended his counsel and declaration of the will of Christ, to the frequent breach of order in public meetings and for acting as a divided body from their pastor and the rest of the brethren, voting their acts as church acts, and publishing them with other particulars presented to the council lately assembled, who determined, and we with them do judge, that such practices are breaches of church order, peace and unity, also you seem to lay the major part of the church under a censure and to deny any further treating with them until they have reconciled themselves to their offended brethren by confessing such faults as you have charged upon them.   To these things thus charged upon us, the major part of the brethren adhering to Jesus Christ and his word do answer, that we do not judge ourselves guilty of those sins as you have publiquely charged upon us, having duly examined our consciences and actions by the word of God, and therefore cannot approve of your proceedings therein, but do conceive that you have proceeded therein beside the rule that Christ hath given his church to walk by, and have exercised lordship over God's heritage by charging the major part of the brethren of the church, as we conceive unjustly, with many sins, which you do not so much as name nor specify in any such way as whereby we may know what they are, much less to be convicted that we are guilty of such sins, but under general heads of sins, as that we know not what they are for the general of them, nor who are actually guilty of them, if any such should be committed by any of the brethren.   Therefore it cannot tend to conviction or reformation of sin, but rather as we conceive it

✻ Town records.   † Colonial records.
11

must proceed from some distemper of spirits, and so to be accounted to cast an odium upon us and upon the cause we maintain. We therefore conceive that that writing is not regular, nor that which will stand with the rule of the gospel, to proclaim before the church and the town that we are sinners and that you are justly offended with us before you have used any due or regular means to convict us, or made any due proof against us that we are such as you have proclaimed us to be, therefore we take it to be a sentence before judgment, the coarsest proceeding among men. We do therefore hereby testify that we are justly offended with your irregular proceeding in casting such public scandals upon us without due cause and besides due order, and we cannot satisfy our consciences, otherwise than to declare our dissatisfaction with your proceedings and shall take into due consideration what God doth farther call for at our hands to bear farther witness against such doings and for the reformation thereof.

'Also we do bear witness against your two sermons out of Matthew 18 : 17 the one presented January thirtieth, and the other February second. We conceive you have not followed the mind of Christ in several things contained in the same sermons, but contrary thereunto, and contrary to the order of the churches established by the general court, contrary to the synod booke, contrary to the practice of all the churches in this jurisdiction, tending to the breach of peace civill and ecclesiastical, and has its tendency to the undermining and destroying of all church order allowed in this jurisdiction.

'This we read as a complaint to the church.'

The court records proceed to state, that 'John Webster is charged with publishing the contents of this paper annexed in the open congregation at Newbury on the Sabbath day after meeting without leave obtained from the elder which was done at or about the thirteenth of February, 1670. Question. Guilty or not guilty?' To which the jury reply, 'we find according to evidence given that John Webster read the contents of this paper annexed in Newbury meeting house.'

The next account I find of the proceedings of the brethren, is the following from the quarterly court files in Salem. It will be recollected that each party claimed to be *the* church, and to have a majority of the members. It is a copy of a paper sent to Mr. Parker by Mr. Woodman and his party. It is as follows:

'The church having seriously considered of the complaint brought to us by Mr. Woodman against our reverend pastor, master Parker and do judge it clearly proved by sufficient evidences, and much of it known to our selves to be true, do judge that you have been instrumental of the divisions and troubles, that have a long time [been] and still are, continued in this church, partly by your change of opinion and practice and several times breaking promises and covenants or agreements with the church, and other things contained in the complaint, therefore we cannot but judge you worthy of blame, and do hereby blame you, and for the restoring of peace to the church we are enforced, though with great grief of heart, to suspend you from acting any thing that doth appertain to your office, in administring seals and sacraments, or matters of government as an officer, until you have given the church satisfaction therewith. We do desire and admonish you in the name of our Lord Jesus Christ speedily to endeavour that God may have his glory by it and the hearts of your grieved brethren in the church may be comforted and *in the mean time as a gifted brother you may preach for the edification of the church if you please.* Your loving but afflicted brethren of the church of Newbury. Signed by us in behalf of the church.

'March sixteenth, 1670.   RICHARD DUMMER.
                                                  RICHARD THORLA.'

'This was brought to Mr. Parker by Archelaus Woodman, William Titcomb, Richard Bartlet and Samuel Plumer, and Samuel Plumer read it.'

Witnesses.

RICHARD KNIGHT. ANTHONY SOMERBY.
NICHOLAS NOYES. SAMUEL LOWLE.

'After sunset William Titcomb, Stephen Titcomb, Stephen Greenleaf, Richard Bartlet and Caleb Moody came with a message to Mr. Parker and told him they were sent from the church to give him notice that the church had chosen two ruling elders, namely, Mr. Dummer and Mr. Woodman, and they were to send to the two neighbouring churches to join with them to ordain them upon this day sevennight. Witnesses to the message of the church, captain Gerrish, Richard Knight, Nicholas Noyes, John Knight, senior, Mr. Woodbridge and Anthony Somerby.'

'We whose names are here underwritten do consent to the writing, which do declare an act of the church laying Mr. Parker under blame, and suspending him from all official acts in the church. Dated sixteenth of March, 1670.

MR. RICHARD DUMMER.	JOHN BAILEY.
MR. EDWARD WOODMAN.	JOB PILSBURY.
ARCHELAUS WOODMAN.	STEVEN SWETT.
WILLIAM MOODY.	BENJAMIN ROLF.
WILLIAM ILSLEY.	JOHN WELLS.
FRANCIS PLUMER.	NICHOLAS BATT.
WILLIAM TITCOMB.	ABRAHAM TOPPAN.
JOHN EMERY, senior.	ANTHONY MORS, senior.
JOHN EMERY, junior.	WILLIAM SAWYER.
RICHARD THORLA.	EDWARD WOODMAN, junior.
JOHN MERRILL.	WILLIAM PILSBURY.
FRANCIS THORLA.	CALEB MOODY.
EDMUND MOORES.	JOHN POORE, senior.
STEPHEN GREENLEAF.	JOHN POORE, junior.
THOMAS BROWNE.	JOHN WEBSTER.
ABRAHAM MERRILL.	ROBERT COKER.
BENJAMIN LOWLE.	JOHN BARTLET, senior.
RICHARD BARTLET.	JOHN BARTLET, junior.
SAMUEL PLUMER.	EDWARD RICHARDSON.
JOSEPH PLUMER.	JAMES ORDWAY.
THOMAS HALE, junior.	41.'

Mr. Parker then sent the following letter to Mr. Woodman and his company.

'*March* 16th, 1670. Having so frequently and seriously testifyed against your irregular actings (determined to be such by the council) it cannot be expected that I should concur with you to promote any disorder and consent to the erecting of any new form of government contrary to the received profession and constant practice of the churches here amongst us.

Your carriages have been such in these transactings, as have reflected great infamy and reproach on me. I cannot consent to agree with you to promote you in your way, till by some publick audience I shall have vindicated myself from any unjust aspersion you have cast upon me. My compliance with you may by others be interpreted a judging of myself guilty, and that therefore I am willing by composition to make up my own errors and miscarriages. Four of the brethren have been publickly complained of and brought before the church to answer for their publick offences, their answer through your meanes and their open refusal hath been interrupted. I shall not willingly consent to any motions from you that may hinder their just conviction, nor do I think that any of your designes are to be attended to till this be duly examined and judged. Once more I earnestly desire you to consider yourselves, and not go on in such irregular courses, which though you seem to justify yourselves in, yet assuredly will prove evil in the end. Do not thinke it a light matter to break the unity and peace of the church, hinder the edification of the church, cast contempt on the ministry, grieve your pastor and brethren, give offence to other churches, and bring up an evil report and cast reproach upon the government of the churches here, and once more I entreat you to think of some way of reconciling our differences, which we think will only be by consenting with us to call a regular council, resolving to submit to their advice.   If we cannot prevail with you by this motion, we shall be forced to consider what courses shall be taken to defend ourselves, and blame us not for using any lawful meanes whereby we redress your sin and our distractions.

THOMAS PARKER.

' The preceding paper Mr. Parker sent to Mr. Woodman and his company by seven of the brethren, who when they had read it to them were desired to absent themselves from them, and towards night they sent the ensuing paper,' namely.

' Reverend sir,
' Mr. Thomas Parker,
' Hearing a bruite about ye towne of an intention of some of your party to complain at Ipswich court of several brethren of their personal and common weakness, we thought good to put you in minde how far it is from the rule of christian love so to practice one against another before court and county, which might be healed at home with a word of reproof from one brother to another according to the mind of God, which saith, thou shalt not hate thy brother in thy heart, neither shalt thou suffer sin upon him.   We would desire you to consider that yourselves are men of infirmity as well as we are, and in case your practice in this kind should provoke us to do the like, what appearance of revengeful doings would there be in the face of the country, and no end could appear but to vent corruption towards one another, and nothing attained thereby of that concernment, to which we pretend ourselves conscientiously engaged, but to vent our stomachs one at another to the great dishonor of God, reproach of religion, and to put advantage into the hands of wicked men to speak reproachfully of religion in general.   More rather we desire that we may be of one mind so far as to cover the shame of each other, when no good end can be obtained in opening of the same, and commit our case as it is conscientious to us to the determination of the general court, to which we must sit down, either active or passive, without which we see no hope of issue, and for the avoiding of offence, what may be, we will state our complaint at home, and you shall have a copy of it in case you will agree there to answer to it which will bee the most likely way to issue our endless and boundless confusions, that we do know of.'

EDWARD WOODMAN
In the name of the church.'

' Received the above the twenty-third of March 1670, read by Samuel Plumer, ferryman, and brought by John Webster.'

The following by Mr. Parker and his friends needs no explanation.

'*March* 19*th*, 1670. It is too wofully known what great and how many contentions have troubled this church for sundry years, what means have been used from time to time for reconciling of them.   We have the testimony of a council of nine churches concurring with us that Mr. Woodman and those that have adhered to him have been the causes of a disturbance.   What patience have been used towards them, yet what opposition have been made by them, how irreverently they have carried themselves in presence of God in sundry church meetings, what impediments they have cast in our way, whereby church administrations have not only wanted their solemnity, but also have been hindred so as that just discipline could not be executed.   These things are all publickly known.   But especially their actings on the Lord's day January twenty-ninth, 1670, which have since bin in several meetings continued by them. We have often minded them and earnestly desired that they would consent with us to call a council as an ordinance of God, commonly practised by the churches of this country as a hopeful meanes of a reconciliation, which motion of ours hath been as often by them refused as by us proposed. In conclusion they have so far proceeded in their irregularities and miscarriages as that March sixteenth they have sent a writing to Mr. Parker their pastor whereby they do signify that they do suspend him from acting any duty of his office. They have chosen two ruling elders imposing them on the pastor and the church contrary to their consent, whereby they would not only deprive this church of the holy ordinances, which Christ hath given them, but have hereby cut themselves off from the communion of the church.

' In consideration of which premises (to mention no more) we the pastor and brethren of the church of Newbury, in the name and fear of the Lord Jesus Christ in way of defence of his poor flock here that they may not be left as sheep without a shepherd, and in vindicating the honor of our Lord Jesus Christ and his ordinances, not knowing any other regular way left according to the rule of the scripture, than to withdraw from them, who walk inordinately and cause division; we do hereby declare that for the future we do renounce communion with all those brethren that have so deeply violated the communion of Christ's church, nor shall we accept them as regular members of the church of Christ among us till God shall give them a mind to see and heart to acknowledge and confess their great offences, which we earnestly desire of him to grant through Jesus Christ.

' At a church meeting March twenty-second 1670.

' Agreed that this paper should be annexed to the vote that was passed the Lord's day March nineteenth 1670 that those brethren that have acted in the paper sent the sixteenth of March 1670 to the pastor, wherein they suspend the pastor from his office, we do renounce communion with them in the communion of the Lord's supper and in the administration of discipline until they give us satisfaction.'

THOMAS PARKER.

The next day, March twenty-third, Mr. Parker and some brethren with him, sent the following paper to Mr. Woodman's party.

' That there may be nothing wanting in us to evidence that love and respect unto you, which brethren ought to have one towards another, and the duty we owe to God binds us to, understanding by your messengers that you intend to ordain two ruling elders, we cannot but once more motion to you, that though you little regard the offence and grief of your pastor, brethren and the churches of God abroad, which we suppose you ought to do, and if you have any bowels of love left, we hope you may do, yet we earnestly intreat you not to despise the Lord Jesus Christ by making his ordinances contemptible. Do you not know how distasteful it will be to him to profane his holy things ? Do you think he will own them for his ordinances, which you make use of to advance your owne humours and divisions ? Do not despise the civil authority above us, we have cause abundantly to thank God that they will countenance and protect us in the enjoying what Christ allows us, but you know that the rule of the scriptures and theirs concurring with it is that elders should be blameless, nor do they allow any to be ordained that are scandalous, and you know that Mr. Woodman, one of them that you have chosen stands publickly charged with several scandals, nor hath he to this day endeavoured to satisfy his brethren. If you should still persist and go on after this our advice, which in love and affection we give unto you, we hope we have discharged our duty and leave you to his judgment, that will in his time judge every thing in truth. In the mean while this shall stand as an evidence for us that we have done our endeavour to prevent your sinne.'

THOMAS PARKER.

'Names of those, who adhered to Mr. Parker and did not act in Mr. Parker's sentence.'

RICHARD DOLE.	JAMES KENT.
JOHN KENT.	RICHARD KENT.
THOMAS HALE, senior.	RICHARD KNIGHT.
JOHN KNIGHT, senior.	JOHN KELLY.
JAMES JACKMAN.	ROBERT LONG.
DANIEL PIERCE, junior.	HENRY SHORT, senior.
NICHOLAS NOYES.	SAMUEL MOODY.
THOMAS TURVILL.	HENRY JAQUES.
Captain WILLIAM GERRISH.	ROBERT ADAMS.
TRISTRAM COFFIN.	JOSEPH MUZZEY.
NATHANIEL CLARK.	WILLIAM CHANDLER.
Captain PAUL WHITE.	Mr. RICHARD LOWLE.
WILLIAM MORSE.	ANTHONY SOMERBY.
JONATHAN MORSE.	ABIEL SOMERBY.
ABEL HUSE.	Mr. HENRY SEWALL.
JOHN DAVIS.	GEORGE LITTLE.

Thirty-two regular members.

Mr. JOSEPH HILLS.	Mr. JOHN WOODBRIDGE.
DANIEL PIERCE, senior.	RICHARD PETTINGELL.
JAMES SMITH.	JOHN SMITH.

Though no members.'

On the nineteenth of April, the ex-parte council, which had assembled November fifth, 1669, met again at Newbury. The following is 'a copy of the request presented by Mr. Woodman and the brethren with him to the council.'

'The major part of the brethren of this congregation doth in all humble wise desire this honored and reverend assembly to take into their serious consideration our sad and distracted condition, who have spent twenty-five years and more in uncomfortable and unprofitable contention and division, whereby God hath been much dishonored, religion much disadvantaged, our souls much impoverished and our credit as a church much impaired, defamed throughout the country for an unquiet people and unreconcilable by the long continuance of our difference and dissension, and now of late the cry hereof hath been more loud in the ears of the churches than in former times, which produced this effect. The messengers of nine churches are come to see whether things are amongst us according to the cry that their ears are filled withal, whom we do heartily wish that God would make instruments for the settlement of peace and truth amongst us, and so throw down the strong hold that Satan has erected against us for the obtaining of which end our impartial request to this reverend assembly is that the ground and causes of our long dissensions may be thoroughly inquired into. Among physicians it is a maxim that when it is known what the disease is and where it is settled, it is half cured. Our earnest desire is that you would grant us three things. First, that you would cancel any hand writing signed by yourselves against us, our case not being heard. Second, that you will be pleased to hear our case and give us your advice, not as a council, (we having had no hand in your call, but in an orderly way the hands of two thirds of the church lifted up against it) but as honored and reverend brethren, giving your advice tending our sad and solemn estate.

'Third, that you will lay aside all prejudice against us, which you may receive by so many private informations and instigations against us and now begin to hear what both parties can say for themselves as to the case in hand, as if you had heard nothing concerning the same.

'It is no small trouble upon our spirits that we should be so ill resented in the hearts, and so ill spoken of amongst many godly and reverend persons (as we conceive) without any just cause at all as unto man, especially when we consider the pretended cause, which is some grand defect in matter of religion as a people declined and fallen from something therein, which maketh our persons offensive and out of favour with many. If there be any thing of that nature, of which we are guilty, it must be in matter of faith or in church order. As for matters of faith, we know not wherein we differ from the godly in general what order soever they are under.

'As concerning church order or discipline we know not what may be against us, for we wholly own that, which the New Testament doth clearly hold forth as the mind of Christ to his church, that which the general court hath established for the synod book, we hold the substance of it. We own Mr. Hooker's Polity, Mr. Mather's catechisme, Mr. Cotton's Keys, for the substance of it. That, which the churches have practised in general with a joint consent as far as we know. Yea that, which hath been New England's glory, in which God hath come nearer to them than to any other people. And the way, in which the Old and New Testament do prove to be the instituted way of God's appointment for his churches to walk in. But indeed we have cause to doubt that the offence here against us here at home is because we abide constant to those principles and will not turn presbyterians. As for our controversy it is whether God hath placed the power in the elder, or in the whole church, to judge between truth and error, right and wrong, brother and brother, and all things of church concernment. It is denied that the fraternity have any thing to do with it, but the minister only; and if his determination be not approved of, the persons aggrieved may appeal to all the ministers in the country. And it is come to that passe that such as do not consent hereto are Corathites, and like the sons of Eli, that make the holy things of God to be despised, and upon this ground is our division and contention. Principles preached and endeavoured to be practised, one contrary to another, have made two sorts of professions, contrary one to another, whereby we differ almost in all things in church and town affairs. And yet we that to this day have stood unmoveable to those principles proved by the scriptures in books of controversy, in catechisms by the synod, by the ecclesiastical laws confirmed, and approved of by the practice of all churches in general, are tost up and down by the mouths of some unworthy persons as decliners to levelism, to Morellianism and are a people that nothing will satisfy.

'Thus having opened to this honored and reverend assembly in general the state and condition of this poore distracted congregation, our earnest desire is that you will be pleased to apply your wisdom to the uttermost for our healing, and not conceit that a slight plaster will heal us, for our wound is festered, our disease is rooted. God did once complain that the wound of the daughter of his people was healed slightly, and so it brake out again. Consider we beseech you that to heal breaches and repair desolations in churches is not a work of an inferior nature, for if peacemakers shall be called the children of God, it doth greatly concern you to improve the opportunity God hath put in your hands to make peace and truth dwell together in this poor distracted congregation. The which that you may do, the God of peace guide both your hearts and lips to create peace for us, so shall we record in our hearts and acknowledge with our lips to the praise of God that under himself he hath delighted to make you instruments of our peace and repairers of the breach in this congregation.

'These things we desire of the honored and reverend assembly, not as of a council, but as above premised, as honored friends and brethren.'

(Before the council returned their answer, the following script was sent in, namely:)

'Honored and reverend friends, this is as an addition to our first request, that in case you will not be pleased to cancel what you have signed against us, that you give us liberty to speak to that case before any other thing be brought in agitation.'

'THE ANSWER FROM THE COUNCIL.'

'To Mr. Woodman and the brethren with him.

'Though we do, and cannot but, assert ourselves as a council, consisting of elders and messengers of churches, yet for the present waving

that consideration, having weighed your affectionate motion, we shall be ready to hear your case, provided that you will engage to submit actively or passively to such advice as we shall commend unto you therein according to the word of God.   THOMAS COBBET
In the name and with the consent of the elders and
messengers of the churches assembled.'

ANSWER.

' We thankfully acknowledge your condescending to hear our case, and do seriously profess that our aim and end is to hear the advice of yourselves therein in order unto practice and do solemnly engage to the utmost of our ability to receive with all readiness, and attend with all diligence whatsoever scripture light you may impart unto us according to the best of our understanding and consciences.

EDWARD WOODMAN,
WILLIAM TITCOMB,
ARCHELAUS WOODMAN,
April nineteenth, 1670.   CALEB MOODY,
In the name of the rest.

' On the nineteenth day in the afternoon Mr. Parker and the brethren with him their grievances were read in publick.
' On the twentieth day Mr. Woodman's twenty-six grievances were read.
' On the twenty-first day another grievance was sent in by Mr. Woodman's partie, signed by William Titcomb and Caleb Moody in the name of the rest.'
' On the twenty-second of April 1670 the council came to the following result.'

'COVENANT.'

' We whose names are underwritten do hereby testify and declare that we do fully consent and agree unto the covenant and agreement contracted and made betwixt Mr. Parker, our reverend pastor, and Mr. Woodman and the brethren that are with him, that is to say that the synod book called the platform of discipline with the other four articles shall be our rule in the church of Newbury for our practice in all administrations, because we take it to be an explanation of the scriptures, and a rule agreed upon as a means to avoid all future divisions and contentions, we mean the agreement made before and by the help of the messengers of nine churches, contained under five heads, signed under the hand of the moderator and scribe of the assembly, in witness whereunto and in witness whereof we the assembly set our hands.'

' Articles of accommodation betwixt Mr. Parker of Newbury, Mr. Woodman
and the brethren with him mutually agreed upon before the council at Newbury April twenty-second, 1670.

'First, that the platform of discipline, established by the general court, practised by the churches of New England, shall be the rule or standard of the congregational way according to which the church of Newbury do resolve both pastor and brethren to act in all church administrations.
' Second, that all matters of controversy being considerable and of moment, not issued before the pastor or elders to mutual satisfaction of parties concerned, shall be brought to the church according to the said platform.'
' Third, that they, who are propounded for admission into the church shall stand some considerable time, at least a fortnight, and public warning given on the Lord's day, when they are to be admitted.
' Fourth, that no difference shall be made in admission of members into the church upon account of their difference of judgment as to the congregational way pro or con, the persons being orthodox and of good conversation.
'Fifth, that, when the providence of God shall give an opportunity of regular call of any other officer, it shall be attended by the church according to what is laid down in the said platform of discipline, chapter the eighth.
THOMAS COBBET, Moderator.
ANTIPAS NEWMAN, Scribe.
Signed by Mr. WOODMAN, ⎫
Mr. DUMMER and 38 others. ⎭

This second attempt of the council, to reconcile the conflicting opinions, and harmonize the discordant feelings, of both parties, was of no avail. The truce was of short duration. Before the close of the year, the 'articles of accommodation' appear to have been entirely forgotten, and the storm, which had apparently subsided, again raged more fiercely than ever; and it was not until the lapse of several years that peace was finally restored. The 'distractions in the military company' still continued.

'On May eleventh, the court, having left it to the care of the major general to make temporary provision for military officers at Newbury, who did appoint Archelaus Woodman lieutenant, and Stephen Greenleaf ensign, confirms their appointment.' Both of these officers were of Mr. Woodman's party.

On March seventh, 'Peter Cheney proposed to the town for half an acre of land on or about the little hill this side the mill, to build a wind mill upon to grind corn for the town, when the water mill fails.' This was granted by the town, 'upon condition that he do build a good mill to answer the end proposed for and so long as the mill is made and maintained for the said service and no longer.'

This mill stood on the 'little hill,' near the mill bridge, or 'four rock,' as it is sometimes called, and remained there till Mr. Cheney removed to Byfield, in the year 1687.

May 21*st.* 'It was voted that the order in the town book, that gives Mr. Woodbridge sixty pounds a year for his preaching is made void.' *

September 19*th.* 'It was voted that the selectmen shall take care that ****** ****** fence in no more [land] than his due.' *

'The town granted to William Titcomb and Amos Stickney the little pine swamp to be their propriety, with skirts of the common, provided they make and maintain a sufficient fence about the hole for the safety of the cattle from time to time.' *

The 'pine swamp' mentioned above, is the tract of land on the south side of Oak-hill cemetery, and was, it appears, surrounded by the common. The town also voted, 'that the selectmen should order Thomas Turvill to his kinsman's, also to be helpful to the poore.' *

This is the first intimation, except the case of John Eels, the bee-hive maker, that the town had any occasion to make provision for the poor. Turvill went to reside with his 'kinsman,' Henry Short, in whose old account book I find the following inventory. It was taken May twenty-second, 1673, when he had made an agreement with the town, to keep Thomas Turvill for three shillings per week.

'The following is an account of what clothes he had and their value, appraised by three of the neighbours.

* Town records.

'*May* 22*d*, 1673.

An old worne out coat and briches with an old lining,	£0	6s.	0d.
A thread bare, tho indifferent close coat and doublet with an old wast coat,	£1	0	0
Two shirts and a band 11s., a pair of shoes, 4s.,		15	0
An old greasy hatt, 6d., a pair of stockings, 1s.,		1	6
An old doublet, an old wast cote and a pair of old sheep skin briches,		4	0
		£2 6s.	6d.
In 1675 his clothes were appraised again by three neighbours and the amount was		£2 12s.	5d.'

' There was a great drought this summer.' *

1671.

At the April term of the court at Ipswich, the following complaint was entered. It needs no explanation, as it is sufficiently clear and explicit.

' To the honored court at Ipswich.

' Having tried all private means and publick ecclesiastical by councils according as we were directed by our honored magistrates, all which since they prove unsuccessful, nor can we see any hope of silencing, much less of curing, our difficulties and fearing lest such miscarriages may have an influence, not only to breed public disturbance in other churches, some sparks whereof already appear, but may break forth into open factions and mutinies, having no other remedy we humbly conceive it our duty, as being necessitated to it, to present our case to civil authority intreating them at least to redress such miscarriages as are contrary to the known laws of the country, and so, contrary to the public peace. Title ecclesiastical section fourteen is forbidden contemptuous behaviour toward the word of God preached, or the messengers of the same, or casting any reproach on their doctrine and persons, to the dishonour of our Lord Jesus, disparagement of his holy ordinances, and making God's ways contemptible and ridiculous, as sect. chapter heresies n. seven. Every person, that shall revile the person or office of magistrates, or ministers, such person, or persons shall be severely whipt or pay the fine of five pounds. Likewise it is provided, chapter first, that no man's honour or good name shall be stained.

' First, as offenders against these laws we humbly present to this honored court, whether all those, that call themselves the church and brethren of the church of Newbury, who have irregularly convened, have publickly read and debated certain articles presented to them by Mr. Edward Woodman against our pastor, Mr. Parker (whose inoffensiveness is generally known) tending to his great reproach and infamy, and have as appears by their publick writing judged and determined the said Mr. Parker to be the cause of their divisions and troubles to have broken several covenants and agreements with the church (as may more fully appear by the articles exhibited by the said Mr. Woodman against him) and therefore do publickly blame him, yea so deeply that they take upon them to suspend him from his office, which articles upon due examination, we doubt not but will appear vanities, yet their publick actings being bruited over the country must need tend to the great reproach of Mr. Parker when they shall hear so many articles and such a censure, and in particular we present to you Mr. Woodman, the plaintiff, and Mr. Richard Dummer, whom they termed the president, Archelaus Woodman, and William Titcomb, moderators, and Samuel Plumer and Richard Bartlet, messengers, who are able to inform of the rest.

* Roxbury church records.

'Second, whether Mr. Edward Woodman, who was formerly convicted of his scandalous reviling Mr. Parker, besides frequent contemptible speeches and threatenings of him be not fallen into the same offence by publickly affirming that Mr. Parker hath broken covenant three times already, and no covenant will stand before him. Likewise in the same law underneath whosoever shall go about to destroy or disturb the order or peace of the churches established in this jurisdiction on groundless conceits and so forth. Now as contrary to this,

'First, whether it be not factious for a part of the church without the knowledge and privity of the pastor and brethren to meet together and carry on church affairs in a way of complaint against their pastor, and whether this may not be accounted an act of conspiracy against their pastor and the church, yet this has been done by them at Stephen Greenleaf's house, where were present Mr. Woodman, Mr. Dummer and many others as we are informed.

'Second, whether it be not a disturbance to the order of the churches for Mr. Woodman at most but a deacon, on a Lord's day immediately after the morning exercise (though he was desired by the pastor to forbear, and not profane the sabbath day by open disturbance and so forbad him to proceed) to desire the church to stay; and when Mr. Parker told him he had broken the agreement, Mr. Woodman replied to him, I speak not to you, but to the church, for I have divers complaints against you, and when Mr. Parker was gone, to tell them that he had several complaints against Mr. Parker, and desired them to appoint a church meeting to hear them (though Mr. Parker immediately before had warned a church meeting) many of them consented to it, and so upward of thirty voted it.

'Third, whether it be not a like breach of the public order and peace of the churches for the said persons solemnly to cause the bell to be rung and repair unto, and observe, such an irregular meeting, to term themselves the church (though not the major part of the church) and in the name of the church to send for the pastor to answer the charges laid against him by Mr. Woodman. And here particularly Mr. Dummer, Archelaus Woodman and William Titcomb were moderators, the rest witnesses and judges.

'Fourth, whether it be not a like breach of the order and peace of the churches when any of the members being publickly warned by the pastor and the persons duly summoned, the said persons shall publickly contest against their pastor, and will not agree so much as to have their charges read, unless their pastor will first put it to vote whether it were the mind of the church that it should be read, and whether after such debate taken, the said charges shall begin to be read there is an uproar and hubbub raised that the church might not hear what was read, and when they are read, they being particularly read and desired to answer, they shall directly refuse to do, yet guilty of such things are Mr. Woodman, Archelaus Woodman, William Titcomb, William Pilsbury.

'Fifth, whether Mr. Richard Dummer, and Richard Thorla signing a paper in behalf of the church, which contained (in their apprehension) an act for the suspension of the pastor from his office, and thereby what in them is, depriving the whole church of the ordinances of Christ, which he hath given to his church, and this without the advice and direction of any other church, are not guilty as leaders in the disturbance of the church but also of falsehood, when it is not the church, nor the major part of the church acting in any lawful meeting, that gives them authority so to do, and whether Archelaus Woodman, William Titcomb, Richard Bartlet and Samuel Plumer in bringing and delivering it, be not alike guilty of promoting the disturbance of the church.

'Sixth, whether it be not a disturbance of the publick peace and order in an organic church for private members contrary to the mind and privity of their pastor and brethren, to elect ruling elders, imposing them on the pastor and brethren without their consent, Mr. Woodman one of them being known to be scandalous in his conversation, and this not by the major part of the brethren either, yet this, William Titcomb, Richard Bartlet, Stephen Greenleaf, and Caleb Moody brought as a message to Mr. Parker from them, whom they called the church, and they are able to give an account who they were that set them to work.

'Seventh, lastly whether in these things (to omit many others that may be mentioned) Mr. Woodman and those who adhere to him, be not guilty as much as in them lies, of erecting a new form of government in the church with a great deal of strife and contention, contrary to the platform of discipline allowed by the general court and the received practice of all the congregational churches in this country, and whether this be not to the breach of the peace both civil and ecclesiastical (n. 11.) Civil authority here established hath power and liberty to see the peace, ordinances and rules of Christ to be observed in every church according to his word ; and our honored magistrates in their letters direct-ed to us, do account themselves bound by all due means to countenance and protect the observers of the congregational government. We present then these things to your wisdoms. At our request you would be pleased to encourage those who desire to be faithful to God and lovers of truth and peace.

Presented by us, RICHARD KENT,
DANIEL PIERCE, senior.'

To the preceding communication the following reply was made.

' To the honored court at Ipswich April eighteenth, 1671.

' Concerning the seven queries put to the consideration of this court, they do involve so many within them that they are from us uncapable of an answer, neither do we know what use the court will make of them against us, seeing they come in as queries and not as charges. We ourselves could trouble the court with many queries, but at this time we shall forbear. In brief we would humbly desire you to consider that most if not all, the particulars mentioned, are such, as will prove good or evil, as we shall appear to be a church regularly acting or not, for if we be a church of Christ according to order then it is lawful for a brother to complain to the church against any brother that doth offend. Then secondly it is lawful for the church to hear and judge. Thirdly, then it is lawful for two brethren also to sign an act of the church as witnesses. Fourth, then it is lawful for them to send messengers to Mr. Parker, or whom it may concerne. Fifth, then it is lawful for them to meet as a church together. Sixth, then it is lawful for them to elect a ruling elder or elders. But we hope your honored court will convict us that we have broken some standing law or laws, that were made by the general court before they blame us, for we do not account ourselves well dealt withal by the authors of those queries and declaration, whom we leave to the Lord.

' Lastly we do profess ourselves to be servants of God and faithful subjects to the commonwealth, lovers of magistrates and ministers, and all the churches and people of the Lord, and do not willingly err from any rule of God, nor of the commonwealth, but we trust such, as shall be found faithful.

' We do therefore desire this court to consider whether it be not against all order, law or custom that complaint should be brought to a court against breth-ren, which from conscience of the rule of Christ do complain to a church against an offending brother, merely because they have complained, when the church hath heard the complaint and acquit the complainer, by owning the complaint to be duly proved, and sentenced the person complained against. So leaving what have been said to your wisdoms to be considered, and yourselves to the God of all wisdom to be directed, with our hearty prayers for you, we rest in the Lord to be commanded.

WILLIAM TITCOMB.
CALEB MOODY.
SAMUEL PLUMER.
STEPHEN GRENLEFE.
RICHARD BARTLET.'

' A declaration of the pastor, and several brethren of the church of Newbury presented to this court at Ipswich.'

' The manifold contentions, that have been among us for sundry years have been matter of continual grief, and ought to be of continual humiliation, that such things should arise among a people, whose beauty consists in their union to Christ and unity one with another.

' To omit all former transactions (which we cannot reflect upon but with grief) so high were the opposites that according to the direction of our honored magistrates, who pitied our distractions, we were forced to desiring help of our neighbouring elders, and churches, who at a council convened November third 1669, whom our brethren would by no means own, or subject unto as a council, though there was as much reason to respect them and accept their advice as most in the country.

' The council hereupon was forced to proceed according to the allegations and proofs presented to them, whereby they found and judged the actings of our brethren to be very irregular, contrary to the peace and unity, which ought to be in the church, tending to confusion, and that which casts reproach on the order of the congregational churches among us, and therefore were offensive, and if they should proceed after such testimony of theirs against their ways it would be much more offensive, sufficiently evidencing to them that there was just cause of complaint against them, as more fully may appear by their testimony left in writing, which was publickly read the next Lord's day after their departure.

' The council having adjourned till the nineteenth of April following, we endeavoured in the mean time to see what composition we could bring our brethren to, and accordingly by publick and private agitations we laboured to reduce our brethren to a right and sober mind, that our contentions might cease, and they might be brought to a right understanding of the congregational way as it was commonly practised by the churches according to the direction of the council, which, if our brethren had consented to, there might have been hopes to have proceeded peaceably, but instead of any composition with us there appears farther ground of distraction, as may be seen by their paper disorderly published in the congregation, the copy whereof stands in record in the court.

' The council returning according to their adjournment found as little acceptance by our brethren as formerly, who though they made their appearance, yet it was with such a spirit and carriage, as did ill befit them before such a reverend assembly, nor would they comply to do any thing till the council agreeing to hear them as friends and not as a council instead of answering the allegations first or last objected against them (which in reason they ought to have done if they could have cleared themselves) they brought in such exceptions as they could against Mr. Parker their pastor, all which we fully heard and answered, nor was there any thing (of twenty-five articles) of moment alleged or proved against Mr. Parker, their pastor, who was sufficiently vindicated by the council, but sufficient on this point to show what spirit they were of.

' On the last day of their setting, about sunset Mr. Woodman with several others with him came into the council, speaking to this purpose (Mr. W. affirming that he was appointed to speak in the name of the brethren, and called for witness to attest it) that now they were convinced by the word of God that they had acted irregularly and came there to acknowledge their offences, which accordingly they did to the great satisfaction of the hearers, sundry of them speaking to the same purpose that they had done ill. The council seeing such a compliance which in all the former part they saw so little ground to expect, readily embraced the appearance of such a temper, and more willing to bring things to a full agreement, they left off what they intended as a council and fell upon the consideration of some articles of accommodation whereby both parties for the future might act peaceably, which articles were agreed unto by Mr. Woodman and many of his party there present who also promised their endeavours to bring the rest to a compliance with them.

' Mr. Woodman notwithstanding such an appearance of a cordial agreement, yet refuses the communion of the church from that day, and within a little while finds occasion to make as much disturbance as ever. We could scarcely have any publick occasions (as for discipline of members and so forth) but there was some publick opposition from some or another, and nothing could be managed with peace, though (as we suppose) there was never any just cause of disturbance.

' Sundry private agitations there were, wherein propositions were made by them tending to a farther ground of difference than any settlement. Some things [were so stated] that Mr. Parker professed he could not in conscience agree to them, yet Mr. Woodman threatened him that he would bring him before authority, before the highest judicature of the country, and again revive the twenty-five articles, which were brought before the council, which they had the hearing of and acquitted Mr. Parker.

'After many debates, and little likelihood and appearance of agreement, there still continuing great murmurings and private surmises cast up and down to Mr. Parker's prejudice through false suggestions, Mr. Parker to testify what things he might, warns a publick church meeting, which convened December eighth, when by reason of the tumultuous carriage of things there was little likelihood of bringing any thing to a fair issue. Omitting many unworthy and disorderly carriages exceeding unsuitable to the solemnity that ought to be in God's presence, towards the end of the meeting Mr. Woodman was charged by one of the brethren for publick offences, one in almost totally absenting himself from the publick worship on the Lord's days, though it was known sufficiently that he was able enough to attend on other occasions, therefore abstaining from the communion of the church. He instead of answering for these offences publickly professed he is offended with Mr. Parker for some miscarriages, and desires the church to appoint a meeting to hear him. Mr. Parker bids him produce his charges, and he was ready there to answer them before the church, but this Mr. Woodman refused to do.

'Not long after he comes accompanied with two brethren, and tells Mr. Parker he comes with two others to deal with him according to the rule in order to bring him to the church, if he refused to hear him.

'Mr. Parker replied to him that his accusations being only such points wherein they differed in their opinions it was not reasonable to think they were meet judges, or that he was likely to satisfy them. But if Mr. Woodman would choose three or four elders, whom he would, of the neighbouring churches, he was ready to answer before them whatsoever they could allege against him, and besides that himself standing charged with several scandals, he was not a meet person to come to deal with him in such a manner till he had answered for his own offences. Mr. Woodman professed he would never call in the help of any elders as long as he lived, but if Mr. Parker refused to hear him he would bring it to the church in order to depose him, and then they would desire the advice of other churches what they were to do in point of farther censure, and this was the issue of that meeting.

'Shortly after (under the notion of a fast, though no such things were observed) most of the opposite brethren convened, but (as we are informed) the substance of their agitation was how to prosecute their design against Mr. Parker, which was ordered to be done the next sabbath day, which Mr. Woodman accordingly though irregularly set on foot. There they (though not the major part by several persons) voted a church meeting though Mr. Parker just before warned a meeting for the whole church. Mr. Parker warned his at one of the clock in the afternoon, they anticipated him by designing theirs at eight o'clock in the morning of the same day. Mr. Parker desiring to prevent their irregular motions, on the lecture day being Wednesday (the meeting being warned to be on the Monday following) publickly appoints another meeting two days after namely, the Friday before the meeting formerly warned, and withal order was taken that four of the brethren should have notice that they were then to appear to answer what should be alleged against them for the irregularities of the last sabbath and other things. The persons were Mr. Woodman, Archelaus Woodman William Titcomb and William Pilsbury. The church appeared at the time, and the persons warned, but instead of answering, they fell to contradicting their pastor, endeavouring what they could that their charges, which were in writing, might not be read or heard. But when the resolution was they should be read, instead of hearkening to them, whereby they might understand what they were charged with, that they might give satisfaction they raised an hubbub, knocking, stamping, hemming, gaping, to drown the reading. Afterwards being demanded whether they would answer to their charges, they all of them (uncivilly enough) refused so to do. Mr. Parker finding little good to be done, but much dishonor to God, dissolved the meeting, and seeing all our endeavours were in vain, on the sabbath day following dissolved the meeting formerly warned also. Yet our brethren kept their motion, and though they fell short of the major part, yet in the name of the church they sent to Mr. Parker, desiring him to come to answer to the church, what Mr. Woodman had against him. Mr. Parker, testifying their irregularities refuses to attend them. They in the meeting house having chosen their moderator and so forth, sit formally as a church. Here Mr. Woodman's complaints to the number of fifteen or sixteen he exhibits and reads against Mr. Parker and also twenty-five more, which formerly he had presented to the council, who found little cause to blame Mr. Parker, but saw sufficiently what temper they were of, to rake up what they could for thirty years, yet had not any thing of value to fasten on him. Some of the brethren there present undertook (though not by Mr. Parker's motion) if they might have liberty presently to answer them. A fair promise they had that they should have liberty, but could get no performance of it either at that or the next meeting.

' The first meeting then adjourned to a second, the second to a third and the third to a fourth. Mr. Parker and others frequently desired them that they would agree to call a lawful and regular council to help settle our distractions, but they resolving to go on in their own way refused all such motions. It is impossible to mention all particulars, nor is it to be thought how many discourses have been to bring them to a right understanding, and it hath been past our skill by any thing we could do (without injuring truth and conscience) to find any way to reclaim them. We have borne their contradictions with patience. Frequently, as we had opportunity we debated with them. The platform of discipline, which they agreed should be their rule, proves nothing to them, unless they may be the judges and interpreters of it. We supposed (unless they deluded the council) that they had ingenuously acknowledged their irregularities, yet are more deeply fallen into them than before. The testimony of a council of nine churches (which we called and maintained at our own charge, and which they contributed nothing to, but contempt and contradiction to linger out the time) is despised by them and counted as an empty paper. The received and approved practice of all the churches in the country is not regarded by them. So that we are at a stand and could not imagine what farther course to take, [with them] who will be content with nothing but their own will, to the subduing of all to their humours and the ruin of the church.

' In the issue it comes to this, that their designs bring forth a monstrous birth. The members cut off the head. Without the advice of any church or churches, without any shew of any just ground and reason (but what their own enraged fancies and violent passions suggest) they take upon them. (and this by a lesser part of the church present, and some of them dissenting, the brethren that were not of their persuasion, were desired to withdraw,) to depose the pastor, to choose two ruling elders, imperiously enough imposing them on their pastor and brethren, were as fit to be respected as others. Whereupon at last for our own defence, for upholding the ordinances of God among us, when we find they despise councils, will not subject themselves to church dealing, or by combination will prevent it, and would rob us of our sacred enjoyments, prostituting all to their confusions, being enforced to it, we saw no remedy but according to the rule of the scripture to withdraw from them that cause divisions, and walk inordinately, as is more fully expressed in our paper, and publickly communicated to them when they were assembled together March twenty-third, 1671.'

The above was written by JOHN WOODBRIDGE.

The next paper, is an answer to the foregoing, and is entitled a ' defence of the persons accused.'

' To the honored court now sitting at Ipswich we humbly present these lines in way of apology to declare the grounds of our late actings as a church to be regular, both by our ecclesiastical liberties, secondly by our late covenant and thirdly correspondent to scripture rule and example.

'*April eighteenth*, 1671.

'First, that a church hath liberty to proceed against an elder, or elders, not only to an act of suspension, but also to expulsion upon due cause. It is without controversy and clear as in law book page twenty-five, section five, every church hath also free liberty of admission, recommendation, dismission, expulsion or deposal, of their officers and members upon due cause with free exercise of the discipline and censures of Christ according to the rules of the word. Second, by our late covenant contained under five articles.

'The first is that the platform of discipline shall be a rule for practice in the church of Newbury in all our administrations, which saith that it is a prerogative that Christ hath given to the brotherhood. Chapter ten, sections five, six, seven. Chapter five, section two. Chapter eight, section seven.

'Second, where it is said chapter tenth, other churches directing thereunto where they may be had, we answer first, that advice is not laid down in the platform as of necessity to be a rule, but where as they may be had. Second, it relates not to the suspension of elders, but to the deposal of them. Third, we have earnestly called upon two churches to have their advice, but one of them refused to come, the other that did come refused to give their advice to the case we had in hand. Fourth, we then sent three questions to the church of Salisbury for their resolution, but they gave us no answer. Then we were forced to take liberty as God hath given us to proceed ourselves as the rule of the word doth lead us. Matthew 18 : 17. Colossians 4 : 17. Romans 16 : 17. Platform chapter ten, sections five, six, seven. Chapter five, section two. Chapter eight, section seven. Law book page twenty-five, section five.

'Third, where a church hath liberty not only to the suspending, but also to the expulsion and deposal, of their officers upon due cause, as is proved before, for the lesser is included in the greater, then also to appoint a church meeting to examine whether be due cause, although the elder offending doth not consent thereunto, for we humbly conceive that no offender is to be active in his own censure, but passive under which he is subject. The contrary seemeth to us to be contrary to law and reason.

'Fourth, the church according to rule may deal with an officer, as is proved already, then a brother that is offended with an officer may deal with him according to rule as Matthew 16 : 17. Platform chapter ten, section five, six, seven, chapter eight, section seven, where it is said to be a power and prerogative given to a brother to deal with any brother, with whom he is offended, and in case he hear him not, to tell it to the church.

'Fifth, if it be the duty of a brother offended after private means used, and he is not satisfied, to tell it to the church, then it is the duty of the church to hear that brother's complaint, and get their judgment upon it in obedience to the rule of Christ Matthew 18 : 17. 1 Corinthians, verse 4.

'Sixth, if this brother offended in a lawful publick meeting upon the Lord's day, doth speak to the whole church to stay and hear him a few words of complaint against a brother, with whom he is offended, and some wilfully go away and do not their duty, but by neglect thereof lose the power and privilege of judgment in what was presented to the church, their refusing their duty is not an obstruction to the major part of the church, that doth stay to do their duty, as they are obliged by the rule Matthew 18 : 17.

'Seventh, Mr. Parker, Mr. Woodbridge and the brethren with him which are forty-five have made a solemn written explicit covenant by the advice of the messengers of nine churches, who as witnesses have subscribed it by the moderator and scribe, that those articles then agreed on should be the rule for practice in the church of Newbury in all their administrations. The which covenant Mr. Parker did refuse to put to the vote of the church, giving the reason that then his party would be engaged to practice it, although himself had covenanted that it should be the rule for practice in the church in all our administrations.

'Eighth, we do conceive that those brethren that consent not unto the covenant made by the pastor and the major part of the brethren, are not in a capacity to act in matters of discipline, in which we shall refer ourselves to the advice of better understanding, the reason of our referring is because our church covenant is lost or burned, and the contents not known, and so under no church covenant until the last covenant made whereby as a congregational church we have no power one over another, but by virtue of this lately made, as is evident by our rule agreed upon, chapter 4, section 1, 3, platform.

'Ninth, it hath been the custom of this church from the beginning not to take notice of the number of brethren, that come to church meeting, but in case the meeting is lawfully warned, if but half the church come together, to carry and end all things by the major part of them that did come, be they few or many, and as far as we know this is the practice of all churches, but notwithstanding we have acted by a major part of the brethren.

'Tenth, we would put it to your serious considerations, whether if none but the brethren, that are in covenant with Mr. Parker, have been desired to stay, seeing the rest own not the covenant by any publick manifestation, our meeting had not been an authentic church meeting, and what we had acted by the major part of them be authentic, yet the whole church was desired to stay without any distinction, therefore no appearance of exception on that account.

'Eleventh, we conceive that every church have an ecclesiastical judiciary amongst themselves to judge of, and give sentence upon, any offences, or upon any persons that are of their combination or society, allowed to every particular church by Christ, Matthew 18, 17, confirmed by our laws, page 25, section 5, by an agreement or covenant as in platform, chapter 10, sections 5, 6, 7. This jurisdiction or judicatory being distinct from the civil power, except we break their laws, or go contrary to the law of God in fundamentals of faith and discipline.

'Twelfth, lastly we would humbly desire you to consider that the major part have the concluding power in all the government and orders of this commonwealth, in our highest court, in the court of assistants, in the county courts, in commissioners' courts, among freemen in their meetings, by towns in their meetings, by military commissioners in their societies, so in choice of all officers from the governor to the constable and way wardens. Also in synods, in councils, in all churches in New England that we know, and how it is come to pass that the poor church of Newbury among the thousands in New England should be opposed in their lawful liberties we cannot but a little wonder. And that it should be commended to this court's consideration whether we are not a people that go about to set up a new government, because we act or allow the act of the major part of the church to be authentic, to us seemeth to be an objection new coined by such as might as well say a church hath no power or privilege whether they be major, or minor, or the whole.

WILLIAM TITCOMB.
CALEB MOODY.
SAMUEL PLUMER.
STEPHEN GRENLEFE.
RICHARD BARTLET.'

In addition to the preceding extracts, there is on file a large number of testimonies, taken before the court in proof of the statements made by the friends of Mr. Parker, in their complaint to the court against Mr. Woodman and his friends. A few of these are here given as a specimen.

TESTIMONY OF ABIEL SOMERBY. '*December* 19, 1670. In the school house Mr. Woodman expressing himself highly, Mr. Parker said, soft, sir, your ways are ungodly, you neglect publick worship and withdraw from the communion of the church. Mr. Woodman said Mr. P.'s ways were ungodly. After further discourse Mr. Woodman began to call for witness of what Mr. Parker said. I said, Mr. Woodman, you said Mr P.'s ways were ungodly, and therefore it is but quid pro quo. Who is that that saith so, Biel? I answered, you, sir. He broke forth with a strange expression, the Lord help us, or the Lord have mercy on us. A man had need to have a care what he speaks before such men.

Sworn to March twenty-eighth, 1671.

'I Abiel Somerby was present when my father in law Richard Knight asked Mr. Woodman for the church book. Mr. Woodman said that he would not let it go till the church sends for it. My father Knight said that Mr. Parker and the church had voted that he should come to fetch it. Mr. Woodman answered I do utterly disown such a church. My father Knight said, is this your answer? Mr. Woodman said yes, that is my answer, only I think you do very sinfully to hold with such a church.   Sworn to April eighteenth, 1671.

'Henry Jaques affirmeth that on January twenty-ninth, 1671 when Mr. Woodman desired the church to stay, that he stayed, but it was not to joyne with them, and speaking to Mr. Woodman he said he thought it unreasonable that Mr. Woodman should desire a church meeting to deal with Mr. Parker, when there was more need for him to be dealt withal for his offences. He also affirmeth that he heard Mr. Woodman publickly affirm that Mr. Parker had broken three covenants already, and that no covenant would stand before him.
                                      Sworn to, April eighteenth, 1671.

'*Deposition of Tristram Coffin and John Knight.*
'On the sixth of February in a publick meeting in the meeting house Mr. Woodman affirmed that when he went to deal with Mr. Parker according to rule and two brethren with him, that Mr. Parker refused to hear him, and told him his ways were ungodly. Tristram Coffin said, sir, you delude the people for those words were spoken the nineteenth of December on another account and it was that day fortnight that Mr. Woodman with others went to deal with Mr. Parker.   Sworn March twenty-eighth 1671.'

As Mr. Woodman's party claimed to be THE church, and to have a majority of the members, it was deemed of consequence on one side to establish that claim, and on the other to prove the contrary.

'There are,' says Mr. John Woodbridge, 'according to just computation, reckoned as members of our church, if Mr. Dummer be left out, seventy-nine, if he be reckoned, eighty. Our brethren of the number of eighty lay claim to forty-one to be with them, if Mr. Dummer be reckoned into them.
Steven Swett, one of their number is a professed anabaptist and hath refused communion with this church several years. Thirty-four only voted with them, which is far from the major part of the church. This being the foundation of all their meetings and actings as a church, if the foundation be tottering, all their meetings being continued by adjournment from one to another, the errors of the foundation must needs convey irregularity to all subsequent motions.'

'John Knight and Tristram Coffin testify that it was a minor part of the church that voted (to sit) for appointing a meeting to hear Mr. Woodman's complaint against Mr. Parker, for thirty-nine have not joyned with them, besides three of forty-one, that Mr. Woodman lays claim to were not present, namely, Mr. Dummer, John Merrill, John Wells, and Mr. Woodman is the complainer, and there remains but thirty-seven. Benjamin Rolf and William Moody did not vote, and Steven Swett ought not to vote, because he is an anabaptist and hath not had communion with this church, and so only thirty-four voted.

'I Joseph Hills aged sixty-nine do hereby testify that on the day of the church meeting appointed on motion of Mr. Woodman, I being in conference with Mr. W. about forbearing all proceeding till it might be cleared up by help of counsel or conference, whether the power of church discipline was in the majority or elsewhere, Mr. Woodman said that Mr. Parker had broken covenant with the church sundry times and it would be to no purpose to make an agreement with Mr. Parker.   Sworn April eighteenth 1671.

'The deposition of Robert Pike aged fifty-three or thereabouts, being desired to give my testimony concerning Mr. Richard Dummer about his being a member of Newbury church, this is that I do testify, that at a meeting many years ago, as I remember upon a sabbath day, there was some thing propounded concerning Mr. Dummer's transmission from the church at Roxbury to the church in Newbury, which seemed to good acceptance with the church, but whether it was by dismission or recommendation I understand not.

ROBERT PIKE.'

'The meeting was in the open ayr under a tree.'

After hearing all the testimony in the case the court came to the following decision, namely :

'Complaint being made unto this court against Mr. Woodman, Mr. Dummer, William Titcomb and a party adhering to them as doth appear in three papers presented by Daniel Pierce and Richard Kent, the said Woodman and divers others complained of, were summoned at the sessions of this court in March last, where the several complaints and charges were read to the said parties then appearing, and their answers required thereunto, when the said Mr. Woodman among other things alleging that their accusations were many and heavy, and that they had many matters to charge upon Mr. Parker and those adhering to him, which they had neither time nor opportunity on the sudden to prepare, the court not willing to surprize them and desiring fully to understand the whole state of a case so extraordinary and of so high a nature, adjourned to the eighteenth of April, allowing them copies of the charges exhibited against them, and advising them to prepare their objections against Mr. Parker and those with him, and to acquaint him with the same that they also might be in readiness to make their defence at the adjournment, and the court might then clearly understand upon hearing the whole case and according to the merit thereof give judgment. The court meeting at the day aforesaid, after a full hearing it did appear that Mr. Woodman, Mr. Dummer, William Titcomb and others adhering to them (not appearing to be the major part of the church at Newbury, although the major part of such as met together) have proceeded to admonish their pastor, Mr. Parker, and to suspend him from the exercise of his office, as appeareth by their act sent unto him the said Mr Parker as signed by Mr. Dummer and Richard Thorlay.

'Second, that the said Mr. Woodman and party as above said did proceed to elect two ruling elders, namely Mr. Woodman himself and Mr. Dummer, appointing a day for their ordination. Third, that this answer was passed against their pastor upon the complaint and solicitation of Mr. Woodman, and that the said Woodman had openly published several falsehoods to animate his party (which lay under some discouragement by the judgment of a council declared against such irregular acting) and to exasperate them against Mr. Parker, who before and at that time of meeting, wherein they suspended him, to prevent so great an evil and scandal, did advise them as became his place, and offered and intreated them to joyne with him to call a council to hear their differences, engaging himself to be concluded thereby, which was not attended by said Woodman and parties, but they proceeded to act as abovesaid, for the defence of which high and irregular practices unheard of in this country, exceedingly scandalous and reproachful to the way of the churches here established, destructive to the peace and order of the gospel, threatening the ruin and desolation of all order. They have alleged nothing but that they were the major part of the church, not charging, much less proving, any offence given by their reverend pastor, Mr. Parker, who for any thing, that doth appear is altogether innocent, though so exceedingly scandalized, reproached and wronged by Mr. Woodman his party. All which clearly and undeniably appearing by the papers, pleas and evidences that are on file, the court as in duty bound being sensible of the dishonor to the name of God, to religion here established and also the disturbance of the peace, the scandalizing of a venerable, loving and pious pastor and an aged father can not but judge the said Woodman, Mr. Dummer, and William Titcomb, the parties joyning with them guilty of very great misdemeanors, though in different degrees, deserving severe punishment, yet being willing to exercise as much lenity as the case is capable of, or may stand with a meet testimony against such an offence, which we are bound in duty to God and our consciences to bear testimony against, do hereby adjudge the said Mr. Woodman and party adhering to him to pay the several fines under written with the charge of the witnesses and fees of court, and that they all stand committed till the said fines, charges and fees be satisfied and paid.'

The sentence of the court was passed May twenty-ninth, 1671. The following is a complete list of Mr. Woodman's party, with the amount of the fines affixed to their names.

'Mr. Edward Woodman, twenty nobles.* Mr. Richard Dummer, Richard Thorlay, Stephen Greenleaf, Richard Bartlet and William Titcomb four nobles each. Francis Plumer, John Emery senior, John Emery junior, John Merrill and Thomas Browne a mark each.† Nicholas Batt, Anthony Morse senior, Abraham Toppan, William Sawyer, Edward Woodman junior, William Pilsbury, Caleb Moody, John Poor senior, John Poor junior, John Webster, John Bartlet senior, John Bartlet junior, Joseph Plumer, Edward Richardson, Thomas Hale junior, Edmund Moores, Benjamin Lowle, Job Pilsbury, John Wells, William Ilsley, James Ordway, Francis Thorla, Abraham Merrill, John Bailey, Benjamin Rolf, Steven Swett, and Samuel Plumer, a noble each.' Robert Coker and William Moody were not fined. The whole number is forty-one.'

The following are the names of Mr. Parker's party.

Mr. JOHN WOODBRIDGE.	Captain WILLIAM GERRISH.
Captain PAUL WHITE.	Mr. PERCIVAL LOWLE.
Mr. HENRY SEWALL.	JAMES KENT.
RICHARD KENT.	ROBERT LONG.
JOHN KENT.	RICHARD PETTINGELL.
HENRY SHORT.	WILLIAM MORSE.
DANIEL PIERCE, senior.	JONATHAN MORSE.
RICHARD KNIGHT.	JOHN DAVIS.
ANTHONY SHORT.	JOHN SMITH.
RICHARD KNIGHT.	JAMES SMITH.
JOHN KELLY.	JAMES JACKMAN.
JOHN KNIGHT.	JOSEPH MUZZEY.
HENRY JAQUES.	RICHARD DOLE.
THOMAS HALE, senior.	ANTHONY SOMERBY.
ROBERT ADAMS.	NATHANIEL CLARKE.
ABEL HUSE.	TRISTRAM COFFIN.
GEORGE LITTLE.	NICHOLAS NOYES, senior.
SAMUEL MOODY.	THOMAS TURVILL.
WILLIAM CHANDLER.	NICHOLAS WALLINGTON.
Mr. NICHOLAS NOYES.	Mr. JOHN GERRISH.
NICHOLAS WALLINGTON.	Whole number 41.

The foregoing completes the transcript from the county court records of all that is deemed necessary to a right understanding of the case, which is in some respects peculiar, and must be deeply interesting, not only to the descendants of those engaged in such a contest, but to all who wish to ascertain the feelings, the views, opinions, and principles, of the early settlers of New England, respecting that vital question in church and state: in whose hands is the power of government rightly lodged? Ought or ought not the majority to govern? On this question, which agitated the church in Newbury for more than a quarter of a century, I make no comments, and

---

* A noble is six shillings and eight-pence.
† A mark is thirteen shillings and fourpence.

offer no opinion. The facts are before the reader. He must draw his own conclusions. Should he, however, suppose, that the action of the county court was a final settlement of the whole affair, and that peace and quietness was once more re-established in the church and among the people of Newbury, he will find his supposition erroneous, as the following extracts from the general court records will show.

' *May* 31, 1671. The present distressed and labouring state of the church of Christ at Newbury being represented to this court, whereof they are deeply sensible, this court doth judge it expedient that some help be sent unto the said church in a way of communion of churches, and therefore do order and appoint that the secretary doe in the name of this court write unto these several churches of Charlestown, the first church of Boston, the church of Dedham, the church of Roxbury, desiring them to send their elders and messengers to the church of Newbury, that they may enquire into their state and offer them their best advice, according to the word of God, for their composure and healing and to make a return of what they shall judge and doe in this matter, unto this court or the council of this commonwealth, and that the secretary doe signify this order unto the reverend Mr. Thomas Parker to be communicated unto both parties there at variance in that church of Newbury; and that Mr. William Stoughton be desired to join with the secretary in writing their letters.'

On June twenty-third, 1671, Mr. William Stoughton addressed the following letter to the reverend Thomas Parker.

' The present state of your church being so uncomfortable and so publickly known, it hath occasioned many and sad thoughts of heart in all that tenderly love the name and interest of the Lord Jesus Christ and seek the good and welfare of these churches with their whole hearts. A solemn grief it is that after such pains and labour heretofore taken by the reverend elders and messengers of several churches that were with you and some hopes of a good success thereof, yet matters in conclusion should come to no better an issue than what of late hath fallen out amongst you. What in this case is incumbent on authority to doe that your divisions may be healed and the scandal of them removed hath been (though under some straits of time) a serious disquisition amongst us. You may please therefore to understand that we have written unto these four churches, namely, of Boston, Charlestown, Roxbury and Dedham, exhorting and desiring them (according to the known and approved practice of communion of churches amongst us) joyntly to send their elders and other meet messengers unto you that they may in such a way of God take knowledge of your present case, and being fully informed give you their best advice an counsel therein as the rules and appointments of our Lord Jesus Christ in his word shall direct. And what these reverend elders and messengers shall find and doe in this your weighty concern they are requested to make a return thereof either to the next general court, that shall be held or to the council of this commonwealth. The messengers of the churches when chosen will give you seasonable notice of the time, which they shall have agreed on, of coming to you.

' And, that there may be that readynesse and preparednesse in you all to receive their coming upon so solemn an errand, as you ought in the Lord, we desire and expect that what we now write unto you may be communicated and read unto your whole church, if it may be assembled together, or at least unto both the parties at variance therein severally. Now, reverend sir and dear brethren we expect and warn you all, and with all earnestness call on you that you would thoroughly and solemnly as in the sight of God reflect upon your doleful and deplorable condition, considering both whence such distractions and disorders spring, and whereunto they tend, none being gainers by them but Satan and his instruments, whilst in the mean time your own souls, and the glory of God and the common interest of these churches are great losers. We beseech you, every one, to be jealous of and judge himself, to humble yourselves greatly before the Lord, to beg that pardon of God and reconciliation with him, without which there can never be any healing among yourselves. That this you may do and that there may be a sovereign and plentiful effusion of grace, love, peace, and a sound mind whereby you may be in every respect framed unto a thankful entertainment of unfeigned submission to such counsels of peace and healing, as may be in the way prososed given in and pressed upon you, is the cordial sincere desire of

WILLIAM STOUGHTON.'

On the second of July, the first church in Boston chose deputy governor John Leverett and five other messengers, ' to go to the church at Newbury, to hear the differences that be there to be a means of healing, if God please.'*

The council assembled at Newbury according to the direction of the general court, but at what precise time we are not informed. The result of their labors was presented to the court, who made a report thereon at the May session, 1672, as the reader will see in its proper place.

From the records of the first church in Rowley, the following letters are extracted.

' Newbury, sixteenth of February, 1671.

' To the church of Christ in Rowley both elder and brethren, grace and peace be with you.

' Reverend and beloved in the Lord,
          ' It is the portion that the God of all wisdom hath allotted this poor church, to pass over the greatest part of her time in this wilderness in great divisions and contentions which cannot but occasion much perturbation of spirit among ourselves, and many thoughts of heart in our sister churches round about us, that we above all others should thus unquietly pass the days of our pilgrimage here, having no other time but the present moment that pass over us, which may be called ours, and the voice of God still sounding in our ears to day if ye will hear his voice then harden not your hearts. And we being conscious that a state of division and contention in the church of Christ is an inlet to much sin and evil occurrences, and that such customs are not to be allowed in the church of Christ, and yet we are commanded to contend for the faith once given to the saints whereby we doe confess that contentions against truth and against rule are only forbidden by the Lord. We therefore considering the aptness that is in men to think well of their own judgments and actions, doe think it expedient, and that, which doth stand with the mind of Christ, and to the rule, to which we have lately agreed, and must have recourse thereto in things wherein we differ, to call upon neighbouring churches for help and advice. We doe therefore earnestly desire that you will send us the messengers, such as be most capable of giving us advice from scripture, or from rule thereunto agreeing, for if it be the good pleasure of the Lord we would once have an end of trouble and contention in his way and according to his will. We shall call in for our help herein at this time only our next two neighbouring churches, Salisbury and Rowley, thereby you may consider what number may be most convenient to send. The time we desire your presence is the last day of February being Tuesday seven night after the date hereof at nine o'clock in the morning. We would desire you to repair to the ordinary, where some of us shall attend to receive you. Once more we do earnestly desire you in the bowels of Christ Jesus not to fail our expectations for our condition itself doth unfortunately call for help and advice, in a case, in which the glory of God and the peace of this church is soe nearly concerned and the rule we are agreed upon

* Boston first church records.

doth direct us to your advice as yourselves are our witness; not doubting but by your advice through God's presence and blessing his name shall have glory and ourselves a benefit. And that it might soe be we commend you to his grace and direction, and rest in love yours to serve you in what we may.

By us signed, whose names are underwritten in the
name of the brethren of the church.

ARCHELAUS WOODMAN.   WILLIAM TITCOMB.
STEVEN GRENLEFE.   CALEB MOODY.
RICHARD BARTLET.   SAMUEL PLUMER.'

ANSWER.

' To Mr. Woodman and the rest of our beloved brethren with him at Newbury, members of the church of Christ there, grace and peace be with you.

'*Rowley, February 20th,* 1671.

' Beloved brethren,
' Your letter, (wherein you desire of this church of Christ at Rowley that we would send messengers to give advice tending to the healing of your long and uncomfortable differences) hath been read before them the nineteenth of this instant. Their answer is that though they are sensible of your uncomfortable condition as things now stand with you and are willing to send the best help God hath given us, yet at present we judge it not seasonable because we are informed by brother Titcomb your messenger to us and by others that you did not by any publick act agree to desire your reverend pastor and the brethren with him to joyne with you in calling a council. We conceive it most agreeable to the rule the fourteenth of Romans seventeen that you desire his concurrence with you in calling a council, and we know noe instance wherein this method has not been attended of such brethren ********** as have at any time called in council in any of these churches. If it be said he will not joyne in calling a council we answer, it may be soe, yet your way is then the clearer to call in help without him. Thus far the whole church.
' Only several of this church do conceive that it were more suitable to your affairs if your church call in some more help than what you mention in your letter, three at least, if not four churches. A covenant breaker is very hardly set, and if nine churches could hardly be instrumental of your peace, how you think two should set you at rights we cannot easily imagine. But we hope if you are willing to call in four or five churches Mr. Parker and the brethren would concur with you therein, whereas if you only mention Salisbury and Rowley to him, we doubt whether he will concur, for he cannot be ignorant that there is not suitable help to be sure of at Rowley as there is in others that you might call in help from. Besides consider that word the eleventh of Proverbs fourteen in the multitude of counsellors there is safety. When are many counsellors needful but in difficult cases, and if yours are not such we cannot readily think of any that are. No more but our prayers to God for you that he would grant you peace by all means. Soe pray your loving brethren,

SAMUEL PHILIPS,
MAXIMILIAN JEWETT,
In the name of the whole church at Rowley.'

'*Newbury, March* 17, 1671.

' The church of Christ which is at Rowley both elder and brethren grace and peace be with you from the Lord Jesus Christ.

' Reverend and dearly beloved in the Lord. After our long and troublesome differences in the church, it is well known unto yourselves that in April the twenty-second last by the help and advice of the assembly of the elders and brethren of nine churches we made an agreement or covenant that the church of Newbury should be governed by a rule then agreed upon in all the administrations contained in five articles. Notwithstanding our troubles being still continued and lengthened out without all hope of remedy in that estate the church stood in having but one elder, and himself so contrary to the church with whom he hath entered into the late covenant or agreement. Insomuch that we are without all orderly proceedings in any church matters, no members admitted, noe censure can pass on offenders, but our condition attended with many evil occurrences to the dishonor of God, to the reproach of congregational churches and especially to this church as not being capable of healing our distempers. In consideration whereof a brother of this congregation hath lately attempted to deal with Mr. Parker as concerning the cause of all our troubles and contentions have proceeded from himself but Mr. Parker refused to hear him saying that none but elders had to doe with him, whereupon this brother made this complaint to the whole church one Lord's day and desired the church to appoint a time to hear him in his complaints, but Mr. Parker forbad the brother to complain to the church and forbad the church to hear him; notwithstanding the church did stay and appointed a time to hear the complaint and have met and heard it. Then considering the weight of the cause in respect to the person concerned in the complaint, agreed to call in two neighbouring churches for advice, but there came to our help but the messengers from Salisbury only, whose advice was that the choice of officers either teaching or ruling elders, such as the church should most unanimously agree upon would most conduce to our peace and quiet. Whereupon three or four of the brethren being sent to Mr. Parker to desire his consent to this advice but he did deny it. The church having adjourned their former meeting, when they heard the complaint, met again at a time appointed and passed their judgment upon it, and being forced thereunto to the great grief and trouble of our hearts and by an act laid Mr. Parker under blame, suspending him from all official acts until he gave the church satisfaction, only to preach as a gifted brother if he please, and having soe done they elected two ruling elders Mr. Richard Dummer and Mr. Edward Woodman, and have appointed Thursday next for their ordination. This is therefore to request that you would be pleased to send your messengers to give their approbation to the work intended, and what help you can to the furtherance of the work. If your reverend pastor would be pleased to preach us a sermon we shall be much obliged unto him. Thus we thought good to lay open to your understanding the order of our proceedings, as not desiring to walk in the dark, or any way to beguile your apprehensions. In case the Lord should stir up your hearts to send us your help in a work that soe much concerns the glory of God, the peace of the church, we hope you shall have no cause to repent of your labour, but to praise the God of peace with ourselves hoping that by such means he will be pleased to create peace for us. Soe commending you to his gracious direction in this and all your concernments we rest in him to serve you in what we may. Signed by us, whose names are underwritten In the name and by the consent of the church.

ARCHELAUS WOODMAN.   WILLIAM TITCOMB.
STEPHEN GRENLEFE.   RICHARD BARTLET.
SAMUEL PLUMER.   CALEB MOODY.'

ANSWER.

'Rowley, March 20, 1671.

' Dearly beloved in the Lord Jesus,
    ' The lecture this week calls for my attendance so that I cannot enlarge, but in brief you may by these understand that your letter hath been read before the church, and their answer is that they judge not meet to send any messengers to encourage or countenance you in what you have done in reference to you reverend pastor, nor in what you are farther about to do in respect to your ordination of elders, as being doubtful of such proceedings, yet neither do they think meet by messengers or by writing to bear testimony against your actings or absolutely to condemn them.
    ' But for myself as one that you were pleased to direct your letters unto, I must needs say that I conceive you are far out of God's way, and therefore doe most earnestly beseech you to desist from such irregular proceedings and unheard of in any church in New England that I know of. The reasons why I conceive your late transactions to be irregular are these.

'First, in that you have not called in counsell in an orderly way by desiring your pastor and the brethren with him to joyne with you in calling in advice. Now it seems to me irrational as well as unbrotherly, that brethren especially a pastor should not have liberty as well as brethren (that bear offence against him,) to chuse such as may hear the matter between them.

'Second, in that he hath offered you to joyne with you in calling in advice, you have not closed with his motion, nor been moved thereby to put any stop to your actings.

'Third, as to your deposing of your reverend pastor, from the exercise of his pastoral office, you mention no advice from the messengers of Salisbury church to encourage you therein, nor doe I believe any church in the colony will stand by you in it. You know what the judgment of the churches is as to that case expressed in the platform. It must be for scandalous evils, not matters controversial. And the whole brotherhood agreeing that called him to office, and therefore not a mere major part, and with the advice of neighbouring churches, the calling in of which you have neither referred to your pastor nor accepted his offer of it to you. For my coming to preach with you on Thursday next if I should soe doe I should think myself much better employed than **** sometimes was when he was not well employed. I have not been unwilling, nor shall be to serve you as God *shall* call and *when* he calls me thereto. In the mean while I beseech the good Lord to direct your work in truth and insure that mercy to you and me that David begs Psalms 19 : 13. Keep back thy servant, and so forth. I rest your grieved brother
SAMUEL PHILLIPS.'

The two following letters were written by the reverend Samuel Phillips of Rowley. They are also transcribed from the Rowley church records and commence thus :

'*January* 16*th*, 1672.

'A reply to a letter sent to S. P. from Mr. John Woodbridge in justification of their practice in coming to the Lord's table notwithstanding the sad divisions among them.'

'Reverend and dear sir,
'Though I have noe great list nor leisure for writings of this nature your long epistle necessitating some reply I doe entreat your consideration of these few lines in way of answer. You doe in yours inform me that the brethren opposite to Mr. Parker doe encourage themselves by something that they have heard from me, as if I profest against your practice in celebrating the Lord's supper in such a time of division. I know not what reports you have heard nor from whom, nor on what ground you receive them, notwithstanding I deny not, but upon occasion I was of your last council's mind in this matter (who advised a cessation at present till your spirits were healed and sweetened with love one towards another) and have expressed noe less to Mr. Parker before the council was sent. But if it be the way of Mr. Woodman and the rest with him to take advantage by any hint (as you say) though never so frivolous, you needed not to take such notice of the taking encouragement from such hints, nor take so much pains to confute them.

'Concerning the question as yourself have stated it, it is easily answered, for yourself confess that if there were any thing chargeable in the reverend pastor and brethren why they should abstain from the use of the sacrament, that then you would acknowledge that the case were somewhat altered, if it were soe. But that I conceive is the case, for the pastor and the brethren stand charged by a council to have acted irregularly in several things. Three are in my mind at present.

'First, that Mr. Parker, contrary to the agreement in the former council, did refuse to admit some into fellowship, because they were of different persuasions from himself, whereas different persuasions on either side was to be noe lett to admissions.

14

' Second, that the articles of agreement (of which the forementioned was one) to which Mr. Parker consented and several principal brethren, yet that he should refuse to publish them and to endeavour a consent to them, was an omission that had sad consequences following amongst yourselves, not to speak how much the former council's pains was made thereby ineffectual and God's name taken in vain whilst solemn thanks were given to God in the churches that he had blessed endeavours and inclined their hearts to such articles of agreement.

' Third, that the pastor and brethren did pass a sentence against Mr. Wood-man's party before calling them to repentance, or advising in soe weighty a matter with other churches, and though you once expressed yourself that these circumstantial omissions (tho' Mr. Parker did not grant so farre) I conceive that they were, especially the former, a substantial omission of attendance to the article that calls upon us to have patience with an heretic, and not reject him presently without using means once and again to convince and reduce him, for it becomes us much more to use means with our brethren to convince and reduce them from the errors of their ways, James 5 : 20, and Timothy 2 : 24 and 25.   In a word I do conceive that if the council's determination when they left you, and the reply to your objections be well considered, there will appear something chargeable on the pastor and brethren, which ought to be acknowledged, (that thereby the hearts of the brethren grieved and offended may be eased) before you came in order to the Lord's table.   And besides it may be feared that your-selves not beginning in this work is the cause why the opposite party are not more forward to attend their duty herein, which duty how much it is incumbent on both, methinks those scriptures the fifth Matthew 23, 24 and James 5 : 16 doe evince.   It is true God will have have his holy ordinances attended, which you strongly plead, but you know that he will have them attended after the due order, otherwise we may expect a breach rather than a blessing 1 Chronicles 5 : 12.   God loves his worship and desires it much but he **** more upon peace and union amongst his people than upon attendance upon him in this or that part of substituted worship, which are means to further us in moral duties and therefore tells us that he is willing to stay for his service till we be reconciled one to another.   If the gift must be left at the altar till personal reconciliation be made, much more when the distance is between so many, not healed by per-sonal acknowledgements.   And as to this you should do as you would be done by.   You will not admit the brethren to that ordinance without confession of their faults, and why should you goe to it without attendance to the duty you call for from them, being there are failings with you as well as greater evils with them.   As for your pleading therefore not guilty, it is not unuseful to con-sider what Mr. Burroughs speaks in his Irenicon, who tells us when our spirits are hot with displeasure one against another, we are apt to be hardened from seeing what is amiss in ourselves as it was with Jonah when his spirit was hot and angry he would hardly be convinced by God himself that he did or spoke any thing amiss.

' Concerning your judgment that no cessation in your case can be grounded on 1 Corinthians, 11, I desire you would a little consider the eighteenth, twentieth, and thirty-third verses.   He tells them that whilst there were divisions and other evils amongst them, this was not to eat the Lord's supper, hence it necessarily follows, that those things, which made it to be noe participation in the Lord's supper, if not amended, ought to be reformed before they came, otherwise why does God set the sword's point at their breast verses twenty-seven and twenty-nine, yea [threaten] them not only with sickness but with death, if they might still meet at that ordinance though those divisions and other evils are not removed.   He that says examine, prepare and soe come, does therein say come not otherwise ; and church reformation, not only personal examination is required in that chapter before they might partake of that ordinance, other-wise they might expect to hear from God this is not to eat the Lord's supper verse twentieth yea and might expect to feel more of his displeasure besides what what they had felt.   I need not tell you, sir, what God required of the Jews as to searching out of leaven before they eat the passover, or what it sig-nified.   The apostle expounds the 1 Corinthians 9 purge out the old leaven that you may keep the feast.   The least sin is worse than a cartload of leaven.

These forementioned failings the scriptures doe condemn as well as the council. The Lord enable you to purge them out by repentance, that soe you may come together to that ordinance of love, joy and prayse purely for the better and not for the worse. Soe prays your unworthy brother,

SAMUEL PHILLIPS.'

'Rowley April 3d, 1672.

' Reverend and good sir,
     ' It was in my purpose, (as it seems it was in yours), not to have troubled you nor myself with any more writing, and therefore having perused your reply to my letter, though I got not satisfaction by it, yet I attempted noe return, judging it meet that yourself should have the last word, but having received another writing from you intimating that I have to great offence admitted one of Newbury church, or more to the Lord's table with us, though under scandal, and having given satisfaction, this does necessitate me to write once more and upon this occasion I shall make a brief reply unto your former large letter. The fifth of Matthew you wave as conceiving it touches not your case, but condemns moral evils, covered with a cloak of devotion towards God, such as open violence, devouring widows' houses and for a pretence making long prayers, but the text saith, if thou rememberest that thy brother hath aught against thee if it be a lesser fault, such as you mention, yet if it be a breach of rule whereby I have offended my brother in word or deed, I ought to acknowledge my fault and be reconciled unto him. It is true as you say a man must remember that his brother hath something against him and if you yourselves can remember nought of that nature, who can help it but only God? whereas you say in your first writing and also in your second that all duties, (if God's worship may), both publick and private must be omitted, I know noe such consequence as that can rationally be gathered from any thing I have exprest. You say that all God's ordinances are of the same nature and alike holy. Though that be granted, yet I conceive a man may and ought to attend upon God in duties of his worship daily in his family and weekly in hearing the word and so forth, though in his sins, loving and allowing himself in them, as suppose a pott companion, and one that has offended many by his ungodly words and ways, and though it is his sin to come with the stumbling block of his inquity before his face yet he may not abstain from the service of God in family and in publick, but for him to come to the Lord's supper in such a condition were a high provocation to God, very sinful in them that suffer it and very dangerous to his own [soul.] The reason is because some duties of God's worship as reading, hearing, prayer and so forth are means appointed for converting and working grace, and therefore to be attended by such as are impenitent offenders, but the sacrament is appointed for comforting the weak brethren, and for strengthening and increasing of grace ; my meaning is not in the least to reflect in all this, but to show the invalidity of such an assertion that if we must abstain from the Lord's supper till we have acknowledged our faults, whereby we have offended our brethren (especially all that are more publick) then by the same reason we must abstain from all duties of God's worship both publick and private. Besides family worship daily and publick worship weekly are stated as to time of attending such duties, but the Lord's supper is not so, but we may come to it seldomer or oftener as we are in capacity for such an ordinance. Old Mr. Shepard administered it once in ten weeks and truly better not once in a year than to come with any allowed leaven (publickly taken notice of) but not removed by repentance. You farther add that the innocent are not be judged with the guilty. I answer,
     ' First, it is hard to conceive that in a church contending and divided there will be many innocent, though some are usually farre more guilty than others. 1 Corinthians 11 : 30 we read not of many clear.
     ' Secondly, if there be particular persons men and women innocent yet till the church be in peace and offences healed in some measure, they are to submit to the affliction to want the Lords supper. At Ipswich there was hot contentions about Mr. Norton's leaving them, some sadly clasht with the reverend Mr. Rogers, and one with another, and though there were divers good men and women that

never meddled in that business, but sat silent, yet the sacrament was not administered. And was it not the duty (think you) of these innocent ones to submit to it (though for a time they wanted that ordinance), the church not being in a capacity to celebrate it till matters were composed.

' As to the three particulars I mentioned I conceived you had and have cause to blame yourselves herein. Time permits not to argue farther with you about them, only a few words as to the third about your censure upon the offending brother. I will not now discourse upon the nullity of that sentence nor how farr ye saying clavis **** non ligat is applicable to your act, yet two things I formerly mentioned were omissions, which I still think cannot be justified.

' First, the not calling upon them to see their sin in such an unheard of act, you tell me you had often warned them to desist from their irregular proceedings and actings, but not a word of any endeavour to bring them to the sense of that sin, or those sins you censured them for, and therefore they could not be looked upon as such as would not hear the church, when the church had not admonished them, nor called upon them for repentance, and as only such as refuse to hear the church are to be censured, or withdrawn from, by the church. And forasmuch as you say what good success could have been expected, if you had endeavoured to bring them to a sight of these evils ? I answer whether they would hear or forbear, yet God's rule is to be attended and therefore your third ingredient to right sentence is namely, to seek a law of God, that will allow them you mention to withdraw from you, obstinate offenders to be censured. I answer not to be withdrawn from till all due means be used for their conviction and bringing them to repentance, neither could they be called obstinate offenders when you had not endeavoured to bring them to a sight of their evils, especially the scandalous one of deposing Mr. Parker.

' It is true what you say it is easier to *find* faults than to *mend* them ; it is also as true it is easier to *make* faults than to *see* them, as appears by your calling this an omission of you know not what, and let what I have said formerly and now as to this matter be accounted a private fancy, I am willing to bear it having a council to bear it with me and what is more the rule will stand by me to my best understanding.

' Second, touching the other omission of calling in council your own words doe evince that it was an unjustifiable omission, in that you once and again say (I think truly) that it was a case the like was never heard of, that you know of in the christian world, the more necessity of serious deliberation and good advice, and you may be sure noe council in the country would have advised you to pass any sentence against them or [them to] withdraw from you till due means had been used by yourselves together with the body of other churches, if need were to bring them to repentance. By this you may perceive that I am farre from that [opinion] that particular churches have absolute power to carry all matters amongst themselves. If some of our church has lisped out something that way, we own it not for a congregational principle, only they say, I own that every particular church organic has power to carry on all affairs and administration in God's house, excepting when they cannot proceed for want of light in difficult cases, or for want of peace and accord.

' As for that passage you mention out of the platform that the power of regular government is in the pastor and the brethren walking in communion, they can't be thought to intend it of a divided and rent church as yours is. Concerning your last writing as to the satisfaction the brethren generally rendered, I judge as you do that it is farre from what the Lord and his people do expect from them. As for the matter of blame you allege against me **** ****** as receiving to the sacrament one or more of your offending brethren scandalous and impenitent, I answer that it is easy to conceive a grievous fault and then to aggravate and lay a load of blame upon it. I am not of that opinion as you intimate, nor has there been any such practice amongst us as yet that we know of. The person that communicated with us was goodman [Thomas] Hale junior. You say our practice therein is episcopal, I wish there were nothing in Newbury that looks of a more episcopal countenance, but to let that pass.

' First, the censure put upon him, namely, goodman Hale and the rest was understood by the council to be null, I answer it was irregular though its true the fault was great.

' Second, he was one that Mr. Parker was willing to accept to the Lord's supper with himself as being satisfied with his acknowledgement (wherein he comes up fully to own his fault according to the sentence of the council in terminis) provided he would come to the sacrament.

' Third, we have it attested by two witnesses that Mr. Parker told them (going to him to acknowledge their faults according to the sentence of the council) that let them go as far as they would in acknowledgement except they would come and join with him at the Lord's table, it would not be taken for satisfaction.

' Fourth, I propounded his desire of partaking to our church, that if any had any thing to object. There was not one that manifested the least dissent.

' I asked the week before advice of Mr. Cobbet in reference to Mr. Dummer and goodman Hale their desire of partaking with us that in case they came up to full acknowledgement of their evil to Mr. Parker and the brethren that they might be admitted, if Mr. Parker do not own that he have submitted to the council's sentence (I mean goodman Hale) to take blame upon him, which they lay upon him, and was unwilling or refused to own as much publickly as he presented to Mr. Parker more privately, then I acknowledge there was a wilful irregularity in admitting him to communion in that ordinance with us for the witnesses I spoke of were not present when goodman Hale offered such full satisfaction to Mr. Parker, which I understood not till a day or two after the sacrament, but the testimony is that they there offered up like full satisfaction, but it was not accepted except they would come to the sacrament. I shall not for the future admit him nor any more of yours till they make it evident by full proof that they have attended their duty in what is before mentioned, and then though they should essay to join with that part of the church with you, which do partake, I do not see how they can be rejected of other churches, yet notwithstanding I shall not be very forward to admit any more of yours till God be pleased to find out some way for issuing the difference amongst you, which might have been obtained before this day, had both parties acknowledged to each other what was amiss. I would not be understood as if I looked upon the offences as equally evil, yet the mote in our eyes should trouble us (if the humble soul may call his sin a mote) as well as in another's, for a less fault is more hurtful to *us*, if not repented of, than the greatest crimes of others can be.

' For my intermeddling as a busy-body in other men's matters, for that is the apostles' expression that you seem to refer to, you cannot be ignorant that I can easily answer it, but I desire not to aggravate, but to love you and delight in you, notwithstanding all reflections, for I cannot but say that you have been and are dear to me and reverend Mr. Parker also, though it may be neither of you are very ready to believe it at present. I do not intend to trouble you with any more writing (but hope we may have opportunity to discourse the matter lovingly together.) In the meanwhile while the God of love and peace direct us in the way thereof.   Pray for your unworthy brother,
                                SAMUEL PHILLIPS.'

The difficulties in the church in Newbury had, it seems, excited a deep interest in almost all parts of the state, and, as usual in times of excitement, a vast deal of falsehood was circulated respecting Mr. Parker. One of these stories was deemed of so much importance by the grand jury, that they sent the following to the county court :

' We present Edward Lumas of Ipswich for publishing these following words, namely, ' that Mr. Parker of Newbury had sent a letter to the lord arch bishop of Canterbury for help and relief about their troubles at Newbury and that *he saw a copy of the letter.*'

' For this offence,' the court records inform us, May first, 1672,

' Edward Lumas and Robert Adams shall audibly make public acknowledgement next lecture day.'

1672.

From the general court records I make the following extracts:

'*May* 19*th*, 1672. The court having perused the return of the messengers of the churches chosen by order of the ecclesiastical court to inspect the differences in the church of Newbury and to offer their best advice according to the word of God for their composure and healing and to make return of what they shall find and do in this matter unto this court or council of the commonwealth and upon our consideration judge meet to declare their approbation of the same and desire it may be attended to accordingly by all persons respectively concerned, the particulars whereof are as followeth.

' First, concerning Mr. Woodman and his company we do judge their actings in withdrawing from the rest of the church, to set up meetings among themselves in the name of the church and to act the power of the church in admonishing and suspending their reverend pastor and choosing elders, appointing a time of ordination, although they be the major part of the brethren and, notwithstanding offences and provocations given them we cannot but bear due witness against them, as a violation of church order in the gospel and usurpation upon the liberties of their brethren, for although the whole church agreeing may censure an officer for gross and scandalous evils in dealing or conversation, impenitently persisted in according to Colossians 4 : 17, Romans 16 : 17, as is alleged in the platform of discipline, yet in a divided state of the church for the major part and that by a very few, and that in a matter doubtful and disputable, to act as is aforesaid is a matter of great disorder and scandalous and contrary to 1 Thessalonians 5 : 13, Gallatians 4 : 13, 1 Corinthians 13 : 4, and therefore is a nullity.

' Second, concerning the act of the reverend pastor and those with him suspending Mr. Woodman and the brethren with him notwithstanding the offence given them, yet to pass such an act or censure suddenly and thereby increasing the rent and occasioning greater divisions and themselves being the minor part of the church and not seeking after healing means and so forth or taking counsel is irregular and null 1 Corinthians 14 : 40, 2 Corinthians 13 : 10. Thus far we have in faithfulness declared our judgments concerning offences and failings each party is guilty of. Some other things that are more dubious in the agitations before us, we shall only give our advice about to avoid unnecessary disputes about them for the future.

' First, whereas our Lord Jesus Christ hath given liberty of voting in all their own concerns to the whole church it necessarily follows that the judgment of the whole church should be clearly manifested and forasmuch the scripture mentioneth the lifting up of hands Acts 14 : 23, we judge that the most clear way and rather to be chosen, and that a sufficient number should appear to discover a major part, the rest being silent.

' Second, we advise Mr. Woodman according to the fourth commandment to attend diligently on the publick worship of God on the Lord's days avoiding offence and evil example in the contrary so far as bodily infirmities will suffer him so to do.

' Third, in reference to the reverend Mr. Woodbridge we advise and entreat that whereas the peace and edification of the church of Christ is much promoted and depends upon the amicable close of spirit and united judgment, between the officers and brethren, the speaker and hearers, the enemy being vigilant to take all advantages to hinder the gracious operation of the holy word of God in the publick ministry thereof, and whereas there doth appear not only some hesitations, but distance in judgment in reference to discipline and of affections and some other provoking words passed in publick in our hearing, we desire, request and advise the reverend Mr. Woodbridge, not to impose himself or his ministry (however otherwise desirable) upon this church, but that they have the liberty that Jesus Christ, gospel rule, and approved church order, doth allow them, to choose their own minister, that all obstruction to edification and ground to temptation may be removed, as was intimated was the mind of the former council, but to wait to see the mind of God in the issue of the reconciliation of the church, if God shall guide their hearts to closing with him.

' Fourth, we advise that hereafter ecclesiastical offences be not too suddenly brought to civil courts without consulting with churches being contrary as we judge to 2 Colossians 5, 6, 7.

' Considering the great age and weakness of reverend Mr. Parker and thereby his unfitness to manage church discipline, we advise it as very suitable and seasonable to this church's case to choose a ruling elder or two, provided they be without just offence to either party, for the healing this great breach and offences, that have brought so much dishonor to God, and the profession of the gospel, and been so destructive of the edification of this church and the people of this plantation. We do advise and most seriously exhort in the name of our Lord Jesus Christ unto these duties, which the Lord requires of this church in such a case.

' First, that this church be sincerely and deeply humbled before the Lord as for their divisions, distances and want of love in general, so also in particular for such failings and evils as we have before mentioned and that according to the nature and scandalousness of the evils any of them have fallen into, then that every one may know and acknowledge the plague of their own heart before the Lord according to the rules of Christ Matthew 8 : 3, Revelations 3 : 5, repent and do the first works and as God shall open their hearts, shall confess to one another according to James 5 : 16.

' Second, we advise and exhort after due humiliation, there be a mutual, hearty and free forgiveness of each other according to the rules of Christ, if thy brother repent, forgive him even to seventy times seven. Matthew 8: 22, Colossians 3 : 13 forbearing one another as God for Christ's sake forgave you Matthew 18 : 15.

' Third, we advise and exhort that this repentance may be manifested by all such acts of reformation and love as is suitable to the grace of true repentance, Matthew 3 : 8, bring therefore fruits meet for repentance, and that hereafter the whole church walk according to the rule of faith, love and the order of the gospel, whereunto you latterly had a seasonable exhortation that soe peace and mercy may be upon you with the whole Israel of God.'

' The court also ordered the following letter to be sent to the church of Newbury.

' Reverend and beloved in our and your Lord.
           ' By these we signify to you that we have received the return of the within messengers of churches, elders and brethren of their travail and pains with you in pursuance of their churches' call upon our desire. Upon reading and considering their result, we have passed our approbation of the counsel therein given unto you, as suitable to your case, which we remit to you with these. And although we might enjoin you, yet for love's sake we beseech you and every one of you as you are concerned therein, pastor and people, preacher and hearers, however before divided, that you jointly attend to the counsel so given you, that we may say of you that though for some time you have been unprofitable one to another, yet now you are become profitable again as in former times, and that the churches of our Lord Jesus Christ which have been saddened by your divisions and contentions, may have cause to rejoice in and before the Lord on your behalf, and the name of the Lord, that hath been dishonored may be honored by your mutual putting forth such acts of faith and repentance as may reach to the recovering of your peace with the Lord and with one another that so you may be found in the more excellent way of charity manifesting yourselves unto all men that you are Christ's disciples by loving one another. Our just expectation is that you delay not in this great concern, but that you apply every one in your respective places unto the furtherance thereof.

Should there be a failure of you or any of you therein (which the Lord forbid) you may not think but that we shall be necessitated to advise what further course is to be taken according to God that contentions may be removed and peace restored among you. Thus we commend you to the Lord and to the word of his grace.'

By the court,

EDWARD RAWSON, *Secretary.*

' To the reverend Thomas Parker,
pastor of the church in Newbury, to be communicated to the church there.'

I shall here give one more extract from the general court records, and relieve the patience of the reader. It is the last notice that I have been able to find on the subject in any record whatever.

'*October 8th*, 1672. Whereas there hath been a complaint exhibited to this court by many of Newbury, whereby it is evident that the council agreed to and sent in May last to be attended to by them hath not been so attended as the court expected, and for that the persons more especially informed against, as obstructing the same have not, appeared personally before the court that they might answer for themselves, this court doth further commend the said advice unto them to be attended by both parties, professing their readiness there to and that the distemper of their contentions may not obstruct in the manner of their coming to the understanding of themselves and one another therein this court doth appoint Mr. Thomas Danforth, Mr. William Stoughton, Mr. Urian Oakes, doctor Leonard Hoar, captain Thomas Clarke, Mr. Henry Bartholomew, Mr. John Elliot and Mr. Joshua Moody as a committee and that the major part of the whole meeting there shall be a quorum, who are to repair to Newbury and call both parties together and persuade with them to attend the same in love and christian submission one to another according to God and in case there shall appear any refractoriness in any amongst them that the persons so sent cannot prevail with them that they then make return to the next court of election what they find and do therein.'

To some of my readers the following transcript from the county court files in Salem, may be interesting.

' I Ann Hills, sometime servant to Abraham Toppan, testify that Abraham Toppan did make sundry voyages to the Barbadoes, of which one or two were profitable, the produce being brought home in sugars, cotton wool and molasses, which were then commodities, rendering great profit, wool being then at twelve pence, sugar at six or eight pence per pound profit, of which he brought great quantities.

'Jacob Toppan testifieth that the last voyage from Barbadoes above mentioned he brought home eight barrels and one hogshead of sugar and two or three thousand pounds of cotton wool.'

Testimonies taken in 1671.

'*April 1st*, 1672, [*old style.*] A great storme of driving snow came out of the north west and drove up in drifts about six feet deep. For the space of fourteen days [after] it was a sad time of rain, not one whole fair day in fourteen and much damage done to mills and other things by the flood, which followed.' *

* Hampton records.

1673.

'*March* 26*th*.   The town was fined five pounds for neglect about Thorlay's bridge and ordered to make it passable for safe traveling, on penalty of ten pounds more.   John Pearson of Rowley to see it made sufficiently and to be done by midsummer,' and so forth.＊

'Richard Kent is freed from trayning by paying four bushels of good mault to the use of the troop.' ＊

September 24*th*.   'There was a storme of raine and snow so that the ground was covered with snow and some of it continued till the twenty-sixth.' †

January 31*st*.   A committee was chosen for building a house 'for the ministry of the same dimensions every way as Nathaniel Clark's is with the addition of a porch.' ‡   'It was also voted to lay out six acres of land behind captain Gerrish's house towards Trotter's bridge for the ministry.' ‡

April 16*th*.   'The town voted that the minister's rate should be made every year in October, one half to be paid in English grain as wheat, barley, rye and pease, the other half in Indian corn.' ‡

July 5*th*.   'The selectmen ordered that John Webster shall pay ten shillings and Peter Toppan five shillings for cutting down trees on the land that is called the burying place.' ‡

When the town of Newbury was first settled, large quantities of sturgeon were taken from the rivers Merrimac and Quascacunquen, which were not only used and highly valued as an article of diet, but pickled and packed in kegs for transportation.

Frequent allusions to this subject are made in the county and state records, old account books, and so forth.   Thus Wood, who visited America in 1633, says, 'that much [sturgeon] is taken on the banks of the Merrimac, twelve, fourteen, eighteen feet long, pickled and sent to England.'

In 1656, 'a keg of sturgeon, ten shillings,' was among the charges for entertaining an ecclesiastical council at Salisbury.   In 1667, Israel Webster testified, 'that he carried twenty-two ferkins and kegs of sturgeon from William Thomas' cellar to send to Boston.'

In 1670, Joseph Coker was licensed by the county court 'to make sturgeon in order to transport.'   In 1680, September twenty-eighth, the records of the county court inform us, that 'Thomas Rogers [of Newbury] is licensed to make sturgeon, provided he shall present the court with a bowle of good sturgeon every Michaelmas court.'   In 1684, 'Caleb Moody and Daniel Pierce were licensed to boil sturgeon in order to a market.'   In 1733, captain Daniel Lunt of Newbury was ordered to sell his sturgeon in Boston at twelve shillings per keg, 'if he could get no more.'   In the same year, Mr. Daniel Pierce exchanged fifteen kegs of sturgeon for a small cask of rum, and a larke cask of molasses.

＊ **County records.**   † **Hampton records.**   ‡ **Town records.**
15

The following petition is copied from the original, now on file among the papers in the state house, Boston.

‘ To the honored general court assembled at Boston May seventh, 1673.

‘ The petition of William Thomas humbly shewing,

‘ That your petitioner after sundry experiments, and travels into foreign countries, upon great expence of his estate, hath through the blessing of God upon his industry herein, attayned unto the art of boyling and pickling of sturgeon, by means whereof it is a commoditie, not only in this countrie, but in England and other parts for transportation and increase of traffique for the procuring of goods more useful and needful for this countrie, and may so continue and increase, if sundry persons, of other callings, unskilful in that mystery, who for lucre of monie and other sinister ends, presume to deal therein, shall not cause it to be debased and of no value for transportation, as indeed by that means it in part already is (as is known to sundry gentlemen and merchants of Boston) to the defamation of your aged petitioner, and damage of the countrie, who now in the seventy-fourth year of his pilgrimage, hath his whole dependance under God for the subsistence of his family upon that employment, who if he were not forestalled and circumvented by others might live comfortably, and also afford some yearly revenue to the countrie, but some there are, that by hooke or crooke, for strong liquors or otherwise, that finger the fish taken for and by the Indians procured and employed by your petitioner, and that oft times upon payments fore made for the same, and if he were not undermined and interrupted therein by interlopers and other unskilful persons, it might be beneficial both to him and the countrie.

‘ His humble petition therefore is that henceforth no man be suffered to pickle or put upp any sturgeon for trade or traffique directly or indirectly within this jurisdiction but such as by lawful authoritie shall be licensed thereto on certain penalties, as title, innkeepers or otherwise and that there may be some skilful men impowered and sworn to search all such sturgeon as shall be packed or putt up in any kind of vessels whatsoever, and to refuse all such as they shall find defective for transportation or continuance at least the year about. And such and such only shall be sufficient in all respects for traffique as aforesaid to mark with the letters of their and the sturgeon boiler's names. And that it may be lawful for any man knowing of any sturgeon put upp as for trade or traffique, that is not so marked, to inform any searchers or constables, and that they may seize upon it as forfeited, one third to the informer, one third to the officer seizing, and the other third to the treasurer of the county where it shall be found.

‘ And your petitioner farther humbly prayeth that he may be licensed for the counties of Essex and Norfolk during his own and his wife's life, being aged and altogether uncapable of any other way of subsistence or service in town or countrie, which favour being granted your petitioner will cheerfully pay to the treasury or otherwise as this honored court shall appoint either ten kegs of sturgeon yearly or every twentieth keg and firken by him made from time to time or the true value thereof at every year's end namely, the twenty-ninth of September annually, and as duty binds him shall daily pray and so forth.

WILLIAM THOMAS.

‘ Newbury, May seventh, 1673.’

Of the result of this petition we are not informed. Probably it was not granted, as we find in 1674 that ‘ Peter Toppan was licensed to make, boyl and sell sturgeon,’ and William Chandler was appointed searcher and sealer of sturgeon, by the county court.

December 2d, 1673. ‘ A committee was chosen for the building of Mr. [John] Richardson's house and to carry it on to the finishing of it.’ *

* Town records.

By this it appears that the town had determined to settle Mr. Richardson as their minister, though he was not ordained till October, 1675. He probably commenced preaching early in this year, and might have been instrumental in settling the difficulties, which had agitated the church and town for more than a quarter of a century, as we hear of no difficulty between the church and minister, subsequent to the autumn of 1672. The situation of the church and people of Newbury, at the time of his arrival here, undoubtedly occasioned the peculiarity of his language in his conditions of settlement, which were : ' first, so long as the people of God here do continue in the profession of the true faith and peace of the gospel as in Acts 11 : 42 ; second, so long as I may have the liberty of my ministry among them ; and third, discharge my duty to my family. Thus I say I do express myself willing to settle among you with a true intention and a true affection.' *

' JOHN RICHARDSON.'

' August fifteenth, 1675.'

' The liberty of the ministry,' says the reverend doctor Popkin, 'is an expression frequently used in the histories of the puritans : and appears to be opposite in signification to that restraint, under which they were held by ecclesiastical authority.'

' Francis Thorlay was presented for striking his brother Thomas and flinging stones at him.' He was fined ten shillings and costs of court. †

1674.

' *March 2d.* It was voted that the finishing of the house for the ministry and the alteration of it is left to the selectmen.' ‡

March 28th. ' It was voted that captain Gerrish, Mr. Daniel Pierce and Tristram Coffin should lay out the six acres formerly granted to build a house on and to make a pasture for the maintenance of the future ministry, that part for the building of the house to be on the side next to captain Gerrish's orchard and the rest of the said six acres to be laid out next Richard Brown's pasture.' ‡

'*December 6th.* Reverend John Richardson was admitted a member of the church in Newbury.' This is the earliest fact recorded in the church book, all the preceding transactions having been destroyed apparently by design. Until the settlement of Mr. Richardson the records are in the handwriting of William Chandler.

In the latter end of this year, a converted Indian, named John Sausaman, acquainted the governor of Plymouth that the profane Indians were plotting mischief againt the English, and expressed his apprehension that they would murder him. This apprehension was realized, as, before the close of the winter, he was murdered by three Indians, who were afterward tried and executed.

---

* Church records.　　　† County records.　　　‡ Town records.

1675.

March 1st. 'A committee of two was appointed to complete the finishing the ministry house and fencing about said house. Warning was also given by the selectmen for every person to appear with carts and oxen and hands, and tools suitable to bring stones and so forth and every person not having oxen is to appear in person to help forward the work and so forth.' *

April 13th. 'It was voted that the piece of meadow above Mr. Sewall's farm, the meadow at Trotter's bridge, a piece at Lob's pound and two parcels of salt marsh about three acres near Pine island should be laid out to the ministry house for the use of Mr. Richardson while he continues our minister, and so forth.' *

May 7th. 'There was laid out to Richard Dole six rods and a quarter upon the point of land that lies between the two gutters, that come from the point of rocks near Watts' his cellar about two rods in breadth bounded by the river on the north to about a foot upon the rock that is there on the south and three rods in length by the water side and so forth adjoyning to the former grant.' *

This piece of land was between the market house in Newburyport and Mr. George T. Granger's store.

June 18th. It was ordered that all non-freeholders should 'pay for every horse going on the commons five shillings, for every neat beast two shillings and sixpence, for every score of sheep five shillings, for every swine twelve pence and for every load of wood two shillings and sixpence for the use of the town.' *

October 5th. The town voted that they would not fortify 'the meeting house, but voted that they would buy a couple of field pieces about seven or eight hundred apiece.'*

October 20th. Reverend John Richardson was ordained. His salary was to be one hundred pounds a year. Each person was to pay 'his proportion as followeth, one half in merchantable barley, the rest in merchantable pork, wheat, butter or Indian corn, or such pay paid unto Mr. Richardson to his satisfaction, as every person may understand upon inquiry of Tristram Coffin,' who was chosen in April 'the town's attorney to gather Mr. Richardson's rates and in case the said Tristram Coffin shall neglect his trust herein, he shall pay forty shillings fine to the selectmen.'*

November 12th. Henry Short was appointed schoolmaster. He is to have five pounds for the first half year and to have sixpence a week for every scholar.

In the month of June this year the three Indians were executed, who murdered John Sausaman. On the twenty-fourth of June was shed the first English blood, in what was afterward called Philip's war. On that day, nine Englishmen were murdered in Swanzy, by the Indians, as they were returning from the meeting house, it being

* Town records.

the day appointed as a day of humiliation and prayer throughout Plymouth colony, who being thus unexpectedly involved in trouble, sent to the other colonies for assistance. On June twenty-sixth, soldiers marched from Boston to Plymouth. On the twenty-ninth, a day of humiliation and prayer was appointed on account of the war. The men prest from Newbury, were as follows, namely :

August 5th. Steven Greenleaf, Thomas Smith, John Toppan, Caleb Richardson, Daniel Rolf, John Hobbs, Daniel Button, John Wheeler, and Henry Bodwell, nine men and fourteen days' provisions.

August 6th. Seven more were prest and fourteen days' provisions.

August 27th. Seven men were prest, fourteen days' provisions, twenty-three horses, saddles, and bridles.

September 23d. Two men and two days' provisions.

September 27th. Five men, ten days' provisions, and twenty-three horses, saddles, and bridles, were pressed for the country's service.

September 29th. Richard Kent's man was pressed.

December, 1675. Twenty-four men were pressed for the country's service, being in all forty-eight men, and forty-six horses, for this year.

The town expenses for this year were very great.

The minister's rate was   103 pounds, 17 shillings, 1 penny.

The expenses for the war, 457   "   18   "   8 pence.

The town debt was   191   "   3   "   9   "

Beside other expenses, not included in the above.

At the battle fought December nineteenth, at the Indians' fort in Narraganset, 'four men were slayne,' of whom Daniel Rolfe was from Newbury, and eighteen wounded, of whom Daniel Somerby, Isaac Ilsley, Jonathan Emery, William Standley, and Jonathan Harvey were from Newbury.

Daniel Somerby was the only son of Henry Somerby. Before he marched against the Indians he made his will, and soon after his return died of his wounds.

1 6 7 6 .

January 2d. Thirteen men were impressed.

June 9th. Town voted to purchase a barrel of powder and fifteen hundred flints.

June 21st. The town appointed Henry Short ' to keep school for this year, from the first of May last, to the first of May next, and the selectmen engage to pay him ten pounds out of the next town rate, and if the number be about twenty scholars, he is to teach them at the watch house.'*

Henry Short taught the grammar school. In his old note book

* Town records.

I find the following account of scholars, commencing thus: 'when I kept school at home and the time they [the scholars] came.' Here follow the names of seventeen scholars, from May tenth to December twenty-fifth.

The following extract from the colonial records presents to the reader as lively a picture of the anxiety and distress among the people of Massachusetts, occasioned by the bold and daring determination of king Philip and his Indian allies to extirpate the English, as can well be imagined. The proposition to erect a fortification of such a length and height, shows the desperation, to which they were reduced, and the dangers to which they felt exposed.

'At a court held in Boston March twenty-third, 1676.

'Whereas several considerable persons have made application to us and proposed it as a necessary expedient for the publick welfare and particularly for the security of the whole county of Essex and part of Middlesex from inroads of the common enemy, that a line or fence of stockades or stones (as the matter best suiteth) be made about eight feet high extending from Charles river where it is navigable unto Concord river from George Farley's house, in Billerica, which fence the council is informed is not in length above twelve miles, a good part whereof is already done by large ponds that will conveniently fall into the line and so forth, and so forth, by which means the whole tract will be environed for the security and safety (under God) of the people, their houses, goods and cattel from the rage and fury of the enemy.'

The court then orders one able and fit man from each of the included towns to meet at Cambridge on March thirty-first, to survey the ground, estimate the expense, and so forth, and so forth, and bring their report in writing how it may be prosecuted and effected, what each town should pay, and so forth.

Nearly all the towns made a report.

That from Newbury is as follows, namely:

'At a meeting of the selectmen of Newbury March 1675-6.

'We having taken it into consideration what the honored council hath propounded unto us as to the fortifying from Merrimack river and so to Charlestown river, we conceive it not feasible nor answering the end propounded, but leave it to the consideration of wiser than ourselves, conceiving this to be difficult in doing it or mayntaining it when done, but rather think it will most conduce to our safety to have a sufficient company of men that may range to and fro as our honored council judge meet. We have ordered several houses to be garrisoned and fortified and men appointed and are about fortifying with a mile or somewhat more from river to river most of our plow lands and houses, if men will own our power (as we hope will be) with their own and our endeavours to compleate our trust.

WILLIAM GERRISH,	STEVEN GREENLEAF,
WILLIAM TITCOMB,	PETER CHENEY,
BENJAMIN ROLFE,	FRANCIS PLUMER,

Selectmen.

1677.

March 5th. ' Captain [Paul] White proposed for about a rod of land at the hanging of the hill before his still house in the street.' *

' Marchant [Richard] Dole proposed for liberty to build a dock about Watts his cellar, and as many of the town as were willing to help him about it, he will accept of their help.' *

March 27th. At the county court at Salem, 'Joshua Richardson, Caleb Richardson, and Edward Ordway were sentenced to be severely whipt or pay a fine of ten pounds each, for breaking into the meeting house, demolishing a pew chairs and so forth.'

It appears by the town records that the selectmen had granted permission to several young women to build ' a new seat in the south corner of the women's gallery.'

This pew or new seat, from some now unknown cause, excited the indignation or anger of these young men, who, having demolished the seat, chairs, and so forth, were tried, convicted, and sentenced.

The following testimonies in the case are copied from the files of the county court in Salem.

' *Testimony of* —— —— *aged forty-five years.*

' I dow testify consarning the [mischief] att the meting hows that the meting hows windowse weare brocken open severall times and the dore was dabid with a sarrowans and the ceay holl [key hole] dabid allso. There was a sarrowans pute in the corne, which was pute in the meting hows lowft for safety, which was in a cask in the chambear.'

' I dow testify that I saw Joshua Richardson uppon Wensday the wery next day after the pue or new seate was brocken doun the last of January last past. I on purpos towck wery good notis of him and to my onderstanding he did goo ass weall att that time ass hee youste to due att other times, without any limping or a going lambe that I could perseaif.'

Another testimony declares, that the window was fastened with ' tow hapsis,' and that the ' glass was broken in pessis.'

April 22d. Seventy-six of the principal inhabitants of Newbury petitioned the court to mitigate their fines.

' We do not know,' say they, ' that any of the young men have been detected of open crimes, have been diligent and laborious to promote and support their parents, who stand in need of their help, they have endured hardships and adventured their lives and limbs for their country, they have openly, ingenuously and solemnly made acknowledgment of their offence before many assembled to that end,' and so forth, and so forth.

April 24th. Reverend Thomas Parker died.

Captain William Gerrish was ordered, April fifteenth, by major general D. Denison to march to Salisbury with forty of his best men, well armed, and so forth, and again, May first, with twenty men to Portsmouth. Expenses were five hundred pounds.

* Town records.

Judge Sewall, in his diary, under date of July eighth, 1677, has the following. 'A female quaker [Margaret Brewster] in sermon time came in a canvass frock, her hair dishevelled, loose like a peri-wigg, her face as black as ink, led by two other quakers, and two other quakers followed. It occasioned the greatest and most ama-zing uproar that ever I saw.' She had previously taken off her stockings and shoes, and left them in the porch of the meeting-house,* under the care of John Easton, son of Nicholas Easton, formerly of Newbury. John was afterward governor of Rhode Island.

September 21st. The town desired captain Gerrish to propose to 'Ipswich court that Thomas Thorla's ordinary may be put down.' †

The town chose a committee 'to hire a schoolmaster,' and voted to give him twenty pounds a year 'for encouragement besides what they shall agree upon for the children that shall come to school to him.' †

From an old account book I learn that this year turnips and ap-ples were a shilling a bushel, a day's mowing, two shillings and two pence, men's wages for a year ten pounds, women's wages from four to five pounds, board four shillings per week, and labor two shillings a day.

Thanksgiving, November third, on account of a plentiful harvest and a cessation of the wrath and rage of the enemy.

1678.

March 4th. 'Concerning building of a dock, it was granted, provided that all boats that belong to the town shall have free liberty of egresse and regress to lie there as occasion may serve.' †

This was probably the dock for which Richard Dole petitioned, as in September 'a committee was chosen to conclude the business between marchant Dole and the town about his dock.'

September 20th. The committee appointed for that purpose laid out 'to Richard Dole senior a parcel of land lying near Watts his cellar, where *he is now building a wharf and dock*' three rods broad from the east side of the west gutter to a stake near to the great rock with the flats adjoining thereto excepting two rods in breadth upon the easterly point of upland, which is to lie for a perpetual high way for the town's use to the dock for to unlade hay, wood, timber, boards, or any thing else, which is produced in or upon the river, it not being imported from or exported to the sea. We also do grant the town's title, right and interest to the point of land on the northerly side thereof, which is commonly known by the name of captain White's point and so forth and the said Dole is to set a wharf against the two rod that is appointed for a way for the town's use.' †

November 22d. Town voted to continue the 'twenty pounds a

year to the schoolmaster,' and 'that Mr. Richardson, so long as he carries on the whole work of the ministry among us, shall have twenty pounds a year added or two contributions, which he pleases to accept.' *

December 22d. Town voted that 'Thorlay's bridge should be built at the town's charge as the court gave them liberty.' *

'Judith Thorla was fined for selling liquor to the Indians on the Lord's day.'

In this year a new brick building was erected at Cambridge as a college building. It was erected by subscription. Newbury gave thirty-three pounds and three shillings. Rowley forty-five pounds, and Ipswich eighty pounds.

November 12th. The town granted to John Emery, junior, twelve acres of land, beginning at Artichoke river, on condition that he build a grist mill.

November 26th. In answer to a petition of the selectmen, Newbury was allowed to build a firm and safe 'bridge.' * The toll 'a penny for a man and three pence for a horse.'

'The wife of John Davis of Lynn was presented for breaking her husband's head with a quart pot and otherways abusing him.'

This year all persons over sixteen years of age were required to take the oath of allegiance. A list of their names from every town in the county of Essex is in the county records. That of Newbury contains the names of two hundred and thirty-six persons, with their ages affixed by Mr. John Woodbridge, who administered the oath in September. In no other list are the ages given.

1679.

March 3d. 'The town granted to John Emery junior twelve acres of land on the west side of Artichoke river provided he build and maintain a corn mill to grind the town's corn from time to time and to build it within one year and a half after the date hereof and so forth.' *

In compliance with the law the selectmen chose fourteen tything men, each of whom had a specific duty to do respecting a designated number of families, generally ten, all living in the same neighborhood, and classed by the selectmen. After making the arrangement, they sent a note to each of the tything men, informing them of their appointment, and of the families committed to their care. A copy of one of these notes, found among the papers of the late deacon Abraham Merrill, is here subjoined.

'To deacon Abraham Merrill.
'At a meeting of the selectmen March thirty-first, 1679.
'You are hereby required to take notice that you are chosen according to court order by the selectmen to bee a tithing man to have inspection into and

* Town records.

look over these familes that they attend the publick worship of God, and do not break the sabbath, and further you are to attend as the court order declares.

'The names of the families are Edward Woodman junior, Samuel Bartlet, Richard Bartlet, Abel Pilsbury, John Stevens, Christopher Bartlet, Thomas Chase, goodman Bailey, John Chase.

By order of the selectmen.
ANTHONY SOMERBY, *Recorder.*'

May 21*st.* A committee of twelve men was appointed, ' to consult of a way for dividing of the upper commons if it be possible so to agree that the town may like of it.' *

May 28*th.* The selectmen petitioned to the general court respecting Plum island, in which they say that the inhabitants ' of Rowley having sold their parts to several of Newbury and some of Ipswich, so that the whole island now is in the occupation of the inhabitants of Ipswich and Newbury, who make improvement by cutting the grass, and some of Ipswich by planting some small parcels thereof, and by reason of the impossibility to part the island by fencing, and the proprietors of Ipswich by reason thereof finding themselves much damnified in that their marshes were trodden to dirt and almost utterly spoiled by a *multitude of horses and other cattle put thereon by those of Newbury in the winter to live of what they can get and suffered there to continue till the middle of May, if not longer* which will unavoidably (as experience hath taught us) be the ruin and utter destruction of the whole island, the horses and cattle eating up the grass, that grows upon the sand hills, which gives a stop to the running of the sands in stormy weather, which otherwise would in a very short space cover all the marshes, as we have found at Castle neck. Wherefore we beseech this honored court to prohibit the putting or going of any horses, cattle and so forth upon the said island and so forth and so forth.'

August 29*th.* ' Town voted to new clapboard and repair the minister's house, and dig a well.' *

December 24*th.* Mr. Daniel Davison proposed to have ' liberty to make a building dock about Watts his cellar.' *

This year is rendered memorable by the commencement of the only recorded case of supposed witchcraft, in Newbury, that was ever subjected to a legal investigation. The principal sufferer in this tragi-comedy, for so it might well be called, was Elizabeth Morse, who, with her husband, William Morse, a shoemaker, resided in a house, still standing, at the head of Market street, in [now] Newburyport. He was then sixty-five years of age, and is said to have been a very worthy, but credulous, unsuspecting man, and consequently a very easy dupe to the impositions practiced upon him. Not suspecting any deception, the good man readily attributed all his troubles and afflictions to the supernatural agency of witchcraft, instead of watching the actions of those around him, especially of a roguish grandson, who lived with him. At that time, especially,

* Town records.

a belief in witchcraft was almost universal, and afforded a ready solution of every thing strange and unintelligible. No one appears to have suspected the boy as the author of any part of the mischief, except one Caleb Powell. Believing from what he had seen, that the whole affair was the result of human agency, with nothing supernatural or marvelous about it, he informed goodman Morse that he believed he could ascertain the cause of his trouble, and develop the whole mystery. The better to conceal his purpose, he affected, as will be hereafter seen, to have a knowledge of astrology and astronomy, and if he only had another learned man, and said *Morse's grandson with him,* the whole truth would come to light. The consequence was, that suspicions of witchcraft, and of dealing in the black art, fell upon him. He was accused, tried, and narrowly escaped with his life, thus affording another proof of the danger arising to any person, in being, or pretending to be, wiser than his neighbors.

That the whole affair may be understood, the evidence, and so forth, taken from the court records in Salem, is here subjoined.

December 3*d*, 1679. ' Caleb Powell being complained of for suspicion of working with the devill to the molesting of William Morse and his family, was by warrant directed to the constable, brought in by him, the accusations and testimonies were read and the complaint respited till the Monday following.'

December 8th, Monday. ' Caleb Powell appeared according to order and farther testimony produced against him by William Morse, which being read and considered, it was determined that the said William Morse should present the case against Caleb Powell at the county court to be held at Ipswich the last Tuesday in March following and in order hereunto William Morse acknowledgeth himself indebted to the treasurer of the county of Essex the full summe of twenty pounds.

' The condition of this obligation is that the sayd William Morse shall prosecute his complaint against Caleb Powell at that time.

' Caleb Powell was delivered as a prisoner to the constable till he find security of twenty pounds for the answering of the sayd complaint, or else he was to be cast into prison.

JOHN WOODBRIDGE, Commissioner.'

The following is a specimen of the testimony against him.

' John Badger affirmeth that Caleb Powell said that he thought by Astrologie, and I think he said by Astronomie too with it he could find out whether or no there were diabolicall means used about the said Morse his trouble, and that the said Caleb said hee thought to try to find it out.'

Anthony Morse's testimony.

' I Anthony Mors ocationlly being att my brother Morse's hous, my brother showed me a pece of a brick, which had several tims come down the chimne. I sitting in the cornar towck the pece of brik in my hand. Within a littell spas of tiem the pece of brik was gon from me I kuow not by what meanes. Quickly aftar, the pece of brik came down the chimne. Also in the chimny cornar I saw a hamar on the ground. Their being no person near the hamar it was sodenly gone ; by what meains I know not, but within a littell spas after, the hamar came down the chimny, and within a littell spas of tiem aftar that, came a pece of woud, about a fute loung, and within a littell after that came down a fiar brend, the fiar being out. This was about ten deays agoo.

Newbury December eighth, 1679.

Taken on oath December eighth, 1679 before me
JOHN WOODBRIDGE, *Commissioner.*'

December 5th, 1679. 'The testimony of William Mors and his wife, which they both saw one last Thursday night my wife and I being in bed we heard a great noies against the ruf with stekes and stones throwing against the hous with great vialanse whereupon I myselfe arose and my wife and saw not anny body, but was forsed to returne into the house againe, the stones being thrown so vilantly aganst us we gooing to bed againe and the same noies in the hus we Lock the dore againe fast and about midnight we heard a grete nayes of A hoge in the house and I aros and found a grete hoge in the huse and the dore being shut. I opened the dore the hoge running vilently out. The next morning a Stek of Lenkes hanging in the Chemney fast I saw Com Down vilintly and not anny body ner to them and Jumped up upon A Chaire before the fire ; I hanged them up again and they Com down again into the fire. The next day I had an Aule in the window, which was taken away I know not how and Com Dune the chimney. I take the same ale and put into a Cubard and fasened the Dore. The same ale Com Down 3 or 4 times. We had a basket in the Chamber Com Doun the Chemney. I tooke it up myselfe and laide it before me, it was Sudinly taken away I know not how and Com dune the Chimney againe. I then took a brick and put into it and said it shold cary that away, if it ded goo up againe. It was taken away I know not how and Com dune the Chemney and the brick a Letel after it. One Saturday next Com stekes on Light fire dune Chimney and stones, and then my awls taken away from me 4 times as I used them and Com Douen the Chemney 4 times. My nailes in a cover of A ferkin Com douen the Chemney againe. The dore being Locked I heard a hoge in the house I let alone until day and found it to bee one of my owne, willing to goo out. The next day being Sabath Stekes and stones were thrown viliantly [down] the Chemney. One Munday next Mr. Richeson and annother saw many things. I sent my boy to se if nothing was amis in my barne. I not being abel to tey my Catel up to nightes but stel being untied with many other strange thinges, the frame being thrown Downe upon the boy : We all run out to help him in.

'When we Com in we saw a Coten whele turned with the Leges upward and many thinges set up on it as a Stale and a Spade Lick the form of a ship. Potes hanging over the fire Dashing one against the other I being forsed to unhang them. We saw A andiron dance up and dune many times and into a pot and out againe up atop of a tabal, the pot turning over and Speling all in it. I saw a tube turn over with the hop fling of it. I sending my boy to fech my toles, which I doe mak Ropes with, so soone as the dore being opened thay Com viliantly Doune of themselves. Againe a tub of bred Com dune from a Shelufe and turned over. My wife went to make the bed the Clothes Ded fly of many times of themselves, and a Chest open and Shut and Dores fli together. My wife going into the Seler thinges tumbling dune and the dore fling together vialintly. I being at prayer my hed being Cufred with A Cloth A Chaire did often times bow to me and then Strike me on the side. My wife Com out of the other rome A wege of Iron being thrown at her, and A spade, but [did] not rech her, and A stone, which hurt her much, I seting by the fire with my wife and to more neighbours with us A stone Struk against the Lampe and struk it out many times, and a shoo, which we saw in Chamber before Com doune the Chemney the Dore being shut and struk me A blow one the hed, which ded much hurte. A mate of A ship Coming often to me and said he much grefed for me and said the boye was the case of all my truble and my wife was much Ronged, and was no wich, and if I would let him have the boye but one day he would warrant me no more truble. I being persuaded to it he Com the nex day at the brek of day, *and the boy was with him untel night and I had not any truble since.*'

The preceding testimony is in the handwriting of William Morse.

1 6 8 0 .

January 5th. ' The town granted liberty to ensign [Stephen] Green-leaf and Mr. [Daniel] Davison to build a wharf at the point of rocks above Watts his cellar, to be threescore feet in front at high water mark and so down to low water mark, provided the inhabitants of the town shall have liberty to land wood or hay or other goods so that the said goods be not above twenty-four hours, neither at any time to do them damage.' *

At the same meeting Nathaniel Clarke, doctor John Dole, Rich-ard Dole, Benjamin Rolf, and Robert Coker in ' the behalf of his son Benjamin Coker, each proposed for a place to make a wharfe.'*

February 6th. ' Joseph Pike was chosen to gather the rest of the contribution for the college.' *

March 1st. The town granted to Nathaniel Clarke a parcel of the flats on the southeast of the point ' of rocks, that was granted to captain White provided it be done within three years.' *

The town also voted to grant the proposition of ' Benjamin Rolf, doctor John Dole and Richard Dole for four or five rods on the flats from Watts cellar spring to ensign Greenleaf's for a place to build a wharf and a place to build vessels upon provided they come not within ten or twelve feet of the spring and make up said wharf within three years' and so forth.*

March 24th. Sixteen tithing men were chosen.*

At the March term at Ipswich court the following additional tes-timony was produced in the case of Caleb Powell, taken February twenty-seventh, 1680.

' Sarah Hale aged thirty-three and Joseph Mirick testify that Joseph Moores hath often said in their hearing that if there were any wizards, he was sure Caleb Powell was one.'

NOTE. This Joseph Moores was the boatswain of the ship, of which Caleb Powell was mate, and Joseph Dole, captain.

' *Deposition of Mary Tucker aged about twenty.*

' She remembereth that Caleb Powell came into their house and sayd to this purpose that he coming to William Morse his house and the old man being at prayer he thought not fit to go in, but looked in at the window and he sayd he had broken the inchantment, for he saw the boy play tricks while he was at prayer and *mentioned some* and *among the rest that he saw him to fling the shooe at the old man's head.*'

The court, after reading all the testimony that could be produced against Caleb Powell, came to the following conclusion.

' Upon hearing the complaint brought to this court against Caleb Powell for suspicion of working by the devill to the molesting of the family of William Morse of Newbury, though this court cannot find any evident ground of pro-ceeding farther against the sayd Powell, yett we determine that he hath given

* Town records.

such ground of suspicion of his so dealing that we cannot so acquit him but *that he justly deserves to beare his owne shame and the costs of prosecution of the complaint.'*
' It is referred to Mr. Woodbridge to hear and determine the charges.'

The court at this time must have been men of profound wisdom and accurate discrimination, as they appear to have determined, first, that he was just guilty enough to pay the expense of being suspected, secondly, that he ought 'to bear his owne shame,' and, thirdly, that they had no reason to believe that he was guilty at all. This somewhat resembles the case, which is not found in the books, where A. sues B. for breaking a borrowed kettle. The defence was, ' first we never had the kettle, secondly, it was broken when we borrowed it, and thirdly, it was whole when we returned it.'

The people, however, were not so lenient as the judges. If Caleb Powell was innocent, some other person must be guilty of ' being instigated by the divil,' for, in their opinion, no agency merely human could produce effects so strange and unaccountable. They accordingly selected Elizabeth Morse, the wife of William Morse, as the guilty person, as we shall hereafter see.

April 13*th.* ' In answer to the proposition of Ipswich inhabitants to prohibit all sorts of cattle from going any more on Plum island winter or summer, the town's conclusion is that they do not consent to such an act.' *

May 17*th.* ' The town granted Mr. Richardson twenty pounds in money, and forty pounds in other pay, to build an addition to the ministry house, and so forth.' *

May 19*th.* On petition of some of the inhabitants ' of Newbury the selectmen were authorised to raise by way of rate sixty pounds per annum to be to the use of the schoolmaster there.' *

June 28*th.* Governor Bradstreet thus writes to England. ' The principal townes of trade within our government are Boston, Charlestown and Salem. Some little trade there is for country people at Ipswich, Newbury and so forth.

' The number of merchants in the colony is nearly forty, and about one hundred or one hundred and twenty ships, sloops, ketches and other vessels.'

' At a court of assistants on adjournment held at Boston May twentieth 1680.

' The grand Jury presenting Elizabeth, wife of William Morse senior. She was indicted by the name of Elizabeth Morse for that she not having the fear of God before her eyes, being instigated by the Divil and had familiarity with the Divil contrary to the peace of our sovereign lord the king, his crown and dignity, the laws of God, and of this jurisdiction, after the prisoner was at the barr and pleaded not guilty, and put herself on God and the country for triall, the evidences being produced were read and committed to the jury.

' The jury brought in their verdict. They found Elizabeth Morse, the prisoner at the barr, guilty according to indictment. The governor on the twenty-seventh of May after ye lecture pronounced ye sentence.

' Elizabeth Morse, you are to goe from hence to the place from whence you

* **Town records.**

came and thence to the place of execution and there to be hanged by the neck, till you be dead, and the Lord have mercy on your soul.

' The court was adjourned diem per diem and on the first of June 1680 the governor and magistrates voted the reprieving of Elizabeth Morse condemned to the next session of the court in October as attests.

EDWARD RAWSON, Secretary.'

It appears from the record, that the reprieve was not agreeable to the deputies, who, on assembling in November, thus complain :

' The deputies on perusal of the acts of the honorable court of assistants relating to the woman condemned for witchcraft doe not understand why execution of the sentence given against her by said court is not executed and that her second repreevall seems to us to be beyond what the law will allow and doe therefore judge meete to declare ourselves against it with reference to the concurrence of our honored magistrates hereto.

WM. TORREY Cleric.

November third, 1680.

Not consented to by the magistrates.
EDWARD RAWSON, Secretary.'

No record gives us any farther information concerning Elizabeth Morse this year.

August 18*th.* ' The selectmen ordered that Anthony Morse should every sabbath day go or send his boy to Mr. Richardson and tell him when he is going to ring the last bell every meeting and for that service is to have ten shillings a year added to his former annuity.' ✱

✱ *October* 22*d.* ' It was agreed that Mr. Burly should keep school in the watch house.' ✱

The Essex regiment was divided into two, to be commanded by major N. Saltonstall, and major D. Denison. Newbury to have two companies, and Ipswich three.

This year, Thorlas bridge was, on the petition of Rowley people, made a county bridge.

1681.

The case of Elizabeth Morse, who had been reprieved by the governor, was again brought before the general court, to whom William Morse, her husband, sent two petitions, the one on May fourteenth, in the elegant handwriting of William Chandler of Newbury, the other on May eighteenth, in the handwriting of major Robert Pike of Salisbury, who was the next year chosen one of the assistants.

His first petition is as follows.

' To the honored generall court now sitting in Boston.

' The humble petition of William Mors in behalfe of his wife, Elizabeth Mors your distressed Prisoner, humbly begging this that you would be pleased to give your petitioner leave to present to your consideration what may clere up the truth in those evidences wch hath bin presented and what is otherwise as first. To Joseph Bayley his testimony. Wee are ignorant of any such thing.

✱ Town records.

Had it bin then spoken of, we might have cleared ourselves. He might have observed some other as my wife, it being a frequent thing for Catle to be at a stand.

'To Jonathan Haines. As to his Catle, or himselfe, not making good work at such a time, when Catle are haggled out, to place it on such account, yt his neglect in not bringing us a bow of mault was the cause, which had it bin spoken of wee might have given full satisfaction.

'To Caleb Moody. As to what befell him in and about his not seeing my wife, yt his cow making no hast to hir calfe, wch wee are ignorant of, it being so long since, and being in church communion with us, should have spoken of it like a christian and yn proceeded so as wee might have given an answer in less time yn tenn yeares. Wee are ignorant yt he had a shepe so dyed. And his wife knowne to be a pretious godly whoman, yt hath oftne spoken to hir husband not to be so uncharitable and have and doe carry it like a christian with a due respect in hir carridge towards my wife all along.

'To John Mighill. About ye loss of his catle was yt he came one day to worke, and would have had him come another day to finish it because ye raine came in so upon us, and his not coming, judges my wife was angry and yrfore had such loss, wch wee never knew of. This being twelve yeares agoe did amaze us now to here of it.

'To Zachariah Davis. To sensure my wife now for not bringing quills aboute sixteen yeares agoe yt his loss of calfes was for that, when his father being in communion with us did profess it to us yt he judged it a hand of God and was farr from blaming us but rather troubled his sonn should so judge.

'To Joshua Richardson loosing a shepe and his taking it forth off our yard, my wife should say you might have asked leave, and whether overdriving it or what, now to bring it in I hope will be considered.

'To John March Test. He heard John Wells his wife say she saw imp o' God into said Morss howse. She being prosecuted would not owne it and was adjudged to pay damages, and now this is brought in.

● To James Browne Test. yt one day George Wheeler going forth, my wife should say for a trifle she knew he should not come in againe, which my wife knowes not of it, nor doth some of ye owners ever remember such a thing as to judge or charge it on hir, but now is brought forth sixteen yeares after when his wife said to goody Hale yt said Browne was mistaken. Hir husband did come home well that voyage; and that James Browne should say to Robert Bedell yt yt Powell, whom wee sued did put in these words and not himselfe in the test and yt said Browne did oune to his unkle Mr. Nicholas Noyes yt he could not sware to such a test; and did refuse to doe it before Mr. John Woodbridge, and Mr. Woodbridge did admire he had sworne to it. And for his seeing my wife amongst troopers. What condition he might be in wee leave it to consideration. Wee are ignorant of such a thing till now brought in so many yeares agoe as he saith.

'To goodwife Ordway. Hir child being long ill, my wife coming in and looking on it, pitting of it, did feare it would dy, and when it dyed Israell Webster our next neighbour heard not a word of it, nor spoken of by others, nor any of ye family, but hir conceite, and now brought in.

'As for William Chandler's test. aboute his wife's long sickness and my wife's visiting hir, she through hir weakness acted uncivilly and yet now to bring in against my wife, when for so many yeares being in full communion with us never dealt with us aboute any such thing, but had as loving converse with him as christians ought, and knew no otherwise till now.

'To widow Goodwin hir having hir child sick, gave forth yt it was bewitched by my wife, as she thought; wee hearing of it dealt with hir aboute it, and she brake forth in teares, craving forgiveness, and said it was others put hir upon it to say as she did, but now urged by Powell to say as she now saith.

'To John Chase so saying yt he saw my wife in the night coming in at a little hole, and ye like, when he himselfe hath said he did not know but he was in a dreame, and yt unto several persons he hath so said, though now as he test., when my wife disowns any such thing.

'To John Glading yt saw halfe of my wife about two a clocke in ye day time, if so, might then have spoken, and not reserved for so long a time, which she utterly denies it, nor know of any such thing, where she should be at yt time as to clere hir selfe.

'To William Fanning should say my boy said the devill was at his howse. Upon Fanning's saying to the boy ye devill was at their howse, and he would have me chide ye boy, which I tould said Fanning ye boy might be instructed to know ye devill was every where though not as at our howse, and should not in time of affliction upbraid him to our griefe.

'To Jonathan Woodman, seeing a catt, and so forth, he struck at it, and it vanisht away and I sending for doctor Dole to see a bruise my wife had by the fall of a peece reching downe some bacan in our chimly, which was many days before this time, as doctor Dole affirms it was no green wound, though neglected to send for said Dole till then.

'To Benjamin Lowle about my boy's ketching a pidgin ; my boy desired of me to see to ketch a pidgin, by throwing a stone, or ye like, and he brought a pidgin, which I affirm was wopnded, though alive.

'To goodwife Miricke about a letter. My wife telling her somewhat of ye letter, which she judges could not be and my wife hearing of it there was a discourse and so forth aboute this love letter, might speake something about it by guess, and not by any such way as she judged, and many have spoken, guessing at things, which might be.

'As to our troubles in ye howse it hath bin dreddfull, and afflictive and to say it ceased upon hir departure, when it ceased before for a time and after she was gone there was trouble againe.

'As to rumors of some great wickedness committed in ye house, which should cause ye divill so to trouble us, our conscience is clere of ye knowledge of any such thing more than our common frailtyes and I reverence the holy sourainty of God in laying such affliction on us, and that God's servants may be so afflicted in this manner as hath bin knowne. And that Mr. Wilson of Ipswich, where she hath bin twenty-eight weekes, did declare to me yt my wife's conversation was christian-like as far as he observed. Thus praying for you in this and all other your concernes, am your distressed servant,

WILLIAM MORSE.

Newbury May fourteenth 1681.'

From the preceding petition of William Morse, and his attempted answers to the accusations and charges brought against his wife Elizabeth, and sent to the general court, it appears that seventeen persons had given in their testimony in writing, stating their reasons why they verily believed goody Morse was really a witch, and ought to be hung, according to the old Mosaic law, which says, 'thou shalt not suffer a witch to live.' Of these testimonies only one is to be found on the files of the general court. If this one is a fair specimen of the whole, the loss of the remainder is not greatly to be regretted, except as a specimen of the logic of that day, and of the manner in which some of our ancestors stated their premises, and drew thence their most profound conclusions. It is here presented entire, and if it does not most conclusively prove that Elizabeth Morse was guilty of witchcraft, and ought not to have been suffered to live, it will only furnish another evidence that belief and demonstration are not identical, and that what is sincerely believed is not for that reason always true. Zechariah Davis thus testifies verbatim and literatim.

'When I lived at Salisbury, William Morses' wife asked of me whether I could let her have a small passell of winges and I told her I woode, so she would have me bring them over for her the next time I came over, but I came over and did not think of the winges, but met goody Morse, she asked me whether I had brought over her winges and I tel her no I did not thinke of it, so I came 3 ore 4 times and had them in my minde a litel before I came over but stil forget them at my coming away so meting with her every time that I came over without them aftar I had promised her the winges, soe she tel me she wonder at it that my memory should be soe bad, but when I came home I went to the barne and there was 3 cafes in a pen.   One of them fel a danceing and roreing and was in such a condition as I never saw on cafe in before, but being almost night the cattle came home and we put him to his dam and he sucke and was well 3 or 4 dayes, and on of them was my brothers then come over to Nubery, but we did not thinke to send the winges, but when he came home and went to the barne this cafe fel a danceing and roreing so wee put him to the cowe, but he would not sucke but rane a roreinge away soe wee gate him againe with much adoe and put him into the barne and we heard him roer severall times in the night and in the morning I went to the barne and there he was seting upon his taile like a doge, and I never see no cafe set aftar that manner before and so he remained in these fits while he died.'

Taken on oath June seventh, 1679.

From the date of the preceding testimony, it is evident it was used in the county court prior to the transfer of the case to the state tribunals.   On the eighteenth of May, William Morse presented the following petition.

'To the honored governor, deputy governor, magistrates and deputies now assembled in court May the eighteenth 1681.

'The most humble petition and request of William Morse in behalf of his wif (now a condemned prisoner) to this honored court is that they would be pleased so far to hearken to the cry of your poor prisoner, who am a condemned person, upon the charge of witchcraft and for a wich, to which charge your poor prisoner have pleaded not guilty, and by the mercy of God and the goodness of the honored governor, I am reprieved and brought to this honored court, at the foot of which tribunal I now stand humbly praying your justis in hearing of my case and to determine therein as the Lord shall direct.   I do not understand law, nor do I know how to lay my case before you as I ought, for want of which I humbly beg of your honors that my request may not be rejected, but may find acceptance with you it being no more but your sentence upon my triall whether I shall live or dy, to which I shall humbly submit unto the Lord and you.

William Morse in behalf of his wife
ELIZABETH MORSE.'

For reasons, which do not appear on the records, the deputies had changed their minds, and, instead of being dissatisfied with her respite, were willing to grant another hearing of the case.   This the magistrates opposed.   In the court record it is thus stated :

'The deputyes judge meet to grant the petitioner a hearing the next sixth day and that warrants goe forth to all persons concerned, from this court then to appear in order to her further triall our honored magistrates hereto consenting.

WM. TORREY, Cleric.

May twenty-fourth, 1681.

Not consented to by the magistrates.
EDWARD RAWSON, Secretary.'

The following additional testimony, taken from the county files, is here presented, as necessary to a full understanding of the whole case. It is in the handwriting of John Woodbridge, esquire, and was undoubtedly copied by him from the original, written by William Morse himself, and should have been inserted in 1679. The curious reader will be much amused in comparing this, and the preceding testimony of William Morse, with the report of the same case, made by Increase Mather in his 'Remarkables,' and especially that made by Cotton Mather, in volume second, pages 391 and 392 of the Magnalia. In that 'wonderful' book, the latter gentleman perverts and amplifies the testimony to a 'prodigious and nefandous' extent. If his 'fourteen astonishing histories' in his 'Thaumatographia Pneumatica,' have been as much indebted to his imagination for the dress which they now wear, as that of William Morse, it is no wonder that Mr. Savage, in his appendix to Winthrop, volume first, page 417, says of him, that 'instead of weighing evidence, [he] had not discretion enough to be trusted to wipe the scales.'

'The testimony of William Morse, which saith together with his wife aged both about sixty-five yeeres, that Thursday night being the twenty-seventh day of November, we heard a great noyes without round the house of knocking the boards of the house and, as we conceived, throwing of stones at the house, whereupon myselfe and wife lookt out and saw no body and the boy all this time with us, but we had stones and sticks thrown at us that we were forced to retire into the house againe, afterwards we went to bed and the boy with us and then the like noyes was upon the roof of the house.

'The same night about midnight the doore being lockt when we went to bed, we heard a great hog in the house grunt and make a noyes, as we thought willing to gett out, and that we might not be disturbed in our sleep I rose to let him out, and I found a hog in the house and the doore unlockt. The doore was firmly lockt when we went to bed.

'The next morning a stick of links hanging in the chimney, they were thrown out of their place, and we hanged them up againe and they were thrown downe againe and come into the fire.

'The night following I had a great awle lying in the window, the which awle we saw fall downe out of the chimney into the ashes by the fire.

'After this I bid the boy put the same awle into the cupboard, which we saw done and the doore shut to, this same awle came presently downe the chimney againe in our sight, and I took it up myselfe. Againe the same night we saw a little Indian baskett, that was in the loft before, came downe the chimney againe and I took the same baskett, put a piece of brick in it, and the baskett with the brick was gone, and came downe againe the third time with the brick in it and went up againe the fourth time and came downe againe without the brick, and the brick came downe a little after.

'The next day being Saturday, stones, sticks and pieces of bricks came downe so that we could not quietly eat our breakfast, and sticks of fire also came downe at the same time.

'That same day in the afternoon my thread four times taken away and came downe the chimney againe ; my awle and a gimlett wanting, came downe the chimney. Againe my leather taken away came downe the chimney. Againe my nailes being in the cover of a ferkin taken away, came downe the chimney.

'The next day being Sunday many stones and sticks and pieces of bricks came down the chimneye. On Monday Mr. Richardson [the minister] and my brother being there, the frame of my cow house they saw very firme, I sent my boy to skare the fowles from my hogs' meat. He went to the cow house and it fell downe, my boy crying with the hurt of the fall.   In the afternoone the potts hanging over the fire, did dash so vehemently one against the other, we sett downe one that they might not dash to pieces.   I saw the andiron leap in to the pott and dance, and leap out, and againe leap in and dance, and leap out againe, and leap on a table and there abide, and my wife saw the andiron on the table. Also I saw the pott turn itselfe over and throw down all the water.   Againe we saw a tray with wool leap up and downe and throw the wool out and saw no body meddle with it.   Againe a tub his hoop fly off, of itselfe and the tub turne over and no body neere it.   Againe the woolen wheele upside downe and stood upon its end and a spade sett on it.   Stephen Greenleaf saw it and myselfe and wife.   Againe my rope tooles fell downe in the ground before my boy could take them being sent for them and the same thing of nailes tumbled downe from the loft into the ground and no body neere.   Againe my wife and the boy making the bed, the chest did open and shutt, the bed clothes would not be made to ly on the bed, but fly off againe.

ɽ 'Thomas Rogers and George Hardy being at William Morse his house affirme that the earth in the chimney corner moved and scattered on them, that Thomas Rogers was hit with somewhat, Hardy, with an iron ladle, as is supposed.   Somewhat hitt William Morse a great blow, but it was so swift that they could not tell what it was but looking downe after they heard the noyes they saw a shoe.   The boy was in the corner at first, afterward in the house.

'Mr. Richardson on Saturday testifyeth that a board flew against his chaire and he heard a noyes in another roome, *which he supposed in all reason to be diabolicall.*

'John Dole saw a large fire stick of candle wood to fall downe, a stone, a fire brand, and these things he saw not whence they came, till they fell downe by him.

'Elizabeth Titcomb affirmeth that Powell sayd that he could find out the witch by his learning, if he had another scholar with him.

'John Emerson affirmeth that Powell sayd he was brought up under Norwood and it was judged by the people there that Norwood studied the black art.'

In another paper entitled ' a farther testimony of William Morse and his wife,' he states that ' we saw a keeler of bread turn over — a chair did often bow to me and rise up againe — the chamber door did violently fly together and the bed did move to and fro and not any body neer them.'

He also states that the cellar door did violently fly down and a drum rolled over it — his ' barn door was unpinned four times, and going to shut the doore, *the boy being with me,* the pin (as I did judge) coming downe out of the aire did fall down neer to me.'

' Againe Caleb Powell came in as before and seeing our spirits very low by the sense of our great afflictions, began to bemoane our condition and sayd that he was troubled for our affliction, and sayd that he eyed the boy, and drawed neere to us with great compassion, poore old man, poore old woman, this boy is the occasion of your griefe, for he does these things and hath caused his good old grandmother to be counted a witch.   Then sayd I, how can all these things be done by him ?   Then sayd he although he may not have done all, yet most of them, for this boy is a young rogue, a vile rogue.   I have watched him and see him do things as to come up and downe.

' Caleb Powell also said he had understanding in Astrology and Astronomy and knew the working of spirits, some in one country and some in another, and looking on the boy said you young rogue to begin so soone.   Goodman Morse, if you be willing to let mee have the boy, I will undertake you shall be freed from any trouble of this kind while he is with me.   I was very unwilling at the first, and my wife, but by often urging me to, and when he told me whither and in what employment and company he should goe, I did consent to it and we have been freed from any trouble of this kind ever since that promise made on Monday night last till this time being Friday afternoone.'

After enumerating a great variety of marvellous exploits, such as ' hearing a great noyes in the other roome,'—' his chaire would not stand still but ready to throw me backward,'—' my cap almost taken off my head three times,'—' a great blow in my poll,' — ' the catt thrown at my wife and thrown at us five times, the lamp standing by us on a chest, was beaten downe,' and so forth, he thus concludes :

' Againe a great noyes a great while very dreadful. Againe in the morning a great stone being six pounds weight did remove from place to place. We saw it. Two spoones throwed off the table and presently the table throwed downe, and being minded to write, my ink horne was hid from me, which I found covered with a rag and my pen quite gone. I made a new pen and while I was writing, one eare of corne hitt me in the face and fire sticks and stones and —— throwed at me, and my pen brought to me. While I was writing with my new pen, my ink-horne taken away. Againe my specticles thrown from the table, and throwne almost into the fire by me, my wife and *the boy*. Againe my booke of all my accounts throwne into the fire and had been burnt presently, if I had not taken it up. Againe boards taken of a tub and sett upright by themselves, and my paper, do what I could, I could hardly keep it, while I was writing this relation. Presently before I could dry my writing, a monmouth hat rubbed along it, but I held it so fast that it did blot but some of it. My wife and I being much afraid that I should not preserve it for the publick use, we did think best to lay it in the bible and it lay safe that night. Againe the next [night] I would lay it there againe, but in the morning it was not to be found, the bag hanged downe empty, but after was found in a box alone. Againe while I was writing this morning I was forced to forbeare writing any more, I was so disturbed with so many things constantly thrown at me.

This relation taken December eighth, 1679.'

On the court records I find nothing more concerning Elizabeth Morse. From an essay on witchcraft, by the reverend John Hale, of Beverly, and published in the year 1697, I make the following extracts.

' She [Elizabeth Morse] being reprieved was carried to her own home and her husband (who was esteemed a sincere and understanding christian by those that knew him) desired some neighbour ministers, of whom I was one, to discourse his wife, which we did, and her discourse was very christian, and still pleaded her innocence as to that, which was laid to her charge. We did not esteem it prudence for us to pass any definitive sentence upon one under her circumstances, yet we inclined to the more charitable side. In her last sickness she was in much trouble and darkness of spirit, which occasioned a judicious friend to examine her strictly, whether she had been guilty of witchcraft, but she said *no*, but the ground of her trouble was some impatient and passionate speeches and actions of her while in prison upon the account of her suffering wrongfully, whereby she had provoked the Lord by putting contempt upon his word. And in fine she sought her pardon and comfort from God in Christ and dyed so far as I understand, praying to, and resting upon, God in Christ for salvation.'

It was owing, we believe, to the firmness of governor Bradstreet, that the life of Elizabeth Morse was saved, and the town of Newbury thus prevented from offering the first victim, in Essex county, to that lamentable spirit of delusion, which twelve years after left so dark a stain on its annals.

The following is a view of the house occupied by William Morse and family, and which, in the language of the excessively credulous Cotton Mather, 'was so infested with demons' in 1679, and where, 'before the devil was chained up, the *invisible* hand did begin to put forth an astonishing *visibility!*' The house is still standing at the corner of Market street, opposite to saint Paul's church. The lot on which it stands was granted to William Morse in 1645, but in what year he erected it, no record informs us; but from all that I can ascertain, the house, or at least a part of it, must have been erected soon after the lot was granted.

March 8th. The town granted the petition of John Badger for 'two rods of land over against his house to set up a mill to make oatmeal.' This mill was kept in operation till 1810. The last proprietor was Mr. Nicholas Lunt, who, between 1763 and 1810, manufactured thirty-seven thousand, five hundred and sixty bushels of oatmeal.

March 8th. 'The selectmen (hearing that Jeremy Goodridge and his family was in a suffering condition) sent up Joseph Pike to know how the case stood with him, and upon his inquirie Jeremy Goodridge told him he was in a way to get a house of his owne and for provision he was in a way also to provide for himselfe, for he had corne paid for, which he hoped he should have. And Joseph Pike told him if he was like to suffer he should come and acquaint the selectmen with it and they would make him supply.' *

* Town records.

'*August* 29*th*. James Merrick chosen sexton, and to have three pounds and ten shillings a year for his service.' *

'*October* 12*th*. It was voted that whereas the scholars are so few that such as come to learne English shall pay three pence a week for their schooling.' *

October 19*th*. The town voted to impower the selectmen to petition the general court to grant Mr. Woodbridge magistratical power. In their petition they say, among many other things, ' by reason of the largeness of the towne and frequent concourse of vessels to trade among us, they wish•to have Mr. Woodbridge, as he is the fittest and most able for such a work in this place.'

'*November* 28*th*. The town voted that henceforth the general towne meeting should be the first Tuesday in March.' *

1 6 8 2 ·

Early this year, a small baptist church was formed in Newbury, as appears from the following extract from the records of the first baptist church in Boston.

' *February* 6*th*, 1681-2. [It was] agreed upon a church meeting that we the church at Boston have assented unto the settling of the church at Newbury.'

The persons who formed this church, were, probably, George Little and Philip Squire, who united with the baptist church in Boston in 1676, Nathaniel Cheney, William Sâyer and wife, Benjamin Morse and wife, Mr. Edward Woodman and wife, John Sâyer, and Abel Merrill, all of whom became members of the same church in 1681. All these were residents in Newbury at that time. This comprises all the information that I can find on the subject.

Among the papers of George Little, above-mentioned, the following petition, in the elegant handwriting of William Chandler, is still to be seen. It has neither date nor signature, but was probably written between the years 1661 and this year. The justness of the sentiments, and the beauty of the style, warrant the insertion of it here.

' To the honored generall court.

' Whereas·wee have these many yeares bin preserved by the good providence of God under a peaceable goverment in this wildernesse and many worthy things have by you bin donne unto and for this people, which we acknowledge with all thankfulnesse, notwithstanding, may it please you to take notice of some greevance of many of the people of God in this country which lieth on their spirits, respecting some streightnes and streightening of yt christian liberty which wee think ought to be allowed unto all christians houlding the foundation and walking orderly, though of different perswations, namely, to worship God according to their owne judgement and consciences without being restrained to the judgements of others by human laws; and forasmuch as our gratious king is pleased in his letter † to declare (as wee apprehend) that a principall end of this plantation granted is yt liberty of conscience may bee heere

---

* Town records.   † September, 1661.

enjoyed. Wee hope therefore it will be noe griefe of mind to you to consider of it, and to repeale such lawes as are a hinderance or restraining in any respect to ye people of God either in their joining together in church fellowship or exercising in the ordinances of God accordinge to ye pure gospel rule. Our humble petition is that all such laws, as occasion or cause any such streightnes, restraint or hinderance may be repealed, and that such christian liberty may bee allowed and confirmed, the which wee believe will tend much to ye glory of God in ye peace and settlement of his people heere. And soe shall wee pray for your peace and remaine (as in duty wee are bound) your faithful and humble petitioners.'

'*March* 22*d.* The selectmen agreed with William Bolton to keep the dry herd and to come upon the first day of May and fetch the cattle and drive them up into the upper commons * and so forth and William Bolton is to have paid him by the owners of the cattle sixpence a head to be paid in malt or Indian corne.'

' And he is to burne the woods and to make up the flatts' fence and for that he shall be paid fourteen shillings.' †

' At a legall meeting of the towne April nineteenth 1682.

' There was voted to go to Ipswich to subscribe according to court order about Mr. Mason's clayme, captain Daniel Pierce, Mr. Richard Dummer, sergeant [Tristram] Coffin, sergeant [Caleb] Moody, Mr. John Woodbridge, Mr. Henry Sewall, Nicholas Noyes.'

In October, the general court renewed the license of Hugh March to keep an ' ordinary.' In his petition to the court, he states, that 'the town of Newbury some years since were destitute of an ordinary and could not persuade any person to keep it. For want of an ordinary they were twice fined by the county and would have been fined a third time had I not undertaken it. It cost me,' says he, ' one hundred and twenty pounds to repair the house, and more than four hundred pounds in building house, barn, stables and so forth.'

March 22*d.* ' It was ordered that all swyne that goes upon the cow commons shall be ringed under the penalty of twelve pence a head and so forth and that all horses and horse kind and dry cattle *shall be cleared out of the commons and Plum island* between this and the first of May next under the penalty of two shillings a head' and so forth. All these were to be driven up into the upper commons, except ' such horses that are kept for the necessary use of their owners.' These were ' to be fettered under a like penalty,' in case of neglect. †

From this extract, from the petition sent to the general court in 1679 by the inhabitants of Ipswich, and from other circumstances and allusions, it is evident that large numbers of cattle and horses were, by the inhabitants of Newbury, for many years after the first settlement of the town, driven on to Plum island in the fall of the year, there to spend the winter and live as they could till the spring of the year, or turned out in the lower commons to shift for themselves. Tradition informs that many of the cattle, especially those

* ' The upper commons,' see March twenty-first, 1642.
† Town records.

on Plum island, became so wild, that it became necessary for their owners to shoot them as they would other wild beasts.

As may be easily supposed, neat cattle were much smaller than those which are kept by our farmers at the present day. At the same time that their cattle were thus neglected, large quantities of hay were sent to Exeter, Portsmouth, Dover, Lynn, and so forth.

March 14*th.* Sergeant Nathaniel Clark was appointed by the selectmen, 'to warne Evan Morris out of the towne of Newbury.' †

In this year, March twenty-second, I find the following regulations concerning sheep.

'It was ordered that all sheep shall be kept in that part of the commons where their owners live. The inhabitants of the old town to keep their sheep there. The next flock to be kept from Lob's pound * and over the mill bridge to Henry Jaques his pasture. And the next flock from thence to James Smith's and over Trotter's bridge. And the inhabitants from James Carrs to Mr. John Sewalls and Jacob Toppans are the frog pond flock and their range shall be the Aps swamp from James Smith to George Marches bridge and dismal ditch and Robin's pound, and Moses Pilsbury and the further end of the towne are to have the plaines for their flock.' †

May 17*th.* 'The towne voted that the selectmen shall have power to take care that the poore may be provided for and to build cottage or cottages for them according to their discretion and so forth.' †

June 20*th.* The highway from Newbury to Andover, was this day laid out, to 'go by James Smiths and so by George March his farme, thence to said George's high field and from thence by marked trees to falls river upon as straight a lyne as the ground will admit, and so forth.' †

In April, twenty-nine men and thirty-one women were 'seated' in five new seats in the gallery.

Mrs. Ann White had her license renewed to keep an 'ordinary.'

November 23*d.* 'Thanksgiving appointed on account of a very plentiful harvest.'

1683.

On the fifteenth of February, the general court ordered, 'that major Sallonstall with the deputies take care to make a division of the soldiers of Newbury into two foot companies in as equall a manner as they can, and that captain [Daniel] Pierce and his commission officers shall have the first choice, and captain Thomas Noyes and his commission officers, the other. Consented to.' ‡

On February ninth, the court of assistants 'order that the port of Boston to which Charlestown is annexed, and the port of Salem,

* 'Crowdero, whom in irons bound,
    Thou basely threwst into Lob's pound.' . . *Hudibras.*

† Town records.   ‡ General court records.

18

to which Marblehead, Beverly, Gloucester, Ipswich, Rowley, New-bury and Salisbury are annexed, as members, shall be the lawful ports in this colony, where ships and other vessels shall lade or un-lade any of the plantation's enumerated goods, or other goods from foreign parts and no where else and so forth.'

This occasioned the following petition:

' To the honored general court now sitting in Boston, the humble petition of some of Newbury.

' Wee humbly crave the favour that your honors would be pleased to consider our little Zebulon and to ease us of that charge, which at present we are forced unto by our goeing to Salem to enter our vessells and thereby are forced to stay at least tow days, before we can unload, besides other charges in going and coming. That some meet person might be appointed to receive the enter of all vessells, and to act and doe according as the law directs in that case and we shall be bound forever to pray for your honors.

May fifteenth, 1683.

HENRY WHEELER,	THOMAS NOYES,	WILLIAM NOYES,
HENRY JAQUES,	JOHN KENT,	WILLIAM TITCOMB,
D. DAVISON,	J. DOLE,	PENUEL TITCOMB.
CALEB MOODY,	BENAYAH TITCOMB,	

Referred to the next general court.'

By referring to the preceding year, it will be seen, that the whole of the 'lower commons,' that is, the territory, south of Artichoke river, was divided by the town into five distinct 'ranges,' or 'sheep walks,' which were to be occupied by five flocks of sheep, each of which must be kept within its own prescribed limits, 'under penalty of twelve pence a head for every sheep so disorderly'* as to be out of place night or day. Each flock was under the care of a shepherd, hired by the owners of the sheep. From an ancient doc-ument, found among the papers of the late deacon Nathaniel Little, of which the following is a copy, we are enabled to ascertain the manner, in which each company managed its concerns. The company here alluded to, resided in the vicinity of the upper green, and comprehended those living within the third 'range.'

'*April 16th*, 1683. At a legall meeting of the company, whose names are here set down [we] have agreed that every man shall take his full turn of fold-ing for this year in order according as their names are set down; and for the next year it shall begin with that man, that had no benefit, or that had not his whole benefit of folding upon his corn and so successively from year to year till every man hath had that benefit of folding upon his corn or otherways in season. And also it is agreed that every man shall bring a sufficient gate for every score of sheep he doth bring or send to the flock belonging to this com-pany according to the number of sheep given in for folding as witness our hands,

RICHARD BROWN,	JOHN WOOLCOTT,
MOSES GERRISH,	THOMAS NOYES,
JOSHUA MORSS,	MATTH. PETTINGELL,
JONATHAN HAYNES for this year,	JAMES SMITH.'

' It is also agreed that Mr. Nois and Mr. Gerrish shall tack account of every man's sheep, and proportion to every man his share of foulding, and to conclude

* Town records.

the end of foulding the fifth of November and let the first share of foulding be the bigest, if they make any difference in every man's two shares.

DANIEL PEIRCE, PETER TOPPAN, JOSHUA MORSS.

'It is agreed that Evan Morris shall keep sheep for this year 1683 and he is to have six shillings a week in pay, and he that have above forty in the fold shall give him one shilling out of the whole in money, and all that are under thirty shall pay sixpence in money a man.' 'They whose sheep are kept shall allow him his dyett besides the said six shillings per week where the sheep are folded.'

The following is a list of the company, and number of their sheep.

Mr. Moses Gerrish,	. 90	Richard Brown,	. . . 24
John Atkinson,	. . . 40	Thomas Noyes,	. . . 40
Cousin Pettingell,	. . 14	Robert Long,	 30
Samuel Pettingell,	. . 30	James Smith,	 44
Captain [Daniel] Peirce,	105	John Woolcot,	. . . 54
Joshua Morss,	 27	John Smith,	 12
Serjeant Trist. Coffin,	55	Widow Stickney,	. . 24
Doctor [Peter] Toppan,	80	John Webster,	 35
	441		263
			441
		Total, . . .	704

Here we find sixteen individuals, in one neighborhood, owning seven hundred and four sheep. How many more there were in the remaining four flocks, we have no means of accurately ascertaining, but estimating the number owned by each individual in town, to be in proportion to the tax he paid in 1685, the whole number of sheep, owned in Newbury this year, would be five thousand six hundred and eighty-five, a number, which is probably not far from the truth.

As there may be some things in the preceding quotations, which will need a little explanation, I will here furnish it from a few other old papers, and an old account book kept by Richard Bartlet, junior. It will be recollected that our fathers found it necessary, on account of the wolves, to have their sheep securely folded every night. This necessity they turned to the advantage of their corn land, by folding the sheep upon it. Having set the day on which shepherd Morris was to commence his services, which this year was the twenty-third of April, and designated the man, who was to have the first 'benefit of folding,' who this year was Richard Brown, each one of the company brought to his corn land his share of the materials, ('a gate * for every score of sheep,') with which they set up the pen. After remaining there the prescribed time, it was taken down and set up on 'Cousin Pettingell's' land, and thus it passed round from one to another, like a mug of flip at an 'ordinary' in

* Thus, 'September ninth, 1702. John Ordway Dr. for your help in carting two load of *sheep gates* into my field.' *Bartlet's account book.*

olden time, each one receiving, 'upon his corn,' or corn land, 'the
full benefit' of the top dressing, which seven hundred sheep could
give.   Wherever the pen was erected, there the shepherd was to
have his 'dyett,' and thus like a menagerie, or traveling circus, he
and his animals were continually in motion.   At other times, and
in other places, the pen was erected on some part of the common
land, and was, after a suitable time, removed, and a crop of turnips
raised, which, in the fall, were divided pro rata among the owners
of the sheep.   Turnips at that time, and for half a century after,
supplied the place of potatoes.   In 1662, the price of a cord of oak
wood, and a bushel of turnips, was the same, namely, one shilling
and sixpence.   In 1702, a cord of oak wood was three shillings, a
cord of walnut five shillings, and a bushel of turnips from one shilling and sixpence to two shillings.*   From Mr. Richard Bartlet's
old journal I take the following.   'In 1676, turnips one shilling per
bushel, hemp and butter sixpence per pound.   In 1687, cotton wool
was one shilling and sixpence per pound.'

The inquisitive reader will excuse the minuteness of these
details, as it gives a picture of some of the customs of our forefathers, which the lapse of more than a century and a half has
either materially changed or entirely effaced.

A negro woman, named Juniper, came to Newbury this year.
She was warned out of town, but, refusing to go, the selectmen
appealed to the county court, 'to be eased of such a burthen.'

1 6 8 4 .

January 2d.   'At a generall legall meeting of the towne it was
proposed and voted on the affirmative, whether or no we think it
expedient and meet to divide a part of the commons, if we can
agree upon a rule to do it by.' †

A committee of fourteen persons were chosen, 'to consult and
consider about a rule.'   It was also voted 'to divide the commons
above the hedge.' † ‡

'*January 16th.*   At a legall meeting of the freemen and freeholders it was voted that six thousand acres of the upper common shall
be lotted out, namely, one thousand acres to the non-freeholders
and soldiers, and five thousand acres to the freeholders, to every
freeholder alike with an addition to some few men that have deserved more and this shall not be a precedent to the future in the
ordering or dividing of any other part of the common.' †

In consequence, however, 'of some, that did manifest dissatisfaction at the votes it was voted that there shall be no further proceed-

---

* John Knight's journal.   † Town records.

‡ 'The hedge,' so called, was near Artichoke river, and was the dividing line between
'the lower commons,' and 'upper commons,' or 'upper woods,' as it was sometimes
called.   The upper commons was appropriated for the pasturage of 'the dry herd.'
The lower commons was divided into 'cow commons, ox commons, steer commons, and
calf commons.'   The sheep pasture covered the same ground, but was differently divided.

ing upon that vote, nor any division of the common until the free-men and freeholders do agree who the persons shall be that deserve any addition, and what they do deserve more than an equall share.' *

On the subject of dividing the commons, nothing more was done until March, 1686, when, as will be seen, the division was made. The cause of the dissatisfaction, which existed among a large portion of the inhabitants, originated in the order passed the seventh of December, 1642, which ' declared and ordered that the persons *only* abovementioned [ninety-one in all] are acknowledged to be freeholders by the towne and to have a proportionable right in *all waste lands, commons, and rivers* undisposed of and such as by, from or under them or their heyrs have bought, granted and purchased from them or any of them theyr right and title thereunto *and none else.*' *

This order of course excluded all the other inhabitants of the town from any right or title to any of the common lands, the river lots, and Plum island. As early as 1680 attempts were made by the non-freeholders to own and occupy the commons equally with the freeholders, using language to the freeholders to this effect.

' We think it hard to be deprived of the right of commonage. We pay according to our property as much as you for the support of public worship, the support of schools, the repairing of the roads, and our equal proportion of all other taxes, and some of us have served as soldiers for your defence, and yet you have rights and privileges, of which we are deprived.' This was at least plausible, and after many meetings, they, in 1686, as we shall see, succeeded, with the assistance of some of the rich freeholders, in partially accomplishing their object, and establishing a rule, by which the division was made.

May 15th. At this session of the general court, Nathaniel Clarke of Newbury was chosen naval officer for Newbury and Salisbury. This was in accordance with the last year's petition of Newbury, and with that of Salisbury, who at this session of the court, preferred a similar petition, stating that they ' had some small trade.'

May 31st. Honorable Nathaniel Saltonstall, of Haverhill, thus writes to captain Thomas Noyes of Newbury. ' In ye major general's letter I have order also to require you, which I herein do, with all convenient speed, to provide a flight of colours for your foot company, ye ground field, or flight whereof is to be green *with a red cross* with a white field in ye angle, according to the antient custome of our own English nation, and the English plantations in America and our own practice in our ships and other vessels. The number or bullets to be put into your colours for distinction, may be left out at present without damage in the making of them.' †

Sr faile not

Your friend and servant,

N. SALTONSTALL.'

---

* Town records.   † Robert Adams's manuscripts.

Thus it appears that the cross in the colors, which Endicott, at the instigation of Roger Williams, had cut out in 1634 as a 'relique of antichrist,' and had been laid aside for many years, was again ordered to be inserted. The scruple, however, against its use, still continued in many minds. ' Judge Samuel Sewall, who in 1685 was captain of the south company of militia in Boston, resigned his commission November eleventh, 1686 on account of an order to put the cross in the colours.' *

In his diary, under date of August twentieth, 1686, he says: ' read tenth Jeremiah, was in great exercise about the cross to be put into the colours, and afraid, if I should have a hand in it, whether it may not hinder my entrance into the Holy land.'

This year, for the first time, a list of the town debts is given in full, from which the following extracts are taken. It is in John Pike's handwriting.

' To Mr. Edward Tomson for keeping school this year, . . . £30 0s 0d
To Richard Hening for sweeping the meeting house, ... 2 10 0
To Anthony Somerby for keeping the town booke, · 1 0 0
To Daniel Lunt an houre glass, ...   1 6
To John Hendrick one day at the hedg, ...   3 0
To Samuel Sawyer burning the woods in olde time, ...   4 0
To Mrs. White tavern expences, ... 5 2 4
To James Brown, watch house glass, ...   9 6
To Samuel Plummer ferriage, ... 10 0
To William Sawyer karting lime to meetting house, ...   2 0
To James Ordway and Jonathan Clark, twenty-eight bushels lime 1 8 0 '

From the same account it appears that the 'coullers' for the troop cost two pounds and fourteen shillings, and for the two foot companies six pounds, six shillings, and seven pence. The whole amount of the town tax for all purposes this year was three hundred and thirty-eight pounds and eighteen shillings, of which one hundred and twenty-eight pounds, six shillings, and sixpence, was the salary of reverend John Richardson.

November 24*th.* Inquest on the body of John Poore, senior.

' We judge that being in the woods and following his game, he was bewildered, and lost himself and in his pursuit plucked off his clothes, and scattered them some good distance one part from another till he had left nothing on save his waistcoat, and drawers, and breeches and hose and shoes.' †

1685.

February 8*th.* ' Sabbath afternoon there was an earthquake.' ‡
January 17*th.* ' Boston harbour frozen over down to the castle, and nine hundred men on the ice at once.' ‡

The following petition was sent in to the town of Newbury by some of the inhabitants at the west end.

* Quarterly register, February, 1841. † County records. ‡ Judge Sewall's diary.

'*March* 10*th*, 1684-5. To the town of Newbury the humble request of some of the inhabitants of this town doe sire and intreat that you would be pleased to grant us your consent, approbation and assistance in geting some help in the ministry amongst us, by reason that we doe live soe remote from the means, great part of us that we cannot with any comfort or convenience come to the publick worship of God; neither can our families be brought up under the means of grace as christians ought to bee, and which is absolutely necessary unto salvation; therefore we will humbly crave your loving compliance with us in this our request.'

The preceding petition is the first recorded intimation, that is to be found, that the people of the west end of the town desired to have public worship among themselves. This was the commencement of a contest, which, as we shall see, involved the whole town, and especially the westerly part of it, in difficulties and quarrels, which were not settled for many years, the injurious consequences of which are even now perceptible.

April 20*th*. King James proclaimed king ' in the market place, Boston, by the governor, deputy governor, eight soldiers and one troop to guard the governor.'

This year, May twentieth, William Bolton was chosen 'to keep the dry cattell in the upper commons above the hedge, and to take care for ye repayring of such breaches as should be in the hedg from time to time,' and so forth.

June 18*th*. The selectmen defined the limits of the five flocks of sheep. They were called 'the old-town flock,' 'Henry Short's flock,' 'captain Pierce's flock,' 'the frogg pond flock,' and 'the Artechoak flock.'

In November the selectmen ordered the names of all the taxpayers to be recorded, with the amount paid by each individual toward Mr. Richardson's salary, which was 'forty pounds in money and seventy pounds in other good pay.' The word 'pay' at this time meant all kinds of grain, and so forth, and sometimes cattle and horses. By a warrant from the state treasurer 'to the selectmen and constables of Newbury, the town was required to collect of the inhabitants eighteen pounds, two shillings and ten pence in money, and thirty-six pounds, five shillings and eight pence to be paid in country pay, wheat at five shillings and sixpence, barley and barley malt and pease at four shillings and sixpence, rye at four shillings, Indian corn at three shillings, and oats at two shillings per bushel, and all other things at money prices, provided no leane cattle or horses be paid, and in case any pay money in lieu of country pay they are to be abated one third,' and so forth.

The whole number of persons rated, was two hundred and thirteen, among whom are the names of eight with the title of ' Mr.,' a mark of distinction at this time, one esquire, three captains, three lieutenants, two ensigns, eight sergeants, three corporals, three deacons, and two doctors.

1686.

'*January* 24*th, Sunday.* So cold that the sacramental bread is frozen pretty hard and rattles sadly into the plates.' *

At the March meeting this year, 'it was ordered that the selectmen shall have twenty shillings apiece for the bearing of their charges and the expence of their time about the towne buisiness and ye commissioner to have ten shillings and what they spend more they are to pay out of their owne estate.' †

March 16*th.* 'The towne being sensible of their great want of another corne mill,' a committee of five persons was chosen 'to view such place or places, as may be most convenient for ye setting up of a mill.' †

'For the preservation of convenient shades for cattle and sheep in ye home commons,' all persons were forbidden, under penalty of twenty shillings a tree, 'apses, birches and alders excepted, to cutt, fall, girdle or lopp any tree in any of the towne's high wayes or in any of ye commons' within certain specified limits. †

'Juniper proposed for a liberty to build a cottage to dwell in upon ye common neer frogg pond. The towne voted in the negative.'†

March 22*d.* 'At a legall meeting of the selectmen twenty tything men were appointed and chosen for the year ensuing.'

'Benjamin Mors was appointed to burn the woods this year above Artichoke river and to have for his pains ten shillings.'

Hugh March and Mrs. Ann White were licensed to keep an 'ordinary.'

'At a county court March thirtieth captain Daniel Pierce, captain Thomas Noyes and lieutenant Stephen Greenleaf are commissioned to be magistrates by the court, as there was no magistrate among them,' that is, the people of Newbury. So says John Badger in his petition.

March 23*d.* 'At a legall meeting of the freemen and freeholders,' another attempt was made to divide a part of the upper commons. Among the votes passed was one, forty-three to thirty-eight, that 'each freeholder should have twenty acres of land laid out in the upper commons on Merrimack river and on the southwest side of the upper commons' and so forth, and 'it was also determined and agreed that if this land in time to come *shall be* improved by fencing or otherwise the improvers of it shall pay to all public towne charges,' and so forth.†

From this and other votes and allusions, it is evident that the larger part of the land lying above Artichoke river, was still common, unfenced, and unimproved except for pasturage. Large quantities of timber in this tract were granted to various individuals to make 'long shingle,' as it was called, 'to cover houses,' for 'pales'

* Judge Sewall's diary.   † Town records.

for 'clapboards,' 'for posts and rayles,' for buildings of various kinds, and for wheelwrights and coopers' use.

In the month of April, complaints were 'made to the selectmen of great spoyle of timber that was made in the towne's commons, constable Moses Pilsbury seized and delivered to Joseph Pike twenty-one red oak trees and sixteen white oak trees at the southeast end near Savages' rock and the westerly end of Long hill near Merrimack river.'

May 5th. A committee of seventeen was chosen, to 'agree upon a meete way of dividing the commons and bring in theyr result and conclusion to the towne,' and so forth.*

On October twentieth, the committee reported, and the 'towne voted that the upper commons be divided in manner following, namely, the six thousand acres, one half of them in quantity and quality be divided among the freeholders, to every freeholder a like share, and the other half of said commons be divided among all such inhabitants of this towne and freeholders as have paid rates two years last past, proportionable to what each man paid by rate to the minister's rate in the year 1685.' *

'And that about eleven hundred acres of the lower commons be divided according to the above method and laid out into five general pastures and so forth, and the rest of the commons to be divided and laid out into wood lots according to the above division and same rule.'*

'*June* 19*th*. James Myricks house burnt down.' †

The committee, who were chosen October twenty-first, to divide and lay out the lands, were captain Daniel Pierce, lieutenant Stephen Greenleaf, serjeant John Emery, Joseph Pike, lieutenant Tristram Coffin, ensign Nathaniel Clark, and Henry Short.

November 26*th*. The freeholders of Newbury met and passed several orders before the lots were drawn. One was, that 'Indian river should be free as far as the tide flows for the passing and re-passing of boats and canoes. Another, that every freeholder should draw his lot as his name is entered in the town booke.* The freeholders' meeting was then adjourned for half an hour to attend the towne meeting then to be.' *

This division of land, which the freeholders had at last agreed to make, was one of the most important transactions in which the town had been called to engage. It had occasioned, as we learn from a protest on record, signed by Margaret Lowle and James Brown, 'great confusions, contentions, inconveniences, and injuries,' and was not settled without much difficulty and opposition. On November twenty-ninth, they again met, and 'agreed that the persons concerned in the rate division of the upper commons shall be drawne into four companyes, then one man of each company shall draw in the name, and for the said company, and he that draweth figure one that company shall have theyr proportions first,' and so on. 'Then every man's name of every company, and the names of the four

* Town records.   † Sewall's journal.

19

companyes shall be putt into four several baggs, and the committee
chosen to lay out the said rate proportion shall take a paper out of
the bagg belonging to the first company, and that man's name, that
first comes to hand shall have his lott first laid out and so all the rest
successively until the whole be laid out and so for the rest of the
companyes.' *

December 1st.   The freeholders again met and voted, that 'they
would begin the division next Mr. John Gerrish's farm next Bradford line,' and so forth.   The lots were accordingly drawn, and the
land was laid out by 'the two lott layers, namely lieutenant Tristram
Coffin and Henry Short,' and thus this perplexing business was
finally settled, in perhaps the only way which could reconcile the
conflicting interests and opinions of the great majority of the people.

December 13th.   A committee was chosen to divide eleven
hundred acres of the lower commons into five general pastures.

December 20th.   Sir Edmund Andros came to New England.

December 21st.   The committee were desired to 'measure the
old towne common and proportion it to the old towne men and
proportion the rest of the land adjacent to the rest of the inhabitants in the same proportion.' *

It may not here be improper to explain the difference between a
'freeholders' meeting,' a 'freemen's meeting,' and a 'town meeting.'
A man might be a freeholder and not a 'freeman,' and vice versa.
He might be a voter in town affairs, and yet neither be a freeholder
nor a freeman.   A freeman was one who had taken the freeman's
oath, and which alone entitled him to vote in the nomination of
magistrates, choice of deputies, alias representatives.   A freeholder
was one, who either by grant, purchase, or inheritance, was entitled
to a share in all the common and undivided lands.   When any
town officers were to be chosen, or money raised by way of rate,
all the inhabitants could vote.   Thus we sometimes find the expression, 'at a meeting of the freemen,' sometimes 'a meeting of the
freeholders,' or 'a meeting of the freeholders and proprietors,' or 'a
meeting of the freeholders and inhabitants,' or 'a generall towne
meeting,' and sometimes 'a legall towne meeting.'   These expressions always indicate the nature and object of the meeting, and
were necessary, as all the transactions were recorded by the town
clerk, in the same book.   In this year, two sets of books began to
be kept, one for the town, and one for the proprietors, and were
kept separate till the final settlement of the proprietors' concerns, in
the sale of Plum island in 1827.   To the division of the land in
the upper commons, on the plan proposed, many were opposed,
some from principle, and some from interest.   The division was at
last settled by a compromise, which evinced a good deal of management, quieting the non-freeholder, and, at the same time, enrich-
ing the wealthy freeholder at the expense of the poorer freeholder.
That a rich freeholder would obtain a larger share by consenting

* Town records.

that the rate-paying non-freeholders should share with him according to 'the rule,' is evident. For example, were one hundred and thirteen acres of land to be divided among the freeholders alone, each would have an acre; but were the same amount to be divided, one half among the freeholders, and the other half among the freeholders and rate payers, a freeholder would have half an acre on the first division, and if he paid a sixteen shillings tax, he would obtain eight times as much on the other half as a freeholder who only paid a two shillings tax.

November 21*st.* 'The three deacons namely, deacon Nicholas Noyes, deacon Robert Long and deacon Tristram Coffin were at the request of the selectmen, chosen standing overseers of the poore for the town of Newbury.'

December 1*st.* 'Captain Daniel Pierce and captain Stephen Greenleaf senior, were added to the deacons as overseers of the poor, and that any three of them shall have power to make a valid act.' * The town also engaged 'to ratify and confirm whatsoever bargain the overseers of the poore shall make, provided alwayes that they do not engage money.' *

December 13*th.* The town empowered a committee 'to lay out a convenient high way of such breadth as they shall see meet thro' the plaines to sergeant Emery's mill.' *

'The first range of lots for the freeholders began at sergeant John Emery's farm [near Artichoke river] and so ran up Merrimack river unto Mr. John Gerrish's farm [near or adjoining to Bradford.']

The committee, consisting of Mr. Daniel Pierce, with Tristram Coffin, and Henry Short, lot-layers, laid out a road 'four rods wide and no more from Artichoke river to Lowell's brook [now Brown's spring] and thence to Bradford line.' *

Joseph Dudley was appointed president of Massachusetts, Plymouth, New Hampshire, and Maine, with a council, but no house of representatives. In six months he was superseded by sir Edmund Andros. He was very arbitrary and oppressive. Five only of the councillors joined with governor Andros in his measures; the greater part refusing to act with him.

1687.

January 5*th*, 1687. A committee was appointed 'to treat with Peter Cheney about setting up a corne mill and a fulling mill upon the Falls river, and to treat with William Moody concerning his Indian purchase and the quantity of land he claims thereby,' * and so forth.

January 8*th.* Town granted Mr. [D.] Davison a 'piece of ground twenty foot wide next Mr. Richard Dole's ware house grant and thirty-five foot long towards doctor Dole's house,' and laid it out second of April.

* Town records.

Town sent a petition to sir Edmund Andros, knight, praying him to appoint and empower some man or men to take the acknowledgment of deeds, and give oaths, and a clerk to issue 'forth all needful writs and warrants, there being not one of your excellencys council within twenty miles.'

February 15*th*, 1687. Peter Cheney proposed to 'build and maintaine a good sufficient grist or corn mill within two years, and a fulling mill within three yeares at ye upper falls, and to full ye towne's cloth on the same terms that Mr. John Pearson doth full cloth, and resign up his interest in Little river on condition that the town give him fifty acres of land joyning to Falls' river,' * and so forth, which the town granted.

March 28*th*. The town granted to eleven young men, 'liberty to build a pew in the hindmost seat in the gallery, that is before the pulpit.' *

October 18*th*. The committee chosen by the town, 'agreed with Mr. Seth Shove to be ye lattin Schoolmaster for ye town of Newbury for the present year.'

April 6*th*. 'A warrant was granted to warne out of ye towne Wm. Nisbett, Edw. Badger and one David that lives at Mr. Thurlos.' *

'This year the worms did much mischief in the summer, eating up trees, grass as though they had been mown, leaving weeds.' †

October 25*th*. A new ferry across the Merrimac was granted by sir Edmund Andros, to captain John March, and was the first ferry granted within the limits of what is now Newburyport. It was situated just where it is now. The first was granted at Carr's island, and, till this year, had monopolized the whole travel of the country, from the mouth of the river to Amesbury ferry. This grant was in consequence of a petition sent by captain March, September twenty-third, 1687. James Carr remonstrated against it, stating that 'the first bridge at Carr's island cost more than three hundred pounds, that the ferry at George Carr's death was worth near four hundred pounds and that the injury to him by March's ferry was fifty or sixty pounds a year.' Mr. March, in a letter to the town of Salisbury, offered to be at one half of the expense of making their part of the road passable to the ferry.

During the vacation of the charter, and the tyrannical administration of Andros, it was asserted that the people had no title to their lands. The following letter from Mr. Robert Mason, who, in consequence of a grant to his father from the council of Plymouth, before the settlement of Massachusetts, claimed all the land from Naumkeag river, [Salem,] to Merrimac, will be read with interest. Mason was one of Andros's council, and resided at Portsmouth, New Hampshire.

* Town records.   † Sewall's journal.

'Great Island, August 13th, 1687.

' To his excellency Edmund Andros,
    ' Sir,
    ' Your excellency may please to remember I proposed some persons as fitting to serve his majesty in the town of Newbury both in civil and military affairs.   In my return to this place I had discourse with several persons, the most considerable of that town, that by want of justices of the peace, nothing hath been done at the meeting of those inhabitants for settling the rates and other concerns of the publick.   Mr. Woodbridge, one of the justices is very ancient and crazy and seldom goes abroad.   Mr. Dummer the other justice lives six miles from the place and therefore very unfit for that service for the town of Newbury, besides his other qualites in not being of the loyal party as he ought to be.   I doe therefore intreat of your excellency, that in the commission of the peace my two friends, Daniel Pierce and Nathaniel Clarke may be put, which I assure myself will be for his majesty's service and to your excellency's satisfaction.   There are no military commissions sent to that place and therefore I doe entreat your excellency's favour that commissions be sent these following persons.   Daniel Davison, captain of horse for Newbury and Rowley.   Stephen Greenleaf junior lieutenant.   George March cornet.   Of the first company Thomas Noyes captain, Stephen Greenleaf senior lieutenant, James Noyes ensign.   Of the second company Nathaniel Clarke captain, John March lieutenant, Moses Gerrish ensign.   I shall desire your excellency that Mr. Davison may have his commission first for raising the troops, there being many young men, that will list themselves under him, if not before listed by the captain's foot.   He is very well beloved and I presume will have the completest troops in the country.
    ' I shall be extream glad to heare of my good lady's safe arrival, which so soon as I shall understand, I will make a speedy journey to Boston to kiss her hands.   I came last night to this place.   *I hope all things will go easy so that I may have no occasion of using the former severities of the law against my tenants.* I had rather see them rich than poor.   I humbly kiss your excellency's hands and am   Your excellency's servant
                                                  ROBERT MASON.'

1688.

January 26*th.*   John Woodbridge, esquire, and eight others, sent in a written prostestation ' against the injurious and unreasonable dealing of some invading and disposing of the town's commons, which (as they suppose) they have no right nor authority to do,' and so forth, and 'demanded that whatsoever is already done to the dividing and impropriating our commons may be made void and nulled,' and so forth.

The town granted ' their interest in the stream of the little river to the mouth of it where it vents into the great river to Henry Short to build a grist mill upon for the towne's use, provided he build it within one year, and if he do not build within one year he is to pay five pounds and the towne to have theyr interest in the stream againe.' *

This summer, the people of Massachusetts, in addition to the grievances, which they suffered under the tyrannical administration of sir Edmund Andros, were again, after a twelve years' respite, afflicted with the horrors of an Indian war.   It was called Castine's war from the baron de saint Castine, a Frenchman, who had mar-

* Town records.

ried a daughter of Madochawando, the Penobscot chief, and whose house, in his absence, had been plundered by the English. The Canadian French also united with the Indians in their depredations, which were continued at intervals till 1698. Notwithstanding all the difficulties, under which the people labored, they were, in general, very patient under the ' new government.' *   There were, however, a few exceptions. ' One John Gould was tried, convicted and fined fifty pounds for treasonable words.' The reverend John Wise and Mr. John Appleton, of Ipswich, were imprisoned for remonstrating against the taxes as a heavy grievance.*

Caleb Moody of Newbury was imprisoned and Joseph Bayley put under bonds of two hundred pounds to answer for an alleged offence, which is best related in Moody's own words.

' Caleb Moody of Newbury aged fifty-two years testifyeth that some time in January 1688 Joseph Baylie of ye same towne gave me a paper, which he told me he had taken up in the king's highway, the title of it was,

> ' New England alarmed,
> To rise and be armed,
> Let not papist you charme,
> I mean you no harme,' and so forth.

' The purport of the paper was to give notice to the people of the danger they were in, being under the sad circumstances of an arbitrary government, sir Edmund Andros having about one thousand of our souldiers, as I was informed, prest out of the Massachusetts colony and carried with him to the eastward under pretence of destroying our enemy Indians (although not one Indian killed by them that I heard of at that time.)   We had no watching nor warding at our towne by order of those yt sir Edmund put in command there.   Justice Woodbridge and Justice Epps sent me a warrant to bring a paper that was in my hands, which I did, and told them I received the paper from Joseph Baylie, who owned it to them, whereupon I was cleared, and they bound said Joseph Baylie in a bond of two hundred pounds to answer it at Salem court ye fifth of March following and they took me for his bondsman.   Notwithstanding this, about a week after the said justices by a warrant brought me before them and then committed me to Salem prison (though I proffered ym bayle) they would not take it but I was to be safely kept to answer what should be charged against me upon the king's account for publishing a scandalous and seditious lybell.   After I had been in prison a whole week then judge Palmer and Mr. Grayham, ye king's attorney came to Salem and examined me and confined me to close imprisonment ordering that neither my friends, or acquaintance nor fellow-prisoners to come to me, which continued for about a week's time, and then judge P. and Mr. G. came againe, and said G. sent for me, and after some discourse he refused any bayle, but committed me to close prison, and after, Charles Redford, the high sheriff, came to prison and told Joseph Baylie and myself that he had orders to examine us, and to put a new mittimus upon us and charge us with treason, and the time came when the court should have sent to try us and there was no court. Afterwards there came news of ye happy arrival and good success of ye prince of Orange, now king of England, and then by petitioning I got bayle.   The time of my imprisonment was about five weeks, and I doe judge my dammage one way and another was about forty pounds.

Boston New England, January ninth, 1689-90.' †
' Caleb Moody appeared personally January ninth, 1689-90 and gave evidence upon oath of the truth of the above written before me

SAMUEL APPLETON

Assistant for ye colony of ye Massachusetts
bay in New England.'

---

* Hutchinson.   † Colonial files.

The 'one thousand souldiers,' mentioned by Moody in the preceding statement, were in fact only seven or eight hundred, whom governor Andros had impressed, and marched at their head in the eastern country in November, a 'measure universally condemned,' as 'not an Indian was killed,' and 'many of the soldiers died with hardships.' The names of those impressed by his order from Newbury, November, 1688, were, captain John March, Charles Stuart, Benjamin Goodridge, William Goodridge, John Cram, Joseph Short, Edward Goodwin.

In the January following, Giles Mills, Nicholas Cheney, Jacob Parker, John Richards, and Andrew Stickney, were impressed.

Joseph Moring, a soldier, in his will, dated November fifth, 1688, says, 'I give to the 'new town' in Newbury twenty pounds to help build a meeting house, *if they do build one*, if they do not build one, then I give twenty pounds towards rebuilding or repairing the meeting-house that is now standing in Newbury.'

In Richard Bartlet's old account book I find, in 1689, the following. 'Bought boards and shingles and nails for the meeting house.' The west parish meeting-house was therefore built in 1689.

1 6 8 9 .

For the last three years, there is nothing of interest to be found on the town records. The reason of this, probably, is, that nothing of consequence was done. Under the tyrannical and arbitrary government of Andros, the people were kept under great restraint.

'Every town was suffered to meet once a year to choose their officers, but all meetings at other times or for other purposes, were strictly forbidden.' *

The body of the people, who had borne with great patience the tyranny of Andros's administration, were determined to bear it no longer. On Thursday, the eighteenth of April, the inhabitants of Boston and the vicinity 'seized and confined the governor and such of the council, as had been most active, and other obnoxious persons and reinstated the old magistrates.' * Some went from Newbury. Among them was Samuel Bartlet, a staunch friend of liberty, a very facetious but decided man. 'He was a basket maker, fidler and farmer. On the first intimation of any difficulty, he armed himself, mounted his horse, and so rapid, it is said, was his flight to Boston, that his long rusty sword, trailing on the ground, left, as it came in contact with the stones in the road, a stream of fire all the way. He arrived in season to assist in imprisoning the governor.' †

The following is the first article on the records for this year.

'*May 6th.* The committee of safety in Boston having desired us to send a man or men for consulting with them what may be

---

* Hutchinson.
† Interleaved almanacs of the late honorable Bailey Bartlet, esquire, Haverhill.

best for the conservation of the peace of the country. Our inhabitants being met this sixth day of May 1689 have chosen captain Thomas Noyes and lieutenant Stephen Greenleaf senior for the end aforesaid,' and on May twentieth the inhabitants of the town met for consultation, and among other things declared that being ' in full expectation of enlargement of privilege and liberty of choyce for the future,' they ' give their consent to the freemen of the towne to make choyce of the governor, deputy governor, and assistants to be our lawful authority.' It was therefore voted ' by the towne and by the freemen,' with only two dissenting votes, that the charter should be reassumed, though nothing had then been heard from England. On May twenty-sixth, news arrived at Boston that William and Mary had been proclaimed king and queen of England. ' This,' says Hutchinson, ' was the most joyful news ever received in New England.'

July 1st.   Town desired ' for the present exigence to have all the military officers, that were in commission May twelfth 1686,' to be reinstated.

' Also we desire and empower the said committee of militia to appoint so many houses to be fortified among us as they shall see cause and to proportion so many families to each fortification according to theyr discretion.'

August 22d.   ' Brig Merrimack of Newbury, captain John Kent, was captured by pirates in Martin Vineyard sound.'

August 24th.   The governor and council and representatives desired the town of Newbury to raise a ' subscription for a loan of money, goods and provisions for the carrying on of the Indian war.' The town, ' in answer thereunto,' say, ' it is our desire to maintaine ye soldiers of our own towne as to provision and wages.' *

September 23d.   Samuel Sâyer was licensed by the court to sell victuals and drink, living conveniently by the road to Bradford and Haverhill.'

December 25th.   Peter Cheney was allowed one year longer to finish his fulling mill.

December 26th.   ' The towne granted all theyr right, title and interest in the stream of the little river to Henry Short so long as he shall build and maintain a sufficient corne mill,' and so forth.

Sometime this year, the first meeting-house in the west end of the town was erected. It was about thirty feet square, and was built at the cost and charge of sixteen persons. It stood on what is called ' the plains.'

1690.

February 25th.   ' Divers of the inhabitants of the new towne having made a proposition unto ye towne in order to their calling of a minister amongst them,

* Town records.

'The towne considering the great weight of such a thing and yt such an affayre may be duly considered the towne have desired [a committee of eight persons] to advise with ye reverend Mr. Richardson about the said proposition and to draw up such proposals to the next meeting of the towne as they shall think may best conduce to peace that the towne may consider farther of it.' *

March 3d. The committee waited on Mr. Richardson, who declined giving 'advice on the one side or the other, knowing he must of necessity give offence.' The committee reported, 'that considering the times as troublesome, and the towne being so much behind with Mr. Richardson's salary, the farmers and the neck men being under greater disadvantages upon many accounts do desire and expect, if such a thing be granted that they should have the same privilege to provide for themselves, which we think cannot conduce to peace, therefore desire the new towne to rest satisfied for the present.' *

'*March* 1690. The committee of Newbury appoint the house of Mr. Abraham Merrill to be a garrison house and request him with all convenient speed to fortify his house.

DANIEL PIERCE *Captain.*'

March 11th. At this meeting, fifteen men, belonging to the west end of the town, after stating that 'it was well known how far they had proceeded as to a meeting house,' left two propositions with the town, one that the town would agree to support two ministers, so that one could preach 'at the west meeting house,' or that the town would consent to have the 'ministry amongst them upon their own charge and that the town would lovingly agree upon a dividing line between them that so they might know what families may now belong to the west meeting house,' and so forth.

This year, Isaac Morrill, a native of New Jersey, came to Newbury, to entice Indians and negroes to leave their masters and go with him, saying that *the English should be cut off, and the negroes should be free.* He was arrested May twenty-ninth, 1690, and sent to Ipswich for trial. What was the result of his examination, I have not ascertained. Their intention was to take a vessel out of the dock at Newbury, and go for Canada and join the French against the English, and come down upon the backside of the country and save none but the negroes and Indians. They intended to come with four or five hundred Indians, and three hundred Canadians, between Haverhill and Amesbury, over Merrimac river, near 'Indian river by Archelaus' hill on the backside of John Emery's meadow and destroy, and then they might easily destroy such small towns as Haverhill and Amesbury. Morrill said that he had viewed all the garrisons in the country and that captain Gerrish's was the strongest.' †

The persons implicated in this scheme to obtain their inalienable

* Town records.　　　　　　　　† Quarterly court files.

rights, were James, a negro slave of Mr. R. Dole, and Joseph, Indian slave of Mr. Moody.

George Major, a Jerseyman, was also implicated. How many slaves, Indian and African, there were at this time in Newbury, we have no means of ascertaining. The number was probably small, as governor Bradstreet, in a letter dated May nineteenth, 1680, to the lords of the privy council, says among other things, ' now and then two or three negroes are brought hither from Barbadoes. In our government [Massachusetts] about one hundred and twenty in all.'

Fifteen soldiers were sent from Newbury to Salisbury, Amesbury, and Haverhill, April twelfth.

April 28th. Sir William Phipps, with a fleet of eight small vessels, sailed against Port Royal, [now Annapolis,] which he took ' with little or no resistance,' and returned the thirtieth of May. His success encouraged the court to attempt the acquisition of Canada, which after much expense and loss of men proved a total failure, which occasioned so great an expense as to induce the government to issue bills of credit from two shillings to ten pounds' denomination. The soldiers were great sufferers by this paper money, the first seen in New England.

The situation of Newbury during the present Indian war may be in part ascertained by the following order, which is similar to the one passed in 1638.

August 7th. ' These are in his majesty's name to require all the soldiers belonging to this towne to bring their arms and ammunition to ye meeting house evary saboth day and at all other publick meetings, and also they ar required to carry their arms and ammunition with them into meadows and places, where they worke, and if any man doe refuse or neglect his dewty as above expressed he shal pay five shillings for every such neglect. *

DANIEL PIERCE, captain,   JONA. MOORES, lieutenant,
THOMAS NOYES, captain,   JACOB TOPPAN, ensign,
STEPH. GREENLEAF, captain,   HENRY SOMERBY.'

July 15th. ' John March is appointed a captain of one of the companies for the Canada expedition, and ordered to enlist a company under him.'

The following letter from Nathaniel Saltonstall, esquire, may not be uninteresting. It is from Robert Adams's manuscripts.

'*Haverhill August 20th,* 1690.

' Captain Noyes,
    ' After you were gone being thoughtfull how yourself and the rest with you last night would get home, I began to have some hopes concerning you, because I did not believe your dinners would ly upon your stomachs so as to indispose you in riding unless in vexation for the want of one ; there being a common saying ; a man after a good dinner is most airy and most agile and readie for riding or such kind of imployments.

' James Sanders just now promised me to call for this letter, which incloses

* Robert Adams's manuscripts.

ye papers, yt are to be improved ye next lecture day about Joseph Bayley and John Chase.

' Fail not of giving me a true account of your management of ye matter, and now it comes just into my mind to propose to you for your farther proceeding; and if you act accordingly hereto it shall be owned by me notwithstanding the issue made; which will without doubt fully be known to all your people. ·It is this, if ye said Joseph or John do carry it submissively and give you thereby ground to hope that their confession was from ye heart, which I for some reason account so to be, you may tell them you will venture to stop their publique appearance on ye lecture day; which if they afterward run into ye like evils will be a great aggravation of their fault.

' I will tell you. Formerly when I had prosecuted several for offences in ye field at court too, and judgment given for their open confession at ye head of ye company, I did abate it and I found I did not offend ye court, but engaged ye person to civility and thankfulness.

' Let me have a punctual return yt I may know what I have to do.

' If they or either of them be insolent let not them or him, yt is so, be abated of ye full extent of what is written in ye judgment.

' Give a little assistance to James Sanders to obtain my lettre, which brother Woodbridge writes me word he sent long since by major Davison. I suppose it was at yt time when – Clark had ye – — to gett a canonical auricular confessor for himself and family.

' Present my service to ye lady Noyes, and ye major the C**** Mr Richardson, and any one else, who will send me a cheap freight of good hay, I care not how cheap. Believe it, sir, and yt I am your servant,

N. SALTONSTALL.'

October. ' Captain Stephen Greenleaf, lieutenant James Smith, ensign William Longfellow serjeant Increase Pilsbury, William Mitchell, Jabez Musgrave of Newbury and four more were cast away and drowned at Cape Breton.' *

Of Jabez Musgrave, mentioned above, Mather, in his Remarka-ables, thus speaks in 1684.

' Remarkable also was that which happened to Jabez Musgrave of Newbury, who being shot by an Indian [in 1676] the bullet entered in at his ear and went out at his eye on the other side of his head, yet the man was preserved from death yea and still is in the land of the living.'

Musgrave was one of the sixteen soldiers from Newbury, who volunteered to go in this disastrous expedition.

This year, major Robert Pike, of Salisbury, thus writes:

' Captain Pierce, captain Noyes, captain Greenleaf, and lieutenant Moores with the rest of the gentlemen of Newbury, whose assistance next under God was the means of the preservation of our towns of Salisbury and Amesbury in the day of our distress by the assaults of the enemy.

' First I give you my hearty thanks for your readiness to adventure yourselves in that service, as always you have been ready to do and so forth.

' Second, to request the like favour of you upon the like occasion, if any such be offered.

' Third, that no *dunt*,† which is common pay in the country, may

---

* Judge Sewall's diary.   † ' I hae a guid braid sword,
                                    I 'll take *dunts* frae naebody.' *Burns.*

hinder any advised man from doing thayr duty, which is the advice that I give to myself, which you cannot but think have and shall have as much *dunt* as I can bear,' and so forth.

Captain John March and Mrs. Ann White were this year licensed as innholders.

This year, Essex soldiers were divided into three regiments.

1691.

March 10*th*.   The selectmen were desired to take care that persons infected with the small pox should be confined, and that their 'families should not suffer, if they were themselves unable.' ✳

May 13*th*.   ' The town voted that from this time forward the moderator shall be chosen by papers, and that it shall not be in the power of any moderator to adjourn a towne meeting but by vote of the towne.' ✳

' The town grants Mr. Seth Shove thirty pounds for the year ensuing, provided he will be our schoolmaster and so forth as followeth namely to teach readers free, Latin scholars sixpence per week, writers and cypherers fourpence per week, to keep the school one third part of the year at the middle of the new towne, one third part at the school house, and the other third part about middle way between the meeting house and oldtown ferry.' ✳

June 21*st*.   The officers of the two militia companies issued an order to Henry Short, requiring him ' in his majesties name to take care of his watch every night.' They were fifty-one in all. ' They are alike required to come to your house to take their charge. You are to order them to go to George Little's garrison, and there one of them is to keep his post all the night. The rest are to walk three in a night to the mill bridge, and from thence to Anthony Morse's house and elsewhere according to your direction. The number of men belonging to your care and charge are under express,' and so forth, and so forth.

July 14*th*.   ' The towne understanding that several of the inhabitants of new towne are about calling of Mr. [Edward] Tompson to be their minister, the towne did by vote manifest their dislike against it, or against any other minister, whom they should call, until ye church and towne are agreed upon it, looking upon such a thing to be an intrusion upon ye church and towne.'

August 21*st*.   The commissioner with the selectmen states the number of ratable polls to be two hundred and fifty.

October.   Several of the inhabitants of the west end of the town petitioned the general court ' to be established a people by themselves for the maintenance of the ministry among them.'

December.   The town did by vote manifest themselves 'against the new town having their petition granted,' and chose a committee to present a counter petition to the general court.

✳ **Town records.**

This year Newbury was allowed by the general court to have another house of entertainment.

1 6 9 2.

In February of this year, commenced the witchcraft delusion, which, for a long time, occasioned so much terror, distress, and suffering, in several towns in Massachusetts. It originated in Salem village, now Danvers, in the family of the reverend Samuel Parris, whose 'daughter and niece, girls of ten or eleven years of age, and two other girls in the neighborhood, began to act very strangely, appeared to fall into fits, would creep into holes, under benches and chairs,' put themselves into odd postures, and, as the physicians who examined them could give no satisfactory name to their apparent disorder, and probably feeling that he must say something, one of them very gravely pronounced them *bewitched*. From this beginning, originating in fraud and imposture, and continued by the grossest superstition and ignorance, combined with great fear, for no one was safe, arose those accusations and 'prosecutions of the people, under the notion of witches, whereby twenty suffered as evil doers, (besides those that died in prison,) about ten more condemned, a hundred imprisoned, and about two hundred more accused, and the country generally in fears, when it would come their turn to be accused.' * In the language of the reverend Charles W. Upham, 'all the securities of society were dissolved. Every man's life was at the mercy of every other man. Fear sat on every countenance; terror and distress were in all hearts; silence pervaded the streets; many of the people left the country; all business was at a stand, and the feeling, dismal and horrible indeed, became general, that the providence of God was removed from them, and that they were given over to the dominion of Satan.' † From this awful scourge, Newbury was wholly exempt, though we have abundant evidence, that the inhabitants participated in the almost universal belief, that witchcraft was a reality. It was a fault of the age, from which the most pious, and, in other respects, learned men, were not free. Sir Matthew Hale was a firm believer in witchcraft, and the celebrated Richard Baxter, in a preface to one of Cotton Mather's sermons, on a case of supposed witchcraft, declares, ' that this instance comes with such convincing evidence, that he must be an obstinate Sadducee, who will not believe it.' It is well observed by governor Hutchinson, that 'in all ages of the world, superstitious credulity has produced greater cruelty than is practised among the Hottentots, or other nations whose belief of a deity is called in question.'

March. Several of the west end people, again made a petition and proposition about calling a minister.

---

* Robert Calef.   † Lectures on witchcraft.

May 14*th*. Sir William Phipps arrived at Boston, with the new charter for the Massachusetts province.

July 14*th*. Thanksgiving appointed on account of peace, the charter, and so forth.

November 1*st*. By special order of Sir William Phipps, twelve soldiers were sent from Newbury to Haverhill.

December 13*th*. Town ordered that ' whosoever shall build any vessels on the towne common shall pay to the town threepence per ton for the use of the building yard, that they shall improve.' *

December 20*th*. The town voted ' that they would call another minister at the west end of the towne.' Against this vote, twenty-two of the 'west end' men entered their dissent. *

December 27*th*. A committee was chosen 'to enquire after a suitable person to preach to the west end and to keep schoole.' *

This year, a petition to divide Essex county was presented to the general court; Newbury was allowed to have another house of entertainment; and the grand jury of Essex county ' presented Joseph Bailey for saying the men appointed by the town to answer the petition of those, who wanted another minister were devils incarnate.'

1693.

April 20*th*. The town 'chose Tristram Coffin treasurer for the poor.' *

May 12*th*. ' Towne voted that Mr. John Clarke be called to assist Mr. Richardson in the work of the ministry at the west end of the towne to preach to them one year in order to farther settlement and also to keep a grammar schoole.' *

May 31*st*. The selectmen of Newbury, in their petition to the general court, state that ' a long difference has existed between the people of Newbury, and those in the west end of the town about calling a minister, that the west end people had called Mr. Edward Tomson to preach to them without acquainting the minister, church or towne with their proceedings in that affair, the which when our town did understand that they were about to bring him into town, the town being met to consider of it by their vote did declare that they were against his coming, or any other until the church and town were agreed, yet they persisted in their design and brought him in, and when he was come in our minister warned him to forbear preaching till the church and town were agreed, yet he presumed to set up a lecture, and preach without any allowance of ministers, church or town, which when the church did understand, they did call him to account, and declared their dislike of his irregular proceeding, yet he hath persisted in these irregularities to the great disturbance of our peace, and since upon the request of severall of the inhabitants of the west end of our towne, called another minister, Mr. John Clark, who hath accepted of the call, and yet

* Town records.

there are severall, who refuse to accept of him, pretending they are bound to said Tomson, which agreement they made when the rest of their neighbors were about to make application to the town, which was since the late law was made to direct the town to call the minister.'

June 15*th.* A committee of the west end people, in their petition, thus reply. They request the governor and council 'to pity and help them,' 'to ease them of a heavy burden of travel on God's day.' ' We have been,' say they, 'endeavoring above these five years to have the publick worship of God established among us on the Lord's day for reasons such as these. The bulk of us live four miles from the ould meeting house, some six or seven. Our number is above three hundred. Few of us have horses, and if we could get down to the ould meeting house, it is impossible it should receive us with them so that many [would] lay out of doors, the house is so little. Some of us have groaned under this burden this thirty years, some grown old, some sickly, and although we were favored with the liberty granted by king James the second and had erected an house to the worship of God, on our own cost and charge, and acquainted the two next justices with our intent before we built the said house. A committee of five were appointed to come on the place, but before they had finished their work, the governor arrived, which caused them to desist. We complained to the governor, who granted us a protection from paying to the ould meeting house, then countermanded it. The town had a meeting — they intend to delude us by granting the help of a schoolmaster at sometimes for one yeare. We believe our neighbours would be glad to see us quite tired out. We beg the honorable court to establish peace among us a rational dividing line.'

' *June* 15*th,* 1693.'

July 5*th.* ' The towne in theyr votes for the choyce of a minister for the west end of the towne in order to a full settlement in the work of the ministry and Mr. John Clarke was then chosen and not one vote against him.' ✳

July 5*th.* Twenty-five persons of the west end entered their dissent against ' calling Mr. Clark. The reason is because the new towne people have a minister already.' ✳

This year, a jury of twelve women held an inquest on the body of Elizabeth Hunt, of Newbury. The following is an accurate copy of their verdict, which was doubtless perfectly conclusive and satisfactory.

' We judge according to our best light and contients, that the death of said Elizabeth was not by any violens or wrong dun to her by any parson or thing, but by som soden stoping of her breath.'

September 26*th.* On this day, the court of common pleas held its first sessions in Newbury. The court was held in the first parish meeting-house.

✳ **Town records.**

1694.

February 21*st*.   Liberty was granted to the petitioners 'to erect between captain Noyes' lane and Mr. Woodbridge's [upper green] a little house for the accommodation of a good and sufficient schoole dame.'   A similar petition was granted to deacon William Noyes, 'to sett up a schoole house upon the towne's land.'

A salary of 'twenty pounds in money and fifty pounds in graine was voted to ye reverend Mr. John Clarke so long as he carry on the worke of the ministry.'   Mr. Clark having declined the call, Mr. Christopher Toppan was invited 'to preach at the new towne.' Mr. Toppan having declined settling, but expressing his willingness 'to help in the work of the ministry for a year,' the town voted 'to give Mr. Toppan forty pounds in money and four contributions a year.'

March 26*th*.   The town granted permission to John Kelly, senior, to keep a ferry over the Merrimac, at Holt's rocks, 'in the place where he now dwells.'   Ferriage, 'sixpence for horse and man, and twopence for a single man.'

September 4*th*.   'Mr. Joseph Pike and Richard Long,' both of Newbury, 'were shot by the Indians as they were traveling near the end of Pond plain,' ※ in Haverhill.

September 5*th*.   A committee, consisting of Joshua Brown, John Ordway, and Samuel Bartlet, petitioned to the general court, 'in behalf of the company, that as they had erected a meeting house, and supplied themselves with a minister yet nevertheless our distresses do continually grow upon us toward an insupportable extremity, since the imprisoning of some of our number for their signifying our desire to enjoy the minister, whom we had formerly invited to preach in the meeting house, which we built at our own cost and charge, and some of us have been fined for not delivering up the key of the said meeting house.'

They conclude by requesting the general court, that they would 'so far interpose in our concerns as to take some effectual care for the relief of your petitioners and for the quiet of the whole town, the peace whereof is now so dangerously interrupted.' †

October 22*d*.   'The town brought in theyr votes by papers,' for a minister for 'the west end of the towne of Newbury and Mr. Christopher Toppan had sixty-five votes and Mr. Tompson seventeen.' ‡

December 21*st*.   A committee of five were chosen 'to draw up articles and proposals in order to setting off part of the west end of the towne' ‡ as a separate parish.

This year, a petition was sent to the governor and council, from Newbury and four other towns, for a division of the county of Essex. 'John and Samuel Bartlet, Abraham Morrill John Emery and

---

＊ Reverend John Pike's journal.   † General court files.   ‡ Town records.

Joseph Bailey were bound over and admonished for opposing their ordained minister, Mr. John Richardson.'

1695.

January 1*st*.   The town met and 'voted that Pipe-stave hill near Daniel Jaques' house *shall be* the place for the meeting house, and those that live nearest to that place shall pay to the ministry there, and those that live nearest to the old meeting house shall pay there, the inhabitants at the west end to choose a minister for themselves, only Mr. Tompson excepted.'   'And the meeting house to stand *where it do*, until the major part of them see cause to remove it.' 'The dividing line shall be from the middle way from the prefixed place in Pipe-stave hill and the old meeting house, to run on a straight line to Francis Brown's house near Birchen meadows and so straight over to the little pond.' *

January 3*d*.   Tristram Coffin, Henry Short, and Abraham Merrill, divided the town into two parishes.

Hugh March, in behalf of himself and brother, captain John March, petitioned the town 'to grant them a piece of ground and flatts to build a wharf and dock near captain March's barn.' * This petition was granted on certain conditions, January sixteenth, provided they are built ' within three years.' *

March 17*th*.   ' Mr. John Woodbridge dies, a good man and a constant attendant upon God in his publick worship on the Lord's day.' †

June 5*th*.   ' Town voted to give Mr. Christopher Toppan twenty pounds yearly in money and three hundred pounds a year in good country pay so long as he carries on one half of the ministry among them, and thirty pounds a year so long as he shall keep a grammar and a writing schoole, the scholars to pay as they did to Mr. John Clarke,' which proposals Mr. Toppan accepted, July seventeenth.

September 9*th*.   ' Twenty-four men at Pemaquid, going to get wood, are shot, four of whom are dead. Serjeant Hugh March, [of Newbury,] George's son, was killed at the first shot.' †

October 7*th*.   On the afternoon of this day, five Indians attacked and plundered the house of John Brown, who lived on the westerly side of Turkey hill, and captivated nine persons; one only of the family escaped to tell the tale. On the same day, colonel Daniel Pierce sent the following letter to colonel Appleton and colonel Wade, of Ipswich.

' Sir, this afternoon there came the enemy to a house in our town and went in and took and carried away nine persons and plundered the house, and as near as we can gather, they went southwestwardly between Boxford and Bradford. We can not gather that there were above five of the enemy, but night came on so that we could not pursue them, but we have lined Merrimac river with about fourscore men to watch lest they should carry the captives over the river, and

---

* Town records.   † Judge Sewall's diary.

21

do design in the morning to pursue them and range the woods with all the force we can make, and think it advisable that you range the woods towards Andover, and that Rowley towards Bradford, for if they escape us it will be an encouragement to them. Sir, I do think the case requires our utmost industry who am your friend and servant,

D. PIERCE.

October 7th, 1695.'

To this letter was appended the following.

' Colonel Gedney,
Honored sir, it is thought advisable on the consideration abovesaid yt it may be beneficial for the several companies in the several townes to range ye woods with all possible speed towards Bradford and Andover and so towards Merrimack river, so that if it might be ye enemy may be found and destroyed, which spoyle our people.
Ipswich, October eighth, at five in the morning.
Your servant,
SAMUEL APPLETON.'

Three hours after this, colonel Thomas Wade thus writes from Ipswich.

' Honored sir,
Just now captain Wicom brings information that the last night captain Greenleaf with a party of men met with the enemy by the river side, have redeemed all the captives but one, which they doubt is killed. Three of the Indians got into a canoe and made escape. and the other two ran into the woods. Captain Greenleaf is wounded in the side and arm, how much we know not, which is all at present from your servant,
THOMAS WADE.'

Judge Sewall, in his journal, says, ' all the captives were brought back, save one boy, that was killed. The Indians knocked the rest on the head, save one infant.'

Reverend John Pike, in his journal, states, that ' the captives were all retaken but some died of their wounds.'

On the fifth of March, 1696, captain Greenleaf addressed the following petition to the general court.

' The petition of captain Stephen Greenleaf of Newbury,
' Humbly sheweth,
' That upon the seventh of October last about three o'clock in the afternoon a party of Indians surprised a family at Turkey hill in said town captivated nine persons, women and children, rifled the house, carrying away bedding and other goods. Only one person escaped and gave notice to the next family and they, the town. Upon the alarm your petitioner with a party of men pursued after the enemy, endeavouring to line the river Merrimack to prevent their passage, by which means the captives were recovered and brought back.
' The enemy lay in a gully hard by the highway and about nine at night made a shot at your petitioner and shot him through the wrist between the bones, and also made a large wound in his side, which wounds have been very painful and costly to your petitioner in the cure of them and have in a great measure utterly taken away the use of his left hand and wholly taken him off from his employment this winter.
' Your petitioner therefore humbly prays this honored court that they would make him such compensation as shall seem fit, which he shall thankfully

acknowledge and doubts not but will be an encouragement to others speedily to relieve their neighbours when assaulted by so barbarous an enemy,

And your petitioner shall ever pray,

STEPHEN GREENLEAF.

'*March* 6*th.* Read and voted that there be paid out of the province treasury to the petitioner the sum of forty pounds.'

From one of John Brown's descendants, William G. White, I learn the following particulars as a family tradition. The Indians had secreted themselves for some time near the house, waiting for the absence of the male members of the family, who, about three o'clock, departed with a load of turnips. The Indians then rushed from their concealment, tomahawked a girl, who was standing at the front door. Another girl, who had concealed herself as long as the Indians remained, immediately after their departure gave the alarm, which resulted as before related. The coat, which captain Greenleaf wore in his pursuit of the Indians, is still preserved by his descendants, together with the bullet, which was extracted from his wound. This, I believe, is the only instance, in which the Indians either attacked, captivated, or killed, any of the inhabitants of Newbury.

From the original document now in my possession, I copy the following.

'*October* 14*th*, 1695. To Abraham Merrill of Newbury.

' These Are In his Majesty's name to will and Requier you to take the Cear to seat the watch of five men A night Begining att Samuel Poores and Job Pilsburyes and all Sàyer's Lean [lane] to Edward Poores and soe Runing by ye Road to Hartichoak river and soe Notherly Except the Boundars. You Are Likewise Required to Ordar two of said watchmen upon Dewty to walke Dowen to Daniel Merrill's and two more to John Ordways att thaier returen Always keeping out a Sentinell upon dewty. You are also to Make return of all defacts unto the Capten to whom they belong forthwith. It is also desiered that you demand and require ye fien for each man's defeact and upon their refusall to make return as aforesaid.'

December 18*th.* The town, ' on the request of the inhabitants of the west end of the towne of Newbury, granted them five acres of land on the east side of Artichoke river for a pasture for the ministry and one acre of land near the west meeting house, and when the major part shall see cause to remove the said meeting house, the land shall be at the disposal of the towne to procure land for the ministry, near the west meeting house, *when removed.*'*

1696.

February 28*th.* A rate was made for payment of building and finishing the west end meeting-house and ministry house. The expense was twenty-two pounds and three shillings in money, and two hundred and eighteen pounds, eighteen shillings, and twopence

* Town records.

in pay. This was due from sixty-four persons. Of this number, twenty-four, namely, Benjamin and Joseph Morse, Thomas, Daniel and Moses Chase, John, senior, John, junior, and Abiel Kelly, Mr. Abraham Annis and Isaac, Joseph Richardson, Abel Huse, Caleb Moody, Benjamin Low, Tristram Greenleaf, Daniel Morrison, Edward Woodman, John Hoag, Hanariah Ordway, Thomas Follansbee, lieutenant John Emerson, Thomas Williams, Francis Willet, and Samuel Sâyer, junior, objected to the continuance of the meeting house on the plains, and wished to have it removed to Pipe stave hill. The contest, thus commenced, continued for many years with an obstinacy and bitterness, to which the annals of Newbury furnish no parallel. Its results we shall hereafter see.

March 1*st*. The town granted to Stephen Greenleaf ' four or five rods on the flatts from Watts' cellar spring to ensign Greenleaf's and Mr. Davison's grant from high water mark to low water mark to build a wharfe and a place to build vessels uppon,' on certain conditions, one was ' that it come not within ten or twelve feet of the spring.'*

July 29*th*. The town offers Mr. Nicholas Webster thirty pounds a year in country pay to keep a ' grammer schoole provided he demand but fourpence per week for Latin scholars and teach the town's children to read, write and cypher without pay.'*

September 9*th*. Reverend Christopher Toppan ordained.

' The winter of this year was the coldest since the first settlement of New England.' *Lewis's history of Lynn.*

1697.

March. Laid out to Stephen Greenleaf a ' parcel of flatts and rocks lying on Merrimack river near Watts' cellar, bounded northerly by the river, easterly by major Davison's grant, southerly by the common land of Newbury and the westerly bound comes within about fifteen foot of the spring.'

'*March* 11*th*. The town laid out to Anthony Somerby a piece of land three rods square, lying at the place knowne by the name of Glading's spring † bounded by the *common or undivided land of Newbury on every side*, bounded with a small rock at every corner, for the convenience of dressing of leather.' *

'*April* 25*th*, *Thursday*. This day is signalized by ye achievement of Hannah Dunstan, Mary Neff and Samuel Lennardson, who killed two men, two women, and six others and brought home their scalps.' ‡

This year ensign James Noyes made a great discovery. It is thus mentioned by Judge Sewall in his diary.

' 1697. Colonel Pierce gave an account of ye body of limestone discovered at Newbury and the order of the selectmen published by

* Town records.
† ' Glading's spring' is a few rods southwesterly from Mr. Silas Noyes's house.
‡ Judge Sewall.

James Brown deputy sheriff, to prohibit any persons from carrying any more away under ye penalty of twenty shillings. It seems they began to come with teams thirty in a day. The town will have a meeting and bring it to some regulation. Our Mumford says 't is good marble. Ensign James Noyes found it out.'

We at the present time can hardly conceive of the excitement occasioned in the town and neighborhood by this discovery. It was deemed by judge Sewall worthy of special notice, as an answer, among other things, to a letter written from New England to Old England, ' discoursing of an impossibility of subsisting here.' He thus writes in his ' Phænomena quædam apocalyptica,' page sixty-fourth, published this year.

' This summer ensign *James Noyes* hath happily discovered a body of marble at *Newbury,* within half a mile of the navigable part of *Little* river, by which means very good lime is made within the province.'

From this extract it would appear that this body of limestone was the first discovered in Massachusetts. Certain it is, that vast quantities of lime of the best quality were annually made in Newbury, for nearly a century, for export as well as for home use. Prior to this time, lime was manufactured from oyster and clam shells. Lewis, in his very minute and accurate history of Lynn, informs us under the year 1696, that ' immense numbers of great clams were thrown upon the beaches by storms. The people were permitted, by a vote of the town, to dig and gather as many as they wished for their own use, but no more ; and no person was allowed to carry any out of the town, on a penalty of twenty shillings. The shells were gathered in cart loads on the beach and manufactured into lime.'

July. ' Sore and long continued drought.'

July 22d. ' Drought continuing many of the towns and churches had days of fasting and prayer.' *

September 12th. ' Our army abroad under the command of major John March [of Newbury] going ashore at a place, called Damaris cove, a small island in the eastern parts, the Indians being there, they waylaid them and killed several of them. Our English fought bravely and drove them off the island.' *

September 22d. The town chose ' major Daniel Davison, corporal George March and ensign James Noyes, as a committee, who shall inspect into all matters concerning the lime stones in any of the undivided lands in the town, who shall have the sole ordering, disposing and importing said lime stones for the town's use in what way and manner they shall judg shall most conduce to the benefit of the towne,' and so forth, and so forth. The committee were to keep accurate accounts of all disbursements and profits, which were to be read once every six months in a public town meeting. All persons were prohibited, under a penalty of twenty shillings the hogshead and proportionable for smaller quantities, who should presume to

* Fairfield's journal.

dig or carry away or dispose of any of the aforesaid limestone, and so forth.

' It was also voted that *the* kiln for burning said lime shall be built at or near the end of Muzzie's lane next Merrimack river.' *

' The kiln ' mentioned above was the kiln in which the lime was burnt by the committee for the benefit of the town. Lime kilns owned by individuals in various parts of the town were numerous.

'*August.* Ordered by the selectmen that the river called by the Indians Quasacuncon and has since been called by divers names, as Newbury river, Oldtown river, be from this time called by the name of the river Parker in remembrance of the worthy, learned, and reverend minister Mr. Thomas Parker, who was a first planter and pastor of ye church of Newbury and learned schoolmaster.' *

November 8th. The town voted that the assessors ' raise the tax on polls one penny on the poll for every penny that they raise upon ye pound.' *

' Also voted that the selectmen procure a flagg for the meeting house to be put out at the ringing of the first bell, and taken in when the last bell is rung.' *

' As I lay in my bed this morning,' says judge Sewall, 'this verse ran in my mind :

' To horses, swine, neat cattle, sheep and deer,
Ninety and seven proved a mortal year.'

1698.

May 4th. ' The towne voted that Mr. George March should be paid for fencing in the burying place.'

July 5th. ' The towne voted that they would build a new meeting house, and for that purpose chose the worshipful colonel Daniel Pierce, captain Thomas Noyes and serjeant Stephen Jaques a committee, who on October fifth made their report.'

December 21st. ' The towne voted that serjeant Stephen Jaques should build a meeting house sixty feet in length fifty feet in breadth and twenty feet in the stud for five hundred and thirty pounds.' The next February, ' the town voted to have the meeting house twenty-four feet post instead of twenty and to pay serjeant Jaques twenty pounds more.'

October 26th. A church was gathered in the west precinct, and on November tenth the reverend Samuel Belcher was ordained their minister.

November. ' Near the close of this month,' says Fairfield, in his diary, ' there was a general contribution in the province for the relief of captives in Mequinez in Morocco.' In a letter to colonel Thomas Noyes on this subject, honorable Andrew Belcher thus writes. ' On the sixth of December 1698 you paid me three pounds

* Town records.

eight shillings and ten pence, it being the collection of some of the inhabitants of Newbury, towards the relief of the captives in Sallee.' *

' This year, Ezra Cottle commenced ship-building, at or near the foot of Chandler's lane [Federal street] where Mr. William Johnson built.' †

The town made some new regulations about the lime stones, and ' voted that four shillings per ton shall be paid for lime stones, transportation, and that no more be sold out of the towne till further order.' †

1699.

' The town,' on certain conditions, ' granted to Ebenezer Knowlton nine rods of land for the setting up a tanning trade.' †

December 18*th*. ' Colonel Daniel Pierce and colonel Thomas Noyes were impowered to employ ye honorable captain Samuel Sewall to procure a good and sufficient meeting house bell for the towne of Newbury, suitable for our towne considering the remoteness of our dwellings.' †

1700.

' This year,' says the reverend Richard Brown, in his diary, ' has been famous for three things, namely :

' First, for yt the winter was turned into summer, or at least we have had little or none, the ground being bare for the most part, though we have had snow at some times, yet very shallow, not exceeding above twelve inches and that by an advance of southerly gales faded away speedily.

' Second, an earthquake on the last of January, which was considerably great.

' Third, another on the last of February passingly considerable.'

April 22*d*. ' Serjeant Stephen Jaques was ordered to hang the old meeting house bell in the new turret.'

September 18*th*. ' The town voted to have the new meeting house composed with seats as the old one was, except ten feet on three sides for pews and alleys.'

October 18*th*. ' Voted that a pew be built for the minister's wife by the pulpit stairs, that colonel Daniel Pierce should have the first choice for a pew and major Thomas Noyes shall have the next choice and that colonel Daniel Pierce esquire, and Tristram Coffin esquire be impowered to procure a bell of about four hundred pounds weight.' †

This year a house was built for the poor to live in.

November 6*th*. Permission was granted to twenty persons ' to build pews on the lower floor for themselves and families.'

In November of this year, Hester Rogers, of Newbury, was

---

* Robert Adams's manuscripts.   † Town records.

arrested on suspicion of murdering her child.   The following is a literal copy of the constable's bill.

'John Pike, constable for ye town of Newbury.'
'His bill of cost for seaseing and securing the body of Hester Rogers of said Newbury apprehended by one of his majestie's justices for murdering her children in ye year 1700.

Item, for procuring of a warrant for seasing her body . . .	£0, 1s.
Item, by guarding of ye body of the said Rogers night and day with two men from ye thirteenth of November 1700 until ye ninth day of December 1700	6, 10
Item, by setting said guard dayly with new men at sixpence per time	0, 13
Item, by conveying of her body to Ipswich gaol	0, 8
Item, for fier wood and attendance during said term of time, . .	1, 12
Item and also for fier wood and trobaling ye house, . . .	1, 00

£10, 04s
JOHN PIKE, constable as abovesaid.'

December 6th.   The committee appointed to 'seat the meeting house,' performed their task.   The number of men and women to whom seats were assigned, were three hundred and thirteen, whose names are all recorded.

From a testimony on file in the quarterly court, it appears, that, so late as this year, only two houses had been erected on the banks of the Merrimac, in Newbury.   One of these, owned by doctor Humphrey Bradstreet, stood near the head of Hale's wharf, the other, owned by Daniel Pierce, was farther south.

1701.

March 18th.   The canopy of the old pulpit was given by the town ' to the west part of Newbury for their pulpit.' *

In Judge Sewall's diary I find the following, by which it appears that Hester Rogers had her trial at Boston.

'*July* 15th.   Esther Rogers was tried and condemned for murder. Mr. Cook pronounced the sentence.'

From Fairfield's journal I make the following extract:

'July thirty-first, a young woman, named Esther Rogers was executed at Ipswich for murdering her child (a mulatto) of whom it may be noted, she was a poor sinful creature, as vile as ordinarily any are under the light of the gospel, and one, who had a child by a negro at Newbury, when she was about seventeen years of age, as she herself confessed, and that she murdered it and buried it in the garden, and four years after had a child again and murdered that, but could not conceal it.   Of her carriage in prison and at the execution there is an account printed with three sermons in Ipswich on occasion thereof.'

Tradition informs us that Esther Rogers drowned her child in the pond behind the first parish meeting-house.

In October, Thomas Mossum, a colored man, was ordered to leave town with his family.

* Town records.

'*October* 15*th*. Voted to give Mr. Richard Brown and Mr. Moses Hale twelve shillings per sermon for every sermon that they preached to us during Mr. Toppan's sickness.' *

December 9*th*. The town voted to abate one half the minister's rate of sixteen persons at 'the falls,' for the coming year. *

1702.

January 13*th*. The town voted to divide according to 'former rule eighteen hundred acres of the lower commons, reserving pasturage for four cows for the ministry in the east end of the towne, three for the ministry in the west end, three for the free school and the herbage of twenty cows for the benefit of the town's poor.' *

July 22*d*. Town voted to give Mr. Richard Brown twenty pounds for his yearly salary, and to have fourpence a week for his Latin scholars.

Town also chose ' the selectmen a committee to consider and report what it will cost to remove the old meeting house farther from the new meeting house and to fitt it up for a court house, towne house and school house.' *

Sometime this year, the people residing within the limits of what was afterward incorporated as Byfield parish, built a meeting-house near the place where the present house now stands. As the parish comprehended a part of Newbury, and a part of Rowley, it was at first called ' Rowlbury.' Mehetabel, wife of William Moody, and daughter of Henry Sewall, who died August second, 1702, aged thirty, was the first person interred in the burying ground there.

1703.

March 9*th*. ' The town voted to pay four pounds to those who killed two wolves at the Ipswich end of Plum island.' *

The town also ' voted to let the ferry over the river Parker for four years at four pounds a year to corporal Richard Jackman, who is to carry all the court officers, going and returning from court, all town officers, when employed by the town, and all the rams, belonging to the town, ferry free.' *

March 17*th*. Town voted that the old meeting-house be repaired and fitted for a court house, ' school house and town house.' *

' Thirty rods of land were granted to Richard Goodwin on the southerly side of the great hill, said Goodwin engaging himself and heyrs, never to keep a dogg, whilst he or they shall dwell on said land.' *

This year ' Benaiah Titcomb's vessel was captured on his voyage from Antigua to Newbury.'

September 28*th*. There was a great snow storm.

* Town records.

22

In November, captain John March petitioned the general court to grant him some compensation for the losses he sustained in his defence of Casco fort. He says, ' I forsook my own habitation at Newbury and removed my family, stock of cattle and so forth to the said fort, upon which upon the perfidious breach made by that barbarous people, your petitioner was in utmost hazard of losing his life, and by a wonderful preservation escaped the hands of those infidels, and did actually lose more than five hundred pounds of his estate.' Among his losses, he mentions 'sloop and furniture, eighty-nine head of sheep and cattle, five and a half acres of wheat, six acres of as good peas as ever I saw, four and a half acres of Indian corn,' and so forth.

'*November* 20*th*. The general court granted to captain John March fifty pounds in consideration of the brave defence of his majesty's fort at Casco bay, when lately attacked by the French and Indian enemy, and of the wounds he then received.' *

1704.

January 5*th*. ' The town voted that two shillings and sixpence per ton shall be paid for lime stone, provided that they that buy them, dig them, and burn them in Newbury.' †

'*January* 19*th*. The town chose a committee to measure and divide the bank against Merrimack river, and voted that two men be hired to watch and ward upon the river until it breaks up.' †

February 24*th*. ' This day the new parishioners met in the house, built for their minister and agree to call the precinct Byfield.' ‡

The following is a copy of a letter from Judge Sewall to his brother, William Moody of Newbury.

'*Boston, April* 1*st*, 1704.

' Loving brother,

    ' After your being here last I writt a letter to colonel Byfield and informed him that you had named your infant parish Byfield, and would from henceforth look upon him as your patron, and be ready gratefully to acknowledge any countenance or favour he should be pleased to afford you. To this effect in more words. This day I received a letter from colonel Byfield, in which are these words :

' I am surprised at the account you give me of the name of a new town upon the river Parker near Newbury. How they hitt upon my name I can't imagine. I heartily wish them prosperity ; and if any respect to me was the cause, it is an obligation upon me (when God shall enable me) to study how I may be serviceable to them.'

' I called it only a parish. What if Mr. Hale should write a letter to colonel Byfield, intimating the matter of fact, that it was in regard to him. You have been informed of his parentage. He has only two daughters, Madam Lyde and Madam Taylor. I believe he is a good man, and a fast friend, very industrious and thorow in promoting what he undertakes.'

                                        SAMUEL SEWALL.

---

    * Province records.   † Town records.   ‡ Judge Sewall's diary.

March 28*th.* The court again confirmed the ferry to colonel John March, which was granted him in 1687.

August 3*d.* Colonel N. Saltonstall thus writes to colonel Thomas Noyes :

'Sir, by his excellency's express direction I command you in her majesty's name forthwith to appoint and set forth one half of your company by name and have them ready, well fixt with arms and ammunition and ten days' provision to march at an hour's warning. The command is strict.'

September 28*th.* He thus writes : 'I desire and order that by tomorrow morning at farthest you press and post at your block houses in Newbury twelve able souldiers, *three at each of your four* [block] houses, to abide there night and day, to watch.'

The expense this year for these block-houses was one hundred and six pounds, ten shillings, and seven pence.

November 11*th.* 'Henry Lunt, Thomas Newman, and Richard Dole,' captains of freighting sloops from Newbury, complained to the general court of the conduct of captain Tuthill, of the castle, who 'brought all their vessels to an anchor, took them out, carried them to the castle, demanded money for a shot, which he said was fired at them, made them pay six shillings and eight pence apiece, one shilling apiece for pass money, and three shillings apiece to carry them back to their vessels again.' *

In 1702, 'walnut wood was five shillings per cord, oak three shillings,' cotton wool one shilling and ten pence per pound, corn two shillings per bushel. In this year, 1704, cider was six shillings per barrel. In 1703, turnips were one shilling and three pence per bushel, and 1708, one and eight pence, and in 1711 sturgeon was two pence per pound.†

1705.

February 6*th.* The town 'voted to apportion the flatts among the proprietors' by lot, and on February thirteenth, 'that they should begin next Mr. Pierce's meadow and that there *should be* a way above said lots two rods broad.' ‡ By this it appears that 'Water street' was not laid out till this year.

The number of the river lots was two hundred and twenty-four.

February 20*th.* Governor Dudley thus writes to colonel Saltonstall : 'I pray you to give direction that your snow-shoe men from Newbury to Andover be ready at a moment's warning till the weather breaks up, and then we may be quiet awhile.'

May 23*d.* The 'old meeting house was granted to Richard Brown with liberty to remove it.' ‡

July 11*th.* The 'ferry over Merrimack river between Newbury and Salisbury near captain Edward Sargent's,' was purchased by the town, of colonel John March, for two hundred and forty pounds,

* Province Records.   † Old account books.   ‡ Town records.

and on March fifth, 1706, 'they sold one half of it to Salisbury for one hundred and twenty pounds.'

June 27th. Governor Dudley orders colonel Saltonstall 'to detach twenty able soldiers of the Newbury militia and have them rendezvous at Haverhill on July fifth.'

On the appearance of these men at Haverhill, colonel N. Saltonstall thus writes to colonel Noyes:

'Haverhill, July 17th, 1705.

'I received your return of ye twenty men ye Governor commanded me to call for, and when ye persons (which I can't call men) appeared, even a considerable number of them, to be but boys, or children, and not fit for service, blind in part, and deaf, and cross-handed, I stopt till I waited on ye governor, ye twelfth instant and upon libertie to speak with him, I with ye major have taken the best care we can to keep the men and children sent hither for ye present, till I may have opportunity to tell you the queen likes it not, to be served in this manner.

'But one in special, Nicholas ******* by name, is blind, and deaf, and small, and not fit to be continued, and therefore to be short, I send Nicholas ******* home to you, and do expect that you will send some able man in his place, if you have an able one in Newbury.

'The other diminutives are sent out to garrison at present, or else you had mett with them to return to you for ye like exchange.

'My heart, if it speaks, is full. I wait a suitable time, to tell you what I have to say on her majesty's behalf. To take boyes for originally prest men, and they hired too, I know not ye regularity of it. I shall be glad to see you, and intend to do it at Haverhill or Newbury or a middle place, as you will desire, if I am able to attend, to see what is right and what is our duty for us to do.

Your very humble servant,

To lieutenant-colonel Thomas Noyes.'   NATHANIEL SALTONSTALL.

In another letter he thus writes :

'August 4th, 1705.

'One Smith came this day with two of his sons in order to get a release for John Danford. I wonder how you concern yourself so much about this man, to get Danford home, and disregard your default and have not yet sent a good man for that pitiful insufficient sick man Nicholas ******* whom I sent off ye sixteenth of July last to you to send a better hand, and he to returne in two days time to me, but he is not yet come, nor other for him. Pray consider what lyes at your doore and do not deale so unhandsomely with your patient friend and humble servant,

N. SALTONSTALL.

To lieutenant-colonel Thomas Noyes.'

1706.

January 4th. 'Voted that the new bell be hanged in the turret of the meeting house with all convenient speede. Also to take care that the bell be rung at nine of the clock every night and that the day of the month be every night tolled.' *

The inscription round the bell is: 'let us love as brethren. Matthew Bagley fundit, 1705.'

'The town granted to twelve persons a piece of ground between

---

* Town records.

the watch-house and the meeting house pond joyning to doctor Toppan's fence to set up a stable.' *

March. ' Many sheep were drowned this month in Newbury, by the overflowing of Merrimack river, the ice being jam'd.' †

October 21st. ' The Newbury part of Byfield was set off for so long a time as they shall maintain an orthodox minister amongst them.' *

October 23d. Henry Short, the town clerk, died.

October 30th. Mr. Richard Brown was chosen to supply his place. At the same meeting, the town voted to employ ' serjeant Joseph Pike to build a bridge over Indian river near his saw-mill.' *

November 17th. Reverend Moses Hale was ordained the minister of the ' falls' parish, but had preached for them about four years.‡

February 28th. ' The town chose a committee of three to proceed and build a meeting house at Pipe-stave hill.' * For a more full account, see under the year 1712.

1707.

January 29th. The ' town voted that there be a gaole or prison built in Newbury, for the ease of the subject, for the restraining of much vice and keeping up of the order of government, provided the county be at one half of the cost and charge.' *

1708.

May 26th. The general court ' ordered that colonel Thomas Noyes [of Newbury] shall for the present ease of her majesty's subjects, whose situation makes it disputable to which of the provinces they belong, notify the gentlemen appointed by Massachusetts and New Hampshire, to meet at such time and place as he shall appoint,' in order to run the line ' that they may not be oppressed by a demand upon them by both governments.'

June 18th. The town ' voted that the nine a clock bell should be rung *at* nine of the clock precisely, nightly for the year ensuing.' *

July 6th. The town's commons ' were divided into four general pastures. The first, the common land at the neck. The second, the old town common to Mr. Short's farm. The third to extend near to the dwelling house of corporal James Smith and to run up by the brook, whereon the new bridge is to Mr. March's farm and by the southerly side of said farm to the birchen meadows and the rest of said common at the new town to be the fourth.' *

'*August.* There was a great drought.' §

This year Joseph Lunt rode post.

August 29th. Joseph Bartlet, of Newbury, was taken captive by the French and Indians in their attack on Haverhill, and carried into

---

* Town records.   † Sewall's diary.
‡ Parish records.   § Fairfield's journal.

Canada, where he remained over four years. See his narrative, appendix G.

Liberty to build a saw mill was ganted to Edmund Goodridge and John Noyes, junior, for twenty-one years on ' cart creek.'

1709.

March 8th. The town ' voted that the selectmen shall take care that the burying place may be fenced.' *

March 15th. ' Voted that the selectmen be impowered to dispose of the lime stones.' *

' Voted also to petition the court of sessions for liberty to hang gates across the country high ways in Newbury where shall be thought needful.' *

March 22d. ' Voted that there should be gates hung across the town high ways, where it shall be thought most convenient for the fencing off the pastures,' * that is, the four general pastures.

' Great drought this year. In October, want of water for men and cattle.' †

' *May.* An expedition was formed against Canada. On the tenth there was an impress for soldiers. Some say every tenth man was taken.' ‡

1710.

March 7th. A committee was chosen by the town ' to discourse with Benjamin Rolfe about purchasing the lane called Rolfe's lane in order to make it a highway for the town's use.' *

In June of this year there was an extreme drought.

October 28th. Byfield parish was incorporated. It was at first called Rowlbury, being formed from a part of Newbury and a part of Rowley.

1711.

April 24th. ' John Kent of the island had his barn burnt by tabacko with six oxen and four calves and a goose, that was bringing young ones.' †

July 30th. Fleet set sail for Canada.

' Cottle's lane,' once so called, now South street, was bought and laid out ' one rod and a half wide from Ezra Cottles to the way by Merrimack.'

The town ' voted that the grammar school be removed to Greenleaf's lane or near thereabouts.' Greenleaf's lane is now State street.

' John Swett was licensed by the court to keep the ferry at Holt's

---

* Town records.   † Sewall's diary.   ‡ Fairfield's journal.

rocks September twenty-fifth. Fare twopence for a man and four pence for a horse.'

The town voted that Benjamin Morse should 'ring the bell at nine o' clock every night, and sabbath days and lecture days, and said Morse is to winge or rub down the principal seats the day after sweeping the meeting house — and to toull the bell till the minister comes.' *

October 9th. Deacon Nathaniel Coffin was chosen town clerk, in room of Mr. Richard Brown, resigned. On leaving town for Reading, where he was ordained as minister, June twenty-fifth, 1712, he left the following on the fly leaf of the town book.

' I have served Newbury as schoolmaster eleven years and as town clerk five years and a half and have been repaid with abuse, contempt and ingratitude. I have sent nigh as many to college as all the masters before me since the reverend and learned Parker. Those I have bred think themselves better than their master (God make them better still) and yet they may remember ye foundation of all their growing greatness was laid in the sweat of my brows.

' I pray that poor unacknowledging Newbury may get them that may serve them better and find thanks when they have done.

' If to find a house for ye school two years when ye town had none, if to take the scholars to my own fire when there was no wood at school as frequently, if to give records to the poor, and record their births and deaths gratis, deserves acknowledgements, then it is my due, but hard to come by.

Est aliqua ingrato meritum exprobare voluptas
Hoc fruar, hæc de te gaudia sola feram.

R. Brown.'

A later writer adds the following lines.

' The lines above do seem to me absurd,
Which by a scholar are left on record
Such boasting as school master is very wrong,
Such boasting don't of right to man belong.'

The town employed Joshua Moody to teach the grammar school the remainder of the year, and voted that the grammar school be removed to Greenleaf's lane, [State street.]

Town also ' voted that the selectmen shall forthwith employ several persons to take care ye boys be kept in order on sabbath days and satisfie said persons out of ye money of ye parish, to which they belong for their sarvice.'

1712.

March 11th. The town ' voted that a house for ye keeping ye grammar school in shall be built and set up near ye middle way between ye old school house and the little old house now standing by the way near frog pond.' *

In the beginning of this year, a few individuals residing near

---

* Town records.

what is called ' the plains,' separated from the church and society, with which they had been hitherto connected, and declared themselves in favor of the episcopal form of worship.   As the causes, which led them to dissent from the accustomed order of the New England churches, have never been fully explained, ' the narrative' of those causes, drawn from authentic documents, ' cannot,' in the language of the reverend doctor Morss, 'fail of being interesting and instructive.'

As early as March, 1685, the people at the west end of the town, on account of the increase of their numbers, and their distance from the ' meeting house,' petitioned the town for ' some help in the ministry amongst' them.   As the reply to this petition was not satisfactory, sixteen persons in 1689 erected a meeting-house on ' the plains.'   In 1695, the town voted that Pipe-stave hill *shall be the place* for the meeting-house, and so forth.   From this time till 1712, those, who lived nearer to the meeting-house on the plains than they did to Pipe-stave hill, acted in opposition to the votes of the town, the authority of the state, and a large part, (forty to twenty-four,) of the worshipers in their own precinct, all of whom had decided that the right place for the meeting-house was Pipe-stave hill, while the other party were as decided that it should stand where it was, and not be moved.   As early as 1696, the reverend Samuel Belcher with his family was residing in the precinct.*   In the same year, a vote was passed to build a ministry house, and to enlarge the meeting-house on ' the plains.'   In January, 1706, the precinct voted that ' they either would remove the meeting house and build an addition to it, or else build a new meeting house.'   February twenty-eighth, ' it was voted that ye inhabitants of ye west end of the town of Newbury will build a new meeting house upon Pipe stave hill, fifty-four feet long and thirty-four feet broad within the space of five years at ye furthest and to meet in the old meeting house five years, not to force any person to pay any money or pay till three years be expired, and then to pay one quarter part yearly until ye whole be paid.'

From this vote twenty persons dissented.

' Captain Hugh March, Caleb Moody and serjeant John Ordway were also chosen a committee to build the new meeting house and enlarge the old meeting house.' *   In February, 1709, the party opposed to the removal of the meeting-house from ' the plains,' to Pipe stave hill, petitioned the general court for relief.   Among other things they say, that, 'having built a meeting house and settled a minister, which hath not been effected above twelve years or thereabouts, there are certain of our inhabitants *since planted* in the upper parts of our precinct, who under the supposing notion of a major vote of our inhabitants have adventured against our declared dissents to make a considerable and chargeable process towards the building of another meeting house, wherein they have proceeded so far as to adventure

---

* Parish records.

upon ourselves to levy a tax upon that account and to employ a collecter to take away our goods, and so forth.' They proceed to state, that, 'if the abovesaid process and design on hand proceed to take effect according to the desire of ye managers thereof, namely, to fix ye meeting house and ministry solely there, *where they have now erected their new meeting house*, it will not only as we apprehend very unreasonably necessitate us to lose ye great charge we have been at, but which is worse, frustrate our good ends therein, which were our own and our children's enjoyment of ye means of grace, and render it in divers respects more difficult and inconvenient than before our separation, and so forth. We therefore pray your excellency and honors to vouchsafe to us a favorable regard to our humble address that our so very hard and costly privileges may be continued to us in such sort as may not be suppressed by our opponents, and so forth. And we humbly pray that if no better method may be found out for our relief that we may be set off so far as may agree with righteousness and religion, to maintain our minister and ministry amongst ourselves, the charge whereof we choose abundantly to undergo rather than have our good ends, desires and endeavours abovesaid frustrated and made voyde.' * Signed by fifty-five persons—eleven Bartlets, six Sawyers, three Merrills, four Browns, three Baileys, Charles and Joseph Annis, two Thurstons, two named Rogers, three Littles, and nineteen others.

From the preceding petition we learn that the meeting-house had been erected on Pipe-stave hill, prior to the date of the petition, probably in the latter part of 1708. Judge Sewall, in his diary, under the date of May tenth, 1709, says, ' visited cousin Jacob Toppan and laid a stone in the foundation of ye meeting house at Pipe staff hill.'

On March twenty-first, 1710, the inhabitants of the precinct voted ' that they accepted of what was already done and authorized the major part of the committee (who were chosen in 1706, February twenty-eighth,) to proceed and finish the meeting house according to the time mentioned in said vote.' †

From this vote twenty-two persons dissented.

Among the papers on file in the state house in Boston, is one written by John Ordway, but without date, giving his reasons why he declined acting with the committee appointed in 1706 to build the new meeting-house. ' First, because the vote was dissented against by many, and more offered their dissent and therefore a great likelihood of contention among us. Second, because we had no land to set it on, nor order to purchase any. Third, because it was so long a time since we were chosen, and I wished to call a meeting of our precinct to see if they were united, and if not, I thought it very unadvisable to proceed in strife and contention, for the building of a meeting house ought to be carried on in love and peace. To what is above written captain March and lieutenant

---

* General court files. † Parish records.

Moody or one of them answered, we have a vote for it, and if you will not goe on with us, we will goe without you and you shall pay for it.'

On June second, 1710, a notification was sent from the general court to the town of Newbury, which was served on them by some of the west end petitioners to the court. On June seventh, the town chose colonel Thomas Noyes to act in their behalf, who, on June ninth, replied to the petition of February ninth, 1709. In his reply he states, that, ' of the fifty-five signers to the petition, thirty-four were at no charge in building their meeting house, several live within a mile of Mr. Toppan's [first parish meeting-house] and ten more to the west and northwest of the new meeting house, so that it is impossible that the major part should be any ways aggrieved by putting down the old, or putting up the new meeting house.' He concludes by saying, among other things, that ' the whole of the western precinct assemble in a house of not above thirty feet square and yet rather than not have their wills they would have two churches.'

This produced a long reply, dated June twentieth, in which they state, ' that we now have one hundred and thirty families, seventy of which do not live two miles from the old meeting house.'

They conclude by saying, ' we must acknowledge ourselves obliged to him in the superlative degree for speaking the very truth concerning us namely, rather than not have our wills, which are not the sparing of our purses but ye propagation of ye gospel and ye promoting ye edification of ourselves and ours, particularly our young ones under the means of grace and ye welfare of immortal souls, we had rather have two churches and meeting houses also, most convenient for the obtaining those good ends. We only pray the general court to prove their servants awhile with their petitioned pulse and water and afterwards as ye shall see and find our countenances, so deal with your humble servants.'

This petition was not granted, and on the twenty-second of June it was ' resolved in council that Pipe-stave hill is the most convenient place, and so forth, and that a committee of the principal inhabitants in the said precinct, do forthwith attend the reverend Mr. Belcher and acquaint him with the desire of this court that when a meeting house shall be erected there and a convenient dwelling house thereto for his reception with suitable accommodations of land and so forth he be content to remove thither.' They also resolved that ' a tax be laid on all the inhabitants.' *

Determined, as it would appear, not to worship in the meetinghouse on Pipe stave hill, twenty-seven of the petitioners signed the following document, which is accurately copied from the original now before me.

'*July ye 12th,* 1710.
' We whos names Are hearto Subscribed doo Agree And oblidge oursealves to

* General court files.

each other to mayntain the publick ministry At the old meeting house in ye west precinct in Newbury Although we are forsed to pay Elswhare what shall be lavid upon us.'

On the next day, July thirteenth, the inhabitants of the west parish held a meeting, and ' voted to observe the direction and resolve of the general court June twenty-second in every particular.' On July seventeenth they had another meeting, in which they ' voted to levy a tax of four hundred pounds to defray part of the charges of building a meeting house ministry house and so forth, to pay back all they had taken by distraint and to confirm all that the building committee, chosen in 1706, had done and gave them full power to finish and so forth.' *

On the nineteenth of April, 1711, the precinct had another meeting, and as the time of five years, during which they had determined, in February, 1706, to meet in the old meeting-house, had expired, the majority proceeded to carry the remainder of the vote into execution. To this end, they chose a committee of three, to dispose of the ministry house and land near the old meeting-house, and obtain a house and land near the new meeting-house, at Pipestave hill. They also voted ' to take the seates and boards and glass out of ye old meeting house to be improved in the new meeting house and also to remove the old meeting house and sett it up att Pipe-stave hill to be *improved for a barn* for the ministry in convenient time.'

It will readily be seen, that, as soon as the 'convenient time' came, to carry the preceding vote into effect, the minority would find it impossible to ' mayntain the publick ministry at the old meeting house,' as they had obligated themselves to do, July twelfth, 1710. The ' convenient time' soon came, but not in the manner contemplated by the vote. Corroborated tradition informs us, that a party of men from the upper part of the parish, came down in a riotous and disorderly manner, in the night, tore down the ' old meeting house,' and carried it off. The parish, however, March fifth, 1712, on account of the ' difference amongst ye inhabitants about pulling down ye old meeting house agreed to leave it to the determination of three men and to sit down satisfied and rest contented with their determination.' *

This, without doubt, increased the opposition of the minority, who, being as determined not to submit, as the majority were to govern, immediately commenced preparations to build a new meeting-house. This undertaking, the majority determined to frustrate, if possible. A committee of six persons, petitioned the general court, in July, to take notice of the matter, and state that ' Samuel Bartlet, Joseph Bailey, lieutenant Samuel Sâyer, Josiah Sâyer, John Bartlet junior, John Bartlet third, Nathan Bartlet, Richard Bartlet third, William Huse, Joshua Brown junior, Stephen Brown and Skipper Lunt, their carpenter, and several others have cut and halled

* Parish records.

timber in order to build a meeting house and intend to raise said meeting house within one fortnight and set it at or near the east end of the west precinct in Newbury as they inform us, not regarding the late resolve of the great and general court,' and so forth, and so forth.

'*July* 19*th*, 1711. The court advised and directed for the preservation of the peace of the town of Newbury that the persons herein named and others concerned, desist their proceeding to the raysing their meeting house until there be a hearing of the matter before the court.'

To this advice and direction the minority paid no attention, but went steadily on with their work. Fervet opus. This caused another petition against them, in which a committee of the majority state, August twenty-fourth, 1711, that 'they, [the minority,] had raised and in part covered a meeting house and set it near the dividing line, notwithstanding the advice and direction of the court.'

The court immediately ordered that 'Samuel Bartlet, John Ordway, deacon Joshua Brown, Joshua Bailey, Skipper Lunt, and Penuel Titcomb be anew served by the sheriff with a process and order of this court of nineteenth July, strictly forbidding them and their associates proceeding in the work of their intended meeting house and so forth, and that said persons be summoned to attend this court on the second Wednesday of their fall session.'

On the twenty-third of October, 1711, they again petition the court, 'to grant them leave to goe on with their meeting house that they have begun, that the farthermost of forty families and about thirty more of our neighbours are not above one and a half miles from the meeting house we are about to erect and prepare and that we *deem it our duty to maintain the reverend Mr. Belcher, (for whom we have a peculiar respect,) until we may be orderly dismist.*' They also request the court 'to set them off as a precinct, making Artichoke river the dividing line, and that there are now ninety-six families above Artichoke river.'

In the general court records, under date of November second, 1711, is the following. 'Upon hearing the case of Newbury referring to the house late pretended to be raised for the publick worship of God on or near deacon Joshua Brown's land, contrary to the direction of this court, of which there is no present necessity. It is ordered that the building of the said house be not on any pretence whatever further proceeded in but that the division of the town into two precincts between the old meeting house and that upon Pipestave hill be the present division of the auditory and is hereby confirmed and established and all persons concerned are to yield obedience accordingly, and that the disorders, that have been in the proceedings about the said house in Brown's land, be referred to the next sessions of peace in Essex.'

On November fourth, 1711, another petition was prepared to be presented to the general court, signed by Abraham Merrill, Joshua Brown, and sixty-five others. In it, among other things, they pray the court 'to indulge us with your favorable grant of liberty to proceed in ye finishing of our meeting house, and to call some orthodox approved person to preach ye word of God to us there, whom (notwithstanding ye usual objections framed on yt account against us) we trust under God's blessing we shall so accommodate as may be approved by your honors and satisfactory and comfortable to himself. Thus praying,' and so forth.

This petition, which is now in my possession, was, of course, not presented, probably on account of the peremptory order of the court, passed November second, two days before their petition was drafted, but which they probably had not seen. Here was a difficulty, which the petitioners knew not how to obviate. They had erected a meeting-house, in which they had intended to settle 'some ortho-dox approved person,' but which the court would not allow them either to use or finish. Up to this time, it is evident, from their own petitions, that they had intended to settle a congregational minister in the meeting-house, which they had erected for that purpose. The manner in which a part of them became episcopalians, is best told in the following extract from a narrative of the proceedings of the precinct, from its commencement to 1734. It was found among the papers of Mr. Nehemiah Bartlet, and was written many years ago.

'Our fathers did not regard what the court sent to them, but had raised said building and had got on to finish it. This honorable court sent on express to forbid us going on under any pretence whatever. Resolved Pipe-stave hill to be the place for the whole parish. Our people went to this court to show their grievances. No relief. *Met with a gentleman Mr. [John] Bridger, churchman, telling a way to protect them, to come under the church of England he would protect them. Some being acquainted with the church complied.* Reverend Mr. Harris came and preached, went home, sent Mr. —— Lampton, chaplain of a station ship, some abiding with him, some went back to Pipe-stave hill,' and so forth.

This Mr. Bridger was 'surveyor of the king's woods,' as I learn from several letters of his, between 1707 and 1715. In the latter year, he was in London. In Judge Sewall's diary, I find the following :

'*December 15th*, 1707. Governor calls a council, reads a letter from Mr. [John] Bridger, complaining of trees cut contrary to char-ter. Mr. Bridger has been here above a twelvemonth.'

On the twenty-first of October, 1711, Mr. Bridger thus writes from Portsmouth, to colonel Thomas Noyes, of Newbury :

'Sir, pursuant to the governor's orders I do apply to you for a guard of six or eight troopers for my guard while doing my duty as surveyor of his majesty's woods for America.

I am your most humble servant,

JOHN BRIDGER.'

From the same diary of Judge Sewall, I make the following extract, namely :

'*Wednesday, February 27th*, 1711–12. Joseph Bailey of Newbury, introduced by Mr. Myles, Mr. Harris and Mr. Bridger presented a petition to the governor signed by Abraham Merrill, Joshua Brown, Samuel Bartlet, John Bartlet, Samuel Sàyer, Joseph Bailey, twenty-two in all, declaring that they were of the pure episcopal church of England, would no longer persist with their mistaken dissenting brethren, had sent to their diocesan, the bishop of London for a minister and desired protection.

' *February* 28*th.*   Governor dates his letter to ye episcopal church at Newbury.'

In another part of the same diary, he says, ' on the twenty-seventh of February last 1711–12 I saw the certainty of what I could not believe before namely deacon Merrill and deacon Brown and twenty-two others and so forth.   Now though it is well enough known what was the spring of yr motion and notwithstanding their aprons of fig leaves they walk naked.'

Their petition to governor Dudley, and his reply, are as follows, namely :

' To his excellency Joseph Dudley, the humble petition of several freeholders and the inhabitants of the town of Newbury.

' Whereas your excellency's petitioners have declared themselves members of the church of England, and have raised a building, for the worship of almighty God according to the manner of service prescribed in the said church we humbly desire your excellency's protection and encouragement in our just and laudable undertakings.   We are convinced that the church of England is a pure orthodox church, and so are resolved to continue no longer in that separation, which has so unhappily prevailed among the mistaken and prejudiced inhabitants of this country.   This resolution has occasioned ye ill will of our dissenting brethren, who levy upon us more than ordinary rates towards the maintenance of their minister, and other purposes of that nature, which act of theirs is a very great hardship and grievance to us, since we have addressed a letter to our right reverend diocesan ye bishop of London to send us a minister, which we shall most gladly receive, but think ourselves under no obligation to any other ; it being a thing unknown in her majesty's dominions yt ye members of the church of England are obliged to contribute to the support of the dissenting teachers.   We therefore pray your excellency's favour, that we may not be molested for the future upon this account and beg leave to subscribe ourselves
                    Your excellency's most dutiful and obedient servants.'

The following is a copy of the reply :

                         '*Boston, February* 28*th*, 1711-12.
' I received yesterday an address and petition, signed by twenty-two freeholders and inhabitants of the town of Newbury, setting forth that they are declared members of the episcopal church of England, as by law established, and that they have raysed a building for the service of God according to the manner of service prescribed in the said church, desiring protection and encouragement therein accordingly, and that they have addressed the right reverend the bishop of London to have a minister sent to them, and that thereupon they may not be obliged to contribute to the subsistence of the other ministers of any other profession as at large is set forth in this petition.

' I am also informed by the reverend Mr. Harris, one of the ministers of the church of England in this place, that at their desire he has visited and preached to that new congregation, and had a very considerable auditory, and that he shall continue so to do, until their said address to the lord bishop of London shall be considered and orders given therein.   I am thereupon of opinion that the said petitioners and others that joyne with them ought to be peaceably allowed in their lawful proceedings therein for their good establishment ; and ought not to be taxed or imposed upon for the support and maintenance of any other public worship in the said town.—Of which I desire all persons concerned to take notice accordingly.   Given under my hand,
                                   J. DUDLEY.'

At what precise time their letter was addressed to the bishop of London, I have found no record. It must have been between November fourth, 1711, and February twenty-eighth, 1712. I have in my possession an original letter from the bishop of London, of which the following is a copy.

' Sir,

' I am very glad of the assurance from you, how well your people are disposed to hold communion with us ; and you need not doubt of all due encouragement so far as the difficulty of the times will allow, and therefore I should be glad to hear what it is particularly, that may suffice for this encouragement ; and in the mean time I shall endeavour to gett the best advice I can in reference to the deed. I pray God prosper your pious endeavours and pray believe me

Sr your most assured friend
and humble servant,

Fulham, April 19th, 1712.' HENRY LONDINI.

As the superscription of this letter is torn off, I am not able to say to whom it was addressed.

The next allusion to the church that I find, is the following extract from a letter, written by the reverend Benjamin Colman, of Boston, to bishop Kennet. It is dated November seventeenth, 1712.

' This last year a difference happened in the town of Newbury about placeing their meeting house. The matter was brought before our general court, who determined it according to the free vote and act of the precinct whereby they had obliged themselves to each other. Whereupon a number of them declare themselves for the church of England. Many of them I will suppose persons of sobriety and virtue only in a pett and to save their rate to their aged and worthy minister, Mr. Belcher, utterly ignorant of the church they declare for, nor offended in the least with the form of worship or discipline, which they turn from ; *and as wide herein from their old pastor's spirit and principles, which are as catholick as can well be found among ministers of any denomination; being till now among the* most narrow and rigid dissenters, who would before this have disowned me in particular for the use of the Lord's prayer, reading the scriptures and a freer admission to the Lord's table, than has been generally practised in these churches.' *

The lines in the above letter, printed in italics, are entirely omitted by the reverend James Morss in his century sermon, delivered December thirty-first, 1837, the words ' difference,' and ' turn from,' are changed to ' difficulty,' and ' had observed,' and the words ' they were,' before ' most narrow,' added.

Since the compilation of the foregoing narrative, the following letter, or part of a letter, written by the reverend Matthias Plant, and published in the Christian Witness, January twenty-eighth, 1842, has been pointed out to me. The date is not given, nor the name of the person, to whom it was addressed. It was obtained, as I am informed, by the reverend doctor Hawkes, during his recent visit to England, and is undoubtedly accurate in its statements.

' NEWBURYPORT. We copy the following from the Church Record ; and, as it gives some interesting incidents in the early history of the ancient church in Newburyport, we presume it will be acceptable to our readers :

* Turell's life of Colman, pp. 124, 5.

' First, the history of building the church, et cetera. It was erected for a meeting-house, in 1711, by the inhabitants, about forty-five families in number, but being opposed by a greater body of people within the same division or parish, who had erected another meeting-house, they complained of them to the justices of the peace, who committed some of them to prison, and others were compelled, for their safety, to appeal to the governor and council, where they met with no better treatment, for erecting a meeting-house contrary to law ; (for, according to the laws of the province, the major part appoints the place where the meeting-house shall be built.) Mr. Bridger, of Portsmouth, in New England, having information of the severity used towards these people, came to Newbury, and told the inhabitants that if they would convert their intended meeting-house into a church, he would engage them protection from the governor. They complying with his motion, (after the perusal of several church books,) he obtained their easement. The salary is weekly contributions by the auditors ; about twenty pounds per annum. The materials with which the church is built are wood. The dimensions of it, fifty feet long and thirty wide, but accommodated with no house or glebe.

' Second, the number of hearers was about one hundred, who at first frequented the church ; (for many who contributed towards building the church never consented to convert it to that use.) Their condition of fortunes is like unto our ordinary farmers, who rent thirty or forty pounds per annum. They commonly add some trade to their farming. In matters of religion, dissenters. Their settlements dispersed after the manner of our cottages, upon commons, some perhaps having thirty to sixty acres of land. Some of my hearers live in the adjacent towns, from two to six miles distance. Marblehead is the nearest church, thirty-two miles remote. My constant auditors are from one hundred and fifty to two hundred, or thereabouts, and daily increase, as doth my salary. Their fortunes are no otherwise improved than by their lands becoming more valuable, which is occasioned by people becoming more numerous in the country.

MATTHIAS PLANT.'

At what time the reverend Mr. Lampton came to Newbury, I have not been able to ascertain. It must, however, have been subsequent to twenty-seventh of February, 1712, as, in the petition to the governor, of that date, we find the expression, ' send us a minister, which we *shall* most gladly receive.'

From a letter in the library of the American Antiquarian Society, at Worcester, written by the reverend Christopher Toppan, to Cotton Mather, November twenty-eighth, 1712, I make the following extract :

' Perceiving that some of the ceremonies were camels too big for them at first to swallow, he [Mr. Lampton] told them they should be left to their liberty as to kneeling at the sacrament, baptising with the sign of the cross and so forth. This has been wonderfully taking with them and a great means to encourage them in their factious proceedings.'

Notwithstanding the ' opinion,' that the petitioners of February twenty-seventh ' ought not to be taxed' for the support of the congregational ministers, the precinct ' voted fourteenth of April that captain Hugh March should go to the general court and ask advice of them about gathering Mr. Belcher's rate and the meeting house rate of those persons that pretend to sett up ye episcopal way of worship,' and on October seventh, desired captain March to proceed in ' that affaire.'

As to what was done ' in that affaire,' no record informs us.

March 5th. The west parish held a meeting, on account ' of the difference among the inhabitants about pulling down the old meeting house, selling the parsonage house and land and so forth, and agreed to leave the above mentioned particulars to lieutenant John White of Haverhill, lieutenant John Foot of Amesbury and Mr. Thomas Kimball of Bradford, promising to set down satisfyed and rest contented with their determination.'*

1713.

' *February* 3*d.* Deacon Abraham Merrill, deacon Joshua Brown [and six others] were requested by a committee of the church to give their reasons for absenting themselves from the communion of the church.' Their reasons were:

' First, we do count that you acted illegally in disposing of a house, that you never built.

' Second, for violently pulling down our meeting house and carrying it away contrary to our minds and consent.

' Third, taking away from our brethren and neighbours part of their estates by distress,' and so forth.†

1714.

January 15*th.* The west parish agreed to concur with the church in calling the reverend John Tufts to settle with them in the ministry.

March 30*th.* The parish ' voted to give the reverend John Tufts eighty pounds a year till he settles and keeps house, and then ninety pounds a year.'

April 2*d.* The parish ' voted to free all that are, or shall be, for the episcopal way of worship and also all quakers.'

April 5*th.* The town ' voted to grant liberty to Mr. Benjamin Woodbridge and Mr. Henry Somerby to cut timber on Plum island to finish two wharfs with.'

June. The ferry at Holt's rocks, was settled for forty years on Newbury and Haverhill by the court.

June 30*th.* Reverend John Tufts ordained.

In judge Sewall's diary, I find the following, which is all I have been able to find on the subject:

' *December* 25*th.* Mrs. Bradstreet of Newbury, her killing her negro woman [is] much talked of.'

In this year, the reverend John Tufts, of the west parish, published a small work on music, entitled, ' a very plain and easy introduction to the art of singing psalm tunes, with the cantus or trebles of twenty-eight psalm tunes contrived in such a manner as

---

* Parish records. † Church records.

that the learner may attain the skill of singing them with the greatest ease and speed imaginable, by the reverend Mr. John Tufts. Price sixpence or five shillings per dozen.'

Small as this book must have been, to be afforded for sixpence per copy, it was at this time a great novelty, it being the first publication of the kind in New England, if not in America. As late as 1700, there were not more than four or five tunes known, in many of the congregations in this country, and in some, not more than two or three, and even those were sung altogether by rote. These tunes were York, Hackney, Saint Mary's, Windsor, and Martyrs'. To publish at this time a book on music, containing the enormous number of twenty-eight psalm tunes, (which were in three parts, and purely choral,) although it was only a reprint of Ravenscroft, which was first published in 1618, was a daring innovation on the old time-honored customs of the country, and the attempt to teach singing by note, thus commenced by Mr. Tufts, was most strenuously resisted, and for many years, by that large class of persons, everywhere to be found, who believe that an old error is better than a new truth. Many, at that time, imagined, that fa, sol, la, was, in reality, nothing but popery in disguise. A writer in the New England Chronicle, in 1723, thus observes. ' Truly I have a great jealousy that if we once begin to sing by rule, the next thing will be to pray by rule and preach by rule and *then comes popery.*'

In 1721, reverend Thomas Walter, of Roxbury, published a book on music, entitled ' the grounds and rules of musick explained, or an introduction to the singing by note fitted to the meanest capacity.'

In the preface, Mr. W. says: ' the tunes now in use in our churches, when they came out of the hands of the composers of them, were sung according to the rules of the scale of musick, but are now miserably tortured and twisted, and quavered in some churches into a horrid medley of confused and disorderly noises. Our tunes are for want of a standard to appeal to in our singing, left to the mercy of every unskilful throat to chop and alter, twist and change, according to their infinitely divers and no less odd humours and fancies. No two churches sing alike. At present we are confined to eight or ten tunes and in some congregations to little more than half that number.'

September 1st. Town 'voted to give forty shillings for every grown wolf and ten shillings apiece for wolf's whelps killed within the towne.'

1715.

March 11th. A highway, of two rods broad, was laid out, from Kent street to Ordway's lane, now Market street.

March 14th. John Emery, Archelaus Woodman, Stephen Emery, and Benjamin Sawyer, petitioned the town to grant them ' liberty to set up a fence across the way to Turkey hill that we may

keep our sheep from running away before we have sheared them.'
The petition was granted.

May 3d. ' Town voted to give five pounds per head for every
grown wolfe, which shall be killed within the town of Newbury.'

May 20th. Mr. John Bridger sent a letter 'to the church wardens
and vestry at Newbury,' from London, by Mr. Henry Lucas, who
had been appointed their minister, and says : ' I have no reason to
doubt he will fully answer your expectation and advance the church
amongst you to the praise and glory of almighty God and to the
edification of many souls,' and so forth.

October 27th. A committee of the west end precinct church,
was appointed, ' to discourse with certain members of the church,
who had withdrawn from their communion and see if something
could not be said or done to draw them to our communion again,
and if we cannot draw them by fair means, then to determine what
means to take with them.' *

1 7 1 6 .

January 24th. A day of humiliation was kept by the church in
the west precinct, for several reasons ; one was, ' that God would
prevent ye spread of errors in this place, especially the errors of the
quakers.' †

We, at the present day, can hardly conceive of the feelings entertained and manifested by our ancestors, against the quakers. In
the law, passed by Massachusetts, in 1658, the fourth section thus
commences. ' Whereas there is a cursed sect of hereticks lately
risen up in the world, which are commonly called quakers,' and so
forth. In 1661, another law was passed, ' to prevent the intrusions
of the quakers, who do like rogues and vagabonds come in upon
us,' and so forth. In 1658, Robert Adams, of Newbury, was indicted for attending a friends' meeting, in Salem, at the house of
Nicholas Phelps, to hear William Brend and William Leddra. In
1680, governor Simon Bradstreet thus writes to ' the right honorable
the lords of his majesty's privy council.' ' We have no beggars
and few idle vagabonds, except a few quakers from Road Island,
that much molest us.' In 1704, Judge Sewall thus writes. ' I told
Mr. [Nicholas] Noyes of Salem of ye quaker meeting at Samuel
Sâyers and of ye profaneness of ye young Hoags professing that
heresy.' These ' young Hoags,' were all sons of John Hoag, and
resided in the west parish of Newbury. In this year, [1716,] says
judge Sewall, there was a ' quakers' dispute at Newbury.'

In the account book of Stephen Jaques, I find the following,
namely :

' *October 21st,* 1716. On the sabath day about eleven of the clock in sarman
time it grue so dark that one could not see a parson from one end of the metting

* West parish records. † Church records.

hous to the other except it was against a window, nor could know another four seats off, nor read a word in a psalm book. It continued near half an hour. Sum ministers sent for candels, sum set still, till it was lighter. Sum was ready to think ye world was at an end ; all seemed to be consarned. It was a time when ye air was very full of smoke. It came dayly down when it was a south west wind, the wind now being as I remember at est, which might bring ye smoak back, and dark clouds pass over, as it being cloudy weather. I was an eie witness of this myself.

Stephen Jaques.'

For a similar account of the same darkness, see Philosophical Transactions, number four hundred and twenty-third.

In October of this year, 'governor Shute went from Boston to Portsmouth, was met by the Newbury troop, conducted to lieutenant governor Dummer's house, where his excellency was finely entertained that night and morning.' *

In judge Sewall's diary, under date of June twenty-second, I find the following. ' I essayed to prevent negroes and Indians being rated with horses and cattle, but could not succeed.'

Instances like the following, were formerly frequent. In the inventory of the estate of Samuel Morgaridge, who died in 1754, I find,

' Item, three negroes, ... £133, 6s. 8d.
' Item, flax, ... 12, 2, 8.'

In the inventory of Henry Rolfe's estate, taken in April, 1711, I find the following, namely,

' Fifteen sheep, old and young, ... £3, 15s.
' An old gun, ... 2
' An old negroe man, ... 10, 0
                                        ———————
                                        £13, 7s.'

In Moses Gerrish's inventory, I find,

' Barley, Indian corn, and oats, ... £10.
' An Indian slave, ... 20.'

From the tax book of William Titcomb, junior, I make the following extract. This year the number of ratable polls in Newbury was six hundred and eighty-five, of which four hundred and thirty-seven were in the first parish, one hundred and ninety-six in the west parish and fifty-two in the falls parish. In August, a valuation of the town's property was taken. Plough land and meadow were estimated at twelve shillings per acre, pasture land at six shillings. The whole valuation of property, real and personal, was nine thousand and sixty-two pounds, and one shilling.

In 1712 and 1713, the number and valuation stood thus :

1712, polls 584, estate £7857.
1713, " 613, " 7790.

The province rate was 5s. per poll, and 6d. on the pound.
The town rate was 2, 3d. " " and 2 1-2 " " "
Mr. Toppan's rate was 2, 6d. " " and 3 " " "

* News Letter.

1717.

This year is rendered memorable, by the unusual quantity of snow, which fell on the twentieth and twenty-fourth of February. In these two storms, the earth was covered with snow, from ten to fifteen feet, and, in some places, to twenty feet, deep. Many one-story houses were covered, and, in many places, paths were dug, from house to house, under the snow. Many visits were made, from place to place, by means of snow shoes, the wearers having first stepped out of their chamber windows, on these excursions. 'Love,' we know, 'laughs at locksmiths,' and, of course, will disregard a snow-drift. Tradition informs us, that a Mr. Abraham Adams, wishing to visit his 'ladye love,' Miss Abigail Pierce, mounted his snow shoes, took a three miles' walk, for that purpose, and entered her residence as he left his own, namely, by the chamber window. He was the first person the family had seen from abroad, for more than a week. Cotton Mather has left in writing a particular account of 'the great snow,' and the many marvels and prodigies attending it.

Stephen Jaques, in his account, thus writes. 'The year 1717–18 aftar this darkness * was the sadest time for sickness. A mortal feaver spred throw ye country and in about three months time it made twenty widows, besides many other parsons swept away.'

1718.

May 11th. 'The selectmen were desired not to grant approbation for above five taverns and not above three retailers of strong drink.'†

Town voted 'to invite the neighbouring towns in the county of Essex to join with us in endeavouring to obtaine a dividing of ye county of Essex into two counties.' †

June 23d. Richard, son of captain Richard Gerrish, of Portsmouth, was drowned at the end of Long wharf.

September 24th. The town granted to Moses Chase, Abraham Annis, Joseph Pike, William Morse, Benjamin Smith, Abiel Kelly, Jonathan Kelly, John Swett, John Carr, and Joshua Bayley, on their petition, 'eighty rods of the flatts above Holt's rocks to fish on, on condition they pay as an acknowledgement to ye town two salmon per year one to Mr. Toppan, ye other to Mr. Tufts, *if they catch them.*'

The value of salmon at this time, may be estimated, by the following letter to Anthony Morse.

'Mr. Morse,
This is to desire ye favour of you to gett me one, two or three or more of ye first sammon yt can be had this year. I am willing to give a good price and

---

* October twenty-first, 1716.   † Town records.

a great price rather than not have it and will pay a man and horse for bringing it to content, but observe he do n't bring for any body else at ye same time.   If there be but one single sammon, send away forthwith.   If more, then it will help ye extraordinary charge, but do n't let them be kept till almost spoiled in hopes of more.   Pray give my sarvice to your father Moody and I desire his help in this affair.   If you have success let ye bearer call at Mr. Woodbridge's and at captain Corney's in his way to me, for they may happen at ye same time to have some.   I shall take it very kindly if you will be mindfull.

I am your friend

H. WHITTON.

Boston, March twenty-first, 1728.'

1 7 1 9 .

March 6*th*.   Cottle's lane, now South street, was laid out, 'one rod and a half wide from High street to Merrimack river.'

March 10*th*.   Town voted to give Mr. John Woodbridge, forty pounds 'for the year ensuing to keep a free school for latin scholars, readers, writers and cypherers, and sixty pounds for maintaining schools in the remote parts of the town.'

This year, potatoes were introduced, by some emigrants from Ireland.   They were raised in the garden of Mr. Nathaniel Walker, esquire, of Andover.   Tradition informs us, that the first which were raised in Newbury, grew on the land, once owned by Henry Sewall, lately by Mr. Stephen Noyes, and now by Mr. William Sargent, but in what year this valuable root first made its appearance in Newbury, no record informs us.   In 1732, I find, in a Mr. Morgaridge's journal, 'half a bushel of pertaters, six shillings,' and in the same year, 'one peak of pertaters.'   In the diary of a farmer of Lynn, he mentions 'patatas,' in 1733.   In 1737, the reverend Thomas Smith, of Portland, says, in his diary, 'there is not a peck of potatoes in the whole eastern country.'   In 1739, Robert Adams chronicles the sale of a bushel and a half of 'pertaters.'   Their introduction into general use, was slow, and, so late as 1750, should any person have raised so large a quantity as five bushels, great would have been the inquiry among his neighbors, in what manner he could dispose of such an abundance.   They were, at first, raised in beds, like onions.

May 12*th*.   The town voted 'that all the country roads should be four rods broad, if they are not now.'

In the latter end of this year, the people of New England were much excited and alarmed, at the appearance of the northern lights, which were to them a novelty, and were supposed to betoken some dire calamity.   In the journal of Mr. Stephen Jaques, under the date of December eleventh, 1719, he thus writes.

' *December* 11*th*, 1719.   Between seven and eight o'clock at night, the moone being neare the full, it might want two days, there appeared in ye north above like a rainbow, but it was white.   It seemed to reach from norwest to northeast, and it was more strait in the middle than a rainbow.   It seemed to be eight foot wide.   It looked like a cloud.   There appeared in the north clouds, which looked very red and seemed to lie up allmost overhead, as if they had been driven with a farse wind and then parted to the east and so vanished away. The white cloud or bow remained an hour or two. Between ten and eleven there appeared a cloud, which came from ye norwest like a mist. We could see the stars through it. It was as red as blood or crimson, but not a thick red. My eies saw it.

STEPHEN JAQUES.'

Lewis, in his history of Lynn, says, 'the northern lights were *first* observed this year on the *seventeenth* of December.' As the moon was 'neare the full,' any person, with an almanac for 1719, can easily ascertain which is correct, December eleventh, or December nineteenth.

1720.

' This year,' says doctor Holmes, in his annals, 'tea began to be used in New England.' It must, however, have been used in small quantities, many years before. The first tea kettles were small articles, made of copper, and first used in Plymouth, in 1702. The first cast iron tea kettles, were made in Plympton, now Carver, between 1760 and 1765. 'When ladies,' says Lewis, 'went to visiting parties, each one carried her tea cup, saucer and spoon. The tea cups were of the best china, very small, containing as much as a common wine glass.' *

From an unpublished letter, written in England, in the year 1740, January first, I extract the following.

' They are not much esteemed now that will not treat high and gossip about. Tea is now become the darling of our women. Almost every little tradesman's wife must set sipping tea for an hour or more in a morning, and it may be again in the afternoon, if they can get it, and nothing will please them to sip it out of but china ware, if they can get it. They talk of bestowing thirty or forty shillings upon a tea equipage, as they call it. There is the silver spoons, silver tongs, and many other trinkets that I cannot name.'

'1720 March ye first about half an hour after eight of ye clock there appeared a thick strack from ye northwest to ye southest allmost right ovar my head like an arch and it seemed to be about eight or ten foot in breadth. It was like a very thick black smoke of a chimney, and seemed very low. It began in ye norwest to vanish and disappear and so by degrees to pass away, the moon about half an hour high a going down.' *Stephen Jaques' journal.*

' *August* 20*th.* 'T is said Mr. Lucas, the church of England minister, cut his own throat at Newbury. However the minister of Marblehead set a good face on it, had the corpse carried into the church and preached a funeral sermon.' †

' *November* 24*th.* There appeared on this day about eight of the clock at night a light in ye north almost like that, which appeared the last year, it being red, but not so much. The Friday night

---

* History of Lynn.   † Judge Sewall's diary.

before there appeared in ye north between seven and eight a light like the day light, when it breaks three quarters of an hour high.'
Stephen Jaques' journal.

1721.

September 20th. The town chose deacon Nathaniel Coffin, ensign William Titcomb, and lieutenant Henry Rolfe, to receive the town's part of the fifty thousand pounds, granted by Massachusetts, thirteenth of July, 1720, and let it out, on good security, in sums not less than ten pounds, nor more than thirty pounds, at five per centum, for no longer period than one year at a time. For the use of this money, the town was to pay the state four per centum. This was the famous 'land bank' scheme, as it was called, which proved so injurious to the estates of many individuals.

In judge Sewall's diary, of this year, I find the following.

' Thomas Hale [was] made a justice. I opposed it, because *there are five in Newbury already* and he had lately kept an ordinary and sold rum. I was answered he had laid it down. I fear it will not be for the honour of the persons, nor of the governor and council, nor for the welfare [of the town] unless perhaps dwelling on the neck he may give check to traveling on the Lord's day.' Within the limits of ' ould Newberry,' there are now forty-four justices.

September 21st. This year, the small-pox prevailed in New England. More than eight hundred died in Boston, where it began. Newbury sent twenty pounds to the poor of Boston, in wood.

1722.

The town's stock of ammunition was, this year, examined, and found to consist of seven bags and two casks of bullets, and eight casks of powder, consisting of five hundred and forty-three pounds of bullets, and three hundred and fifty-seven pounds of powder.

' The fever began at Rowley and many peopel dyed. The like was not known in that town.' *

September 17th. The first parish in Newbury, gave their assent to the formation of another parish, in Newbury, which was formed September nineteenth, and was called the third parish in Newbury, now first in Newburyport.

1723.

' *February 25th.* An unusual high tide, higher by twenty inches than was ever known before. At the same time the sea at Hampton broke over its banks for some miles together and continued running for several hours.' †

* Stephen Jaques' journal.   † Cotton Mather.

February 25th. ' Second parish bought of deacon William Morss for seven pounds ten shillings half an acre of land near Swett's ferry, and a quarter of an acre of Ezekiel Hale for a burying place.' Swett's ferry was near Holt's rocks, now Rock's bridge.

' *March* 12*th.* A committee of three was chosen to compute the cost of an alms house and to view a place' to set it, and so forth.*

April 19*th.* Mr. Daniel Holbrook died. He had been called to assist in the work of the ministry, and would have been ordained, had his life been spared. ' He was taken sick in the pulpit on Sunday April fourteenth, after he had commenced preaching and was obliged to leave the meeting house.' †

' This year,' says Stephen Jaques, in his journal, ' was the sadest year as ever was known in Newbury, for in ye month of April there died near forty parsons, most of them grown up, sometimes two a day, sometimes three a day, young men and wimmen. About the twenty-fourth day of the month the town capt a fast. There was nine parsons lay dead that day and I do believe fifty or sixty or more lay sick and it pleased God to hear the prayers of his people and to ansar them in a wonderfull mannar, for the nues was the next morning they were all better, and so it was, for very fue dyed aftarward. O that men would praise the Lord for his goodness and his wonderfull works to ye children of men.'

' *May* 3*d*, 1723. Newbury. Time of health now. No person that I know of having been lately seized with the distemper that hath proved so mortal.' †

On occasion of this mortality, John Calef, son of John Calef of Newbury, aged nineteen, wrote and published three elegies, which a writer thus notices, in the New England Chronicle, of August fifth, 1723.

' It is with the utmost concern I would now represent to you the hard fate, which our countrymen are like to suffer, who happen to die with a good name. The dead have been long enough abused and the living disturbed by the very dregs of the college and the plough in their elegiac performances insomuch that some considerable persons among us have been constrained to do but little good and appear useless all their lifetime, to avoid the *persecution* of an elegy at their death. We have indeed flattered ourselves that it would be better living and better dying for all honest men in New England than it has been for a hundred years past, but to our mortification we find that this spirit of versification has spread itself among the *neat cattle*, no less than three *elegies* having been lately wrote and published by Mr. John Calf of Newbury, one of which is *upon* the *death of the reverend Mr. Daniel Holbrook of Newbury*, who was taken *sick on the day* he *designed* to preach madam Fryer's funeral sermon ; and how well this *bleating Calf* has performed his task and embalmed the memory of the deceased the following lines may shew.

' On sabbath day he went his way,
As he was used to do,
God's house unto, that they might know
What he had for to shew.
When he came there he went to prayer,
But very faint he spoke,

* Town records. † New England Chronicle.

25

His mortal wound inclosed round,
And gave a fatal stroke.
His hat he took, his head he shook,
A mournful sigh he gave,
A shepherd true, the flock went through,
Not daunted to the grave.
He often said, when that he laid,
His dying bed upon,
Distracted he should surely be,
Before his breath was gone.
God's holy will he must fulfil,
But it was his desire
For to declare the sermon rare
Concerning madam Fryer.
A man in pain doth pray in vain,
Unless he prays to God
To him let's pray both night and day,
To ease his heavy rod.'

'His second performance is a mournful elegy occasioned by the great mortality in the family of *Mr. Henry Clark* of Newbury, which is chiefly made up of the days of the month and ages of the persons deceased. And after he has barbarously buried the dead one after another as they were born, he cries out in a rapture

'If such vines wither well may we,
Whose bodies so corrupted be.

'His third set of jingles is called a funeral elegy occasioned by the death of Mr. Edmund Titcomb, at the close of which he has a few lines to shew that death is certain, but the time when very uncertain, and to make his argument good, he mentions the death of Sampson and says '*no body can deny but that he died.*' But methinks this is but a poor way of arguing for allowing it to be true that Sampson did die, yet it is as true that he died by his own hands and some are of opinion that if he had not been so foolishly heroic as to pull his house down about his ears he might have lived till this time.

'To omit any further remarks on this elegiographer, I think it necessary to inform the world that since the publication of his elegies he has been inspired with a great desire of *learning*, and in order to prepare himself for college he has made a vigorous attempt upon his *accidence* and could boast before two credible witnesses that he had got it all by heart *twice* in a week.

'I hear his next trial of skill will be on Cole's dictionary, and that he promises to get that by heart in three months' time, which if he does, it will be the interest of all *gentlemen* and *ladies, deacons* and ministers to beware of dying in good terms with his *calve's head* and pluck, for then no doubt

'*His brains will issue forth and as they fly*
Congeal into a mournful elegy,
The sense of which, if mortal man can dive in
His verse may raise the dead or kill the living.

Tibullus.'

This year there was a ship-yard, and ships were built, by Thorla's bridge.

1724.

The war with the Norridgewock Indians, which began in 1721, was this year ended, by the death of Sebastian Rallè, the French jesuit. He was killed by lieutenant [Richard] Jaques, of Newbury. This information we obtain from Hutchinson, who obtained from 'captain [Jeremiah] Moulton a minute and circumstantial account of the' battle. He says, 'captain Moulton, with about eighty men reached Norridgewock about three P. M. August twelfth and commenced the attack. After driving the Indians (about sixty men and one hundred women and children) over the river and killing many, they returned to the town and found the jesuit in one of the wigwams firing upon a few of our men, who had not pursued after the enemy. Moulton had given orders not to kill the jesuit, but by his firing from the wigwam one of our men being wound, a lieutenant Jaques stove open the door and shot him through the head. Jaques excused himself to his commanding officer, alleging that Rallè was loading his gun and declared that he would neither give nor take quarter.'

On July sixth of this year, reverend Christopher Toppan, of Newbury, wrote a long letter to Cotton Mather, who, if any thing strange, prodigious, or unnatural happened, was sure to obtain an account of it. From this letter, now in the library of the American Antiquarian Society, in Worcester, I make the following extract.

'Concerning the amphisbena,* as soon as I received your commands I made diligent enquiry of several persons, who saw it after it was dead, but they could give me no assurance of its having two heads, as they did not strictly examine it, not calling it the least in question because it seemed as really to have two heads as one. They directed me for further information to the person I before spoke of, who was out of town, and to the persons, who saw it alive and killed it, which were two or three lads, about twelve or fourteen, one of which a pert sensible youngster told me yt one of his mates running towards him cryed out there was a snake with two heads running after him, upon which he run to him, and the snake getting into a puddle of water, he with a stick pulled him out, after which it came towards him, and as he went backwards or forward, soe the snake would doe likewise. After a little time, the snake upon his striking at him, gathered up his whole body into a sort of quoil, except *both heads*, which kept towards him, and he distinctly saw *two mouths* and two *stings* (as they are vulgarly called) which stings or tongues it kept putting forth after the usual manner of snakes, till he killed it. Thus far the lad. This day understanding the person mentioned before was returned, I went to him, and asked him about the premises, he told me he narrowly examined the snake being brought to him by the lads after it was dead and he found two distinct heads *one at each end*, opening each with a little stick, in each of which he saw a sting or tongue, and that each head had two eyes, throwing it down and going away, upon second thoughts he began to mistrust his own eyes, as to what he had seen, and therefore returned a second time to examine it, if possible, more strictly, but still found it as before. This person is so credible that I can as much believe him as if I had seen him myself. He tells me of another man yt examined it as he did, but I cannot yet meet with him.

'*Postscript.* Before ensealing I spoke with the other man, who examined the amphisbena (and he is also a man of credit) and he assures me yt it had really two heads, one at each end, two mouths, two stings or tongues and so forth.

'Sir I have nothing more to add but that he may have a remembrance in your prayers, who is,   Sir, your most humble servant

CHRISTOPHER TOPPAN.'

' A smart close winter, ending February twenty-eighth, 1725.' †

* Amphisbena, a snake with two heads, one where the tail should have been.
† Reverend T. Smith's diary.

1725.

This year, the third parish in Newbury, now first in Newburyport, erected their meeting-house, of which, the earliest notice that
I find, is the following, from a letter, written by William Moody,
of Byfield, to his brother, judge Sewall, dated seventeenth of February, 1725. He thus writes : 'our people at towne are going to
build another meeting house, but intend to set it so nigh to Mr.
Toppan's, that I fear it will make great contention. Newbury are
great sufferers this day for what have happened by contending about
the place of a meeting house.'

February 25th. The town 'voted that a towne house should be
built and should be set at the upper end of Greenleaf's lane,' *
[now State street.]

June 25th. On this day, the third parish meeting-house, now first
in Newburyport, was dedicated. The sermon was preached by the
reverend John Tufts, of Newbury. The house was at first forty-five
by sixty feet, in length and breadth, but, in 1736, was enlarged, thus
making it sixty by eighty feet. It stood in what is now the market
place, in Newburyport, the steeple fronting the river. The pulpit,
which was on the westerly side, standing near where the town
pump now stands.

August 3d. The reverend John Lowell was called to the work
of the ministry, having preached to the people from June twenty-
seventh.

August 31st. 'About midnight a company of rioters assembled
on horseback and with crow bars broke the doors, bolts and locks
of the gaol in Newbury and took off on spare horses, Isaac Brown
and Hugh Ditson charged with capital offences. Governor William
Dummer offered a reward of fifty pounds for their apprehension.' †

November 30th. A committee, consisting of 'lieutenant colonel
Richard Kent, major Joseph Gerrish, deacon Caleb Moody, lieutenant Charles Pierce and captain John March were appointed to use
all proper means with others of other towns for to get the county of
Essex divided into two counties.' *

In November, the general court 'ordered a committee to view
the situation of the westerly end of the first parish.' This committee
met December first, and reported December eighth.

December 29th. 'The third parish voted to give Mr. John Lowell one hundred and thirty pounds yearly salary and two hundred
to build him a house.'

The general court confirmed the dividing line of the third parish,
which was 'Chandler's lane, [now Federal street,] thence to captain
John March's farm, [now Samuel Thurlow's,] thence to the line of
the second parish,' with this condition, that those who wished, might
remain with the first parish. About thirty remained. Eight families, south of Chandler's lane, wished to belong to the new society.

* Town records.   † News Letter.

1 7 2 6.

January 12*th.* The third congregational church in Newbury, was this day gathered, by the reverend Caleb Cushing, of Salisbury. Twenty-two of the male members had been dismissed, January second, from the first church in Newbury, for that purpose. The day was observed as a day of fasting and prayer. A sermon was preached by the reverend Moses Hale, of Byfield.

January 19*th.* The reverend John Lowell was ordained pastor of the third church in Newbury. Sermon by the reverend Thomas Foxcroft, of Boston.

1 7 2 7.

January 17*th.* The town 'voted that a work house and a house of correction should be built.' *

March 22*d.* First parish 'voted to give the third parish the old bell.'

May 10*th.* A highway, of two rods wide, was laid out, 'from ye country road near to his honor the lieutenant governor Dummer's house to the parsonage land in Byfield parish on the land of John Dummer esquire, Mr. Richard Dummer and Mr. Joseph Noyes.' *

May 23*d.* The third parish 'voted to get a bell weighing about four hundred pounds.'

July 25*th.* 'Town voted to make a good and sufficient way over Ash swamp — said way to be covered with suitable wood of thirteen feet in length and the wood to be well covered with gravel all across the swamp,' * and so forth.

September 16*th.* 'A mighty tempest of wind and rain, which did much hurt by land and sea.' †

'In the month of September,' says Stephen Jaques, 'on Saturday in ye afternoon ye wind began to be very strong and increased more in the night. It blew down and brake six trees in my ould orchard and trees all over ye woods. There never was ye like known. It twisted young walnut trees in ye midst. It raised a great tide, which swept away near two hundred load of hay, that was in swath.'

As the earthquake, which happened in October of this year, was one of the most violent ever felt in New England, and as, according to Hutchinson and other writers, 'the shock was greater at Newbury and other towns on Merrimack river than in any other part of Massachusetts,' I shall be a little more minute, in my extracts from accounts written in Newbury at the time. From the records of the episcopal church in Newburyport, kept by the reverend Matthias Plant, I make the following extract.

'*October* 29*th*, 1727. Being the Lord's day at forty minutes past ten the same evening, there was a most terrible, sudden and amazing earthquake, which did

* Town records.　　　　　　† Reverend Mr. Phillips.

damage to the greatest part of the neighbourhood, shook and threw down tops of chimnies and in many places the earth opened a foot or more. It continued very terrible by frequently bursting and shocking our houses and lasted all that week (the first being the loudest shock, and eight more that immediately followed, louder than the rest that followed) sometimes breaking with loud claps six times or oftener in a day and as often in the night until Thursday in the said week and then somewhat abated. Upon Friday in the evening and about midnight, and about break of day and on Saturday there were three very loud claps. We also had it on Saturday, the sabbath, and on Monday morning about ten, tho' much abated in the noise and terror. Upon the Tuesday following, November seventh, about eleven o'clock a very loud clap upon every day or night more or less three, four, six times each day or night and upon the twelfth being the Lord's day twice from betwixt three to half past four, in all which space of time some claps were loud, others seemingly at a distance and much abated. Upon Monday two hours before day a loud burst and at half past two in the afternoon another burst was heard somewhat loud. On the nineteenth about ten at night a very loud shock and another about break of day, somewhat *here* abated, but at Haverhill a very loud burst, making their houses rock, as that over our night did with us. It was Lord's day in the evening. It hath been heard twice since much abated. The very first shock opened a new spring by my father Samuel Bartlet's house in the meadow and threw up in the lower grounds in Newbury several loads of white sand. After that some loud claps, shocking our houses. On December seventeenth, about half an hour after ten being Lord's day at evening a very loud burst, shocking our houses. Another about four the next morning abated.'

The next account, is one written by Stephen Jaques, and is as follows, namely :

' On the twenty-ninth day of October between ten and eleven it being sabath day night there was a terabel earthquake. The like was never known in this land. It came with a dreadful roreing, as if it was thunder, and then a pounce like grate guns two or three times close one after another. It lasted about two minits. It shook down briks from ye tops of abundance of chimnies, some allmost all the heads. Knight's and Toppan's fell. All that was about ye houses trembled, beds shook, some cellar walls fell partly down. Benjamin Plumer's stone without his dore fell into his cellar. Stone wals fell in a hundred plasis. Most peopel gat up in a moment. It came very often all ye night aftar, and it was heard two or three times some days and nights, and on the sabath day night on ye twenty-fourth of December following between ten and eleven it was very loud, as any time except ye first, and twice that night aftar but not so loud. The first night it broke out in more than ten places in ye town in ye clay low land, blowing up ye sand, sum more, sum less. In one place near Spring island it blew out, as it was judged twenty loads, and when it was cast on coals in ye night, it burnt like brimstone.'

The following is a copy of a letter, written by Henry Sewall, of Newbury, to his kinsman, judge Samuel Sewall, of Boston. It is printed in the Boston News Letter.

' *Newbury, November 21st*, 1727.

' Honored sir :
' Thro' God's goodness to us we are all well and have been preserved at the time of the late great and terrible earthquake. We were sitting by the fire and about half after ten at night our house shook and trembled as if it would have fallen to pieces. Being affrighted we ran out of doors, when we found the ground did tremble and we were in great fear of being swallowed up alive, but God preserved us and did not suffer it to break out, till it got forty or fifty rods from the house, where it broke the ground in the common near a place

N. Emmons pinx.   O. Pelton.

The Hon.ble Samuel Sewall, Esq.r.

Late Chief Justice of His Maj.s Province of Massachusetts Bay in N.E.

And Judge of Probate for the County of Suffolk.

Æ. 77. 1728.

Auris, mens, oculus, manus, os, pes; munere fungi.
dum Pergunt, Praeftat discere velle mori.

called Spring island, and there is from sixteen to twenty loads of fine sand thrown out where the ground broke, and several days after the water boiled out like a spring, but is now dry and the ground closed up again.   I have sent some of the sand that you may see it. Our house kept shaking about three minutes.'

December 7th.   The church connected with the third parish, in Newbury, met, and chose a select number of the members, ' to meet once a month and consider what may be for the good of the town in general, especially the churches in it and more particularly their own church.   The other churches proceeded in the same method and upon the same design.' *

1 7 2 8.

The reverend Mathias Plant thus continues his account of the earthquakes this year.

' January third, about nine at night an easy clap.   Saturday night and day five claps.   From about six at night to four Sunday morning some people said it continued for half an hour without ceasing burst upon burst.   Upon Wednesday January twenty-fourth about half an hour after nine at night one loud burst followed in half a minute by another much abated.   Upon Lord's day January twenty-eighth another easy burst about half after six in the morning, another about ten same morning easy.   At the same night about one o'clock a loud burst.   Monday January twenty-ninth it was heard twice.   Tuesday the thirtieth about two in the afternoon there was a very loud clap equal to any but the first for terror, shaking our houses so that many people were afraid of their falling down, pewter and so forth was shaken off dressers at considerable distance. Another shock much abated about half an hour afterwards.   February twenty-first about half after twelve at midnight a considerable loud burst.   February twenty-ninth about half after one P. M. another.'   Mr. P. also mentions shocks as having occurred ' March seventeenth about three A. M.   March nineteenth about forty minutes past one P. M. and at nine the same night.   April twenty-eighth about five P. M.   May twelfth Sunday morning about forty minutes past nine a loud and long clap.   May seventeenth Friday about eight P. M. a loud and long clap.   May twenty-second several claps in the morning, and about ten the same morning a very loud and long clap.   May twenty-fourth about eleven at night June sixth about three in the morning.   June eleventh at nine A. M.   July third A. M. and July twenty-third about break of day a very loud clap.'

January 30th.   ' About two o'clock a shock of an earthquake.'
' *March* 18th.   The third parish voted to add thirty pounds to the thirty pounds granted by the town,' † for the schools.
April 16th.   ' The town received of the State one thousand three hundred and twenty-eight pounds, and fifteen shillings, being their proportion of the sixty thousand pounds, raised by the state to be loaned to raise a revenue.' ‡
May 13th.   The town ' voted not to build a town house or an alms house in a short time.' ‡
' In July there was a great drought in Maine.' §

---

* Third parish church records.   † Third parish records.
‡ Town records.   § Reverend T. Smith's diary.

November 26*th*.   The third parish chose a committee ' to select a place for a school house and also for a burying place.'   This was the commencement of the burying place near Frog pond.

1729.

January 28*th*, 1729, died Daniel Emery, aged thirty-six.   In his will, he gave sixty pounds for the use of the ministry, of which, ten pounds was for communion plate, twenty pounds more for the first church, which should be gathered at Chester, and a minister ordained, twenty pounds for Nottingham, twenty-five pounds to the parish in which he belonged, twenty-five pounds to Mr. Tufts, fifty pounds to his kinsman at college, and one thousand pounds to his brothers and sisters, besides providing liberally for his widow.

April 15*th*.   The inhabitants of the upper part of the west parish, on this day made an agreement ' to build a meeting house fifty feet by thirty-eight and twenty foot stud.'

August 28*th*.   The people in the upper part of the west parish, petitioned the general court, to divide the west parish into two precincts.   They state, among other things, that they ' have near eight score dwelling houses, besides churchmen and quakers.'

From an accurate map of the west parish of Newbury, taken by John Brown, esquire, and dated September fifteenth, 1729, on which is drawn, a representation of every house in the parish, and the name of each occupant, it appears that the number of houses was at that time one hundred and eighty-four, and number of families one hundred and eighty-three.

' March nineteenth betwixt two and three P. M. earthquake very loud.   September eighth at half past three P. M. another shock.   September twenty-ninth about half past four P. M. another.   October twenty-ninth the earthquake was heard twice that night, one of the times being about the time of night it was the first time we heard it two years past.

' November fourteenth about eight A. M. it was loud being attended with two cracks like unto two sudden claps of thunder and shook the house.   November twenty-seventh, about eight P. M. a very loud noise and a large shock of the earthquake.   It was heard at Ipswich.' *

1730.

February 19*th*.   ' The earthquake was pretty loud before day.'

March 10*th*.   Town voted not to approbate more than six persons to keep houses of public entertainment.

March 17*th*.   ' The third parish voted to set their school house

* Reverend Matthias Plant's journal.

by Frog pond about two thirds of the way between Fish street [now State street] and Green street.' *

This year the 'burying place,' now burying hill, near Frog pond, was inclosed with a board fence.' *

In this year, shocks of an earthquake were noticed and recorded, on ' February eighth about eight P. M. and at midnight. February twenty-sixth two shocks a quarter before two A. M. April twelfth about eight P. M. July twenty-eighth about nine A. M. August fifteenth two shocks about eight A. M. November sixth about eleven A. M. a loud shock. November fourteenth about nine A. M. another. November twenty-fifth another about twenty minutes past eight P. M. December eleventh at a quarter before seven P. M. December nineteenth about half past ten P. M. a very heavy shock. It was perceived at Boston and Portsmouth about equal to ours here.'

1731.

February 22d. The town voted this day 'to build a town house in Chandler's lane,' now Federal street. From this vote fifty-seven persons dissented.†

' *March 9th.* Mr. John Woodbridge was chosen a grammer school master for the year ensuing and shall have forty-five pounds for his service and *shall have none but Latin scholars.*' †

March 9th. ' The town granted liberty to William Johnson and nine others to build a wharf at the foot of Chandler's lane [now Federal street] on condition it be built within four years and that the inhabitants of Newbury may fasten their hay boats or gondolas to said wharf without paying for it.'

Liberty was also given to Abiel Somerby and others, to build a wharf at the foot of Queen street, now Market street, on similar conditions.

' *March 22d.* William Ilsley and Joseph Morse junior were chosen and appointed to tune the psalm in ye meeting house in time of publick worship and take their turn in that work that it may be done with ye more ease and cheerfulness. And the said Morse is appointed to sit in the fore seat of ye south body with ye said Ilsley for ye managing said work.' ‡

March 29th. The second parish voted to desire the general court, to confirm the setting off the fourth parish, from the second, which was done by a committee, on February twenty-second, according to a vote passed by the second parish, January sixth, consenting to the division.

May 10th. ' Town voted to give to the first parish in Kittery fifty pounds towards building a meeting house.' †

Shocks of the earthquake were this year noticed by Mr. Plant, as happening 'January seventh, about seven P. M. January elev-

---

* Third parish records.   † Town records.   ‡ First parish records.

enth about midnight. March seventh five P. M. May twenty-eighth nine A. M. July fifth about sunrise. August twenty-first, evening. October twenty-first about eleven P. M. loud and long.'

On February first, a subscription paper was circulated, for the purpose of raising money to build a town house, ' to be set where will be best entertaining for horses, for strangers and so forth,' provided ' any person will give the land to set said house upon between the meeting house and Archelaus Adams' tavern house.'

It was finished, and conditionally deeded to the county, February eighteenth, 1735, reverting to the town and parish, should no court be held in it for nine months. The original cost of the building was five hundred and thirty pounds, and ten shillings, of which the county paid two hundred pounds, and individuals contributed the remainder. It was occupied as a court house, town house, school house, and so forth, and stood on land, given by Benjamin Morse, opposite the head of Marlborough street, where captain Amos Knight's house now stands. It remained there till March fifth, 1780, when it was bought at auction by John Mycall, esquire.

1732.

' *January 5th.* This day died in Dedham that noted Indian, Samuel Hyde in the one hundred and sixth year of his age. He was a faithful soldier to the English. It was said by himself, and of him by others that he killed nineteen of the enemy Indians (he kept the account on his gun) and would fain have made up the number twenty.' *

This ' noted Indian' was for some time a resident in Newbury, of whom many anecdotes are still told, indicative not only of his wit and shrewdness, but of his incorrigible mendacity. The phrase, ' you lie like Sam Hyde,' or, ' you lie like old Hyde,' expresses to a native of Newbury, the *ne plus ultra* of lying. Among the testimonies on file, among the county papers, is one concerning him, in a complaint against a citizen of Newbury, which is quite characteristic, but not suitable for publication. In a petition to the general court, August twenty-fifth, 1676, Daniel Gookin, senior, testifies, ' that Sam and Jeremy Hyde have acquitted themselves well both for courage and fidelity, especially Sam Hyde, whom they have witnessed to be one of the best and most active of them all,' and that ' he took at Bridgewater one young man, and five young women and children at other places, and he slew one lusty young man and brought his hand to captain Hunting at mount Hope.'

May 12th. The town voted, that ' the school be kept at the town's house by the meeting house in the first parish this year.' This was probably the watch house.

' *September 5th,* at eleven P. M. there was a small shock of an earthquake.' †

* News Letter.   † Parish records.

1733.

'The winter of 1732–3,' says Stephen Jaques, 'was very severe. The snow fell about ye fourteenth of November and lay until April. Hay was three pounds a load. Peach trees began to blossom ye eleventh of May,' [old style.]

March 13*th.* A committee was appointed 'to procure a frame and other materials for a town house,' which, on May eleventh, the town granted 'liberty to the first parish to build within two years on their own cost and charge near lieutenant John March's house,' * and which, on December fourth, the first parish 'voted should be for the use of the county.' †

'*October* 19*th,* Friday about midnight,' says Mr. Plant, 'there was a long and loud noise of the earthquake.'

'*November* 4*th.* Moses Bradstreet killed on Plum island in a violent storm sixty wild geese with a club.' ‡

November 25*th.* A moose, seven feet high, was killed in Salisbury.

1734.

'*January* 16*th,* about twenty minutes past ten A. M. there was an earthquake long and loud.' §

'*January.* Mr. John Stickney, aged forty-one, a noted coaster, fell overboard from his sloop and was drowned.'

'The winter of 1733–4 was very moderate.'

May 7*th.* The town granted, on certain conditions, 'liberty to have a bridge built over the river Parker provided it may be built and maintained without being a charge to this town of Newbury and within ten years from ye date hereof.'

'*June* 29*th,* at a quarter past three P. M. there was another earthquake.' §

'*August.* A great storm. Much hay carried off and Indian corn damaged.'

September 13*th.* Town 'voted that the town house shall be finished with the remainder of the interest money of ye first bank, and that said house shall be made sure to the town and county.'

September 23*d.* A committee was chosen to comply with 'the order of court July thirtieth to build a prison.'

'*October* 9*th,* about twenty minutes past ten A. M. an earthquake.' §

'*November* 12*th,* about one A. M. we had the loudest noise and greatest shock (except the first of all) very awful and terrible and long. November sixteenth at six A. M. a severe shock.' §

* Town records.　　† Parish records.　　‡ Boston paper.　　§ M. Plant.

1735.

'*February* 2*d*, about six P. M. there was a shock of the earthquake pretty loud.' *

'*March* 11*th*. The town voted thirty pounds to make Rolf's lane a town way.'

'*March* 21*st*, about half past ten A. M. there was a loud noise of the earthquake.' *

In May this year, a disorder, called the throat distemper, appeared in Kingston, New Hampshire. The first person who took the disease, was a Mr. Clough, who, having examined the swelled throat of a dead hog, died suddenly with a swelling in his throat. In about three weeks, three children, about a mile from Mr. Clough's, were attacked, and died in thirty-six hours. In fourteen towns in New Hampshire, nine hundred and eighty-four died between June, 1735, and July sixteenth, 1736. In Massachusetts, the mortality was nearly as great as in New Hampshire. A particular account of the number in each town in the two states, was published, by the reverend Mr. Fitch, in Portsmouth, and the reverend John Brown, of Haverhill. Of the mortality in Newbury, Stephen Jaques thus writes :

'A sickness began by the water side about September at Thomas Smith's, which carried off two of his children and prevailed among the children, so that by the middle of February there died from Chandler's lane [Federal street] with the falls eighty-one persons. John Boynton lost eight children. Benjamin Knight had three buried in one grave.' Mr. John Boyton had four children buried in one grave, two on Saturday, and two on Sunday, December twentieth and twenty-first. In another place, Stephen Jaques writes as follows.

'*Thursday, October* 29*th*. My wife went into a chamber, that was locked, to fetch candels, that was in a bushel under a bed, and as she kneeled down and took her candels and laid them on the bed and thrust back the half bushel, there came out a child's hand. She saw the fingers, the hand, a streked boy's cote or sleeve, and upon sarch there was no child in the chamber. On Thursday a fortnite aftar, my Steven's son Henry died. The next Thursday Ebenezer died. The next Monday morning his eldest son Stephen died.'

July 24*th*. Town 'chose Joseph Gerrish and Henry Rolfe esquires to use proper means to have ye county of Essex divided into two counties.'

'In September a Newbury sloop, Offin Boardman, master, with a cargo of rafts at her stern was overset on her passage from Casco bay to Boston and thirteen persons drowned.'

1736.

February 2*d.* There was an earthquake.

March. The third parish 'voted to enlarge their meeting house thirty-five feet back.' It was, when erected, in 1725, forty-five by

* M. Plant.

sixty feet. It was now eighty by sixty feet. They also 'voted to petition the general court to have liberty to raise money in order to keep a grammar school for themselves, as the first parish has petitioned, and be freed from paying to any other school.' On the twenty-fifth of March, the first parish had petitioned for the same liberty.'*

'*July* 13*th*. About three quarters past nine in the forenoon, there was a loud shock of the earthquake.' †

September. The ways for landing of ferry boats was settled by court.

September 21*st*. A committee of three 'was appointed to treat with his majestie's justices about moving the gaol now standing in Newbury.' ‡

September 21*st*. 'The town leased March's, now Newbury port, ferry to Benjamin Woodbridge and Moses Gerrish for seven years at thirty-six pounds a year.' ‡

'*October* 1*st*. About half past one A. M. there was a great and very loud shock of the earthquake.' †

'*November* 12*th*. About two A. M. another shock, and about six the same morning another.' †

'*December* 29*th*. There was a surprising bloody appearance in the heavens.' §

In this year thirteen families in Byfield buried all their children with the 'throat distemper.'

' In the year 1734 a few caterpillars of a peculiar kind appeared on the oak trees as soon as the leaves began to grow. In 1735, a much larger number, one hundred to one, were seen, but in this year the number of caterpillars was astonishing. Almost all the woods in Haverhill and Bradford, some part of the east end excepted, the easterly part of Chester and Andover, many thousand acres of thick woods had their leaves and twigs of this year's growth entirely eaten up. They cleared off every green thing so that the trees were as naked as in the depth of winter. They were larger than our common caterpillar and made no nests. No river or pond could stop them. They would swim like dogs, and travel in unaccountable armies and completely cover whole houses and trees. Cart and carriage wheels would be dyed green from the numbers they crushed in their progress.' ‖

Richard Kelly, of Amesbury, in his diary, says, 'they are larger than the orchard caterpillar, but smooth on the back with a black streak with white spots. They are thought by many to be the palmer worm.'

1737.

'*February* 6*th*. About a quarter past four P. M. there was a considerable shock of an earthquake.' †

' In ye spring of this year,' says Richard Kelly, 'was an extraordinary scarce time for hay. Many cattle in the country were lost and many others brought very low, and the summer after was the scarcest time for corn that ever I knew.'

* Parish records.   † M. Plant.   ‡ Town records.
§ Reverend Mr. Parkman's manuscripts.   ‖ Honorable Bailey Bartlet's almanacs.

March 15*th.*   Humphrey Richards was chosen sexton of the first parish in Newbury, a post which he occupied without interruption till his death in March, 1785, a period of forty-eight years.   His successor was Moses Short, who was annually chosen to the same office, from 1789, till a short time before his death, July sixth, 1841, a period of nearly fifty-two years.

June 15*th.*   The general court impowered the inhabitants of the first parish to support a grammar school, and exempted them from paying elsewhere.

August 10*th.*   On this day the assembly of New Hampshire met at Hampton falls, and that of Massachusetts, at Salisbury.   A large cavalcade was formed at Boston, which with a troop of horse escorted the governor.   At Newbury ferry he was met by another troop, and at the supposed divisional line between the states by three more, who escorted him with great pomp to the George tavern in Hampton falls, where he held a council and made a speech to the New Hampshire assembly.   The object, which both assemblies had in view in thus meeting within five miles of each other, was to settle the line, a subject, which had created great interest in both provinces.   The governor's cavalcade occasioned the following pasquinade.

> ' Dear paddy you never did behold such a sight,
> As yesterday morning was seen before night.
> You, in all your born days saw, nor I neither,
> So many fine horses and men ride together.
> At the head, the lower house trotted two in a row,
> Then all the higher house pranced after the low.
> Then the governor's coach galloped on like the wind,
> And the last that came foremost were the troopers behind.
> But I fears it means no good to your neck, nor mine,
> For they say tis to fix a right place for the line.' *

From November seventeenth, 1735, to October sixth, 1737, one hundred and ninety-nine persons died with the throat distemper in Haverhill, Massachusetts.

'*December* 7*th.*   A little before eleven at night the earth quaked very much.' †

1738.

The regular increase of the mercantile interest among ' the water side people,' especially in ship building, and the consequent addition to the population, not only from other parts of the country, but from Europe, made it extremely inconvenient for the congregationalists to worship either in the first or second parish, or for the episcopalians to worship in Queen Anne's chapel, ' on the plains.'   The former, as has been noticed, had erected their house of worship in the centre of business, as early as 1725, and had been obliged to make what had been a breadth of forty-five feet, a length of eighty feet in 1736, and though a portion of the latter had, according

* Belknap.   † M. Plant.

to a statement made by Mr. Plant in his diary, begun to agitate the subject of building a new church on a more convenient spot, as early as 1725, nothing effectual was done till this year, when saint Paul's church was erected on the spot, which its successor now occupies. The same cause, which induced many of the builders of the congregational meeting-house on the plains, to become episcopalians, and to name their house of worship, Queen Anne's chapel, namely, the distance they had to travel, soon produced a division among themselves. The original founders of the society, who had been unwilling to go 'to meeting,' up river as far as Pipestave hill, were equally unwilling to go 'to church,' down river as far as Market street, while the 'water-side people' had objections equally valid against worshiping at 'the plains.'

They, therefore, as soon as practicable, took the necessary steps to obviate the difficulty. 'Joseph Atkins, esquire, offered to give fifty pounds towards building a new church by the water side and I,' says Mr. Plant, 'proposed to give the same sum. Here was laid the foundation of a new church,' and so forth, which, though raised in 1738, was not sufficiently finished for public worship till 1740. In February, 1742, eleven persons gave Mr. Plant a written invitation to preach at saint Paul's church. This, with the consent of the people at 'the plains,' he agreed to do, every other Sunday, but in December, regret having been expressed, that such an invitation had been given to Mr. P., a vote was passed, that he should deliver up the instrument, inviting him down from queen Ann's chapel. This was accordingly done, April twenty-first, 1743, and virtually excluded him from saint Paul's church. The contest now, was between Mr. Plant and the water side people, they desiring to manage the affairs of saint Paul's church in their own way, independent of him, and he, on the other hand, demanding, that they should give him induction into saint Paul's church. This they refused to give, and the difficulty thus commenced, was not settled till June twenty-fourth, 1751, when, in the language of the reverend doctor Morss, 'the independence of the gentlemen at the water side was relinquished and Mr. P. was legally inducted into saint Paul's church.' In his private diary, of which I have a copy, he details with great minuteness, all the difficulties between himself and the water side people, in letters to doctor Bearcroft, which are very interesting, but of which we have no room, even for an abstract. He appears to have been a man of strict integrity, and great benevolence, and encountered the difficulties which beset him, with firmness and discretion. On December twenty-third, 1751, he made choice of Mr. Edward Bass, to assist him in the work of the ministry, and died April second, 1753, aged sixty-one, having officiated from April, 1722, a period of thirty-one years.

February 26th. On this day a council was called, in the second parish, to take into consideration 'the distressed state and condition of ye second church of Christ in Newbury by reason of their reverend pastor Mr. John Tufts being charged by a woman or women of his indecent carriage and also of his abusive and unchristian behavior towards them at several times and so forth.' *

The council, consisting of ten ministers and twenty delegates, met, but Mr. Tufts refused to unite with the council, vehemently opposed the swearing of the witnesses against him, and in this unsettled state of affairs, he asked and obtained a dismission from the church and people, March second, the church refusing to recommend him as a christian minister, and stating, among other things, that, as Mr. T. had never been admitted a member of the second church, a recommendation and dismission from the church would not be proper.

May 18*th.* The town granted permission to Joseph Atkins, and sixty-four others, to build a wharf at the foot of Queen street, now Market street.

This year there was published in Boston, a pamphlet of seventeen pages of rhyme, concerning the ravages of the throat distemper. The two following verses are a sufficient specimen.

> To *Newbury* O go and see
> To *Hampton* and *Kingston*
> To *York* likewise and *Kittery*
> Behold what God hath done.
>
> The bow of God is bent abroad
> Its arrows swiftly fly
> Young men and maids and sucking babes
> Are smitten down thereby.

1739.

January 10*th,* was the first snow this winter that lay.

January 31*st.* Reverend Thomas Barnard ordained pastor of the second church and parish in Newbury. At this time, the church contained two hundred and twenty members.

April 11*th.* Mr. William Coker, of Newbury, and Mr. Samuel Green, of Boston, were drowned in Merrimac river.

August 2*d,* about half past two, a great shock of the earthquake.†

December 9*th.* No ice on Merrimac river, no frost in the ground.

December 29*th.* The town chose two persons 'to prosecute any person, who should kill any buck, doe or fawn contrary to law.'

December 29*th.* General court passed a law, restraining cattle and horses from going on Plum island, under a penalty, forbidding the cutting of bushes, and so forth.

1740.

In May, Mr. Samuel Long, of Newbury, buried his wife and four children, (all his family,) with the 'throat distemper.'

---

* **Letter missive.**   † **M. Plant.**

September 10*th.* The reverend George Whitefield preached on this day, for the first time in Newbury. At one of his subsequent addresses, in front of the meeting-house, which then stood on the east side of High street, a few rods south of Federal street, a stone was thrown at him, which nearly struck the bible from his hand. His answer to this unprovoked assault, was the following. ' I have a warrant from God to preach. His seal, (holding up the bible,) is in my hand and I stand in the King's high way.' *

The summer and fall of this year, were as remarkable for the rain, which fell and flooded the country, as the subsequent winter was, for the severity of the cold. It was probably the most severe winter ever known, since the settlement of the country. Reverend Mr. Plant, Stephen Jaques, honorable Nathaniel Coffin, and many others, recorded some of the most remarkable events that occurred, from which I shall make a few extracts.

' The summer of 1740 was a wet summer. In October gathered our corn, one third very green. We could not let it stand by reason of rain. On November fourth, the winter set in very cold. On the fifteenth a foot of snow fell, about the twenty-second of the month it began to rain and it rained three weeks together. The stars in the evening seemed as bright as ever, but the next morning rain again, which occasioned a freshet in Merrimack river, the like was not known by no man for seventy years. It rose fifteen feet at Haverhill and floated off many houses. It was said that a sloop might pass between Emery's mill and his house, and that the water was twelve feet deep on Rawson's meadow at Turkey hill.' †

' It washed away all the wood and timber for building of ships so that for fourteen days every inhabitant was fishing for wood in the river. It was commonly supposed that upwards of two thousand cords were taken up on Plum island.' ‡

' Our corn,' says Stephen Jaques, ' moulded as fast as six hogs could eat it.'

' *December* 12*th.* The river was shut up again by the severity of the weather. Before the first of January loaded teams passed from Haverhill, Newbury, Newtown, Amesbury, sometimes twenty, thirty, forty in a day having four, six, eight oxen in a team and landed below the upper long wharf nigh to the ferry. People ran upon the ice for several days to half tide rock. Shipping was all froze in and this severity extended to New York government. On December fourteenth about thirty-five minutes past six there was a loud noise of the earthquake.' ‡

1741.

' January tenth there was a thaw, which held three days. January eighteenth about four A. M. and on January twenty-fifth about

---

* Reverend S. P. William's historical discourse. † Stephen Jaques.
‡ Reverend M. Plant.

ten minutes before four P. M. there was an earthquake. February third about a foot more of snow fell, February ninth another great snow, and on February — another. In February the streets were full of snow to the top of the fences and in some places eight or ten feet deep. The river all the time was frozen over to colonel Pierce's farm. March twenty-eighth the sleighing was good on the river to colonel Peirce's farm and Plum island. April seventh there fell about a foot of snow so there now lay about four feet deep in the woods. From December fifth 1740 till March twenty-seventh 1741 Plum island river was frozen over. On the nineteenth and twentieth of March the river was frozen to the lower end of Seal island. In Plum island river the ice broke about thirtieth of March. There were twenty-seven snows this winter, the hardest winter that ever was known.' 'The people of Newbury had the principal part of their corn ground at Salisbury mills. From February third till March thirty-first Pearson's mill was stopped by the ice. February twenty-eighth the ice at Deer island the strongest place of the tide was thirty inches thick.'

Some time this year, commenced in this county and town, the remarkable revival of religion, which, commenced under the preaching of the reverend Jonathan Edwards, in 1735, and continued by Whitefield, Tennent, and many others, agitated not only New England, but the whole country. An accurate account of the 'great awakening' in this vicinity, the effects of which are to this day everywhere visible, would require a volume. To other sources, therefore, must the inquisitive reader look, on this interesting subject. The following hitherto unpublished letter, will doubtless gratify some of my readers.

'To Nathaniel Coffin, esquire, at Newbury.

Kittery, October 14th, 1741.

'Honored Sir,
    'This may inform you that we had a comfortable time home and found all in health.
    'But the chief design is to give you a short representation of the mighty work of God at York. The reverend Mr. Willard of Biddeford took a journey the last week up as far as our town to visit the brethren and see how they did, preached at every town as he came; on Tuesday twice at York, on Wednesday at our parish from these words: 'Lo they that are far from thee shall perish,' showed very plainly in what respects we were far from God and the certainty of our perishing, if taken away in that state: some few only much affected. Upon his return to York on Thursday he preached from Hebrews third, seventh and eighth verses: 'wherefore (as the Holy Ghost saith) to-day, if ye will hear his voice, harden not your hearts, as in the provocation, in the day of temptation in the wilderness.' Where God was pleased in a most wonderful manner to set home his word by his spirit on the hearts of the hearers. Being much desired to preach to them on Friday and Saturday, he did with the same power and the same influence of the spirit of God accompanying his sermons. Mr. Moody seeing that God had so blest his preaching at York desired him to tarry the sabbath which he did and preached three sermons on said day, the blessing still following. Mr. Moody supplied Mr. Willard's pulpit. The news reached us on Saturday night. On Monday Mr. Rogers with thirty or forty of his hearers went to York to see this marvellous work, father Bartlett and myself in company (to my great amaze and surprize) for the one half was not told us,

neither indeed is it possible for my pen to express it to you. A universal concern about their souls and what they shall do to be saved. More than forty that no doubt are truly converted, about thirty of whom have received comfort and are full of the love of God and Christ, perfectly in a rapture of joy being in full assurance of faith, whose mouths are filled with praises to God and the riches of his free grace in Christ manifested so clearly to them. Most of them young persons under twenty-five and down to the age of five and six years. Some middle aged and a few old persons. To hear these little children of six, seven and eight years old talk so powerfully, wonderfully and experimentally of the things of God and Christ and particularly of the doctrine of free grace is unaccountable were it not truly by the spirit and power of the Almighty. The finger of the Lord is most certainly in this matter.

'It would be almost endless to give you a particular account of those I talked with, both of those new converts and also of them under strong and hopeful conviction. The like was never seen in New England. The conversion of those at Northampton [1734, 5 and 6,] according to Mr. Edwards' account is not comparable to this. The Lord is pleased to make quick work of it. Some convinced, humbled to the dust and converted in a minute, others in an hour — others in a night and others longer — to see them under convictions and in such an extraordinary concern, so that the most acute or most sharp pain of body that ever I saw is any way comparable to it — and how should it be, since Solomon tells us that the spirit of a man sustaineth his infirmity, but a wounded spirit, who can bear — they are indeed pricked in their heart and cry out what shall we do. They admit of no meat, drink or sleep till they find rest for their souls in Christ.

' Mr. Rogers preached to a very numerous congregation on the same day at York and the spirit accompanied his sermon as well as Mr. Willard's. Three persons in particular that were mocking and scoffing on sabbath evening were wonderfully convinced at this sermon — altho' there was not the least terror in it, but altogether on comfort and joy. Mr. Rogers, as he expressed, had a far more clear manifestation of the love of God upon his own soul than ever he had before. He was moved to preach upon this text in the eleventh chapter of Acts and twenty-third verse, 'who when he came and had seen the grace of God was glad;' and exhorted them all, that with purpose of heart they would cleave unto the Lord.

' May God of his infinite mercy and free grace visit our town and yours with the like influence of his holy spirit and the whole land and world of mankind, which is the prayer and heart's desire of your dutiful son,

EDMUND COFFIN.

' Love and duty and respects to all as due.

' P. S. Young Mr. Moody, 't is thought, will come speedily out of his dark and despairing condition in this day of God's mighty power and visitation. He is become very rational in his discourse, and mightily composed in his mind to what he hath been for these four years past, and 't is to be hoped will shortly appear strong in the cause of Christ.'

1742.

' *March 27th*, a quarter before 7 A. M. the noise of the earthquake was very loud, but it did not make any shaking, as I could perceive, although I was alone and seated in my little house. One thing I took notice of namely, at all times before, when we heard the noise, which way our faces were, that way the noise always seemed to be, but now the noise seemed to be behind me, and my family took notice of it that the noise seemed to be behind them.'*

* Reverend M. Plant.

This was indeed a phenomenon, which the observer could not explain, and on which the compiler does not feel competent to make any comments.

‘ *September* 13*th,* about half past five an earthquake.’ *

This year, the excitement on the subject of religion, which had for some time prevailed over a large part of New England, was evidently, in this region, on the increase. Every church, and every parish, was more or less affected, and in some places to a degree, of which the present generation can have but a faint idea. In a letter to doctor Bearcroft, of March second, 1742, reverend Mr. Plant thus writes. ‘ I do not know but before these six months to come most of my hearers will leave me for all the country near me is taken with this new scheme (as they call it.) Within one month fifty-three have been taken into communion in one dissenting meeting house. Some of them belonged to another meeting house, and the dissenting teacher not approving of said scheme they forsook him to [attend] at the other meeting house.’ In another letter, of July twenty-third, he says, ‘ in my last to you I hinted to you something of the commotion that the new scheme of methodism made amongst us. I was under a great surprize at the time, for I thought that all my people would be withdrawn from church, for they began to flock after the itinerants and told me in a full body that if they did not get good by them it was because they had bad hearts, but how strangely is the scene changed.’

In the Boston Evening Post, of May third, is an anonymous article, charging ‘ the reverend N. Rogers of Ipswich, Mr. Daniel Rogers and Mr. Buel, candidates for the ministry with having come into Newbury formed a party and taken possession of Mr. Lowell’s meeting house without his knowledge, or asking leave of the proprietors of the house, or the consent of the church or congregation and so forth and that an attempt of the like factious nature was made upon the reverend Mr. Toppan’s meeting house, but Mr. Toppan being present the party was repulsed,’ and so forth.

This article caused a reply from Mr. John Brown, dated May seventh, denying the truth of part of the charges, and then another article, of May twenty-second, signed J. Lowell, affirming the truth of the first statements. This caused another reply from Mr. Brown, in the Boston Gazette, dated June twenty-ninth, and two other articles, signed Henry Rolfe, Abraham Titcomb, and Humphrey Richards. To these papers I refer the curious reader for further information, merely observing, that I have not the space to give even the title pages of the sermons, dialogues, tracts, and so forth, on religious subjects, with which the neighborhood was filled.

‘ Since my last of July 1742,’ says Mr. Plant, February fifteenth, 1743, ‘ a new meeting house was built by the new schemers.’ This must have been the meeting-house in High street, just below Federal street, where the presbyterian society first worshiped.

* Reverend M. Plant.

1743.

May 16*th.* 'Town chose a committee to consult about building a work house, and to build a powder house.'

'*August* 10*th*, about five P. M. a pretty loud shock of the earthquake.' *

'About the twenty-sixth of June the worms came upon the corn and eat the grass in ye low ground, and did much damage. Many people saved their corn by ditching. They lasted about eight or ten days and went away as strangely as they came.' †

'*October* 15*th.* An exceeding high tide, which did much damage.'†

December 13*th.* Town voted to sell all the old law books belonging to the town, to the highest bidder. Also to build a gaol and a work house.

In this year, a large number of the members of the churches, under the pastoral care of the reverend Mr. Lowell and the reverend Mr. Toppan, separated from them, and, soon after, formed another church, after having had a long controversy, both oral and written, with their respective pastors, without coming on either side to any satisfactory result. Having a transcript of all the letters to and from the reverend Mr. Toppan, I copy the following as a specimen.

'The reverend Mr. Toppan's conduct in this remarkable day of divine visitation having occasioned great uneasiness in his church and parish, divers, who were aggrieved thereat from time to time went to discourse him on divers matters, till at length he declared he would talk no more with them and that if any were uneasy they should write to him and he would answer them by writing, whereupon divers who were aggrieved met together and wrote a letter to him, containing the matters of their grievances, which Mr. Toppan hearing of sent the following letter.

'*Newbury, June* 10*th*, 1743.

'To Charles Pierce esquire in Newbury.
    'Sir,
    'I have been informed that some yt are called schemers, by others new light men (for Satan being now especially transformed into an angel of light hath transformed his followers into his likeness in regard of the new light they pretend unto) have drawn up some articles against me, some respecting my doctrine, taught in publick, some respecting my belief in several articles of religion, and some respecting my practices and I have been told you have the original by you. I have long desired to see it, but could never yet obtain it. This is therefore to desire of you to send me the original, or a copy of it attested, for I am obliged to go to York superior court ye next week and would carry it with me to shew to the superior judges for their judgment upon the whole as to my doctrines whether they be right or no, for which I purpose to carry my sermons reflected upon, as to my principles whether they be right or no, (though in the paper before mentioned I believe there are many things false, for I never yet knew a schemer that would not lie.) As to my practices whether right or no, I shall leave them to judge and determine. I purpose to carry with me a copy of what I now send to you to shew it to them; if you answer not my request in sending me the original or an attested copy.
        Sir, I am yours to serve in what I may,
            CHRISTOPHER TOPPAN.'

---

* M. Plant.   † Stephen Jaques.

1744.

February 7th. The town voted to give the county a piece of land, on which to build a prison and prison keeper's house, which were this year built in Federal street.

' *May* 13*th*, in the morning, and on May sixteenth at a quarter past eleven A. M. there was an earthquake.'

June 2*d.* War was proclaimed at Boston, by England against France.

' *June* 3*d.* Sabbath a quarter past ten we had a terrible shock of the earthquake. It made the earth so shake that it made myself and many others run out of the church.' *

June 28*th.* Public fast, and in the evening an earthquake. *

This summer, the society of friends in Newbury, erected a meeting-house in what is now called Belleville. It is thirty-five feet in length, and twenty-five in breadth, and is now used as a vestry for the congregational society there, the friends having erected a new meeting-house, near Turkey hill.

July 24*th.* The aggrieved brethren of the first church, having been unable to come to any satisfactory result, in their controversy with Mr. Toppan, an ex parte council of eight churches was this day held in Newbury, to examine the charges against him, which were nine in number, and which, having been written June seventh, had been presented to Mr. T. June tenth, 1743. The council, in their report, justify the aggrieved brethren, and condemn Mr. Toppan, and advise the aggrieved brethren ' to hearken to any reasonable method, whereby your final separation from the church and parish may be prevented,' and conclude by saying, that ' however we utterly disapprove of unnecessary separations as partaking of great guilt and accompanied with great scandal, yet looking upon your circumstances as extraordinary and deplorable we cannot think you blameworthy, if with good advice you seek more wholesome food for your souls and put yourselves under the watch of a shepherd, in whom you can confide.'

August 31*st.* This day, another ex parte council met in Newbury, called by the friends of Mr. Toppan, the charges against whom they examined, and in their result, acquit him of nearly all the allegations contained in them, and censure the aggrieved brethren for their ' disorderly walking and advise them to return to the bosom of the church and to the pastoral care of him, who has been so faithful and useful a pastor over you for near fifty years,' and so forth.

November 7*th.* Captain Donahew sailed from Newbury, in a small privateer, belonging to Boston, with sixty men, took a sloop with live stock eight days after he sailed, and in three days after, at Newfoundland, took a French ship with three thousand quintals of fish, and so forth.

* M. Plant.

1745.

In the reverend Thomas Smith's journal, I find the following.

'*February* 2*d*. Great talk about Whitefield's preaching, and the fleet to cape Breton.' These two subjects, war and religion, were at this time in every body's mouth. The enthusiasm in favor of the expedition against Louisburg was extraordinary, and almost unanimous, whilst on the subject of the religious tenets and practices of Whitefield and his adherents, the community was divided, and almost every man was either an ardent advocate, or a decided opponent. The consequence of this state of things, was divisions and contentions in all the churches, and many years elapsed before the storm became a calm. In the midst of this excitement, news came that Louisburg had been taken by the New England troops, June sixteenth. In the reduction of this place, which was one of the most remarkable events in the history of North America, a large number of Newbury soldiers were engaged. Among the most noted of these, was major Moses Titcomb. Of him Hutchinson thus speaks. 'Major Titcomb's readiness to engage in the most hazardous part of the service, was acknowledged and applauded. He survived the siege, was colonel of a regiment when general Johnson was attacked by Dieskau, and there lost his life in the service of his country. Of the five fascine batteries that were erected in the reduction of Louisburg, the last, which was erected the twentieth of May and called Titcomb's battery, having five forty-two pounders, did as great execution as any.' Among the natives of Newbury, who were engaged in that memorable siege, was the reverend Samuel Moody, of York, who went as chaplain, and so confident was he of success, that he took with him a hatchet, to cut the images in the catholic churches. Moses Coffin, afterward of Epping, was also there, and officiated in the double capacity of drummer and chaplain, a 'drum-ecclesiastic.' On returning to the camp after one engagement, he found a bullet had passed nearly through a small pocket bible, which he always carried with him, and which in this case was the means of saving his life. This incident I give on the authority of the honorable William Plumer, senior, of Epping, New Hampshire.

November 10*th*. Reverend John Tucker was settled as colleague with the reverend doctor Toppan. Of the difficulties which preceded, attended, and followed his settlement, something will be said hereafter.

The difficulties still continuing, and rather increasing, in the first church and parish, between the reverend Mr. Toppan and his people, notwithstanding all the attempts that had been made to satisfy both parties, the parish voted, May eleventh, to concur with the church in setting 'apart a day to be kept by solemn prayer and fasting to seek to heaven for a blessing on our endeavours in calling a pious and orthodox man to assist in the ministry.'

'*July* 16*th*. Mr. John Tucker was called to the work of the ministry by the first church and parish in Newbury,' which, after long and anxious deliberation, he accepted, and was ordained November twentieth. This, however, was not effected without great opposition, the majority in the parish in his favor being twelve, and that in the church being two. The minority sent in to the ordaining council, a long but unavailing protest against his ordination. On December twentieth, they sent a letter to the first church, which concludes in these words.

'Wherefore brethren on these considerations, for the peace of our consciences, our spiritual edification and the honor and interest of religion as we think, we do now withdraw communion from you and shall look upon ourselves no longer subjected to your watch and discipline, but shall, agreeable to ye advice given us, speedily as we may, seek us a pastor, who is likely to feed us with knowledge and understanding and in whom we can with more reason confide.

'And now brethren that the God of a full light and truth would lead both you and us into the knowledge of all truth as it is in Jesus, is and shall be the desire and prayer of your brethren, and so forth.

CHARLES PIERCE, and twenty-two others.

Difficulties somewhat similar also occurred in the church and parish under the pastoral care of the reverend John Lowell, which resulted in the withdrawal of 'a considerable number of persons' from the society. This induced the church, on May first, 1743, to vote 'to keep the eleventh of May as a day of fasting and prayer upon this sad occasion.' * From their church records I extract the following.

'May eleventh, 1743, was observed as a day of fasting and prayer in pursuance of the vote above. The same day the separatists held a public assembly in Mr. John Brown's barn in Mr. Toppan's parish at which deacon Beck was present.'

The barn here mentioned, stood in the field nearly opposite to Mr. Silas Noyes's house. Long and able letters ·to and from the reverend John Lowell, of the following dates, October thirty-first, November first, November fourth, December sixteenth, 1743, and January third, 1744, are now on file among the state records, Boston.

1746.

January 3*d*. This day, nineteen of the persons, who, on the twentieth of the last month, had formally withdrawn from the first church, formed the presbyterian church. In their petition to the general court, are these words :

'After this on the third of January 1746 we embodyed into a church and entered into a covenant, whereof we gave the church notice by letter under our hands of the twenty-second of the same month and then proceeded to give the reverend Mr. Jonathan Parsons a call to the ministerial office,' and so forth.

* Third church records.

March 28th. The separate brethren, thirty-eight in number, who had for nearly three years withdrawn from the communion of the third church, petitioned for a dismission and recommendation to the presbyterian church. This the church refused to grant. On April sixth, a committee of the 'separatists' sent a petition to the church, commencing thus, 'reverend and beloved in those points of christianity wherein we can agree,' desiring the church to favor them with 'the reasons for not granting their request.' * This was of no avail, and they were finally admitted to the new church without a recommendation.

The following is the covenant of the presbyterian church.

'We the subscribing brethren, who were members of the first church in Newbury, and have thought it our duty to withdraw therefrom, do also look upon it our duty to enter into a church estate; specially as we apprehend this may be for the glory of God, and the interest of the Redeemer's kingdom, as well as for our own mutual edification and comfort.

'We do therefore, as we trust, in the fear of God, mutually covenant and agree to walk together as a church of Christ according to the rules and order of the gospel.

'In testimony whereof we have hereunto set our hands and seals this third day of January, 1746.

CHARLES PIERCE,	THOMAS PIKE,
MOSES BRADSTREET,	DANIEL WELLS,
EDWARD PRESBURY,	JOSEPH HIDDEN,
JOHN BROWN,	NATHANIEL ATKINSON, junior,
RICHARD HALL,	JONATHAN PLUMMER,
BENJAMIN KNIGHT,	DANIEL GOODWIN,
WILLIAM BROWN,	SILVANUS PLUMER,
BENJAMIN PIERCE,	SAMUEL HALL,
DANIEL NOYES,	CUTTING PETTINGELL.'
MAJOR GOODWIN,	

January 14th. The parish of Byfield voted to build a new meeting-house, fifty-six feet long and forty-five feet wide, which was completed the next summer.

March 6th. First parish voted five hundred pounds, old tenor, to reverend John Tucker, to build a house.

' *August 2d,* just before sunrise, there was a considerable loud and long earthquake.' †

' *August 21st and 22d,* there was a heavy frost.' †

September 10th. A fleet of nearly forty ships of war, besides transports, bringing between three and four thousand troops, with veteran officers, and all kinds of military stores, under the command of the duke d'Anville, arrived from France, in order to retake Louisburg. This attempt, however, in consequence of a violent storm, on September first, and a variety of remarkable incidents, was rendered entirely abortive, to the great joy of the people of New England.

' *October 17th.* Friday about nine A. M. it began to snow and continued snowing until three P. M. the next day. I and my wife went to church in the sleigh and it was very good sleighing, the snow being two feet upon the level and lasted four days.' †

* Third church records.   † M. Plant.

1747.

'*January* 6*th*, about midnight there was an earthquake.' *

'*February* 6*th*. Three deer went through Stephen Morse's land in the west parish of Newbury and disappeared in Amesbury.' †

'*December* 3*d*, at half past four P. M. and on December sixth at four P. M. there was an earthquake. *

1748.

March 8*th*. The town granted to John Crocker, on his petition, liberty to erect a rope walk 'along by the windmill and to improve said place for ten years for making of ropes and for no other use.' ‡

NOTE. The wind mill stood near where the south brick school house now stands by Frog pond, and was erected in 1703. This rope walk was probably the first which was established in Newbury, and stood on the margin of the pond.

'*March* 11*th*, about a quarter before seven A. M. there was an earthquake.' *

This year no rain fell from the last of May till August first.

October 7*th*. Peace was established between England and France, at Aix la Chapelle. By this treaty, Louisburg was restored to the French.

November 5*th*. Charles Pierce and one hundred and twenty-five others, petitioned the general court to be freed from paying taxes to the first and third parishes.

November 10*th*. Governor Shirley, having received the petition, says, among other things, 'I am always averse to any thing grievous upon any people on account of their religious sentiments. I desire you would once take this *repeated* application of the petitioners into your serious consideration.' The petition was not granted.

1749.

March 4*th*. Mr. Joseph Coffin was chosen town clerk.

June 1*st*. One hundred and seventy-nine persons belonging to Mr. Parsons's society, petitioned the general court to be freed from paying taxes to the first and third parishes. August eleventh, having heard the answers of the first and third parishes, they dismissed the petition *nem. con.*

This summer there was a very severe drought. This, attended as it was with swarms of caterpillars, and other devouring insects, caused great distress in New England. 'Many brooks and springs were dried up.' Not more than a tenth of the usual crop of hay was cut, and much was imported from Pennsylvania and England. 'I mowed,' says Richard Kelly, 'several days and could not cut

* M. Plant.   † S. Morse's manuscripts.   ‡ Town records.

more than two hundred pounds a day, and people were fain to kill abundance of cattle because they could not get hay to winter them.'

October 29*th*. Reverend Thomas Barnard resigned his pastoral office, in the second church and parish.

The winter of 1749–50 was a very severe one. Cattle had to be browsed in the woods.

1750.

January 18*th*. Town authorized Daniel Farnham, esquire, to prefer a petition to the general court, for a lottery, to build a bridge over the river Parker.' *

April 1*st*. Province bills, first issued in 1702, ceased to pass. This currency was called 'old tenor.' In 1748, there were three kinds of bills : old tenor, which passed at seven and a half for one; that is, seven shillings and sixpence in bills, was equal to one shilling lawful; middle, or three fold tenor, and new tenor. The redemption of the old tenor bills, occasioned the celebrated Joseph Greene to write a poem, entitled, ' a mournful lamentation for the sad and deplorable death of Mr. Old Tenor, a native of New England, who after a long confinement by a deep and mortal wound, which he received about twelve months before, expired on the thirty-first of March 1750.'

' The winter of 1750–51 was remarkably mild.'

May 20*th*. ' The third church voted nemine contradicente that the scriptures be read in publick the Lord's day.' †

1751.

February 20*th*. Reverend Moses Hale ordained pastor of the second church and parish.

March 12*th*. Several citizens of the town petitioned, that 'several ways and landing places might be confirmed to the town.' This the proprietors' committee opposed, declaring that the town had no power to act in the affair. Here commenced a contest between the town and the proprietors, which was finally settled in favor of the latter, in 1826.

March 22*d*, 1751. Third parish ' voted to choose one or more parsons to take care of the boyes that plays at meeting.' ‡

' 1745, *October* 28*th*. Ephraim Lunt was chosen,' in the first parish, ' to set in the gallery to and take special care that ye boys do not play in service time and correct those boys that do not give due attention,' and so forth.

1752.

' *March* 27*th*. Town voted to build for the use of the town a house near the upper end of Plum island.' *

---

* **Town records.** † Church records. ‡ Third parish records.

This winter was a very cold one.

This year the British parliament made an alteration in the style. From 'Job Shepherd's almanack,' published in Newport, by James Franklin, I make the following extract.

'Kind reader,

'You have now such a year as you never saw before, nor ever will see hereafter. The king and parliament have thought proper to enact that the month of September 1752 shall contain but nineteen days so that we are not to have two beginnings to our years, but the first of January is to be the first day and first month of the year 1752. Eleven days are taken from September and begin one Tuesday, two Wednesday and fourteen Thursday. Be not much astonished, nor look with concern, dear reader, at such a deduction of days, nor regret as for the loss of so much time, but take this for your consolation that your expences will appear lighter and your mind be more at ease. And what an indulgence is here for those, who love their pillows, to lie down in peace on the second of this month and not perhaps awake, or be disturbed till the fourteenth in the morning. Now, reader, since 't is likely you may never have such another year, nor such another almanack, I would advise you to improve the one for your own sake, and recommend the other for the sake of your friend,

POOR JOB.'

'*May* 26*th*. Proprietors lease to Jonathan Pearson for twelve years all the stream of water from Rowley line to Peter Cheney's grant, (which was made fifteenth February 1687) on condition he would grind for Newbury before he would for other towns.'

'*May* 7*th*, 1752. The members of the second church in Newbury met to deal with our brother Richard Bartlet for the following reasons.

'First, our said brother refuses communion with the church for no other reason but because the pastor wears a wigg, and because the church justifies him in it, setting up his own opinion in opposition to the church, contrary to that humility, which becomes a christian.

'Second, and farther in an unchristian manner he censures and condemns both pastor and church as anti-christian on the aforesaid account and he sticks not from time to time to assert with the greatest assurance that all who wear wiggs, unless they repent of that particular sin before they die will certainly be damned, which we judge to be a piece of uncharitable and sinful rashness.'

This opposition to wigs was not peculiar to Mr. Bartlet, though he was probably one of the last, who took so decided a stand against that article of dress. From their first introduction in New England, till the tyranny of fashion had sanctioned their almost universal use, the wearing of wigs had been violently opposed by our fathers, who considered the manner of wearing the hair, as a subject of grave and serious consequence. In many places in judge Sewall's diary, he alludes to this subject. I make a few extracts.

'1685, *September* 15*th*. Three admitted to the church, two wore periwigs.'

'1696. Mr. Sims told me of the assaults he had made on periwigs, seemed to be in good sober sadness.'

' 1697. Mr. Noyes of Salem wrote a treatise on periwigs,' and so forth.

' 1704, *January.* Walley appears in his wig having cut off his own hair.'

' 1708, *August* 20*th.* Mr. Cheever died. The welfare of the province was much upon his heart. *He abominated periwigs.*'

The venerable John Elliot, the apostle to the Indians, believed that the sufferings endured by the people of Massachusetts in Philip's war, were inflicted on them as a judgment from heaven for wearing wigs!

Even the members of the society of friends, were troubled with the wig question. From the minutes of the monthly meeting, I make the following extracts.

' 1721, *November* 16*th.* At this meeting we received an account from ye quarterly meeting, in which we are desired to consider the wearing of wigges and give in our judgment at the next quarterly meeting to be held at Salem.'

' 1721, *December* 21*st.* Hampton. The matter above mentioned consarning ye wearing of wigges was discoursed and it was concluded by this meeting *yt ye wearing of extravegent superflues wigges is altogether contrary to truth.*'

1753.

' *March* 13*th.* Town granted the petition of Nathan Hale and others about a fire engine.'

' *May* 23*d.* Town granted liberty to Samuel Titcomb and John Harris to build a substantial engine to weigh hay to stand where the old engine stood, near the head of Fish street.'

1754.

' *March* 12*th.* Town voted to build a powder house.'

' *September* 19*th.* The town taking into consideration the bill entitled an act for granting to his majesty an excise upon wines and spirits distilled and sold by retail or consumed in this province, voted that they are of opinion that that part of said bill, which relates to the consumption of distilled spirits in private families (which was referred to the consideration of the towns) *is an infringement on the natural rights of Englishmen* and ought not to pass into a law,' and so forth.

1755.

' *January* 21*st.* Town voted, first, that the town will act on an act lately made relating to an excise on the private consumption of distilled spirits, wines, lemons, limes and oranges.

' Second, voted that the petitioners namely captain Michael Dalton and others and any other gentlemen, who are willing to join them should on their own cost and charge apply home in order to prevent said acts obtaining the royal assent.'

'*May* 22*d.* Reverend John Lowell preached a sermon from Deuteronomy 20 : 4 at Newbury at the desire and in the audience of colonel Moses Titcomb and many others enlisted with him in an expedition against the French,' at Crown point, where he was slain, September eighth. ' In the battle of lake George he commanded his regiment on the extreme right wing of general Johnson's line. He got behind a large pine tree about one rod distant from the end of the breast work, where he could stand up and command his men, who were lying flat on the ground, and where he could have a better opportunity to use his own piece. Here he was insensibly flanked by a party of Indians, who crept around a large pine log, across a swamp about eighty yards distant, and shot him. Colonel Titcomb and lieutenant Baron stood behind the same tree and both fell at the same fire. This was about four o'clock in the afternoon of Monday the eighth of September 1755.'

The preceding particulars I give on the authority of Mr. Henry Stevens, junior. In the preface to a funeral sermon preached on the occasion, by the reverend John Lowell, from Joshua 1 : 2, he says, ' being more especially called to take notice of colonel Titcomb's death, and in a religious way publickly to improve it, as he was one of the church under my pastoral care, and his family and relations are with us : and as many had their friends gone from my parish under him, the following sermon in the height of our passionate resentment of the affecting providence, I hastily composed and preached immediately after the news of it; as what I then thought seasonable.'

By a census taken this year, Newbury had fifty slaves, negroes, and Indians; thirty-four males, and sixteen females.

November 1*st.* A great and destructive earthquake destroyed Lisbon.

' *November* 18*th*, about four o'clock A. M. was the most violent earthquake ever known in North America. It continued about four and a half minutes. In Boston, about one hundred chimneys were leveled with the roofs of the houses and about fifteen hundred, shattered and thrown down in part. There was a shock every day till the twenty-second.'

' *December* 19*th.* There were two or three shocks about ten P. M.' *

1756.

' *March* 11*th.* About three P. M. a small shock of earthquake.'

April 16*th.* A great gale of wind commenced, which lasted three and a half days. Sixteen vessels were lost. †

---

* Richard Kelly.   † Caleb Greenleaf's almanacs.

From May eighteenth till June nineteenth there was no rain.

The meeting-house now standing in Federal street was this year erected. From almanacs kept by Mr. Caleb Greenleaf, I make the following extracts.

'*July 5th.* We began to raise our meeting house and finished it the seventh, and not one oath heard and nobody hurt.' The house is one hundred feet long, by sixty broad.

' On the seventh the reverend John Morehead of Boston preached the first sermon in it from 2 Chronicles 7 : 12. The first sermon preached in our new meeting house was on August fifteenth. The text was the whole of the one hundred and twenty-second psalm.'

' *August* 19*th and* 20*th*, we pulled down our old meeting house.'

This house, as has been observed, stood on the easterly side of High, formerly Norfolk street, a few rods south of Federal street. From a letter to doctor Bearcroft, written February fifteenth, 1743, by the reverend M. Plant, it appears that it was erected in 1742. He says, ' *since* my last of July twenty-third 1742 a new house was built by the people called the new schemers and their dissenting teacher received fifty-three into their communion in one day of those, who are of their way of thinking.' The 'dissenting teacher' above mentioned, was the reverend Joseph Adams, who was afterward settled in Newington, New Hampshire.

October 2*d.* The number of quakers in Newbury, was, at this time, twenty-five men.*

' *November* 16*th*, at ten minutes before four A. M. there was an earthquake.' A remarkably open winter.†

1757.

January 13*th.* The town granted the petition of four persons, to build a grist and saw mill at Pine island.

' *July* 8*th*, at twenty minutes past two P. M. there was a small earthquake.'

1758.

This year, another difficulty occurred in the second parish. As the meeting-house, in consequence of the setting off of the fourth parish, in 1729, was no longer in a central place, and was very much dilapidated, the parish had voted, November thirtieth, 1756, to rebuild it at the ' southerly end' of Hanover street. In February and June, nineteen persons petitioned the general court to be set off from the second to the fourth parish, ' on account of distance, badness of the road, badness of the meeting house, and on account of a vote to remove the meeting house half a mile farther east.' They conclude a long petition in the following figurative strain.

' Thus your excellency and honors may justly see that we are afloat in an ocean of difficulty, and must unavoidably without your excellency and honor's

* Robert Adams's manuscripts. † Reverend Peter Coffin's almanacs.

interposition be wafted from our much desired church and congregation into
the bosom of our mother church, into which nothing but a long and tedious
quarrel, a shattered, doleful and uncomfortable house to worship our divine
master in, together with a total despair of being extricated out of our misery,
would bring us.'

May 23d. A committee was chosen by the town, 'to sell the
town's part of the prison house and land in Newbury, and to buy
or build a convenient house for the poor.'

The successes of the French, down to nearly the close of 1757,
had very much depressed and dispirited the colonies; but they
soon began to feel the effect of the energetic measures of the immortal Pitt, who, in the autumn of 1757, became prime minister of
Great Britain, the success or defeat of whose arms, especially in
North America, excited the deepest interest. July twenty-sixth,
Louisburg was taken. August twenty-seventh, fort Frontenac
surrendered, and, on November twenty-fifth, fort Du Quesne, afterward called fort Pitt, now Pittsburg, was wrested from the French.
In all these engagements, the New England people contributed their
full proportion; New Hampshire, Connecticut, and Massachusetts
furnishing fifteen thousand troops, of whom a large proportion went
from Newbury.

September 14th. There was a public thanksgiving, on account
of the reduction of cape Breton.

The bridge over the river Parker was erected this year.

1759.

This year, the British arms were triumphant in all their engagements in North America. July twenty-fourth, Niagara was taken,
and on the twenty-seventh, Ticonderoga, and when the news arrived
in Massachusetts, that, on September thirteenth, the army under
general Wolfe was victorious, on the plains of Abraham, and that,
on the eighteenth of the same month, Quebec had surrendered, the
joy and enthusiasm of the people seemed to know no bounds.

The citizens of Newbury had a day of rejoicing. An ox was
split and broiled on a huge gridiron, at the west end of the reverend
Mr. Lowell's meeting-house. Songs, commemorative of the victo-
ries of this year, were everywhere sung. Every stanza of one
of the songs, ended with the words, 'the year fifty-nine. So, deacon Benjamin Colman, aged ninety-two, now living, [December
twenty-third, 1844,] informs me, who saw the ox broiled, and re-
members the following lines of the song, which was then sung.

'De la C— had a squadron so nimble and light,
On meeting Boscawen like a Frenchman took fright;
But running too fast on some mighty design,
He lost both his legs in the year fifty-nine.

'With true British valour we broke every line,
And conquered Quebec in the year fifty-nine.'

March 13*th.* The town granted the petition of James Knight and nine others, 'to erect another engine to weigh hay near the head of Muzzey's lane,' now Marlborough street.

May 25*th.* The second parish commenced tearing down their old meeting-house, and this year raised their new meeting-house, which was fifty-four feet long and forty-four broad.

June 28*th.* 'A public fast on account of the expedition to Canada.'

July 8*th.* ' At a quarter past two there was an earthquake.'

August. The houses of Anthony Gwynn and Mr. Somerby, of Newbury, and Mr. Greenleaf, of Newbury new town, were struck with lightning.

September 10*th.* ' Mr. Samuel Pettingell fell from the steeple of the reverend Mr. Parson's meeting house, (which was this year erected) and was killed instantly.' *

October 25*th.* ' Public thanksgiving on account of the surrender of Quebec.'

In November of this year, the small-pox made its appearance on ' the plains,' so called, and was for some time called the eruptive fever.

Some time this year, Mr. Enoch Noyes, a self-taught mechanic, commenced, without instruction, making horn buttons and coarse combs, of various kinds, and continued the business till 1778, when he employed William Cleland, a deserter from Burgoyne's army, a comb-maker by profession, and a skillful workman. This was the commencement of the comb-making business in Newbury, and various other places.

1760.

' *February* 3*d,* at three o'clock A. M. there was an earthquake at Newbury.'

May 20*th.* The town acted on the petition of doctor Nathan Hale, and others, and voted that they would not repair or remove the town house, and, on May twenty-sixth, 'voted not to build a new town house.'

Pine island grist and saw mill erected this year.

May 21*st.* Twenty-two members of the ' old church,' namely, queen Ann's chapel, in consequence of the discontinuance of public worship in that building three sabbaths in every month, united with several others, in an agreement to build a new meeting-house, and again become congregationalists, for the same reason that some of their ancestors became episcopalians, namely, distance from the meeting-house, and petitioned the general court to form a new parish.

In July, the small-pox ceased in Newbury. During its continuance, the selectmen fenced in the infected district, from the school-house to Emery's hill, and sent to Boston for physicians and nurses,

---

* Mr. Caleb Greenleaf's almanacs.

29

who, as the custom then was, greatly aggravated the disease, by shutting up the sick in small and heated rooms. About eighty persons had the disorder, of whom thirty-six, all adults but two, died.

September 8th. Montreal was taken by the English, as also Detroit and Mackinaw.

October 29th. There was a 'public thanksgiving on account of the entire reduction of Canada.'

1 7 6 1.

February 6th. Second and third parishes opposed the formation of a new parish at ' the plains.'

March 10th. ' Town chose a committee to use their best endeavours to remove the inferior court held in Salem to Ipswich, and one of the other courts from Ipswich to Newbury inasmuch as they pay a greater tax to the province charges than any other town in ye province save Boston.' *

March 10th. A ferry was granted from Newbury to Salisbury, ' about the middle of Bartlet's cove.'

March 12th, at twenty minutes past two, A. M., there was an earthquake. ' It was divided,' says one writer, ' into two shakes with a pause between.'

April 5th. The fifth parish was incorporated. The parishioners having held a meeting in queen Ann's chapel, bishop Bass wrote their committee the following letter.

' *June 9th*,1761.

' Gentlemen,

' I am informed that you with a number of people whose committee I hear you are, broke into the old church the other day. I shall be very glad to find that I am misinformed, for if it be really so I think you have used me in a very uncivil and ungentlemanlike manner, and without any provocation and not a little exposed yourselves. If you had business to transact, or any grave matters to talk over near the church and it was necessary or convenient that you should go into the church for that purpose I do n't know of any body that would have been against it, but certainly you ought to have done it in an orderly manner by asking leave of me, who am the proper guardian of that church.

EDWARD BASS.'

September 8th. The committee addressed the members of the old church, ' and after stating the incorporation of the parish, and that they had no convenient house for the worship of God at present,' conclude thus: ' we therefore as neighbours and friends desire your consent to improve the said church in the vacancy of Mr. Bass not attending there until we are accommodated with a new house. We are,' and so forth.

September 9th. The preceding request was granted by the proprietors of the ' old church.'

May. A fire engine, the second in Newbury, was imported from

* Town records.

London this month, by Michael Dalton, esquire, and others,* and a fire company of twenty-four men formed.

November 1st, between eight and nine P. M. there was an earthquake.

This summer there was a great drought.

1762.

March 2d. A committee was appointed in Byfield parish, to appoint a grammar-school master, according to the will of governor Dummer, and the academy was erected.

March. The county appropriated two hundred pounds, toward defraying the expense of building a court house, 'for the use of the county and town,' but in consequence of the refusal of the town, March twenty-ninth, to unite with the county, in the erection of such a building, 'the water side people' generously gave the money to build the court house, purchased, July seventh, eleven and a quarter rods of land, at the corner of Essex street, where the museum now stands, of Joseph Clement, shipwright, for sixty-nine pounds. Said building, when erected, was to be used as a court and town house, 'and to no other use, intent or purpose whatsoever.' It was built this year.

'*July 28th.* There was a day of fasting and prayer on account of the grievous drought,' and on August twelfth, a day of thanksgiving, on account of the capture of Havana by the English.

This summer, the church in connection with the fifth parish was constituted, and the reverend Oliver Noble ordained their pastor, September first.

1763.

February 27th, Monday. Dummer academy opened. Mr. Samuel Moody, preceptor. The number of pupils on this day was twenty-eight, of whom, one only, deacon Benjamin Colman, born in 1752, is still living. Reverend Moses Parsons preached a sermon on the occasion, from Isaiah, 32: 8. 'The liberal soul deviseth liberal things.'

May 12th. Town 'voted to build a pest house in the great pasture thirty-eight feet long by twenty-eight wide and one story high.' *

At the June session of the general court, two hundred and six of the 'water side people,' so called, sent in a petition, praying, that, for certain reasons, they might be set off from Newbury, and incorporated into a town by themselves. In this petition, signed, in behalf of themselves and the memorialists, by William Atkins, Daniel Farnham, Michael Dalton, Thomas Woodbridge, and Patrick Tracy, they enumerate a long list of grievances, as reasons

---

* Town records.

why their request should be granted. The substance of it is, that between them, 'the merchants, traders, and mechanics,' and the husbandmen, 'there is a certain jealousy as to their public affairs and a high spirit of opposition,' and so forth. They complain of 'the want of schools by the water side,' a want of fire engines, that 'they are unreasonably taxed,' that 'there is no town treasurer,' that 'they do not have their due proportion of the selectmen,' and, finally, as an instance of the prevailing spirit of jealousy and opposition, they say, that 'the town has not met, and we suppose will not meet, in the new court house lately built at the water side by the county and the people there—and that it is a sufficient objection with them to any measure proposed, or thing done, tho' ever so just and reasonable in its nature, that ye water side people proposed, or did it. Wherefore,' and so forth.

This summer there was a severe drought.

October 20*th.* 'The town voted unanimously three only excepted, that they were opposed to the division of the town. Also voted to build a house for the grammar school at or near the head of Fish street, and to build a small house behind the work house to keep crazed and distracted persons in.'

December 2*d.* The first parish, on account of the supposed weakness of the turret of the old meeting-house, took down the bell, and hung it in a bell-house opposite the meeting-house.'

1764.

January 27*th.* The town authorized the selectmen 'to provide a suitable gate at old town bridge and at Thorla's bridge and employ one man to keep each gate and also to fence across any road to prevent any person infected with the small pox coming into town,' and 'that no vessel shall come up above Hook's point till an examination is made.'

NEWBURYPORT.

January 28*th.* That part of Newbury now called Newburyport, was incorporated as a separate town. The act of incorporation commences thus.

'An act for erecting part of the town of Newbury into a new town by the name of Newburyport.

'Whereas the town of Newbury is very large, and the inhabitants of that part of it, who dwell by the water side there, as it is commonly called, are mostly merchants, traders and artificers, and the inhabitants of the other part of the town are chiefly husbandmen, by means whereof many difficulties and disputes have arisen in managing their public affairs,
Be it enacted,' and so forth.

Here follows a description of the boundary lines of the town, which can be more easily understood by reference to the map. In regard to size, it is the smallest town in the commonwealth, containing about six hundred and thirty acres, less than a mile square. Of its population, business, trade, advantages, and so forth, I shall speak more fully hereafter. I shall here only make one quotation from that inimitable book, written by the late Timothy Dexter, entitled 'a pickle for the knowing ones.' With the exception of the punctuation, I give it verbatim and literatim.

'fourder, frinds. I will tell the a tipe of mankind. what is that? 35 or 36 years agone A toun called Noubry, all won the Younited states, Noubry peopel kept together quiet till the Larned groued strong. the farmers was 12 out of 20. thay wanted to have the offesers in the Contry, the Larned in the see port wanted to have them there. geering A Rose, groued warme, fite thay wood, in Law thay went the Jinrel Cort to be sot of. finely thay got there Eands Answered, the see port caled Newburyport, 600 Eakers of Land out of 30000 Eakers of good land, so much for mad, people of Larning makes them mad. if thay had kept together thay wood have been the sekent toun in this state about half of Boston.'

Among the conditions of the act of incorporation, were these: that Newbury should hereafter send but one representative to the general court, and Newburyport one, and that 'the inhabitants of Newburyport shall from time to time amend and repair a certain bridge over the river Artichoke which they will have occasion to pass and repass, although the same bridge is not included within the limits of Newburyport.'

March 15th. The 'committee chosen by the town of Newburyport report that at least three large schools should be provided and maintained in said town,' and conclude by saying: 'as the inhabitants have now the long desired privilege of being well served with schools, and, as they have heretofore been liberal in supporting private schools, we think it proper that the public schools should be honorably supported.'

To the suggestion of the committee, the town gave a hearty response, and from that time to the present, the public schools have been 'honorably supported,' and it is believed by competent judges, that no town in the commonwealth has done more for the cause of education, in proportion to its means, than the town of Newburyport. In the language of Timothy Dexter, 'the larned groued strong.'

May 25th. 'Newburyport voted to petition the general court to have their limits and bounds enlarged,' and also voted, two hundred and sixty-two against fifty-four, '*not* to petition to be reunited to the town of Newbury.'

1765.

On March twenty-second, an act, passed by the British parliament, for raising a revenue by a general stamp duty through all the American colonies, received the royal assent, and was to take effect November first. It was called the stamp act, was everywhere disapproved, and in many places met with great opposition. On August twenty-sixth, a mob entered the house of William Story, deputy register, and destroyed the records and files of the admiralty court, ransacked the house of Benjamin Hallowell, comptroller of the customs, and destroyed the house of lieutenant governor Hutchinson,* much property, and many valuable books and papers.

September 30th. The town of Newburyport voted that 'the late act of parliament is very grievous, and that this town as much as in them lies endeavour the repeal of the same in all lawful ways, and that it is the desire of the town that no man in it will accept of the office of distributing the stampt papers, as he regards the displeasure of the town and that they will deem the person accepting of such office an enemy to his country.'

October 21st. Each of the towns, Newbury and Newburyport, on this day held a town meeting, and each voted to give instructions to their representative, 'relating to his acting in the general court.' The instructions given to Joseph Gerrish, representative of Newbury, were passed unanimously, and ordered to be kept on file, but are now lost. From the instructions given by Newburyport to their representative, Dudley Atkins, the following extracts are taken.

'After adverting to the right of the people to instruct their representatives, and remarking upon the liberality of the English constitution, the instructions proceed :

'We have the most loyal sentiments of our gracious king, and his illustrious family ; we have the highest reverence and esteem for that most august body, the parliament of Great Britain ; and we have an ardent affection for our brethren at home ; we have always regarded their interests as our own, and esteemed our own prosperity as necessarily united with theirs. Hence it is that we have the greatest concern at some measures adopted by the late ministry, and some late acts of parliament, which we apprehend in their tendency will deprive us of some of our essential and high-prized liberties. The stamp-act, in a peculiar manner, we esteem a grievance, as by it we are subjected to a heavy tax, to which are annexed very severe penalties ; and the recovery of forfeitures, incurred by the breach of it, is in a manner, which the English constitution abhors, that is, without a trial by jury, and in a court of admiralty. That a people should be taxed at the will of another, whether of one man or many, without their own consent, in person or by representative, is rank slavery.

*   *   *   *   *   *   *

'That these measures are contrary to the constitutional rights of Britons cannot be denied ; and that the British inhabitants of America are not in every respect entitled to the privileges of Britons, even the patrons of the most arbitrary measures have never yet advanced.

'We have been full and explicit on this head, as it seems to be the fundamental point in debate ; but was the tax in itself ever so constitutional, we cannot think but at this time it would be very grievous and burdensome.

'The embarrassments on our trade are great, and the scarcity of cash arising therefrom is such, that by the execution of the stamp-act, we should be drained in a very little time of that medium : the consequence of which is, that our commerce must stagnate, and our laborers starve.

'These, sir, are our sentiments on this occasion ; nor can we think that the distresses we have painted are the creatures of our own imagination.

*   *   *   *   *   *   *

* In Boston.

' We therefore the freeholders and other inhabitants of this town, being legally assembled, take this opportunity to declare our just expectations from you, which are,

' That you will, to the utmost of your ability, use your influence in the general assembly that the rights and privileges of this province may be preserved inviolate ; and that the sacred deposit, we have received from our ancestors, may be handed down, without infringement, to our posterity of the latest generations :

' That you endeavor that all measures, consistent with our loyalty to the best of kings, may be taken to prevent the execution of the above grievous innovations ; and that the repeal of the stamp-act may be obtained by a most dutiful, and at the same time most spirited, remonstrance against it.

' That you do not consent to any new or unprecedented grants, but endeavor that the greatest frugality and economy may take place in the distribution of the public monies, remembering the great expense the war has involved us in, and the debt incurred thereby, which remains undischarged.

' That you will consult and promote such measures, as may be necessary, in this difficult time, to prevent the course of justice from being stayed, and the commerce of the province standing still :

' That if occasion shall offer, you bear testimony in behalf of this town against all seditions and mobbish insurrections, and express our abhorrence of all breaches of the peace ; and that you will readily concur in any constitutional measures, that may be necessary to secure the public tranquillity.'

The stamp distributors were everywhere compelled to resign, and in many places they were hung in effigy. In Newburyport, the effigy of a Mr. I—— B——, who had accepted the office of stamp distributor, was suspended, September twenty-fifth and twenty-sixth, from a large elm tree which stood in Mr. Jonathan Greenleaf's yard, at the foot of King street, [now Federal street,] a collection of tar barrels set on fire, the rope cut, and the image dropped into the flames. At ten o'clock, P. M., all the bells in town were rung. ' I am sorry to see that substitute,' said a distinguished citizen of Newburyport, ' I wish it had been the original.' Companies of men, armed with clubs, were accustomed to parade the streets of Newbury and Newburyport, at night, and, to every man they met, put the laconic question, 'stamp or no stamp.' The consequences of an affirmative reply, were any thing but pleasant. In one instance, a stranger, having arrived in town, was seized by the mob, at the foot of Green street, and, not knowing what answer to make to the question, stood mute. As the mob allow no neutrals, and as silence with them is a crime, he was severely beaten. The same question was put to another stranger, who replied, with a sagacity worthy of a vicar of Bray, or a Talleyrand, ' I am as you are.' He was immediately cheered and applauded, as a true son of liberty, and permitted to depart in peace, wondering, no doubt, at his own sudden popularity.

' The uneasiness,' says the reverend N. Appleton, ' in all the colonies was universal. All as one man rising up in opposition to it, such a union, as was never before witnessed in all the colonies,' so that, in the language of doctor Holmes, ' by the first of November, when the act was to take effect, not a sheet of stamped paper was to be had throughout New England, New York, Pennsylvania, and the two Carolinas.'

June 5th. There were several shocks of an earthquake.

December 4th. ' Great numbers of wild geese were caught alive, many were shot, or killed with clubs, and many were found dead.'

1 7 6 6.

On March eighteenth, the stamp act was repealed. The joy of the people, on hearing the intelligence, was as great, as their indignation had been at its passage. The twenty-fourth of July was kept as a day of public thanksgiving, on account of its repeal. ' Our people,' says the reverend Thomas Smith, of Portland, ' were almost mad with drink and joy. A deluge of drunkenness.'

May 20th. A town meeting, in Newburyport, was called, ' by beat of drum and word of mouth.' The upper part of the town house was ordered to be illuminated, at the town's expense, and that ' the selectmen deliver out of the town's stock of gunpowder six half barrels thereof to be used in the public rejoicings of this day.' One half of this was used at the upper long wharf, the other half at the lower long wharf, under the supervision of Mr. John Harbert, and captain Gideon Woodwell.*

The ecclesiastical difficulties which had arisen in the first parish, under the ministry of the reverend Christopher Toppan, were, it appears, far from being settled under his successor, the reverend John Tucker, notwithstanding so large a secession had taken place, from the church and parish, at the time of his settlement. On February eleventh, the parishioners held a meeting, to decide the question, whether to build a new meeting-house, on land owned by John Brown, esquire, or repair the old one. They voted to repair the old meeting-house. This called forth, at a meeting, held March twenty-seventh, a protest from John Brown, and seventeen others, ' forbidding them to lay out one farthing of *their* interest towards the repairs of the meeting house, and demanding their proportion of the parish funds.' At the same time, Joseph Coffin, esquire, and forty-three others, some of whom attended, and some did not attend, the reverend Mr. Tucker's preaching, sent a petition to the parish, stating, among other things, that ' as we cannot adhere to his principles manifest in his preaching, especially of late, we cannot think it our duty to ask the favour to be freed from paying any further taxes towards his support, or any other parish charges. We therefore your petitioners, subscribers hereto humbly pray that you would take our case jointly into your serious and most impartial consideration and grant us the relief we might rationally expect in a nation where liberty of conscience is indulged to every sect and denomination of christians whatever, and in a land where a love of, and an ardent desire after, liberty is born with us, and prevails against all opposition even in civil, much more in religious, affairs. We think that every rational

* Town records.

person must be convinced after about twenty years' trial, that we cannot enjoy any lasting peace in the parish while we thus continue. We therefore,' and so forth. Of this protest and petition, no satisfactory notice was taken. Accordingly, those who felt aggrieved, formed a new society, which they called the union society, and commenced preparations to erect a meeting-house, which, it is said, they first intended to build at the northwest corner of Marlborough street, but finally determined to place it opposite to the old meeting-house, on land which they purchased of John Brown, esquire, February twenty-eighth. This occasioned another parish meeting, April twenty-eighth, at which 'a committee of three was chosen to send to the general court to forbid their building a house so near the present house.' In July, however, the house was raised, and boarded, but was, for some cause, never finished. Tradition asserts, that Mr. Nathan Pierce was once overheard to pray, that 'Dagon, [the old house,] might fall before the ark of the Lord.' This induced the wags of the parish, to call the old meeting-house, 'old Dagon,' and the new meeting-house, 'young Dagon,' and when, on the ninth of February, 1771, in a violent storm of thunder, lightning, wind, and rain, the new house was blown down, one of them exclaimed, as he saw it lifted by the wind, 'I snare, you, young Dagon is agoing!'

We at the present day, can have but faint conceptions, of the feelings which at that time actuated the 'legalists,' and the 'new lights,' as they were then called. This intensity of feeling, was principally owing to the virtual union of church and state, which then deemed conscience a geographical matter, and made it the duty of every man within certain limits, whether he believed the doctrines of the preacher, or not, to assist in his support. A large portion of the people had been, for many years, in the habit of supporting two ministers; one by compulsion, whom they would not hear; the other, whose doctrines accorded with their own, and whom, of course, they heard, and voluntarily maintained. This grievance was, after many years' endurance, finally removed, thus proving the truth of the assertion, 'that liberty is born with us, and *prevails against all opposition* even in civil, *much more in religious affairs.*'

May 28*th.* Captain Joshua Coffin and Nathan Pierce, were chosen by the union society 'a committee to petition the general court for liberty for the inhabitants of the first parish to attend upon and support ye publick worship where they please *in* said parish and not be taxed elsewhere.'

June 2*d.* The union society chose a committee, to treat with the court's committee, June tenth, with respect to the points of difference in the first parish. The founders of the union society, held their first meeting January second, and on January thirtieth, chose a committee of seven to build a meeting-house.

The division of the Newbury regiment, this year, by governor Bernard, caused great excitement and opposition among the militia, as, in their language, 'it deprived the second regiment of its dignity and station and degraded it to the rank of the seventh and last regiment in the county without any regard to justice or the honor of a soldier.' The soldiers would not train, the officers resigned, those who accepted commissions were mobbed, and all attempts to reconcile them to the new arrangement, proved utterly abortive.

1767.

January. It should be mentioned, as a gratifying circumstance, that the separation of the third from the first society, was made in the most amicable manner. Messrs. Cary and Marsh had both been candidates for settlement in the first parish. About one third of the church preferred Mr. Marsh. The majority then observed to the minority, 'you prefer Mr. Marsh, we, Mr. Cary. If you wish to settle Mr. Marsh and build a meeting house we will assist you and give you your part of the church plate,' and so forth. This was accordingly done; the house was built, fronting on Brown's square, and Mr. Marsh and Mr. Cary both settled; one over the first church and parish, the other over the third.

This year Benjamin Lunt built a wharf, at the foot of Muzzey's lane, [now Marlborough street,] 'as there was no wharf convenient to land lumber, and so forth, upon in the town of Newbury.' *

March 10th. Permission given to Stephen Cross, to set up a distillery in Newburyport.*

June 24th. Parliament laid a tax on paper, glass, painters' colors, *teas,* and so forth.

December 17th. Newburyport granted the petition of Cutting Moody, Edmund Bartlet, and others, for the use of the town house, for Mr. Christopher Bridge Marsh to preach in, whose hearers, soon after, formed the third church and society in Newburyport.

1768.

January 15th. A slight shock of an earthquake.†

January 18th. The third church formed, by a separation from the first church.

April 20th. Young ladies met at the house of reverend Mr. Parsons, who preached to them a sermon from Proverbs, 31 : 19. They spun, and presented to Mrs. Parsons two hundred and seventy skeins of good yarn. They drank liberty tea. This was made from an herb called rib wort.

'*May 10th.* An exceeding full market, [in Newburyport,] on account of the ordination tomorrow.' †

'*May 11th.* Reverend Thomas Cary ordained.' †

'*May 23d.* Commenced framing Mr. Marsh's meeting house, which was dedicated September fifteenth and Mr. Marsh ordained October nineteenth.' †

---

* Newburyport records.   † Mr. Samuel Horton's diary.

A quantity of bohea tea, so called, which grew in Pearson town, Maine, 'was received in Newburyport the day that he was ordained. In the afternoon a dish was made and handed round to a circle of gentlemen and ladies, who pronounced it to have all the character-istics of genuine bohea tea.' *

'*June* 20*th.* A shock of an earthquake.' †

September 10*th.* On this day, as we learn from the Salem Ga-zette, one 'Joshua Vickery ship carpenter was seized by a mob in Newburyport, carried by force to the public stocks, and there com-pelled to sit from three to five o'clock on a sharp stone till he fainted. He was then carried round town in a cart with a rope round his neck, with his hands tied behind him, pelted with eggs, gravel and stones and was much wounded. At night he was carried into a dark ware house, hand-cuffed with irons, and there compelled to remain without bed or clothing through the Lord's day till Monday morning, and no person but his wife allowed to visit him. On Monday morning the rioters seized a Frenchman, named Francis Magro, stripped him naked, tarred and feathered him, placed him in a cart and compelled Vickery to lead the horse about town.' The cause of these outrages, was, Magro's giving information to the officers of the customs at Portsmouth, against a vessel, the owners of which, he supposed were engaged in smuggling. Vick-ery was suspected, but was afterward proved to be entirely innocent. This was the second mob in Newburyport, the first occurring in September, 1765.

October 6*th.* A fast was kept by the churches of Newbury and Rowley, according to a vote of the towns, 'on account of the crit-ical situation of the province.' ‡

'*December* 5*th.* Mr. Richard Noyes fell from his cart and was killed by the wheel's passing over him.' †

In the autumn of this year, the merchants of the province mutu-ally bound themselves, not to import, nor to purchase if imported, any British goods, before January, 1770, or until parliament repealed the revenue laws.

1769.

March 14*th.* Town of Newbury voted, to lend James Hudson twenty pounds, to assist him in completing his salt works.

April 19*th.* First church in Newbury voted, that 'it is agreeable that the scriptures be read in publick.'

'*April* 16*th.* Two boats were overset at Newbury bar and eight persons drowned, namely, Enoch Stickney, Diamond Currier, Nathaniel Moulton, and Simeon Woodman of Newburyport, and Samuel Blaisdell, Philip Gould, John Gould, and Moses Currier of Amesbury.' †

April 23*d.* Byfield church voted to make trial of Watts's psalms and hymns.

---

* Salem Gazette.　　　† Mr. Samuel Horton's diary.　　　‡ Town records.

'*July* 13*th*, about six minutes before seven o'clock there was an earthquake.'

'*July* 19*th*. This evening the northern lights made an unusually splendid appearance.'

September 4*th*. Town of Newburyport approved of the non-importation agreement, and, on September twentieth, voted to return the 'thanks of the town to the merchants and others of Boston for their patriotic resolution of nonimportation of goods from Great Britain,' and so forth.

1770.

From the Massachusetts Spy, January seventeenth, I extract the following reprint from an English paper.

'The Newbury, captain Rose, from Newbury, in New England, lies at the Orchard house, Black wall. The above is a raft of timber in the form of a ship, which came from Newbury to soundings in twenty-six days and is worthy the attention of the curious.'

This was one of the three or four ships, built in the same manner, for Mr. Levi, a Jew, one of which was launched December eleventh, 1769, and another October ninth, 1771.

'*February* 24*th*. An earthquake in a smart snow storm.'

March 13*th*. Fifty citizens of Newbury petitioned the town, requesting them to choose a committee, and order them to offer the inhabitants 'a subscription to sign against purchasing any goods,' of certain importers, and also against 'purchasing or using any foreign tea in our families upon any account,' and so forth. They also petition, 'that the names of such persons as shall refuse to sign said subscription may by a vote of the town be recorded in the town book that posterity may know, who in this day of public calamity are enemies to the liberties of their country and their memorial be had in everlasting detestation,' * and much more to the same purpose. 'The petition was read and accepted and the measures herein requested were adopted by an unanimous vote of the town,' and a committee 'of sixteen persons chosen to offer a subscription to ye inhabitants of the town to sign.' * The following is an exact copy of this patriotic pledge, which I find in the handwriting of Joshua Coffin, esquire, one of the sixteen.

'Whereas it evidently appears to be absolutely Necessary for ye Political welfare of this Province to Discourage and by all Lawful Means Endeavour to prevent ye Transportation of Goods from Great Britain, and Encourage Industry, Oeconomy and Manufactures amongst our Selves

'We, therefore, ye Subscribers being Willing to Contribute our Mite for the Publick Good, do hereby promise and Engage to and with each other, That we will as much as in us lies promote and Encourage ye use and Consumption of all useful Articles Manufactured in this Province, and that we will not (Knowingly) on any pretence whatever, purchase any Goods of, or have any Concerns by way of Trade with John Bernard, James McMasters, Patrick McMasters,

* Newbury records.

John Mein, Nathaniel Rogers, William Jackson Theophilus Lillie, John Taylor And Ame and Elizabeth Cummin, all of Boston, or Israel Williams Esquire and Son of Hatfield, or Henry Barns of Marlborough, or any Person acting by or under them or any of them, or any other person or persons whomsoever that shall or may import Goods from Great Britain contrary to ye Agreement of ye United Body of Merchants, or of any Persons that purchases of or Trades with them, or any of them ye sd Importers before a General Importation takes place (Debts before Contracted only excepted.)

'And if it doth or may hereafter appear, that there is any Ship Builder in Newbury Port, or any other Town wheresoever in New England, that has so little Regard for ye Publick welfare, as to undertake to Build any Ship Schooner, or Sea-faring Vessel for any Foreigner, or any other Person And take ye pay for ye Same, or any part thereof, in Goods Imported Contrary to ye Agreement of sd Merchants, We promise and Engage not to have any Connection by way of Trade and Commerce (Debts before Contracted only excepted) with any Such Ship Builder, nor sell them any Materials for Building any Such Vessels. But we will look upon all such Ship Builders (as well as Importers and Traders with Importers) as persons Destitute of ye principles of Common Humanity (Sway'd only by their own Private Interest) Enemies to their Country and worthy of Contempt. And whereas a great part of ye Revenue arising by virtue of ye Acts of Parliament, is produc'd from the duty paid on Tea. We do therefore Solemnly Promise not to purchase any Foreign Tea, or Suffer it to be us'd in our Families upon any Account untill ye sd Revenue Acts are Repeal'd or a General Importation takes place, And we will each one of us, as we have proper Opportunitys Recommend to all persons to do ye same. And we do hereby of our Own free will and Accord Solemnly promise to and with Each Other, That we will without Evasion or Equivocation Faithfully and truly Keep and Observe all that is above written, And whosoever shall or may Sign these Articles, And afterwards (Knowingly) break ye same shall by us be esteem'd as a Covenant Breaker, an Enemy to his Country, a Friend to slavery, Deserving Contempt.

'All and Singular of these Articles to Continue and Remain in Force untill ye sd Acts be Repeal'd, or a General Importation takes place.

'As Witness our Hands.'

March 23*d.* Town of Newburyport voted 'that this town will not use or buy any foreign tea and do what they can to discourage it in others,' and, on April third, voted 'to refrain from all foreign or India tea,' and also 'voted to choose a committee of ten men as a committee of inspection to inspect the transactions of this town respecting the importation of goods into the town contrary to ye agreement of the merchants of Boston and elsewhere.' This committee prepared a subscription paper, 'for all those to sign, who are determined not to buy or sell or use any tea in their families,' and were desired 'to lay before the town the names of those, who refuse to sign,' and 'if there should be any others, who sign the agreement and do n't duly regard it.'

The honorable Caleb Cushing, in his history of Newburyport, says, that the meeting of April third, was called on suspicion 'that a wagon load of tea had been brought into town.'

April 12*th.* The duties on all articles, were repealed by parliament, except *that on tea.*

May 24*th.* The town of Newbury petitioned the general court, to pass an act to prevent the destruction of bass in the river Parker.

This is the first petition of the kind that I have seen from Newbury.

May 24th. The town of Newbury voted to grant the petition of Benjamin Pettingell, and ninety-nine others, who desired, in substance, that they might attend public worship in any part of Newbury or Newburyport, 'where they choose,' 'and pay where they attend and no where else.' The town also, at the same meeting, 'chose Nathan Pierce, Joshua Coffin and Samuel Greenleaf esquires a committee to petition the general court to confirm the above vote by a law of the province.' The town also voted ' that Stephen Brown be added to the tea committee, and the time for subscribing be lengthened until the autumn.' *

July. This summer, the country was visited with immense armies of worms, supposed to be the same species with those that came in 1736. ' This worm,' says doctor Dwight, ' was a caterpillar nearly two inches in length, striped longitudinally with a very deep brown, and white; its eyes very large, bright and piercing, its movements very rapid, and its numbers infinite. Its march was from west to east. Walls and fences were no obstruction to its course, nor indeed was any thing else, except the sides of trenches, which were plowed, or dug before it, and in which immense multitudes of these animals died.' Multitudes of these trenches were dug in Newbury, and many fields were in this way preserved. There was also a drought this summer, and, on July nineteenth, ' Benjamin Poor's barn in Newbury new town was consumed by lightning.'

September 30th. Sunday morning, about six o'clock, died the reverend George Whitefield, in Newburyport, at the house of the reverend Jonathan Parsons. From the seventeenth to the twentieth, he had preached every day in Boston. On the twenty-first, he went to Portsmouth, where he preached daily, from the twenty-third to the twenty-ninth; once at Kittery, and once at York. On Saturday, the twenty-ninth, he preached nearly two hours, at Exeter, in the open air. In the afternoon, he rode to Newburyport, as he had engaged to preach in Newburyport the next morning. He had preached in Newburyport, September tenth and eleventh, and perhaps at other times, as Mr. Samuel Horton says, in his diary, ' I subscribed five pounds old tenor to be remitted to Mr. Whitefield in consideration of his abundant labours in Newburyport.' It was owing to the labors of Mr. Whitefield, that the first presbyterian church in Newburyport was formed, and, in the language of Mr. Cushing, ' whatever may be thought of the peculiar opinions of Mr. Whitefield certain it is that his eloquence as a preacher was unrivalled; and his zeal for the cause he taught, of the highest character. The fruits of his ministration here were great and striking; and the establishment of the society under consideration afforded proof of the permanency of its effects.' † He was buried beneath the pulpit, in the church in Federal street, in which a cenotaph was erected to his memory, in 1829, by the munificence of the late William Bartlet, esquire.

---

* Newbury records.   † History of Newburyport.

Whitefield

NORTH WEST VIEW OF THE FIRST PRESBYTERIAN CHURCH,
NEWBURYPORT, MASS.,
IN WHICH ARE DEPOSITED THE REMAINS OF
REV. GEORGE WHITEFIELD.
INCLUDING A DISTANT VIEW OF THE HOUSE IN WHICH HE DIED.

1771.

March 12*th.* A great freshet, and great destruction of bridges, and so forth.

March 29*th.* Abraham Larkin, an Irishman, was crushed to death, while examining the machinery in the top of the windmill, at the south end of Frog pond.

May 28*th.* The town again voted, that Joshua Coffin, esquire, and others, who were chosen May twenty-fourth, 1770, to prefer a petition to the general court, 'be now instructed to use their utmost influence to get the said vote passed into a law of the province at the next sessions of the general court.' ✳

✳ Newbury records.

1772.

January 30*th*.   Sloop Three Friends, captain Mark Foran, from Greenock, in Scotland, was cast away on Plum island.

February 10*th*.   Captain Thomas Parsons sailed from Newburyport, in a schooner, for the West Indies; was wrecked at St. Mary's, Nova Scotia.   It was supposed, that he, with all his crew, eight in number, were massacred by the inhabitants there, after plundering the vessel, and setting it on fire.

March 26*th*.   First parish voted to erect a steeple on the meetinghouse, to hang the bell in.

June 18*th*.   Snow fell in Newbury.

July 6*th*.   The first parish 'voted to put up a copper weather cock on the top of the pyramid' of the meeting-house.   This was substituted for the iron one, which was made at the time the meetinghouse was erected, from colonel Thomas Noyes's old iron dripping pan.   So Mr. Robert Adams was informed, by Mr. Joseph Noyes, then ninety years of age.

Newburyport held a meeting, December twenty-third, and Newbury, December twenty-ninth, and chose committees, the former of twelve persons, the latter of sixteen, 'to take under consideration our publick grievances,' and 'the infringement of our rights and liberties,' and to report, and so forth.   In both meetings, allusion was made to the able pamphlet 'received from Boston,' and of their proceedings at a meeting, November twentieth.

'*December*.   The whole of this month very warm, rain every three or four days.   On the thirtieth there was no more ice in the river than in June.' *

1773.

January 1*st*.   Newburyport held an adjourned meeting, to hear the report of their committee, whose 'letter was read and accepted,' a copy ordered 'to be sent to the committee of correspondence of the town of Boston.'   The town also 'voted that captain Jonathan Greenleaf, our representative, be acquainted that it is the desire and expectation of this town that he will persevere with steadiness and resolution in conjunction with his brethren in the honorable house of representatives to use his utmost endeavours to procure a full and complete redress of all our publick grievances, and to do every thing in his power in order that the present and succeeding generations may have the full enjoyment of all those privileges and advantages, which naturally and necessarily result from our glorious constitution.'

January 4*th*.   Town of Newbury held a meeting, and voted, unanimously, 'to accept the report of their committee and that it be entered among the records of the town, there to stand as a last-

* Reverend Moses Hale's diary.

ing memorial of the sense they have of their invaluable rights and of their steady determination to defend them in every lawful way as occasion may require.'

The report of the committee, which may be found on the town records, is an able and spirited document, but is too long for publication. Both Newbury and Newburyport most cordially thank the inhabitants of Boston, 'for their vigilance and patriotic zeal,' and chose a committee of correspondence, 'to correspond with the town of Boston and such others as they shall think proper,' and so forth.

February 4th. The first parish 'voted not to release any of the pretended churchmen,' [from paying taxes.]

'*August 14th.* About eight o'clock there was in Salisbury and part of Amesbury the most violent tornado, or short hurricane, perhaps ever known in the country. It continued about three minutes, in which time it damaged, or entirely prostrated, nearly two hundred buildings. It removed two vessels one of them of ninety tons, twenty-two feet from the stocks. The vein of the tempest was about a quarter of a mile in width on the river and about a mile and a half in length.'

September 23d. Dudley Colman chosen town clerk of Newbury.

September 28th. Inferior court held in Newburyport. From the Salem Gazette, I make the following extract.

October, 1773. Extract of a letter from Newburyport. October tenth. ' We have lately had our court week when the novel case of Cæsar against his master in an action of fifty pounds lawful money damages for detaining him in slavery was litigated before a jury of the county, who found for the *plaintiff eighteen pounds damages and costs.*' The defendant was Mr. Richard Greenleaf. For a more full account of this case in particular, and of the transactions concerning slavery in Newbury, see appendix, H.

' *November 26th.* Town of Newbury chose a committee of five persons to prevent the inoculation of the small pox at the house of Moses Little esquire, and also voted not to suffer inoculation in the town.'

December 4th. On this day, the first number of a paper, called the Essex Journal and New Hampshire Packet, was published, in Newburyport, by Isaiah Thomas and Henry Walter Tinges. This was distributed gratis. The next number was published December twenty-ninth.

December 22d. Town of Newbury met and voted, unanimously, ' not to receive the tea sent by the East India company to America upon the terms, we are informed it is now sent upon.

' Voted unanimously that this town will use their utmost endeavours to hinder the importation of tea in America so long as the duty shall remain thereon either by the East India company, or in any other way whatever.

' Voted to choose a committee to draw up what shall appear to them the sense of this town and make report at an adjourned meeting.'

31

' *December 9th.* At a numerous [informal] meeting of the people
of Newburyport and others, a committee of five was chosen, who
reported the following, which was accepted. ' We have taken into
consideration the late proceedings of the town of Boston relating
to the importation of tea by the East India company into America,
and do acquiesce in their proceedings and are determined to give
them all the assistance in our power *even at the risque of our lives
and fortunes.*' '

December 15th. On this day, the people of Boston, having previously tried, without success, to send back the three tea ships that
had arrived, and, determined that it should not be used, a party of
armed men, disguised as Indians, boarded the ships, and threw their
whole cargoes into the docks.

> ' As the Mohawks kind of thought,
> The Yankees *had n't ought,*
> To drink *that are tea.*'

December 16th. At a legal meeting of the freeholders, and other
inhabitants of Newburyport, the committee chosen for that purpose,
' reported the following draft of a letter to be sent to the committee
of correspondence of the town of Boston,' which was adopted at
an adjourned meeting, December twentieth.

' Gentlemen, it is with astonishment that we reflect on the unremitted efforts
of the British ministry and parliament to fasten ruin and infamy upon these
colonies. They not only claim a right to control and tax us at their pleasure,
but are practising every species of fraud as well as violence their deluded
minds can suppose feasible to support and establish this absurd and injurious
claim. A fresh instance we have in the plan lately adopted for supplying the
colonies with tea. If the money thus unconstitutionally taken from us was to
be expended for our real benefit and advantage it would still be grievous, as the
method of obtaining it is of a dangerous nature and most fatal tendency. But
we lose all patience when we consider that the industrious Americans are to be
stript of their honest earnings to gratify the humours of lawless and ambitious
men and to support in idleness and luxury a parcel of worthless parasites their
creatures and tools, who are swarming thick upon us and are already become a
notorious burden to the community. We are sorry that any, who call themselves Americans are hardy enough to justify these unrighteous proceedings.
They surely deserve the utmost contempt and indignation of all honest men
throughout the world, for our part we shall endeavour to treat them according
to their deserts. By the public prints we are favoured with the sentiments of
several respectable towns in the province, expressed in a number of manly,
sensible and spirited resolves with respect to the evils immediately before us.
We are under great obligations to our worthy friends and brethren, who have
nobly stood forth in this important cause. We assure them that should they
need our assistance in any emergency we determine most readily to exert our
utmost abilities in every manly and laudable way, our wisdom may dictate for
the salvation of our country, even at the hazard of our lives and trusting through
the favour of a kind providence we shall be able to frustrate all the designs of
our enemies.' *

December 28th. Great freshet in Merrimac river.

* Newburyport town records.

1774.

January 4th.   The town of Newbury met, according to adjourn-ment, and unanimously adopted a long and able report, embracing fourteen resolutions, of the most spirited and determined tone, con-cluding as follows.

‘ And whereas our brethren address us with religious solemnity, and conde-scend to ask our advice, the committee take leave to offer to the consideration of the town, the following short address, as appearing to them proper upon the present important occasion.

‘ Beloved brethren, let us stand fast in the liberty, wherewith God and the British constitution in conjunction with our own, have made us free, that neither we, nor our posterity after us (through any fault of ours) be entangled with the yoke of bondage.’ *

During this period of apprehension and excitement, which were preparing the people for the arduous conflict before them, they found opportunities for amusement, peculiar to their situation. Many cases like the following might be given, which I relate on the testimony of an eye witness, the late Mr. Caleb Greenleaf, of Haverhill, and the public papers.

February 15th.   One Holland Shaw, having been detected in stealing a shirt, was immediately taken before a sort of ex tempore court, convened for the occasion, was sentenced as follows, namely, ‘ that he parade through the principal streets of the town, accompa-nied by the town crier with his drum.’   The sentence was forthwith put into execution.   The town crier, William Douglass, with his brass barreled drum, and the thief with the shirt, headed the proces-sion, which took up its line of march.   The paper of that day informs us, ‘ that he was compelled to proclaim his crime and pro-duce the evidence, which was the shirt with the sleeves tied round his neck, the other part on his back.’   The proclamation, which he was compelled to utter with a loud voice, was, ‘ I stole this shirt, which is tied round my neck from Mr. Joseph Coffin’s house in Salisbury, and I am very sorry for it.’   Having been thus marched through the principal streets, and satisfied the demands of this new court of justice, he was dismissed, and never, after that night, was he seen in Newburyport.   Another person, who had stolen a quan-tity of salt fish, was compelled to make atonement for his offence, by parading through the streets, holding a salt fish in his hand, above his head, and proclaiming his crime in a similar manner : ‘ I stole this fish and five quintals more.’   An English sailor was also marched round the town, with a pair of stolen breeches tied round his neck, informing the people what he had, and how he obtained them.

April 19th.   Battle at Lexington.

Intelligence having been received in England, on March seventh,

* Newbury records.

of the manner in which the Bostonians had disposed of the East India company's tea, passed an act, which went into operation June first, by which the harbor of Boston was closed against the entrance, or departure, of any vessels. It was called the 'Boston port bill.'

June 17th. Battle of Bunker hill.

June 23d. 'The town of Newbury met to take into consideration certain letters sent from the committee of correspondence in Boston to the committee of correspondence in Newbury, the following answer was taken by yeas and nays without one dissenting voice.'

'As there is a general congress of the colonies proposed to consider and advise on the present distressed state of our civil and commercial affairs, we cannot think it safe, decent or suitable to go into any decisive binding engagements previous to that, but to assure our brethren through the continent of our hearty good wishes to the common cause of liberty and our country, do now testify that we can with the utmost freedom and cheerfulness agree to discontinue all commerce with Great Britain and with all importers of goods from thence, or those who shall refuse to comply with these, or any other measures, that shall be determined by the said congress so long as shall by them be judged expedient and necessary for the opening Boston harbor and recovering and perpetuating all our just rights and liberties.'*

August 3d. The town of Newburyport held a meeting, and, among other things, 'voted unanimously that this town will stand by the result of the congress even if it be to the stopping of all trade.' 'Voted also to send two hundred pounds for the relief of indigent persons in the town of Boston.'

August 9th. 'Town of Newbury voted to send two hundred pounds to purchase provisions to be sent and given to the suffering inhabitants of the town of Boston.'

September 22d. 'The town of Newbury chose the honorable Joseph Gerrish esquire as their representative and voted that he be directed and instructed not to be qualified for his seat in the house by any of the councilors, who have received their commission by mandamus from his majesty but by the council chosen by the house of representatives agreeable to the charter of this province.' *

October 3d. The town of Newburyport met, and gave instructions to captain Jonathan Greenleaf, their representative, of the most derermined and decided character. I have only room for the following extract. 'Armed ships and armed men are the arguments to compel our obedience and the more than implicit language that these utter is that we must submit or die. But God grant that neither of these may be our unhappy fate. We design not madly to brave our own destruction, and we do not thirst for the blood of others, but reason and religion demand of us that we guard our invaluable rights at the risque of both,' and so forth.

October 24th. The town of Newburyport held a meeting, and 'voted that all the inhabitants be desired to furnish themselves with arms and ammunition and have bayonets fixed to their guns as soon as may be.

* Newbury records.

' Voted also that no effigies be carried about or exhibited on the fifth of November or other time only in the day time.'

December 28th. Town of Newburyport chose Tristram Dalton, esquire, captain Jonathan Greenleaf, and Mr. Stephen Cross, ' to represent this town in the provincial congress to be held at Cambridge in February next.'

1775.

The people of Newbury and Newburyport, having made all necessary preparations, and taken all needful precautions, for their protection, and the preservation of their invaluable rights and privileges, and given utterance to their feelings, in the most determined and decided tone, prior to the commencement of this year, soon discovered that nothing short of a severe and bloody contest, or unconditional submission, was before them. With them, submission was out of the question, and events soon transpired, which made it manifest, that they must buckle on their armor, and summon all their energies, for the coming conflict. For this, they were with great unanimity prepared, come when it might. On the twenty-sixth of February, general Gage sent colonel Leslie from castle William to Salem, to seize some military stores. This, the people would not permit him to do, and, had it not been for the prudent interposition of the reverend Thomas Barnard, of Salem, (formerly of Newbury,) and others, the war of the revolution would have begun at Salem, instead of Lexington. The fight at Lexington, the skirmish at Concord, April nineteenth, and the battle at Bunker hill, June seventeenth, precluded all hope of an amicable settlement of the controversy. The spirits of the people rose with the occasion. In the midst, however, of their excitement, an event occurred, which, whether arising from accident, or a regular preconcerted plan, it is impossible to say, occasioned, for a time, great anxiety and distress among the people, and in which, on a review of all the circumstances connected with it, there appeared such a curious commingling of the comic, the ludicrous, and the distressing, as would afford ample materials for a volume of amusement. Those who witnessed the scene, can never forget it, and those who did not, can have but a faint idea of it from any description. I allude now, to what has been usually called ' the Ipswich fright,' which happened on this wise. On Friday afternoon, April twenty-first, the second day after the Lexington fight, the people of Newburyport held an informal meeting, at the town house, and, just as the reverend Thomas Cary was about opening the meeting with prayer, a messenger rushed up stairs, in breathless haste, crying out, ' for God's sake, turn out! turn out! or you will all be killed! The regulars are marching this way, and will soon be here. They are now at Ipswich, cutting and slashing all before them!' The messenger proved to be Mr. Ebenezer Todd, who stated that he had been sent from Rowley, to warn the people of their impending destruction.

The news spread like wildfire, and being generally credited, the consternation became almost universal, and as a large part of the militia had marched to the scene of action, early the next morning after the fight at Lexington, the terror and alarm among the women and children, was proportionably increased, especially, as, from all quarters, was heard the cry, 'the regulars are coming! They are down to Old town bridge, cutting, and slashing, and killing all before them! They'll soon be here!' It is remarkable, that the same story, in substance, was simultaneously told, from Ipswich to Coos. In every place, the report was, that the regulars were but a few miles behind them. In Newbury New town, it was said, they had advanced as far as Artichoke river, at Newburyport they were at Old town bridge; there, they were said to be at Ipswich, while, at the latter place, the alarm was the same. Mr. Eliphalet Hale, of Exeter, was at the latter place, and waited to ascertain the correctness of the report. Learning that it was without foundation, he made haste to undeceive the people, by riding from Ipswich to Newbury in fifty minutes. In the mean time, all sorts of ludicrous things were done, by men and women, to escape impending destruction. All sorts of vehicles, filled with all sorts of people, together with hundreds on foot, were to be seen, moving with all possible speed, farther north, somewhere, to escape the terrible 'regulars.' Their speed was accelerated, by persons who rode at full speed through the streets, crying, 'flee for your lives! flee for your lives! the regulars are coming!' Some crossed the river for safety. Some in Salisbury, went to Hampton, and spent the night in houses vacated by their owners, who had gone on the same errand farther north. The houses at Turkey hill, were filled with women and children, who spent the night in great trepidation. One man yoked up his oxen, and, taking his own family, and some of his neighbor's children, in his cart, drove off to escape the regulars. Another, having concealed all his valuable papers, under a great stone, in his field, fastened his doors and windows, and, having loaded his musket, resolved to sell his life as dearly as possible. One woman, having concealed all her pewter and silver ware, in the well, filled a bag with pies and other edibles, and set off with it and her family for a safer place, but having traveled some distance, and deposited her bag, to make some inquiry, she found, on her return, that there had been 'cutting and slashing,' not, indeed, by the regulars among the people, but by the irregulars among her provisions. Another woman, as I am informed, having run four or five miles, in great trepidation, stopped on the steps of the reverend Mr. Noble's meeting-house, to nurse her child, and found, to her great horror, that she brought off the cat, and left her child at home. In another instance, a Mr. ——, having placed his family on board of a boat, to go to Ram island, for safety, was so annoyed with the crying of one of his children, that he exclaimed, in a great fright, 'do throw that squalling brat overboard, or we shall all be discovered!' A Mr. J—— L——, seeing Mr. C—— H——, a very corpulent man, standing at his door, with his musket loaded, inquired of him if he was not going. 'Going? no,' said he, 'I am going to stop and shoot the devils!' Propositions were made by some persons, to destroy Thorla's, and the river Parker, bridges, while many acted a more rational part, and resolutely refused to move a step, or credit the whole of the flying stories, without more evidence. How, or by whom, or with what motives, the report was first started, no one can tell. It lasted in Newbury and Newburyport, but one night, and in the morning, all who had been informed that the rumor was without foundation,

> ' Returned safe home, right glad.to save
> Their property from pillage ;
> And all agreed to blame the man,
> Who first alarmed the village.'

As was previously remarked, the fight at Lexington was on Wednesday, April nineteenth, and, as soon as the news reached Newburyport and Newbury, which was about midnight, a large number of soldiers were on their march to the field of action. Two companies from Newbury, and two from Newburyport, were soon on the ground, ready for any emergency which might occur. In another place, something more will be found, concerning the part which Newbury and Newburyport took, during the trying scenes of the revolution, and the names of some of the actors ; also a brief summary, of some of the events connected with the privateering business, in which the people of Newburyport were very extensively engaged.

From a journal of every day's proceedings, kept by lieutenant Paul Lunt, I make a few extracts.

' May tenth, 1775, marched from Newburyport with sixty men, captain Ezra Lunt, commander, and May twelfth at eleven o'clock arrived at Cambridge. June fourteenth, some ships and transports arrived at Boston with two hundred horse and three thousand troops. June sixteenth, our men went to Charlestown and intrenched on a hill beyond Bunker's hill. They fired from the ships and Copps' hill all the time. June seventeenth, the regulars landed a number of troops and we engaged them. They drove us off the hill and burned Charlestown. July second, at night general Washington came into the camp. July third, turned out early in the morning, got in readiness to be reviewed by the general. July eighteenth. This morning a manifesto was read by the reverend Mr. Leonard, chaplain to the Connecticut forces upon Prospect hill in Charlestown. Our standard was presented in the midst of the regiments with this inscription upon it : APPEAL TO HEAVEN, after which Mr. Leonard made a short prayer and there we were dismissed by the discharge of a cannon, three cheers, and a war-whoop by the Indians.' 'July thirty-first. At four P. M. they [the British,] sent out a flag of truce, desiring a cessation of arms for three hours, but it was not granted. One of the riflemen shot at the flag staff of the truce and cut it off above his hand.'

General Washington, having projected an expedition against Quebec, determined to send out a detachment, from his camp, at Boston, to march by the way of the Kennebec river, through the wilderness. As that detachment passed through Newbury and Newburyport, and encamped here on its way to Canada, a short account of it will not be unacceptable. In lieutenant Paul Lunt's journal, I find the following.

'*September* 10*th.* Twenty of our company enlisted to go to Canada under the command of captain Ward. September thirteenth. In the afternoon the regiment marched from Cambridge to Newburyport, there to embark for Canada under the command of colonel [Benedict] Arnold, lieutenant colonel [Christopher] Greene [of Rhode Island,] and Major [Timothy] Bigelow [of Massachusetts.] Captain Ward commanded the company that the Newbury men enlisted in.'

One of the men from Newburyport, who was a soldier in this disastrous expedition, was Mr. Caleb Haskell, who kept a journal of the march, and of the hardships and privations endured by the troops. This journal, I have never been able to obtain, though it has been read by many with thrilling interest. I shall therefore make a few extracts from major Return J. Meigs's journal.

'1775, *September* 16*th.* In the morning continued our march and at ten o'clock A. M. arrived at Newburyport and encamped. *
'*Seventeenth, Sunday.* Attended divine service at the reverend Mr. Parsons's meeting. Dined at Mr. Nathaniel Tracy's.
'*Eighteenth.* Dined at Mr. Tristram Dalton's.
'*Nineteenth.* Embarked our whole detachment consisting of ten companies of musketmen, and three companies of riflemen, amounting to eleven hundred men on board ten transports.† I embarked myself on board the sloop Britannia. The fleet came to sail at ten o'clock A. M. and sailed out of the harbour, and lay to till one o'clock P. M. when we received orders to sail for Kennebeck fifty leagues from Newburyport,' and so forth.

In addition to the names already given, of persons who accompanied the army, may be mentioned the late reverend Samuel Spring, of Newburyport, who officiated as chaplain, Matthew Ogden and Aaron Burr, of New Jersey, John I. Henry, afterward judge Henry, of Pennsylvania, captain, afterward general Henry Dearborn, of New Hampshire, captain Daniel Morgan, commander of the riflemen, with captains William Kendricks and Matthew Smith, of Pennsylvania, and many others less known. From the following letters,‡ from general Arnold, it appears that he arrived at Fort Western, as early as September twenty-seventh. The transports landed the men at Pittston, Maine, where the batteaux were built. The result of this expedition, which arrived at Quebec, November ninth, is well known.

'*Fort Western,* 27*th September,* 1775.
' To captain Moses Nowell,
          Newburyport:
     ' Sir:
' You are hereby ordered to receive from captain James Clarkson, one James McCormick, a criminal condemned for the murder of Reuben Bishop, and him safely convey under a proper guard, to his excellency general Washington at head quarters.
               I am your humble servant,
                              B. ARNOLD.'

* The riflemen under captain Morgan, encamped in the field at the corner of Rolfe's lane. The other troops occupied two of the rope walks in town.
† The following are the names of some of these vessels: schooner Broad Bay, captain Clarkson; sloop Britannia; sloop Admiral.
‡ Maine Historical Society's Collection, volume first, page 358.

'Fort Western, 28th September, 1775.

Mr. Nathaniel Tracy :

' Dear Sir :

' This will be handed you by captain Clarkson who will acquaint you with the particulars of our voyage, which has been very troublesome indeed.

' To captain Clarkson I am under many obligations for his activity, vigilance and care of the whole fleet, both on our passage and since our arrival here ; for which he may very possibly be blamed by some of the other captains ; but he has really merited much, and it will always give me a sensible pleasure to hear of his welfare and success, as I think him very deserving.

' I must embrace this opportunity to acknowledge the many favours received from you at Newbury ; and am with my best respects to Mrs. Tracy, your brother and Mr. Jackson, and so forth,

Dear sir, yours, and so forth,

B. ARNOLD.'

NOTE. Some writers, among whom are judge Marshall and reverend doctor Holmes, mistake in stating that a company of artillery under captain John Lamb, accompanied Arnold's expedition. Setting aside the impossibility of transporting heavy cannon and balls, and so forth, and so forth, through the wilderness, between the Kennebec and the Chaudiere, we have the positive assertion of contemporary journals,* that captain Lamb, with a company of artillery, was, August twenty-eighth, 1775, posted on the battery, in New York city, and that, on the eighteenth of September, captain L., (having gone by the way of the Hudson river, to join general Montgomery,†) arrived at Cumberland bay, fifty miles from Montgomery's camp at isle aux Noix.

For the above note, copies of the preceding letters, and other information, which I have been under the necessity of abridging, I am indebted to the politeness of reverend William S. Bartlet, now of Chelsea. I regret that I have not room for the whole communication. Other facts and incidents demand a passing notice. Among them, may be mentioned, the annual celebration of an event, which, from the first settlement of New England, till this year, was deemed worthy of public commemoration. I allude to the discovery of the 'gunpowder plot,' which took place November fifth, 1605. The last public celebration of ' pope day,' so called, in Newbury and Newburyport, occurred this year. ' To prevent any tumult or disorder taking place during the evening or night,' the town of Newburyport voted, October twenty-fourth, 1774, ' that no effigies be carried about or exhibited on the fifth of November only in the day time.' Motives of policy afterward induced the discontinuance of this custom, which has now become obsolete. This year, the celebration went off with a great flourish. In the day time, companies of little boys might be seen, in various parts of the town, with their little popes, dressed up in the most grotesque and fantastic manner, which they carrried about, some on boards, and some on little carriages, for their own and others' amusement. But the great exhibition was reserved for the night, in which young men, as well as boys, participated. They first constructed a huge vehicle, varying, at times, from twenty to forty feet long, eight or ten wide, and five

* New York Gazette and Weekly Messenger, September eleventh, 1775, and † October fifth, 1775.

or six high, from the lower to the upper platform, on the front of
which, they erected a paper lantern, capacious enough to hold, in
addition to the lights, five or six persons.   Behind that, as large as
life, sat the mimic pope, and several other personages, monks, friars,
and so forth.   Last, but not least, stood an image of what was designed to be a representation of old Nick himself, furnished with
a pair of huge horns, holding in his hand a pitchfork, and otherwise
accoutred, with all the frightful ugliness that their ingenuity could
devise.   Their next step, after they had mounted their ponderous
vehicle on four wheels, chosen their officers, captain, first and second
lieutenant, purser, and so forth, placed a boy under the platform, to
elevate and move round, at proper intervals, the movable head of
the pope, and attached ropes to the front part of the machine, was,
to take up their line of march through the principal streets of the
town.   Sometimes, in addition to the images of the pope and his
company, there might be found, on the same platform, half a dozen
dancers, and a fiddler, whose

> ' Hornpipes, jigs, strathspeys, and reels,
> Put life and mettle in their heels,'

together with a large crowd, who made up a long procession.   Their
custom was, to call at the principal houses in various parts of the
town, ring their bell, cause the pope to elevate his head, and look
round upon the audience, and repeat the following lines.

> ' The fifth of November,
> As you well remember,
> Was gunpowder treason and plot;
> I know of no reason
> Why the gunpowder treason,
> Should ever be forgot.
> When the first king James the sceptre swayed,
> This hellish powder plot was laid.
> Thirty-six barrels of powder placed down below,
> All for old England's overthrow:
> Happy the man, and happy the day,
> That caught Guy Fawkes in the middle of his play.
> You 'll hear our bell go jink, jink, jink;
> Pray madam, sirs, if you'll something give,
> We 'll burn the dog, and never let him live.
> We 'll burn the dog without his head,
> *And then you 'll say the dog is dead.*
> From Rome, from Rome, the pope is come,
> All in ten thousand fears;
> The fiery serpent 's to be seen,
> All head, mouth, nose, and ears.
> The treacherous knave had so contrived,
> To blow king parliament all up all alive.
> God by his grace he did prevent
> To save both king and parliament.
> Happy the man, and happy the day,
> That catched Guy Fawkes in the middle of his play.
> Match touch, catch prime,
> In the good nick of time.
> Here is the pope that we have got,
> The whole promoter of the plot.
> We 'll stick a pitchfork in his back,
> And throw him in the fire.'

After the verses were repeated, the purser stepped forward, and took up his collection. Nearly all on whom they called, gave something. Esquire Atkins and esquire Dalton, always gave a dollar apiece. After perambulating the town, and finishing their collections, they concluded their evening's entertainment with a splendid supper; after making, with the exception of the wheels, and the heads of the effigies, a bonfire of the whole concern, to which were added, all the wash tubs, tar barrels, and stray lumber, that they could lay their hands on. With them, the common custom was, to steal all the stuff. But those days have long since passed away. The last exhibition of the kind, took place this year. The principal cause of its discontinuance, was, an unwillingness to displease the French, whose assistance was deemed so advantageous during the revolution.

1776.

February 3d. Newburyport gave to the town of Boston, two hundred and two pounds, ten shillings, and two pence, Mr. Parsons's parish gave ten pounds, sixteen shillings, and four pence, Mr. Tucker's parish, in Newbury, gave forty-six pounds, four shillings, and two pence, and Mr. Noble's gave nine pounds and six pence. These were in addition to the four hundred pounds given by the two towns.

January 15th, Monday. The brig Sukey, captain Engs, ninety tons, from Ireland, was taken by the Washington, privateer, and brought into Newburyport, laden with provisions, destined for Boston. On the morning of the same day, a British ship appeared off Newbury bar. As she lay off and on, several miles from the land, shewing English colors, and tacking often, the wind being easterly, with appearance of a storm, it was conjectured by some persons who observed her from town, that the captain had mistaken Ipswich bay, for that of Boston, which was then in possession of the British. On this supposition, several individuals determined to proceed to sea, and make a closer examination. Accordingly, seventeen persons embarked, in three whale boats, and, as they approached the ship, being satisfied, by the movements on board, that they were right in their conjectures, they determined to offer their services as pilots. For this purpose, they rowed within speaking distance, when captain Offin Boardman, whom they had previously selected to act as commodore of their little fleet, hailed the ship, inquiring whence she came and where bound. The answer was, from London, bound to Boston, with the inquiry, where are you from, and what land is this? The reply was, from Boston, do you want a pilot? Being answered in the affirmative, he told them to heave the ship to, and he would come on board. This being immediately done, his boat was rowed to the ship's gangway, and he, passing up, unarmed, proceeded to the quarter deck, shook hands with the captain, inquiring his passage, the news from London, and so forth, by which time, those in the boats had reached the deck, with their arms, and were paraded across the gangway, most of the crew being forward. Captain Boardman then left the quarter deck, and, to the great surprise of the English captain, and his crew, ordered the ship's colors struck. This order, the English captain told his mate, he supposed he must obey. He then observed to his captors, that the ship and cargo were their own, but, at the same time, hoped that neither he nor his crew would receive any injury.

Thus, by a correct conjecture in regard to the ship's situation, and a well managed finesse in making their approach, they found themselves in quiet possession of a ship, mounting four carriage guns, a crew of nearly their own number, and containing fifty-two chaldrons of coals, eighty-six butts and thirty hogsheads of porter, twenty hogsheads of vinegar, sixteen hogsheads of sour crout, and twenty-three live hogs, intended for the use of the troops quartered in Boston. Having placed the officers and crew under safe keeping, and having a fair wind and tide, they arrived at the wharf, in Newburyport, in less than six hours from the commencement of their expedition. The ship was called the Friends, was owned in London, and commanded by captain Archibald Bowie.

The only names of those who composed the party in the whale boats, which can be ascertained with certainty, are, Offin Boardman, Joseph Stanwood, John Coombs, Gideon Woodwell, Enoch Hale, Johnson Lunt, and Cutting Lunt. It ought to be mentioned, that another company manned the town barge, and proceeded down river on the same design, but, starting at a later hour, met the ship within the bar, on her way up to the wharf. These two vessels, the brig Sukey, and the ship Friends, were the first prizes brought into Newburyport. Captains Bowie and Engs, boarded for some time at Davenport's tavern. The former returned to England, while the latter concluded to stay in New England, and afterward commanded a privateer from Newburyport.

The preceding information is derived from various sources, but principally from a communication from Benjamin Hale, esquire, postmaster of Newburyport, whose father was one of the party who captured the ship.

February 16*th.* The Yankee Hero, captain ——, took, and brought into Newburyport, a bark of three hundred tons, loaded with coal, pork, and flour.

March 1*st.* The Yankee Hero, captain Thomas, brought into Newburyport brig Nelly, captain Robinson, from White Haven, bound to Boston, having two hundred tons of coal, and ten tons of potatoes.

March 13*th.* A committee, consisting of Daniel Spofford, Eliphalet Spofford, Thomas Noyes, Joseph Brown, and Daniel Chute, petition the governor and council, to be restored to the second regiment, and conclude by saying, 'that your petitioners congratulate themselves that the military arrangement is now in the hands of a government, which will pay a sacred regard to justice and the honor of a soldier, which ought ever to remain inviolate, for insult and disgrace damp his spirits, blast his vigor and unnerve his arm,' and so forth.

April 9th. Edmund Sawyer chosen town clerk.

'*April 22d.* Council determined the regiment composed of the towns of *Newburyport*, Amesbury and Salisbury shall take rank as the second regiment.' So far, therefore, as it respected Newbury, the petition was not granted.

May 8th. Newburyport voted to erect a fort on Plum island, and, May sixteenth, voted to hire a sum, not exceeding four thousand pounds, to defray the expense, and, on May twenty-third, Newbury appropriated two hundred pounds for the same purpose.

May 27th. Newbury voted to instruct their representatives 'that they after having seriously weighed the state and case of independence, act their best judgment and prudence respecting the same.'

May 31st. Newburyport 'voted that if the honorable congress should for the safety of the united colonies, declare them independent of the kingdom of Great Britain, this town will with their lives and fortunes support them in the measure.'

June 7th. The Yankee Hero, captain James Tracy, had an engagement with the Milford frigate, of twenty-eight guns. It lasted near two hours, but, as the frigate was vastly superior in force, the Hero struck.

July 14th. Mr. Oliver Moody was drowned from a wharf.

July 19th. The declaration of independence was published in Newburyport, and, on the same day, died the reverend Jonathan Parsons, in his seventy-first year.

'*August 11th.* Independency read in all the meeting houses.'*

In August, there was a state fast.

In the Newburyport town records, September second, I find the following, in the handwriting of Nicholas Pike, esquire, town clerk.

'This meeting was illegal, because the venire for calling it was in the name of the British tyrant, whose name all America justly execrates.'

1777.

March 24th. Town of Newbury this day put it to vote, 'to see if the town would settle in the seventh regiment of militia and it passed in the negative,' notwithstanding it was stated in the warning that '*a speedy settlement of the militia is a matter of the greatest importance to our political salvation.*' This refusal to do military duty in the seventh regiment, to which they had been degraded by governor Bernard, in March, 1766, as has been mentioned, the soldiers of Newbury continued to manifest, throughout the whole of the revolutionary contest. The consequence of this refusal, was, an entire absence of all military subordination, so far as regimental

---

* S. Horton's journal.

musters, and so forth, were concerned. This arose, not from any unwillingness to serve their country, but from a resolute determination, not to train under any officers, till they should be restored to their former rank, as soldiers of the *second*, and not the *seventh* regiment. This restoration was effected about the year 1793. This caused the duty which would otherwise have devolved on the militia officers, to be performed by the selectmen, and is, perhaps, the only instance in the state, where the selectmen were obliged to perform such a service.

May 21st. The town of Newburyport voted 'to impower Jonathan Boardman to procure and exhibit the evidence that may be had of the inimical disposition of any person or persons towards this, or any of the United States,' and, on June thirtieth, the town of Newbury chose Samuel Noyes, to do the same service.

June 29th. The Hessian prisoners came to town.

June 30th. Town of Newburyport 'voted to allow the soldiers stationed at Plum island candles, and sweetening for their beer.'

August. Some time this month, the old church, called queen Anne's chapel, having been unoccupied as a meeting-house after 1766, fell down. It was on the sabbath, a calm and sultry day. The pews and galleries had been removed some time before, and other parts had disappeared, piece by piece, till there was not enough left to hold the frame together.

'*August 21st.* Captain William Friend in a sixteen gun ship, called the Neptune, built in Mr. Cross's yard, sailed, and, when about a league from the bar, overset and sunk in sixteen fathoms of water, having on board sixty hands, only one drowned.' *

'*October 23d.* Great numbers of cannon were fired on account of Burgoyne's defeat, which was October seventeenth, and on December twenty-eighth a thanksgiving throughout the United States, on the same account.' *

1778.

February 12th. Newbury voted, nem. con., 'we the inhabitants of the town of Newbury do hereby give our representatives instructions to acquiesce in and comply with the articles of confederation, as we have received them from the honorable continental congress.'

March 26th. The town of Newburyport 'voted that this town are of opinion that the mode of representation contained in the constitution lately proposed by the convention of this state, is unequal and unjust, as thereby all the inhabitants of this state are not equally represented, and that some other parts of the same constitution are not founded on the true principles of government; and that a convention of the several towns of this county by their delegates, will have a probable tendency to reform the same agreeably to the natural rights of mankind and the true principles of government.'

* Mr. Samuel Horton's diary.

' Voted that the selectmen be desired, in behalf and in the name of the town, to write circular letters to the several towns within the county, proposing a convention of those towns, by their delegates to be holden at such time and place as the selectmen shall think proper: in said circular letters to propose to each of the towns aforesaid, to send the like number of delegates to said convention, as the same towns have by law right to send representatives to the general court.'

' Accordingly the most eminent citizens of this ancient and leading county assembled at Ipswich and instituted an elaborate examination of the intended constitution, which was printed with the title of the Essex Result.   The effect of this pamphlet, which is attributed to the mighty mind of Theophilus Parsons, [a native of Newbury,] then resident in Newburyport, was perfectly decisive of the question.   The town unanimously voted to reject the proposed form of government; and suggested the expediency of calling a new convention for the sole purpose of framing a constitution more worthy of Massachusetts.' *

March 30*th*.   Town of Newbury voted to grant the petition of several of the inhabitants of the 'westerly part of the town, who are desirous of being set off into a separate township.'

From March tenth, 1777, to August twenty-second, 1778, the town of Newbury passed, considered, and reconsidered, many votes respecting inoculation for the small pox, and were much divided and excited on the subject.   A hospital was for some time kept, on Kent's island, but, on August twenty-second, the town voted to petition that ' the small pox may be discontinued in Newbury by inoculation.'

December 30*th*.   Thanksgiving through the United States.

1 7 7 9 .

March 9*th*.   The town voted that ' the unanimous thanks of the town be given to Samuel Moody esquire for his generous donation of one hundred pounds at this time, and of twenty pounds some time past for the purpose of a growing fund for a grammar school being kept in the town for the instruction of youth.'

July 25*th*.   An armament, consisting of twenty sail, besides twenty-four transports, appeared off Penobscot, destined to dislodge the enemy, but proved exceedingly disastrous.   The Pallas, Sky Rocket, and so forth, sailed from Newburyport.   Colonel Moses Little, of Newbury, was at first appointed to command the expedition, but declined, on account of ill health.   ' August fifteenth, British recruits came to Penobscot.   American forces ran up river and burned their own shipping.' †

In this year, the business of chaise making was introduced into Newbury, by James Burgess.   The first regular builders, were Nathaniel and Abner Greenleaf. In Belleville, the business was commenced by Samuel Greenleaf, in 1792, by Joseph Ridgway, in 1793, by Robert Dodge, in 1795, and by Samuel Rogers, in 1796.

November 11*th*. ' The town of Newbury voted unanimously that they approve of and accept the proceedings of the late convention held at Concord in October regulating the prices of merchandise and country produce.'

This alludes to an unavailing attempt, to fix a price on labor, provisions, and all kinds of commodities, by legislative enactments. In the preceding year, the general court had passed, from the best of motives, ' an act to prevent monopoly and oppression,' and the towns of Newbury and Newburyport, had, in pursuance of this act, adopted and published a scale of prices, affixed to all the articles they had for sale, and also all kinds of labor. These prices were never to be exceeded. No imported goods, except hemp and warlike stores, should be sold at more than two hundred and fifty pounds sterling, on one hundred pounds prime cost, and no retailer should make an advance of more than twenty per centum on the wholesale price. All these regulations, were, of course, entirely futile, as they could not be enforced. They were therefore abandoned. The price of cotton, for instance, was established at ' three shillings per pound by the bag and three shillings and eightpence by the single pound. Barbers, once shaving threepence. Dinner boiled and roasted without wine one shilling and sixpence. Supper or breakfast one shilling. Lodging fourpence.' A pound of cotton, would, at this time, purchase two dinners, one night's lodging, once shaving, and leave one penny overplus. How many pounds of cotton would it take now, 1845, to procure the same amount?

December 9*th*. Thanksgiving in all the states.＊

December 15*th*. Earthquake very loud abou' half past eleven o'clock.＊

Some time this year, a wolf came into captain Israel and Liphe Adams's yard, and killed five sheep. He was killed by Moses Adams. No wolf has since been seen in Newbury.

1780.

The winter of 1780, was unusually severe. For forty days, thirty-one of which were the month of March, there was no perceptible thaw on the southerly side of any house, and so deep and hard was the snow, that loaded teams passed over walls and fences, in any direction.

March. The constitution of Massachusetts was framed. The first article in the declaration of rights, is, ' all men are born free and equal.' This was inserted, with the intent, and for the purpose, of entirely abolishing slavery. Prior to the revolution, several slaves

＊ S. Horton's journal.

had sued their masters for detaining them in slavery, one in Cambridge, in 1770, and one in Newburyport, Cæsar against his master, Richard Greenleaf, in September, 1773. In all these cases, the courts decided in favor of the slave. In 1781, a case occurred in Worcester, in which the supreme federal court decided, that slavery was abolished by the constitution.

May 29th. The committee of twenty-five chosen on the fifteenth instant, made their report concerning 'the frame of government now offered to the people and the town after proposing a few amendments and adopting nearly every article, unanimously conclude by saying, ' they have such a sense of the excellency of the constitution in general, that if the amendments proposed cannot be obtained, they are of opinion that the constitution be accepted in its present form.'' *

Newburyport held a meeting on the same subject, and, after proposing amendments, conclude by saying, 'esteeming it in general a wise and good one; the town do vote and declare their approbation of the same in its present form.' †

'*May 19th.* This day the most remarkable in the memory of man for darkness. For a week or ten days the air had been very thick and heavy, which made the sun look uncommonly red. On the morning of the nineteenth the sun was visible for a short time very early, but was soon overcast and very black clouds were seen to rise suddenly and very fast from the west, the wind what there was of it (tho' hardly enough to move the leaves on the trees) at south west. The forementioned clouds mixing with the vast quantities of smoke, occasioned by a general burning of the woods, caused, in the opinion of many this unusual alarming darkness, which began about twenty minutes before eleven o'clock A. M. and lasted the whole day, tho' not equally dark all the time. It was the darkest from about twelve to one o'clock. Afterwards there was a larger glin at the horizon, which made it somewhat lighter. It was however at the lightest, darker, I think than a moonlight night. The sky had a strange yellowish and sometimes reddish appearance. The night following was the darkest I remember to have seen, till about midnight, when a small breeze sprung up from the north or north west, upon which it soon began to grow light. At Falmouth, Casco bay, it was not dark at all. Upon Piscataqua river, Berwick, Dover, and so forth, it was very rainy, (very little of which we had here, which fell a little before it began to grow dark) but not uncommonly dark, as I am told by a person, who travelled there that day. I hear of the darkness as far as Danbury in Connecticut. It did not extend to North river. The forementioned darkness was no doubt occasioned by an unusual concurrence of several natural causes, but to pretend fully and clearly to account for it, argues perhaps too great confidence.' *Bishop Edward Bass's manuscripts.*

In the memoirs of the American academy, I find the following. ' Candles were lighted up in the houses; the birds having sung their evening songs disappeared and became silent; the fowls retired to roost; the cocks were crowing all around, as at break of day; objects could not be distinguished but at very little distance and every thing bore the appearance and gloom of night.' On account of the remarkable darkness, it is still called ' the dark day.'

November 18th, twelve o'clock at night, there was an earthquake.

---

* Newbury town records.   † Town records.

December 7th. Thanksgiving in all the states.

September. This month, the most flagrant instance of treachery that occurred during the revolutionary war, was discovered, by the apprehension of Major Andre, a British officer, who was executed as a spy, October second. The treachery was, an attempt, by general Arnold, to deliver up West Point to the enemy. From a journal kept by a Newbury soldier, I extract the following. 'September twenty-fourth. Pleasant weather, hard duty, poor beef. Our men are not allowed but six cartridges per man but good barracks. Twenty-fifth, pleasant weather. This day about one o'clock general Washington, general Knox, marquis La Fayette came to West Point to take a view of the fort. They stayed about two hours, and then left the point. We had thirteen pieces of cannon discharged. This night Arnold's plot was discovered. He had news of the British officer being taken. He told his wife he was a dead man. He took his horse and rode to the ferry as soon as he could to his barge, when he made the best of his way to a British ship. The ship made the best of her way to York. He carried off John Brown and Samuel Pilsbury of our company. September twenty-sixth. This morning at one o'clock we manned our lines and got in readiness for action. Each man received twenty rounds. This morning at three o'clock colonel Meigs's regiment of continental troops arrived. Twenty-seventh. This day making ready to receive the enemy as soon as they come. This night lay on our arms. Large piquet out.' *

1781.

In January, captain William Friend was cast away on Boon island, and drowned, with six men.

March 12th. Newburyport ' voted that the selectmen be directed to cause one of the bells to be rung at one of the clock in the day and at nine of the clock at night during the ensuing year.'

1782.

February. A Newburyport vessel, captain Calef, from the West Indies, was cast away on Plum island. Seven hands were lost, in consequence of leaving the vessel, and three saved by staying on board.

'*March* 18th. Town of Newburyport voted to accept of Union street and Fair street as laid out and that the same be recorded.'

March 28th. Green street ditto.

'*June* 23d. Mr. Edward Burbeck, formerly of Salem, was this day, sabbath afternoon, instantly killed by lightning,' while standing near a clock in his chamber. The house in which he died, stood on the spot, now occupied by Messrs. Richard and Daniel S. Tenny's house.

* Joshua Davis's journal.

August 9th. Mr. Nathaniel Tracy's new house, old dwelling house, and barn, were consumed by fire.

1783.

'*February 20th.* No snow on the ground, which is as dry as summer.'

March 12th. Newburyport accepted of Orange street as laid out.

September 3d. On this day, a treaty of peace was signed, at Paris, between Great Britain and the United States, by David Hartley and John Adams, esquires, and, on October thirteenth, congress issued a proclamation for disbanding the army.

November 29th. There was a small earthquake.

December 30th. Notice was given in the public journal, that two beacons had been erected on Plum island, for the benefit of vessels.

1784.

'*March 10th.* Newburyport voted to build a new work house, where the present work house stands, unless they can procure a more suitable place.'

April 7th. Reverend Oliver Noble was dismissed from his church and parish, at his own request.

'*July 7th.* Daniel Berry of Chester and Nathaniel Ober of Wenham, were drowned at Newbury bridge by the upsetting of a wherry.'

July 17th. General Jonathan Titcomb was chosen naval officer for this year.

This summer, there was a severe drought.

The bridge over the river Parker, which was built in 1758, under the direction of Mr. Ralph Cross, was this year repaired. It is eight hundred and seventy feet long, twenty-six feet wide, has nine solid piers, and eight wooden arches.

'*November 26th.* A twelve hours' storm raised the highest tide within the memory of the oldest man.'

1785.

May 13th. The town of Newburyport petitioned the general court as follows, namely:

'That in the years 1775 and 1776 the said town in order to guard and defend themselves and the neighbouring towns from the apprehended invasions and attacks of the enemy then infesting the sea coasts, and making depredations on the maritime towns of the state, prepared and sunk a number of piers in the channel of Merrimac river, near the mouth thereof; they have also built a fort on the Salisbury side of said river and another fort on Plum island near the entrance of the harbor; they constructed a floating battery, built a barge and made a number of gun carriages: the whole expense whereof amounted to the sum of two thousand, four hundred and thirty-three pounds, eight shillings and two pence.'

The petition concludes as follows.

' And as your petitioners are still laboring under a very heavy debt, contracted for the general service and defence of the country during the late war, and in addition thereto have been paying interest for the whole sum above mentioned, and are still paying interest for the same, they pray that your honors will be pleased as soon as possible to take the premises into your wise consideration, and order the aforementioned sum to be paid them out of the public treasury, and thus far relieve them under their distresses.'

Signed by the selectmen, ' by order and in behalf of the town of Newburyport.'

April 13*th.*   Merrimac river passable on the ice.   April sixteenth, snow two feet deep, and frozen so hard, as to bear cattle, and, on the nineteenth, a snow storm.

October 21*st.*   A Dutch ship, bound from Amsterdam to New York, was cast away on Plum island.   Crew saved, vessel and cargo lost.

November 16*th.*   Robert Laird and James Ferguson, advertise that they have established a brewery opposite Somerby's landing.

1786.

January 9*th.*   In the morning an earthquake.

July 11*th.*   Mr. Stephen Gerrish had his skull fractured, and Mr. Samuel Kezer, his limbs, by the falling of some rocks, while stoning Mr. Oliver Putnam's, now the Messrs. Ilsleys', well, which was immediately covered, and so remained till August twelfth, when Mr. Abraham Thurlow, on descending it, fell to the bottom, and expired before he could be rescued.   His death was occasioned by the foul air in the well.

December 6*th.*   A slight shock of an earthquake, at a quarter past four, P. M.

This year is rendered memorable, by an insurrection, in the western part of Massachusetts, headed by Daniel Shays.   One company, fifty-five in all, commanded by captain Edward Longfellow, went from Newbury.   They enlisted for sixty days, and left home December twelfth.   Two of the company are still living — deacon Moses Brown, and Silas Moulton, West Newbury.

November 14*th.*   The town of Newbury ' voted to settle the militia in said town, *provided that they be styled the independent regiment.*'

1787.

'The west wind blew steadily from November thirtieth 1786 to March twentieth of this year with only four slight interruptions.' *

This year, the Hessian fly, so destructive to wheat, made its first appearance in New England, entering Connecticut from New York.*

April 4th. This day, there was a 'spinning match' at the house of the reverend Mr. Murray, to whom were given two hundred and thirty-six skeins of thread and yarn. The meeting was in the 'parsonage house, every apartment of which,' says the Essex Journal, was full. The music of the spinning wheel resounded from every room. It was truly a pleasing sight. Some spinning, some reeling, some carding the cotton, some combing the flax. The labors of the day were concluded about five o'clock. Public worship was attended, and a discourse delivered by the pastor, from Exodus 35: 25. 'And all the women that were wise hearted did spin with their hands.'

May 15th. Town of Newburyport voted, that 'Fish street' shall hereafter be called 'State street.'

This year, congress made a grant for lights on Plum island, and, on September fifteenth, Newburyport granted permission to William Bartlet, and others, to appoint a man to live on Plum island, to take care of the fort.

September 17th. Federal constitution unanimously accepted.

1788.

From the Essex Journal I transcribe the following, namely:

'*Newburyport, February 13th,* 1788. On Thursday last we had the pleasing account of the ratification of the new constitution by the convention of this commonwealth. A general joy diffused itself through all ranks of people in this town on this glorious news. We heartily congratulate our readers on this auspicious event, rendered peculiarly happy in the prospect it affords that our sister state of New Hampshire, whose interests and whose dispositions are so similar to our own, will have an additional inducement to add a seventh pillar to the great federal edifice already so far advanced.

'On Friday afternoon the principal gentlemen of the trade and officers of the militia of the town, being informed that the delegates from this town and Newbury were on their way home, and being disposed to show some mark of their satisfaction at the adoption of the constitution, and of their warm approbation of the conduct of those honorable and worthy gentlemen in convention, met them at Newbury green, and escorted them into town, where they were received amidst the acclamations of a numerous collection of their applauding fellow-citizens.'

This year, a deer was tracked from Ash street, in west Newbury, to cape Ann woods, by Messrs. Silas Moulton and Abraham Adams, who were unable to find him. In the same year, the same persons killed one hundred and eighty common foxes, and two silver gray foxes.

* Dwight's travels.

March 26*th.*   ' Kent street was allowed and approved as laid out,' by the town of Newburyport.

1789.

October 28*th.*   The town of Newburyport this day held a meet-ing, to make suitable arrangements for the reception of the president of the United States, general George Washington.   They published a handbill, commencing thus:

' *Newburyport, October* 28*th,* 1789.

' As this town is on Friday next to be honored with a visit from ' the man who unites all hearts,' THE ILLUSTRIOUS PRESIDENT OF THE UNITED STATES, the inhabitants thereof this day in town meeting assembled, have agreed to the following order of procession.'

Here follow the names of thirty-five classes of persons, with di-rections as to the manner in which the procession should move. From the Essex Journal and New Hampshire Packet, of November fourth, I make the following extract.

' *Newburyport, November* 4*th.*   Friday last the beloved PRESIDENT of the UNITED STATES made his entry into this town ; and never did a person appear here, who more largely shared the affection and esteem of its citizens.   He was escorted here by two Companies of Cavalry, from Ipswich and Andover, Marshall Jackson, the High Sheriff of the County of Essex, the Honorable Tristram Dalton, Esquire, Major General Titcomb, and a number of other officers, as well as several gentlemen from this and some neighbouring towns. On his drawing near, he was saluted with thirteen discharges from the Artillery, after which, a number of young gentlemen placed themselves before him, and sang as follows :

' He comes! He comes! The HERO comes !
Sound, sound your Trumpets, beat, beat your Drums:
From Port, to Port, let Cannons roar,
He 's welcome to New-England's shore.
Welcome, welcome, welcome, welcome,
Welcome to New-England's shore !

' Prepare ! Prepare ! your Songs prepare,
Loud, loudly rend the echoing air:
From Pole to Pole, his praise resound,
For Virtue is with glory crown'd.
Virtue, virtue, virtue, virtue,
Virtue is with Glory crown'd ! '

' The lines in the first verse, which call for the beating of drums and roaring of cannon, were instantly obeyed after the pronunciation of each word ; and to the vocal was joined all the instrumental music in both choruses, which were repeated :—Then the PRESIDENT, preceded by the several companies of Militia and Artillery of this town, the Musicians, Selectmen, High Sheriff, and Mar-shall Jackson, passed the Ministers. Physicians, Lawyers, Magistrates, Town-officers, Marine Society, Tradesmen and Manufacturers, Captains of Vessels, Sailors, School-masters, with their Scholars, and so forth, and so forth, who had paraded and opened to the right and left for that purpose, each of whom, as the PRESIDENT passed, closed and joined in procession, which was terminated by about four hundred and twenty Scholars, all with Quills in their hands, headed by their Preceptors — Their motto, '*We are the free-born subjects of the United States.*'

'After the PRESIDENT had arrived at the house prepared for his reception, a Feu-de-joy was fired by the several companies of Militia; and in the evening some Fire-works and excellent Rockets were played off opposite thereto. Much praise is due to the citizens of Newbury-port, and others, assembled on the occasion, for their orderly behaviour through the day and evening.

'Saturday morning the PRESIDENT sat out for Portsmouth under the same escort which conducted him to this town, to which were added, a large number of military and other gentlemen of Newbury-port, who accompanied him to the line of New-Hampshire, where he was met by his Excellency General Sullivan, President of the State of New-Hampshire, with four companies of Light-horse, who conducted him to Portsmouth.

'The PRESIDENT passed through the towns of Amesbury and Salisbury, where several companies of Militia were paraded, which saluted as he passed.

'The Marine-Society of this town prepared and decorated a handsome Barge, for the purpose of carrying the PRESIDENT across Merrimack River, which was previously sent (commanded by one of the society) opposite to Amesbury Ferry, where it waited his arrival. The Barge-men were all dressed in white.

'On the PRESIDENT's crossing the river at Amesbury, he was paid, by *Captain Joseph A. de Murrietta*, of Teneriffe, the Salute of his Nation, (twenty-one guns) his ship being elegantly dressed. We cannot but admire, among the many amiable traits in the PRESIDENT's character, that of his politeness to Foreigners, which was repeated on this occasion.

'Soon after the PRESIDENT's arrival in this town, he was presented with the following Address.

'*To the President of the United States.*'

'SIR: When, by the unanimous suffrages of your countrymen, you were called to preside over their public councils, the citizens of the town of Newbury-port participated in the general joy, that arose from anticipating an administration conducted by the man, to whose wisdom and valor they owed their liberties.

'Pleasing were their reflections, that he, who, by the blessing of Heaven, had given them their independence, would again relinquish the felicities of domestic retirement, to teach them its just value.

'They have seen you, victorious, leave the field, followed with the applauses of a grateful country; and they now see you, entwining the Olive with the Laurel, and, in peace, giving security and happiness to a people, whom in war, you covered with glory.

'At the present moment, they indulge themselves in sentiments of joy, resulting from a principle, perhaps less elevated, but, exceedingly dear to their hearts, from a gratification of their affection, in beholding personally among them, the Friend, the Benefactor, and the Father of their country.

'They cannot hope, Sir, to exhibit any peculiar marks of attachment to your person; for, could they express their feelings of the most ardent and sincere gratitude, they would only repeat the sentiments, which are deeply impressed upon the hearts of all their fellow-citizens: but, in justice to themselves, they beg leave to assure you, that, in no part of the United States, are those sentiments of gratitude and affection more cordial and animated, than in the town, which, at this time, is honored with your presence.

'Long, Sir, may you continue the ornament and support of these States, and may the period be late, when you shall be called to receive a reward, adequate to your virtues, which it is not in the power of your country to bestow.'

'To the foregoing Address the PRESIDENT was pleased to reply as follows.

'*To the Citizens of the town of Newbury-port.*

'GENTLEMEN: The demonstrations of respect and affection which you are pleased to pay to an individual, whose highest pretension is to rank as your fellow-citizen, are of a nature too distinguished not to claim the warmest return that gratitude can make.

'My endeavours to be useful to my country have been no more than the result of conscious duty. Regards like yours, would reward services of the highest estimation and sacrifice : Yet, it is due to my feelings, that I should tell you those regards are received with esteem, and replied to with sincerity.

'In visiting the town of Newbury-port, I have obeyed a favorite inclination, and I am much gratified by the indulgence. In expressing a sincere wish for its prosperity, and the happiness of its inhabitants, I do justice to my own sentiments and their merit.

G. WASHINGTON.'

President Washington came into town, over the river Parker bridge. On reaching the upper green, he left his carriage, and mounted his horse. At South street, he was stopped, and the preceding ode sung. He was then escorted to Newburyport, where he received the address, which was written by John Quincy Adams, then a student at law, in the office of Theophilus Parsons, esquire, who had been appointed by the town of Newburyport to prepare it.

'*November* 16*th*. This has been a day of much animation, for carriages and foot people have been constantly passing to see a whale, which some fishermen found at sea and towed up to Old town bridge.' * It was about sixty feet long.

1790.

According to the census this year, Newbury had five hundred and thirty-eight houses, seven hundred and twenty-three families, and three thousand, nine hundred, and seventy-two inhabitants.

Newburyport had six hundred and sixteen houses, nine hundred and thirty-nine families, and four thousand, eight hundred and thirty-ty-seven inhabitants. At this time, the town owned six ships, forty-five brigantines, thirty-nine schooners, and twenty-eight sloops. Total, eleven thousand, eight hundred and seventy tons.

In this year, only four chaises were owned in the first parish of Newbury, and were in the possession of the reverend John Tucker, Silas Little, esquire, Silas Pearson, and deacon Daniel Hale.

March 9*th*. Newburyport voted to build a school-house about thirty feet by forty, 'near the hay scales.'

April. John Wheelwright was drowned from a vessel at the wharf.

Stephen Cross was this year appointed collector, Jonathan Titcomb naval officer, and Michael Hodge surveyor of the port of Newburyport.

1791.

March 22*d*. Newburyport voted to accept the following report.

' The committee have supposed it necessary, and therefore report that three or four women's schools shall be opened in some rooms hired for the purpose,

* Miss Alice Tucker's diary.

at convenient distances from each other, in different parts of the town ; and that some well instructed school dames shall be appointed for each to take charge of the younger classes of the female children, to learn them good manners, and proper decency of behaviour, and to teach them their letters how to put them together in syllables, to learn them to spell, and finally to read with clearness and precision any chapter in the bible. To these instructions perhaps may be well added, where the parents shall desire it, the teaching plain or common needle work and knitting.' April, 1790.

The scholars were to be between five and nine years of age.

June 1st. Nathaniel Carter, of Newburyport, and eight others, petition for liberty to build a bridge over Merrimac river, at Deer island. June thirteenth, order of notice was given.

June and July. A canal, one mile and a quarter long, to connect two rivers, was dug, to promote inland navigation between Newburyport and Hampton, New Hampshire.

In October of this year, a bear was seen in Bradford woods. On Saturday night, he visited the west parish in Newbury, crossed Ilsley's hill, and was killed, on sabbath morning, by Amos Emery, on Emery's hill.

November 4th. Town of Newbury opposed building of a bridge over the Merrimac river, at Deer island, and, on November thirtieth, reconsidered that vote, and, on December fifteenth, reconsidered their reconsideration, and instructed their representative to oppose it.

From May twenty-fifth, 1790, to November nineteenth, 1791, the number of vessels cleared from Newburyport, was one hundred and seventy-nine.

In the Newburyport Herald, of January twelfth of this year, I find an account of the establishment of Sunday schools in Philadelphia, by some benevolent persons in the city, with this comment. ' Pity their benevolence did not extend so far as to afford them tuition on days when it is lawful to follow such pursuits, and not thereby lay a foundation for the profanation of the sabbath.'

1792.

January 9th. Town of Newbury sent a long remonstrance to the general court, against the erection of a bridge over Merrimac river.

May 10th. ' Newburyport voted not to have arithmetic in the two extremes of the town, but in the centre grammar school only.'

May 16th. Newburyport again voted to send a petition to the general court, praying ' that the town may be reimbursed the expences of sinking piers, building a fort,' and so forth.

September 10th. Town of Newburyport ' voted not to grant the petition of Anthony Mors and others requesting leave to make use of the town house for the reverend Charles W. Milton to preach in.'

November 26th. On this day, Essex Merrimac bridge was opened for the public. ' It consisted in fact of two bridges resting on Deer island in the midst of the river.' It was, when finished, one thousand and thirty feet long, thirty-four wide; height of arch above high water mark, thirty-seven feet, and contained six thousand tons of timber. It was built in seven months, under the direction of Mr. Timothy Palmer, of Newburyport, a native of Boxford.

1 7 9 3 .

March. A cod fish was sold in Newburyport, weighing ninety-eight pounds, five feet and a half in length, and girth at the thickest place, three feet four inches.

April 1st. Newburyport 'voted to build a new work house.'

May 7th. Newbury 'voted that no person be allowed to put a seine, hedge, weir, or drag net into the river Parker at any season for the purpose of fishing for, or catching of, any bass, shad or ale-wives in said river, and that no person catch any of said fish with a dip net or any other way from December first to April first.'

March 13th. Reverend John Murray died.

June 11th, 1793. A meeting-house was this day raised, sixty-seven feet by sixty, in Temple street, for a society gathered by the labors of the reverend Charles W. Milton.

July 4th. 'This day,' says the Essex Journal, 'Timothy Dexter delivered an oration at Essex Merrimac bridge, which for elegance of style, propriety of speech, and force of argument, was truly Ciceronian.'!!

July 6th. The town of Ipswich was visited by a severe hail storm, which broke, in a few moments, four thousand, nine hundred and forty-six panes of glass. Many of the stones were as large as hens' eggs.

October 18th. Captain Timothy Newman, of Boston, son of doctor John Newman, of Newburyport, was taken by an Algerine corsair, chained, handcuffed, and allowed nothing but bread and water.

In December, doctor William B. Leonard offers his services, as a physician, to the good people of Newburyport. He states, that he has been a physician thirty-five years, and that 'a kind Providence has enabled him to spring out of the iron chains of tyranny, horror, devastation and murder to the only summit of liberty under the sun and where the diadem of a despot was hurled down to the bottom-less abyss.'!!

This year, a hospital was built, in common pasture, by Newbury-port, in which the inhabitants were admitted, by classes, in order to be inoculated for the small pox, under the care of doctor Charles Coffin, junior.

August 7th. Newburyport 'voted unanimously that in the opinion of this town the neutrality of the United States during the war now waged by the several belligerent powers in Europe is consistent with the honor and good faith of our government, and not repugnant to any of the treaties now existing between the United States and any of those powers.'

1794.

February 19*th.* Town voted to set off the three north westerly parishes, into a separate town, by themselves, and to choose a committee of nine persons, to see it equitably done, and, on April seventh, voted to choose a committee, to petition the general court to set them off, and, April twenty-third, reconsidered it, one hundred and eighty to five.

In June of this year, the first incorporated woolen factory in Massachusetts, was erected, at the falls of the river Parker, in Newbury. The machinery was made in Newburyport, by Messrs. Standring, Armstrong, and Guppy.

' Very dry summer. The brooks did not begin to fill up till October twenty-seventh, nor the grist mills to grind corn.' *Stephen Brown's journal.*

May 13*th.* Newburyport ' unanimously past a resolution to this effect. That in their opinion the embargo ought to be continued, and it was their wish it might be, as long as the public exigencies require it.'

July 19*th.* Eight persons, belonging to the third parish of Newbury, now second in West Newbury, were drowned, while crossing the Merrimac in a boat. Their names were, Edmund Kendrick, who left a wife and three children, Sarah Brown, Mercy Pilsbury, Mehetabel Brown, Nabby Hale, Polly, Rebecca, and Joshua Chase. The last four were children of Joshua Chase. Six of them were carried to the grave in one procession. A sermon was preached on the occasion, by the reverend David Toppan.

September 18*th.* Newburyport passed two by-laws, the one to prohibit any person from smoking any pipe or cigar in any street, lane, or alley, under a penalty of two shillings for every offence, the other inflicting a like penalty on the owner of ' every duck or goose, gander or drake found in Frog pond.'

This year, the fourth religious society in Newburyport, was incorporated. It originated with a few individuals, who separated from the first presbyterian society, in order to attend the ministry of the reverend Charles W. Milton, who had been invited to visit Newburyport by the reverend John Murray, pastor of the first presbyterian church, as the following letter and extract will show.

' *Newburyport, April* 12*th*, 1789.

' Reverend sir : the news of your mission by that truly venerable mother in Israel made my heart to leap for joy. The success that has attended your labors and those of your worthy colleague since your arrival in New Brunswick has drawn out the gratitude and praises of many to Him with whom the residue of the spirit is. Both these things have conspired to induce me to wish a visit from you to this town. In this I was encouraged by an overture in a letter from our pious and worthy mutual friend, doctor Calef, last winter, accompanied by a very agreeable present of books from yourself. In reply to the doctor I pressed him to prevail with you to come this way in the spring, that I might enjoy your good assistance at our sacrament in May, and have the comfort of having you with my people, while I pursue a journey intended (D. V.) at that time. My hopes were sanguine that captain Lovett would have brought you with him this last trip, but he is returned without you, and without any news of you or my friend. I am the more afflicted with the disappointment because it has pleased God to awaken a number in my congregation and another in this town, besides sundry places in the vicinity. In this state of things who can tell what might be the consequence if you should be moved of the Holy Ghost to come over and help us ? I sincerely long for that privilege, and if your other engagements will permit it I should be very happy to receive you from captain Lovell's hands when he returns.

'Although I have dated my letter at Newburyport I am now writing at Amesbury, snatching an opportunity of sending it on board by an unexpected chance, lest the vessel should be gone before I get home : this prevents my sending you three poor sermons of mine which I lately printed.

' Please to make my kind salutations to doctor Calef and his lady. Tell him, had I been at home, my disappointment should not have prevented my writing to him.

' May the presence of Him, who dwelt in the bush be ever with you. I am with genuine feelings of fraternal love and esteem, reverend sir,
          Your unworthy fellow servant in the dear Immanuel,
                                                  JOHN MURRAY.'

In another letter, dated July twenty-eighth, 1791, Mr. Murray thus writes :

' From your principles, connections, and character, many of my people, as early as they heard of your coming to St. Johns began to long for a personal acquaintance with you.

' My own hearty concurrence with their desires, induced me once to trouble you with a letter, requesting a visit from you. Since that request was known, my people have cherished expectations of seeing you here. After these had been so long frustrated, it gave them and me very sensible pleasure to find the Centinel announce your arrival in Boston last week. Since that time we have not been without hopes of your giving us an earlier opportunity of bidding you welcome to Newburyport as well as to New England.'

In consequence of these invitations, Mr. Milton came to Newburyport, preached for Mr. Murray, and was invited to settle in Amesbury, but his friends, unwilling to lose his ministrations, determined to settle and support him.

October 6th. Newburyport voted to have four conduits, ' in case of fire and to have a town watch to consist of four men for the first six months, and two men for the remainder of the year.'

Newbury and Newburyport were this year surveyed, and maps were taken, which were deposited in the office of the secretary of state.

November 6th. An organ was put up in first congregational church in Newburyport.

November 19th. Reverend Daniel Dana was ordained pastor of the first presbyterian church and congregation in Newburyport. This caused a secession of a considerable number of persons, who formed the second presbyterian church in Newburyport.

1795.

March 10*th.* Town voted, that the inhabitants of Newbury have liberty to attend public worship where they choose, and be exempt from taxation elsewhere, and to petition the general court to confirm the above vote.

In July of this year, the reverend John Boddily came to Newburyport, and was installed pastor of the second presbyterian church, in 1797. He was born in Bristol, England, April twelfth, 1755, began to preach in London, 1778, ordained at Westbury, November eighth, 1780; thence he went to Walsal, thence to Wallingford, where he preached till 1795. On September nineteenth, 1802, he preached his last sermon, and died November fourth, 1802, in his forty-eighth year.

This summer was remarkably moist. 'Throughout ten weeks, commencing from the middle of June, it rained during a greater or less part of half the days. The peas in the pod germinated six inches, and several other seeds proportionally, and more rain fell during the season than had been known for the preceding eighty years.' *

July 2*d.* Newburyport 'voted unanimously the thanks of the town be given to Mr. Timothy Dexter for the generous offer he has this day made to the town of building a market at his own expense.'

In this year, the second presbyterian society was formed, by a number of persons, for the purpose of attending the ministry of the reverend John Boddily.

November 26*th.* This day, the bridge erected at 'Holt's rocks,' between Newbury and Haverhill, and which is called the 'Rock's bridge,' was opened for travelers. It was one thousand feet in length, and was the longest bridge over the Merrimac. It had four arches, a draw, and was supported by five piers and two abutments. It was swept away by the ice, in 1818.

1796.

March 13*th.* 'Newburyport voted to accept of 'Harris street' and 'Pleasant street' as laid out by the selectmen,' and, on April fourth, 'voted to accept of 'Broad street' and 'Essex street,' and to build a brick school house at the southerly end of the mall.'

May. In the Newburyport Herald of this month, appears the confession and acknowledgment of one Solomon Tole, who asks pardon for his imposition, having pretended, during a part of his fourteen years' absence from home, that he was John Pike, the son of John and Martha Pike, of Newburyport, and had called himself by that name. His intended imposition, and the discovery of the whole plot, by the late John Mycall, esquire, would furnish ample

* Dwight's travels.

materials for an interesting pamphlet. He was a native of Epping, New Hampshire.

In June of this year, the yellow fever commenced its ravages in Newburyport, and between that time and the fifth of October, forty-four persons died.

December 22d. Second presbyterian church dedicated. The corner stone was laid May sixteenth, and the frame of the building raised June second.

1797.

May 8th. Beck street and Ship street accepted by Newburyport, as laid out, and, on September twenty-first, Spring street, and, on October twelfth, Lime street.

May 9th. A large house on Carr's island was destroyed by fire.

This year, captain Carter, of brig Katy, of Newburyport, was taken by a French privateer, who took out all the crew, except the captain and two men, and ordered her to a French port. They re-took the vessel, and arrived safe in Boston, July eleventh.

August 28th. Mr. William Noyes, aged twenty-three, was thrown from his horse, and so severely wounded, by a sythe which he was carrying, that he survived the accident but twenty-four hours.

November 8th. The dwelling house of Mr. Moses Savery, who was out of town, was destroyed by fire, about one o'clock at night, and his two apprentices, Spencer Bailey and —— Currier, were consumed in the flames.

December 5th. The grist and saw mills at Pine island, were destroyed by fire.

1798.

' From November twenty-eighth 1797 till March twenty-ninth of this year, the river Merrimac was frozen over above Amesbury ferry.'

In January, John Foss, who had been taken by the Algerines, in the Polly, commanded by captain Michael Smith, in 1793, published an interesting narrative of his captivity.

April 30th. Newburyport, by their appointed committee, addressed a complimentary letter to president Adams, ' pledging their lives and fortunes to support the measures judged necessary by the president and congress, to preserve and secure the happiness, the dignity, and the essential inrerests of the United States,' and so forth, to which the president made an appropriate reply, May eighth.

On June first, a number of the inhabitants of Newburyport, addressed a letter to the honorable Bailey Bartlet, member of congress, commencing thus :

' Sir, a number of the inhabitants of this town have agreed to build and equip a ship of three hundred and fifty-five tons burthen to be mounted with twenty six pound cannon, and to offer to the government of the United States for their use,' and so forth, and so forth.

The proposal was accepted, the keel laid July ninth, and, on October twelfth, she was launched, having been completed in seventy-five working days, and sent to sea, under the command of captain Moses Brown. She was called the Merrimac, and having 'run about five years, was sold to the merchants, and was soon after wrecked on cape Cod.' *

December 4th. 'This night Mr. Richard Jackman and his son about eleven years of age, who went to Plum island on the preceding day after wood and were not able to get home with their boat by reason of the wind and coldness of the night, made an attempt to come home by land, but being chilled with the cold, died with his son in his arms, after having got within half a mile of his own house.' †

1799.

December 14th. George Washington died.

1800.

January 2d. Agreeably to previous arrangements, a procession was formed in Market square, and moved thence, through State, Pleasant, Green, Water, Merrimac, and Federal streets, up to the reverend Daniel Dana's meeting-house, where an eulogy was delivered by Thomas Paine, A. M., who afterward took the name of Robert Treat Paine, being desirous, as he expressed it, ' of having a *christian* name.'

The stores in town were closed and all business suspended. The colors of the shipping were at half mast, and minute guns were fired, during the march of the procession to the meeting-house, which was crowded with an attentive audience.

February 22d. This day was observed, according to a previous vote by the parish of Byfield, in commemoration of the death of Washington, by the tolling of the bell one hour in the morning, an oration, and so forth.

April 9th. Washington street was laid out.

May 22d. The corner stone of saint Paul's church was laid, with masonic ceremonies. Underneath it, were deposited a variety of medals and coins, with a plate, engraven in Hebrew and masonic characters, and another, with this inscription: 'this corner stone of saint Paul's church (founded A. D. 1738) was laid by the right reverend brother Edward Bass, D. D. bishop of Massachusetts and rector of this church assisted by the M. W. Samuel Dunn esquire, G. master, the D. G. master, the grand wardens and brethren of the G. lodge of Massachusetts, on the feast of the holy ascension in the year of grace MDCCC, and of the United States XXIV.'

This year, Mr. Timothy Palmer was chosen surveyor of the high-

---

* Cushing's history of Newburyport.   † Davis's journal.

ways, in Newburyport. Under his skillful supervision, the roads
and lanes of the town assumed a new and greatly improved appearance. The first improvement of any note, was in High street, near
Frog pond. Time was, when at the lower end of the mall, as it
now stands, there was an eminence, on which a windmill was erected, in 1703, and remained till 1771. Afterward, on the margin
of the pond, stood Crocker's rope walk, and, at the upper end, a pot-
ash manufactory. At the head of Green street, there were the old
gun house, and a ravine or gully, one hundred and eighty feet in
length, and fifteen feet deep in the deepest place. The other incum-
brances having been successively removed, captain Edmund Bartlet
began, on June twenty-sixth, to fill up the gully, and in August, the
mall as it now stands was completed, at an expense of about eighteen hundred dollars, of which fourteen hundred were generously
given by captain Bartlet. For this munificence, he received the
thanks of the town, and the mall is called ' Bartlet mall.' On July
tenth, Newburyport voted to purchase the ground on which then
stood the first parish meeting-house. This was effected at an expense
of eight thousand dollars, of which the town paid four thousand and
four hundred. The remaining three thousand and six hundred dollars was collected by voluntary contributions, and by an assessment
on the owners of the land near the meeting-house. The land thus
purchased, received the name of Market square.

1 8 0 1 .

May. A bell was given to the second presbyterian church in
Newburyport, by Timothy Dexter.

September 27th. On this day, the reverend Thomas Cary
preached for the last time in the meeting-house in Market square.
The next day, the building was demolished, a well dug through
the solid rock, and the town pump erected, near the spot where the
pulpit formerly stood.

October. The new meeting-house, erected in Pleasant street,
for the use of the first church and society, was this day dedicated.
Sermon by the reverend John Andrews.

1 8 0 2 .

January 24th. ' This day,' says the historian of Haverhill, ' the
weather was so warm that the ice in the Merrimac moved with the
tide, and there was but little snow till February twenty-second.'
From this day, for nearly a week, an unusual quantity of snow and
hail fell, so that, in the opinion of doctor Dwight, had it been as
light as the snow in 1717, which was six feet deep, the snow would
have been eight feet deep. So hard was the crust, that loaded
sleighs passed any where over the fences. The honorable Bailey

Bartlet, Ichabod Tucker, and some others, rode to Ipswich over the fences in a large double sleigh.

May 11th. Town of Newbury 'voted unanimously that the erection of a bridge across Merrimac river from Salisbury to any part of Newbury will not be beneficial to the public at large, but a public injury,' and so forth, and also voted to oppose the turnpike road going through Newbury.

May 31st. Newburyport voted, that the proposed bridge and turnpike road to New Hampshire line, 'would be of great public utility and convenience,' and so forth. Each town voted to instruct their representatives accordingly.

In March and October, Roberts street and Spring street were laid out and accepted.

September 22d. There was a violent tornado, the wind blowing from south west to north east, in a vein of about eighty rods wide. It swept away entirely from its foundation, the house of Mr. David Bartlet in the west parish.

December 13th. Newbury voted to lay out a four rod way, from Essex Merrimac bridge to Water street, at an expense of one thousand and eighty-two dollars.

Merrimac Humane Society was instituted this year.

1 8 0 3 .

March 1st. Active Fire Society formed in Newburyport.

May. Mail stage commenced running from Haverhill to Newburyport.

December 31st. The shipping of Newburyport consisted, at this time, of nine ships, thirty-two brigs, thirty-four schooners, and sixteen sloops.

August 23d. On this day, the directors of the Newburyport turnpike commenced operations. The number of shares was nine hundred and ninety-five, which, at nearly four hundred and twenty dollars a share, amounted to more than four hundred and seventeen thousand dollars. It was completed in 1806.

Female Charitable Society was instituted June eighth.

1 8 0 4 .

October 2d. Newburyport 'voted unanimously that the town will concur with the honorable court of sessions in placing a new court house on land between Frog pond and the mall directly fronting Green street.'

October 10th. There was a severe storm. Nearly one hundred head of cattle were killed. Thirty were found dead in a small compass.

1805.

In this year, the new court house was erected.

May. Newbury appropriated two hundred dollars, to build two engine houses.

August. Charter street laid out and accepted.

This summer there was a severe drought.

Plum island turnpike, and the bridge over Plum island river, were made this year.

In November, there belonged to Newburyport forty-one ships, sixty-two brigs, two snows, two barques, and sixty-six schooners, besides sloops.

1806.

May 4th. On this day, the reverend John S. Popkin preached for the last time in the old meeting-house in the first parish, New-bury. It was torn down May sixth.

June 16th, the day of the total eclipse of the sun, the sills of the new meeting-house were laid, and, on September seventeenth, the new house was dedicated.

This summer there was a severe drought.

The amount of tonnage in the shipping of Massachusetts, this year, was four hundred and fifty thousand and sixty-one tons, of which, thirty-one thousand, nine hundred, and forty-one tons, was owned in Newburyport.

1807.

September 21st. Newburyport 'voted that the generous donation made to the town by the late Mr. Timothy Dexter of two thousand dollars, the interest of which he directed the overseers of the poor annually to distribute to such of the poor of the town, as are the most necessitous, who are not in the work house, is an act of benev-olence, which the town accept, and acknowledge with gratitude and thankfulness.'

November 9th. Newburyport purchased the county's interest in the court house, for seven hundred and fifty dollars.

December 22d. Congress passed an act of embargo, by which all the ports of the United States were closed against the clearance of all vessels. Whatever may have been said or thought of the propriety or impropriety of this act of the general government, it is certain that the enforcement of the law occasioned great suffering everywhere, but particularly in commercial places. 'Thousands of seamen were thrown out of employment and the harbors of our sea-ports were filled with dismantled vessels.' In the language of Fairfield, 'the grass-grown wharves were beaten with their decaying hulks, and the timid land-bird rested on their rotting shrouds.' The people of Newburyport were great sufferers by this measure, which

met, both in Newbury and Newburyport, with great opposition, a
large majority in both towns being opposed to the policy of the
general government. The votes in Newbury were this year three
hundred and fifty-five for Caleb Strong, and for James Sullivan one
hundred and seventy-one, and in Newburyport, five hundred and
ninety-two to two hundred and fifty-one.

1808.

June 15th. Baptist meeting-house in Newburyport was dedicated.
June 27th. Violent tornado, which did great damage.
August 2d. The town of Newbury met, and, on August ninth,
the town of Newburyport met, to take into consideration 'the distressing situation of our country occasioned by the general embargo,' and so forth. Each of the towns unanimously voted, to send
a petition to the president of the United States, which was done.
These petitions may be found in the town records, but are too long
for insertion here.
September 28th. The Andover institution was this day opened.
Mr. William Bartlet having previously given twenty thousand dollars, Mr. Moses Brown ten thousand dollars, and Mr. John Norris
ten thousand dollars, as a capital fund. The two former were of
Newburyport, the latter of Salem.

1809.

January 12th. Town of Newburyport had a meeting, and, after
having passed a series of resolutions, they presented a memorial to
the general court respecting the embargo, and other matters. On
January twenty-third, the town of Newbury took the same course,
with resolves and a memorial of like tenor. These resolves and
memorials are of great length, and are written with much spirit and
ability. They are too long for publication, and an abbreviation
would not do them justice.
February 9th. Newburyport 'voted to establish one or more
soup-houses for the relief of the poor.'
March 1st. The embargo was repealed, but all trade and inter-
course with France and England were interdicted.
May 13th. The old town house in Newburyport was torn down.
December 20th. Merrimac Bible Society was instituted.
This year the baptist meeting-house was built, in Liberty street.

1810.

September 14th. There was another tornado in the westerly part
of Newbury, with much rain. It carried off Mr. David Ordway's
barn, and did much damage in Mr. Joseph Newell's wood lot.

November 9th.   In the evening, there was a severe shock of an earthquake.

In this year, there were built on the Merrimac river, twenty-one ships, thirteen brigs, one schooner, and seven others, the total tonnage of which, was above twelve thousand tons.*

Newburyport Athenæum was incorporated, and the town hall built.   The Essex Merrimac bridge was rebuilt this year by a Mr. Templeman.   It was the first chain bridge in New England.

1811.

February 2d.   A great snow storm commenced, and continued three days.   It was piled up in reefs, in some places more than fifteen feet.†

February.   First Baptist Society in Newbury and Newburyport was incorporated.

May 31st.   Friday.   On this evening, about half past nine o'clock, commenced one of the most disastrous fires, with which Newburyport, or perhaps any town in the state, was ever visited. From a pamphlet, dated Newburyport, June fifth, 1811, I make the following extract.

'DREADFUL FIRE!

' On Friday evening last, at half past nine o'clock, the citizens of this town were alarmed with the cry of fire, which proved to have taken effect at the place where they have so repeatedly been summoned in the course of the present season on a similar occasion; and where it has for some time past been anxiously feared some vile incendiary intended to accomplish the purpose which is now effected.   The fire commenced in an unimproved stable in Mechanic row, owned by David Lawrence, which at the moment when the fire was discovered was found to be completely enveloped in flames.   It soon extended to the market and to State street, and spread in such various directions as to baffle all exertions to subdue it.   In a few hours, it prostrated every building on the north side of Cornhill, and both sides of State street from Cornhill to the market; it then proceeded into Essex street, on the north east side, to the house of captain James Kettle, where it was checked — into Middle street as far as Fair street on the north-east side and within a few rods thereof on the south-west side — into Liberty street within one house of Independent street, and down Water street as far as Hudson's wharf, sweeping off every building within that circle.   The whole of Centre street was laid in ashes, and the whole range of buildings in Merchant's row on the Ferrywharf, also all the stores on the several wharves between the market and Marquand's wharf, including the latter: thus clearing a large tract of land of sixteen and a half acres in a part of the town the most compact, and containing a much larger proportion of the wealth of the town than any other part.

' It is estimated that nearly two hundred and fifty buildings were burnt, most of which were stores and dwelling-houses; in which number nearly all the dry goods stores in town are included; four printing offices, being the whole number in town; and including the Newburyport Herald office; the custom house; the surveyor's office; the post office; two insurance offices, (the Union and the Phenix;) the baptist meeting-house; four attorney's offices; four bookstores, the loss in one of which is thirty thousand dollars, and also the town library.

* Newburyport Herald.   † Lewis's History of Lynn.

'Blunt's building and the Phenix building, two large four story brick buildings, seemed to present a barrier to the destructive element, and great hopes were entertained for a time that they would effectually restrain its rage; but by a sudden change of the wind the flames were carried directly upon these immense piles, which they soon overtopped, and involved in the calamity, which threatened to become general. State street at this time presented a spectacle most terribly sublime! The wind soon after its change blew strong: these buildings which were much the highest in the street threw the fire in awful columns many yards into the air, and the flames extended in one continued sheet of fire across the spacious area!

'The large brick baptist meeting-house, in Liberty street, in which many had deposited their goods, furniture, &c. as (from its distance and construction) a place of undoubted safety, with its contents shared and increased the awful calamity.

'At two o'clock in the morning the fire seemed to rage in every direction with irresistible fury, and the inhabitants saw very little prospect of preserving any portion of the town. Every thing was accomplished which intelligent and ardent exertion could effect: but they were disheartened by perceiving those efforts apparently without success. About four the danger diminished, and at six the fire had in a great degree spent its fury.

'The scene, says a gentleman, who was present during the night, was the most truly terrible I have ever witnessed. At the commencement of the fire, it was a bright moon light night, and the evening was cool and pleasant. But the moon gradually became obscured and at length disappeared in the thick cloud of smoke which shrouded the atmosphere. The glare of light throughout the town was intense, and the heat that of a sultry summer noon. The streets were thronged with those whose dwellings were consumed, conveying the remains of their property to places of safety. The incessant crash of falling buildings, the roaring of chimneys like distant thunder, the flames ascending in curling volumes from a vast extent of ruins, the air filled with a shower of fire, and the feathered throng fluttering over their wonted retreats, and dropping into the flames; the looing of the cows, and the confused noise of exertion and distress, united to impress the mind with the most awful sensations.

'The loss of property is immense, and cannot fall short of one million of dollars. Upwards of ninety families are driven from their habitations with the loss of a very considerable part of their furniture and clothing, and many of them deprived of the means of furnishing themselves with the necessaries of life. The scene of horror presented to view by the ravages of one night, beggars all description.'

'Within a few months after the fire, the sufferers received in donations, about one hundred and twenty-eight thousand dollars.' *

A splendid comet was seen on the eleventh of October between Arcturus and Lyra, and continued visible several months.

1812.

The baptist meeting-house was built this year in Congress street.
April 4th. An embargo for ninety days was passed by congress, and on June nineteenth, war was declared by the United States against Great Britain. On June twenty-fifth the town of Newburyport held a public meeting 'to express their sentiments on the subject of a war with Great Britain,' and on June twenty-ninth the

* Holmes's annals.

town of Newbury held a public meeting for the same purpose. The latter town 'passed at a very full meeting without a dissenting vote,' a series of resolutions in decided opposition to the war. The former reported an address 'to the executive department and the legislature of the commonwealth, expressive of their readiness to support them in any constitutional measures, which they might adopt for the safety and welfare of the people of the commonwealth and also expressive of their disapprobation of the late declaration of war.' The committee, chosen by Newburyport to draft the memorial, were Nessrs. Jeremiah Nelson, John Pierpont, Joseph Dana, William Bartlet, and William Fans.

This year the Franklin library was instituted, and the Newburyport bank, and the Mechanic's bank, incorporated. The Merrimac bank was incorporated June twenty-fifth, 1795, which was the first in town.

1813.

January 31*st.* Town of Newbury voted to petition the legislature for some relief from the ruinous effects of the unconstitutional embargo law, forced and imposed on us by the general government.

March 26*th.* Merrimac river was frozen over and so continued about two hours.

June 12*th.* The grist mills of Mr. Silas Pearson, Newbury, were destroyed by fire. It was supposed to be the work of an incendiary. Loss between three and four thousand dollars.

'*June* 14*th.* Newburyport voted that the selectmen be requested to cause the bells of the town to be rung from eleven o'clock to twelve on the day of the fifteenth of June in commemoration of the great events in Europe.'

1815.

February 13*th.* News that a treaty of peace had been made at Ghent, arrived in Newbury this day, and on the seventeenth it was ratified by the president.

September 23*d.* American missionaries, Messrs. Bardwell, Richards, Meigs, and Poor, sailed from Newburyport for Ceylon.

1816.

April 1*st.* The meeting-house in Newbury, Belleville, was this day struck by lightning and consumed.

This summer was an unusually cold one.

1817.

July 12*th.* James Monroe, president of the United States, passed through Newbury and Newburyport. He was received with all those marks of honor and respect due to his personal worth as well as his exalted station.

1818.

March 4th. Newbury voted to procure a lot of land to build a town house on.

February 13th. The Howard Benevolent Society of Newburyport was formed.

1819.

The west part of Newbury was this year set off into a separate township, and incorporated by the name of Parsons, which was afterward changed to that of West Newbury.

1820.

The Newburyport Savings bank was incorporated.

1821.

May 10th. Stephen M. Clark, of Newburyport, aged about seventeen years, was executed at Salem for the crime of arson.

This year, the town of Newbury was divided into nine school districts, and, for the first and only time since the settlement of the town, the selectmen received no pay for their services. In 1822, the Marine Bible Society was formed in Newburyport, and in 1823, the Market hall was erected. It stands on what was once called the 'middle ship yard.'

1824.

March. The town of Newburyport voted that the thanks 'of the town be given to John Porter, esquire, for his unparalleled exertions in collecting the whole taxes committed to him the past year.'

August 31st. The marquis Lafayette passed through Newbury and Newburyport. He arrived late in the evening in the midst of a heavy shower to town, where great preparations had been made to welcome the illustrious guest. The next day thousands went to see him, and were highly gratified to see and grasp the hand of the man with whose name and history many of them had been so long familiar.

1826.

This year the difficulty, which had so long existed between the town of Newburyport and the 'proprietors'' committee, was adjusted, the latter giving the former a deed of all the land owned by them within the limits of Newburyport for twelve hundred dollars.

July 4th. John Adams, in his ninety-first year, and Thomas Jefferson, in his eighty-third year, died this day — a remarkable coincidence. A eulogy on the characters of these distinguished men was delivered in Newburyport, by Caleb Cushing, esquire.

1827.

February 6th. This morning, about one o'clock, as Mr. David Jackman and Mr. Frederick Carlton were driving a heavily loaded team, drawn by four oxen and a horse, over Essex Merrimac bridge, the chains broke and precipitated them into the river. Both the men with the horse were saved, but the oxen were drowned. The morning was very cold, and the bridge had on it a large quantity of snow and ice.

This summer the new bridge, connecting Newburyport with Salisbury, was erected. It was passable August twenty-seventh, but was not completed till October. The whole cost was sixty-six thousand dollars.

June 9th. John Tilton, aged nearly eight years, son of Mr. Daniel L. Tilton, Marlborough street, was instantaneously killed by lightning, while standing near a window.

1828.

Merrimac bridge, connecting West Newbury with the Rocks' village in Haverhill, was finished this fall. It is nine hundred feet in length, has four stone piers, two abutments and a draw. The bridge before this was carried away by a freshet in April, 1818.

1829.

This year a 'breakwater,' for which an appropriation of thirty-two thousand dollars had been made in 1828 by congress, was commenced across Plum island river. It is nineteen hundred feet in length, and runs in a northwest direction. It was not completed till 1831, after another appropriation had been made by congress. The main object, for which it was erected, has not been accomplished, though it has been in some respects beneficial.

1830.

April 5th. Newbury voted not to grant licenses to any persons to sell ardent spirits.

1831.

The first number of the Liberator, an anti-slavery paper, was published in Boston, by two natives of Newburyport, William Lloyd Garrison and Isaac Knapp.

1832.

January 6th. The New England Anti-slavery society was formed by twelve persons, of whom two were from Newburyport and one from Newbury. The following is the preamble to the constitution of the society.

' We, the undersigned, hold that every person of full age and sane mind has a right to immediate freedom from personal bondage of whatsoever kind, unless imposed by the sentence of the law for the commission of some crime. We hold that man cannot, consistently with reason, religion, and the eternal and immutable principles of justice, be the property of man. We hold that whoever retains his fellow man in bondage is guilty of a grievous wrong. We hold that mere difference of complexion is no reason why any man should be deprived of any of his natural rights, or subjected to any political disability. While we advance these opinions as the principles on which we intend to act, we declare that we will not operate on the existing relations of society by other than peaceful and lawful means, and that we will give no countenance to violence or insurrection.'

January 13th. About four o'clock, P. M., Mr. Henry Page, harness maker, was found dead in his shop in Liberty street, Newburyport, having been twice stabbed by some person or persons unknown. All attempts to discover the murderer have hitherto proved ineffectual.

1833.

Ocean bank of Newburyport incorporated.

1835.

May 26th. This day, according to previous arrangements made by the citizens of the three towns that once constituted ' ould Newberry,' the two hundredth anniversary of the settlement of the town was celebrated. A salute of twenty-four guns was fired at sunrise, and a similar salute at sunset. At ten o'clock a procession was formed at the town house in Newbury, which moved at half past ten, escorted by the Newburyport artillery company, and the Byfield rifle company; went down the turnpike to High street, thence down High street to Federal street, thence down Federal to Middle street, thence through Market square, Broadway, and Merrimac street, up Market street, through Berry street and Brown's

square to Pleasant street church, where an address was delivered
by the honorable Caleb Cushing, and an ode and hymn written for
the occasion by the honorable George Lunt, were sung. After the
services of the church were concluded, about seven hundred persons dined at the pavilion, erected for the purpose near the Newbury town house. The sentiments and speeches on the occasion,
were, it is said, of a superior order. Lieutenant governor Armstrong, the honorable Messrs. Everett, Phillips, Cushing, and Lunt,
colonel Winthrop and colonel Swett of Boston, judge White of
Salem, and several other gentlemen, addressed the company, which
did not separate till sundown. In the evening the ladies gave a
splendid tea party at the town hall in Newburyport, which was
numerously attended, and which added no little eclat to the festivi-
ties. The newspapers of the day furnish us with a long account
of the toasts, sentiments, speeches, anecdotes, and so forth, which
the celebration elicited, but I have no room for the narration. I
can find room only for the following ode.

PILGRIM SONG.

Over the mountain wave,
　See where they come;
Storm-cloud and wintry wind
　Welcome them home;
Yet where the sounding gale
　Howls to the sea,
There their song peals along,
　Deep-toned and free:
　　Pilgrims and wanderers,
　　Hither we come;
　　Where the free dare to be —
　　This is our home!

England hath sunny dales,
　Dearly they bloom;
Scotia hath heather-hills,
　Sweet their perfume;
Yet through the wilderness,
　Cheerful we stray;
Native land, native land,
　Home, far away!
　　Pilgrims and wanderers,
　　Hither we come;
　　Where the free dare to be —
　　This is our home!

Dim grew the forest-path,—
　Onward they trod;
Firm beat their noble hearts,
　Trusting in God!
Gray men and blooming maids,
　High rose their song;
Hear it sweep, clear and deep,
　Ever along:
　　Pilgrims and wanderers,
　　Hither we come;
　　Where the free dare to be —
　　This is our home!

Not theirs the glory-wreath
Torn by the blast;
Heavenward their holy steps,
Heavenward they past;
Green be their mossy graves!
Ours be their fame;
While their song peals along,
Ever the same:
Pilgrims and wanderers,
Hither we come;
Where the free dare to be—
This is our home!

Thus ended the second centennial celebration of the settlement of Newbury; the completion of the first century, in 1735, having been, according to tradition, duly noticed in the front yard of colonel Joseph Coffin's house, where his great grandson, the compiler of this work, now resides.

1 8 3 7 .

May 24th. The town of Newbury voted to loan to the state, at five per centum, their portion of the surplus revenue. This was accordingly done, and though many attempts have been made to appropriate it to some other purpose, no motion to that effect has been successful.

1 8 4 0 .

The population of Newbury, Newburyport, and West Newbury, has been, according to the census, as follows, namely:

	1764	1790	1800	1810	1820	1830	1840
Newbury,		3972	4076	5176	3671	3771	3389
Newburyport,	2282	4837	5946	7634	6858	6741	7124
West Newbury,					1279	1448	1553

1 8 4 3 .

The winter of 1843 was very severe, and the spring unusually backward. As late as the middle of April the snow in many places was several feet deep.

April 13th. On this day in 1755 as well as this year, the ice broke up in the Merrimac.

June 15th. Abner Rogers, a native of Newbury, who had been in the state's prison in Charlestown two years, and who had again been sentenced five and a half years from March twenty-eighth, 1838, rushed upon the warden of the prison, Mr. Solomon Lincoln, and killed him with a shoe knife. After a long and patient investigation, the jury rendered their verdict, 'not guilty by reason of insanity.' He was then sent to the Worcester insane asylum.

October 19th. 'This morning, about half past six o'clock, an hour after the workmen had commenced operations, the boiler of a six horse power engine in the patent cordage manufactory of

Michael Wormsted & Son, on South and Marlborough streets, exploded. Mr. John Green, the engineer, who was probably standing in front of the furnace, was instantly killed, his head being crushed into an almost shapeless mass. Mr. Lorenzo Ross, who was standing in the doorway of the engine room, was badly scalded, and his body completely blackened. He was taken up senseless, but afterward revived, and it is thought may recover. The engine house was completely demolished, and the bricks, timbers, and boards thickly scattered around, to the distance of eighty or a hundred yards. The boiler was twenty feet long, and weighed over a ton and a half. The main body of it, being eight of the ten joints or plates, and weighing, probably, near twenty-eight hundred pounds, was forced in a straight line, through a pile of heavy anthracite coal, eight or ten feet in thickness, and also the end of the building against which the coal was piled, passing over the vacant lot between the ropewalk and the dwelling-house and out buildings next below it, on Marlborough street, and after striking the ground three or four times, prostrated a small shed, and leveled the fence on the street, which checked its progress so that it turned round and rested on the sidewalk, nearly on a parallel line with Marlborough street, and at a distance of nearly three hundred feet from the engine house.

'A fragment of the boiler, straightened out, and weighing two hundred pounds or more, was thrown about forty yards in the field on the lower side of the engine house, and a smaller fragment, weighing seventy-five or a hundred pounds, was projected about forty yards in a straight line in the rear towards South street, and the head of the boiler weighing probably one hundred pounds, must have been elevated to a great height as it fell on the opposite side of the ropewalk, and within a few feet of the building, having passed over the roof.' *Newburyport Herald.*

This was the first steam engine erected in Newbury, and had been in use five or six years.

1844.

May 19*th*. This day, Abner Rogers, whose insanity caused the death of Mr. Lincoln, lost his own life, undoubtedly from the same cause. The manner was this. ' Near the close of the evening exercises he became impatient and requested his attendant to permit him to retire. His attendant replied that the services would soon be over, when not a moment elapsed before he sprang through the window with great force, taking out four panes with the sash.' The fall was about sixteen feet. He was taken up senseless and so remained until he died, which was the third day after his fall.

Stuart Chase, esquire, was this year chosen town clerk of Newbury. Deacon Ezra Hale, who had for thirty-seven years officiated in that capacity, declined a re-election. A unanimous vote of thanks was given by the town ' for his long and faithful services as clerk, and so forth, and voted that it be entered on the town records by his successor in said office.'

There are four cotton mills in Newburyport, built in 1836, 1839, 1841, and 1844, of which I shall speak more particularly in the appendix.

November 19*th*. This afternoon, the reverend Daniel Dana preached to a numerous audience, in the church in Federal street, a sermon in commemoration of his having been ordained the pastor of that church and congregation a half century before.

The evening of this day was made the occasion of one of those festive meetings known in modern times by the name of 'donation visits.' Preparations had been making, for some time before, among the venerable pastor's numerous friends, to exhibit some substantial testimony of their regard. On this occasion, his house was literally crowded with those of all ages, who gladly came to show their respect for the good and eminent man, who, for half a century, had devoted himself, with untiring zeal, to his master's great business. Drawing toward the close of his labors, nothing could have been more gratifying to him, than to witness the respect and good will of the few, who had listened to his earliest instructions, mingled with the many, who had been favored by his later ministrations. It was, indeed, a cheerful and happy meeting. All were in good spirits. Plentiful refreshments were provided by the friends of him, who had thus been made a respected guest in his own house, and the music of the choir agreeably diversified the entertainment. The numerous party left behind them, in the hands of the committee, ample evidence of their sincere interest in the excellent pastor. They separated to their several homes, at a seasonable hour. All were sorry to leave, and none can ever forget the pleasing circumstances of so interesting a scene.

In token of his gratitude, the doctor puublished in the Newburyport Herald the following card.

'Doctor Dana presents his grateful acknowledgments to those numerous friends of various congregations, who were pleased to honor his house with a visit on the evening of the fiftieth anniversary of his ordination. So extensive a manifestation of interest in his person and his ministerial labors, is cheering to his heart, and its memory will cease only with his life.

'The plan of a friendly congratulation was made subservient to the purpose of *generous beneficence*, a plan conceived with so much secrecy and executed with so much liberality, has rendered the kindness of his friends almost oppressive. He can never cease to implore for them that they may be rewarded in the richest blessings of time and eternity.'

December 27*th*. A meeting-house for the first christian union society of Newburyport, was this day raised in Court street, Newburyport, seventy-five feet in length, and forty-five in breadth. The church was formed May seventh, 1841.

This page, gentle reader, closes, as you perceive, the annals of 'ould Newberry,' and should you, without the perplexity that I have sometimes experienced, receive a tithe of the pleasure, in reading the preceding pages, that I have had in collecting, arranging, and abridging, the materials of which they are composed, I shall feel highly gratified with the result of my labors, and you will, for a short time at least, be quite a happy man. If, on the contrary, your anticipations have not been realized, and you are disappointed in the history, and dissatisfied with the manner in which it has been arranged, you can alter it to your liking, as there still exists an abundance of unpublished materials, amply sufficient for you to make another volume, for your own gratification, and the amusement of the public. You can also omit reading the following appendix, which is served up, as a kind of dessert, for those who have not left the table, either in satiety or disgust.

'DOLAVI UT POTUI.' CICERO.

APPENDIX.

A. *Page* 19.

The following are the names of the most wealthy of the grantees, with the number of acres, which were granted them, affixed to their names. To each of the first settlers was granted a house lot of at least four acres, with a suitable quantity of salt and fresh meadow.

Mr. Richard Dummer,	. .	1080	Mr. James Noyes,	. . .	124
Mr. Henry Sewall,	. . .	630	Mr. Thomas Parker,	. . .	90
Mr. John Clark,	. . .	540	Captain Edmund Greenleaf,	.	122
Mr. John Woodbridge,	. . .	237	Mr. James Browne,	. .	159
Mr. Edward Rawson,	. .	581	Mr. Edward Woodman,	. .	120
Richard Kent, junior,	. . .	134	Mr. Nicholas Easton,	. . .	89
William Moody,	. . .	92	Mr. Stephen Dummer,	. .	386
John Merrill,	. . . .	96	Stephen Kent,	. . . .	84
Mr. John Cutting,	. . .	220	Nicholas Holt,	. . . .	80

To the other grantees, the number of acres varied from ten to eighty. Many of the later settlers were wealthy, who obtained the principal part of their land by purchase, such, for instance, as George Little, Robert Adams, captain William Gerrish, Richard Dole, Mr. John, Mr. Richard, and Mr. Percival Lowle, and a few others.

B. *Page* 33.

A SHORT CATECHISM

COMPOSED BY MR. JAMES NOYES, LATE TEACHER OF THE CHURCH OF
CHRIST IN NEWBURY, IN NEW ENGLAND. FOR THE USE
OF THE CHILDREN THERE.

Question. How do the Scriptures prove themselves to be true?
Answer. By the holiness of the matter, by the majesty of the style, by the accomplishment of the Prophesies, by the efficacy of their power on the hearts of men, besides the holy Ghost beareth witness, helping us to discern the truth of them.

John 7, 46: 14, 29.
1 John 2, 20.
2 Tim. 2, 16 17.
Rom. 16, 25; 10, 9.
1 John 5, 1.
John 17, 2.
Acts 8, 37.

Q. What is the sum of the Scriptures?
A. A Doctrine of a godly life.
Q. Wherein consists a godly life?
A. In the obedience of Faith.

John 6, 40.

Q. What is Faith?
A. Faith is an effectual assent to the Doctrine of the Scriptures, especially concerning the Grace of God in Christ.

1 John 4, 15; 3, 6.

Q. What doth the Scripture reveal concerning God?
A. His Nature, and his Acts.
Q. What is revealed concerning his Nature?
A. His Essence, and his Persons.
Q. How is the Essence of God made manifest?

A. By his Names, and Attributes.

Q. What are his Attributes?

A. His Independency, Unity, Immutability, Eternity, Infiniteness, Omnipresence, Omnipotency, Wisdom, Omnisciency, Holiness, Blessedness, Soveraignty, Goodness, Mercy, Meekness, Clemency, Justice and Verity.

Q. How many Persons are there in the Godhead?

1 John 5, 7.
Mat. 28, 19.

A. Three, Father, Son, and Holy-Ghost; and every one of these is God, and yet there is but One God.

Q. How many fold are the acts of God?

2 Cor. 13, 14.

A. Twofold, eternal and temporal.

Job 1, 1.

Q. What are the eternal acts of God?

Acts 5, 3 4.
1 Cor. 8, 6.

A. His Decrees.

Q. How many fold are his Decrees?

A. Twofold, general and particular.

Q. What is the general Decree of God?

A. An eternal act of God whereby he did determine to make the World, and dispose of all things therein.

Q. What are the particular Decrees of God?

A. Election and Reprobation.

Q. What is Election?

Eph. 1, 4 5 6.

A. An eternal act of God, whereby he did determine to glorifie himself in saving a certain number of persons through Faith in Christ.

Rom. 9, 22.
1 Pet. 2, 8.
Jude 4.

Q. What is Reprobation?

A. An eternal act of God, whereby he did determine to glorifie himself in condemning a certain number of persons for their sins.

Q. What are the Temporal acts of God?

A. Creation, Preservation and Government.

Q. How many-fold is his Government?

A. Twofold: general and special.

Q. What is the general Government?

Mat. 10, 29, 30.
Acts 17, 28.

A. A temporal act of God, whereby he doth dispose of all creatures according to a general Providence.

Jer. 31, 31 32.

Q. What is the special Government of God?

A. A temporal act of God whereby he doth dispose of the reasonable creature according to a special Covenant.

Q. How many Covenants hath God made with man?

A. Two: The Covenant of the Law, and the Covenant of the Gospel.

Q. What is the Covenant of the Law?

Gal. 3, 11 12.

A. A promise of Life on perfect and personal Obedience.

Q. What is the Covenant of the Gospel?

Mark 16, 16.

A. A promise of Life upon Faith in Christ.

Q. What is the Occasion of the Covenant of the Gospel?

Rom. 5, 17.

A. Adams Sin.

1 John 3, 4.

Q. What is Sin?

A. A breach of Gods Law.

Q. How many kinds of Sin are there?

A. Two: Original and Actual.

Eph. 4, 22.

Q. What is Original Sin?

A. A *Being* contrary to Gods Law.

Rom. 7, 23.
1 John 3, 4.

Q. What is Actual Sin?

A. A *Doing* contrary to Gods Law.

Q. What are the effects of Sin?

A. Guilt and Punishment.

Q. What is Guilt?

Rom. 3, 19 23.

A. A liableness to Punishment.

Q. What is Punishment?

Rom. 5, 12; 6, 23.

A. An infliction of evil for Sin; namely, Death temporal and eternal.

Q. How may we escape eternal Death?

Rom. 3, 23 24.

A. By the covenant of the Gospel only.

Q. Can we not escape death by the Covenant of the Law?

Heb. 12, 20.
Rom. 3, 20.
John 15, 5.

A. No: because we cannot perform the condition of it, which is perfect Obedience: yea by reason of the Fall of *Adam*, we cannot do any good thing.

Q. Can we perform the condition of the Covenant of the Gospel?

A.   Yes: because God has shewed us in his Scriptures, that he will help us through Faith in Christ to perform the condition of it.   Jer. 31, 33.

Q.   What is Christ?   John 1, 14.

A.   The Eternal Son of God, and both God and Man.   Heb. 2, 16.

Q.   What are we to consider in Jesus Christ?   Isaiah 9, 6.

A.   His Natures, his personal Union, and his Offices.   Rom. 9, 5.

Q.   How many Natures hath Christ?

A.   Two: the Nature of God, and the Nature of Man; otherwise called the Divine Nature and the Humane.

Q.   What is the personal union of Christ?

A.   The Subsistence of the Humane nature in the second person of the Deity.   Phil. 2, 6 7 8.

Q.   What are the Offices of Christ?   1 Tim. 2, 5.   Zech. 9, 9.

A.   His Mediatorship, Kingship, Priesthood and Prophetship.   Psalm 110, 4.   Deut. 18, 15.

Q.   What is the work of Christs Office.

A.   Redemption.

Q.   What is Redemption?

A.   A deliverance of the Elect from Sin and misery, by the price of Christs Obedience.   Titus 2, 14.

Q.   How many fold is Christs Obedience?

A.   Twofold, active and passive.

Q.   What is his active Obedience?

A.   A *Doing* the will of God.   Rom. 8, 4.

Q.   What is his passive Obedience?   Mat. 3, 15.

A.   His *Suffering* the Will of God, even to the Death of the Cross.   Isa. 53, 12.

Q.   What is the Application of Redemption?

A.   A giving of the Spirit, in and with the graces of the Spirit.   Eph. 2, 5 6.

Q.   What are the graces of the Spirit?   2 Tim. 1, 9.

A.   Vocation, Justification, Adoption and Glorification.

Q.   What is Vocation?   Rom. 8, 30.

A.   A grace of the Spirit, whereby God doth give Faith and Repentance unto his elect ones.

Q.   What is Faith?

A.   A sight of the grace of the Gospel whereby we come to cleave to God in Christ above all things for Salvation.   Mat. 16, 28.

Or else a belief that God will pardon our sins in the way of Repentance for Christs sake.   Acts 2, 38.   Mark 1, 15.

Q.   What is Repentance?   Psalm 37, 27.   Zech. 12, 10.

A.   An overcoming purpose to forsake sin, with sorrow for sin.   Hos. 14, 2 3.

Q.   What is Justification?

A.   A grace of the Spirit whereby God doth accept and pronounce all those that are called, to be just unto eternal life.   Rom. 8, 30.

Q.   What is Adoption?

A.   A grace of the Spirit, whereby God doth accept and pronounce all those that are called, to be His Children, and heirs unto eternal life.   Rom. 8, 14 15 16 17

Q.   What is Glorification?

A.   A grace of the Spirit, whereby God doth translate a man out of the misery of sin, into blessedness.   Rom. 8, 30.

Q.   How is the Application of Redemption made known?

A.   By the experiencing of the graces of the Spirit, and by the witness of the Spirit helping us to discern the truth of them.   1 Thes. 1, 4 5 6 7.   Rom. 8, 15.

Q.   What is the subject of Redemption?

A.   The Church.

Q.   What are the means of applying Redemption?

A.   They are especially publick Ministry and private duties.   Rom. 10, 13 14 15.

Q.   What are the Ministerial Acts?   Mat. 28, 19.

A.   Preaching of the Word, Prayer, Administration of the Sacraments, and Discipline.   1 Tim. 2, 1.   Mat. 18, 17; 16, 19.

Q.   What is a Sacrament?

A.   A visible sign instituted by God for the confirmation of the Covenant.

Q.   How many Sacraments are there?

A.   Two, Baptism and the Lords Supper.

Q.   What is the sign signifying in Baptism?

A.   Water, and the washing with water.

Q.   What is the thing signified?   1 Pet. 3, 21.

A.   The blood of Christ washing away our sins unto eternal life.   Rom. 6, 4.

Q. What is the sign signifying in the Lords Supper ?

A. The Bread and Wine : the Bread broken, and the Wine poured out, the giving and receiving of it.

Q. What is the thing signified in the Lords Supper ?

1 Cor. 11, 23 24 25 26
John 6, 51.

A. The Body of Christ broken on the Cross, his Blood shed for our sins, offered to sinners in the way of believing and received by Faith, for assurance of eternal life.

Mat. 18, 17.

Q. What is Discipline ?

A. A Correction of scandalous Professors by Church Censures.

Acts 20, 7.

Q. What is the season of attending the Publick Ministry ?

A. Especially on the first day of the week, or Lords Day.

Q. When is Redemption consummated ?

Mat. 24, 2.
Hos. 13, 14.
Isai. 63, 34.

A. In the Resurrection at the last Judgment, at the second coming of Christ.

Q. How many Commandments are there ?

A. Ten.

Q. Into how many Tables are the Commandments divided ?

A. Into two Tables.

Deut. 4, 13.
Mat. 22, 37 38.

Q. What doth the first Table contain ?

A. Our duties towards God, or Duties of Religious Worship, in the four first Commandments.

Mat. 22, 39 40.
Rom. 13, 9.

Q. What doth the second Table contain?

A. Our Duties towards the Creature, in the six last.

Q. What is contained in the first Commandment ?

A. Natural Worship; in Faith, Hope, Love, Fear, hearing the Word and Prayer.

Psalm 73, 25.
1 Cor. 13, 13.

Q. What is Hope ?

A. A cleaving to God as our chiefest good, for Blessedness.

Deut. 6, 5.

Q. What is Love ?

A. A cleaving to God as the chiefest good, and deserving all Glory.

Q. What is Fear ?

Deut. 6, 13.
Heb. 12, 28.

A. An admiring and adoring of Gods Holiness, and all his perfections.

Eph. 4, 11 12.
Mat. 28, 19.

Q. What is contained in the second Commandment ?

A. Instituted Worship; in Ministry, Sacraments, and Discipline.

1 Cor. 11, 23 24.
Mat. 28, 17.

Q. What is contained in the third Commandment ?

A. A due manner of Worship, in reverence, devotion and alacrity.

Q. What is contained in the fourth Commandment ?

Heb. 12, 28.
Psalm 132, 7 ; 110, 3.

A. A due time of Worship, as all due seasons, Morning and Evening, especially on the Lords Day.

Q. What is contained in the fifth Commandment ?

Psalm 141, 2; 55, 17.
Acts 20, 7.

A. A due respect to the good name or dignity of our Neighbour, in humility, gratitude and obedience.

1 Pet. 5, 5.
Phil. 2, 3.

Q. What is Humility ?

A. A grace which moderateth the love of excellency.

Rom. 12, 16.

Q. What is Gratitude ?

A. A grace which disposeth us to recompense benefits.

1 Sam. 30, 26 31.

Q. What is obedience?

2 Sam. 9, 1.

A. A grace which disposeth us to honour all such as are in authority, by being subject.

1 Pet. 2, 13.

Q. What is contained in the sixth Commandment ?

A. A due respect to the life of our Neighbour, in goodness, mercy, meekness, and patience.

1 Cor. 13, 4.
Luke 6, 36.

Q. What is Goodness?

A. A grace which disposeth us to shew kindness to all.

Q. What is Mercy ?

A. A grace which disposeth us to relieve all such as are in misery.

Numb. 12, 3.

Q. What is Meekness ?

A. A grace which moderateth anger and revenge.

1 Pet. 3, 4.
Luke 21, 19.
Col. 1, 11.

Q. What is Patience ?

A. A grace which moderateth grief in Affliction.

Q. What is contained in the seventh Commandment ?

A. A due respect to the purity of our Neighbour, in temperance, chastity, modesty, gravity.

Q. What is Temperance ?

Tit. 3, 3.

A. A grace which moderateth affection to all sensual pleasures.

Q. What is Chastity ?

A. A grace which regulateth the lusts of the flesh.   1 Thess. 4, 3 4 5.

Q. What is Modesty?   1 Tim. 2, 9.

A. A grace which restraineth us from wantonness.

Q. What is Gravity?   1 Pet. 3, 2 3.

A. A grace which inclineth us to purity.

Q. What is contained in the eighth Commandment?

A. A due respect to the goods of our Neighbour, in righteousness, liberality, and frugality.

Q. What is Righteousness?   Rom. 13, 7.

A. A grace which inclineth us to give all men their due.   Mic. 6, 8.

Q. What is Liberality?

A. A grace which inclineth us to communicate our goods freely to   Rom. 12, 13.
our Neighbour.

Q. What is Frugality?

A. A grace which inclineth us to be provident and diligent in our   Prov. 31, 27.
Calling.

Q. What is contained in the ninth Commandment?

A. A due respect to the innocency of our Neighbour in verity and fidelity.

Q. What is Verity?

A. A grace which inclineth us to speak the truth for our Neigh-   Zech. 8, 16.
bours good.

Q. What is Fidelity?

A. A grace which inclineth us to keep our Promises.   Psalm 15, 4.

Q. What is contained in the tenth Commandment?

A. A due respect to the prosperity of our Neighbour, in rejoycing   Rom. 12, 15.
in his prosperity, and accepting our own portion with contentation.

Q. What is Contentation?

A. A grace which inclineth us to accept our own portion, whether   1 Tim. 6, 6.
good or evil, with Thanksgiving.   Heb. 13, 5.
   Phil. 4, 11.

The preceding catechism is an exact transcript from the edition of 1714, published in Boston by Bartholomew Green. It is the only copy I have ever seen in Newbury, and was found among the papers of Mr. Ichabod Coffin. As it was undoubtedly composed more than two hundred years ago, I have thought it worth preservation as a specimen of the style of the 'olden time,' and of the principles then inculcated on the rising generation. Its author, Mr. James Noyes, died the twenty-second of October, 1656, in his forty-eighth year.

C. *Page* 38.

For the list of graduates, and other information, see letter I.

D. *Page* 38.

LIST OF GRANTEES, AND GENEALOGY OF THE FIRST SETTLERS
FROM 1635 TO 1700.

From the proprietors' book of records, folio forty-four, I make the following extract.

Mr. Richard Dummer,	Mr. Thomas Parker,
Mr. Henry Sewall,	Mr. James Noyes,
Mr. Edward Rawson,	Mr. John Lowle,
Mr. Stephen Dummer,	Mr. Percival Lowle,
Mr. Edmund Greenleaf,	Mr. John Spencer,
Mr. John Clarke,	Mr. John Woodbridge,
Mr. John Cutting,	Mr. James Browne,
Henry Short,	Thomas Cromwell,

Nicholas Holt,
Henry Rolfe,
John Merrill,
Thomas Hale,
Joseph Peasley,
William Mors,
John Goff,
John Stevens,
Anthony Short,
John Pemberton,
John Pike, senior,
John Musselwhite,
John Emery,
Anthony Somerby,
Richard Bartlet,
William Moody,
William Franklin,
Abraham Toppan,
Henry Somerby,
Walter Allen,
Thomas Silver,
Henry Travers,
Archelaus Woodman,
Richard Knight,
Mrs. [John] Oliver,
Stephen Kent,
Richard Badger,
William Thomas,
Widow [William] Stevens,
John Kelly,
Francis Plumer,
Robert Coker,
William Palmer,
Thomas Coleman,
Nathaniel Badger,
William Berry,
Mr. [Edward] Woodman,
Richard Kent, junior,

Richard Littlehale,
Giles Badger,
Samuel Scullard,
John Osgood,
Abel Huse,
Joseph Carter,
John Knight,
Henry Lunt,
Thomas Browne,
John Hutchins,
Daniel Thurston,
John Poor,
John Pike, junior,
Henry Palmer,
William Titcomb,
Nicholas Batt,
Thomas Smith,
William White,
Thomas Davis,
William Ilsley,
Samuel Gile,
Thomas Dow,
John Swett,
Christopher Bartlet,
Richard Browne,
John Cheney,
Anthony Morss,
Nicholas Noyes,
Nathaniel Weare,
John Fry,
John Bartlet,
Richard Fitts,
Thomas Blumfield,
George Browne,
John Bond,
John Russ,
Mr. [John] Miller.
Ninety-one in all.

'It is declared and ordered hereby, December seventh, 1642, according to the former intentions of the towne that the persons only abovementioned are acknowledged to be freeholders by the towne and to have proportionable right in all waste lands, commons and rivers undisposed, and such as by, from, or under them, or any of them or their heirs, have bought, granted and purchased from them, or any of them their right and title thereunto and none else.'

The number of proprietors, ninety-one originally, was subsequently increased, either by grant or purchase, to one hundred and thirteen, to whom, and their heirs, belonged all unappropriated lands, and so forth, including Plum island, which was sold, in 1827, by the proprietors, to Moses Pettingell, esquire. Of the original proprietors, some returned to England, some removed to other towns, and some, who remained, sold their 'privilege of freehold,' as it was called, to others.

Those, who are desirous of more minute information respecting the first settlers of Newbury, whether grantees or not, and do not place implicit faith in the almost universal tradition, that they are descended from one of just 'three brothers,' who came over with the first settlers, may gratify that curiosity, by examining the subsequent genealogy. It contains all the names, which are to be found on record in any of the town books prior to 1700, with much additional information, which has been collected from various sources, with more care and labor, and attended with greater perplexity, than any other part of the book. Many people, I suppose, will look on the whole collection of names, as so much labor lost, and refer me to Paul's excellent advice to Titus, to 'avoid foolish questions and genealogies, which are unprofitable and vain.' His advice to Timothy is more in accordance with my plan, for I have neither 'given heed to fables,' nor 'endless genealogies,' for mine end in 1700, sometimes in the middle of a family. Some, I presume, will be disappointed in not finding the facts agree with their tradition, and others, perhaps, will be as much disappointed in not finding their ancestors' names at all. Such as I could find, I have inserted with as much correctness as the materials I have been able to obtain, would permit.

Among such a mass of names and dates, mistakes must be expected, for accidents, we are told, will happen in the best families, all imaginable pains to the contrary, notwithstanding. Those, who would be better pleased with a short, comprehensive genealogy of the whole human race, and one, at the same time, free from error, must read the ninth chapter of Genesis: 'Shem, Ham and Japheth, and of them was the whole earth overspread.' As I have not room enough to trace the whole line of descent of the first settlers of Newbury from these 'three brothers,' the reader must be content with that portion of it, which he will find in the subsequent pages.

ACREMAN, STEPHEN m. Sara Stickney 17 Dec. 1684.
ACRES, HENRY m. Hannah Silver 13 March, 1671. Chil.—Catharine, 17 March, 1675. John, 2 Oct. 1678.
ADAMS, ROBERT, tailor, from Devonshire, Salem 1638, Newbury 1640. His wife Eleanor d. 12 June, 1677. He d. 12 Oct. 1682, ag. 81. His second wife Sara, widow of Henry Short he m. 6 Feb. 1678. She d. 24 Oct. 1697. Chil.—Abraham, b. 1639, Isaac, 1648, Jacob, 23 April, 1649, another Jacob, 13 Sept. 1651, Hannah, 25 June, 1650, Robert, Elizabeth, Joanna, Mary, and John.
ADAMS, ABRAHAM son of Robert, m. Mary Pettingell 16 Nov. 1670. Chil.—Robert, 12 May, 1674, Abraham, 2 May, 1676, d. 8 April, 1763 ag. 87, Isaac, 26 Feb. 1679, Sara, 15 April, 1681, Matthew, 25 May, 1686, Israel, 25 Dec. 1688, Dorothy, 25 Oct. 1691, Richard, 22 Nov. 1693. He d. 14 June, 1714, ag. 75.
ADAMS, JACOB son of Robert, m. Anna Ellen 7 April, 1677. Chil.—Dorothy, 26 June, 1679, Rebecca, 26 Aug. 1680. He d. in Suffield, Conn. Nov. 1717 ag. 63.
ADAMS, ROBERT son of Robert, m. Rebekah Knight in 1695. Chil.—Abraham, 8 July, 1696, Rebekah, 28 Jan. 1698, Mary, 3 March, 1700, Robert, 20 Nov. 1702.
ADAMS, ARCHELAUS son of   m. Sara March 18 March, 1698. Chil.— Sara, 22 Jan. 1699, Mary, 29 Oct. 1701, John, 11 Oct. 1704.
ALLEN, CHARLES m. Joanna Scott 1703.
ALLEN. JOHN Chil.—John, 28 Aug. 1656, Samuel, 8 April, 1658, Joseph, 18 March, 1660, Benjamin, 30 Jan. 1662.
ALLEN, WILLIAM, Salem, 1638. Salisbury from 1639 to 1650.
ALLEN. WALTER Chil.—Abigail, 1 Oct. 1641, Benjamin, 15 April, 1647. A Walter Allen d. in Charlestown 8 July, 1681.
ALLY, THOMAS m. Sara Silver 9 Feb. 1671.
'ALFORD, EDWARD was killed 14 July, 1683, by a fall in the ship that John Rolfe built.'
ANNIS, CURMAC alias Charles, b. in Enniskellen, Ireland, in 1638, came to Newbury, m. Sara Chase 15 May, 1666. Chil.—Charles ——, Priscilla, 8 Nov. 1677, Hannah, 15 Nov. 1679, Anne, 28 Dec. 1681, and probably others unrecorded.
ANNIS, ABRAHAM m. Hannah ——. Chil.—Charles, 10 Feb. 1694. Hannah, 19 Nov. 1698, John, 1 May, 1700, Stephen 1 Feb. 1702, Sara, 9 Sept. 1705.
ANNIS, JOSEPH m. Dorothy ——. Chil.—Dorothy, 1 Nov. 1692, Sara, 14 March, 1694, Aquila, 14 June, 1695, Seaborn, 1 Jan. 1697, Hannah, 19 Nov. 1696, Abigail, 25 Sept. 1700, Joseph, 14 Jan. 1703.
APPLETON, SAMUEL of Ipswich, m. Mary Oliver of Newbury 8 Dec. 1656.
ASLETT, JOHN m. Rebecca Ayres 8 Oct. 1648.
ATKINSON, JOHN hatter, son of Theodore Atkinson of Bury in Lancashire, Eng. He was b. in Boston in 1636, was in Newbury 1663, and m. Sara Mirick 27 April, 1664. Chil.—Sara, 27 Nov. 1665, Thomas, 27 Dec. 1669, Theodore, 23 Jan. 1672, and

drowned 24 July. 1685, Abigail, 8 Nov. 1673, Samuel, 16 Jan. 1676, Nathaniel, 29 Nov. 1677, Elizabeth, 20 June, 1680, Joseph, 1 May, 1682.

ATKINSON, JOHN jun. probably son of John, sen. m. Sara ——. Chil.—Thomas, 16 March, 1694, John, 29 Oct. 1695, Theodore, 8 Oct. 1698. He m. widow Hannah Cheney 3 June 1700, who d. 5 Jan. 1705. Chil.—Sara, 6 Nov. 1700, Hannah, 21 Jan. 1703.

AYER, JOHN m. Ruth Browne 31 Oct. 1698. Edith b. 8 April, 1702.

AYER, OBADIAH had a son John b. 2 Mar. 1663.

AYER, THOMAS had a son John b. 12 May, 1657.

AYER, SAMUEL m. Abigail ——. His son Stephen b. 13 March, 1689.

AYER, SAMUEL m. Sara ——. His son Jabez b. 27 Dec. 1690.

AYER, THOMAS m. Hannah ——. Chil.—Abraham, 18 June, 1688, Sara, 29 Aug. 1690, Mehetabel, 5 April, 1693.

BACHILER, REV. STEPHEN b. in England in 1561, came to Boston 5 June, 1632, went to Lynn, thence in Feb. 1636 to Ipswich, thence to Mattakeese, now Yarmouth, in 1637, thence to Newbury in 1638. thence to Hampton in 1639. From 1647 to 1650 he lived in Portsmouth, thence to England, where he died at Hackney aged about 100 years. Chil.—Theodata, who m. Mr. Christopher Hussey, Deborah, who m. John Wing of Sandwich, ——, who m. a Sanborn, (and had three sons, John, Stephen, and William,) Nathaniel, Francis and Stephen. See Lewis's History of Lynn.

BACHILER, JOHN of Reading. m. Sara Poore 10 Nov. 1696.

BADGER, GILES Newbury, 1635. He d. 10 July, 1647. His wife Elizabeth was daughter of capt. Edmund Greenleaf. His son John was born 30 June, 1643.

BADGER, RICHARD and NATHANIEL brothers to Giles, were in Newbury 1635. Nathaniel's wife was Hannah.

BADGER, JOHN son of Giles, m. Elizabeth ——, who d. 8 April, 1669. His second wife Hannah Swett he m. 23 Feb. 1671. He d. 31 March, 1691, aged nearly 48. Chil.—John, b. 4 April, 1664, and d. 29 July, John, b. 26 April, 1665, Sara, 25 Jan. 1667, James, 19 March, 1669, Stephen. 13 Dec. 1671, Hannah, 3 Dec. 1673, Nathaniel, 16 Jan. 1676, Mary, 2 May, 1678, Elizabeth, 30 April 1680, Ruth, 10 Feb. 1683, Abigail, 29 June, 1687, Lydia, 30 April, 1690.

BADGER, JOHN son of John, m. Rebecca Brown 5 Oct. 1691. Chil.—John, 20 Jan. 1692, James, 10 Jan. 1693, Elizabeth, 5 Feb. 1695, Stephen, 1697, Joseph, 1698, Benjamin, 15 June, 1700, Dorothy, 5 June, 1709.

BADGER, STEPHEN son of John, m. Mercy ——, and moved to Charlestown and had six children.

BADGER, NATHANIEL probably son of John, m. Mary Lunt 27 March, 1693. Chil.—John, 3 Jan. 1694, a son [probably Joseph] 29 Nov. 1695, Daniel, 27 March, 1698, Mehetabel, Aug. 1700, Edmund, 2 April, 1703, Mary, 8 Sept. 1705, Mary, 13 1708, Samuel, 14 Aug. 1710, Anne, 25 Jan. 1712, Enoch, probably in 1714. He then moved to Norwich, Conn. where Henry was born 23 March, 1717.

BAILEY, JOHN sen. weaver, from Chippenham, England, was shipwrecked at Pemquid, now Bristol, Me. 15 Aug. 1635, went to Salisbury, thence to Newbury in 1650, where he died 2 Nov. 1651.

BAILEY, JOHN jr. son of John sen. was born in 1613, came to Salisbury and Newbury, mar. Eleanor Emery, sister of John Emery sen. He died March 1691 aged 78. Chil.—Rebecca, 1641, John, 18 May, 1643, and d. 22 June, 1663, Joshua d. 7 April, 1652, Sara, 17 Aug. 1644, Joseph, 4 April, 1648, James, 12 Sept. 1650, Joshua, 17 Feb. 1653, Isaac, 22 July, 1654, Rachel, 19 Oct. 1662, Judith, 3 Aug. 1665, and d. 20 Sept. 1668, Rebecca.

BAILEY, JOSEPH son of John, jun. m. Priscilla ——. About 1700 he moved to Arundel, Me. left in 1703, returned in 1714, and was there killed by the Indians, Oct. 1723, aged 75. Chil.—Rebecca, 25 Oct. 1675, Priscilla, 31 Oct. 1676, John, 16 Sept. 1678, Joseph, 28 Jan. 1681, Hannah, 9 Sept. 1683, Daniel, 10 June, 1686, Mary, 9 June, 1688, Judith, 11 Feb. 1690, Lydia, 25 Nov. 1695, Sarah, 14 Feb. 1698.

BAILEY, MR. JAMES son of John, jun. m. Mrs. Mary Carr 17 Sept. 1672. Chil.— Mary, 6 July, 1673, Isaac, 22 Oct. 1681. See appendix, letter C.

BAILEY, ISAAC son of John, jun. m. Sara Emery 13 June, 1683, who died 1 April, 1694. He m. Rebecca Bartlet 5 Sept. 1700. Ch.—Isaac, 30 Dec. 1683, Joshua, 30 Oct. 1685, David, 12 Dec. 1687, Judith, 11 Feb. 1690, Sara, 11 Feb. 1692.

BAILEY, JOHN son of ——, m. Mary Bartlet 2 July, 1700. Ch.—John, 10 March, 1701, Joseph, 11 Oct. 1702.

BAKER, JOHN was dismissed from Boston church 24 Nov. 1640, thence to Acomenticus, thence to Boston again. See Winthrop, vol. 2, p. 29.

BARBER, THOMAS m. Anne Chase 27 April, 1671. His son Thomas b. 16 Feb. 1672.

BALLARD, WILLIAM b. in

BARTLET, JOHN sen. with four others of the same sirname came to Newbury 1635. He had a son John. His wife Joan d. 5 Feb. 1679. He died 13 April, 1678.

BARTLET, JOHN jun. son of John, sen. m. Sara, daughter of John Knight 5 March, 1660. Ch.—Gideon, 18 Dec. 1660, Mary, who d. 29 March, 1682.

BARTLET, RICHARD sen. shoemaker, brother to John, sen. He died 25 May, 1647. Ch.—John, Christopher, Joanna, Samuel b. 20 Feb. 1646, Richard.

BARTLET, RICHARD jr. son of John, sen. or Richard sen. m. Abigail ——. She d. 1 March, 1687. He d. 1698, aged 77. Ch.—Richard, 21 Feb. 1649, Thomas, 7 Sept. 1650, Abigail, March, 1653. John, 22 June, 1655, Hannah, 18 Dec. 1657, and d. 17 June, 1676, Rebecca, 23 May, 1661.

BARTLET, CHRISTOPHER brother to Richard, jr. m. Mary 16 April, 1645. Martha, 7 March, 1653. She d. 24 Dec. 1661. His second wife, Mary Hoyt, he m. 17 Dec. 1663. He died 15 March, 1670, aged 47. Ch.—Mary, 15 Oct. 1647, who d. young, Anne, 28 Sept. 1650, Martha, March, 1653, Christopher, 11 June, 1655, Jonathan, 5 July, 1657, and d. 7 Dec. 1759, John, b. 13 Sept. and d. 28 Dec. 1665.

BARTLET, SAMUEL son of Richard, sen. m. Elizabeth Titcomb 23 May, 1671, and d. 15 May 1732, aged 87. Ch.—Elizabeth, 13 May, 1672, Abigail, 14 April, 1674, Samuel, 28 March, 1676, Sara, 7 July, 1678, Richard, 13 Feb. 1680, Thomas, 13 Aug. 1681, Tirzah, 20 Jan. 1684, Lydia, 5 Nov. 1687. His wife Elizabeth d. 26 Aug. 1690.

BARTLET, RICHARD son of Richard, jun. m. Hannah Emery 18 Nov. 1673. Ch. —Hannah, 8 Nov. 1674, Richard, 20 Oct. 1676, John, 23 Sept. 1678, Samuel, 8 July, 1680, and d. 20 Nov. 1685, Daniel, 8 Aug. 1682, Joseph, 18 Nov. 1686, Samuel, 2 May, 1689, Stephen, 21 April, 1691, Thomas, 14 July, 1695, Mary, 15 Sept. 1697.

BARTLET, RICHARD m. Margaret Woodman, 12 April, 1699. Ch.—Richard, 27 June, 1700, Joseph, 18 Feb. 1702.

BARTLET, THOMAS son of Richard, jun. m. Tirzah Titcomb 24 Nov. 1685. He d. 6 April, 1689. Ch.—Elizabeth, 7 Aug. 1686, and d. 15 Oct. 1689, Tirzah, 29 March, 1689.

BARTLET, JOHN son of Richard, jr. called 'John the tanner,' m. Mary Rust 29 Oct. 1680. He d. 24 May, 1736, aged 81. Ch.—Mary, 17 Oct. 1681, and d. 29 March, 1682, John, 24 Jan. 1683, Mary, 27 April, 1684, Nathaniel, 18 April, 1685, Dorothy, 23 Aug. 1686, Sara, 27 Nov. 1687, Hannah, 13 March, 1689, Nathan, 23 Dec. 1691, Abigail, 12 Aug. 1693, Alice, 18 March, 1695.

BARTLET, NATHANIEL m. —— ——. Ch.— James and Mary, Dec. 1679.

BARTLET, RICHARD 3d m. Mary Ordway 18 Nov. 1702.

BARTLET, CHRISTOPHER jun. m. Deborah Weed 29 Nov. 1677. Ch.—Christopher, 26 Feb. 1679, Deborah, 23 June, 1680, Mary, 17 April, 1682. He d. 14 April, 1711.

BARTLET, JOHN the 4th m. Prudence Merrill 25 Nov. 1702.

BATT, MR. CHRISTOPHER, tanner, came from Salisbury, England, to Newbury about 16 , thence to Salisbury, where he resided from 1640 to 1650, thence to Boston, where he was accidentally shot by his own son, who was firing at a mark in his orchard 10 Aug. 1661. In his will, written in 1656, is the following remarkable expression : 'knowing that I am at all tymes and in the most secure places and employments subject to many accidents that may bring me to my end,' and so forth. Ch.—John, b. in Salisbury 1641, Paul and Barnabas, 18 Feb. 1643, Christopher, Ann, who m. Edmund Angier. Rev. Samuel, who was a minister in England, Jane, who m. Dr. Peter Toppan of Newbury, Sarah, Abigail, Thomas, Timothy, Ebenezer, who d. 16 Aug. 1685, and Elizabeth, who died 6 July, 1652. Mr. Batt was sixty years old in 1661. His widow Ann was living in 1679.

BATT, NICHOLAS 'linnen weaver from Devizes,' England, came with his wife Lucy in the James to Boston, June 3, thence to Newbury. He d. 6 Dec. 1677. His widow Lucy d. 26 Jan. 1679. Ch.—Sara, 12 June, 1640, and two other daughters.

BEEDLE or BEDELL, ROBERT was b. in 1642. Ch.—Thomas, 30 April, 1668, Elizabeth, 22 Nov. 1669, Judith, 29 March, 1671 and d. 10 July, 1673, Robert, 5 Jan. 1675, Judith, 8 March, 1676, and d. 22 March, 1677, John, 23 April, 1678, Hannah d. 13 Nov. 1678.

BELCONGER, JOHN m. Mary or Sarah Kelly 12 April, 1666. His daughter Mary b. 7 Dec. 1666.

BENTE, ROBERT d. 30 Jan. 1648.

BERRY, WILLIAM Piscataqua 1632, Newbury 1635.

BISHOP, JOHN carpenter, m. Rebecca, daughter of Richard Kent, and widow of Samuel Scullard, Oct. 1647. Ch.—John, 19 Sept. 1648, Rebecca, 15 May, 1650, Joanna, 24 April, 1652, Hannah, 10 Dec. 1653, Elizabeth, 31 Aug. 1655, and d. 6 Dec. 1656, Jonathan, 11 Jan. 1657, Noah, 20 June, 1658, David, 26 Aug. 1660. He removed to Woodbridge, N. J. and there died in Oct. 1684.

BLANCHARD, JOHN d. of the small pox 24 July, 1678.

BINGLEY, WILLIAM m. Elizabeth Preston 27 Feb. 1660. His son William, 24 Feb. 1662.

BLUMFIELD, THOMAS sen. an early settler, died in 1639. Ch.—Thomas and a 'lame daughter.'

BLUMFIELD, THOMAS jun. son of Thomas, sen. Ch.—Mary, 15 Jan. 1642, Sarah, 30 Dec. 1643, John, 15 March, 1646, Thomas, 12 Dec. 1648, Nathaniel, 10 April, 1651, Ezekiel, 1 Nov. 1653. Rebecca, 1656, Ruth, 4 July, 1659, Timothy, 1 April, 1664. In 1665, he moved to Woodbridge, N. J. Gov. Joseph Bloomfield, of that state, was one of his descendants.

BOLTON, WILLIAM b. in 1630, m. Jane Bartlet 16 Jan. 1655. Ch.—Mary, 25 Sept. 1655. His wife Jane d. 6 Sept. 1659. He m. Mary Dennison, 22 Nov. 1659. William, b. 27 May, 1665, Ruth, 1 Aug. 1667, Elizabeth, 23 May, 1672, and d. 17 June, 1671, Elizabeth, 8 Nov. 1674, Sara, 5 April, 1677. Hannah, 18 July, 1679, Joseph, 8 July, 1682. William d. 30 March, 1694, Sara d. 30 March, 1694.

BOND, JOHN m. Hester Blakely 5 Aug. 1649. After 1660 he was in Rowley, thence to Haverhill, where he d. 1675. Ch.—John, 10 June, 1650, Thomas, 29 March and d. 23 May, 1652, Joseph, 14 April, 1653, Hester, 3 Sept. 1655, Mary, 16 Dec. 1657, Abigail, 6 Nov. 1660.

BOYNTON, CALEB m. Mary Moore 24 June, 1672. His son William b. 24 July, 1673.

BOYNTON, JOSHUA m. Hannah Barnet 9 April, 1678. His son William b. 26 May, 1690.

BOYNTON, JOSHUA m. Sara Browne, April, 1678. Ch.—Joshua, 4 May, 1679, and d. 29 Oct. 1770, aged 92, John, 15 July, 1683.

BRABROOK, JOHN came from Watertown, was nephew to Henry Short, d. in Newbury 28 June, 1662. His two sons were b. in Watertown in 1642 and 1643.

BRADING, JAMES m. Hannah Rock 11 Oct. 1659. Son James b. 1662.

BRADLEY, HENRY m. widow Judith Davis 7 Jan. 1696.

BRADSTREET, DR. HUMPHREY from Rowley, m. Sara ———. Ch.—Dorothy, 19 Dec. 1692, Joshua, 24 Feb. 1695, Sara, 14 Jan. 1697, Daniel, 13 Feb. 1701, He d. 11 May, 1717, aged

BRICKET, NATHANIEL m. ——— and had ch. Nathaniel, 20 Dec. 1673, John, 3 May, 1676, James and Mary, 11 Dec. 1679, Nathaniel, 23 Sept. 1683, and was drowned 17 Oct. 1687.

BRITTAIN, FRANCIS m. Hannah ———, son John b. 25 Dec. 1695.

BODWELL, HENRY b. in 1654, m. Bithia Emery, daughter of John Emery 4 May, 1681. Bithia b. 2 June, 1682.

BRYER, RICHARD m. Eleanor Wright 21 Dec. 1665. She d. 29 Aug. 1672. Ch.— Richard, 19 Aug. 1667, Elizabeth, 11 May, 1669, Ruth, 27 Dec. 1670.

BUSBY, NICHOLAS went from Newbury to Boston where he d. 28 Aug. 1657.

BURBANK, JOHN m. Susanna Merrill 15 Oct. 1663.

BROWNE, THOMAS weaver, came to Newbury in 1635 from Malford, England. His wife Mary d. 2 June 1655. Ch.—Mary, 1635, Isaac and Francis. He d. by a fall 8 Jan. 1687, aged 80.

BROWNE, FRANCIS son of Thomas, m. Mary Johnson 21 Nov. 1653. Ch.— Elizabeth, 17 Oct. 1654, Mary. 15 April, 1657, and d. 4 April, 1679, Hannah b. and d. 1659, Sara, 10 May, 1663, John, 13 May, 1665, Thomas, 1 July, 1667, and d. 2 March, 1689, Joseph, 28 Sept. 1670, Francis, 17 March, 1674, Benjamin, 22 April, 1681.

BROWNE, FRANCIS son of Francis, m. 31 Dec. 1679. He d. 1691 aged 59.

BROWN, JOSEPH son of Francis m. Sara ———. Ch.—Abigail, 6 April, 1695, Nathan, 18 June, 1697, Sara, 22 June, 1698, Nathaniel, 1 Aug. 1700.

BROWN, JOHN son of Francis, m. Ruth Huse 20 Aug. 1683. Ch.—John, 27 Oct. 1683, Isaac, 4 Feb. 1685.

BROWNE, RICHARD Newbury, 1635. His wife Edith d. April, 1647. He m. widow Elizabeth Badger, 16 Feb. 1648. He d. 26 April, 1661. Ch.—Joseph b. and d. young, Joshua, 10 April, 1642, Caleb, 7 May, 1645, Elizabeth, 29 March, 1649, Richard, 18 Feb. 1651, Edmund, 17 July, 1654, Sara, 7 Sept. 1657, Mary, 10 April, 1660.

BROWNE, GEORGE brother to Richard, d. 1 April, 1642.

BROWNE, MARGERY d. 26 March, 1651.

BROWN, RICHARD son of Richard, m. Mary Jaques 7 May, 1674. His only son Richard b. 12 Sept. 1675.

BROWN, REV. RICHARD son of Richard, m. Mrs. Martha Whipple 22 April, 1703. Ch.—Martha, 19 Feb. 1704, John, 2 March, 1706, William, 24 Jan. 1708, Mary, 31 Dec. 1709.

BROWN, JOHN son of ———, m. Mary Woodman 20 Feb. 1660. Ch.—Judith, 3 Dec. 1660, Mary, 8 March, 1662.

BROWN, JOSHUA son of Richard sen. m. Sara Sawyer 15 Jan. 1669. Ch.—Joseph,

18 Oct. 1669, Joshua, 18 May, 1671, Tristram, 21 Dec. 1672, Sara, 5 Dec. 1676, Ruth, 29 Oct. 1678, Samuel, 4 Sept. 1687.

BROWN, ISAAC son of Thomas, m. Rebecca Bailey 22 Aug. 1661. He d. 13 May, 1674. Ch.—Ruth, 26 May, 1662, Thomas, 15 Sept. 1664, Rebecca, 15 March, 1667.

BROWN, THOMAS sen. m. Elizabeth ——. Ch.—Isaac b. and d. June, 1696, Sara, 26 April, 1697, Mary, 14 Feb. 1699, Hannah. 29 June, 1700.'

BROWN. JOSEPH m. Lydia Emery 1696. Ch.—Joseph, 1 Nov. 1699, Francis, 23 June, 1702.

BROWN, JAMES m. Hannah ——. Ch.—Benjamin, 21 March, 1681, Abraham, 1683, and d. 13 Jan. 1684, Joseph, 19 May, 1685, Hannah, 16 Nov. 1687, John d. 18 Dec. 1690.

BROWN, JAMES jun. m. Mary Edwards 28 April, 1694, who d. 5 May, 1700. He m. Rebekah Brown for his second wife. Ch.—Elizabeth. 14 Oct. 1696, Sara, 8 Nov. 1701.

BROWN, MR. JAMES came from Southampton in 1634. In 1656 he is called 'late teacher at Portsmouth.'

BROWN, JAMES jun. son of ——, m. and had ch. Mary 25 May, 1663, Abigail, 24 Oct. 1665, Martha, 22 Dec. 1667.

BROWN, JOSHUA jun. son of Joshua sen. m. Elizabeth ——. Daughter Elizabeth, 27 July, 1700.

BROWN, JOSEPH m. Sara ——. Son Nathaniel, 1 Aug. 1700.

CALEF, MR. JOHN m. Deborah King of Boston, 1702. Ch.—John, 3 June, 1703, Deborah. 21 Jan. 1705.

CARR. JAMES b. 28 Apr. 1650, son of George Carr of Salisbury, who died in 1682. He m. Mary Sears 14 Nov. 1677. Ch.—Mary, 15 Dec. 1678, Hannah, 16 Oct. 1680, Sarah, 8 May, 1682, John, 26 Aug. 1684, Katharine, 24 Nov. 1686, James, April, 1689, Hepzibah, 24 April, 1692, Elizabeth, 24 March, 1694.

CARTER, JOSEPH Newbury. 1636.

CHADDOCK or CHADWICK, THOMAS m. Sara Woolcott 6 April, 1675. Daughter Sara b. 3 Oct. 1675.

CHANDLER, WILLIAM cooper, m. Mary ——, who d. 29 Oct. 1666. He m. Mary Lord 26 Feb. 1667. Ch.—Hester, 28 Jan. 1652, William, Dec. 1667, Joseph, 19 Nov. 1669, Samuel, 29 Feb. 1672, Mary. 18 May, 1674. His wife Mary d. 3 Oct. 1676. He d. 5 March, 1701 in his 85th year. His third wife Mary Carter he m. 16 April, 1677.

CHANDLER, SAMUEL son of William, m. Mercy ——, daughter Elizabeth b. 5 Aug. 1695.

CHANDLER, WILLIAM son of William, m. Hannah Huntington 29 Nov. 1692. Ch.—John, 21 Nov. 1693, Joseph, 19 Oct. 1694, Mary, 5 Oct. 1696.

CHANDLER, JOSEPH son of William, m. Mary Hall 10 Feb. 1700. Ch.—Joseph and John. 23 April, 1701, Samuel, 3 March, 1703.

CHASE. AQUILA mariner, from Cornwall, England, was in Hampton 1640, Newbury 1646. He m. Anne Wheeler of Hampton. He d. 27 Dec. 1670 aged 52. Ch.—Sarah, ——, Anne, 6 July, 1647, Priscilla, 14 March, 1649, Mary, 3 Feb. 1651, Aquila, 26 Sept. 1652, Thomas, 25 July, 1654, John, 2 Nov. 1655, Elizabeth, 13 Sept. 1657. Ruth, 18 March, 1660, and d. 30 May 1676, Daniel, 9 Dec. 1661, Moses, 24 Dec. 1663.

CHASE, THOMAS son of Aquila, m. Rebecca Follansbee 22 Nov. 1677. Ch.—Thomas, 15 Sept. 1680, Jonathan. 13 Jan. 1683. James, 15 Sept. 1685, Aquila, 15 July, 1688, Ruth. 28 Feb. 1691, Mary. 15 Jan. 1695, Rebecca, 26 April, 1700.

CHASE, AQUILA son of Aquila, m. —— ——. Ch.—Esther, 18 Nov. 1674, Joseph, 25 March. 1677. Priscilla, 15 Oct. 1681.

CHASE, MOSES son of Aquila, m. Ann Follansbee 10 Nov. 1684. Ch.—Moses and Daniel, 20 Sept. 1685, Moses, 20 Jan. 1688, Samuel. 13 May, 1690, Elizabeth, 25 Sept. 1693, Stephen, 29 Aug. 1696, Hannah, 13 Sept. 1699, Joseph, 9 Sept. 1705.

CHASE, JOHN son of Aquila, m. Elizabeth Bingley 23 May, 1677. Ch.—William, 3 Jan. 1679. Philip, 23 Sept. 1688, Charles,

CHASE, DANIEL son of Aquila, m. Martha Kimball 25 May, 1683. Ch.—Martha, 18 Aug. 1684, Sarah, 18 July, 1688, Dorothy, 24 Jan. 1689, Isaac, 19 Jan. 1691, Lydia, 1693, Mehetabel, 19 Jan. 1695, Judith, 19 Feb. 1697, Abner, 15 Oct. 1699, Daniel, 15 Oct. 1702.

CHASE, JOSEPH son of   m. Abigail Thurston, 8 Nov. 1699.

CHASE, THOMAS jr. m. Sara ——. Ch.—Thomas, 20 Nov. 1700, Abel, 25 Feb. 1702. Jonathan, 19 May, 1703.

CHASE, JONATHAN, m. Joanna Palmer of Bradford, 1703.

CHEATER, JOHN Newbury, 1644, thence to Wells, Maine. Ch.—Hannah, 7 Aug. 1644, Lydia. 12 Jan. 1648.

CHISEMORE, DANIEL m. Cyprian ——. Ch.—Sara, 10 Sept. 1696. Abigail, 15 May, 1699.

38

CHENEY, JOHN shoemaker. Roxbury 1635. Newbury 1636. His wife was Martha. Ch.—Daniel, 1635, Sara, Feb. 1637, Peter, 1639, Hannah, 16 Nov. 1642, Nathaniel, 12 Jan. 1645, and d. 24 April, 1684, Elizabeth, 14 Jan. 1648, John, Mary, and Martha.

CHENEY, DANIEL son of John, m. Sara Bailey 8 Oct. 1665. Ch.—Sara, 11 Sept. 1666, Judith, 1668. Daniel, 31 Dec. 1670, Hannah, 3 Sept. 1673, Joseph, 10 July, 1676, Eleanor, 29 March, 1679, James, 6 April, 1685, Daniel, sen. d. 10 Sept. 1694.

CHENEY, PETER son of John, m. Hannah Noyes 14 May, 1663. Ch.—Peter, 6. Nov. 1663, Nicholas, 23 Dec. 1667, Mary, 2 Sept. 1671, John, 10 May, 1666, Nathaniel, 2 Oct. 1675, and d. 30 July, 1677, Jemima, 29 Nov. 1677, Eldad, 24 Oct. 1681, Hannah, 13 Sept. 1683, Ichabod, 22 Sept. 1685.

CHENEY, JOHN son of John, m. Mary Plumer 20 May, 1660. He d. 7 Jan. 1673. Ch.—Mary, 29 March, 1661, Martha, 11 Sept. 1663, John, 29 Jan. 1669.

CHENEY, JOHN m. Mary Chute 7 March, 1694. Ch.—Edmund, 29 June, 1696, Martha, 30 July, 1700, Mary, 14 Nov. 1701, John, 23 May, 1705.

CHENEY, PETER, jr. m. Mary ——. Ch.—Nicholas, 14 March, 1693, and d. 7 Aug. 1774, Benjamin, 6 Jan. 1699.

CHENEY, DANIEL son of Daniel, jr. m. Hannah ——. Son Daniel b. 16 July, 1699.

CHENEY, JOHN m. Mary Chute 7 March, 1694. Ch.—Edmund, 29 June, 1696, Mary, 14 Nov. 1701.

CHENEY, JOSEPH m. Sarah Wiswall 1702.

CHUTE, LIONEL of Rowley, m. Ann Cheney 1702.

CLARK, DR. JOHN b. in England 1598, came to Newbury 1638, moved to Boston 1651, where he died in 1664 aged 66. His son John was also a physician in Boston.

CLARK, MR. NATHANIEL sen. merchant, m. Elizabeth, daughter of Henry Somerby, 23 Nov. 1663. Ch.—Nathaniel, 5 Dec. 1664, and d. 6 June, 1665, Nathaniel, 13 March, 1666, Thomas. 9 Feb. 1668, John, 24 June, 1670, Henry, 5 July 1673, Daniel, 16 Dec. 1675, Sarah, 12 Jan. 1678, Josiah, 7 May, 1682, Elizabeth, 15 May, 1684, Judith, Jan. 1687, Mary, 25 March, 1689. Having been wounded on board of the ship ' Six Friends ' in the expedition to Canada, he there died 25 Aug. 1690 aged 46. His widow Elizabeth m. Rev. John Hale of Beverly, 8 Aug. 1698.

CLARK, NATHANIEL son of Nath. sen. m. Elizabeth Toppan, 15 Dec. 1685. Daughter Elizabeth b. 27 July, 1686.

CLARK, THOMAS son of Nath. sen. m. Sara ——. Ch.—Sara, 25 Dec. 1690, Thomas, 2 Sept. 1692, Nathaniel, 23 Oct. 1694, Martha, 12 April, 1696, Mary, 16 Aug. 1698, Daniel, 26 Jan. 1701.

CLARK, MR. HENRY, son of Nath. sen. m. Mrs. Elizabeth Greenleaf 7 Nov. 1695. Ch.—Stephen, 21 Feb. 1697, Henry, 21 Nov. 1698, Judith, 15 Aug. 1700, Sara, 7 May, 1702.

CLARK, JONATHAN m. Lydia Titcomb, 15 May, 1683. Ch.—Oliver, 6 Feb. 1684, Samuel, 18 March, 1688, Jonathan, 24 May, 1689, Lydia, 17 May, 1691, Elizabeth, 10 May, 1694.

CLEMENS, ABRAHAM m. Hannah Gove 10 March, 1683. Son Edmund b. 3 March, 1684. He then removed to Hampton, N. H. and had seven other children.

COATES, THOMAS and Martha had a son Philip b. 28 March, 1699.

COLEMAN, THOMAS laborer, or ' Coultman ' as he himself wrote it, was born in 1602, came from Marlboro, Wiltshire, England, to Newbury in the James, which arrived at Boston, 3 June 1635. His first wife Susanna d. 17 Nov. 1650. The same year he removed to Hampton and m. Mary, widow of Edmund Johnson 11 July, 1651, who died in Hampton 30 Jan. 1663. His third wife was Margery. After 1680 he moved to Nantucket, where he died in 1685 aged 83. Ch.—Benjamin, 1 May, 1640, Joseph, 2 Dec. 1642, Isaac, 20 Feb. 1647, Joanna, John and Tobias. The last was the son of the third wife.

COLEMAN, SUSANNA d. in Newbury, 2 Jan. 1643.

COLEMAN, THOMAS m. Phebe Pearson, who d. 28 June, 1754. Ch.—Dorcas, b. 26th, and d. 27th April, 1703, John, 8 March, 1704.

COLEMAN, EPHRAIM m. Susanna ——. Ch.—Ephraim, 3 June, 1701, Hannah, 10 March, 1703.

COOPER, JOHN m. Sarah Salmon, 6 Jan. 1703.

COFFIN, MR. TRISTRAM was born in 1609 in Brixham parish, town of Plymouth in Devonshire, Great Britain. He was the son of Peter and Joanna Coffin. Tristram m. Dionis Stevens, and after the death of his father, he came to New England in 1642, bringing with him his mother, who died May 1661, ag. 77, his two sisters, Eunice and Mary, his wife and five children, Peter, Tristram, Elizabeth, James and John. He at first came to Salisbury, thence to Haverhill the same year, thence to Newbury about the year 1648, thence in 1654 or 5 he removed, to Salisbury, where he signs his name ' Tristram Coffyn, commissioner of Salisbury.' In 1659, a company was formed in Salisbury, who purchased nine-tenths of Nantucket, whither he removed in 1660 with his wife, mother and four of his children, James, John, Stephen, who was born in Newbury 11 May, 1652, and Mary, who was born in Haverhill 20 Feb. 1645. He died 1681 aged 72.

His son Peter was born in 1630, and resided, the principal part of his life, at Dover, N. H. In the Boston News Letter, I find the following:

'On Monday 21 March 1715 died at Exeter Hon. Peter Coffin esquire in the 85th year of his age, late judge of his majesty's superior court of judicature, and first member of his majesty's council of the province, a gentleman very serviceable both in church and state.'

Hon. Peter Coffin had nine children.

COFFIN, TRISTRAM b. in 1632, son of Tristram, merchant tailor, lived in Newbury, m. March 2, 1653, Judith Somerby, widow of Henry Somerby, and daughter of captain Edmund Greenleaf. Ch.—Judith. b. 4 Dec. 1653, Deborah, Nov. 10, 1655, Mary, Nov. 12, 1657, James, April 22, 1659, John, Sept. 8, 1660, and d. May 13, 1677, Lydia, April 22, 1662, Enoch, Jan. 21 1663, and d. Nov. 12, 1675, Stephen, Aug. 18, 1664, Peter, July 27, 1667, Nathaniel, 22 March, 1669. Tristram, jr. d. 4 Feb. 1704, aged 72. Judith, his widow, died 15 Dec. 1705, aged 80, leaving 177 descendants.

COFFIN, JAMES son of Tristram, sen. 12 Aug. 1640, m. Mary Severance, of Salisbury, 3 Dec. 1663, moved to Nantucket and had fourteen children. He d. 28 July, 1720, aged 80 years wanting 14 days.

COFFIN, JOHN son of Tristram, sen. b. in Haverhill 13 Oct. 1647, (his first son John having died in Haverhill 30, 1642,) m. Deborah Austin, and had seven children in Nantucket. He d. 1711, aged 64.

COFFIN, STEPHEN son of Tristram, sen. b. in Newbury 10 May, 1652, m. Mary Bunker and had eight or nine children, and was living in May, 1728. He d. 1735, aged 83.

COFFIN, MARY dau. of Tristram, b. in Haverhill, m. Nathaniel Starbuck of Nantucket and had six children. She died in 1717.

COFFIN, ELIZABETH, daughter of Tristram, sen. b. in England, and m. Stephen Greenleaf.

Tristram Coffin's sister Eunice m. William Butler, and sister Mary m. Alexander Adams of Boston.

COFFIN, JAMES son of Tristram, jun. m. Florence Hook, Nov. 16 1685. Ch.—Judith, 7 Oct. 1686, Elizabeth, ——, Sarah, Aug. 20, 1689, Mary, Jan. 18, 1691, Lydia, 1692, Tristram, 19 Oct. 1694, Daniel, May 10, 1696, Eleanor, May 16, 1698, Joanna, 2 May, 1701, James and Florence, Jan. 1, 1705.

COFFIN, STEPHEN son of Tristram, jun. m. Sarah Atkinson, 1685, and d. 31 Aug. 1725. Ch.—Sarah, May 16, 1686, Tristram, 14 Jan. 1688, Tristram, 6 March, 1689, Lydia, 21 July, 1691, Judith, 23 Feb. 1693, John, 20 Jan. 1695.

COFFIN, PETER son of Tristram, jun. m. Apphia Dole, and moved to Gloucester. Ch.—Hannah, March 3, 1688, Judith, Oct. 9, 1693. Tristram, Aug. 10, 1696, Richard, ——, Sarah, August 24, 1701, Apphia, ——, Apphia, ——.

COFFIN, HON. NATHANIEL son of Tristram, jun. m. Sarah Dole, March 29 1693. He died 20 Feb. 1748. Ch.—John, Jan. 21, 1694, Enoch, 7 Feb. 1696, Apphia, June 9, 1698, Brocklebank Samuel, 24 Aug. 1700, Joseph, Dec. 30, 1702, Jane, 5 Aug. 1705, Edmund, 19 March, 1708, Moses, 11 June, 1711. The posterity of Tristram, jun. in 1705, was 177, in 1722, 319, and in 1728, 446.

The family of Tristram Coffin, sen. and their descendants, have been unusually prolific. 'The first grandchild of Tristram Coffin was Stephen Greenleaf, who was born 15 Aug. 1652. He well remembered his great grandmother, and lived to see his great grandchildren, and transmitted the following account of the increase of said family at two different periods, from August, 1652, to August, 1722, and from August, 1722, to May, 1728, a period of five years and nine months, 'reckoning only children by blood.'

	1722		1728	
Peter, - - - - - - - -	118	83	50	102
Tristram, - - - - - - - -	319	225	127	336
Elizabeth Greenleaf, - - - - -	251	206	89	259
James, - - - - - - -	187	162	106	241
Mary Starbuck, - - - - - -	119	90	36	117
John, - - - - - - - -	64	52	17	69
Stephen, - - - - - - -	19	53	19	64
	1138	871	444	1128
	444			
	1582			

The first column shows the number, who were born before August, 1722, the second, the number then living, the third, the number, which had been added between August, 1722, and May, 1728, and the fourth, the number living in May, 1728. The whole number of his descendants, which were born between 1652 and 1728, was 1582, of which 1128 were living in May, 1728.

COKER, ROBERT yeoman, born in 1606, came to Newbury with the first settlers and d. 19 May, 1680, aged 74. His wife Catherine d. 2 May, 1678, Ch.—Joseph, 6 Oct. 1640. Sara, 24 Nov. 1643, Benjamin, 30 June, 1650, Hannah. 15 Jan. 1645.

COKER, JOSEPH son of Robert, m. Sara Hathorne 13 April, 1665. Ch.—Sara, who d. 30 Nov. 1667, Benjamin, 11 March, 1671, Sara, 28 Nov. 1676, Hathorne, 25 April, 1679. His wife Sara d. 8 Feb. 1688.

COKER, BENJAMIN son of Robert, m. Martha Perley 31 May, 1678. Ch.—Benjamin, 13 Sept. 1680, Hannah, 10 March, 1683, Moses, 4 Aug. 1686, Sara, 13 April, 1688, Mary, 18 Sept. 1691, Mercy, 22 Oct. 1693, John, 9 June, 1698, Judith, 9 June, 1701.

COKER, MR. BENJAMIN jr. son of Joseph, m. Mrs. Ann Price 24 Nov. 1692. Ch.—Mary, 14 May, 1693, Joseph, 23 Dec. 1694, Elizabeth, 2 Feb. 1699, Sara, 19 Feb. 1701, Anne, 3 March, 1703.

COTTLE, WILLIAM son of Edward, of Salisbury, came to Newbury. Ch.—Ezra, 5 May, 1662, Ann, 12 July, 1663, Susanna, 16 Aug. 1665. He d. 30 April, 1668.

COTTLE, EZRA son of William, m. Mary Woodbridge 6 July, 1695. Ch.—William, 27 July, 1696. Mary, 31 March, 1698, Edmund, 15 Feb. 1700.

COURTEOUS, WILLIAM d. 31 Dec. 1654.

CROMLON alias CROMWELL, GILES an early settler in Newbury. His first wife —— d. 14 June, 1648. He m. Alice Wiseman 10 Sept. 1648, who d. 6 June, 1669. Ch.—Argentine, who m. Benjamin Cram 25 Nov. 1662, and Philip, who was a butcher in Salem. Giles d. 25 Feb. 1673.

CROMWELL, JOHN born in 1636 m. Joan Butler 2 Nov. 1662.

CROMWELL, THOMAS born in 1617, was in Newbury in 1637, moved to Hampton in 1639, and died in Boston in 1649.

CUTTING, CAPT. JOHN from London, settled in Charlestown, thence to Newbury, about 1642. He d. 20 Nov. 1659. His widow, Mary Miller, d. 6 March, 1663. Ch.—Sarah, wife of James Brown, and Mary, wife of Samuel Moody.

DAVIS, THOMAS sawyer of Marlborough, Eng. m. Christian —— in England, was in Newbury in 1641, in 1642 in Haverhill, where he died in 1683, aged 80. His posterity are numerous.

DAVIS, JOHN an early settler, married —— ——. Ch.—Mary, 6 Oct. 1642, John, 15 Jan. 1645, Zachary, 22 Feb. 1646, Jeremy, 21 June, 1648, Mary, 12 Aug. 1650, Cornelius, 15 April, 1653, Ephraim, 29 Sept. 1655. He d. 12 Nov. 1675.

DAVIS, JOHN son of John, m. Sara Carter 8 April, 1681. Ch.—Mary, 23 March, 1683. Sara, 13 July, 1685, John, son of John and Mary, b. 29 July, 1692.

DAVIS, CORNELIUS son of John, m. Sara ——. Ch.—Samuel, 11 April, 1689, Judith, 2 June, 1691, Cornelius, 9 Oct. 1693, James, 5 April, 1695 and d. in 1697, Elizabeth, 15 July, 1697. His wife Sara d. 6 March, 1696. He m. Elizabeth Hidden in 1696.

DAVIS, EPHRAIM son of John, m. Elizabeth ——. Ch.—Elizabeth, 7 April, 1690, John, 17 May, 1692, Mary, 20 July, 1694, Ephraim, 20 March. 1697, Joseph, 16 Nov. 1699.

DAVIS, ZACHARY son of John, m. Judith Brown, 4 Feb. 1681. Ch.—Judith, 7 Sept. 1684 and d. 9 Dec. 1702. Elizabeth, 26 April, 1687.

DAVIS, WILLIAM of Haverhill, m. Mary Kelly 31 Dec. 1700.

DANFORTH, WILLIAM was born in London in 1653, and came to Newbury as early as 1667. He m. —— ——, who died 18 Oct. 1678. His second wife was Sarah Thurlow. Ch.—William, Mary, Richard, 31 Jan. 1680, John, 8 Dec. 1681, and d. Oct. 1, 1772, aged 92, Jonathan, 18 May, 1685, Thomas, 11 Sept. 1688, Francis, 15 March. 1691, Joseph. 12 May, 1694.

DAVISON, MR. DANIEL came from Ipswich to Newbury, m. Mrs. Abigail Coffin, of Dover. Ch.—Nicholas, 16 May, 1680, Sara, 1 Feb. 1682, Daniel, 23 May, 1686, Mary, 21 May, 1689, Peter, 20 Oct. 1692.

DELANE, PHILIP probably a Frenchman, came to Newbury from Portsmouth in 1694 with his wife Margery and two children. His wife died 26 Aug. 1694. In 1695 he m. Jane Atkinson. Ch.—Daniel, 24 June, 1694, Charles, Oct. and died in Dec. 1698, Paul, 16 Oct. 1699, Joseph, 22 June, and died Nov. 16, 1702, Eve, 10 July and d. 18 Sept. 1701, James, 16 Aug. 1704.

DOGGETT, JOHN m. 22 June, 1697.

DOLE, RICHARD merchant, b. in Bristol, England, 1624, came to Newbury 1639 He m. Hannah Rolfe 3 May, 1647, who d. 16 Nov. 1678. His second wife was Han nah, widow of Capt. Samuel Brocklebank, of Rowley. whom he m. 4 March, 1679. His third wife was Patience Walker, of Haverhill. Ch.—John. 10 Aug. 1648, Richard, 6 Sept. 1650, Anna, 26 March, 1653, Benjamin, 14 June, 1654, Joseph, 5 Aug. 1657, William, 10 April, 1660, Henry. 9 March, 1663. Hannah, 23 Oct. 1665, Apphia, 7 December, 1668, Abner, 8 March, 1672. Richard, sen. d.

DOLE, MR. JOHN son of Richard, was a physician. He m. Mrs. Mary Gerrish, 23 Oct. 1676. Ch.—Hannah, 16 Aug. 1677, Benjamin, 16 Nov. 1679, Mary, 14 Nov. 1681, Sara, 11 Dec. 1683, John, 16 Feb. 1686, Moses, 24 Dec. 1688, Elizabeth, 16 Aug. 1692.

DOLE, RICHARD son of Richard, m. Sara Greenleaf 7 June, 1677. Ch.—Richard, 28 April, 1678, d. Aug. 1764, aged 86, Elizabeth, 21 Dec. 1680, Sara, 14 Feb. 1681, Hannah, 5 Dec. 1682, John, 2 Feb. 1684, Stephen, 2 Dec. 1686, Stephen, 1687, Joseph, 5 Dec. 1689, Mary, 1 July. 1694.

DOLE, MR. BENJAMIN son of Richard, was a physician in Hampton, N. H. He m. Frances, daughter of capt. Samuel Sherburne, 11 Dec. 1700. Ch.—Jonathan, Mary, and Love. He d. in 1707, aged 53. She died 15 Aug. 1744, aged 67.

DOLE, WILLIAM son of Richard, m. Mary Brocklebank 13 Oct. 1684. Ch.—William, 12 Jan. 1685, Hannah, 28 March, 1686, Mary, 1 Feb. 1688. Richard, 31 Dec. 1689, Jane, 23 Jan. 1692. Patience, 8 April, 1694. Apphia, 13 May, 1696, Samuel, 1 June, 1699, Benjamin, 2 July, 1702.

DOLE, HENRY son of Richard, m. Sara Brocklebank. Ch.—Apphia, 28 Feb. 1688, and d. 9 Oct. 1694. Sara, 12 Feb. 1690.

DOLE, ABNER son of Richard, m. Mary Jewett 1 Nov. 1694, who d. 25 Nov. 1695. He m. Sara Belcher, of Boston, 5 Jan. 1679. Ch.—Henry, 28 Oct. 1695, Nathaniel, 29 March, 1701, Sara, 14 Jan. 1703, Abner, 19 May, 1706.

DOW, THOMAS an early settler, m. Phebe ——. Ch.—Stephen, 29 March, 1642, Mary, 26 April, 1644, Martha, 1 June, 1648, John and Thomas. He died in Haverhill, 31 May, 1654.

DOWNER, JOSEPH m. Mary, daughter of John Knight 9 July, 1660. Ch.—Mary. 18 March, 1662, Joseph, 25 March, 1666, Andrew, 25 July, 1672.

DOWNER, JOSEPH son of Joseph, m. Hannah ——. Ch.—Joseph, 29 Sept. 1693, John, 15 March, 1695, Andrew, 14 May, 1697, Samuel, 12 April, 1699, Richard, 11 Feb. 1702, Hannah, 16. Feb. 1704, Benjamin, 24 Feb. 1706.

DOWNER, ANDREW son of Joseph, m. Susanna Huntington 28 Dec. 1699. Ch.— John, 22 Oct. 1700, Mary, 22 May, 1702, Gideon, 5 Sept. 1703.

DOW, MOSES m. Sara ——. Daughter Mary, 13 Aug. 1694.

DUMMER, MR. RICHARD came from Bishopstoke, England, in 1632, to Roxbury, thence to Newbury, 1636. His second wife, Mrs. Francis Burr; he married about 1643. Ch.—Shubael, 17 Feb. 1636, Jeremiah, 14 Sept. 1645, Hannah, 7 Nov. 1647, Richard, 13 Jan. 1650, William, 18 Jan. 1659, Richard sen. d. 14 Dec. 1679, aged 88. Frances, his wife d. 19 Nov. 1682, aged 70.

DUMMER, JEREMIAH son of Richard, moved to Boston, where he died 25 May, 1718, in his 73d year. His son Jeremy was a most distinguished scholar, and the agent for Massachusetts in England. He died in Plaistow, England, 19 May, 1739.

DUMMER, MR. RICHARD son of Richard, m. Mrs. Elizabeth Appleton 12 Nov. 1673. He d. 4 July, 1689, aged 44. Ch.—Hannah, 12 Aug. 1674, John, 8 Aug. 1676, Richard, 21 July, and d. Sept. 1678, Richard, 22 June, 1680, Elizabeth, 28 July, 1682, Nathaniel, 1685, and d. 27 Feb. 1767, Shubael, 10 Jan. 1687.

DUMMER, THOMAS and STEPHEN brothers to Richard, sen. Thomas lived in Salisbury. Stephen m. Alice Archer. Ch.—Mehetabel, 1. Jan. 1640, and Jane, who m. Henry Sewall.

DUMMER, REV. SHUBAEL son of Richard sen. See list of graduates.

DUNKIN, SAMUEL Newbury, 1638.

EASTMAN, PHILIP m. Mary Morse 22 Aug. 1678.

EASTON, MR. NICHOLAS tanner, came from Wales, was in Ipswich 1634, and in Newbury in 1635. In 1639, he moved to Portsmouth, R. I. thence to Newport. He d. 1675, aged 83.

EASTON, JOHN son of Nicholas, died in 1705, in Rhode Island, in his 85th year.

EASTOW, WILLIAM came to Newbury, thence to Hampton in 1639. He died 23 Nov. 1655. Ch.—Sara, who m. Maurice Hobbs, and Mary, who m. Thomas Marston.

EELS, JOHN 'bee-hive maker,' came to Newbury, 1645, and died 25 Nov. 1653, aged 78.

ELDREDGE, REBECCA d. 15 Nov. 1657.

EMERY, ANTHONY carpenter, came from Romsey, England, in June, 1635, in the ship James to Newbury, thence to Dover as early as 1644, thence to Kittery.

EMERY, JOHN carpenter, brother to Anthony, came with him to Newbury in 1635.

He died 3 Nov. 1683, aged 85.   Ch.—John, born in England, about 1629.   'Ebenezer, a daughter, 16 Sept. 1648, being Monday morning two houres before day,' Jonathan, 13 May, 1652.

EMERY, JOHN son of John, sen. m. Mary Webster, widow of John Webster, of Ipswich, 29 Oct. 1650.   Ch.—Mary, 24 June, 1652, Hannah, 26 April, 1654, John, 12 Sept. 1656, Bethia, 15 Oct. 1658, Sarah, 26 Feb. 1661, Joseph, 23 March, 1663, Stephen, 6 Sept. 1666, Abigail, 16 Jan. 1669, Samuel, 20 Dec. 1670, Judith, 5 Feb. 1673, Lydia, 19 Feb. 1675, Elizabeth, 8 Feb. 1680, Josiah, 28 Feb. 1681.   John Emery, d. in 1693, aged 65.   Mary, his widow, d. 28 April, 1694.

EMERY, JONATHAN son of John, sen. m. Mary Woodman 29 Nov. 1676.   Ch.— Mary, 25 Sept. 1677, Jonathan, 2 Feb. 1679, David, 28 Sept. 1682, Anthony, 13 Nov. 1684, Stephen, 13 Jan. 1687, and d. 8 Oct. 1688, Sara, 18 Dec. 1688, Stephen, 24 June, 1692, Edward, 10 Nov. 1694.

EMERY, JOHN son of John, jun. m. Mary Sawyer 13 June, 1683.   Ch.—Mary, 25 Dec. 1684, John, 29 Sept. 1686, Josiah, 19 Dec. 1688, Daniel, 15 June, 1693, Lydia, 29 April, 1698, Samuel, 25 Oct. 1699.   His wife Mary died 3 Nov. 1699.   He then m. Abigail Bartlet, 27 May, 1700.

EMERY, STEPHEN son of John, jun. m. Ruth Jaques, 29 Nov. 1692.   Ch.—Anna, 10 Oct. 1693, Sarah, 1 Jan. 1696, Ruth, 16 June, 1698, Mary, 15 Dec. 1700, Judith, 25 Feb. 1703, Abigail, 4 May, 1705.

EMERSON, LT. JOHN m. Judith ——.   Ch.—John, 25 June, 1690, Daniel, 15 Jan. 1693, Benjamin, 2 March, 1696, Samuel, 2 Nov. 1699, Jonathan, 10 Aug. 1702.

EWILL, JOHN d. 31 July, 1686.

EVANS, PHILIP m. Deborah ——.   Ch.—William, 13 Oct. 1687, Elizabeth, 8 Nov. 1689, John, 30 April, 1692, born in Ipswich.

FANNING, WILLIAM m. Elizabeth Allen, 24 March, 1668.   Ch.—Joseph, 1 Jan. 1669, Benjamin, 2 April, 1671, William, 10 Nov. 1673, James, 24 July, 1676, Elizabeth, 6 March, 1681.

FAY, HENRY weaver d. 30 June, 1655.

FOLLANSBEE, THOMAS m. Sara ——.   Ch.—Francis, 22 Oct. 1677, Hannah, 10 April, 1680.

FOLLANSBEE, THOMAS jun. m. Abigail ——.   Ch.—Mary, 4 April, 1695, Thomas, 28 March, 1697, Francis, 13 June, 1699, William, 14 March, 1701.

FOLLANSBEE, SARA d. 6 Nov. 1683.

FIELD, JOHN m. Sara ——.   Son John b. 19 Jan. 1695.

FIFIELD, WILLIAM came early to Newbury, and in 1639 removed to Hampton, where he 'died 18 Dec. 1700, aged above 80.'

FITTS, alias FITZ, came from Ipswich, to Newbury.   He m. Sara Ordway 8 Oct. 1654.   He died 2 Dec. 1672.   She died 24 April, 1667.

FORMAN, JOHN had children, Abigail, 10 Nov. 1676, John, 5 Oct. 1678.

FLOOD, PHILIP came from Guernsey to New Jersey, thence to Newbury about 1680.   He m. Mary ——.   Ch.—Joseph, 12 May, 1684, Hester, 15 May, 1686, Mary, 18 July, 1688, Henry, 14 Aug. 1689, John, 11 Nov. 1693, Richard, 25 Feb. 1696, Rachel, 18 March, 1698, Philip, 24 April, 1700, Benjamin 2 May. 1705.

FRAZER, COLLIN m. Anna Stuart 10 Nov. 1685.   Ch.—Symon, 19 Aug. 1686, John, 1 April, 1688, Hannah, 31 Aug. 1692, John, 12 June, 1694, Ebenezer, 27 July, 1696, Gershom, 8 Aug. 1697, Nathan, 8 Jan. 1700, Abigail, 21 April, 1701, Lawson, 14 Sept. 1704.

FRYER, MR. NATHANIEL of Boston in 1657, then in Portsmouth, N. H. m. Mrs. Dorothy Woodbridge of Newbury Oct. 1679.

FRY, JOHN wheelwright, came early to Newbury, thence to Andover in 1645, where he died in 1698, aged 92 years and 7 months.   Ch.—John, Samuel, James, Benjamin, and Elizabeth.

FREEZE, JOHN m. Mary Merrill, 2 June, 1697.

FRANKLIN, WILLIAM blacksmith, in Ipswich, 1634, Newbury, 1635, in Boston, 1642 or 3, in Roxbury, 1644, and was hung for murder the same year.   He m. Alice, daughter of Robert Andrews.   Ch.—William, John, Benjamin, Eleazer and Elizabeth.

GARLAND, JACOB son of John, of Hampton, m. Rebecca Sears, 17 June, 1682. Ch.—Jacob, 26 Oct. 1682, Rebecca, 3 Dec. 1683, and eleven others born afterward in Hampton.

GAGE, SARA widow, died 7 July, 1680.

GALE, DANIEL of Salem, m. Rebekah Swett, 1700.

GERRISH, CAPT. WILLIAM came from Bristol, England, to Newbury, about 1640. He m. Mrs. Joanna Oliver, 17 April, 1645, widow of Mr. John Oliver.   In 1678 he moved to Boston, and died in Salem, 9 Aug. 1687, aged 70.   His wife Joanna d. 14 June, 1677.   Ch.—John, 15 May, 1646, Abigail, 10 May, 1647, William, 6 June, 1648. Joseph, 23 March, 1650, Benjamin, 13 Jan. 1652, Elizabeth, 10 Sept. 1654, Moses, 9 May, 1656, Mary, 9 May, 1658, Anna, 18 Oct. 1660, Judith, 10 Sept. 1662.

GERRISH, MR. MOSES son of capt. William, m. Jane Sewall, 24 Sept. 1677. Ch.—
Joanna, 3 Oct. 1678, Joseph, 20 March, 1682, Sara, 25 Dec. 1683, Elizabeth, 27 Dec.
1685, Mary, 20 Sept. 1687, John, 2 April, 1695. He died 4 Dec. 1694, aged 38.

GERRISH, DR. WILLIAM son of capt. William, m. Ann ——, in 1671. He was a
physician in Charlestown, and there died, 10 May, 1683, aged 35. His son William
was born in Newbury, 21 Jan. 1674.

GILE, SAMUEL an early settler in Newbury, removed to Haverhill in 1640. He m.
Judith Davis, 1 Sept. 1647. Ch.—John, Samuel, Ephraim, and Sara. He died in
Haverhill. 21 Feb. 1684.

GILMAN, MR. NICHOLAS of Exeter, m. Mrs. Sarah Clark, 9 June, 1697.

GILMAN, MAVERICK m. Sara Mayo, 16 June, 1702.

GODFREY, PETER m. Mary Browne, 13 May, 1656. Ch.—Andrew, 3 March, 1657,
Mary, 21 Oct. 1659, and d. 3 Nov. Mary, 23 Jan. 1661, Margaret, 9 Oct. 1663, Elizabeth,
8 Feb, 1667, Peter, 14 Nov. 1669, Joanna, 16 Nov. 1672, James, 9 March, 1677, Sara, 7
April, 1680. He d. 5 Oct. 1697, aged 66. She died 16 April, 1716, in her 81st year.

GODFREY, JAMES son of Peter, m. Hannah Kimball, 10 Feb. 1700.

GOFFE, JOHN came to Boston with Gov. Winthrop, in 1630, lived in Watertown,
thence to Newbury, where he died 9 Dec. 1641. His wife's name was Amy, children,
Susan and Hannah.

GOODALE, RICHARD from Yarmouth, England, came to Newbury about 1638.
In 1640 he moved to Salisbury, and there died, Oct. 1666. Ch.—Ann, who m. William Allen, and Richard, who moved to Boston.

GOODALE, MRS. ELIZABETH from Yarmouth, died in Newbury, 8 April, 1647.
Ch.—Susanna, who m. Abraham Toppan, Joanna, who m. Mr. John Oliver.

GOODRIDGE, WILLIAM had sons Benjamin, Joseph, and Jeremiah, who were sons
in law to John Hull.

GOODRIDGE, BENJAMIN son of William, m. Mary Jordan, 8 Sept. 1663. Ch.—
Joseph, 6 July, 1667, Daniel, 3 Mar. 1670, John, 1 Jan. 1674, son of Deborah, his
second wife, who d. 8 Nov. 1676. On the 16th of November, 1678, he m. Sarah
Croad. Son Samuel b. 15 Aug. 1681.

GOODRIDGE, JOSEPH son of William, born in 1640, m. Martha Moores 28 Aug.
1664. Ch.—Hannah, 27 July, 1665, John, 13 Sept. 1667, d. 9 Mar. 1756, ag. 89, Edmund, 14 June, 1672, Abigail, 17 Sept. 1675, Martha, 2 Feb. 1681, Margaret, 11 Oct.
1683, Joseph. 21 Oct. 1688.

GOODRIDGE, JEREMIAH son of William, m. Mary Adams 15 Nov. 1660. Ch.—
Mary, 21 Nov. 1663, William, 2 Aug. 1665, Philip, 23 Nov. 1669, Elizabeth, 27 Feb.
1679, Hannah, 15 Nov. 1681, John, 26 May, 1685.

GOODRIDGE, EDMUND m. Hannah Dole, 16 Nov. 1702. His son Edmund b. 2
Sept. 1703.

GOODRIDGE, PHILIP son of Jeremiah, m. Mehetabel Woodman 16 April, 1700.
Ch.—Benjamin, 3 Feb. 1701, John, 2 Aug. 1702.

GOODRIDGE, DANIEL m. Mary Ordway, 1698. His daughter Mary b. 19 Sept.
1699.

GLADING, JOHN m. Elizabeth Rogers 17 July, 1666. Ch.—Susanna, 6 Oct. 1668,
John, 11 Oct. 1670, William, 25 July, 1673, Elizabeth, 15 Sept. 1676, Mary, 14 Jan.
1679, Hannah, 8 November, 1681.

GOODWIN, EDWARD of Salisbury m. Susanna Wheeler 5 June, 1668.

GOODWIN, EDWARD m. Martha ——. Ch.—Sara, 30 April, 1703, Lazarus, 11
July, 1705.

GOODWIN, RICHARD m. Hannah Major 26 March, 1692. Ch.—Hannah, 18 Jan.
1693, George. 21 July, 1695, Richard, 8 May, 1698, Susanna, 15 Jan. 1701.

GRANT, JOHN m. Sarah ——. Ch.—Sarah, 10 April, 1691, William, 1 Nov. 1694,
Joanna, 2 April, 1697, Abraham, 2 Jan. 1702.

GRANTHAM, ANDREW d. 15 Dec. 1668.

GREENLAND, DR. HENRY was born in 1628. He resided in Newbury from 1662
to 1675.

GRANGER, LAUNCELOT m. Joanna, daughter of Robert Adams, 4 Jan. 1654.
Ch.—John, 15 Jan. 1655, George, 28 Nov. 1658, Elizabeth, 13 March, 1662, Dorothy,
17 Feb. 1665, Samuel, 26 July, 1668, Abraham, 17 April, 1673.

GREENLEAF, MR. EDMUND dyer, came early to Newbury, with his wife Sara.
About 1650 he removed to Boston, and there died, 1671. Ch.—Judith, b. 1628, who
m. Henry Somerby, and then Tristram Coffin, jun. Stephen, 1630, Elizabeth, who m.
Giles Badger, and then Richard Brown, a son Enoch, and a daughter, who m.

GREENLEAF, DANIEL died 12 Oct. 1654.

GREENLEAF, STEPHEN son of capt. Edmund, m. Elizabeth Coffin, daughter of
Tristram Coffin, sen. 13 Nov. 1651. Ch.—Stephen, 15 Aug. 1652, Sarah, 16 Oct.
1655, Elizabeth, 9 April, 1660, John, 21 June, 1662, Samuel, 30 Oct. 1665, Tristram,

11 Feb. 1668, Edmund, 10 May, 1670, Judith, 13 Oct. 1673, and d. 19 Nov. 1678, Mary, 6 Dec. 1676. Mrs. Elizabeth Greenleaf died 19 Nov. 1678. Capt. Greenleaf m. Mrs. Esther Swett, 31 March, 1679, who d. 16 Jan. 1718, aged 89. He d. 1 Dec. 1690, aged 60.

GREENLEAF, STEPHEN son of Stephen, m. Elizabeth Gerrish 23 Oct. 1676. Ch.—Elizabeth, 12 Jan. 1678, Daniel, 10 Feb. 1680, Stephen, 31 Aug. and d. 15 Oct. 1688, William, 1 April, and d. 15 April, 1684, Joseph, 12 April, 1686, Sara, 19 July, 1688, Stephen, 21 Oct. 1690, John, 29 Aug. 1693, Benjamin, 14 Dec. 1695, Moses, 24 Feb. 1698.

GREENLEAF, JOHN son of Stephen, m. Elizabeth Hills, 12 Oct. 1685. Ch.— Elizabeth, 30 July, 1686, Jane, 10 Nov. 1687, Judith, 15 July, 1689, and d. 30 Sept. 1690, Daniel, 24 Dec. 1690, Parker, 20 Feb. 1695, Martha, 23 April, 1699, Benjamin, 21 Nov. 1701. He died 24 June, 1734, ag. 72.

GREENLEAF, SAMUEL son of Stephen, m. Sara Kent 1 March, 1686. Ch.— Daniel, 28 Feb. 1687, John, 13 Oct. 1688, Stephen, 27 Aug. 1690, Sarah, 3 Nov. 1692. He d. 6 Aug. 1694, aged 29.

GREENLEAF, TRISTRAM son of Stephen, m. Margaret Piper 12 Nov. 1689. Ch.—Nathaniel, 25 Jan. 1692, and d. 19 Dec. 1775, ag. 84, Elizabeth, 16 March, 1693, Stephen, 16 April, 1694, Edmund, 24 June, 1695, Sarah, 27 March, 1697, Judith, 28 Sept. 1698, Mary, 28 Sept. 1699.

GREENLEAF, EDMUND son of Stephen, m. Abigail Somerby 2 July 1691. Ch.— Judith, 15 Dec. 1692, Rebecca, b. and d. 29 Sept. 1693, Abigail, 6 March, 1695, Mary, 10 Sept. 1697, Rebecca, 22 Feb. 1700, Edmund, 10 Feb. 1703.

GREELEY, JOHN m. Elizabeth ——. His son Parker b. 20 Feb. 1695.

HALE, THOMAS glover, with his wife Tamosin, alias Thomasine. came to New-bury in 1635. He d. 21 Dec. 1682, aged 78. She d. 30 Jan. 1683. Ch.—Thomas, b. 1633, John, 1636, and Samuel.

HALE, THOMAS jun. son of Thomas sen. m. Mary Hutchinson of Danvers, 26 May, 1657. He died 22 Oct. 1688. Ch.—Thomas, 11 Feb. 1658, Mary, 15 July, 1660, Abigail, 8 April, 1662, Hannah. 29 Nov. 1663, Lydia, 17 April, 1666, Elizabeth, 16 Oct. 1668, Joseph, 20 Feb. 1671, Samuel, 6 June, 1674.

HALE, JOHN son of Thomas, sen. m. Rebecca Lowle 5 Dec. 1660, who d. 1 June, 1662. He m. Sarah Somerby 8 Dec. 1663. who d. June, 1672. His third wife was Sarah Symonds, who d. 19 Jan. 1699. Ch.—John, 2 Sept. 1661, Samuel, 15 Oct. 1664, and d. 1672, Henry, 20 Oct. 1667, Thomas, 4 Nov. 1668, Judith, 5 July, 1670, Joseph, 24 Nov. 1674, Benjamin, 11 Aug. 1676, and d. Aug. 1677, Moses, 10 July, 1678.

HALE, SAMUEL son of Thomas, sen. m. Sarah Ilsley, 21 July, 1673.

HALE, JOHN jun. son of John, sen. m. Sarah Jaques 10 Oct. 1683. Ch.—Rebecca, 18 Feb. 1684, John, 24 June, 1686, Richard, 21 April, and d. Sept. 1688, Henry, 28 Aug. 1689, and d. 1692, Richard, 9 Nov. 1690, Stephen, 12 April, 1693, Anne and Mary, 3 Jan. and d. 6 Jan. 1701, Anne, 24 Oct. 1703.

HALE, CAPT. THOMAS son of Thomas, jun. m. Sarah Northend 16 May, 1682. Ch.—Thomas, 9 March, 1683, Edna, 21 Nov. 1684, Mary, 28 April, 1687, Ezekiel, 13 May, 1689, Nathan, 2 June, 1691, Sarah, 9 March, 1693, Ebenezer, 21 April, 1695, Daniel, 22 Feb. 1697, Hannah, 7 June, 1699. Joshua, 17 March, 1701.

HALE, HENRY son of John, m. Sarah Kelly 11 Sept. 1695. Ch.—Thomas. 15 Nov. 1696, Sarah, 21 Oct. 1698, Enoch, 11 Oct. 1702. Enoch and Edmund, 7 Oct. 1703. Edmund m. Martha Sawyer 16 May. 1728, and d. May, 1788, aged 85.

HALE, MR. JOHN alias REV. JOHN of Beverly, m. Mrs. Sarah Noyes 31 March, 1684, and Mrs. Elizabeth Clark of Newbury, 8 Aug. 1698. She was widow of Nathaniel Clark, and daughter of Henry Somerby.

HALE, JOSEPH son of John, m. Mary ——, who d. 16 Apr. 1753, aged 75. Ch.— Judith, 22 Sept. 1700, Mary, 25 March, 1703. He d. 24 Jan. 1755, aged 80.

HALE, MR. MOSES m. Mrs. Elizabeth Dummer 1704.

HALL, JOSEPH m. Mary Moody 1700. Judith was born 22 Sept. 1700.

HAYNES, JONATHAN m. Mary Moulton Jan. 1674. Ch.—Mary, 14 Nov. 1675, Mary, 2 Oct. 1677, Thomas, 14 May, 1680, Jonathan, 3 Sept. 1684. He afterward removed to Haverhill, and was there killed by the Indians 22 Feb. 1698.

HART, MR. LAWRENCE m. Dorothy Jones 12 Feb. 1679. Ch.—Lucy, 31 Dec. 1679, Marv, 17 July, and d. 2 Aug. 1681, Anne, 20 Sept. 1682, Charles, 12 May, 1684, Anne, 12 Oct. 1685, Lawrence, 16 April, 1687, John, 18 April, 1689.

HARDY, or HARDIE, GEORGE m. Mary ——. Ch.—Mary b. 2 Feb. 1693. He d. 6 Dec. 1694.

HAZELTINE, SAMUEL of Bradford m. Emma Kent, Jan. 1, 1701.

HEATH, BARTHOLOMEW was born in 1600. His son John was born 15 Aug. 1643.

HEARD, LUKE Newbury, thence in 1640 to Salisbury, thence to Ipswich. He m. Sarah Wyatt of Assington in England. He d. in 1647 leaving sons Edward and John.

HENING, RICHARD had a son Shubael b. 7 Dec. 1671.

HEWES, SOLOMON m. Martha Calef of Boston 1700.

HILLS, MR. JOSEPH born in 1602, New England, 1638, in Charlestown, 1639 thence to Malden from 1647 to 1656, thence to Newbury, and m. Anne, widow of Henry Lunt, 8 March, 1665. He died 5 Feb. 1688, aged 86. His first wife was Hannah ——. His second, Helen Atkinson, he m. Jan. 1656. Ch.—Samuel, Wayt, Gershom, Hannah, and three other daughters, who. m. a Blanchard, a Green, and a Vinton.

HILLS, MR. SAMUEL son of Joseph, m. Abigail Wheeler 20 May, 1679. Ch.— Samuel, 16 Feb. 1680, Joseph, 21 July, 1681, Nathaniel, 9 Feb. 1683, Benjamin, 16 Oct. 1684, Abigail, 2 Sept. 1686, and d. 11 Aug. 1688, Henry. 23 April, 1688, William, 8 Oct. 1689, Josiah, 27 July, 1691, John, 20 Sept. 1693, Abigail, 27 June, 1695, James and Hannah. 25 Feb. 1697, Daniel, 8 Dec. 1700.

HILTON, WILLIAM came to Plymouth, from London, in 1621, thence to Dover in 1623, with his brother Edward, thence in 1641 to Newbury. Ch.—Sarah, June, 1641, Charles. July, 1643, Ann, 12 Feb. 1649, Elizabeth, 6 Nov. 1650, William, 28 June, 1653. A William Hilton, probably the same person, d. in Charlestown 7 Sept. 1675, leaving two other sons, Nowell, 4 May, 1663, and Edward, 3 March, 1665.

HOBBS, MAURICE Newbury, thence between 1640 and 45 to Hampton. He m Sarah Eastow and d. 5 August, 1700, 'aged above 80.' He left ten children.

HOBBS, RICHARD was drowned in Newbury 18 Aug. 1665.

HOTON or HORTON, JOSEPH m. Sara Haynes 13 Nov. 1651.

HOLT, NICHOLAS tanner. came from Romsey, England, in the James, in June, 1635, to Newbury, thence to Andover, in 1645, where he died, 1685, aged 83. Ch.—Elizabeth, 30 March, 1636, Mary, 6 Oct. 1638, Samuel, 6 Oct. 1641. Henry, Nicholas, James, and John, were born in Andover.

HOVEY, LUKE m. Susanna Pilsbury 25 Oct. 1698.

HOAG, JOHN weaver, was born in 1643, came to Newbury and m. *Ebenezer*, the daughter of John Emery, 21 April, 1669. He died in 1728, aged 85. Ch.—John, 20 Feb. 1670, Jonathan, 28 Oct. 1671, Joseph, 10 Jan. 1677, Hannah, 3 Jan. 1683, Judith, 20 April, 1687.

HOOKE, MR. HUMPHREY of Salisbury, m. Mrs. Judith March, 10 July, 1700. Jemima born July, 1703.

HOAG, BENJAMIN m. Sara Norris, of Exeter, 23 June, 1702.

HOAG, JONATHAN m. Martha Goodwin 15 Sept. 1703.

HOLMES. ROBERT m. Esther Morse 26 Feb. 1669. He died 18 Sept. 1673. Ch.— Robert, 3 Nov. 1670, Esther, 22 Feb. 1673.

HOWLET, REBECCA widow, d. 1 Nov. 1680.

HENDRICK, JOHN m. Abigail ——. Ch.—John, 23 Oct. 1678, Daniel, 6 Feb. 1684 William, 15 March, 1688.

HUIT, EPHRAIM of Bridgewater, m. Catharine Acres, 1698. Ch.—Hannah, 23 Sept. 1699.

HUDSON, ELEAZER died in Newbury April, 1736, 'a noted shopkeeper.'

HULL, JOHN d. 1 Feb. 1670. His widow Margaret d. 3 Feb. 1683.

HUSE, ABEL came from London to Newbury in 1635. His wife Eleanor d. 27 March, 1663. He m. Mary Sears 25 May, 1663. He d. 29 March, 1690, aged 88. Ch.— Ruth, 25 Feb. 1664, Abel, 19 Feb. 1665, Thomas, 9 Aug. 1666, William, Oct. 1667 Sarah, 8 Dec. 1670, John, 20 June, 1670, Amy, 9 Sept. 1673, and d. 18 May, 1675 Ebenezer, a daughter, 10 Aug. 1675.

HUSE, ABEL son of Abel, m. Judith ——. Ch.—Abel, 18 Nov. 1696, Stephen, 16 Nov. 1702, Samuel, 30 March, 1705.

HUSE, THOMAS son of Abel, m. Hannah ——. Ch.—Mary, 23 March, 1691, Israel, 23 Oct. 1693, Ebenezer, 16 Jan. 1696, James, 29 June, 1698, Hannah, 5 Nov. 1700, Ruth, 14 Feb. 1703.

HUSE, WILLIAM son of Abel, m. Anne Russell, 1699. Ch.—Anne, 22 May, 1700, William, 30 Oct. 1701.

HUSSEY, MR. CHRISTOPHER came from Dorking, Surrey, England, to Lynn, 1630, thence to Newbury, 1636. He m. Theodata Bachiler, who d. Oct. 1649. In 1639, he moved to Hampton, where he d. 6 March, 1686, aged nearly 90. Ch.—Stephen, 1630, who m. Martha Bunker, and d. in 1718, aged 88. John, Joseph, Mary, Huldah, and Theodata.

HUTCHINS, JOHN and wife, Frances, came to Newbury. He d. in Haverhill, in 1674, aged 70. Ch.—William, Joseph, 15 Nov. 1640, Benjamin, 15 May, 1641, Love, 16 July, 1647, Elizabeth, and Samuel.

HOLMAN, SOLOMON and wife, Mary, came to Newbury about 1693 or 4. Ch.—Mary, 24 Feb, 1695, Solomon, 25 Nov. 1697, Edward, 26 Jan. 1700, Elizabeth, 24 Oct. 1701.

HORNE, ELIZABETH d. 6 May. 1672.

ILSLEY, WILLIAM yeoman, came from Wiltshire, England, to Newbury, in 1635

39

His wife was Barbara. He d. 22 July, 1681, aged 73. Ch.—John, 11 Sept. 1641, William, 23 Feb. 1648, Joseph, 30 Oct. 1649, Isaac, 23 June, 1652, Sara, 8 Aug. 1655, Mary, and Elisha.

ILSLEY, JOSEPH son of William, m. Sara Little 1 March, 1682, only daughter of George Little. Ch.—Sarah, 20 Jan. 1683, Joseph, 14 May, 1684, Lydia, 15 June, 1687, Sarah, 16 July, 1689.

ILSLEY, ISAAC son of William, m. Abigail ——. Ch.—Sarah, 3 Oct. 1683, William, 25 April, 1685. Isaac, 3 July, 1689, Lydia, 18 June, 1691, Hannah, 26 Dec. 1693, Elizabeth, 25 Oct. 1695, Abigail, 22 Aug. 1698, Judith, 2 Feb. 1703.

ILSLEY, ELISHA son of William, m. Hannah Poor 14 March, 1668. Ch.—Elisha, 21 Nov. 1668, William, 10 Nov. 1672, Sarah, 22 Dec. 1675, and 8 Jan. 1691, William or Benjamin, 19 March, 1680, Hannah, 8 Dec. 1681, Barbara, 26 March, 1685, Mary, who d. 9 Nov. 1690. He d. 16 Jan. 1691.

ILSLEY, JOSEPH jr. m. Hannah Pike, 1701.

IVIE, JOHN son of John, b. Nov. 1643.

JACOB, MR. SAMUEL d. 16 June, 1672.

JACKMAN, JAMES nephew of Henry Short, came, it is said, from Exeter, England. His wife was Joanna. He d. 30 Dec. 1694, aged 83. Ch.—Sara, 18 Jan. 1648, Hester, 12 Sept. 1651, James, 12 June, 1655, Joanna, 14 June, 1657, Richard, 15 Feb. 1660.

JACKMAN, JAMES son of James, m. Rachel Noyes. Ch.—Joanna, 20 April, 1683, Joanna, 25 May, 1687, John, 3 Feb. 1691, and d. 3 Dec. 1769, Mary, 23 Jan. 1695, Sara, 19 May, 1697, Esther, 5 Nov. 1699.

JACKMAN, RICHARD son of James, m. Elizabeth Plumer 26 June, 1682. Ch.— Richard, 17 Aug. 1684, James, 5 Sept. 1686, Elizabeth, 12 May, 1689, Joseph, 17 April, 1698.

JACKMAN, RICHARD jun. m. Elizabeth Major 1703.

JAFFREY, GEORGE was born about 1637, m. Elizabeth Walker 7 Dec. 1665. Sarah b. 26 Feb. 1667. He moved to Great Island, [New Castle,] N. H.

JAMES, EDMUND d. in 1672 or 1673. Ch.—Edmund, Feb. 1670, Benjamin, 15 April, 1673.

JAQUES, HENRY carpenter, came to Newbury in 1640, m. Anna Knight 8 Oct. 1648. He d. 24 Feb. 1687, aged 69. She d. 22 Feb. 1705. Ch.—Henry, 30 July, 1649, Mary, 12 Nov. 1651, and d. 23 Oct. 1653, Mary, 23 Oct. 1653, Richard, 1658, Stephen, 9 Sept. 1661, Sara, 20 March, 1664, Daniel, 20 Feb. 1667, Elizabeth, 28 Oct. 1669, Ruth, 14 April, 1672, Abigail, 11 March, 1674, Hannah.

JAQUES, HENRY son of Henry, m. —— and d. before 1687, leaving one son Henry.

JAQUES, RICHARD son of Henry, m. Ruth Plumer 18 Jan. 1682, and was drowned 28 May, 1683. Ch.—Richard, 5 Dec. 1682, Richard, 6 Jan. 1684.

JAQUES, SERJ. STEPHEN son of Henry, m. Deborah Plumer 13 May, 1684. Ch. —Stephen, 28 July, 1686, Samuel, 19 March, 1692, Mary, 26 Sept. 1694, Sarah, 23 Sept. 1697, Richard, 1 April, 1700, Benjamin, 23 Sept. 1702. Ann, 25 Feb. 1705.

JAQUES, DANIEL son of Henry, m. Mary Williams 20 March, 1693. His second wife was Susanna ——. Ch.—Daniel, 27 Dec. 1693, Richard, 2 Feb. 1696.

JEPSON, JOHN of Boston, m. Apphia Rolfe 1 April, 1696.

JEWEL, THOMAS m. Ruth Badger 17 Feb. 1702.

JONES, THOMAS Newbury, 1637, Hampton, 1639. A Thomas Jones was in Kittery, 1652. A Thomas Jones d. in Gloucester, 1671.

JORDAN, STEPHEN d. 8 Feb. 1670. His two daughters m. Robert Cross and John Andrews.

JORDAN, SUSANNA widow, d. 25 Jan. 1673.

JOHNSON, MR. WILLIAM shipwright, came from Charlestown to Newbury after 1690. He m. Mrs. Martha Pierce 9 Nov. 1702. Ch.—Elizabeth, 17 Aug. 1703, Martha, 17 Nov. 1704.

KENRICK, JOHN m. Lydia Cheney 12 Nov. 1657.

KELLY, JOHN came from Newbury, England, to Newbury, Mass. in 1635, and died 28 Dec. 1644. Ch.—Sarah, 12 Feb. 1641, John, 2 July, 1642.

KELLY, JOHN son of John. m. Sarah, daughter of deac. Richard Knight 25 May, 1663. Ch.—Richard, 28 Feb. 1666, John, 17 June, 1668, Sarah, 1 Sept. 1670, Abiel, 12 Dec. 1672, Rebecca, 15 May, 1675, Mary, 24 May, 1678, Jonathan, 20 March, 1681, Joseph, 1 Dec. 1683, Hannah, 17 Nov. 1686. He d. 21 March, 1718, aged 75.

KELLY, RICHARD son of John, m. Sarah, daughter of Lt. James Smith 1692. His second wife was Hannah Greenough, schoolmistress. He died 18 June, 1734, aged 68.

KELLY, ABIEL son of John, m. Rebecca Davis 5 Jan. 1697. Ch.—Richard, 24 Oct. 1697, Sara, 14 Aug. 1699, Rebecca, 26 Sept. 1705, and five others. He removed to Methuen.

KELLY, JONATHAN son of John, m. Hester Morss July 6, 1702. Ch.—Ruth, 15 April, 1704, Jonathan, Samuel, and Benjamin.

KELLY, JOSEPH son of John, m. Jane Heath, of Haverhill, where he settled.
KELLY, JOHN son of John 2d, m. Sara ——. His second wife Elizabeth Emery he
m. Nov. 1696. Ch.—Abigail, 5 March, 1691, John, 9 Oct. 1697, (who d. in Atkinson,
N. H. 27 April, 1783, aged 85,) and five daughters, Daniel, Richard, 8 March, 1704.
KEYES, SOLOMON m. Frances Grant 2 Oct. 1653. Ch.—Hannah, 12 Sept. 1654,
Sarah, 24 Aug. 1656, Mary, 26 Sept. 1658, Jane, 25 Oct. 1660, Judith, 16 Sept. 1662.
KEYES. ROBERT perhaps of Watertown 1633. He d. 16 July, 1647. Daughter
Mary b. 16 June, 1645.
KIMBALL. JOHN m. Mary Hobbs 24 Feb. 1665. He d. Oct. 1668. Ch.—Mary, 19
July. 1667. John, 15 Oct. 1668.
KINGSBURY, JOHN m. Hannah ——. Son John b. 8 April, 1689.
KNIGHT, DEA. RICHARD, merchant tailor, came from Romsey, England, to New-
bury in 1635, in the James. He m. Agnes Coffley, who d. 22 March, 1679. He d. 4
Aug. 1683, aged 81. Ch.—Rebecca, 7 March, 1643, Sara, 23 March, 1648, Anne, and
Elizabeth.
KNIGHT, JOHN sen. mercer or merchant tailor, and brother of dea. Richard Knight,
and came with him in June, 1635. He m. Elizabeth —— who d. 20 March, 1645.
He d. May 1670. His second wife was Ann Ingersoll, widow of Richard Ingersoll of
Salem.
KNIGHT, JOHN jun. b. in 1622, probably son of John sen. m. Bathsua, dau. of Rich-
ard Ingersoll, 1647. Ch.—John, b. 16 Aug. 1648, Joseph, 21 June, 1652, Elizabeth, 18
Oct. 1655, Mary, 8 Sept. 1657, Sarah, 13 April, 1660, Hannah b. 22 March, 1662, and d.
30 July, 1664, Hannah, 30 Aug. 1664, Richard, 26 July, 1666, Benjamin, 21 Aug. 1668,
Isaac, 31 Aug. 1672, and d. 29 July, 1690, John, jr. d. 25 Feb. 1678, ag. 56. His widow
Bathsua d. 25 Oct. 1705.
KNIGHT, JOHN son of John jr. m. Rebecca Noyes 1 Jan. 1672. Ch.—James, 3
Sept. 1672, Rebecca, 27 April, 1674, John, 3 April, 1676, Sarah, 25 Feb. 1679, Eliza-
beth, 13 April, 1681, Joseph, 9 Oct. 1683, Nathaniel, 22 Dec. 1688.
KNIGHT, BENJAMIN son of John, jr. m. Abigail Jaques. Ch.—Benjamin, 8 Feb.
1693, Isaac, 15 Jan. 1695, Abigail, 15 April, 1697, Daniel, 4 Dec. 1699, Daniel, 11 Jan.
1702, George, 31 Jan. 1704.
KNIGHT, CAPT. RICHARD son of John, m. Elizabeth Jaques. Ch.—Henry, 6
July, 1697, Elizabeth, 11 March, 1702.
KNIGHT, JOSEPH son of John m. Deborah Coffin, 31 Oct. 1677. Ch.—Judith, 23
Oct. 1678, John, 20 Jan. 1680, and d. 11 March, 1696, Joseph, 16 Feb. 1682, and d. 2
Dec. 1683, Deborah. 26 April, 1684, Sarah, 3 Nov. 1686, Elizabeth, 18 April, 1690,
Joseph, 16 Feb. 1692, Mary, 3 Sept. 1693, Tristram, 9 June, 1695, John, 10 Dec. 1696,
Stephen, 9 Oct. 1699.
KNOWLTON, EBENEZER m. Sarah Lowle, 14 Feb. 1699.
KENT, RICHARD sen. maltster, came to Ipswich in 1635, thence to Newbury the
same year. He d. 14 June, 1654. Ch.—Rebecca. (who m. Samuel Scullard, then
John Bishop,) John, b. 20 July, 1645, Sarah, whom he left in England, and other
daughters.
KENT, STEPHEN brother to Richard Kent, sen. Newbury, 1635, thence to Haverhill
thence to Woodbridge, N. J. His second wife Ann d. in 1660. He then m. Eleanor
widow of William Scadlock, 9 May, 1662. Ch.—Elizabeth, 1 March, 1642, Hannah,
20 March, 1644, Steven, 6 March, 1648, Rebecca, 3 Aug. 1650, and Mary.
KENT, RICHARD jr. Newbury, 1636, m. Jane ——, who d. 26 June, 1674. He m. his
second wife, Mrs. Joanna Davison, 6 Jan. 1675. He d. 25 Nov. 1689.
KENT, JAMES brother to Richard, jr. He d. 12 Dec. 1681. John Kent was 'his only
son and heir,' who was born in 1641, and d. 30 Jan. 1718. ag. 77.
KENT, JOHN son of James, m. Mary Hobbs 24 Feb. 1665. Ch.—John, 8 April, 1665,
and d. 24 June, Sarah, 1 Aug. 1666, Sarah, 30 Aug. 1667, John 23 Nov. 1668, John, 16
July, 1675, and d. 24 March, 1703, James, 3 Sept. 1679, Mary d. 17 March, 1703.
KENT, JOHN jr. son of ——, m. Sarah Woodman 13 March, 1666. Mary, 10 Sept.
1668, Richard, 25 June, 1670. Richard, 17 Jan. 1673, Mary, 24 Oct. 1674, Emma, 20
April, 1677, Hannah, 10 Sept. 1679, Rebecca, 20 Feb. 1684, James, 5 March, 1686.
KENT, JOHN jr. son of ———, m. Rebekah Somerby. Ch.—Rebekah 4 May,
1696, John, 4 Sept. 1698, Emma, 28 Feb. 1701, Sarah, 7 March, 1704, Mary, 30 March,
1707, Richard, 3 June, 1710.
KENT, JOHN m. Sarah Little 14 Jan. 1703.
KENT, EMMA widow, d. 10 Jan. 1677.
LANE, CAPT. JOHN m. Mrs. Joanna ——. Ch.—Abigail, 15 Aug. 1693, Living, his
son, b. 13 Nov. 1704.
LAVENUKE, STEPHEN a Frenchman, m. Mary Diual 25 Sept. 1672. Ch.—Isabella, 22 Dec. 1673, Judith, 1677, and d. 22 April, 1758, ag. 81, Stephen, 1678, and d. Jan.
1, 1764, aged 85.

LEWIS, ROBERT came from Bristol, England, to Salem, thence to Newbury, and d. 4 March, 1643.

LITTLE, GEORGE tailor, came from Unicorn street, London, to Newbury, in 1640. He m. Alice Poor. Ch.—Sarah, 8 May, and d. 19 Nov. 1652, Joseph, 22 Sept. 1653, John, 28 July, 1655, and d. 20 July, 1672. Moses, 11 March, 1657, Sarah, 24 Nov. 1661. His wife Alice, d. 1 Dec. 1680. His second wife, Eleanor Barnard, of Amesbury, he m. 19 July, 1681. He was living 15 March, 1693, and d. before Nov. 27, 1694, as Amesbury records say ' widow Eleanor Little d. 27 Nov. 1694.'

LITTLE, MOSES son of George, m. Lydia, daughter of Tristram Coffin. Ch.—John, 8 Jan. 1680, Tristram, 9 Dec. 1681, Sarah, 28 April, 1684, Mary, 13 Jan. 1687, Elizabeth, 25 May, 1688, Moses, 26 Feb. 1691, and d. 19 Oct. 1780, aged near 90, Moses, sen. d. 8 March, 1691, aged 34.

LITTLE, JOSEPH son of George, m. Mary Coffin, sister of Lydia, 31 Oct. 1677. Ch. —Judith, 19 July, 1678, Joseph, 23 Feb. 1680, and d. 14 Aug. 1693, George, 12 Jan. 1682. Sarah, 23 Oct. 1684, Enoch, 16 Dec. 1685, Tristram, 7 April, 1688, Moses, 5 May, 1690, Daniel, 13 Jan. 1692, Joseph, 27 Dec. 1693.

LITTLEHALE, RICHARD m. Mary Lancton 15 Nov. 1647. He died in Haverhill 18 Feb. 1664. He had twelve children, John, b. 27 Nov. 1650.

LONG, DEA. ROBERT lived in Charlestown from 1637 to 1642. He m. Alice Stevens in 1647, who d. 17 Jan. 1691. He d. 27 Dec. 1690, aged 69. Ch.—Mary, 24 Feb. 1648, Abiel, 19 Feb. 1649, Susanna, 4 Nov. 1656, Shubael, 14 April, 1661, Martha, John, and Rebecca.

LONG, ABIEL son of Robert, m. Hannah Hills 27 Oct. 1682. He d. 13 April, 1743, aged 95. Ch.—Abiel, 24 July and d. 10 Nov. 1683, Hannah, 6 Nov. 1, 1684, Benjamin, 1 Sept. 1691.

LONG, SHUBAEL son of Robert, m. Hannah Merrill 26 Aug. 1695. Ch.—Robert, 20 May, 1696, Abigail, 3 Jan. 1697, and d. 29 Jan. Abigail, 31 Jan. 1699, John, 2 Nov. 1701.

LONGFELLOW, WILLIAM born in 1651, in Hampshire, England, came to Newbury, m. Anne Sewall 10 Nov. 1676. He was drowned at Anticosti, 1690. Ch.—William, 25 Nov. 1679, Stephen, 10 Jan. 1681, and d. 13 Nov. 1683, Anne, 3 Oct. 1683, Elizabeth, 3 July, 1688, Nathan, 5 Feb. 1690.

LT. STEPHEN, b. 1685, and d. 17 Nov. 1764, ag. 79.

LOWLE, MR. PERCIVAL d. 8 Jan. 1665. His wife, Rebecca, died 1645, Dec. 28.

LOWLE, MR. RICHARD came from Bristol, England, in 1639, to Newbury. His second wife was Margaret ——. His first wife died in 1642. He died 5 Aug. 1682, aged 80. Ch.—Percival, 1639, Rebecca, 27 Jan. 1642, Samuel, 1644, Thomas, 28 Sept. 1649.

LOWLE, MR. JOHN brother to Richard, and came with him to Newbury. Ch.— Joseph, 28 Nov. 1639, John, Peter, Mary, and James. His second wife was Elizabeth Goodale, who d. April 1651. He d. 29 June, 1647. His other children were Benjamin, 12 Sept. 1642, Thomas, 4 June, 1644, Elizabeth, 16 Feb. 1646.

LOWLE, BENJAMIN son of John, m. Ruth Woodman 17 Oct. 1666. Ruth, 4 Sept. 1667, Elizabeth, 16 Oct. 1669, Benjamin, 5 Feb. 1674, Sarah, 15 March, 1676, Joseph, 12 Sept. 1680, John, 25 Feb. 1683.

LOWLE, PERCIVAL son of Richard, m. Mary Chandler 7 Sept. 1664. Ch.—Richard, 25 Dec. 1668, and d. 29 May, 1749, aged 80, Gideon, 3 Sept. 1672, Samuel, 13 Jan. 1676, Edmund, 24 Sept. 1684.

LOWLE, GIDEON son of Percival, jun. m. Mary ——. Daughter Mary b. 1 March, 1693.

LOWLE, RICHARD m. Sara Brown 8 April, 1695. Ch.—Hannah, 11 March, 1696, Sarah, 10 April, 1705.

LUNT, HENRY came to Newbury in 1635, m. Anne ——. He d. 10 July, 1662. Ch. —Sarah, 8 Nov. 1639, Daniel, 17 May, 1641, John, 30 Nov. 1643, Priscilla, 16 Feb. 1646, Mary, 13 July, 1648, Elizabeth, 29 Dec. 1650, Henry, 20 Feb. 1653.

LUNT, DANIEL son of Henry, m. Hannah Coker 16 May, 1664, who d. 29 Jan. 1679. His second wife was Mary Moody, widow of Samuel Moody. Ch.—Hannah, 17 May, 1665, Daniel, 1 May, 1667, Henry, 23 June, 1669, John, 10 Feb. 1672, Sarah, 18 June, 1674, Mary 24 July, 1677, Joseph, 4 March, 1681, Anne, 28 Jan. 1683, Benjamin, 15 March, 1686.

LUNT, JOHN son of Henry, m. Mary Skerry, 19 Nov. 1668. He d. 17 Sept. 1678. Ch.—John, 22 Oct. 1669, Elizabeth, 12 Oct. 1671, Henry, 22 Feb. 1674.

LUNT, HENRY son of Henry, m. Jane ——. Ch.—Skipper, 29 Nov. 1679, Mary 16 Jan. 1682, Abraham, 10 December, 1683, John, 1 Feb. 1686, William, 4 July, 1688, Daniel, 1 Jan. 1691, Jane, 9 November, 1693, Samuel, 26 March, 1696.

LUNT, HENRY 3d, m. Sarah Bricket, 1 Jan. 1701.

LUNT, THOMAS m. Opportunity Hoppin, of Roxbury, 17 Jan. 1679.

LUNT, HENRY jr. m. Mary ——. Ch.—Daniel, 15 June, 1695, Benjamin, 21 June, 1700.

MATTOX, JOHN a sawyer, came from Stepney parish in the ship Planter, 1635. He died in Newbury, 24 April, 1643.

MACKENETENE, MATTHEW m. Grace Mitchell 10 Feb. 1700.

MACY, THOMAS came from Chilmark, England, to Newbury, thence to Salisbury, thence to Nantucket, in 1659. He m. Sarah Hopcot, who d. in 1706, aged 94. He d. 19 June, 1682, aged 74. He had six children.

MARCH. MR. HUGH carpenter, m. Judith ——, who d. 14 Dec. 1675. His second wife, Dorcas Blackleach, he m. 29 May, 1676, who d. 22 Nov. 1683. His third wife, Sarah Healy, he m. 3 Dec. 1685, who d. 25 Oct. 1699. He died 12 Dec. 1693, aged 73. Ch.—George, 1646, Judith, 3 Jan. 1653, Hugh, 3 Nov. 1656, John, 10 June, 1658, James, 11 Jan. 1664.

MARCH, MR. GEORGE son of Hugh, m. Mrs. Mary Foulsham 12 June, 1672. Ch. —George, 6 Oct. 1674, John, 18 Aug. 1676, Mary, 28 Aug. and d. 15 Nov. 1678, Stephen, 19 Sept. 1679, and d. 10 Feb. 1684. James, 19 June, 1681, Israel, 4 April, 1683, Sarah, 6 July, 1685, Stephen, 16 Nov. 1687, Henry, 31 July, 1697, George, 24 April, 1698, Jane, 8 May, 1699.

MARCH, MAJ. JOHN son of Hugh, m. Jemima True 1 March, 1679. Ch.—Judith, 21 March, 1682, Mary, b. 2 April, 1684, Joseph, 8 May, 1687, John, 26 Sept. 1690, Abigail, 4 Sept. 1693, Hugh, 8 Jan. 1696, Elizabeth, 6 Sept. 1698.

MARCH, MR. JOHN m. Mrs. Mary Angier, of Watertown, 1700. Son John b. 27 Feb. 1702.

MARCH, CAPT. HUGH son of Hugh, m. Mrs. Sarah Moody 29 March, 1683. Ch. —Sarah, 27 April, 1684, Henry, 22 Sept. 1686, Samuel, 2 March, 1689, Elizabeth, 27 Oct. 1691, Hannah, 4 Sept. and d. 6 Oct. 1694, Daniel, 30 Oct. 1695, Mehetable, 3 Jan. 1703, Trueman, 14 Nov. 1705.

MARCH, LIEUT. JAMES son of Hugh, m. Mary ——. Ch.—Benjamin, 23 Nov. 1690, Nathaniel, 2 Sept. 1693, Tabitha, 20 June, 1696.

MARTIN, RICHARD son of Richard, b. 8 Jan. 1674.

MAJOR, GEORGE came from the parish of St. Lora, in the island of Jersey, to Newbury, and m. Susanna —— 21 Aug. 1672. Ch.—Hannah, 18 May, 1673, George, 20 Nov. 1676.

MARSTON, WILLIAM Salem 1637, thence to Newbury, thence to Hampton, 1640, where he died 30 June, 1672. His wife was Sabina. He left five children.

MARVYN, THOMAS d. 28 Nov. 1651.

MATTHEWS, HUGH m. Mary Emerson 28 Aug. 1683. Ch.—John, 26 Feb. 1688, Judith, 30 April, 1689, Joanna, 19 April, 1690, Hugh, 15 May, 1691, Hugh, 19 May, 1696.

MARSHALL, EDMUND shipwright. Ch.—Edmund. 5 Oct. 1677, John, 7 July, 1682.

MARSHALL, MR. PETER m. Mrs. Abigail. Ch.—Thomas, 1 July, 1689, Ruth, 31 Dec. 1690.

MAYO. JOSEPH m. Sara Short, 29 May, 1679. Ch.—Sarah, 9 July, 1679, Thomasine, 10 June, 1689.

MERRILL, JOHN one of the first settlers. m. Elizabeth ——, who d. 14 July, 1682. He d. 12 Sept. 1673. He left a daughter Hannah, who m. Steven Swett.

MERRILL, NATHANIEL brother to John, m. Susanna Jordan. Ch.—Nathaniel, 1638, John, Abraham, Susanna, Daniel, 20 Aug. 1642, Abel, 20 Feb. 1644. He d. 16 March, 1655.

MERRILL, NATHANIEL son of Nathaniel, m. Joanna Kinney, 15 Oct. 1661. He d. 1 Jan. 1683. Ch.—John, 16 Feb. 1663. Nathaniel, 8 Feb. 1665, Peter, Aug. 1667, Hannah, 12 July, 1672, Mary, 18 Sept. 1675.

MERRILL, MR. JOHN son of Nathaniel, m. Lucy ——. Ch.—Nathaniel, 26 July, 1687, John, by second wife Mary, b. 27 Feb. 1702.

MERRILL, ABRAHAM son of Nathaniel, m. Abigail Webster 1 Jan. 1661. Ch.— Abigail, 13 Aug. 1665, Mary, 5 July, 1667, Prudence, 26 April, 1659, Hannah, 9 Jan. 1671, John, 15 Oct. 1673, Jonathan, 19 Jan. 1676, David, 20 Feb. 1678, Sara, 9 Oct. 1679, Susanna, 6 Dec. and d. 15 Dec. 1681, Prudence, 1 Oct. 1683.

MERRILL, ABEL son of Nathaniel, m. Priscilla Chase 10 Feb. 1671. Ch.—Abel, 28 Dec. 1671, Susanna, 14 Nov. 1673, Nathan, 3 April, 1676, Thomas, 1 Jan. 1679, Joseph, 12 July, 1681, Nathaniel, 6 Feb. 1684, Priscilla, 13 July, 1686, James, 27 Jan. 1689.

MERRILL, DANIEL son of Nathaniel, m. Sara Clough 14 May, 1667. Ch.—John, 7 Oct. 1674, Sara, 15 Oct. 1677, Ruth, 7 Feb. 1681, Moses and Martha, 3 Sept. 1683, Stephen, 16 Sept. 1688.

MERRILL, ABEL son of Abel, m. Abigail Stevens 19 June, 1694. Ch.—Samuel, 13 Sept. 1695, Abel, 20 March, 1698, Abigail, 22 Jan. 1700.

MERRILL, NATHAN son of Abel, m. Hannah Kent 6 Sept. 1699. Ch.—Hannah, 7 July, 1700, John, 30 Nov. 1701, Priscilla, 16 Oct. 1703.

MERRILL, NATHANIEL son of Nathaniel, jun. m. Rebecca ——, who d. 9 Dec. 1689. His second wife was Sarah ——. Ch.—Nathaniel, 23 Nov. 1688, Hannah, 30 Dec. 1692, Sarah, 26 Oct. 1694.

MERRILL, PETER son of Nathaniel, jun. m. Mary ——. Ch.—Mary, 13 Jan. 1693, Peter, 10 March, 1696.

MERRILL, ABRAHAM jun. m. Abigail Bartlet 1696. Ch.—Abraham, 23 Aug. 1698, Abigail, 5 May, 1701, Elizabeth, 2 May; 1705.

MILLER, MARY d. 6 May. 1664.

MILLER, JOSEPH d. 21 July, 1681.

MIRICK, JAMES was born in 1612. Ch.—Hannah, 6 Feb. 1657, Abigail, 5 Sept. 1658, Joseph, 27 April, 1661, Isaac, 6 Jan. 1665, Timothy, 28 Sept. 1666, Susanna, 20 Aug. 1670.

MIRICK, TIMOTHY son of James, m. Mary Lancaster, 1696. Ch.—Ezra, 31 March, 1697, Abigail, 26 Nov. 1698.

MIRICK, JAMES son of James, jr. b. 16 April, 1683.

MIRICK. JAMES jr. m. Hannah ——. Ch.—Benjamin, 16 April, 1683, James, 16 July, 1684, John, 10 Sept. 1686.

MITCHELL, WILLIAM m. Mary Sawyer 7 Nov. 1648. He d. 6 July, 1654. His widow m. Robert Savory. Ch.—Mary, 31 Aug. 1649, John, 21 May, 1651, William, 1 March, 1653, Elizabeth, 15 March, 1655.

MITCHELL, JOHN son of William, m. Hannah Spafford 20 May, 1680, who d. 24 April, 1689. He m. Constance Moores 15 Nov. 1697. Ch.—Hannah, 12 April, 1681, Sara, 26 Sept. 1682, John, 17 June, 1685, Sara, 10 April, 1689.

MILWARD, MR. THOMAS, mariner, came to Newbury 1636 or 7, was in cape Ann 1640, and d. in Boston, 1 Sept. 1653, aged 53. Ch.—Ann, Nov. 1642, Rebecca and Elizabeth.

MINGO, ROBERT m. Elizabeth ——. Ch.—Thomas, 2 June, 1689, Robert, 11 Oct. 1697.

MOODY, WILLIAM saddler, came from Ipswich, England, to Ipswich, 1634, then Newbury. 1635. His wife was Sarah. Ch.—Joshua, Caleb, William, and Samuel.

MOODY, REV. JOSHUA son of William, graduated, settled in Portsmouth, moved to Boston and there died. See appendix.

MOODY, CALEB son of William, m. Sara Pierce 24 Aug. 1659, who d. 25 Aug. 1665. His second wife, Judith Bradbury, he m. 9 Nov. 1665, who d. 24 Jan. 1700. He d. 25 Aug. 1698, aged 61. Ch.—Daniel, 4 April, 1662, Sara, 23 July, 1664, Caleb, 9 Sept. 1666, Thomas, 20 Oct. 1668, Judith, 23 Sept. 1669, and d. at Salisbury 28 Jan. 1679, Joshua, 3 Nov. 1671, William, 15 Dec. 1673, Samuel, 4 Jan. 1676, Mary, 23 Oct. 1678, Judith, 12 Feb. 1683.

MOODY WILLIAM son of William, m. Mehetabel Sewall 15 Nov. 1684. Ch.—Mary, 30 May, 1685, deac. Samuel, 21 March, 1689, and d. 25 May, 1767, Mehetabel, 15 Feb. 1691, and probably others. William, son of lt. Wm. died 23 Feb. 1700.

MOODY, SAMUEL son of William. m. Mary Cutting 9 Nov. 1657. He died 4 April, 1675. Ch.—Mary, 16 Nov. 1658, William, 22 July, 1661, Sara, 20 June, 1663, Mary, 18 Feb. 1665, Lydia, 5 Aug. 1667, Hannah, 4 Jan. 1700, Samuel, Dec. 1671, Cutting, 9 April, 1674, William, John and Sarah.

MOODY, SAMUEL son of Samuel, m. Sarah Knight 16 April, 1700.

MOODY, JOHN son of Samuel, m. Hannah ——. Ch.—Apphia, 23 June, 1693, Sarah, 7 March, 1697.

MOODY, CUTTING son of Samuel, m. Judith Little 25 March, 1696. Ch.—Hannah, 16 March, 1699, Joseph, 26 April, 1701.

MOODY, DANIEL son of Caleb, m. Elizabeth Somerby 29 March, 1683. Son Daniel b. 27 Feb. 1684.

MOODY, THOMAS son of Caleb, m. Judith Hale. Ch.—Ezra, 11 April, 1693, Sara, 11 Feb. 1695, Caleb, 10 March, 1697, Judith, 6 Aug. 1699, Oliver, 7 Oct. 1701, Thomas, 11 Jan. 1704.

MOODY, CALEB son of   m. Ruth Morse 9 Dec. 1690. Daughter Judith, 16 Sept. 1691.

MOODY, MR. JOSHUA son of Caleb, m. Mrs. Mary Greenleaf 1696. Ch.—Mary, 26 June, 1697, Elizabeth, 4 Dec. 1698, Joshua, 11 Nov. 1700, Abigail, 30 Sept. 1703, Judith, 26 Oct. 1705.

MOORING, JOSEPH d. 8 May, 1689.

MOORES, EDMUND was born in 1614, came to Newbury 1640, m. Ann ——, who d. 7 June, 1676. Ch.—Martha, 12 Dec. 1643, Jonathan, 23 April, 1646, Mary, 30 Nov. 1648, Edmund, who died 8 Nov. 1656, Richard, 3 Nov. 1653, Sarah, 1 April, 1661.

MOORES, EDMUND jr. m. Sarah C—— 3 Jan. 1677. He d. 19 April, 1699. Ch.—

Edmund, 5 Dec. 1677, Sarah, 9 Dec. 1681, Mark, 9 Feb. 1689, Martha, 20 Aug. 1691, Edmund, 3 April, 1693.

MOORES, SAMUEL m. Hannah Plumer 3 May, 1653, who d. 8 Dec. 1654. His second wife, Mary Ilsley, he m. 12 Sept. 1656.

MOORES, MATTHEW m. Sara Savory 27 March, 1662. Ch.—Sara, 15 Dec. 1663, William, 26 May, 1664, William, 10 Feb. 1666.

MOORES, JONATHAN son of Edmund, m. Constance Longhorne, 10 May, 1670. Ch.—Richard, 24 July, 1683, Samuel, 20 Feb. 1686, Thomas, 6 Nov. 1688, Dorothy, 8 Dec. 1690.

MOORES, HANNAH d. 25 March, 1665.

MORSS, ANTHONY shoemaker, came from Marlborough, England, in the ship James to Newbury, 1635. His wife's name was Mary. His second wife Mary Barnard, whom he m. 16 Nov. 1669. He died 25 Feb. 1678, aged 60. Ch.—Benjamin, 4 March, 1640, Sara, 1 May, 1641, Lydia d. May, 1645, Lydia, 7 Oct. 1647, Mary, 9 April, 1649, and d. 14 June, 1662, Hester, 3 May, 1651, Joshua, 24 July, 1653, Joseph, John, Peter, and Anthony.

MORSS, WILLIAM shoemaker, brother to Anthony, came with him to Newbury. He m. Elizabeth ——. He d. 29 Nov. 1683, aged 69. Ch.—Hannah, 6 March, 1641, Timothy, 10 June, 1647, and d. 27 Dec. 1659, Abigail, 14 Feb. 1652, Jonathan, Obadiah, and Elizabeth.

MORSS, ANTHONY jun. m. Elizabeth Knight 8 May, 1660, who d. 29 July, 1667. He also m. Ann ——, who d. 9 March, 1680. He d. 12 Oct. 1686. Ch.—Ruth, 20 May, 1661, and d. 24 July, Joseph, 29 July, 1665, Elizabeth, 29 July, 1667, John, 13 Sept. 1670, Peter, 14 Nov. 1674, Sara, 23 November, 1676, Mary, 31 Aug. 1672.

MORSS, ROBERT m. Ann Lewis 30 Oct. 1654. Ch.—Elizabeth, 25 Sept. 1655, Mary, 25 Feb. 1658, and d. 23 Nov. Lydia, 13 July, 1662, Sara, 28 April, 1666.

MORSS, BENJAMIN son of Anthony, sen. m. Ruth Sawyer, 27 Aug. 1667. Ch.— Benjamin, 24 Aug. 1668, Ruth, 8 Dec. 1669, Joseph, 5 Feb. 1672, William, 23 Jan. 1674, Sara, 13 Jan. 1676, and d. Jan. 1679, Philip, 19 Oct. 1677, Sara, 19 Jan. 1680, Ann, 27 March, 1681, Mary, 15 May, 1686, Samuel, 7 Dec. 1688.

MORSS, ANTHONY m. Sara Pike 4 Feb. 1686. Ch.—Sara, 27 Oct. 1686, and d. 13 Nov. Anthony, 26 May, 1690, Joseph, 3 April, 1694, Stephen, 28 Dec. 1695, Thomas, 25 March, 1702.

MORSS, BENJAMIN jun. son of Benjamin, m. Susanna Merrill 28 Jan. 1692. Ch.— Abel, 5 Oct. 1692, Ruth, 25 Sept. 1694, Priscilla, 22 April, 1697, Judith, 13 March, 1699, Stephen, 30 March, 1701, Margaret, 14 April, 1702.

MORSE, JOSEPH son of Anthony, jun. m. Lydia ——, who d. 8 Nov. 1689. His second wife was Elizabeth ——. Ch.—Lydia, 2 Nov. 1689, Joseph, 28 Oct. 1693, Daniel, 8 March, 1695, John, 22 Oct. 1696, Mary, 10 Jan. 1699.

MORSE, JOSHUA m. Joanna ——, who d. 10 April, 1691. He d. 28 March, 1691. Ch.— Hannah, 15 Feb. 1681, Joshua, 11 April, and d. 1 July, 1656, Anthony, 15 April, 1688.

MORSE, WILLIAM m. Sara Merrill 12 May, 1696. Ch.—Daniel, 26 April, 1697, Ruth, 4 March, 1699.

MORSE, JONATHAN m. Mary Clarke, 3 May, 1671.

MORSE, BENJAMIN tertius m. Susanna ——. Ch.—Joseph, 26 Aug. 1691, Mary, 29 Jan. 1694, Hannah, 20 Jan. 1696. Joshua, 1 March, 1698, and d. 26 June, 1699, Joshua, 30 March, 1700, Margaret, 14 April, 1702, Mary, 8 Sept. 1703.

MORSE, JOSEPH, jun. m. Sarah Merrill, 1696. Ch.—Sarah, 30 Dec. 1697, Joseph, 30 April, 1700, Abigail, 30 Dec. 1702.

MORSE, ANN wife of Anthony, d. 9 May, 1681.

MORRISON, DANIEL m. Hannah ——, who d. 9 Oct. 1700. Ch.—Daniel. 1 Aug. 1691, John, 28 March, 1693, Hannah, 27 Jan. 1696, Ebenezer, 6 Oct. 1697, Mary, 20 March.

MOULTON, THOMAS Newbury, 1637. Hampton, 1639, where he died 18 Feb. 1665.

MOULTON, JOHN Newbury, 1637, Hampton, 1639, and there died 1651. Ch.— William, Thomas, Henry, Bridget and Jane, twins, who d. the same day, 19 March, ——, aged 64. .

MOULTON, WILLIAM m. Abigail Webster 27 May, 1685. Ch.—Abigail, 13 June, 1686, Batt, 4 July, 1688, Jonathan, 7 Sept. 1692, Joseph, 25 Nov. 1694, Margaret, 21 Feb. 1699, and d. 25 Sept. 1701, Sarah, 4 July, 1701, Mary, 2 Aug. 1705.

'MUSSILOWAY, DANIEL alias ROGER WALDRON,' an Irishman, was born in 1645, m. Anne Chase 14 June, 1672, who d. 21 April, 1687. His second wife was Mary ——. Ch.—Daniel, 16 May, and d. 19 May, 1688, Daniel, 9 Sept. 1690, John, 13 Feb. 1693. The name is now Siloway. He died 18 Jan. 1711.

MUFFET, WILLIAM m. Mehetabel ——. Ch.—William, 14 Feb. 1693, John, 18 June, 1695, Mehetabel, 17 Dec. 1700, Joseph, 11 July, 1703.

MUSSELWHITE, came from Langford in the ship James, to Newbury, in 1635. He died 30 Jan. 1671, leaving estate to sister Eda, brother Thomas, and brother John, in Beaverstock, in Wiltshire.

MUSSEY, JOSEPH son of Robert, of Ipswich, was born in 1628, m. Esther Jackman 9 Feb. 1671. He d. 30 Dec. 1680. Ch.—Mary, 25 Nov. 1672, Esther, 8 Jan. 1675, Joseph, 21 Dec. 1677, Benjamin, 17 Aug. 1680.

MUSSEY, JOSEPH son of Joseph, m. Joanna Pettingell, 1700. Ch.—Joseph, 1 March, 1703, Mary, 2 Aug. 1705.

NEFF, WILLIAM Newbury, thence to Haverhill, m. Mary Corliss 23 Jan. 1665. He died Feb.'1689, aged 47. Mary Neff was with Mrs. Hannah Dunstan, when she killed the Indians, in 1697.

NELSON, PHILIP of Rowley, m. Elizabeth Lowle 1 Jan. 1667.

NISBITT, MR. WILLIAM m. Hannah Woodman 5 June, 1690. Daughter Sarah b. 14 March, 1691.

NOYES, REV. JAMES was born in Choulderton, Wiltshire, in 1608, m. Miss Sarah Brown, of Southampton, Eng. came to New England 1634, and to Newbury 1635. He d. 22 Oct. 1656, ag. 48. Ch.—Joseph, 15 Oct. 1637, James, 11 March, 1640, Sarah, 12 Aug. 1641, and d. 21 Feb. 1653, Moses, 6 Dec. 1643, John, 3 June, 1645, Thomas, 10 Aug. 1648, Rebecca, 1 April, 1651, William, 22 Sept. 1653, Sarah, 25 March, 1656.

NOYES, COL. THOMAS son of rev. James, m. Martha Pierce 28 Dec. 1669, who d. 3 Sept. 1674. He then m. Elizabeth Greenleaf 24 Sept. 1677. Ch.—Sara, 14 Sept. 1670, Martha, 24 Feb. 1673, Daniel, 30 Aug. 1674, James 3 July, 1678, Thomas, 2 Oct. 1679, Parker, 29 Oct. 1681, Elizabeth, 29 Feb. 1684, Joseph, 5 Aug. 1688, Moses, 29 Jan. 1692, Rebekah, 19 April, 1700, Judith, 17 April, 1702.

NOYES, NICHOLAS brother to rev. James, b. in 1614, m. Mary Cutting, sister of capt. John Cutting. He died 23 Nov. 1701, aged 83. Ch.—Mary, 15 Oct. 1641, Hannah, 30 Oct. 1643, John, 20 Jan. 1646, Nicholas, 22 Dec. 1647, Cutting, 23 Sept. 1649, Sarah, 13 Sept. 1651, Sarah, 22 Aug. 1653, Timothy, 23 June, 1655, James, 16 May, 1657, Abigail, 11 April, 1659, Rachel, 10 May, 1661, Thomas, 20 June, 1663, Rebecca, 18 May, 1665. and d. 1 Dec. 1683.

NOYES, JOHN son of Nicholas, m. Mary Poore 23 Nov. 1668. Ch.—Nicholas, 18 May, 1671, Daniel, 23 Oct. 1673, Mary, 10 Dec. 1675, John, 15 Feb. 1678, Martha, 24 Dec. 1679, Martha, 19 Dec. 1680, Nathaniel, 28 Oct. 1681, Elizabeth 15 Nov. 1684, Moses, 22 May, 1688, Samuel, 5 Feb. 1692.

NOYES, MR. WILLIAM son of rev. James, m. Sara Cogswell 6 Nov. 1685. Ch.— John, 27 July, 1686, William, 1 Sept. 1688, Sarah, 10 May, 1691, and d. 3 Dec. 1703, Moses, 27 Jan. 1694, and d. 16 Feb. Susanna, 25 Feb. 1696, Mary, 24 May, 1699, and d. 16 Dec. 1703, Sarah, 5 Dec. 1703, Parker, 17 Jan. 1705.

NOYES, CUTTING son of Nicholas, m. Elizabeth Knight, 25 Feb. 1674. Ch.— John, 15 Dec. 1674, Cutting, 28 Jan. 1677, Elizabeth, 2 Jan. 1679, Nicholas, 22 May, 1681, and d. 5 Dec. 1694, Joseph, 21 Jan. 1689, Mary, 27 March, 1693.

NOYES, TIMOTHY son of Nicholas, m. Mary Knight 13 Jan. 1681. Abigail, 28 Feb. 1685, Mary, 8 Dec. 1686, Sarah, 26 March, 1789, Timothy, 25 Jan. 1691, Rachel 8 Feb. 1694, John, 19 Feb. 1696. Martha, 14 March, 1697, Nicholas, 7 March, 1701.

NOYES, JAMES son of Nicholas, m. Hannah Knight 31 March, 1684. Ch.—Rebecca, 12 Jan. 1685, Joseph, 20 Sept. 1686, Hannah, 13 March, 1688, Nicholas, 9 Feb. 1690, Nathan, 5 Feb. 1692, Ephraim, 20 Nov. and d. 19 Dec. 1694, Lydia, 30 Nov. 1695, Ephraim, 25 Dec. 1698, Benjamin, 22 Feb. 1701, Mary, 13 March, 1703, James, 19 Aug. 1705.

NOYES, THOMAS jun. son of Nicholas, m. Sarah ——. Ch.—Bethia, 20 Oct. 1691, Rebecca, 20 Jan. and d. 28 Jan. 1694.

NOYES, NICHOLAS jun. son of John, m. Sara Lunt 1695. Ch.—John, 21 July, and d. 7 Aug. 1696, Sarah, 15 Sept. 1697, John, Dec. 6, 1699.

NOYES, DANIEL m. Judith Knight 29 Dec. 1703.

NOYES, JOHN m. Mary Noyes 1700.

NOYES, CUTTING m. Elizabeth Toppan 8 Jan. 1703.

OLIVER, MR. JOHN born in Bristol, England, in 1613, came to Newbury 1639, m. Mrs. Joanna Goodale. He d. in 1642, aged 29. His widow m. capt. William Gerrish, and daughter Mary born in 1640. m. Samuel Appleton, of Ipswich 8 Dec. 1656.

ORDWAY, JAMES came, tradition says, from Wales to Newbury. He was born in 1620, mar. Ann Emery 23 Nov. 1648, who d. 31 March, 1687. Ch.—Ephraim, 25 April, 1650, James, 16 April, 1651, Edward, 14 Sept. 1653, Sarah, 14 Sept. 1656, John, 17 Nov. 1658, Isaac, 4 Dec. 1660, and d. 16 Jan. 1669, Jane, 12 Nov. 1663, Hananiah, 2 Dec. 1665, Anne, 12 Feb. 1670, Mary, 5 April, 1670. He died after 1702.

ORDWAY, JOHN son of James m. Mary Godfrey 5 Dec. 1681. Ch.—Mary, 18 Sept. 1682, John, 29 Oct. 1684, James, 4 July, 1687, Peter, 15 Sept. 1691, Hannah, 20 Nov. and d. 5 Dec. 1693, Hannah, 6 March, 1695, Stephen, 8 April, 1697, Ann, 15 May, 1699, Nathan, 28 April, 1703.

ORDWAY, JAMES jun. son of James, m. Tirzah ——. Ch. 12 Oct. 1691, who d. 10 Jan. 1696. His second wife, Sarah Clark, of Rowley, he m. May, 1696. Ch.—Lydia, 12 July. 1693, Lydia, 14 July, 1696, Joanna, 22 May, 1697, John, 22 June, 1699, Mary, 28 April. 1703.

ORDWAY, EDWARD son of James, m. Mary Wood 12 Dec. 1678. Ch.—Joanna, 28 Nov. 1685, Rachel, 14 Jan. 1688, Jacob, 14 Jan. 1690, Isaiah, 28 Jan. 1692, Daniel, 13 Jan. 1694.

ORDWAY, HANANIAH son of James, m. Abigail ——. Ch.—Rebecca, 2º Dec. 1690. Abigail, 2 Aug. 1693, Nathaniel, 3 July, 1695, Joanna, 15 April, 1698, Elizabeth, 15 Feb. 1702.

ORDWAY, SAMUEL m. ——. His son Isaac b. 4 Feb. 1680.

OSGOOD. JOHN was born in Andover, England. 23 July, 1595, came to Ipswich, thence to Newbury, thence to Andover-1645. and there died in 1651, aged 56. Ch.— John, Stephen, Mary, and Elizabeth.

PALMER, HENRY came to Newbury about 1637, moved to Haverhill, and there died 15 July, 1680. He had two daughters.

PALMER, WILLIAM came to Newbury about 1637, removed to Piscataqua. His daughter Martha m. John Sherman of Watertown.

PALMER, JOSEPH m. Sara Jackman 18 March, 1665. Ch.—Sara, 5 Dec. 1665, James, 18 Dec. 1667. Joseph, 8 July, 1670.

PALMER, JOSEPH son of Joseph. m. ——. His second wife was Hester ——. Ch. —Joseph, 24 Oct 1696, William, May. 1700, Joseph, 10 Nov. 1702.

PARKER, NATHAN came early to Newbury, thence to Andover in 1645, m. Sara Short 10 Nov. 1648. He died in 1685.

PARKER, JOSEPH came early to Newbury, thence to Andover. Ch.—Joseph, 15 May, 1642. Stephen, John. and Samuel.

PARKER, NATHAN m. Mary Browne 15 Dec. 1675. Daughter Mary was born and d. 6 April, 1679.

PARKER, NATHANIEL had a daughter Mary b. 11 July, 1678.

PARKER, REV. THOMAS only son of rev. Robert Parker, of Wiltshire, was born in 1596, came to Ipswich May, 1634, thence to Newbury in 1635, and there died unmarried 24 April, 1677.

PEARSON. BENJAMIN son of John, of Rowley. m. Hannah Thurston. Ch.—Phebe, 14 July, 1682. Daniel, 25 Dec. 1684, Abigail, 1 March, 1689. Benjamin, 12 Aug. 1690, and d. 5 April, 1774, Sarah. 10 Dec. 1691, Mehetabel, 18 May, 1695, Joseph, 4 Dec. 1699. David, 18 Jan. 1702, Oliver, 14 Aug. 1704.

PEARSON, SAMUEL m. Poor 6 Dec. 1670.

PEASLEY, JOSEPH an early settler in Newbury, thence to Salisbury. now Amesbury, where he died 3 Dec. 1660. Ch.—Sarah, 20 Sept. 1642, Joseph, 9 Sept. 1646, Elizabeth.

PENGRIN, MOSES married Abigail ——. Daughter Abigail. 11 Nov. 1695.

PEMBERTON. JAMES was in Newbury in 1646. Ch.—John b. in Newbury 16 Feb. 1648. Thomas and Joseph were born in Boston, where a James Pemberton died 11 Oct. 1696.

PEMBERTON, JOHN was dismissed from Boston to Newbury church 24 Nov. 1640. His wife died 22 Feb. 1646.

PERKINS, BENJAMIN had a son Daniel b. 18 Dec. 1684.

PERKINS, LYDIA of Newbury, m. Eliakim Wardwell, of Hampton, 17 Oct. 1659.

PENUEL. WALTER m. Anne 15 April. 1700.

PERRY, JOHN and wife Damaris were in Newbury in 1651. He sold his farm to Samuel Plumer.

PETTINGELL. RICHARD born in 1621. came, tradition says, from Staffordshire to Wenham. where he was in 1648. In 1652 he came to Newbury with his wife Joanna, (who was daughter of Richard Ingersoll, of Salem,) and several children. Mary was born in Newbury 6 July, 1652, Nathaniel, 21 Sept. 1654.

PETTINGELL, NATHANIEL son of Richard, m. Hannah Goodridge 1703. Ch.— Mary, died 3 March, 1698.

PETTINGELL, SAMUEL son of Richard, m. Sarah Poore 16 Feb. 1674. Ch.— Samuel, 3 Feb. 1676, Richard, 26 Aug. 1677, Richard, 24 Jan. 1679, John, 20 Sept. 1680, Mary and Sara, 20 Jan. 1686, Joanna, 10 Feb. 1689, Benjamin, 18 Dec. 1692.

PETTINGELL. MATTHEW son of Richard, m. Sam. Noyes 13 April, 1674. Ch.— Nathaniel, 21 Jan. 1676, Matthew, 18 Sept. 1678, Joanna, 27 Jan. 1681, Nicholas, 15 Nov. 1685. Sarah, 19 April, 1688, John, 16 Feb. 1694, Abraham, 23 Sept. 1696, Abigail, 17 Oct. 1699, Mary, d. 3 March, 1698. His second wife Jemima French he m. in 1703.

PETTINGELL, MATTHEW jr. m. Joanna ——. His son Abraham b. 4 Dec. 1704.

PETTINGELL, DANIEL m. Mary Stickney 13 Nov. 1699. Son Daniel b. 5 Jan. 1705

PETTINGELL, RICHARD son of Samuel, m. Jemima Cheney, 10 Oct. 1701

PETTINGELL, NATHANIEL jr. m. Margaret Richardson 1702. Daughter Anne b. 22 Dec. 1703.

PHELPS, EDWARD m. Elizabeth Adams. Son John b. 15 Dec. 1657. He moved to Andover.

PIKE, JOHN laborer, came from Langford, England, in the ship James, to Newbury, in 1635. He d. in Salisbury 26 May, 1654. Ch.—Robert, b. in 1615, John, Dorothy, Ann, Israel, a daughter, Sarah, who d. Nov. 1659, Dorothy, who m. Daniel Hendrick. 'The worshipful maj. ROBERT PIKE,' son of John, died in Salisbury 12 Dec. 1706, in his 92d year.

PIKE, JOHN son of John, m. Mary ——. Ch.—Joseph, 26 Dec. 1638, John, 12 Jan. 1641, and d. 28 May, 1649, Hannah, 26 April, 1643, Mary, 11 Nov. 1647, John, 30 Mar. 1650, Ruth, 17 July, 1652, Sarah, 13 Sept. 1655, Thomas, 7 Dec. 1657, Samuel.

PIKE, JOSEPH son of John, jr. m. Susanna Kingsbury 29 Jan. 1662. Ch.—Sarah, 12 Oct. 1666, Mary, 19 April 1670, John, 28 Dec. 1671, Joseph, 17 April, 1674. He died 1694, aged 73. Benjamin, 21 Sept. 1676, Hannah, 24 March, 1679, Thomas, 4 Aug. 1681. He was probably the Joseph Pike killed by the Indians in Haverhill, 4 Sept. 1694.

PIKE, JOSEPH son of Joseph, m. Hannah Smith Dec. 1695 Ch.—Joseph, 4 Nov. 1696, John, 24 Feb. 1699, Thomas, 25 Sept. 1700, James, 1 March, 1703, Sarah, 2 April, and d. 20 June, 1705. Joseph, d. 1757, aged 84.

PIKE, JOHN son of John jr. m. Lydia, widow of Moses Little, 18 March, 1695. Ch. —Judith, 4 Dec. 1695, Susanna, 3 April, 1697, Lydia, 23 Dec. 1698, Joanna, 17 Dec. 1700, Dorothy, 23 Sept. 1702.

PIKE, HUGH m. Sarah Brown, 17 June, 1685. Son Hugh b. 28 May, 1686.

PILSBURY, WILLIAM came, tradition says, from Staffordshire. He m. Dorothy Crosby, in Dorchester, about 1641, thence to Newbury, where he d. 19 June, 1686. Ch.—Caleb, 28 Jan. 1654, and d. 4 July, 1680, William, 27 July, 1656, Experience, 10 April, 1658, Increase, 10 Oct. 1660, Thankful, 22 April, 1662, Joshua, 20 June, 1674, Moses, Job, Abel.

PILSBURY, WILLIAM son of William, m. Mary Kenny 13 Dec. 1677. Ch.—William, 22 March, 1680, Experience, 16 April, 1682, William, 7 July, 1687, Lydia, 25 Dec. 1689, Increase, 5 Jan. 1695, Apphia, 8 May, 1700.

PILSBURY, MOSES son of William. m Susanna Worth, 1668. Ch.—Joseph, 6 June, 1670, Dorothy, 9 April, 1675, Susanna, 5 Feb. 1677, Judith, 16 March, 1679, Caleb, 27 July, 1681, Hannah, 3 May, 1686.

PILSBURY, JOB son of William, m. Katharine Gavet 5 April, 1677. Ch.—Daniel, 20 Sept. 1678, Josiah, 17 April, 1686.

PILSBURY, ABEL son of William, m. Mary ——. Ch.—Joshua, 12 April, 1679, John, 13 Sept. 1682, Jacob, 20 March, 1687, Abel, 12 April, 1690, Elizabeth, 20 March, 1694.

PILSBURY, DANIEL m. Sarah Allen 1703.

PILSBURY, CALEB m. Sarah Morse 1702.

PILSBURY, JOSEPH son of Moses, m. Sarah ——. Ch.—Joseph, 16 Jan. 1695, Moses, 19 Sept. 1697, Nathan, 3 June, 1699.

PILSBURY, MOSES jun. m. Abigail Rolf 1698. Ch.—Moses, 16 Jan. 1699, Abigail, 9 Aug. 1700.

PIERCE, DANIEL blacksmith, came from London to Watertown, thence to Newbury about 1637. His first wife was Sarah. He m. Anne Milward, 26 Dec. 1654. She d. 27 Nov. 1690. He d. 27 Nov. 1677. Ch.—Joshua, 15 May, 1643, Martha, 14 Feb. 1648, Daniel, 15 May, 1642, and 'son in law Thorpe.'

PIERCE, DANIEL son of Daniel, m. ——. Ch.—Joanna, who d. 16 Sept. 1690, Daniel, 20 Dec. 1663, who d. 2 Sept. 1690, Anne, 22 May. 1666, Benjamin, 26 Feb. 1669, Joshua, 16 Oct. 1671, Martha, 26 Feb. 1677, Sara, 3 Oct. 1679, George, 5 March, 1681, Mary, 14 April, 1685, John, 16 Oct. 1687. Catharine, 18 Sept. 1690.

PIERCE, MR. THOMAS m. Mehetabel Frost 5 Jan. 1698. Son John b. 5 Nov. 1698.

PIERCE, BENJAMIN son of Daniel. jun. m. Lydia ——. Ch.—Daniel, 6 Aug. 1693, and d. 25 Aug. Charles, 3 Feb. 1695, Elizabeth, 14 Nov. 1696, Daniel, 11 Oct. 1698, Benjamin, 13 June. 1700, John, 7 Nov. 1703.

PIERCE, MR. JOSHUA m. Mrs. Joanna. Daughter Anne, 14 Oct. 1704.

PEABODY. WILLIAM m. Mary Browne 8 Dec. 1680.

POORE, JOHN came from Wiltshire to Newbury in 1635. He d. 23 Nov. 1684, aged 69. Ch.—Jonathan, John, 21 June, 1642, Hannah, 14 Oct. 1645, Elizabeth, 8 Nov. 1647, Mary, 15 July, 1648, Hannah, 25 March, 1649, Henry, 13 Dec. 1650, Mary, 6 March, 1652, and d. 8 Sept. Joseph, 4 Oct. 1653, Mary, 12 Dec. 1654, Sarah, 5 June, 1655, Lydia, 5 Dec. 1656, Edward, 4 April, 1658, Abigail, 26 March, 1660, Abigail, 5 Aug. 1661.

POORE, JOHN son of John, m. Mary Titcomb, 27 Feb. 1666. Ch.—John, 7 May, and d. 4 Oct. 1668, Mary, 9 Aug. 1669, Sarah, 27 Oct. 1671, Elizabeth, 26 July, 1674, Hannah, 16 Aug. 1677, Jonathan, 5 Feb. 1679, Judith, 22 May, 1681, John, 26 June, 1683. He died 15 Feb. 1701, ag. 59.

POORE. JONATHAN son of John, m. Rebecca ——. Daughter Rebecca b. 10 May, 1705.

POORE, HENRY son of John, m. Abigail Hale 12 Sept. 1679. Ch.—Abigail, 9 Sept. 1680, Henry, 31 Jan. 1682, Jeremiah, 10 Jan. 1684, Mary, 10 April, 1686, Mary, 20 Sept. 1687, Hannah, 19 July, 1692, Sarah, 18 Jan. 1694, Benjamin, 1696, Daniel, 1700.

POORE, HENRY jr. of Rowley, m. Mary Holmes 1703.

POORE, SAMUEL perhaps a brother to John, sen. m. —— ——. Ch.—Rebecca, 7 Feb. 1649, Mary, 21 March, 1651, Samuel, 14 Oct. 1653, Edward, 27 May, 1656, Elizabeth, 21 Jan. 1659, Joseph, 10 June, 1661, Sarah, 4 June, 1664, Benjamin, 22 Feb. 1667, Mary. 21 Feb. 1671. He died 31 Dec. 1683, aged 60.

POORE, JOSEPH son of Samuel, sen. m. Mary Wallington 6 Aug. 1680. Ch.—Joseph, 25 April, 1685, Benjamin, 7 Nov. 1687, Sarah. 12 May, 1690, Mary, 12 Aug. 1692, Abigail, 1 Aug. 1695, Hannah, 3 April, 1698, John, 1 Aug. 1701, Lydia, 14 March, 1704.

POORE. BENJAMIN, son of Samuel, sen. m. widow Mary Hardy 13 April, 1696. Ch.—Sarah, 6 Sept. 1697, Ann, 31 Oct. 1700. She d. 8 Aug. 1707.

POORE, SAMUEL son of Samuel, sen. m. Rachel Bailey 16 Feb. 1680. Ch.—Rebecca, 18 Jan. 1681, Samuel, 3 June, 1682, and d. 11 July, 1769, aged 85, Judith d. 12 Dec. 1683, Sarah. 12 July, 1686, Eleanor, 23 Dec. 1689, Rebecca, 1 March. 1694.

POORE, EDWARD, m. Elizabeth ——. Stephen, 20 April, 1688, Elizabeth, 21 March, 1690, Joseph, 15 April, 1704.

POORE, JOSEPH jun. m. Anna Johnson 1698. Ch.—Katherine, 18 Feb. 1699, Joseph, b. 9 April. 1701.

POORE, SARAH widow of John, d. 3 Dec. 1702.

PLUMER, FRANCIS ' linnen weaver,' came. some say from Woolwich, Eng. others from Wales, about 1633. He was in Newbury 1635. His first wife Ruth d. 18 Aug. 1647. He m. widow Ann Palmer 31 March, 1648 or 9, who d. 18 Oct. 1665. He then m. Beatrice, widow of William Cantlebury, of Salem. 29 Nov. 1665. He d. 17 Jan. 1673. Ch.—Samuel. b. 1619, Joseph, 1630, and Mary, who m. Cheney.

PLUMER, SAMUEL son of Francis. m. Mary ——. Ch.—Samuel. 20 April, 1647, Mary. 8 Feb. 1650, John, 11 May, 1652, Ephraim, 16 Sept. 1655, Hannah, 16 Feb. 1657, Silvanus, 22 Feb. 1658, Ruth, 7 Aug. 1660, Elizabeth, 19 Oct. 1662, Deborah, 13 March, 1665, Joshua, Lydia, 2 July, 1668, Bathshua, 31 July 1670. He died 1702 aged 83.

PLUMER, JOSEPH son of Francis. m. 23 Dec. 1652. Ch.—Joseph, 11 Sept. 1654, Benjamin, 23 Oct. 1656, Sarah, 13 May, 1660, Francis, 23 April, 1662, and d. 5 Dec. 1663, Francis, 25 Feb. 1664, Nathaniel, 31 Jan. 1666, Jonathan, 13 May, 1668, Abigail, 16 July, 1669, and d. 11 Dec. 1683.

PLUMER, EPHRAIM son of Samuel, m. Hannah Jaques 15 Jan. 1680. Ch.—Mary, 19 Feb. 1681, Hannah, 12 Oct. 1682, Samuel, 27 Oct. 1684, Elizabeth, 21 Nov. 1686, John, 7 Nov. 1688, Ruth. 5 Nov. 1690, Daniel. 10 March, 1693, Richard, 3 Aug. 1695, Bitfield, 12 June, 1697, Sarah, 26 July, 1699, Emma, 21 June, 1704.

PLUMER, SILVANUS son of Samuel, sen. m. Sarah Moody 18 Jan. 1682. Ch.— Mary, 22 Oct. 1683, Samuel, 12 Nov. 1684, and d. 2 Aug. 1685, Samuel, Lydia, Sarah, and Benjamin.

PLUMER, JOSEPH jun. son of Joseph, sen. m. Hannah Swett 20 Jan. 1685. Ch.— Samuel. 4 May, 1686, Abigail, 11 Dec. 1687, Miriam, 16 June, 1690, Aaron, 16 Jan. 1693, Eleazer, 29 Jan. 1694, Joseph, 12 Jan. 1695, David, 16 March, 1696, Sampson. 14 March, 1699, Hannah, 17 July, 1700, Sarah, 17 April, 1702, Deborah, 19 Dec. 1703, Eliphalet, 1 April, 1705.

PLUMER, JOSHUA son of Samuel. m. Elizabeth Dole 6 Nov. 1699. Ch.—Samuel, 3 Sept. 1700, Stephen, 6 Dec. 1702, Joshua, 22 Aug. 1705, Nathaniel, 19 June, 1708, Enoch, 3 Dec. 1711. Elizabeth. 22 March, 1716.

PLUMER, SAMUEL son of Samuel, sen. m. Joanna Woodbery 5 Dec. 1670.

PLUMER, JOHN of Rowley, m. Elizabeth Smith 1700.

PLUMER, FRANCIS son of Joseph, m. Mary Ellitrop. Daughter Mary b. 15 May, 1701.

PLUMER, JONATHAN son of Joseph, m. Sarah Pearson 16 June, 1696. Ch.—John, 25 March, 1697, Daniel, 7 Jan. 1699, Mary, 6 Dec. 1701, Jonathan, 14 Aug. 1705.

PRICE, WALTER born 17 May, 1620, lived in Salem.

RANDALL, WILLIAM was born in 1618, m. Elizabeth —— 2 Oct. 1649. Ch.—Elizabeth, 13 May, 1650, William, 2 March, 1653, John, 5 March, 1655, Mary, 26 March, 1656, Hannah, 7 Jan. 1659.

RANDALL, WILLIAM jun. m. Rebecca ——, who d. 18 Feb. 1677. Son Enoch b. Dec. 1676.

RAWSON, MR. EDWARD came from Gillingham. Dorsetshire, was in Newbury about 1636 or 7, and removed to Boston 1650. He m. Rachel Perne. Ch.—Edward, Rachel, David, 6 May, 1644, Perne, 1646, Susan. who d. in Roxbury, 1654. Grindal, 23 Jan. 1649, William, born in Boston, 1651, Rebecca, and John. He d. 1693, ag. 77.

REMINGTON, JOHN was in Newbury, 1637, thence to Andover and Rowley, and finally to Roxbury or Boston. His wife's name was Abigail.

RICHARDS, JOHN m. Hannah Goodridge 22 March, 1694. who died 29 Jan. 1695. He then m. Sarah Cheney 16 July, 1696. Ch.—Sarah, 13 Sept. 1697, Mehetabel, 25 June, 1699. Sarah. 10 Feb. 1702.

RICHARDSON, WILLIAM m. Elizabeth Wiseman 23 Aug. 1654. He d. 14 March, 1658. Ch.—Joseph, 18 May, 1655, Benjamin. 13 March, 1657.

RICHARDSON, EDWARD m. ——. Ch.—Edward, 21 Dec. 1649, Caleb, 18 Aug. 1652, Ruth, 23 Nov. 1655, Moses, 4 April. 1658, Mary, 2 Sept. 1660. He died 14 Nov. 1685. Another Edward Richardson died 25 March, 1655.

RICHARDSON, EDWARD jr. m. Elizabeth Hale 11 Dec. 1696.

RICHARDSON, EDWARD jun. m. Anne Bartlet, 28 Oct. 1673. Ch.—Mary, 25 Oct. 1673, and d. 3 April, 1678. Edward, 2 Sept. 1674. Mary, 25 Aug. 1676, Moses, 22 Jan. 1680, Margaret, 7 July, 1682. He d. 14 Nov. 1682.

RICHARDSON, JOSEPH m. Margaret Godfrey 12 July. 1681. Ch.—Mary, 16 April, 1682, William. 22 March, 1684, Joseph, 31 Dec. 1686, Elizabeth, 28 Feb. 1689. Daniel, 4 April. 1692, Sarah. 19 June, 1694, Thomas. 15 Feb. 1697, Caleb, 9 June. 1704.

RICHARDSON, JOSHUA m. Mary Parker 31 Jan. 1679. who died 7 March, 1685. He then m. Jane ——. Ch.—Esther, 15 March, 1683. Judith. 25 June, 1688, Hannah, 9 Oct. 1690. Abigail, 6 Aug. 1692, Elizabeth, 4 Nov. 1694, Joanna, 6 March, 1697, Joshua, 20 May, 1702.

RICHARDSON, CALEB m. Mary Ladd 31 July, 1682. Ch.—Mary, 12 Jan. 1685, Ruth, 1 March, 1683.

RICHARDSON, MR. JOHN m. ——. Ch.—Sarah, 9 Sept. 1674. Mary, 22 July, 1677, Elizabeth, 29 April, 1680, Katharine. 15 Sept. 1681, and a son John.

ROBINSON, ROBERT b. 1628, m. Mary Silver 26 Oct. 1664. Ch.—Mary. 18 Nov. 1665, Daniel, 9 Oct. 1667, John, 12 Dec. 1669, Samuel, Thomas, Sarah, Hannah, 21 Dec. 1683. Robert, 5 May, 1686.

ROBINSON, JOHN m. Susanna ——. Ch.—John. 6 Sept. 1690, Samuel, 2 Dec. 1692, Daniel, 14 March, 1695. He died March, 1699.

RIDGE, JOHN d. 30 Dec. 1666.

ROBBINS, THOMAS m. Priscilla Mallard 1703. Son Thomas b. 12 March. 1704.

ROGERS, ROBERT m. Susanna ——, was in Newbury in 1651. He died 23 Dec. 1663. Ch.—Robert, 28 April, 1650, Thomas, 9 July, 1652, John, 13 March, 1654, Susanna. 6 Feb. 1657, Joshua, 1 Aug. 1658.

ROGERS, THOMAS son of Robert. m. Ruth Brown 18 May, 1677. Ch.—Thomas, 14 Aug. 1678, Ruth, 16 April, 1680, Susanna, 17 March, 1682. Robert, 5 April, 1684, John, 11 July, 1686, Isaac, 21 June, 1691, Stephen, 20 Aug. 1693, Daniel, 14 Nov. 1695, Jonathan, 18 June, 1702.

ROGERS, THOMAS m. Hannah Long 18 Aug. 1702.

RAWLINS, NICHOLAS m. Rebecca Long 31 Oct. 1679. Ch.—John. 1 Dec. 1680, Daniel, 21 March, 1682. Mary, 10 April, 1683, Joseph. 25 March, 1685, Benjamin, 2 March, 1687, Rebekah, 1 Oct. 1689, Martha, 5 Nov. 1692.

RAWLINS, JOHN m. Mary Thomas. of Exeter, 9 Oct. 1702.

ROLFE, HENRY son of Honour Rolfe, came to Newbury among the first settlers. He d. 1 March, 1643. His only son, John, died before him. His grandson Benjamin was born in 1640.

ROLFE, JOHN brother to Henry, m. Mary Scullard 4 Dec. 1656. Ch —Mary, 16 Jan. 1660, Rebecca, 9 Feb. 1662, Mary, 2 Nov. and d. 10 Dec. 1658. He d. 8 Feb. 1664.

ROLFE, SAMUEL m. Sarah Jepson of Cambridge, 1699. Son Samuel, 16 Aug. 1703.

ROLFE, BENJAMIN m. Apphia —— 3 Nov. 1659, who d. 24 Dec. 1708. He died Aug. 1710. Ch.—John, 12 Oct. 1660, Benjamin, 13 Sept. 1662. Apphia. 8 March, 1667, Mary, 16 Sept. 1669, Samuel, 14 Jan. 1672. Mary, 11 Nov. 1674, and d. 18 June, 1677, Henry, 12 Oct. 1677, Elizabeth, 15 Dec. 1679, Nathaniel, 12 Nov. 1681, Abigail, 5 May, 1684.

ROLFE, JOHN m. Dorothy ——. Son John b. 24 March, 1691, Jonathan, 2 Aug. 1695.

ROLFE, JOHN d. 30 Sept. 1681.

RUSS, JOHN born in 1611, came early to Newbury, thence to Andover in 1645, where he d. 1692. Ch.—John, 24 June, 1641, Mary, 16 Feb. 1644, Jonathan, Thomas, Josiah, and Joseph.

SADLER, ANTHONY had a son Abiel b. 2 Nov. 1650.

SALMON, WILLIAM m. Anne Webster 29 Sept. 1700.

SAMPSON, JONATHAN m. Mary Chandler 16 Nov. 1695. Son John b. 17 Aug. 1696.

SAMPSON, WILLIAM m. Christian Elwell, of Gloucester, 1702.

SAUNDERS, JOHN born in 1625, in Weeks, county of Wiltshire, was in Newbury in 1645. Ch.—Sarah, 20 Aug. 1647, Mary, 12 June, 1649, Abigail, 12 April, 1651, Joseph, 1653. and d. 1654, Elizabeth, 26 Jan. 1655.

SAVORY, ROBERT m. widow Mary Mitchell 8 Dec. 1656. Ch.—Sarah, 12 Nov. 1657, William 15 Sept. 1659, Samuel, 18 March, 1662, Rebecca, 20 Jan. 1664, Robert, 8 Aug. 1666.

SARGENT, WILLIAM one of the twelve men who settled Ipswich in 1633, thence to Newbury, thence to Amesbury in 1643, where he died about 1675, aged 73. Ch.— Thomas, William, Mary. and Elizabeth.

SAYER, now SAWYER, WILLIAM was in Wenham 1643, thence to Newbury. He m. Ruth ——. Ch.—John, 24 Aug. 1645, Samuel, 22 Nov. 1646, Ruth, 16 Sept. 1648, Bitfield, ——, Mary, 7 Feb. 1650, and d. 1659, Sarah, 20 Nov. 1651, Hannah, 23 Feb. 1654, and d. 1660, William, 1 Feb. 1656, Francis, 24 March, 1658, and d. 7 Feb. 1660, Mary, 29 July, 1660, Stephen, 25 April, 1663, Hannah, 11 Jan. 1665, and d. 28 Aug. 1683, Francis, 3 Nov. 1670.

SAWYER, WILLIAM son of William, m. Mary Emery 10 March, 1671. Ch.—Mary, 20 Jan. 1672, Samuel, 5 June, 1674, John, 15 March, 1676, Ruth, 20 Sept. 1677, Hannah, 12 Jan. 1679, Josiah, 20 Jan. 1681.

SAWYER, JOHN son of William, m. Sarah Poore 18 Feb. 1676. Ch.—Ruth, Sept. 1677, William, 29 April, 1679, Sarah, 20 May, 1681, John, 25 April, 1683, Jonathan, 4 March, 1685, Daniel, 13 Jan. 1687, John, 10 Sept. 1688, and died 19 March, 1689, John, d. 30 May, 1689, aged 44.

SAWYER, STEPHEN son of William, m. Ann ——. Ch.—Ann, 1 Aug. 1687, Daniel, 28 Jan. 1689, Enoch, 22 June, 1694.

SAWYER, JOHN m. Mary Merrill 25 Dec. 1700.

SAWYER, WILLIAM m. Lydia Webster 7 Jan. 1703. Daughter Elizabeth b. 1 Oct. 1702.

SARGENT, CAPT. EDWARD m. Elizabeth ——. Ch.—Edward and Ebenezer, b. at Saco, 2 Dec. 1684, Nathaniel, Saco, 16 Jan. 1687, Elizabeth, Portsmouth, 3 Oct. 1689, Elisha, 24 Oct. 1695, Rachel, 10 Oct. 1698, Ichabod, 5 Aug. 1701, Abigail, 26 June, 1704.

SEERS. THOMAS m. Mary Hilton, alias Downer, 11 Dec. 1656. Ch.—Mary, 30 Oct. 1657. Rebecca, 5 Nov. 1661. He d. 26 May, 1661.

SEWALL, HENRY sen. b. in Coventry in 1576, m. Anne Hunt, came to Newbury, and in 1646 removed to Rowley, where he died March, 1657, in his 81st year. He had one son. Henry, jun.

SEWALL, HENRY jr. only son of Henry Sewall of Coventry, Eng. came to Ipswich 1634, Newbury 1635, m. miss Jane, daughter of Stephen Dummer, 25 March, 1646, who d. 13 Jan. 1701, aged 74. He died 16 May, 1700, aged 86. Ch.—Hannah, 10 May, 1649, Samuel, 28 March, 1652, John, 10 Oct. 1654. Stephen, 19 Aug. 1657, Jane, 25 Oct. 1659. Ann, 3 Sept. 1662, Mehetabel, 8 May, 1665. Dorothy, 29 Oct. 1668. The last three were born in Newbury, the others in England.

SEWALL, MR. JOHN son of Henry, m. Hannah Fessenden, of Cambridge, 27 Oct. 1674. He died 9 Aug. 1699, aged 45. Ch.—Hannah, 21 Dec. 1675. and d. 4 July, 1677, Hannah, 26 Dec. 1677, John, 10 April, 1680, Henry, 7 Sept. 1682, Steven, 17 Jan. 1684. Samuel, 9 April, 1688, Nicholas, 1 June, 1690. Thomas, 5 March, 1693.

SCULLARD, SAMUEL an early settler, m. Rebecca, daughter of Richard Kent, and d. 1647. Ch.—Mary, 9 Jan. 1642, Rebekah, 4 Feb. 1644, Sarah, 18 June, 1645, Martha Scullard d. 6 March, 1645.

SHATSWELL, RICHARD of Ipswich, m. Eleanor Cheney 17 Dec. 1696. Son Richard b. 1 Feb. 1698.

SHORT, ANTHONY Ipswich 1634, Newbury 1635. He d. childless 4 April, 1670.

SHORT, HENRY brother to Anthony, m. Elizabeth ——, who d 22 March, 1648. He m. a second wife. Sarah Glover. 9 Oct. 1648. Ch.—Sarah, 18 Dec. 1649. Henry, 11 March, 1652, John, 31 Oct. 1653, and d. 1654. Sarah, 28 Jan. 1660. He died 5 May, 1673.

SHORT, HENRY son of Henry, m. Sarah Whipple ,30 March, 1674, who d. 28 Dec. 1691. He m. Anne Longfellow 11 May, 1692. He d. 23 Oct. 1706, aged 54. Ch.— Henry, 22 Aug. 1675, Sarah, 1 Aug. 1677, John, 14 Dec. 1679, and d. 1684, Hannah. 28 March. 1682, John, 13 Oct. 1685, Matthew, 14 March, 1688, Lydia, 7 May, 1690, and d. 1691, Jane, 4 March, 1693, Samuel, 18 Nov. 1694, and d. 1698, Mehetabel, 12 Jan. 1696, Samuel, 16 Feb. and d. March. 1698, Samuel, 22 Feb. 1699, Hannah, 2 March, and d. April, 1701, Joseph, 8 April, 1702.

SILVER, THOMAS Ipswich 1637, then Newbury. His second wife, Katharine C—, he m. 1S Aug. 1649. who d. 23 July, 1665. He died 6 Sept. 1682. Ch.—Mary, 1645, Elizabeth and Martha, 14 March, 1651, Thomas, 26 March, 1653, and d. 1656, Thomas, 26 March, 1658, John, 24 Aug. 1660, Samuel, 16 Feb. 1662, Hannah and Sarah, 1S Oct. 1655.

SILVER. THOMAS born in 1632, m. Mary Willliams 4 Jan. 1682, and d. 1695. Daughter Sarah b. 2 Oct. 1682.

SIMMONS, SAMUEL was killed with the fall of a horse, 18 June. 1682.

SLOWMAN. SYMON, son of Symon and Hannah, b. 14 July, 1691.

SINGLETERRY, RICHARD was born in 1585, was in Salem 1638, thence to Newbury, Salisbury. and Haverhill. He d. 25 Oct. 1687, in his 102d year. He had a son John. and perhaps others.

SMITH. THOMAS weaver, from Romsey. England, came to Newbury, 1638, from Ipswich. His wife was Rebecca. Ch.—Thomas, 1639, and drowned in 1648, Dec. 6. Rebecca, 20 Feb. 1640, James, 10 Sept. 1645, John, 9 March, 1648, Matthias, 27 Oct. 1652, Thomas, 7 July. 1654, and was killed by the Indians at Bloody Brook, in 1676. Thomas Smith, sen. d. 22 April. 1666. A Thomas Smith d. 14 May, 1653. Another Thomas Smith had a son John, b. 14 Sept. 1668.

SMITH, LIEUT. JAMES son of Thomas, m. Sarah Coker 26 July, 1667. He was drowned at Anticosti Oct. 1690. Ch.—Sarah. 12 Sept. 1668, James, 16 Oct. 1670, Thomas. 9 March, 1673, Hannah, 23 March, 1675, Joseph, 8 June, and d. 19 July, 1677, John, 1 Nov. 1678. Samuel, 31 Jan. 1680, Benjamin, 21 Aug. 1681, Mary, 27 Feb. 1684, and d. 15 Dec. 1685.

SMITH, JAMES son of James, m. Jane ——. Ch.—James, 25 Nov. 1696, Sarah, 21 June, 1699. Mary, 23 May, 1701, Hannah, 1 March. 1704.

SMITH, RICHARD m. Mary Chandler, 17 Oct. 1666.

SMITH, JOHN m. Rebecca Poore 26 Nov. 1667. Ch.—John, 14 Sept. and d. 14 Oct. 1668, Rebecca, 1 Aug. 1669, John, 20 Oct. 1671, and d. 31 Aug. 1677, Mary, 29 Dec. 1673, John, 17 March, 1678, Samuel, 31 Jan. 1680, and d. Nov. 1685, Josiah, 28 March, 1687, Hannah, 27 Jan. 1690, Dorothy, 20 Aug. 1692.

SOMERBY, ANTHONY schoolmaster, son of Richard, who was son of Henry Somerby of Little Bytham, in Lincolnshire, came to Newbury, in 1639, in the ship Jonathan. His wife Abigail d. 3 June, 1673. He d. 31 July, 1686, aged 76. Abiel, his only child. was born 8 Sept. 1641.

SOMERBY, ABIEL son of Anthony, m. Rebecca, daughter of deac. Richard Knight, 13 Nov. 1661. He died 27 Dec. 1671. aged 30 years. Ch.—Henry, 13 Nov. 1662, Abiel, 20 Dec. 1664, Abiel, 24 Aug. 1667, Abigail, 25 Jan. 1670, Anthony and Rebecca, 7 June, 1672.

SOMERBY. HENRY son of Abiel, m. Mary Moody, 26 June, 1683.

SOMERBY, ABIEL son of Abiel, m. Jane Brocklebank, 26 Jan. 1693. Ch.—John, 7 July, 1693, Sarah, 23 Jan. and d. 8 March, 1695, Sarah, 12 Feb. 1696, Jane, 8 Dec. 1698, Abiel, 3 Jan. 1702.

SOMERBY, ANTHONY son of Abiel, m. Elizabeth Heard, of Ipswich, 1696. Ch.—Elizabeth, 28 March, 1699, Anthony, 12 March, and d. 22, 1700, Abiel, b. in Feb. and d. in March, 1703, Elizabeth, 29 June. 1704.

SOMERBY, HENRY brother to Anthony, sen. m. Judith, daughter of capt. Edmund Greenleaf. He d. 2 Oct. 1652. His widow m. Tristram Coffin. Ch.—Sarah, 10 Feb. 1645, Elizabeth, Nov. 1646, John, 24 Dec. 1648, and d. 14 Dec. 1650, Daniel, 18 Nov. 1650, and d. in the army in 1676.

SNELLING. DR. WILLIAM came from Chaddlewood, county of Devon. He m. —— —— in September, 1646. In 1648, July 5, 'he m. Margaret, eldest daughter of Giles Stagge. of Southwark, Barnaby street, at the sign of the Christopher.' Ch.—William, 24 June, 1649, Ann, 2 March, 1652. He removed to Boston about 1654, and there died.

SPENCER, MR. JOHN came from London to Ipswich in 1634, thence to Newbury, in 1635. He died in England about 1650. In his will he mentions nephew John Spencer, brother Thomas Spencer, and cousin Ann Knight. His nephew and heir, John Spencer. sold his farm to his uncle, Daniel Pierce, in 1651.

SQUIRE, PHILIP m. Mary ——. His son Thomas b. 31 Oct. 1694.

STAPLES, THOMAS m. Elizabeth ——. His daughter Mary b. 6 Jan. 1702.

STEVENS, WILLIAM m. Elizabeth —— 19 May, 1645. He died 19 May, 1653. Ch. —Bitfield, b. 16 March, 1649, John, 19 Nov. 1650, Samuel, 18 Nov. 1652.

STEVENS, JOHN came early to Newbury, thence to Andover in 1645, where he died, April, 1662. Ch.—John, 20 June, 1639, Timothy, 23 Sept. 1641, Nathan, Joseph, Ephraim, and Benjamin.

STEVENS, THOMAS m. Martha Bartlet 15 April, 1672. A Thomas Stevens m. Mary Mighill 13 Oct. 1681.

STEVENS, JOHN m. Mary Chase March 9, 1670. Ch.—Mary, 6 Feb. 1671, Thomas, 3 July, 1676.

STEVENS, widow ANN died July, 1650.

STICKNEY, AMOS son of William, a native of Hull, England, came to Boston, thence to Rowley, thence to Newbury, and m. Sarah Morse 24 June, 1663. He d. 29 Aug. 1678. Ch.—John, 23 June. 1666, Andrew, Dec. 1657, Amos, 3 Aug. 1669, Joseph, 14 April, 1671, Benjamin, 4 April, 1673. d. 5 Mar. 1756, Sarah, 19 Oct. 1674, and d. 1675, Hannah, 31 March, 1676. Moses, 26 Nov. 1677.

STICKNEY, JOHN son of Amos, m. Mary Poor 10 Dec. 1689. Ch.—Mary, 1 July, 1691, John, 30 July. 1693, Sarah, Sept. 1698, Joseph, 19 Dec. 1700.

STICKNEY, ANDREW son of Amos, m. Rebecca ——, who died 30 Jan. 1693. Daughter Rebecca b. 16 Jan. 1693.

STEWART or STUART, DUNCAN ship builder, m. —— ——. He removed to Rowley prior to 1680, and was the ship builder in that place. He d. 1717, aged 100. Ch.—Martha, 4 April, 1659. Charles, 5 June, 1661, James, 8 Oct. 1664, Henry, 1 May, 1669, all born in Newbury, and three others born in Rowley.

STUART, JAMES son of Duncan, m. Elizabeth ——. Ch.—James, 29 July, 1688, Charles, 16 Jan. 1690.

STUART, JOHN m. Elizabeth ——, who d. 20 Dec. 1689. Daughter Elizabeth b. 11 Dec. 1689.

SUTTON, WILLIAM m. Mary Gaffell 27 Oct. 1679. He d. 7 May, 1690.

SWETT, STEVEN cordwainer, was born in 1620, m. Hannah Merrill 24 May, 1647, who d. 4 April, 1662. He then m. Rebecca Smith 4 Aug. 1663, who d. 1 March, 1670. Ch.—John. 20 Oct. 1648, and d. 13 Jan. 1652, Steven. 20 Aug. and 24 Sept. 1650, Hannah, 7 Oct. 1651, Steven, 28 Jan. 1654, Elizabeth. 16 Jan. 1656, Joseph, 28 Nov. 1657, Mary, 17 March, 1662, Benjamin, 20 May, 1664, Rebecca, 4 Dec. 1665, and d. 31 May, 1666, Rebecca, 27 Feb. 1670.

SWETT, widow PHEBE d. May, 1665.

SWETT, SARAH d. 11 Dec. 1650.

SWETT, JOSEPH m. —— 1650.

SWETT, JOHN son of Steven, m. Mary Plumer 6 Dec. 1670. Ch.—Mary. 10 April, 1672, Hannah, 15 June, 1674, John, 20 Feb. 1677, Samuel, 10 Sept. 1680, Steven, 27 Jan. 1684, Joseph, 2 Feb. 1687, Benjamin, 11 April, 1688.

SWETT, JOHN jr. m. Susanna Page. His son John b. 31 Dec. 1699.

SWETT, CAPT. BENJAMIN m. Hester, sister of Nathaniel Weare, Nov. 1647, who m. ensign Steven Greenleaf 31 March, 1679, and d. 16 Jan. 1718, aged 89. Ch.— Hester, 7 June, 1648, Sarah, 7 Nov. 1650, Mary, 7 Jan. 1652, Mary, 2 May, 1654, Benjamin, 5 Aug. 1656, Joseph. 21 Jan. 1659, Moses, 16 Sept. 1661. Prior to 1664, he moved to Hampton, and had five other children. ' He was slain at Black Point by the barbarous Indians 29 June, 1677.'

SYLE, MR. RICHARD m. Hannah Scott Aug. 1697.

TEWKSBURY, HENRY m. —— ——. Ch.—Hannah, 1 Sept. 1662, Henry, 15 Dec. 1664, Naomi, 18 Jan. 1667, Ruth, 10 March, 1669.

TOMPSON, MR. EDWARD m. Sarah ——. Ch.—Samuel, 1 Sept. 1691, Edward, 14 May, 1695.

THOMPSON. SYMON m. Rachel Glover 21 Aug. 1656.

TILLOTSON, JOHN m. Dorcas Colman, sister of Thomas Colman, 14 July, 1648, who d. 1 Jan. 1655. He m. Jane Evans 24 May, 1655. Ch.—Mary, 13 Feb. 1650, John, 21 Feb. 1651, James, 19 Dec. 1652, Philadelphia, 28 Sept. 1656, Joseph, 11 Jan. 1658. Jonathan. 6 July, 1659.

TITCOMB, WILLIAM came early to Newbury, m. Joanna Bartlet, daughter of Richard, sen. He also m. Elizabeth Stevens 3 March, 1654. He d. 24 Sept. 1676. Ch.—Sarah, 22 June, 1640. Hannah, 8 Jan. 1642, Mary, 17 Feb. 1644, Milla, 7 June, 1646, William, 18 March, 1648, and d. 2 June, 1659, Peniel, 16 Dec. 1650, Benaiah. 28 June. 1653, Elizabeth, 12 Dec. 1654, Rebecca, 1 April, 1656, Tirzah, 21 Feb. 1658, William, 14 Aug. 1659, Thomas, 11 Oct. 1661, Lydia, 13 June, 1663, John, 17 Sept. 1664, Ann, 7 June. 1666.

TITCOMB, MILLESENT d. 20 Jan. 1664.

TITCOMB, PENUEL son of William, m. Lydia Poore 8 Jan. 1684. Ch.—Sarah, 22 Dec. 1684, Sarah, 14 Dec. 1685, William, 8 April, 1687, John, 24 Sept. 1689.

TITCOMB. BENAIAH son of William. m. Sarah Browne 24 Dec. 1678. Ch.—Be- naiah, 24 Oct. 1679, Joseph, 25 Jan. 1681, Edmund, 9 Dec. 1682. Sarah, 2 March, 1688. Joseph, 2 April, 1691, Enoch, 1 April, 1695, Mary, 17 Feb. 1698.

TITCOMB. WILLIAM son of William, m. Ann Cottle 15 May, 1683. Ch.—Jedidiah, 17 Jan. 1684, Joanna, 15 July, 1686. Daniel, 22 April, 1691, Sarah, 17 Dec. 1693, Elias, 27 Feb. 1696, Joseph and Benjamin, 30 March, 1698, Moses, 19 June, 1700, Joanna, 3 Sept. 1702.

TITCOMB. THOMAS, son of William, m. Mary Dam 30 Nov. 1693. Ch.—Hannah, 5 Sept. 1695. Judith, 30 July, 1698, Mary, 17 Aug. 1700, Anne, 27 Jan. 1703.

TOPPAN, ABRAHAM cooper, came to Newbury in 1637, m. Susanna Goodale of Yarmouth. England, who d. 20 March, 1689. He d. 5 Nov. 1672, aged 64. Ch.—Peter. b. in 1634. Abraham. 1644, Jacob, 1645, Susanna, 13 June, 1649, John, 23 April, 1651. Isaac, Elizabeth. 16 Oct. 1665.

TOPPAN, DR. PETER son of Abraham, m. Jane, daughter of Mr. Christopher Batt, 3 April, 1661. Ch.—Peter, Dec. 1662. Elizabeth. 16 Oct. 1665, Peter, 22 Dec. 1667, Samuel, 5 June 1670, Christopher, 15 Dec. 1671, Jane, 4 Jan. 1674.

TOPPAN, ABRAHAM son of Abraham, m. Ruth Pike. He d. 1704, without issue.

TOPPAN. JACOB son of Abraham, m. Hannah Sewall 24 Aug. 1670, who d. 11 Nov. 1699. He d. 13 Dec. 1717. Ch.—Jacob, 20 May, 1671. Samuel, 30 Sept. 1672, and d. 25 Aug. 1691, Jane, 28 Sept. 1674, John, 29 Jan. 1677, Hannah, 4 March, 1679, Elizabeth, 20 Dec. 1680, Abraham, 29 June, 1684. Ann, 16 May, 1686.

TOPPAN, JOHN sen. son of Abraham, m. Martha ——. He was wounded by the Indians at Bloody Brook in 1676, and d. in Salisbury 26 Dec. 1723, aged 72, leaving a son James, b. 15 March, 1702.

TOPPAN, JACOB jr. son of Jacob, m. Sarah Kent, 1696. Ch.—Sarah, 23 Sept. 1697, Hannah. 23 Nov. 1699, Samuel, 6 Jan. 1702.

TOPPAN. PETER jun. m. Sarah Greenleaf 28 April, 1696. Ch.—Peter and Timothy, 2 Feb. 1698. Jane. 24 Jan. 1700, Elizabeth, 25 April. 1702.

TOPPAN. SAMUEL son of Peter, sen. m. Abigail Wigglesworth in 1702. Son Samuel. 24 Nov. 1702.

TOPPAN, MR. CHRISTOPHER son of Peter, sen. m. Mrs. Sarah Angier, of Cambridge, who d. 20 Feb. 1739, in her 64th year. He died 23 July, 1747, in his 76th year. Ch.—Christopher, 24 Feb. 1700, Edmund. 7 Dec. 1701, Bezaleel, 7 March, 1705.

THOMAS, WILLIAM an early settler, m. Susanna, widow of Robert Rogers, 8 March, 1666, who d. 29 March, 1677. He died without issue 30 Sept. 1699, aged 80.

THORLA, RICHARD came from Rowley to Newbury, 1651. His wife Jane d. 19 March, 1684. He d. 10 Nov. 1685. Ch.—Francis b. 1630, Thomas, 1632.

THORLA, FRANCIS son of Richard, m. Anne Morse 5 Feb. 1655. He died 26 Nov. 1703, aged 73. Ch.—Elizabeth, 3 June, 1656. Mary, 14 May, 1658, and d. 26 Aug. 1659, John, 25 March, 1660, Jonathan, 14 March, 1662, a son and daughter, 20 July, 1664, Richard, 25 Nov. 1665, Thomas and Francis, 20 April, 1669.

THORLA, THOMAS son of Richard, m. Judith March 1670, who d. 11 July, 1689. He d. 23 June, 1713, aged 82. Ch.—George, 12 March, 1671, Simon, 20 Feb. 1673, and d. 4 July, 1690, a daughter, 13 Dec. 1675, Judith, d. 29 July, 1677, Judith, 12 Nov. 1679, Mary, 1 May, 1682, Judith, 14 April, 1685.

THORLA, JONATHAN son of Francis, m. Mary Merrill 22 Dec. 1685, who d. 11 Oct. 1703. He d. 22 Sept. 1703. Ch.—Elizabeth, 20 Nov. 1686, Abraham, 20 Oct. 1688, Francis, 20 April, 1692, Richard, 20 June, 1694, Abigail, 10 Feb. 1696, Mary, 1 July, 1698, Jonathan, 29 August, 1699, Prudence, 4 Sept. 1701, John, 4 March, 1703.

THORLA, GEORGE, son of Thomas, m. Mary ——. He d. 17 Jan. 1714. Ch.—Judith, 6 Sept. 1696, Mary, 11 April, 1699.

THORLA, JOHN son of Francis, m. Sarah How, 2 March, 1685. Ch.—Mary, 10 Feb. 1687, Sarah, 3 Oct. 1689, Anne, 29 Feb. 1692, and d. 11 Sept. 1703, Lydia, 20 Aug. 1695, Bethia, 3 March, 1698, Hannah, 9 Sept. 1701.

THRESHER, ARTHUR m. Mary Goodridge, 21 April, 1684. Daughter Dorothy, 4 Feb. 1692.

THURSTON, DANIEL sen. an early settler, m. Anne Lightfoot 29 Aug. 1648, for his second wife, his first wife having died 25 May, 1648. He d. 16 Feb. 1666, without issue, leaving his estate to his 'kinsman, Daniel Thurston.'

THURSTON, DANIEL jun. m. Anne Pell, 20 Oct. 1655. He died 19 Feb. 1693. Ch.—Daniel, 2 July, and d. 3 Nov. 1659, Hannah, 20 Jan. 1659, Danie', 18 Dec. 1661, Sarah, 8 Jan. 1664, Stephen, 25 Oct. 1665, Joseph, 14 Sept. 1667. Anne, 6 Sept. 1669, James, 24 Sept. 1670, Stephen, 25 Oct. 1672, Stephen, 5 Feb. 1674, Abigail, 17 March, 1678.

THURSTON, JAMES son of Daniel, m. Mary ——. Ch.—Hannah, 15 Nov. 1694, and d. 8 Nov. 1701, Dorcas, 20 Oct. 1696, Abner, 28 Feb. 1699, Phebe, 20 June, 1702.

THURSTON, DANIEL jr. son of Daniel, m. Mary ——. Ch.—Daniel, 26 June, 1690, John, 12 June, 1692, Mary, 7 Jan. 1694, Benjamin, 4 May, 1695, Hannah, 20 Jan. 1698, Martha, 27 Nov. 1700, Jonathan, 16 March, 1701.

THURSTON, JOSEPH son of Daniel, m. Mehetabel Kimball 1695.

TRAVERS, HENRY an early settler, m. Bridget ——. Ch.—Sarah, 1636, James, 28 April, 1645.

TRUEWORTHY or TREWORGY, MR. JOHN m. Mrs. P—— Spencer 15 Jan. 1646. Son John b. 12 Aug. 1649. He removed to Saco.

TROTTER, WILLIAM m. Cutbury Gibbs 9 Dec. 1652. Ch.—Mary, 22 Jan. 1653, Rebecca, 5 July, 1655, Samuel, 5 June, 1657, Abigail, 1 Feb. 1664. Sarah, 3 May, 1665.

TUCKER, MR. JOHN m. Mary Richardson 11 July, 1670. Ch.—Mary, 13 May, 1677. Mary, 25 Jan. 1679, Richard, 9 March, 1681, John, 29 July, 1683.

TURRILL, THOMAS tanner, d. 22 May, 1677. Judith his wife d. 11 July, 1689. He left no issue.

WAKEFIELD, WILLIAM Hampton 1639, came to Newbury in 1646.

WALLINGTON, seaman, m. Sarah Travers 30 Aug. 1654. He was taken captive at sea and never returned home. Ch.—John. 16 Sept. 1655, and d. 6 Jan. 1656, Nicholas, 2 Jan. 1657, John, 7 April, 1659, Sarah, 20 May, 1661, Mary, 29 August, 1663, James, 6 Oct. 1665, Hannah, 27 Nov. 1667, William, 7 Feb. 1670.

WARRANT, JOHN d. 28 Oct. 1666.

WARHAM, WILLIAM sometimes Worm, b. 1654, m. Hannah Adams 10 Feb. 1682. Son Paul, b. 2 Oct. 1683.

WARNER, DOROTHY d. 12 Nov. 1689.

WASS, MR. THOMAS schoolmaster, d. 18 May, 1691.

WATSON, WILLIAM m. Sara Perley 6 Dec. 1670.

WEARE, PETER d. 12 Oct. 1653.

WEARE, NATHANIEL m. Elizabeth Swain 3 Dec. 1656. Ch.—Nathaniel, 5 Jan. 1658, Peter. 5 Nov. 1660, and six others born in Hampton, whither he removed about 1663. He d. 13 May, 1718, aged nearly 87.

WEBSTER, JOHN son of John of Ipswich was born 1632, came to Newbury with his mother and brothers, m. Anna Batt 13 June, 1653. Ch.—John, 11 Feb. 1656, Mary, 29 March, 1658, Sarah, 1 July, 1659, Abigail, 16 March, 1662. Lucy, 19 Dec. 1664, Mary, 24 May, 1667, Stephen, 8 May, 1669, Anna, 7 Sept. 1671, Nicholas, 19 Oct. 1673, Jonathan, 21 May, 1676.

WEBSTER, ISRAEL brother to John, was born in 1624, m. Elizabeth Brown 3 Jan. 1666, who d. 10 Oct. 1668. He d. 7 Dec. 1683. Ch.—Elizabeth. 7 Oct. 1668, Anna, July, 1672, Joseph, 15 March, 1676, and d. 2 May, 1689, Mary, 18 May, 1679, Lydia, 20 Dec. 1681. His second wife, Elizabeth Lunt, he married 9 Nov. 1669, who d. 3 Aug. 1688.

WEBSTER, STEVEN probably son of John, m. Sarah Clark, 1 Nov. 1698. Ch.—Joanna and Sarah, 10 Dec. 1701.

WEBSTER, MARY d. 4 May, 1658.

WELLS, THOMAS m. Sara Browne 1696. Ch.—Sarah. 9 March, 1699.

WELLS, THOMAS m. Mary Parker 3 March, 1673. Son John b. 4 Feb. 1676.

WEED, NATHANIEL of Amesbury, m. Sarah Stickney 27 Oct. 1701.

WHITE, CAPT. PAUL came from Pemaquid, now Bristol. Maine, to Newbury, about 1653, m. Mrs. Ann Jones, widow, 14 March, 1665. Mrs. Bridget White, probably his first wife, d. 11 Dec. 1664. He died 20 July, 1679, aged 89.

WHITE, WILLIAM Ipswich, then Newbury, then Haverhill, where he d. 28 Sept. 1690, aged 80. Son James b. about 1649.

WHITTIER, THOMAS born in 1620, went to Haverhill from Newbury about 1650, and d. 28 Nov. 1696. Ch.—Richard. b. 1663, John, 23 Dec. 1669, and others. A John Whittier d. in Newbury 20 Feb. 1699. A Thomas Whittier died at sea 20 Feb. 1679.

WILLET, FRANCIS b. in 1634, m. Martha Silver 20 Dec. 1669. Ch.—Martha, 24 Feb. 1670, Francis 22 Feb. 1671, Sara, 19 Jan. 1673, Joseph, 11 May, 1674, William, 12 Feb. 1681, Thomas, 24 Dec. 1682, Hannah, 5 Aug. 1685, John, 9 July, 1687.

WILLET, FRANCIS son of Francis. m. Elizabeth Lowle 29 Jan. 1696. Ch.—Mary, 20 Sept. 1698, Judith, 10 May, 1702, Ruth, 2 May, 1704.

WILLIAMS. JOHN Ch.—Mary, 20 Sept. 1641, Lydia, 15 March, 1643.

WILLIAMS, JOHN m. Rebecca Colby, 1661. He d. 1674.

WILLIAMS, JOHN d. 30 April, 1698.

WISWALL, THOMAS of Cambridge m. Hannah Cheney 17 Dec. 1696.

WILLIAMS, THOMAS m. Mary, daughter of Benjamin Lowle 15 Jan. 1696.

WINGET, JOSHUA of Hampton m. Mary Lunt 19 Nov. 1702.

WHEELER, DAVID born in Salisbury, England, 1625, came from Hampton to Newbury 1645. He m. Sarah Wise 11 May 1650. Ch.—John, 5 Dec. 1653, Abigail, 2 Feb. 1656, Jonathan, 6 Jan. 1658, Nathan, 27 Dec. 1659, Lydia, 7 May, 1662, Jethro, 26 March, 1664.

WHEELER, GEORGE m. Susanna Stowers 30 April, 1660. Ch.—Ephraim, 21 Oct. 1662, Samuel, 15 June, 1661, and d. 27 Dec. 1663, Samuel, 15 Sept. 1664.

WHEELER, ROGER m. Mary Wilson 7 Dec. 1653, who d. 27 Dec. 1658. Ch.—Mary, 12 Feb. 1655, Joseph, 29 Aug. 1656, and d. 13 Oct. 1659.

WHEELER, NATHAN son of David, m. Rebecca ——. Ch.—Sarah, 4 July, 1692, Rebecca, 11 Sept. 1694, Mercy, 30 Aug. 1696. Abigail, 16 Dec. 1698.

WHEELER, JOHN came from Salisbury, England. Ch.—Adam, Edward, and

41

William, whom he left in England, David, who m. Sarah Wise, and Anne, who m. Aquila Chase. He d. 1670, and his wife, Anne, 15 Aug. 1662.

WHEELER, JOSEPH son of Roger, m. Sarah Badger 24 Sept. 1685. Daughter Mary. 22 Sept. 1686.

WOODBRIDGE, MR. JOHN was born in Stanton, Wiltshire, in 1613, came to N. E. in 1634, to Newbury, 1635. He m. Mercy Dudley, daughter of Gov. Thomas Dudley. He d. 17 March, 1695. Ch.—Sarah, 7 June, 1640, Lucia, 13 March, 1642, Mary, 1652, Thomas, 1649, John, Benjamin, Dorothy, Anne, Timothy, Joseph, Martha, and one more name unknown. These last were born in England.

WOODBRIDGE, MR. JOSEPH son of John, m. Mrs. Martha Rogers 20 May, 1686. He died   Ch.—Joseph, 7 May, 1687, John, 13 Feb. 1690, Nathaniel, 28 Jan. 1696, Margaret, 1698.

WOODBRIDGE, MR. THOMAS son of John, m. Mrs. Mary Jones, only daughter of Mrs. Ann White, 12 June, 1671. He died 30 March, 1681, aged 33. In Judge Sewall's diary is the following: ' Thomas Woodbridge is so burnt in his own fire that he dieth of insupportable torment in about 12 hours time.' Ch.—Paul, 12 Feb. 1673, Mary, 20 Feb. 1675. Thomas, 28 Jan. 1677, John and Benjamin, 24 Feb. 1679.

WOODMAN, ARCHELAUS mercer, came from Malford, England, to Newbury, in the James, June, 1635. His wife Elizabeth died 17 Dec. 1677. He m. Dorothy Chapman 1ᴐ Nov. 1678. He d. 7 Oct. 1702.

WOODMAN, MR. EDWARD came from Malford with his brother Archelaus. Ch. —Sarah, 12 Jan. 1642, Jonathan, 5 Nov. 1643, Ruth, 28 March, 1646, and perhaps others.

WOODMAN, EDWARD jr. was born in 1628, m. Mary Goodridge 20 Dec. 1653. Ch.—Mary. 29 Sept. 1654, Elizabeth, 11 July, 1656. and d. 27 Dec. 1659, Edward, 1658, Rebecca, 17 Sept. 1661, Rebecca, 29 July, 1663, Sarah, 18 July, 1665, Judith, 18 Nov. 1667, Edward, 20 March. 1670, Archelaus, 9 June, 1672, Margaret, 31 Aug. 1676.

WOODMAN, JOSHUA m. Elizabeth Stevens 22 Jan. 1666. Ch.—Mehetabel, 20 Sept. 1677, Jonathan.

WOODMAN, JOHN m. Mary Field 15 July, 1656.

WOODMAN, JONATHAN m. Sarah Mighill of Rowley 1700.

WOODMAN, JOSHUA m. Mehetabel Wicomb 1703.

WOODMAN, ARCHELAUS jr. m. Hannah ——. Ch.—Mary, 26 Feb. 1696, Edward, 12 May, 1698, Archelaus, 15 May, 1700.

WOODMAN, EDWARD m. Mary Sawyer 29 June, 1702.

WOODMAN. JONATHAN ship builder, m. Hannah Hilton, 2 July, 1668. Ch.— Hannah, 8 March, 1669, Sarah, 19 Oct. 1670, Ruth, 11 July, 1672, Jonathan, 16 April, 1674, Ichabod, 26 April, 1676, Mary, 25 April, 1678, William, 29 March, 1681.

WOODMAN, JONATHAN jr. son of Jonathan, sen. m. Abigail Atkinson, 1696. Daughter Hannah, 24 Aug. 1696.

WOOLCOTT or WOLCOTT, carpenter, born in 1632, m. Mary Thorla 20 Nov. 1653. Ch.—Mary, 1654, Sarah, 23 Aug. 1657, John, 25 Oct. 1660, Joseph, 2 Feb. 1664, Elizabeth, 24 Feb. 1667, Martha, 13 Sept. 1670, Lydia, 15 Jan. 1674, Hannah, 18 April, 1679.

WOOLCOT, JOHN m. Mary Emerson 4 Jan. 1685.

WORSTER, TIMOTHY m. Huldah ——. Son Samuel b. 23 Oct. 1691.

WOOLERY, RICHARD m. Hannah Huggins 24 Dec. 1678. Ch.—A daughter 1 Feb. 1680, Hannah, 10 Feb. 1681, Mary, 22 Feb. 1683.

WOOLSWORTH, RICHARD, weaver, Newbury, 1679.

WORTH, LIONEL m. Susanna, daughter of John Whipple. He d. 29 June, 1667. The widow Susanna m. Moses Pilsbury 1668. Ch.—Susanna, Mary, Judith, Sarah, Oct. 1656, John, 18 Sept. 1664, and perhaps others.

WORTH, RICHARD m. Mary Pike 11 Sept. 1667.

WORTH, JOHN son of Lionel, m. Elizabeth Webster 17 March, 1687. Ch.—Elizabeth, 17 Aug. 1688, John, 7 Feb. 1690, Joseph, 7 Aug. 1693, Edmund, 22 Oct. 1695.

WRIGHT, JOHN had ch. Jonathan, 7 Dec. 1650, Ruth, 31 May, 1652.

YOUNG, MATTHEW m. Eleanor Hayes 23 April, 1696.

YOUNG, EDWARD m. Hannah ——. Ch.—Thomas, 17 Jan. 1691, Richard, 7 Sept. 1693.

WYATT, JOHN m. Mary Badger 15 Dec. 1700.

WEBSTER, JOHN jun. son of John, m. Bridget Huggins 9 March, 1681. Ch.— Anne, 9 June, 1682, John, 2 Nov. 1683, Sarah, 28 Dec. 1685, Israel, 9 April, 1688, Hannah, 5 Oct. 1692, Stephen, 11 Jan. 1698.

WELLS, JOHN m. Mary Greenleaf 5 March, 1669. Ch.—Mary, 16 Dec. 1669, and d. 1670, Mary, 16 Feb. 1673, William, 15 Jan. 1675.

E. *Page* 47.

As a specimen of the manner, in which history, so called, is sometimes written, I am induced to make an extract from the first number of the 'Reminiscences' of the right reverend Philander Chase, formerly bishop of Ohio, but now bishop of Illinois, a descendant from Aquila Chase. To this extract, I shall append a few notes (indicated by figures,) designed to correct some of the mistakes, into which the bishop has fallen. As these mistakes are not of any great consequence, it really seems a pity to spoil so good a story, but, as the bishop has on the authority of others, asserted in his 'reminiscences,' circumstances that no person ever remembered, for the very conclusive reason that they never happened, I have thought proper, for the honor of 'ould Newberry,' to state that there is nothing in the town or church records, which 'put together,' affords any materials for the following 'singular story,' as it is very properly styled. On the church records the name of Aquila Chase is not found, and the following grant comprises all that the town records say concerning him. Who the person might be, whom the bishop employed to examine the town records I know not; he must have been of that class, who prefer fiction to fact, and find it easier to invent, than to examine. The following is a copy of the grant.

'Granted to Aquila Chase anno 1646 four acres of land at the new towne for a house-lott, and six acres of upland for a planting lott, where it is to be had and six acres of marsh, where it is to be had also, on condition that he do goe to sea and do service *in the towne* with a boate for four years.' Proprietors' records, page 67.

The following is the extract from the 'Reminiscences,' published in 1841.

'AQUILA CHASE, according to a tradition among his descendants, was a native of Cornwall, in England, and was born in 1618. It is certain from the (1) records of the town of Newbury, at the mouth of Merrimack river, that he was the first captain who in a regular vessel ever sailed into that port. By reason of his nautical skill and enterprising character, he received an invitation from the inhabitants of that infant settlement to bring his family from Hampton, not far off, where they had lived a few years on coming to America, and make his home among them ; and to ensure his compliance, the 'select men,' who acted as (what is called in other places than New England) a *town council*, tendered him the donation of several lots of land and some other immunities. (2) He complied with their wishes and became an inhabitant of that then promising maritime village. (3)

'It appears from the records (4) which the writer caused to be examined in Newburyport in 1826, that captain Aquila Chase had several children and an affectionate wife, who made home to him more than ordinarily agreeable. Connected with these facts and circumstances there are recorded on the town books (5) many events, which, being put together, fully justify in its main features the truth of the following singular story of this venerable ancestor of most of the New England Chases.

'It appears that the captain and his industrious family had improved the lots, which had been presented to him by the 'select men,' into a pretty garden ; (6) and while the enterprising and hardy parent was at sea, buffeting the waves and enduring the hardships of a voyage across the Atlantic, the wife and children felt that they could do no less than try to make him comfortable on his return and during his stay (short enough always) on shore.

'It happened on a year of peculiar vernal (7) forwardness in gardening, after the captain had been absent a great part of the winter, and had delayed his return beyond the expected time, that this most affectionate family mutually conferred together on the great question how they could most acceptably, by their skill in gardening, welcome his return whom of all earthly beings they loved most. The boys proposed to force forward the potatoes; (8) the girls thought that the sweet flowers of May would please him best; but the mother observed that she knew of something which would gratify him more than all. ' Green peas are your father's favorite,' said she; 'and it is my wish that we try to force them forward to the utmost of our power.'

' There was something more than that which met the eye in this expression. Mrs. Chase had often heard her husband complain of the danger to bodily health, in long voyages at sea, from the want of vegetable diet; for acids (9) at that era were not known as means to obviate this evil. She therefore could not but mingle with the motives which prompted her to treat her husband with kindness, in presenting him with the first fruits of her garden on his arrival, something beside the mere pleasure of seeing him regale his appetite, and that was a settled conviction that the same would be for his health. ' He must have been a long time at sea,' said she to her children, when cultivating the favorite bed of peas; 'and who knows but this precaution may not prevent some deadly disease ?'

' Never were children more mindful of a parent's commands than were those of captain Chase in all things relating to the cultivation of the garden peas meant to greet him on his expected arrival. The dark green vines of this delicious vegetable grew apace; the flowers put forth, and the pods formed and swelled; and, just as they were ready to pluck, a vessel was seen crowding all her sails to get into port.

' It was Sunday morning. The news came that she had passed the bar; then that captain Chase himself had been descried as if giving cheerful orders to his men; again it was reported that he had arrived and laid his ship 'long side of Newbury old wharf.' (10)

' This indeed was a reality, and the grateful father was soon on shore, surrounded by his sons,—full of talk, of questions, and of glee. ' But it is the Sabbath,' said the youngest boy; ' we must not talk loud; the deacon will hear us if we do.' ' Suppose he do, my child,' said the father, tenderly embracing him; ' God hears us, too, and knows our hearts and thoughts, and how thankful we all are for being permitted, after so long a voyage, to meet in peace and health.'

' As they were walking to their home, another of his sons said, 'dear father, it will give mother a great deal of pleasure to see you.' ' I hope so, my son.' ' But she will be additionally happy when she sees you eat her *green peas*.' ' What green peas,' said the captain. ' Some that we have all been raising. at mother's particular request, to regale you on your arrival. No one else in Newbury has any half so forward. Yes, they are ready, mother said, to pick this moment; and when we came away she said she wished you had come on a week day, for then you should have them for dinner.' ' Suppose we were yet to have them ?' said the father. ' Did not the disciples of our Lord pluck the ears of corn, and rub them in their hands, and eat them too, on the Sabbath day; and may we not pick and eat the green peas without incurring the divine displeasure ?'

' This was reported to the ears of the mother, and consent was obtained to prepare the peas. And now comes the difficulty. Some one who was going home from 'meeting,' (for it was thought sinful to say, 'going home from *church*' in those days, saw the captain's family in the garden on the Sabbath day, and that they were gathering peas! (11) The next day he was cited to appear before the minister. The captain pled his own cause,—it seems one against many,—and cited the passage alluded to in his justification. At the close he alleged that he had been long at sea, and that the peas were necessary to his bodily health, and would be adjudged so by the physicians. It was unfortunate for him that he attempted to draw a contrast between his accusers and the ancient Scribes and Pharisees. This shut the door of mercy on him, and they pronounced him 'guilty.' (12) They did not punish *him* corporeally, as in those days was common, ' with forty stripes save one,' but they laid a heavy fine upon him, and compelled him to pay. (13.)

' It does not appear that captain Chase retained any ill will toward the people of Newbury on account of this treatment: on the contrary, all his descendants have had and still have a traditionary affection for the place and its inhabitants, where that venerable ancestor was invited to reside, and where he spent so many of his happiest days.'

NOTE (1.) Nothing of the kind is on the records, nor is there the slightest evidence that Aquila Chase was ever master of a vessel. Had that been the case, he would have been called on the records, captain, or master, especially in those days, when a title of any kind was a mark of distinction, and never omitted.

NOTE (2.) This is a mistake. There were no ' other immunities,' than the grants of land above mentioned.

NOTE (3.) ' Promising maritime village.' At this time there was no village in what is now Newburyport. As late as 1700, fifty-four years after Aquila Chase came to Newbury, there were but two dwelling houses and one fish house between Mr. Daniel Pierce's farm, and Chandler's lane on Water street. One of these houses was Mr. Daniel Pierce's, and the other, doctor Humphrey Bradstreet's, which stood near Hale's wharf. Newburyport market was then an alder swamp, and boats came up near where the town pump now stands.

NOTE (4) and (5.) The town 'records,' so far from 'fully justifying in its main features the truth of the' preceding 'singular story,' contain no allusion to any 'event,' in any way connected with it except the grants and condition on which they were given.

NOTE (6.) 'Improved the lots into a pretty garden.' If this were the fact, the 'garden' must have been large as well as 'pretty,' as the lots contained sixteen acres, of which six were 'salt marsh.'

NOTE (7.) 'Peculiar *vernal* forwardness.' The county records state '*September* 1646, Aquila Chase and wife and David Wheeler of Hampton were presented for gathering peas on the Sabbath day.' David Wheeler was brother to Aquila Chase's wife.

NOTE (8.) 'The *boys* proposed to force forward the *potatoes*.' This cannot be true, as there was not a potato raised in New England till 1719, which was seventy-three years after Aquila Chase's family are said to have tried their skill in gardening. There is another difficulty. 'The boys,' at that time were not in being. Aquila Chase's oldest son, Aquila, was born 26 Sept. 1652, and his oldest daughter, Sarah, was probably, at the time of 'gathering pease,' about a year old.

NOTE (9.) This is an error. Acids were as well known 'as means to obviate the evil' of which he speaks, as they are now. See Winthrop, volume first, page forty-fifth, anno 1630, and several other places.

NOTE (10.) '*Long side of Newbury old wharf*.' This cannot be true, as the first wharf in Newbury, now Newburyport, was not erected till 1655, which was nine years after the 'peas were gathered.'

NOTE (11.) 'Cited to appear before the minister.' There are two objections to this statement, supposing all the remaining parts of the story are true. First, Aquila Chase was not a member of the church in Newbury, and consequently, he was not amenable to an ecclesiastical tribunal. Secondly, if he had been a member, 'the minister' was not the person to settle the difficulty with the offending brother, but the brethren. See Matthew, ch. 18, v. 15, 16, 17.

NOTE (12) and (13.) 'They pronounced him 'guilty,'' 'laid a tax on him and compelled him to pay.' These statements are not correct. As the case was a civil one, they, i. e. his accusers, had no power to do either. The county records state, that Aquila Chase was ordered to be 'admonished,' but the usual fines for such an offence were 'remitted.'

It will readily be seen, that the evidence, on which the bishop founded his story, and which he presumed was correct, will not bear a very rigid examination. It is proper to add, that the errors were pointed out to the bishop, who expressed his gratitude for the information, and declared that the mistakes would be corrected in a second edition, should one be printed. Mistakes, in some respects similar to the preceding, are very numerous in historical works, and authors and compilers will find it difficult, if not impossible, in all cases to avoid them. Thus, for instance, there was published many years ago an amusing account of an interview between the reverend Nathaniel Ward, of Ipswich, and the reverend Cotton Mather, of Boston, the writer probably not knowing that Mr. Ward died in England, several years before Mr. Mather was born. In Abbott's history of Andover, page 150, it is stated that John Kittredge was grandson of John Kittredge, 'a physician from Germany.' Now it so happens that this German doctor was born in Billerica, in 1666, who married at the age of nineteen, and died in 1714.

I once received a letter from a descendant of one of the first settlers in Newbury, in which he in minutely tracing his pedigree back to old England, made his New England ancestor five years older than his English father, the latter being born in 1609, and his son in 1604, a very forward youth, certainly. In a printed book, now before me, the writer, in one case, makes the father about 120 years of age, when his first son was born. In the life of president Holley, there is an anachronism of a hundred years, which makes the genealogy of his family utterly worthless, because it cannot be true. Other instances might be pointed out, and perhaps some in this very book, which will remind the reader of the assertion made by the insane patient, mentioned by doctor Rush. He declared that his father was Alexander the great, his mother was queen Elizabeth, and that he was born in Philadelphia. Persons, who are not insane, sometimes make ludicrous mistakes, and should the compiler of this work be found in that class, the reader, as in all other instances of the kind, must be as charitable as the case will admit.

F. *Page* 63.

The following ballad is the one alluded to page 63, and was first published some years ago, in the North Star, a Philadelphia annual. Its republication will, I doubt not, gratify many of my readers, who will have an opportunity of comparing and contrasting the facts of the historian with the beautiful embellishments of the poet.

The goodman sat beside his door
  One sultry afternoon,
With his young wife singing at his side
  A quaint and goodly tune.

A glimmer of heat was in the air,
  The dark green woods were still;
And the skirts of a heavy thunder cloud
  Hung over the western hill.

Black, thick and vast arose that cloud
  Above the wilderness,
As some dark world from upper air
  Were stooping over this.

At times the solemn thunder pealed,
  And all was still again,
Save a low murmur in the air
  Of coming wind and rain.

Just as the first big rain drop fell,
  A weary stranger came,
And stood before the farmer's door,
  With travel soiled, and lame.

Sad seemed he, yet sustaining hope
  Was in his quiet glance,
And peace, like autumn's moonlight clothed
  His tranquil countenance.

A look, like this his Master wore
  In Pilate's council hall:
It told of wrongs, but of a love
  Meekly forgiving all.

'Friend! wilt thou give me shelter here?'
  The stranger meekly said;
And leaning on his oaken staff,
  The goodman's features read.

'My life is hunted — evil men
  Are following in my track;
The traces of the torturer's whip
  Are on my aged back.

And much I fear 't will peril thee
  Within thy doors to take
A hunted seeker of the truth,
  Oppressed for conscience' sake.'

O, kindly spoke the goodman's wife,
  'Come in, old man!' quoth she,
'We will not leave thee to the storm,
  Whoever thou mayst be.'

Then came the aged wanderer in,
  And silent sat him down;
While all within grew dark as night
  Beneath the storm cloud's frown.

But while the sudden lightning's blaze
  Filled every cottage nook,
And with the jarring thunder roll
  The loosened casements shook,

A heavy tramp of horses' feet
  Came sounding up the lane,
And half a score of horse or more
  Came plunging through the rain.

'Now, goodman Macy, ope thy door,
  We would not be house breakers;
A rueful deed thou'st done this day,
  In harboring banished quakers.'

Out looked the cautious goodman then,
  With much of fear and awe,
For there with broad wig drenched with rain,
  The parish priest he saw.

'Open thy door, thou wicked man,
  And let thy pastor in,
And give God thanks, if forty stripes
  Repay thy deadly sin.'

'What seek ye?' quoth the kind goodman,
  'The stranger is my guest;
He is worn with toil and grievous wrong—
  Pray let the old man rest.'

'Now, out upon thee, canting knave!'
  And strong hands shook the door,
'Believe me, Macy,' quoth the priest,
  'Thou'lt rue thy conduct sore.'

Then kindled Macy's eye of fire,
  'No priest, who walks the earth,
Shall pluck away the stranger guest
  Made welcome to my hearth.'

Down from his cottage wall he caught,
  The match-lock, hotly tried
At Preston-pans and Marston-moor
  By fiery Ireton's side;

Where puritan and cavalier,
 With shout and psalm contended;
And Rupert's oath, and Cromwell's prayer
 With battle thunder blended.

Up rose the ancient stranger then;
 'My spirit is not free
To bring the wrath and violence
 Of evil men on thee;

And for thyself, I pray forbear
 Bethink thee of thy Lord,
Who healed again the smitten ear,
 And sheathed his follower's sword.

I go, as to the slaughter led;
 Friends of the poor, farewell!'
Beneath his hand the oaken door,
 Back on its hinges fell.

'Come forth, old gray beard, yea and nay,'
 The reckless scoffers cried,
As to a horseman's saddle bow
 The old man's arms were tied.

And of his bondage hard and long
 In Boston's crowded jail,
Where suffering woman's prayer was heard
 With sickening childhood's wail,

It suits not with our tale to tell,
 Those scenes have passed away —
Let the dim shadows of the past
 Brood over that evil day.

'Ho, sheriff!' quoth the ardent priest —
 'Take goodman Macy too;
The sin of this day's heresy
 His back or purse shall rue.'

And priest and sheriff both together
 Upon his threshold stood,
When Macy, through another door
 Sprang out into the wood.

'Now, good wife, as thou lovest me, haste!'
 She caught his manly arm:
Behind, the parson urged pursuit,
 With outcry and alarm.

Ho! speed the Macys, neck or nought,
 The river's course was near:
The plashing on its pebbled shore
 Was music to their ear.

A gray rock, tasseled o'er with birch,
 Above the waters hung,
And at its base with every wave
 A small light wherry swung.

A leap — they gain the boat — and tnere
 The goodman wields his oar;
'Ill luck betide them all,' he cried —
 'The laggards upon shore.'

Down through the crashing underwood
 The burley sheriff came: —
'Stand, goodman Macy — yield thyself;
 Yield, in the king's own name.'

' Now out upon thy hangman's face !'
    Bold Macy answered then,
' Whip *women* on the village green,
    But meddle not with men.'

The priest came panting to the shore,
    His grave cocked hat was gone;
Behind him, like some owl's nest, hung
    His wig upon a thorn.

'Come back — come back,' the parson cried,
    ' The church's curse beware.'
' Curse an' thou wilt,' said Macy, ' but
    Thy blessing prithee spare.'

'Vile scoffer !' cried the baffled priest, —
    ' Thou'lt yet the gallows see.'
' Who's born to be hanged, will not be drowned,'
    Quoth Macy merrily;

And so, sir sheriff and priest, good bye !
    He bent him to his oar,
And the small boat glided quietly
    From the twain upon the shore.

Now in the west, the heavy clouds
    Scattered and fell asunder,
And feebler came the rush of rain,
    While fainter growled the thunder.

And through the broken clouds the sun
    Looked out serene and warm,
Painting its holy symbol-light
    Upon the passing storm.

Oh, beautiful ! that rainbow span,
    O'er dim Crane neck was bended;
One bright foot touched the eastern hills
    And one with ocean blended.

By green Pentucket's southern slope
    The small boat glided fast,
The watchers at the block house saw
    The strangers as they passed.

That night a stalwart garrison
    Sat shaking in their shoes,
To hear the dip of Indian oars —
    The glide of birch canoes.

They passed the bluffs of Amesbury,
    And saw the sunshine glow
Upon the Powow's winding stream,
    And on the hills of Po.

The fisher-wives of Salisbury
    (The men were all away)
Looked out to see the stranger-oar
    Upon their waters play.

Deer island's rocks and fir trees threw
    Their sunset shadows o'er them,
And Newbury's spire and weathercock,
    Peered o'er the pines before them.

Around the Black rocks on their left
    The marsh lay broad and green,
And on their right with dwarf shrubs crowned,
    Plum island's hills were seen.

42

With skillful hand and wary eye,
  The harbor bar was crossed;
A play thing of the restless wave,
  The boat on ocean tossed.

The glory of the sunset heaven
  On land and water lay, —
On the steep hills of Agawam,
  On cape, and bluff and bay.

They passed the gray rocks of cape Ann
  And Gloucester harbor bar;
The watch-fire of the garrison
  Shone like a setting star.

How brightly broke the morning,
  On Massachusetts bay!
Blue wave and bright green island,
  Rejoicing in the day.

On passed the bark in safety,
  Round isle and headland steep;
No tempest broke above them,
  No fog-cloud veiled the deep.

Far round the bleak and stormy cape,
  The venturous Macy passed,
And on Nantucket's naked isle
  Drew up his boat at last.

And how in log-built cabin,
  They braved the rough sea-weather;
And there, in peace and quietness,
  Went down life's vale together;

How others drew around them,
  And how their fishing sped,
Until to every wind of heaven,
  Nantucket's sails were spread;

How pale Want alternated
  With Plenty's golden smile;
Behold, is it not written
  In the annals of the isle?

And yet that isle remaineth
  A refuge of the free,
As when true-hearted Macy
  Beheld it from the sea.

Free as the winds that winnow
  Her shrubless hills of sand;
Free as the waves that batter
  Along her yielding land.

Than hers, at Duty's summons,
  No loftier spirit stirs:
Nor falls on human suffering,
  A readier tear than hers.

God bless the sea-beat island!
  And grant for evermore, .
That Charity and Freedom dwell,
  As now, upon her shore!

G. *Page* 174.

Joseph Bartlett, the author of the following narrative, was a native of Newbury. He was the fifth son of Richard and Hannah Bartlett, and was born 18 November, 1686, and died 1754, aged 68. For a copy of the pamphlet, which was published in 1807, I am indebted to one of his descendants, doctor Levi S. Bartlett, of Kingston, N. H.

NARRATIVE.

' In the year 1707, in November, I Joseph Bartlett, was pressed, and sent to Haverhill. My quarters were at the house of a captain Waindret. August 29, 1708, there came about 160 French and 50 Indians, and beset the town of Haverhill — set fire to several houses; among which was that of captain Waindret.* The family at this time were all reposing in sleep; but Mrs. Waindret waking, came and awaked and told me that the Indians had come. I was in bed in a chamber, having my gun and ammunition by my bed-side. I arose, put on my small clothes, took my gun, and looking out at a window, saw a company of the enemy lying upon the ground just before the house, with their guns presented at the windows, that, on discovering any person, they might fire at them. I put my gun to the window very still, and shot down upon them, and bowed down under the window; at which they fired, but I received no harm. I went into the other chamber, in which was Mrs. Waindret, who told me, we had better call for quarter, or we should all be burnt alive. I told her we had better not; for I had shot, and believed I had killed half a dozen, and thought we should soon have help. After re-loading my gun, I was again preparing for its discharge, when I met with a Mr. Newmarsh, who was a soldier in that place. He questioned me concerning my destination. I answered, that I was going to shoot. He told me if I did shoot, we should all be killed, as captain Waindret had asked for quarter, and was gone to open the door. I asked him what we should do in this situation. He said we must go and call for quarter; and, setting our guns in the chamber chimney; we went down and asked for quarters. The entry was filled with the enemy, who took and bound us, and plundered the house. They killed no one but captain Waindret. When they had done plundering the house, they marched off; and at no great distance coming into a body, I had a good view of them, so that I could give a pretty correct account of their number, expecting to escape.

' After a short stop, they proceeded. When they had travelled a short distance, the Indians knocked in the head one of their prisoners, whose name I think was Lendall, a man belonging to Salem. They then marched on together, when captain Eains with a small company waylaid and shot upon them, which put them to flight, so that they did not get together again until three days after, as the French afterwards informed me. The small company which had me in keeping, I believe did not fire a gun.

' At first I was taken by the French, and was with them till this fight was over; during which an Indian came to me in great fury, with his hatchet, I suppose to take away my life; but, through the mercies of God, the French put him by; and so I was spared. I heard many bullets hum over my head, as we marched away. After the fight was over, the French gave me to the Indians — for the Indians killed their prisoners. How many were killed in the fight I do not know. I saw one Indian that had his thigh broken, whom two of them carried away to a pond of water, where I thought they put him in, but after a great while the French told me that another Indian staid with and took care of him, and about three months after he brought him to Montreal; but he was ever after lame. We travelled hard all that day till nearly sun-set, when they camped for the night. They tied me down, and laid each side of me upon the strings; and so they did almost every subsequent night. The next morning they arose very early, and led me — my arms being tied behind me, and another squaw-line about my neck. I was led by an Indian, who had a hatchet in his hand, and a pistol in his girdle. In this manner I was led the most part of the way. They travelled hard the three first days. I had not as yet eaten hardly any thing, for they had little besides horse-meat; and, carrying a heavy pack, I was very much fatigued. Ascending a steep hill a little before we came to Winnipesocket pond. I was almost ready to give out; but, through the goodness and help of God, I was enabled to proceed this third day; but at night I was extremely faint. The Indians made a little water pottage without salt or sweetning, and gave me some to drink. I drank a little draught; and with the

* Captain Simon Wainwright.

blessing of God, it very much revived me, and proved the best cordial I ever took in my life. I slept very well that night, and the next morning was very cold, and so hungry that I could eat almost any thing. Marching a short distance, we came to the pond, where the French and Indians all took their canoes. which were a little way from the pond. Here the French and Indians parted; the former going northerly, and the latter westerly. Before we had crossed the pond, we saw a bear swimming, which they killed, and hauled to shore. We then fared sumptuously, and tarried at the pond, about a day and a half. Leaving their canoes a little way off, we travelled for five days, with very little sustenance, except a small quantity of pounded corn, which they had procured. In these five days the Indians scattered, so that there were but fourteen or fifteen with me. From Winnipesocket pond we came to a river which runs into the lake. Here the Indians in a day and a half made canoes, in which we proceeded down the river three days; having nothing to eat but a few sour grapes and thorn plumbs for four days. They then killed a hawk. which they boiled, and parted among fifteen — giving the head for my share, which was the largest meal I had in these four days; but with the blessing of God I was strengthened, and had my health. The Indians, when much reduced by hunger, would gird up their loins with a string, which I found very useful when applied to myself.

' Going down the river to the lake, we met several companies of Indians, who gave us some corn and pompkins; and when we came to the lake we met ten Frenchmen, who came to give us provisions. After this, the Indians killed five sturgeons, which gave us a good supply of food. One of the Indians being taken sick, we camped for two or three days. They then set out for another island in the night; and the wind and waves were very high, so that the water beat into the canoes. Sitting on the bottom of one of these, I was very wet and cold. When they came to the shore, we camped for a short time; and in about three days we proceeded to Chamblee, a French fort upon the river that runs from the lake into the St. Lawrence, or Canada river — where we obtained an additional supply of food. I here saw an Englishman, whose name was Littlefield — taken I think from Wells. We had a little talk with the Indians, and tarried there three or four hours. We made two encampments within a short distance; the last of which continued four days, in consequence of the indisposition of one of the Indians. Some of the Indians carried those who were sick upon their backs. Before we reached Montreal, we came to Capredia, a French fort I think about fifteen miles from Chamblee — where the Indians cut the hair from one side of my head — greased the remainder and my face, and painted the latter.

' We then went over the river to the governor — where they examined and questioned me concerning the affairs of our land — whether the English talked of invading Canada or not. Afterwards we went to the seminary, that is, the priest-house, where we tarried that night. Next morning we set out for the Indians' fort, which the French called Sadrohelly, and which was about nine miles from Montreal. When they had proceeded about half-way, they made a stop, and marked a tree with the picture of a man's hand and some scalps. They then led me along a little further to a place where was a fire and about fifteen Indians and thirty boys. Here they made a stop, and tied me for a short time; during which I believe they held a counsel whether to burn me or not. But God, who hath the hearts of all in his hands, spared my life. The Indians that took me and the boys marched away, and left me with the others, who led me along a little way, and permitted a squaw to cut off one of my little fingers, and another to strike me severely with a pole. Passing through a large company of Indians, we entered the fort, where they bound up my finger with plantain leaves, and gave me some roasted pompkin to eat. Here there came together a great company that filled the wigwam, which was nearly forty feet in length, where they sung and danced a greater part of the night, as many at a time as could stand from one end of the wigwam to the other. In this manner they danced round their fires. They often invited me to dance; but I refused from time to time. However, they pulled me up, and I went around once with them. Next day they came together again with their scalps, which they presented their squaws. One of them then took me by the hand, and, after a lengthy speech, gave me to an old squaw, who took me into another wigwam. Here, after a little crying and whimpering, she made me put off my Indian stockings and my blanket, and gave me others; and she warmed some water, and washed the red paint and grease from my face and hands. There was another family lived in the same wigwam. An English woman. who belonged to one of the French nuns, came in, and told me I need not fear, for I was given to this squaw in lieu of one of her sons, whom the English had slain; and that I was to be master of the wigwam; — but she being a papist, I placed little reliance on her assertions. The old squaw was very kind to me. I staid here about two weeks; and then went to another fort about eighteen miles distant. While I was there, the Indians brought an English lad, whom they had taken at Quabog, whose name was John Willet. He was very glad to see me; and I tarried with him about a fortnight, when I returned to the fort from whence I came. The poor boy was sensibly affected at my departure, and was very loth to part with me; but I spake as comfortably to him as I could, and told him that he should hope and trust in God for deliverance; for he was able to keep us, and return us again to our homes. I bade him farewell, and told him I hoped we should see each other in happiness in another world.

'After I had been a short time at the other fort, there was brought in by the Indians an Englishman, named Martin Kelcock, who lived in the same wigwam with me. I found him of great benefit to me, as he understood and could well explain their language. He had been taken by them some years previous; but escaped, and was afterwards re-taken. We lived together till February; but we endured much from the severity of the weather, being poorly clad, and destitute of proper food. They would sometimes soak corn, and break it between two stones; then boil it with the flesh of beaver — sometimes with the inwards of cattle obtained from the French; and frequently they would kill a dog, and cut and boil the flesh with squatted corn; of which they would make a feast. They had a meeting-house in the fort, and a French priest: they made me attend their meeting at times; but I could understand nothing that was said.

'Sometime in February after I was taken, I went to live with the French. The man with whom I resided they called Mr. Delude: he was a captain, and a rich man. He being incapable of walking, by reason of a gout sore, it was allotted to a Frenchman and myself to attend upon him. At times of leisure, I wrought at shoe-making. I lived here about fifteen months, during which time I fared well for food. I had a great deal of talk on the subject of religion, and the different modes of worship. My mistress used to ask me why I did not attend meeting. I answered, that I could not understand what they said. She said she could not. I asked her what she went for. She answered, to say her prayers. I asked her why she could not understand them. She said, because they speak in Latin. For what they say the most in Latin, I do not know. The mass commences the services: after which they attend to praying, reading and singing; the priest receiving the sermon with abundance of bowing and kneeling. The altar is built up in the meeting-house, and makes a fine appearance; at one end of which they have a small cupboard, where they keep their sacramental bread and wine. While the mass is saying, their bread is formed into little wafers about the size of our copper pence. They then put one of them into a thing about the bigness of the palm of the hand, which has a handle, and is covered with a glass. When they say mass, the priest takes this out of the altar, and turns around, making a sign of a cross to the people, who all fall upon their knees and say their prayers. The priest tells the people that this bread or water is Christ's body — flesh, blood and bone, after it is consecrated. Hence they worship it as much as if Christ came bodily among them. The priest, when he says mass, has two boys, one on his right hand and the other on his left; one of them rings a bell when the priest is going to take that which they call Christ, to give notice of his approach.

'They were very civil to me, not compelling me to kneel. On my coming to reside with the French, Mr. Meriel, a French priest, came and brought me an English bible. As I sat at shoe-making, he came and sat down beside me, and questioned me concerning my health, and whether I had been to their meetings. I told him I had not. On his asking the cause, I answered (as I had done before) that I could not understand what they said. He said he wished to have me come and witness their carryings on. I told him it was not worth my while. But he was very earnest that I should come to his meeting; and advised me to try all things, holding fast that 'which is good. Who knows (said he) but that God hath sent you here to know the true way of worship. I told him I believed ours was the right way. Says he, we hold to nothing but what we can prove by your own bible. After considerable conversation, I told him I did not know but that I should come to their meeting, and see how they carried on; which after a little while I did. Now in their meeting-house there stood a large stone pot of their holy water; into which every one that came in dipped their finger, making a sign of a cross, putting their fingers first to their foreheads, then to their stomachs, afterwards to their left shoulder, and then to their right shoulder, saying, 'Father, Son, and Holy Ghost — amen;' and kneeling down, they say a short prayer to themselves. They have pulpits in their houses for public worship; in which the priests sometimes preach. After a short time, the priest came again to visit me, and asked me how I liked their manner of worship. I told him it seemed strange to me. He said this was generally the case at first, but after a while it would appear otherwise. I told him he had said that he would hold to no doctrine but what he could prove by the bible: what proof (said I) have you of such a place as Purgatory, or a middle place for departing souls? He said in Luke xvi. 22 — And he died, and was carried by angels into Abraham's bosom. I said I supposed Abraham had gone to heaven. I asked him what was done in Purgatory. He said they tarried there awhile to be purged from their sins, and afterwards go to heaven. I told him, it was appointed unto men once to die, and after death is the judgment, Hebrews ix. 27; and in Eccl. xi. 3 — If the tree falls towards the south or towards the north, in the place where the tree falls there it shall lie; — and that I believed as death leaves us so judgment will find us. He said there were some little sins which were not unto death, if not repented of; and that there were some little sinners; and asked if I thought all should fare alike. I said all willful sins were unto death, if not repented of; and that I believed there were different degrees of torments. I told him I understood that they prayed to angels and saints, and asked him what scripture authority they had for that. He said nature and reason would teach us to do so; for, said he, had you any great business with the king, you would get some great man to speak for you. I said the cases were not similar, for we are invited to come to Christ. Hebrews iv. 16 — Let us therefore come boldly to the throne of grace, that we may obtain mercy and find grace to help in time of need. We are forbidden to pray to saints and angels, or to give divine worship to any creature. In Rev. xxii. 2 and 9, John was forbidden to fall down and worship before the feet of the angels. It is said of Cornelius, Acts x. 2, He prayed to God always; and if he prayed to God always, he did not pray to saints.

'I set out on my return from captivity on Sunday, October fifth, 1712. We went from Chamblee on the ninth of the same month, and came to Albany on the twentieth, where we tarried seven days, and two at Kinderhook, which was one day's march from Albany. We were two days in travelling from Kinderhook to Westfield; from thence to Springfield one day. From Springfield to Quabog one day — from Quabog to Marlborough one day, and from Marlborough to Boston one day. My arrival at Boston was on the fourth of November. Here I tarried four days; and came to Newbury the eighth of November, 1712 — after a captivity of four years, two months and nine days.'

After his return the general court ordered that 'the sum of twenty pounds and fifteen shillings be allowed and paid to Joseph Bartlett in full of his petition of charges and expences to obtain his liberty from the Indians, being taken prisoner by the Indians at Haverhill, when in her majesties' service in the year 1708, and for his support during four years' captivity and for the loss of his arms.'

In this attack on Haverhill, sixteen inhabitants of that place were killed, and some others, not inhabitants. The reverend John Pike in his journal says 'that many soldiers belonging to Salem were slain.' On the general court records I find the following:

'*November 3d*, 1708. Resolved that the sum of five pounds be allowed and paid out of the publick treasury to the petitioner, Mrs. Sarah Coffin, on account of the remarkable forwardness and courage, which her husband, William Coffin of Salem, distinguished himself by, in the action at Haverhill where he was slain.'

The reverend Benjamin Rolfe, pastor of the church in Haverhill, who with his wife and one child was slain on that eventful day, was a native of Newbury. For a more particular account of him see list of graduates.

H. *Page* 241.

In selecting and arranging the materials, used in the preceding compilation, I soon discovered that a more extended account of the transactions in 'ould Newberry,' concerning slavery, than the brief notices I could conveniently give in the annals, would be necessary. I have therefore thought proper to insert in this note an abstract of such facts, as would be deemed appropriate and interesting. Justice to our forefathers requires that the lights and shades of their character on this subject, as well as all others, should be given as accurately as possible, and to omit all allusion to any of their marked peculiarities, would lead to erroneous conclusions, and do both them, and their posterity injustice. A 'suppressio veri' is in fact a 'suggestio falsi,' or, in the language of Cicero, 'nam, qui nescit, primam esse historiæ legem, ne quid *falsi* dicere audeat, ne quid *veri* non audeat, ne qua suspicio *gratiæ* sit in scribendo.'

Slaves, we know, were introduced into Virginia in 1620, and into Massachusetts in a very few years after its settlement, but the number was very small. In the 'Body of Liberties, composed by [the reverend] Nathaniel Ward of Ipswich, author of the Simple Cobbler of Agawam, and adopted by the Colony of Massachusetts in 1641, which was the first Code of Laws established in New England,' I find the following:

'There shall never be any bond slaverie, villinage or captivitie amongst us unles it be lawfull captives taken in just warres, and such strangers as willingly selle themselves, or are sold to us. And these shall have all the liberties and christian usages, which the law of God established in Israell concerning such persons doeth morally require. This exempts none from servitude, who shall be judged thereto by authoritie.' *

'If any man stealeth a man or mankinde he shall surely be put to death.' Ex. 21:16.

In 1646, in consequence of transactions on the coast of Guinea, by one James Smith, a member of the church of Boston, who brought home two negroes, and was the means of killing near one hundred more, the general court passed the following order, namely:

'The general court conceiving themselves bound by the first opportunity to bear witness against the heinous, and crying sin of man stealing, as also to prescribe such timely redress for what is past, and such a law for the future, as may sufficiently deter all others belonging to us to have to do in such vile and odious courses, justly abhorred of all good and just men, do order that the negro interpreter with others unlawfully taken, be by the first opportunity at the charge of the country for the present, sent to his native country (Guinea) and a letter with him of the indignation of the court thereabouts, and justice thereof desiring our honoured governor would please put this order in execution.'

Among the papers on file in the court records, I find the following petition. It is also printed in Savage's Winthrop, vol. 2, page 379-80. Though not relating to Newbury, it is worth inserting here.

'To the honored general court.

'The oath I took this yeare att my enterance upon the place of assistante was to this effect: That I would truly endeavour the advancement of the gospell and the good of the people of this plantation (to the best of my skill) dispencing justice equally and impartially (according to the laws of God and this land) in all cases wherein I act by virtue of my place. I conceive myself called by virtue of my place to act (according to this oath) in the case concerning the negers taken by captain Smith and Mr. Keser; wherein it is apparent that Mr. Keser gave chace to certaine negers; and upon the same day tooke divers of them; and at another time killed others; and burned one of their townes. Omitting several misdemeanours, which accompanied these acts abovementioned, I conceive the acts themselves to bee directly contrary to these following laws (all of which are capitall by the word of God; and two of them by the lawes of this jurisdiction.)

'The act (or acts) of murder (whether by force or fraude) are expressly contrary both to the law of God, and the law of this country.

'The act of stealing negers, or of taking them by force (whether it be considered as theft, or robbery) is (as I conceive) expressly contrary, both to the law of God, and the law of this country.

* See 'Remarks on the Early Laws of Massachusetts Bay: with the Code adopted in 1641 and called the BODY OF LIBERTIES now first printed By T. C. Gray, LL. D. A. A. S. S. H. S.' in vol. VIII. third series of the Historical Society's collections. 1843.

'*The act of chaceing the negers (as aforesayde) upon the sabbath day (being a servile worke and such as cannot be considered under any other heade) is expressly capitall by the law of God.*

These acts and outrages being committed where there was noe civill government, which might call them to accompt, and the persons, by whom they were committed beeing of our jurisdiction, I conceive this court to bee the ministers of God in this case, and therefore my humble request is that the severall offenders may be imprisoned by the order of this court, and brought into their deserved censure in convenient time ; and this I humbly crave that soe the sinn they have committed may be upon their own heads, and not upon ourselves (as otherwise it will.)

Yrs in all christean observance,
RICHARD SALTONSTALL.'

' The house of deputs thinke meete that this petition shall be granted, and desire our honnored magistrats concurrance herein.

EDWARD RAWSON.'

From a letter addressed by governor ' Simon Bradstreet 18 May 1680 to the lords of his majestie's privy councill, containing 'answers to their inquiries,' ' I extract the following :

' There hath been no company of blacks or slaves brought into the country since the beginning of this plantation, for the space of fifty yeares, onely one small vessell about two yeares since after twenty months' voyage to Madagasca brought hither betwixt forty and fifty negro's, most women and children, sold here for ten, fifteen and twenty pounds apiece, which stood the merchants in neer forty pounds apiece one with another : now and then, two or three negro's are brought hither from Barbados and other of his majestiess' plantations, and sold here for about twenty pounds apiece, so that there may bee within our government about one hundred or one hundred and twenty, and it may be as many Scots brought hither and sold for servants in the time of the war with Scotland, and most now married and living here, and about halfe so many Irish brought hither at several times as servants.'

From these extracts it appears that slaves, though not numerous in Massachusetts, were, notwithstanding the law, introduced without difficulty, and bought and sold without scruple, by all classes of people.

At how early a period, and in what numbers, slaves, either African or Indian, were introduced into Newbury, no record informs me, but I have reason to believe that, prior to 1700, the number was small, although a large proportion of the wealthy families had one or more. This is ascertained by reference to their wills, inventories, and so forth. Thus in the inventory of captain Paul White, 1679, I find, ' one negrow = £30.'

In the will of Henry Jaques, dated 1687, I find this sentence : ' my will is that whereas Jasper, my Indian, hath been a good servant to me my will is that he shall serve my executor faithfully after my decease six years and then he shall be free.'

In the inventory of Richard Dummer's estate, I find, ' a negro = £60.' In Richard Dole's will, 1698, he gives to one of his children, ' my great bible, fowling piece, musket, and also my negro boy Tom.' To son William, ' negro boy Mingo,' to daughter Hannah, ' my negro maid, named Lucy.' ' My negro Grace shall have her freedom, if she will accept of it.' ' My negro servant Betty shall serve two years, and then she shall be free.' .

In 1702, Samuel Plumer, ferryman, gives freedom to his Indian servant Kate.

Many of the slaves in Massachusetts were Indians imported from the south. Thus, in 1708, ' Thomas Steel sells to John Farnum of Boston for thirty-five pounds an Indian boy called Harry, imported into the province from South Carolina.' In 1725, Theophilus Cotton, of Hampton, deeds to Jonathan Poore, of Newbury, 'all that my Indian boy Sippai aged about sixteen.' As early as 1649, December twenty-ninth, William Hilton, of Newbury, 'sells to George Carr for one quarter part of a vessel, James-my Indian with all the interest I have in him to be his servant forever.'

The following receipt, in the hand-writing of Stephen Jaques, I give verbatim.

'Reseved of Richard Kelly of Newbry the sum of thorty eayght pound in full mony for a Spanish Ingnn boy nemed sesor, by our judgment under ten eyr old in the eyr of 1714, reseved by me this day of ienry, being the fifteenth of ienry, 1718, I say by me.
CUTTING NOYES.'

In 1716, Rice Edwards, of Newbury, shipwright, sells to Edmund Greenleaf, 'my whole personal estate with all my goods and chattels as also *one negro man*, one cow, three pigs with timber, plank and boards.'

'*November 4th*, 1725. I, the subscriber do one and acknowledge that I have sold to Mr. Richard Kelly a nagrow man, caled Reuben, for which I have received an hundred pounds in bills of credit,' and so forth. '**JONATHAN POORE.**'

In the honorable Nathaniel Coffin's account book, I find the following:

'1731. An account of some things my son Edmund had of me.

'Paid for his learning, and his books and his medicine,   £70
To Jack, a negro man,   50
To 8 sheep, 2 hogsheads of lime, a half bushel of oatmeal, and 29 lb. of flax,   £2 18s.'

In 1738, Ezekiel Chase sells and delivers to John Merrill, for forty pounds, 'my negro boy named Titus about one year and a half old during his natural life.'

In the settlement of colonel Joseph Coffin's estate, I find the following, namely:

'1771, *Nov.* 27. Daughter Sarah, Dr.
     To part of negro girl Lucy,   £45, old tenor.
1771, *Nov.* 27. Daughter Susanna, Dr.
     To part of negro girl Lucy,   £45, old tenor.'

In March, 1739, William Johnson, shipwright, gave, granted, bargained and sold for thirty-five pounds, 'to Moses Titcomb to his heirs and assigns forever a certain negro-man called by the name of Cambridge of the age of about twenty-one years — and that the said Moses Titcomb, his heirs, executors, and administrators shall by virtue of this deed have, hould, use and improve said negro man Cambridge during the whole term of his natural life,' and so forth.

These deeds were sometimes of great length, and written with as much formality and minuteness as the deeds to an estate worth a million of money, and, with few exceptions, all classes of people, merchants, farmers, mechanics, professors of religion, and ministers of the gospel, bought and sold slaves, apparently without the slightest idea of the enormity of the sin, and on the same principle that they would purchase a horse, a sheep, or a piece of land. They thus necessarily sanctioned the slave trade, and all its unspeakable abominations.

The reverend Matthias Plant, in his diary, June twenty-second, 1735, says, ' I wrote to Mr. Salmon of Barbadoes to send me a negro.'

About the year 16   , I find the following :

' A count of dets from ye town to saveral parsons.'

' Serj. Jacob Tapin to driving sheep one day.'
' And to timber for ye high way.'
' Abal Marel a two year bull.'
' *James Ordway for his negro being lost.*'
' Mr. William Moulton a two year old bull.'

This state of things was not always to last. As early as May twenty-sixth, 1701, the 'representatives were desired to promote the encouraging the bringing of white servants and to put a period to negroes being slaves.'

About 1710, judge Sewall wrote and published a tract against slavery, entitled, 'the selling of Joseph.' In 1716, he says in his diary, ' I essayed to prevent negroes and Indians being rated with horses and cattle, but could not succeed.' A few years after this, Elihu Coleman, of Nantucket, wrote and published a tract against slavery. Excepting these two persons, there appears to have been no public advocate for the slave in Massachusetts, till a short time prior to the revolution. Then an examination of their own rights induced hundreds to examine the subject of slavery, who could not avoid seeing and feeling the gross inconsistency of contending for their own liberty, while at the same time they were holding thousands in abject bondage. It became everywhere a subject of discussion. Many essays appeared in the public papers, in favor of emancipation. In 1765, the celebrated Granville Sharpe, of England, espoused the cause of the Africans with great zeal, and, through his instrumentality, it was decided in 1772, that the moment a slave touched the soil of England, that moment he was free.

In 1766, the controversy concerning slavery in Massachusetts began, and in 1767, an attempt was made in the legislature to abolish the slave trade. A bill was brought into the house of representatives 'to prevent the unnatural and unwarrantable custom of enslaving mankind and the importation of slaves into this province,' but the council, then the upper house, non-concurring, it failed. On March second, 1769, the reverend Samuel Webster, of Salisbury, Massachusetts, published ' an earnest address to my country on slavery.' I give an extract.

' Now keep your eye upon the Christian *law* of *love*, or upon the *golden rule* in their most plain and obvious sense (after *all* possible *limitations* and *exceptions, which do not absolutely destroy them*) and reconcile common slavery therewith and I will undertake to reconcile *light* with *darkness*, and *Christ* with *Belial*. Let a *man love his neighbour and do as he would be done by*, and if he makes a slave upon this plan, I will venture to be his slave forever. I fear, I greatly fear that it is want of *honesty* more than want of *light*, which continues it in the world. This is too plain a case for men always to deceive themselves in. I must believe that most, who desire to see, *can here see* what is right, and *do see and feel*, if they have any understanding, and any bowels and mercies. What then is to be done ? Done ! for God's sake break every yoke and let these oppressed ones *go free without delay* — let them taste the sweets of that *liberty*, which we so highly prize, and are so earnestly supplicating God and man to grant us : nay, which we claim as the natural right of every man. Let me beseech my countrymen to put on bowels of compassion for these their *brethren* (for so I must call them,) yea, let me beseech you for your own sake and for God's sake, *to break every yoke* and let the oppressed go free.'

In 1770, James, a servant of Richard Lechmere, of Cambridge, brought an action against his master for detaining him in bondage, which was decided in favor of the plaintiff. In all subsequent suits of the same nature, 'the juries invariably gave their verdict in favor of liberty,' and so great was the change in public opinion, in consequence of the exertions of those who were favorable to emancipation, that in seven years slavery was abolished in six of the then thirteen colonies; namely, Vermont, in 1777, Massachusetts and Pennsylvania, in 1780, New Hampshire, in 1783, Connecticut and Rhode Island, in 1784. The society of friends was the first religious body that took up the subject, and so efficiently did they act, that in 1787 not a single acknowledged member of the society was the owner of a slave.

At the annual commencement at Cambridge, July 21, 1773, a forensic disputation 'on the legality of enslaving the Africans,' was held by two candidates for the bachelor's degree;, namely, Theodore Parsons and Eliphalet Pearson, both of whom were natives of Newbury. This was published the same year, in a pamphlet of forty-eight pages. The question was, 'whether the slavery, to which Africans are in this province, by the permission of law, subjected, be agreeable to the law of nature.'

In October of 1773, an action was brought against Richard Greenleaf, of Newburyport, by Cæsar [Hendrick,] a colored man, whom he claimed as his slave, for holding him in bondage. He laid the damages at fifty pounds. The counsel for the plaintiff, in whose favor the jury brought in their verdict and awarded him eighteen pounds damages and costs, was John Lowell, esquire, afterward judge Lowell. This case excited much interest, as it was the first, if not the only one of the kind, that ever occurred in the county.

In this same year, another attempt was made in Massachusetts to prohibit the slave trade. In January, 1774, a bill for that purpose passed both houses, but the governor, (Hutchinson,) refused his assent. 'His instructions,' he said, 'forbad.' Governor Gage refused for the same reason. On this important subject the people of Massachusetts were not idle. The pulpit and the press were not silent, and sermons and essays in behalf of the enslaved Africans were continually making their appearance. Of this class of writers, no one entered more deeply into the cause of the suffering and the dumb, and displayed more zeal and ability than deacon Benjamin Colman, of Newbury. He wrote, and talked, and prayed on the subject, was instant in season and out of season, and it is owing to the exertions of such men, that public opinion was so soon prepared for a general emancipation, which was virtually done at the adoption of the constitution of Massachusetts, in 1780.

His first essay that I have seen, was published July twentieth, 1774, in the Essex Journal, of Newburyport, and contains two columns, from which I take the following extract.

'I pray that we may refrain at present from any bitter reflection on the British ministry and search among ourselves and see if we cannot find an Achan, an accursed thing, that is the troubler of our land and for which God is at this day contending with us. Among the innumerable evils, that abound among us I look upon the oppression, bondage and slavery exercised upon our poor brethren the Africans to be a God-provoking and a wrath-procuring sin. I call them brethren because God has told us so in his word that he has made of one blood all nations, that dwell on the earth. They are as free by nature as we, or any other people have a natural right to liberty and freedom as much as we and it is only by power and tyranny that they are brought and kept under this cruel yoke of bondage and this iniquity is established by law in this province and although there have been some feeble attempts made to break the yoke and set them at liberty yet the thing is not effected, but they are still kept under the cruel yoke of bondage.

'Shall we, my fathers and brethren, or can we lift up our faces with confidence before God, by solemn prayer, that he would remove the yoke of bondage from us and set us at liberty from the bondage that lays upon us, while we keep a tenfold heavier yoke on the necks of our brethren, the negroes? I confess I blush, when I hear of a proposal for a provincial fast (although I am as desirous of it as others) when I read the fifty-eighth chapter of Isaiah, where the people are represented as keeping days of fasting and prayer and yet obtained no gracious answer from God. I do not say that our grievances will not be redressed until we break the yoke of bondage from our negroes' necks, but I must needs say I do not expect it. But that we, all as one, may be enabled to search out and put away every thing from among us whereby God is dishonored and offended, to break every yoke of oppression, so that he might cause light to rise in obscurity, is I trust the prayer of every friend to New England.   B. C.'

On June fifth, 1774, two discourses on liberty were delivered at the North church in Newburyport, by Nathaniel Niles, M. A., an able and zealous advocate for emancipation. These discourses were printed in a pamphlet of thirty-eight pages, and are written with great ability. In his preface, the author says that ' his general design is to awaken in his countrymen proper sentiments and emotions respecting both civil and religious liberty. The former without the latter is but a body without a soul.' His texts were from 1 Corinthians, chapter 7, verse 21, and John, 8 chapter, verse 36. From the sermon on civil or personal liberty I take the following extract.

' We have boasted of our liberty and free spirit. A free spirit is no more inclined to enslave others than ourselves. If then it should be found upon examination that we have been of a tyrannical spirit in a free country, how base must our character appear! And how many thousands of thousands have been plunged into death and slavery by our means!

' When the servant had nothing to pay, and his master had frankly forgiven him all, and he had gone and cast his fellow servant into prison, there to remain till he should pay the last farthing; the master justly punished his ingratitude and severity with the like imprisonment. Hath not our conduct very nearly resembled the conduct of that servant? God gave us liberty and we have enslaved our fellow men. May we not fear that the law of retaliation is about to be executed on us? What can we object against it? What excuse can we make for our conduct? What reason can we urge why our oppression shall not be returned in kind? Should the Africans see God Almighty subjecting us to all the evils we have brought on them, and should they cry to us, O daughter of America, who art to be destroyed, happy shall he be that rewardeth thee as thou hast served us; happy shall he be that taketh and dasheth thy little ones against the stones; how could we object? How could we resent it? Would we enjoy liberty? Then we must grant it to others. For shame, let us either cease to enslave our fellow men, or else let us cease to complain of those, that would enslave us. Let us either wash our hands from blood, or never hope to escape the avenger.'

In the Essex Journal and New Hampshire Packet of March eighth, 1776, I find the following letter, addressed to —— ——, and was 'inserted by desire of some of the customers' of the paper.

' *Newbury, September* 16*th*, 1775.
' Dear sir,
        ' As the judgments of God are a great deep, and the footsteps, or designs of his providence are not fully known to us, so I think it becomes us to study sobriety, and fear in the application of the same. But when the Lord doth so clearly reveal himself, and shew forth such an evident resemblance between men's sin and their stroke of correction as he doth at this day; I think it cryeth aloud for a serious observing thereof. And I beg leave to say that the calamitous distressed circumstances we are in at this day, in my apprehension, do bear such a resemblance with our notorious crime, that he that runs may read; I mean the oppression of our brethren the negroes; a crime so

unscriptural and unreasonable that I should be ready to think that every rational person, and especially every christian American would detest the thought of keeping their brethren in bondage; especially when they themselves are struggling for liberty, and deliverance from oppression brought upon them by their brethren. But such is the infatuation, with which this idol god, gain, has overcome this people; that although we unitedly say, we will spill our blood, and lose our lives in the defence of liberty; yet we don't grant it to those poor oppressed brethren of ours, who have been under the yoke of slavery (themselves and their ancestors) this one hundred years past; think sir, if you please, how inconsistent your practice is with your profession, how long halt you between two opinions, if oppression and slavery be right, why do you fight against it? but, if it be wrong why do you allow of it?—Happy is he saith the apostle Paul that condemneth not himself in that thing which he alloweth Rom. 14, 22. But here I must make an apology, for I write not to you sir, as an individual that approves of, or practices this detestable crime yourself, for I never heard you did either; but I write to you as a member of our honorable general court, by whom this idolatry should be thrown down, and a reformation take place by the authority of that legislative power. I call it idolatry because covetousness which is at the bottom of it, and by which it is maintained, is idolatry; so says the apostle Paul, Coll. 3. 5. mortify your members, your members which are upon the earth, fornication, and so forth and so forth and covetousness which is idolatry. Here I would say the covetous man does not believe his money to be God; but by his inordinate love of it, and trusting in it, he is as truly guilty of idolatry as if he bow'd his knee to it; for God more regards the internal acts of the mind, than he doth the external acts of the body. In like manner the idolatrous papists do not believe the saints and angels to be gods, but by praying to them, and trusting in them for relief and help, they give them the inward worship of the soul, which is idolatry. As to what any man may say in vindication of slavery, upon that text in Leviticus 25, 45, 46, you may buy of the children of the strangers, and so forth — I refer you to what I have published in the Newbury-Port paper in July 1774, upon that subject for an answer. But to go on sir, some ignorant persons may be ready to object and say these negroes are men's private property, their masters have bought them with their money, and such men traders may think it would be wrong for the general court to deprive them of their property; this is taking men's estates from them, say they;—good God! what do such men mean? to talk of private property in the human species, creatures made in the image of God and endowed, with all the rational faculties and immortal principles as we are, and differing in nothing from us except in color and education, to call such people, men and women private property, shocking indeed to a human mind! What if I had bought you sir, of some person that pretended a right to sell you, and had paid a large sum of money for you, and kept you still in slavery and bondage, and should plead the authority of the general court, and the common and constant custom of the people in behalf of my conduct towards you, would you not be ready to curse that body that maintained such a law, or indulged one man to act so unreasonably towards another?—Matthew 7, 12. Therefore all things whatsoever ye would that men do unto you, do ye even so them. I must need say I wonder, notwithstanding all the prejudices people labour under through long custom, and a gainful practice in this man trade, that their eyes are not opened so as to lay it aside, especially when God in his providence so plainly testifies against it as he does at this day. Will not Joseph's brethren (Gen. 42, 21,) rise up in judgment against us, who when they were brought into distressing circumstances, humbly confessed, 'we are verily guilty concerning our brother, in that we saw the anguish of his soul when he besought us, and we would not hear, therefore is this distress come upon us.' Will not Adonibezek (recorded judges 17,) rise up in judgment and condemn us? who said 'threescore and ten kings having their thumbs and great toes cut off, gathered their meat under my table, as I have done so God hath requited me.' Shall heathens, and such as never had the advantages that we have had, see and generously acknowledge their sins against God and their fellow creatures, (for sin is the cause of natural as well as moral evil) and shall we who have the clear light of the gospel refuse to confess ours? God forbid! let us bethink ourselves, let's attend to the groans of these enslaved people; I doubt not but their complaints have reached Heaven, and whatever others think, I believe God is coming down to deliver them. Woe to us if we withhold them when God challenges them as his. But methinks I hear some say, we believe the British troops are near taking their departure, and then we hope to live in peace and safety, and to possess and enjoy as we did before they came. But stop my friends, your rejoycing;—God's arm is strong, he has many arrows in his quiver; if the controversy between him and us be not taken up, we have reason still to fear, for he has his choice of all his manifold judgments, to punish a stubborn incorrigible people by. Did the Almighty bring ten dreadful plagues upon Egypt before Pharaoh would let his slaves go? witness the consequence. Did he also punish the children of Israel with seventy years captivity in Babylon, to cure them of their idolatry? and did he ever take up his rod of correction, and exercise it upon any people, and lay it down without accomplishing his design? And will he now think you, let us go till he has brought us to his terms? His commands and demands are plain in the 58th chapter of Isaiah, viz. loose the bands of wickedness, undo the heavy burdens, let the oppressed go free, and break every yoak, &c. To which the gracious promise is connected, viz. then shall ye call, and the Lord shall answer, thou shall cry, and he shall say here am I. Has not our great Superintendant permitted a formidable host to come against us, with all their dreadful artillery of war? Has he not at the same time made our army a defence to us, and a terror to our enemies, and withheld the sword from going thro' the land? I'm persuaded sir, you are ready to ascribe our preservations and salvations to the most High. Shall not the merciful interpositions of Providence excite in us gratitude to God, our kind preserver; but, let us at the same time search and see wherefore he thus contendeth with us. And here the divine word is plain for our conviction, viz. Revelations 13, 10, He that leadeth into captivity shall go into captivity, he that killeth with the sword must be killed with the sword.* God is mercifully at present holding back the sword from going through the Land, and waiting to see what we will do; he seems unwilling to execute judgment on us. Pray let us return to him, for if we do not speedily put away the violence that is in our hands and let the oppressed go free, I dread the next stroke. The poor oppressed negroes are waiting with wishful expectations that the Almighty in this day of our calamity will open our eyes and set them at liberty. God grant it may be so for his name's sake and for this land's sake.

' But, sir, you may be readily too hastily to conclude from this writing that my mind is so fastened upon the slave trade, as if it were the only crime that we were chargeable with, or that God was chastening us for. As I have said before, so say I again, our transgressions are multiplied but yet this crime is more particularly pointed at than any other. Was Boston the first port on this continent that began the slave trade, and are they not the first shut up by an oppressive act, and brought almost to desolation, wherefore, sir, tho' we may not be peremptory in applying the judgments of God, yet I cannot pass over such providences without a remark. But to conclude. I entreat and beseech you by all the love you have for this town, by all the regard you have for this distressed, bleeding province, as for the American colonies in general, that you exert yourself, and improve your utmost endeavours at the court to obtain a discharge for the slaves from their bondage. If this was done, I should expect speedy deliverance to arise to us, but if this oppression is still continued and maintained by authority, I can only say, my soul shall weep in secret places for that crime.

' I am, Sir, your friend and humble servant,
BENJAMIN COLMAN.'

In the records of the church at Byfield, there is a long account of a controversy between the reverend Moses Parsons and deacon Benjamin Colman, on the subject of slavery. From this account it appears that on the twenty-first of December, 1780, a church meeting was held to hear the charges made against Mr Colman by Mr. Parsons, and the complaint of Mr. Colman against Mr. Parsons. The articles of charge were three : first, ' that Mr. Parsons was guilty of the wicked practice of man-stealing,' second, 'that deacon Colman had repeatedly called him a thief,' and third, ' that he had offered to sell [Violet] his slave, (as he called her) for a large sum of money.'

In subsequent meetings, held January twenty-ninth, February twelfth, and March twelfth, 1781, the church sustained the pastor, and at the last meeting, suspended deacon Colman ' from the fellowship and communion of the church till he does by repentance and confession give christian satisfaction for the offence he had committed.' July tenth, 1782, another attempt was made, and November third, 1784, a council was called, to settle the difficulty, but without success. As Mr. Parsons deceased the eleventh of December, 1783, nothing further was done, till the church had another meeting June thirtieth, 1784. On

---

* Thus saith the Lord by the Prophet, if ye walk contrary unto me, I also will walk contrary unto you; with the froward he will shew himself froward, and with the upright he will shew himself upright.

the twenty-sixth of October, 1785, the deacon was restored to the church on his acknowledgment 'that in his treatment of the reverend Moses Parsons the late worthy pastor of the church, that he urged his arguments against the slavery of the Africans with excessive vehemence and asperity without showing a due concern for his character and usefulness as an elder, or the peace and edification of the church,' and so forth, and so forth.

The three following communications are a sufficiently full expression of deacon Colman's views on the subject of slavery, and need no comment or explanation.

'The Declaration and Testimony of Benjamin Colman, together with his Complaint against the Reverend Moses Parsons, pastor of the Church in Byfield is as follows.

'Viz. That God has a controversy with the people of this Land I suppose no judicious person will pretend to deny; The bloody, dreadful sword of War has been drawn against us by our brethren, and has prevailed for more than five years; whereby great numbers of our brethren the inhabitants of this Land have been slain, many Towns made desolate, the Dwelling places of our people consumed by fire, the Inhabitants, many of them, Slaughtered, and others driven away and reduced to extream poverty and sore distress. The widows and fatherless are multiplied amongst us and the hand of God lies heavy upon us still. The hand of God is lifted up; the War continues; our enemies are powerful and numerous; and they, flushed with their success, are expecting shortly to make a compleat conquest of America; and if God do n't appear for us and stop their progress, we may rationally expect they will conquer our country. It is time for us to look about us, to search and try our ways, to consider what we have done to provoke our God, to send our unprovoked brethren, and make them his severe rod of correction to chastise us in this manner.

'We have been called upon, by our Continental Congress, to humble our selves before God by fasting and prayer, to implore the mercy, and help of our God, that we may be delivered out of the hands of our cruel Oppressors. We have observed those days set apart for prayer in the manner we have done. But as acts of Justice and Righteousness have not been Joined with our humiliations and petitions, it seems the Lord has not heard our requests for help. Isaiah 38th, 6th. 'This is the fast that I have chosen, to loose the bands of Wickedness, undo the heavy burdens, and let the oppressed go free, and break every yoke.' When we keep such a fast as he has prescribed, then we may call and the Lord will answer. Then shall our light rise in Obscurity; then may we cry and he will say here I am, &c. for the Lord has promised to do so; and his Word stands firmer than heaven and earth.

'I confess the Continental Congress have taken one good step towards reformation; as they have come into a resolution not to import any more slaves. But still the bands of Wickedness are not loosed; many thousands of this poor oppressed people are held down under oppression by Tyranny. And as we have come into a partial reformation, so the Lord has granted a partial deliverance; but as we have stayed our hand as to a thorough reformation, so he has stayed his hand from granting us compleat Deliverance; his Word is fulfilled, as he has said, 'with the froward he will shew himself froward, and with the upright he will shew himself upright.' And can we wonder that God shuts out our prayer, and turns a deaf ear to our cries for help against our foes? Our Land is defiled with blood, we have slain many of our brethren, in taking and captivating them; and our fingers with iniquity in making merchandise of others: we have committed violence upon our brethren; and violence is still in our hands. We have turned a deaf ear to the cries of the oppressed; and this law which supports Oppression reaches through the whole of these *United States.* The Slaves in this State have petitioned for Liberty and Freedom from bondage, since our Troubles began, in the most importunate and humble manner; yet they are not set free in a general way. We have taken them, by cruel hands; rending parents from children, and children from parents; and, by violence, brought them from their own native country, (the Land that their God, and our God, had given them to possess and enjoy,) and subjected them to the most abject slavery and bondage. Magistrates, Ministers, and common people have had a hand in this Iniquitous Trade.

'But in order to open people's eyes to see the horridness of this *Man-trade,* this Oppression and cruelty that has been exercised on our brethren, I beg leave to give a short sketch of the way and manner how our people come by these slaves, when they transport them from their own country.

'And the account I shall give shall be from printed histories concerning the carrying on of this slave-trade and these historical accounts I have had confirmed by persons that have been eye-witnesses to these horrid transactions upon the spot. And it is as follows. When a ship of ours arrives in one of their harbours, some of the people there come on board the ship, and ask what they want? They tell them they want a cargo of slaves. They ask the master what he has to pay for them? he shews them Wine, Brandy, Rum, Clothing, fire arms, and ammunition; as they carry all such articles as they know are most tempting to those people. And when they have agreed upon a price, by the head, or poll; they furnish out a company with arms and ammunition, to go and take a sufficient number of captives to load their ship. So they go out into their country, some twenty, some thirty, sometimes more than sixty miles; say my authors, till they come to little, defenceless towns and villages Inhabited by these poor defenceless people; and there they take as many, and of such an age as they like; others they slaughter without compassion to age or sex. The strong ones they confine with Irons: the younger ones they bind with cords; and drive them before them in droves to the Sea port; where they have a great Pound built to confine them till the Ship is ready to take them. In this situation, say my authors, some are so dismayed, at the thoughts of what they are coming to, that they refuse to eat what they feed them with; and choose to die there rather than live such a life as they expect. When their keepers perceive them refuse to eat, they sometimes take one, and torture him, or her before the rest; sometimes they kill one, and cut him to pieces before their eyes; and tell the others they will do so to them, if they will not eat.

'When the ship is ready they carry them on board with their boats: some try to throw themselves overboard and drown, and so forth. Those they get on board they thrust into the hold of the ship, fasten them in, and feed them with something to support their lives during the passage; there they lie, in their filth and stench, till the ship arrives at her home.

'Some ships bring one hundred, some one hundred and fifty, and some near two hundred of these poor people at once. Upon taking them out, they commonly find ten, fifteen, or twenty dead in the hold, and often a number of children born on their passage, some dead, and some alive. But this is not all; there is what they call *seasoning*, to fit these wretched mortals for severe slavery, to be done to them yet; and their method is to feed them with coarse and mean food, a scant allowance, to try and prove their constitutions; in this experiment many of them die; so that the merchants that import them lay their accounts thus, viz. if six in ten live through their transportation and seasoning, they make a saving voyage. And now they sell these poor people to any one that will give them the most money for them.

'Horrid manstealing! sordid gain! violent oppression and cruelty!

'And has this deadful, this horrid practice been supported, or tolerated by the law of this land through the United States of America for twenty years past? and are there not many thousands of these wretched mortals, in this land, under the cruel yoke of oppression at this day? What shall we say for ourselves as a people? are not our hands defiled with blood? and our fingers with iniquity? and how can we with confidence, lift up our prayer, to that God, who is a God of knowledge, and by whom actions are weighed, for deliverance from oppression, till we have loosed the bands of wickedness, proclaimed liberty to our captives, and let the oppressed go free? do not our crimes stare us in the face? and is not our God rising up out of his holy place, to retaliate our doings upon us? is he not laying righteousness to the line, and judgement to the plummet? Three, if not four, of our states are already fallen into the hands of our cruel enemies; and we have no reason to expect but that the rest will shortly fall a prey to them, if repentance and reformation do n't prevent it. Had we taken these slaves captives in a just war with them, we might have had some excuse for our doings; but now we have none: for as they never molested us, our sin of oppression is aggravated; and God is now requiting blood for blood, oppression for oppression, according to his Word. Revelations 13, 10th, he that leadeth into captivity, shall go into captivity; he that killeth with the sword, must be killed with the sword.

'And now, reverend sir, I entreat your candid attention to what I have to offer to you, at this time, by way of complaint; the substance of which I have offered to you as my grievous complaint for many years in private. And as these grievances increase upon my mind, and our iniquities of this kind stare us in the face, and as the Lord, by his severe corrections, seems to point directly to this our sin of unrighteousness, oppression and violence upon our brethren; I think I may be allow'd to speak my mind without giving just cause of offence, to plead the cause of the oppressed, to bear my testimony against sin, and to take God's part, in visiting this land with judgements, as at this day. And, as I have said before, I look upon this oppression as the CAPITAL SIN of these states, as it has been supported by the law of the land. And although I am sensible our transgressions are multiplied, I think that *this* sin of oppression and violence, is more peculiarly pointed at than any other, in the dispensations of providence. But here I would first observe, that in applying the judgements of God to a person or people, it becomes us to be modest, and cautious; as it may sometimes happen to wicked men according to the work of the righteous. But, on the other hand, it is a sure truth that God is known by the judgements he executes; and in every age he doth point out sin to the world, by some remarkable strokes, some great examples of judgements wherein men may read their sin in their punishment; as in the case of Adoni-bezek Judges 1st, 7th and Ahab 1 Kings 21, and others.

You tell us, sir, and I think very truly, that God has no unmeaning providences; that judgements tread on the heels of sin; pray, sir, what meaning do you affix to God's designs in bringing this judgement of violent oppression upon us by the hand of our brethren, if it be not to convince and humble us for the like violent oppression on our brethren? When there is so plain, so exact a resemblance, between a people's sin and God's judgements, I think it would be an argument of stupidity in us not to apply them to our selves. You tell us that unbelief is the *Damning* sin under the Gospel; I grant the truth of it; but pray, sir, What resemblance, or connection is there, between the sin of unbelief, and the Sword of violent oppression by our brethren, to take away our money, and deprive us of all our temporal enjoyments? No, Sir, the present Dispensation points us to a Sin against the Second table, viz. against our neighbour, our brethren: for thus stands the Controversy, they Demand our properties; we tell them we will not Yield up our rights; We will not be Slaves to them; for Liberty and property are our Just rights; we will die Sooner than we will be Slaves. Well, if liberty and property are so valuable to us, are they not as valuable to our *Neighbours?*

'As to the toleration granted, by Moses, at God's direction to the Jews of old, viz. that they might buy of the heathen Captives, and keep them as their Inheritance, I have answered it before in the publick newspapers, and so need not to mention it here.

' And now, Reverend Sir, I would humbly ask, have *you* had no hand in this Iniquitous, Man-stealing, or Slave-trade? have you not bought divers of these people for money; (people made of the same flesh and blood with yourself and your Children;) And kept them in Bondage? One of Which, if I Mistake not, you have Baptized, and received as a Member of the Church of Byfield; And Afterwards offered to Sell the Same Slave for a large sum of money. Pray, Sir, is this teaching the way of Righteousness? is this doing as you would be done by? is this practising the great command of our Redeemer, according to that Sacred rule of equity Delivered by our Saviour's own mouth, Matthew 7: 12, Therefore all things Whatsoever ye would that men should do to you, do ye even so to them; for this is the law and the prophets? have you never attended to what our Redeemer has told you, in that Same Memorable Sermon on the Mount, Matthew 5: 19, Whosoever shall break one of the least of these Commands; and shall teach men so, shall be called the least in the Kingdom of heaven? and can you say, Sir, that you have not violated that Sacred universal rule? and have you not taught others to do so, by your example? have you considered that text in Corinthians 6: 9th, know ye not that the unrighteous shall not inherit the Kingdom of God? have you been so long a preacher of the Gospel, and not learnt Righteousness? Pray, Sir, look on that text, Jeremiah 22: 13, Wo unto him that buildeth his house by Unrighteousness, and his Chambers by Wrong; that useth his Neighbour's Service without Wages, and giveth him not for his Work. Has not this been your practice, as you have kept Slaves? I beseech you, Sir, to consider who these men-stealers are Ranked with, whom We find in the first Epistle to Timothy first Chapter and ninth verse, for the law was not made for the Righteous, but for the ungodly, and for Sinners, and so forth, for murderers of fathers, and murderers of mothers, for man-slayers, for manstealers, and so forth. Here we find man-stealers Ranked amongst the most enormous crimes that Scripture gives us any account of. But, Sir, this Wicked practice of yours is not all that I Complain of; I intreat you to consider the melancholy Consequences of this your practice; for hereby, you have rendred your self incapable of discharging the duty of a faithful Watchman; for your mouth is shut; you can't reprove others, or bear publick testimony against this horrid crime, without condemning your self, and your own practice; so that others, by your neglect are hardened in their Sin, and emboldened to commit the like. I pray you sir, to consider what the Lord Saith by the Prophet Ezekiel Chapter 33, verses 2d and downward, Son of man, Speak to the Children of thy people, and say unto them, When I bring the Sword upon the land, if the people of the Land take a man of their coasts and set him for their Watchman, and so forth, and so forth, if the watchman see the Sword come, and blow not the trumpet, and the people be not warned, if the Sword come and take any person from among them, he is taken away in his iniquity, *but his blood will I require at the Watchman's hands.* O, Sir! are you not set for a Watchman in this place, and for the people of this Land? and have you ever blown the trumpet to give warning of this horrid Sin of Manstealing; this *Capital Sin* of this people, for which our Land bleeds and

44

mourns at this day ? is not the hand of God lifted up ? and does he not threaten to retaliate and visit our Iniquities of this kind upon this people ? And do *you* keep Silence, and not call upon this people to put away the violence that is in their hands ? And do you, Sir, when you view the dispensations of providence, at this day, acquit your self as a faithful Watchman ?

' But if you Say you do not view this iniquitous practice in the Same light that I, and others do, I pray you to look into the fourteenth Chapter of Ezekiel, where the Lord Saith by that prophet, if any man come to enquire of the Lord having the Stumbling block of his iniquity before his face ; I. the Lord will answer that man by my self. I intreat you to consider whether this Stumbling block of your Iniquity, has not blinded your eyes; and, if so, are you a Qualified Watchman ? I confess, Sir, you cry aloud against Some Sins ; If men ask or take an exorbitant price for their Corn, Meat, Butter, or Wood and so forth, you say ' is this doing as you would be done by ? is this loving your Neighbour as your self ?' But When men buy or Sell their brethren, (for I confess I know not Which is the most criminal, the buyer, or the Seller,) and make merchandise of human flesh, here you are silent ! and why, but for the reason given above, that is you are afraid to condemn your self ?

' And should you plead, Sir, the Law of the land, or the practice of the people, as an excuse in your favour; I answer, that neither the Law of the land, nor the commonness of the people's practice in this affair, alters the nature of the Crime at all : for that which is Wrong in its own nature, can never be made right by any law or practice of men. But, to conclude at this time, tho' more might be said against this wicked practice, I intreat you to consider What the Word of God Says; but if you refuse still to hearken, I can only Say my soul shall weep in Secret places for you, and the people of this bleeding Land. I am, Reverend Sir your humble Servant,

' BENJAMIN COLMAN.

' Byfield in Newbury, November 7th, 1780.'

Deacon Colman's letter to a Church member for selling a slave.

' *Newbury, February 9th,* 1782.

' Dear Sir,

' As the affair I now write to you upon has been talked over between us from year to year are no stranger to my sentiments on this subject; but although I have been unsuccessful with you as to your conviction of your error, I don't despair of success now. The subject is interesting, yea of the last importance to you ; for if you are condemned at the bar of the Supreme Judge of right and wrong, you must know there is no appeal and no repealing his sentence. Therefore in the bowels of love, and in tender compassion to your immortal soul, I beseech you to give me leave, not only as a fellow mortal with you, but as a brother in covenant, and fellow servant, who expects to stand at that tremendous bar, and hear my own sentence and yours from the mouth of Jesus Christ, at whose tribunal we must all appear and answer for all our conduct here.

' The sacred text, which I make the subject of my present argument with you, is recorded in the eighteenth of St. Matthew's gospel from the twenty-third verse to the end of said chapter, which I entreat you to read with attention and application to yourself.

' I have inserted the parable at large, because I am very desirous to draw your attention to the subject as I look upon you as peculiarly concerned in it. I am one of your fellow servants that am very sorry for what you have done : and in love to your immortal soul, in faithfulness to my covenant-obligations to you as a brother, I give you this warning, and now humbly ask you to view this parable and think with yourself whether your picture is not truly drawn in the character of the wicked servant mentioned in that parable. I now as a fellow servant suppose the following things are true.

' 1. You are the person that was arrested by force of the divine law, and found to owe ten thousand talents to the King of Kings.

' 2. You suppose that by falling down at the foot of divine justice, you have obtained a pardon for the same, upon your submission to his government and sentence, so as to obtain forgiveness.

' 3. You are the person that afterwards have gone out and laid hold of your fellow servant Peter, took him by the throat, and by your advertisement cast him into prison for something, though I suppose he owed you nothing; for I verily believe that instead of his owing you one hundred pence you were in his debt for past services.

' 4. You sold him in prison, and all that he had into perpetual slavery and bondage. Now, dear Sir, though I may have missed drawing the lines of your picture in some circumstance attending this affair, I presume you can't deny the substance to be facts viz. That you have sold your brother Peter, who was brought up at the same table with you, for money or something else; and have done this thing against our sovereign the King of Kings and his plain laws in such cases made and provided; as in Matthew 7 : 12, Matthew 18 : 23, and as I think against the whole plan of the gospel dispensation.

'Now, Sir, I entreat you to consider what account you will be able to give of this your conduct at that tremendous bar, when death takes hold of your soul and you are summoned to answer for your breach of this divine law, when the dreadful sentence shall be pronounced ' *O thou wicked servant, I forgave thee all that debt, because thou desiredst me, and shouldest thou also have had compassion on thy fellow servant, even as I had pity on thee?* What will you say for yourself to the King? Will you apologize and say I thought no harm? Will you plead the law of the State, or the law and practice of this land! Will you plead in your favour the old Jewish abrogated law, with which you had not any thing to do, as you are a Gentile by nature and profess to be under the law to Jesus Christ? Will you plead the example of our father Abraham, who you say kept servants? (Tho' you read not that he sold any of them as slaves.) Will you plead that your pastor and teacher did the like as you have done? Will you plead that you were not friendly and faithfully warned of your sin and danger by what you have done? No, Sir, this parable is sufficient to stop your mouth; for this is the rule he has told you, by which he will proceed with you at the tremendous assize. And you can't plead ignorance because the book of the divine laws you have always had in your house. Moreover you can't plead that you had not brotherly warning, for I, your fellow servant, soon after you committed this trespass against the law of Christ, friendly admonished you and entreated you to consider and do justice to Peter, by redeeming him and set him at liberty. Afterwards I warned you when you were on your sick bed, which we all feared would prove your death bed; but still you refused to hearken to the warning; you made light of it and called it a small matter. Since that I dealt with you by two of our brethren, and brought you to hearken to the counsel of God's word and do justice to the said Peter, but you have hitherto refused to hearken. Now Sir this letter stands as a witness and warning of your hazard. I beseech you again to consider and repent before that dreadful day comes, before the judge becomes inexorable, and divine vengeance and wrath are unappeasable. If I may be allowed to speak my solid sentiments in your case, I must say, I would not sleep one night under your guilt for a million worlds, unless I was come to a full determination to go or send, as soon as possible, and redeem that slave and set him at liberty. Will you, Sir, attend upon God's house and worship. and say as some wicked people of old time said we are delivered to do all these abominations?

'Now, Sir, I say, had you done this deed in times of former ignorance it might have been winked at, or more easily excused; but as it was perpetrated in the time when we were all struggling for liberty from slavish oppression, it looks to me inexcusable. But what seems to complete your character as the wicked servant, mentioned in the parable under consideration, is this as I have been credibly informed: Peter in Rhode Island gaol, fell down at your feet, and virtually, in effect, either before your face or by an advocate pleaded with you to have patience with him, and he would come home with you and be your servant or slave. But you turned a deaf ear to his complaint and cries for mercy and you sold him into perpetual bondage and slavery, where I suppose he is groaning under the oppressor's yoke. if living, to this day. And if his complaints do n't pierce your conscience now I believe they will one day be felt with aggravated horror and remorse. I subscribe your faithful monitor, aggrieved brother and fellow servant

B. C.'

'A Remonstrance offered by Benjamin Colman to the Reverend Moses Parsons Pastor, and the Chh in Byfield, from the second Book of the Cronicles 16th, 10th vs. Then Asa was Wroth with the Seer and put him in a prison house, for he was in a rage with him, because of this thing. And Asa oppressed Some of the people the Same time.

'Persecution is one of those dreadfull effects of mans Apostacy that has not only made its discovery in the first man that was born of a Woman; but has discovered its self in the practise of the degenerate race ever since. Cain was the first man that was born, and he was a persecutor even unto deth, and the apostle John 1 epistle 3 : 12, Says not as Cain who was of that Wicked one and slew his brother: and wherefore slew he him, because his own Works were evil, and his brothers righteous. Here is the dreadfull Source of all persecution; Enmity against God, and hatred to holiness; and the enmity between the Seed of the Woman and the Seed of the Serpent, will never be reconciled. Yet the enemies to truth and Righteousness have always the pharisees excuse ready in their mouths, viz. for a good work we stone thee not: for noth'withstanding man has lost all that part of God's image upon his soul, which consisted in Righteousness, and true holiness; yet God has left such an impress, of what is right. upon men's consciences and of what is Wrong, that but few Wicked men dare to Say, boldly, and deliberately, they are not afraid to practice that which is wrong. But although the restraints of God's grace, the happy effects of a good education, and some Selfish worldly motives, may cause even wicked men for a time to shew much respect to the people of God. Yet when Temptation comes, when their Idol God Self is touch'd, when their Worldly honour or interest are like to clash with truth : they will act out the natural enmity of their hearts rather than loose what is dear to them in this World. For there is something that lays nearer the hearts of Carnal men then God or his truth. But let us take a view of the Character of King Asa as it stands upon Sacred record. And I confess there are severall things to be taken notice of in his Character that look favourably, for he was a great reformer in the Worship of God. and did much in throwing down Idolatrous Worship. He put down his Mother from being Queen, because she was an Idolater. Yea, it is said of him that his heart was perfect all his days. Which may mean that he retained an abhorrence to Idol Worship, and kept up good externall government all his days in his Kingdom. He was verry Sucksessfull in his Wars with the Ethiopians and Lubims, who came against him with a huge host of a Thousand Thousand and three hundred chariots, and he obtained a compleet victory over them. Upon which he was congratulated by the prophet Azariah, who said to him in the name of God; the Lord is with you While ye be with him, and if ye seek him he will be found of you; but if ye forsake him he will forsake you. Upon which he was much annimated and stirred up to promote reformation work for a long time.

'But in the thirty-sixth year of his Reign, Baasha King of Israel, made War with Asa King of Judah, and here he turned aside from putting his trust in the Lord, and put his trust in the King of Syria. He robbed the treasures of the house of the Lord, and the Kings house, to hire a heathen King to assist him in the War, in this he did foolishly, as the prophet afterwards told him, and reproved him for not putting his trust in the Lord. For the Lord says by the prophet Jeremiah chapter 17: 5 Cursed be the man that trusteth in man, and maketh flesh his arm, and whose heart departeth from the Lord and so forth.

'Herein he did Wickedly; in robbing the house of the Lord of its treasure, to bribe, and perswade a heathen Idolatrous King to break his Solemn League and Covenant with the King of Israel to assist him. (For Leagues or Covenants were look'd upon to be Sacred, even among heathens.) Whereupon the prophet Hanani comes to him with a message from God, and tells Asa the King, verse 17, because thou hast relied on the King of Syria, and not relied on the Lord thy God, therefore is the Host of the King of Syria escaped out of thine hand. Were not the Ethiopians, and the Lubims a huge Host, with very many chariots and horsemen? Yet because thou didst rely on the Lord, he delivered them into thine hand. For the eyes of the Lord run to and fro throughout the whole earth to shew himself strong in the behalf of them whose heart is perfect towards him. Herein thou hast done foolishly; therefore from henceforth thou shalt have Wars. Now comes in the Words of the text. Then Asa was wroth with the Seer, and put him in a prison house; for he was in a rage with him because of this thing. And Asa oppressed, or as the margin reads it crushed some of the people the same time. And here I would remark, that if King Asa was a good man as I would fain hope he was, he is the only one of that Character on Sacred record that turn'd a persecutor; or at lest I do n't recollect any other instance of the like kind. It may be so that he was the only one. For as one Divine well observes, there is one Instance of a Conversion at the eleventh hour of his life, viz. the thief upon the Cross, that none may despair; So there is but one that none may presume. So this instance before us may be left on record, for the encouragement of any, who have been left to persecute the Godly; to turn to God by repentance while there is hope. But to return to the text; he was Wroth with the Seer, and shut him up in a prison house for he was in a rage with him because of this thing. As much as if he had said to the prophet Hanani : Are you one of the Kings Councill, will you who are my Subject presume to direct your Sovereign prince what he shall do. Will you tell me that I have done foolishly : in hiring Assistance when I needed help and so forth. No if you will preach, you shall preach in a prison house, and not before your King; and so he put him in a prison house. And we do n't read that he ever set him at Liberty till his own deth, which was at lest four years after. O the pride and haughtiness of mans heart when left to himself; and left to forsake God; And as the prophet Azariah told him Chapter 15: 2, if ye forsake him he will forsake you, So the Lord fulfilled his word sent by that prophet. But was not the prophet Hanani rash and insolent to tell the King he had done foolishly? might he not have softned, or polished his Message by Saying : I think you have not done so well as you might have done, I am sorry you did not rely on the Lord and so forth: I answer, no. God's Messengers must be bold, plain and faithfull in delivering his Messages, or els they would incurr their Masters displeasure: they may not in his cause give flattering titles, lest their maker take them away. But here I would remark the very great difference between the temper of this King Asa, and his predecessor David; concerning reproof; David Said, let the Righteous smite me it shall be an excellent oil which shall not break mine head. And when the prophet Nathan came to reprove him for his murder and Adultry, 2 Samuel 12: 13, how, meekly, and readily did he acknowledge his fault, I have Sinned Said he, and God immediately gave him news that he was pardoned. But what can such haughty ones expect who when they are Justly reproved for their faults, do rage at the Messenger, and despise the Message. But King Asa also gave further proof of his having forsaken God; when he was visited with a painfull Disease in his feet; he sought not to the Lord but to the Physitians for help. Vers, 12 Things look dark respecting him in his latter dayes, for the Lord Says expressly by the prophet Ezekiel, Chapter 33: 13, when I shall say to the righteous that he shall surely live; if he trust to his own Righteousness and committ iniquity: all his righteousness shall not be remembred, but for his iniquity that he hath committed, he shall die for it. And so verse 18 of the same Chapter. From the time that King Asa forsook the Ways of the Lord, his Kingdom was upon the decline, he was exercised with wars and tumults, and a very painfull disease; and although he had a pompuous burial, yet his sun seemed to set in a cloud, for we read not that he return'd to God by repentance. But here I would remark how dangerous it is to tell great men of their faults. John baptist lost his head by telling King Herod of his faults. And saint Paul was comanded to be smitten on the mouth for reproving the proud high priest. And what numberless instances have we upon record in Ecclesiastical history, of the faithfull people of God Suffering persecution, for the faithfull discharge of their duty in reproving Sin in their Superiours.

' But I would now address myself to the Reverend pastor of Byfield Chh. Reverend Sir you have been my pastor and teacher for many years. We took Sweet Counsel together and went to the house of God. I rejoyced in your preaching the great Doctrines of grace and Salvation through Jesus Christ. I trust I have been instructed and edified by your Ministry from time to time. But permit me Reverend Sir to Complain to you that you are turn'd a persecutor like the King Asa of whom I have been Speaking. I brought you a Message from the word of God concerning the Wicked practise of Slave keeping, and you were angry with me, and put me in prison, and have confined me for more than two years. If you ask what I mean by being imprisoned? I answer you have by your Chh. Censure Shut me up from the Society and fellowship of God's people in Gospel Ordinances; which I take to be as really persecution as to be confined to a local prison house. If you Say you have not Shut me up from communion with any but Byfield Chh. I answer according to your principles you have from all Churches: for had I applyed to another Chh. and been received to communion with them, you would have been angry with that pastor and Chh. for so doing. If you ask how I know this I answer, because the case has been tried in a like instance, for in time past when a Member of your Chh. who was dissatisfied with you, and applied to a Neighbour Chh. and was received to their Communion, you found fault with that pastor, and Maintained a Quarrel with him, for a number of years. For that and the like things, have I not importunately requested Counsel ever since the dispute began, according to the Congregational platform, upon which you took your Ordination Office, but have hitherto been denied yt. privilege. You may remember Reverend Sir that I did not Wish to Stand in a Wrong, or false cause, and told you if you would Answer my paper of Complaint, and point me to any thing, or things that Stood wrong in S'd paper, according to the Word of God I would immediately retract them, and in the humblest manner acknowledge my fault and ask forgiveness both of God and man. But your Answer to me then was, (if I rightly remember, in the following words,) I can't Answer you, the Chh. may Answer you, but I can't Sit down with you Deacn. Colman. And so you call'd upon the Brethren of the Chh, to vote me out of your communion. And this you Said as it appeared to me, with a good deal of Warmth and temper. Sir I do n't pretend to be vested with the Authority of a prophet, or publick teacher, yet if my message in the paper referr'd to Stands right with the Rule of Gods word; it ought to be regarded by you as if it had been delivered to you by the Mouth of a prophet, for Since the Canon of Scripture is Compleeted, God has given us in the Bible, one perfect unerring rule of faith and practise. So that whatever is plainly deducible from Scripture, is Scripture, and ought to be received as of Divine authority, whoever is the Messenger, for all truth is Christs, who is the truth its self, emphatically, as well as the way and the life. And now Reverend Sir that you and I may be convinc'd of every thing we ought to be convinc'd of, and have the path of truth and duty made plain before us, and that we may receive grace from Christ Jesus, whereby we may Sincerely comply with the Will of God as revealed in his Word, is the prayer of your Abused friend, and humble Servant.

Benjamin Colman.

' But before I conclude this remonstrance, I beg leave to make a short address to the brethren of the Chh. in Byfield;

' Dear brethren you can't but remember that from the time the controversey between Mr. Parsons and I began, I was desirous of Councill in our case; I offered Several times to refer it to a councill of Mr. Parsons own chusing, but was denied by the Pastor. Since I have offered to Joyn in Councill, and consented that he Should Nomina'e and choose two thirds of the Councill; and if I was found to be the faulty cause of the Trouble and charge, I would pay the expenses thereof. but Still I am denied. I now put it to your Consciences whether you do by me as you would be Willing to be done by, were you in my case, for I know no other rule perfectly right but this, which Christ has given us as the universal Rule of equity.——

' I confess the paper I Offered to our pastor is of a rough draft, it is not polished with learning or retorick as it might have been, but I suppose it contains nothing but truth. And if it is an unanswerable Testimony against Slave keeping, it is what I designed it to be.——

' And as it pleased God to open my eyes at that time to see the Abominable Wickedness of that practise, I believe Silence in me would have been a Crime.

' But my brethren, there is one Text upon Sacred record which I beg leave to offer to your Serious consideration. it is recorded in St. Matthews gospel, 5th Chapter 23 and 24 verses. ' Therefore if thou bring thy gift to the Altar, and there rememberest that thy brother hath ought against thee, leave there thy gift before the Altar, and go thy way, first be reconciled to thy Brother, and then come and offer thy gift.' How you Satisfy your Consciences in attending the Ordinance of the Lords Supper I can't See, if you remember that you, and the pastor, have Shut me out of your Communion, for bearing Testimony against the Detestable practise of Slave keeping, and making Merchandise of human people? people made of the Same flesh and blood as we are and differ from us only in colour. This as I understand is the true Stating my case. This is verry Wide from what I am well informed is the practise of the purest Chhs. in the Jersey State, they will not admit Members to their Communion, who hold their Slaves. But I am shut out for bearing Testimony against that Wicked practise You can't but be Sensible the practise of Slave keeping is Reprobated, and Abhorr'd by the most Godly people through this State, but to add no more, that truth may appear and Justice take place in every instance, is the prayer of your Agrieved brother,

Benjamin Colman.

Byfield November 3d 1783.'

Letter I, *instead of* C, *page* 38.

LIST OF GRADUATES FROM NEWBURY.

Benjamin Woodbridge, whose name stands first on the Cambridge catalogue, was of course the first person, who received a degree at Cambridge College, as from the first commencement in 1642 till 1773, degrees were conferred on the students, and their names arranged in the catalogue, not according to age, or scholarship, or the alphabet, but according to the rank their families held in society. Thus the son of a captain preceded him who was only the son of a lieutenant, and in one instance, where this order was reversed, great offence was taken. The apology was that the lieutenant was the more respectable man, and would have been a captain too, had his health permitted.

In the following list, which comprises the names of those graduates who were, or are, natives of Newbury, Newburyport and West Newbury, the alphabetical arrangement will be used, with the exception of the name of Mr. Woodbridge. The names of those who were born in England, but came to Newbury when young, will be indicated by an asterisk. Among them was Benjamin Woodbridge. He was a son of the Rev. John Woodbridge, of Stanton in Wiltshire, a brother to the Rev. John Woodbridge, with whom he came to America in

1634, and a nephew to the Rev. Thomas Parker and the Rev. James Noyes, the first ministers of Newbury. He is called by Dr. Calamy, ' the first fruits of the college in New England, as Arch Bishop Usher was at that in Dublin.' He had been a member of Magdalen College in Oxford, but chose to complete his collegiate education in Massachusetts. He soon after returned to England. He at first preached at Salisbury, on the river Avon, thence after a few years, he was called to succeed the Rev. William Twiss D. D. in Newbury, England, where he shone as a scholar, a preacher, a casuist, and a christian. In August, 1662, he was silenced by the act of uniformity, and as he could not preach publicly, he maintained a private meeting at Newbury, whither he had returned after an absence of a year or two. In 1671 he was permitted to resume his public labors, and died at Inglefield in Berkshire, November first, 1684, in his sixty-third year.

Mr. Woodbridge was also a poet. From his eulogy on the Rev. John Cotton, who died in 1652, I make the following extract.

> A living breathing *Bible;* tables where
> Both *covenants,* at large, engraven were;
> *Gospel* and *law,* in 's heart, had each its column
> His head an index to the sacred volume.
> His very name a *title page;* and next,
> His life a *commentary* on the text.
> O, what a monument of glorious worth
> When in a *new edition,* he comes forth
> Without *erratas,* may we think he 'll be
> In *leaves* and *covers* of eternity.'

Dr. Calamy says of him ' He was a universally accomplished person; one of a clear and strong reason, and of an exact and profound judgment.' Anthony Wood says of him that ' he was accounted among his brethren a learned and mighty man.'

ADAMS, REV. BENJAMIN b. 8 May, 1719, Harv. 1738, ord. in Lynn, 5 Nov. 1755, and died 4 May. 1777, aged 58.

ADAMS, REV. JOSEPH twin brother to Benjamin, Harv. 1742. was a zealous 'new-light' so called, and preached for some time to the society which afterward settled the Rev. Jonathan Parsons in Newbury, now Newburyport. Mr. A. was settled in Stratham. N. H. 24 June. 1756. and died 24 Feb. 1785, aged 66.

ADAMS, ISAAC b. 15 Feb. 1777, Harv. 1798, studied medicine, but his health failed and he died 4 June, 1807.

ADAMS, FREEBORN b. 30 Sept. 1774, Dart. 1801, was a physician in South Carolina, Newbury District.

ADAMS, JOSEPH   Bowd. 1827, and resides in Gardiner. Maine.

ANDREWS, EDWARD W. b. 2 Aug. 1790, Harv. 1810. died in Nov. 1825, in Philadelphia.

ATKINS, MR. DUDLEY b. 1731, Harv. 1748, and died 24 Sept. 1767. aged 36.

ATKINS, MR. DUDLEY Harv. 1816, was a physician in N. Y. and died 7 Apr. 1843.

ATKINSON, REV. JONATHAN   Dart. 1787, ord Oct. 1794, in Limington, Me. and was living in 1821.

ATKINSON, THOMAS b. 27 Dec. 1669. Harv. 1691, and died before 1699.

ATKINSON, MOSES LITTLE Dart. 1838. and is a physician in Newbury, Mass.

ATKINSON, CHARLES M. b. 17 June, 1819. Amh. 1844.

ATKINSON, GEORGE H.   Dart. 1843.

ALLEN, WILLIAM STICKNEY 1803, Dart. 1824, and now resides in St. Louis.

ALLEN. REV. EPHRAIM W. brother to William S. b. 1816, Amh. 1838, ord. North Reading, Mass. May. 1843.

BAILEY. REV. JAMES b. 12 Sept. 1650, Harv. 1669, was a preacher for some time in Salem village, now Danvers, and died in Roxbury 17 Jan. 1707.

BAILEY, ISAAC b. 2 Oct. 1681. Harv. 1701.

BAILEY. REV. ABNER b. 15 Jan. 1716, Harv. 1736, ord. at Salem, N. H. 30 Jan. 1740, and died 10 March, 1798, aged 82.

BAILEY, ENOCH brother to Abner, b. 20 Sept. 1719, Harv. 1742, after preaching some time he entered the army as chaplain, and died at Albany, in Aug. 1757, aged 38.

BAILEY, REV. JOSIAH b. 26 Jan. 1734, Harv. 1752, ord. at Hampton Falls, N. H. 19 Oct. 1757, and died 12 Sept. 1762, aged 29.

BAILEY, EBENEZER b. 25 June, 1794, Yale, 1817, was a distinguished teacher in Boston, and died in Lynn, 5 Aug. 1838.

BAILEY, REV. JOSEPH H. b. 15 Sept. 1808, Amh. 1839, ord. in N. Dighton, Mass. 31 Dec. 1843, and died Nov. 1844.

BAILEY, REV. KIAH   Dart. 1793, ord. in Newcastle, Me. in Oct. 1797, now in Hardwick, Vt.

BARTLET, WILLIAM   Harv. 1801.

BARTLET, JOSIAH   Harv. 1795, a teacher in Newburyport.

BRADSTREET, EDWARD M. D. Harv. 1834, and died 13 Dec. 1844.

BARNARD, REV. THOMAS D. D. b. 5 Feb. 1748, Harv. 1766, ord. in Salem, Mass. 13 Jan. 1773, and died 1 Oct. 1814, aged 67.

BOARDMAN, REV. JOHN b. 8 Nov. 1795, Dart. 1817, settled in West Boylston, 28 Feb. 1821, resigned Feb. 1834, resettled in Douglas, 25 Feb. 1835, and died 8 Nov. 1842, aged 46.

BOYD, WILLIAM b. 20 March, 1776, Harv. 1796, and studied medicine and died in Boston, 13 Jan. 1800, aged 24.

BRADBURY, THEOPHILUS b. 13 Nov. 1739, Harv. 1757, practised law in Newburyport, was a Senator, Representative, and Judge of the Supreme Court. He died 6 Sept. 1803, aged 63.

BRIGGS, JOHN A. M. D.   Harv. 1835, is a physician in Newburyport.

BROWN, REV. RICHARD b. 12 Sept. 1675, Harv. 1697, was town clerk and schoolmaster in Newbury for several years, ord. in Reading, 23 June, 1712, and died 12 Oct. 1732. His widow, with her children, returned to Newbury.

BROWN, REV. SAMUEL b. 4 Sept. 1687, Harv. 1709, ord. in Abington, 17 Nov. 1718, and died 12 Sept. 1749, aged 62.

BROWN, JOHN B. b. 2 March, 1706, Harv. 1725, and died in Newbury, 11 Aug. 1770, aged 65.

BROWN, JOHN S.   Dart. 1836.   He died 13 Jan. 1842.

CALDWELL, SAMUEL L.   Waterville, 1841.

CALDWELL, WILLIAM W.   Bowd. 1843.

CARY, REV. SAMUEL b. 4 Nov. 1785, Harv. 1804, ord. in Boston colleague pastor with Dr. James Freeman, 1 Jan. 1809, and died at Rayston in England, 22 Oct. 1815, aged 30.

CARY, THOMAS b. 5 Aug. 1777, Harv. 1798, and died in Greenland, N. H. 14 June, 1820, aged 43.

CARTER, THOMAS D. b.   Harv. 1817, and died at sea.

CARTER, REV. HAMDEN S. b. 1807, Athens, Geor. about 1826 or 7, is a Presbyterian clergyman.

CHASE, CALEB   1766, Nassau Hall, was a teacher in Concord, N. H. some years, then removed to Thornton.

CHASE, REV. STEPHEN b. 26 Oct. 1705, Harv. 1728, ord. in Lynn, now Lynnfield, 24 Nov. 1731, left Lynnfield, and was resettled in Newcastle, N. H. 5 Dec. 1750, where he died Jan. 1778.

CHASE, REV. JOSIAH b. 20 Nov. 1713, Harv. 1738, ord. at Spruce Creek, Kittery, 19 Sept. 1750, and died 17 Dec. 1778. Having attended a wedding, he missed his way, and perished near his own house.

CHASE, SIMEON b. 1745, Harv. 1767, was a teacher of youth more than half a century in Newbury, where he died 13 Sept. 1829, aged 84 1-2 years.

CHASE, REV. MOSES B.   Bowd. 1831, and is now a chaplain in the navy.

CHASE, REV. PLUMER b. 13 March, 1794, Bowd. 1821, and settled in Carver, Mass. 15 Oct. 1828, and died 1837, ag. 43.

CLARK, REV. JOHN b. 24 June, 1670, Harv. 1690, ord. in Exeter 21 Sept. 1698, and died 25 July, 1705, aged 35.

CLARK, REV. THOMAS M. b. 4 July, 1812, Yale 1831, ord. rector of Episcopal church, Boston, 5 Nov. 1836, now rector of St. Andrews' church, Philadelphia.

CLARK, REV. RUFUS W. b. 17 Dec. 1813, Yale 1838, ord. in Portsmouth, N. H. Nov. 16, 1843.

CLARK, GEO. H. 7 Nov. 1819, Yale 1843, studying divinity.

COFFIN, REV. ENOCH b. 7 Feb. 1695, Harv. 1714, was a preacher, received a call to settle in Dunstable, but his want of health prevented. He died 7 Aug. 1728.

COFFIN, BROCKLEBANK SAMUEL brother to Enoch, b. 24 Aug. 1700, Harv. 1718, and died 14 June, 1727.

COFFIN, DR. NATHANIEL b. 1716, Harv. 1744, and died in Falmouth 12 Jan. 1766, aged 50.

COFFIN, REV. PAUL D. D. b. 16 Jan. 1737, Harv. 1759, ord. in Buxton Me. 16 March, 1763, and died there 6 June, 1821, aged 84.

COFFIN, CHARLES M. D. brother to Paul, b. 17 Aug. 1741, Harv. 1759, was a physician in Newbury and Newburyport, and died 30 April, 1821, nearly 80.

COFFIN, CHARLES M. D. b. 4 Sept. 1765, Harv. 1785, was a physician, a teacher in Portsmouth, N. H. and died in Beaufort, S. C. 8 Sept. 1820. Principal of the academy in that place.

COFFIN, REV. EBENEZER brother to Charles, b. 16 Feb. 1769, Harv. 1789, ord. in Brunswick, Me. 23 June, 1794, dismissed 1802, and died in Newbury 26 Jan. 1816.

COFFIN, JOSHUA b. 12 Oct. 1792, Dart. 1823, resides in Newbury.

COFFIN, REV. CHARLES b. 15 Aug. 1775, Mr. D. D. at Wms. 1807. Pres. of Greenville college in Tennessee.

COFFIN, CHARLES HECTOR 24 April, 1804, Green. coll. 1824.

COFFIN, GEORGE b. 1802, Bowd. 1829, was a student in Andover, and died in Newbury, Sept. 1830.

COKER, THEODORE b. 16 Oct. 1707, Harv. 1726.

COKER, ROBERT A. 19 March, 1807, Harv. 1831, and d. 8 March, 1833.

COLMAN, DUDLEY b. 13 Aug. 1745, Harv. 1765, was town clerk in Newbury, was an adjutant in the army, removed to Boston, thence to Brookfield, N. H. where he died 16 Nov. 1797.

COLMAN, THOMAS brother to Dudley, b. 8 March, 1751, Harv. 1770, and was drowned at Newbury bar 28 Oct. 1784.

COLMAN, H. CHARLES Bowd. 1844.

CONNER, PHINEHAS S. 22 August, 1813, Dart. 1835, is a physician.

CROSS, ROBERT b. 3 July, 1799, Harv. 1819, is a lawyer in Michigan.

COUCH, REV. PAUL, b. 20 June, 1803, Dart. 1823, ord. in West Newbury 21 March, 1827, resigned 14 Aug. 1828, then settled in Bethlehem, Conn. 1830, and again settled 7 Oct. 1836, in North Bridgewater, Mass. where he now resides.

CUSHING, CALEB b. in Salisbury, Harv. 1817, was a tutor in Harv. coll. memb. of congress, and late minister to China, resides in Newburyport.

CUSHING, WILLIAM Harv. 1843.

DUMMER, REV. SHUBAEL b. 17 Feb. 1636, Harv. 1656, preached at York 1662, ord. there 3 Dec. 1672, and was there killed by the Indians as he was mounting his horse at his own door 25 Jan. 1692.

DUMMER, NATHANIEL 14 Feb. 1724, Harv. 1745, and was drowned on his return from a voyage at sea.

DALTON, TRISTRAM b. 28 May, 1738, Harv. 1755, resided in Newburyport, where he died 30 May, 1817, aged 79.

DALTON, JOHN C. M. D. b. Harv. 1814, was a physician in New Boston, N. H. and died Jan. 1830, aged 35.

DANA, REV. WILLIAM C. b. 13 Feb. 1810, Dart. 1828, settled in Charleston, S. C.

DODGE, ALLEN W. b. 9 April, 1804, Harv. 1826, resides in Hamilton, Mass.

DOLE, REV. GEORGE T. Yale, 1838, ord. in Beverly, Mass. 6 Oct. 1842.

DUTTON, ALFRED Bowd. 1842.

EMERY, REV. SAMUEL b. 20 Dec. 1670, Harv. 1691, ord. in Wells, Me. 29 Oct. 1701, and died 28 Dec. 1724.

EMERY, ANTHONY b. 5 Sept. 1713, Harv. 1736, was a physician in Chelmsford, Mass. then Hampton, N. H. where he died 19 Aug. 1781, aged 67.

EMERY, REV. STEPHEN b. Harv. 1730, settled in Nottingham, N. H.

EMERY, THOMAS b. 1750, Harv. 1768, died 21 Nov. 1770.

EMERY, REV. SAMUEL M. 10 April, 1804, Harv. 1830, settled as an episcopal clergyman in Portland, Conn.

EMERY, REV. SAMUEL H. 1815, Amh. 1834, now in Taunton, Mass.

EMERY, JOSHUA jr. b. 1807, Amh. 1831, settled in Fitchburg, now in N. Weymouth.

EMERSON, JOHN E. Amh. 1844.

EUSTIS, JOHN b. 21 April, 1790, Harv. 1810.

EMERSON, REV. JOHN b. Harv. 1726, ord. in Topsfield, and died 11 July, 1774, aged 64.

FELTON, CORNELIUS C. Mr. tutor and prof. in Harvard university, b. Harv. 1827.

FELTON, SAMUEL M. Harv. 1834.

FLANDERS, CHARLES b. Harv. 1808, and is a lawyer in Plainfield, N. H.

FARNHAM, JOHN HAY b. 22 July, 1791, Harv. 1811, studied law, resided in Salem, Indiana, where he died 10 July, 1833.

GERRISH, REV. JOSEPH b. 23 March, 1650, Harv. 1669, ord. in Wenham 12 Jan. 1675, and died 16 Jan. 1720, aged 70.

GERRISH, MOSES b. 10 June, 1744, Harv. 1762, was a school teacher, and removed to Grand Menan, where he died in 1825.

GERRISH, JOSEPH b. 5 March, 1775, Dart. 1797, studied law, afterward went to sea as commander of a ship for several years, and died in Newbury 6 Dec. 1839.

GILMAN, EZEKIEL 24 Jan. 1817, Harv. 1839.

GREENLEAF, REV. DANIEL b. 10 Feb. 1680, Harv. 1699, ord. in North Yarmouth, 1708. He removed to Boston, where he died 27 Aug. 1763, aged 83.

GREENLEAF, STEPHEN b. 4 Oct. 1704, Harv. 1723, was sheriff of Suffolk Co. and died Jan. 1795, aged 91.

GREENLEAF, BENJAMIN b. March, 1732, Harv. 1751, was judge of probate, and judge of common pleas. He died 13 Jan. 1799, aged 67.

GREENLEAF, SIMON Mr. LL. D. b.   Bowd. 1817, practiced law for some years in Portland, and is now prof. of law in Harvard university.

GREENLEAF, REV. JONATHAN brother to Simon,   Bowd. 1824, ord. in 1815, Wells, Me. then preacher to the seamen in N. Y. for some years, and settled in Brooklyn, Long Island, 8 March, 1843.

GREENLEAF, CHARLES H. b.   Dart. 1832, and died

GREENLEAF, ALFRED   Dart. 1838, teacher of the High school in Brooklyn, Long Island.

GREENLEAF, JAMES b.   Dart. 1834.

GORDON, WILLIAM A. Mr. M. D. Harv. 1826, is a physician in Hingham, Mass.

GOULD, BENJAMIN A.   Harv. 1814, was for many years teacher of the Latin school in Boston.

HALE, REV. MOSES b. 10 July, 1678, Harv. 1699, ord. in Newbury, Byfield, Oct. 1706, and died Jan. 1743, ag. 66.

HALE, REV. MOSES b. 1703, Harv. 1722, ord. in Chester, N. H. 20 Oct. 1731, and dismissed 4 June, 1735.

HALE, REV. MOSES b. 18 Jan. 1715, Harv. 1734, settled in Newbury, west parish, 20 Feb. 1752, and died 15 Jan. 1779, aged 64.

HALE, REV. MOSES son of the preceding, b. in Rowley 19 Feb. 1749, Harv. 1771, ord. in Boxford   and died 26 May, 1786.

HALE, NATHAN b. 1 March, 1720, Harv. 1739, and died in Newbury.

HALE, SAMUEL b. 24 Aug. 1718, Harv. 1740. In 1745, he commanded a company of provincials at Louisburg, and for more than thirty years was a distinguished teacher of youth in Portsmouth, N. H. He died 10 July, 1807, aged 89.

HALE, REV. BENJAMIN, Mr.   Bowd. 1818, and at Dart. 1827, tutor and prof. and now president of Geneva college, N. Y.

HALE, EBENEZER M. D.   Dart. 1829.

HILLS, WILLIAM   Oberlin Ins. 1844.

HODGE, NICHOLAS b. 20 May, 1719, Harv. 1739, and died in 1743, aged 24.

HODGE. MICHAEL b. 9 Sept. 1780, Harv. 1799, and died 6 July, 1816, aged 36.

HOOPER, REV. HEZEKIAH b. 1769, Harv. 1789, ord. in Boylston, 12 March, 1794.

HOOPER, THOMAS W. b. 25 Jan. 1771, Harv. 1789, died in the naval service.

HOOPER, STEPHEN b. 7 April, 1785, Harv. 1808, practiced law, removed to Boston, and there died in 1825. He had been representative and senator of Essex co. Massachusetts.

HORTON, REV. WILLIAM   settled in Dover, N. H.

HOWARD, REV. WILLIAM G.   Amh. 1835.

HUSE, STEPHEN b. 16 Nov. 1702, Harv. 1726.

HUDSON, HENRY I.   Harv. 1843, studying divinity, in Cambridge.

INGALLS, WILLIAM b. 3 May, 1769, Harv. 1790, M. D. and prof. at Brown. He now resides in Boston.

JACKSON, JUDGE CHARLES b. 31 May, 1775, Harv. 1793, resides in Boston.

JACKSON, JAMES MR. M. D. prof. b. 2 Oct. 1777, Harv. 1796, is a physician in Boston.

JEWETT, REV. CALEB b.   Dart. 1776, ord. in Gorham, Me. 5 Nov. 1783, and dismissed and died in 1800.

JAQUES, STEPHEN b. 5 Feb. 1685, Harv. 1707, resided in Newbury, was a notary public, and a teacher of youth. He died about 1779.

JAQUES, REV. RICHARD b. 1 April, 1700, Harv. 1720, ord. in Gloucester, 3 Nov. 1725, and died 12 April, 1777, aged 77.

JOHNSON, JONATHAN G.   Harv. 1810, is a physician in Newburyport.

KELLY, REV. WILLIAM b. 31 Oct. 1744, Harv. 1767, ord. in Warner, N. H. 5 Feb. 1772, and dismissed 11 March, 1801, and died 18 May, 1813.

KENT, AMOS b. 16 Oct. 1774, Harv. 1795, was a lawyer in Chester, N. H. and died 18 June, 1824, aged 49.

KENT, MOODY   Harv. 1801, is in the practice of law in Concord, N. H.

KIMBALL, EDWARD b. 16 Aug. 1793, Harv. 1814, resides in Wenham.

KNAPP, JACOB NEWMAN 7 Nov. 1773, Harv. 1802, resides in Walpole, N. H.

KNAPP, SAMUEL LORENZO LL. D. at Paris, b. —— Dart. 1804, was a lawyer in Newburyport, thence to Boston, and died in Hopkinton, Mass.

KNAPP. PHILIP COOMBS   Dart. 1840.

LE BRETON, EDMUND L.   Harv. 1824, practices law in Newburyport.

LITTLE, SILAS b. March, 1754, Dart. 1776, resides in Newbury.

LITTLE, MOSES b. 3 July, 1766, Harv. 1787, was a physician in Salem, Mass. and died 13 Oct. 1811.

LITTLE, MICHAEL b. 14 March, 1771, Dart. 1792, and died in Newbury, 29 March, 1830.

LITTLE, EDWARD brother to Michael, b. 12 March, 1773, Dart. 1797, and now resides in Danville, Me.

LITTLE, JOSIAH brother to the two preceding, b. 13 Jan. 1791, Bowd. 1811, resides in Newbury.

LITTLE, JOSIAH S. b. in Minot, Me.   Bowd. 1825, is a lawyer in Portland, Me.

LONGFELLOW, STEPHEN b. 1723, Harv. 1742, moved to Portland 1745, was a school teacher, parish, and town clerk 22 years, register of probate 15 years, clerk of the court 16 years, and died 1 May, 1790, aged 67 years.

LONGFELLOW, EDWARD b. 1758, Dart. 1780, was a teacher. commanded a company in the expedition against Daniel Shays, and died 5 Sept. 1794.

LORD, REV. THOMAS N. b. 19 Aug. 1807, Bowd. 1835, and ord. in Topsham, Me. 10 Aug. 1837.

LOWELL, JOHN LL. D. b. 17 June, 1743, Harv. 1760, commenced the practice of law in Newburyport, removed to Boston, and there died 6 May, 1802, aged 58.

LOWELL, JOHN LL. D. b. in Newburyport, Harv. 1786, was a lawyer in Boston, where he died.

LOWELL, FRANCIS C. brother to John, b. 7 April, 1775, Harv. 1793, and died in Boston, 1818. He studied law, became a manufacturer, and in

LUNT, JOSEPH b.   Harv. 1737, and died at sea.

LUNT, REV. WILLIAM P. b. 2 Ap. 1805, Harv. 1823, ord. in Quincy, 3 June, 1825.

LUNT, GEORGE b. 31 Dec. 1803, Harv. 1824, is a lawyer in Newburyport.

McGAW, THORNTON born in Newburyport, Dart. 1820, and is a lawyer in Bangor, Me.

MARCH, REV. EDMUND b. 1703, Harv. 1722, ord. in Amesbury, 3 July, 1728, resigned 19 March, 1743, and died in Newbury, 6 March, 1791, aged 88.

MARCH, REV. JOHN C. b. 9 Oct. 1805, Yale, 1825, ord. in Newbury, Belleville, 1 March, 1832.

MERRILL, REV. NATHANIEL b. 1 March, 1713, Harv. 1732, ord. at Nottingham West, now Hudson, 30 Nov. 1737, and died 1796, aged 83.

MERRILL, REV. NATHANIEL b.   1743, Harv. 1767, ord. in Boscawen, 19 Oct. 1768, dismissed 1 April, 1774. and died in Poultney, Vt. Oct. 1791, aged 48.

MERRILL, JOHN b. 3 Jan. 1793, Bowd. 1811, resides in Woodbury, N. J.

MERRILL, REV. THOMAS 4th, b. 9 May, 1814, Waterville, 1841.

MERRILL, DAVID b. 7 Oct. 1806, Yale, 1827, lives in Newburyport.

*MOODY, REV. JOSHUA b. 1632, Harv. 1653, ord. in Portsmouth, N. H. 1671, was minister of the first church in Boston, from 23 May, 1684, till 1692, and died in Boston, 4 July, 1697, in his 65th year.

MOODY, REV. SAMUEL b. 4 Jan. 1675, Harv. 1697, ord. in York, 20 Dec. 1700, and there died 13 Nov. 1747.

MOODY, SAMUEL b. 1700, Harv. 1718, commanded the fort at Pemaquid, then fort George, was a physician in Brunswick, where he died in 1758.

MOODY, REV. JOHN b. 1705, Harv. 1727, ord. in Newmarket, 25 Nov. 1730, and died 15 Oct. 1778, aged 73.

MOODY, REV. AMOS b. 20 Nov. 1739, Harv. 1759, ord. in Pelham, N. H. 20 Nov. 1765, dismissed in 1792, and died 22 March, 1819, aged 79.

MOODY, REV. SILAS b. 28 April, 1742, Harv. 1761, ord. in Arundel 9 Jan. 1771, and died April, 1816.

MOODY, STEPHEN b.   Harv. 1790, was a lawyer in Gilmanton, N. H. where he died.

MOODY, SAMUEL b.   Dart. 1790, moved to Hallowell, Me. where he died.

MOODY, NATHAN b.   Dart. 1795, resided in Hallowell, Me.

MORSE, REV. JOHN b. 13 Sept. 1670, Harvard, 1692, ord. in Newton on Long Island in 1697.

MORSE, REV. JOSEPH b. 10 Feb. 1672, Harv. 1695, ord. in Stoughton, now Canton, 30 Oct. 1717, and died 29 Nov. 1732.

MORSE, PARKER b. 20 April, 1715, Harv. 1734.

MORSE, HUMPHREY b. 1808, Amh. 1834, and died in Newbury, April, 1836.

MORSS, REV. JAMES D. D. b. 25 Oct. 1779, Harv. 1800, ord. rector of St. Paul's church in Newburyport, where he died 26 April, 1842.

MOSELEY, REV. WILLIAM OXNARD Harv. 1836, b. 27 April, 1815, and is settled in Scituate, Mass.

NEWMAN, SAMUEL jr.   Amh. 1840, now in Newbury.
NORTHEND, WILLIAM DUMMER   Bowd. 1843, is studying law.
NORTON. STEPHEN S. 6 Feb. 1788, Harv. 1805, and died young.
NOYES, REV. JAMES b. 4 March, 1640, Harv. 1659, was a preacher in Stonington,
    Conn. 1664, ord. there 10 Sept. 1676, and died 30 Dec. 1719.
NOYES, REV. MOSES b. 6 Dec. 1643, Harv. 1659, was the first minister in Lyme,
    Conn. and died there 10 Nov. 1726, aged 83.
NOYES, REV. NICHOLAS b. 22 Dec. 1647, Harv. 1667, preached in Haddam, Conn.
    13 years, ord. in Salem 14 Nov. 1683, and died 13 Dec. 1717, aged 70.
NOYES, REV. EDMUND b. 29 March, 1729. Harv. 1747, ord. in Salisbury, 20 Nov.
    1751, and died 12 July, 1809.
NOYES, EBENEZER b. 1739, Nassau 1759, was a physician in Dover, where he
    died 11 Aug. 1767, aged 28.
NOYES, REV. NATHANIEL b. 12 Aug. 1735, Nassau Hall 1759, ord. in Southamp-
    ton, N. H. 23 Feb. 1763, dismissed 8 Dec. 1800, and died in Newburyport, Dec. 1810,
    aged 75.
NOYES, REV. THOMAS b.   Harv. 1795, and died in Newbury.
NOYES, NATHAN M. D. b.   Dart. 1796, was a physician in Newburyport,
    and died Sept. 1842.
NOYES, REV. JEREMIAH   Dart. 1799, ord. 16 Nov. 1803, in Gorham,
    and died 15 Jan. 1807.
NOYES, MOODY   Harv. 1800.
NOYES, DANIEL b. 29 Jan. 1739, Harv. 1758, was register of probate for Essex, and
    died in Ipswich 21 March, 1815, aged 77.
NOYES, JOSHUA b. 1739. Nassau, 1759, was pastor elect of the church in Kingston,
    N. H. and died 8 July, 1773, aged 34.
NOYES, JOHN b. 9 May, 1709, Harv. 1753.   He died 13 Aug. 1759, aged 50 years.
NOYES, REV. GEORGE R. b. 6 March, 1798, Harv. 1818, ord. in Brookfield, Mass.
    31 Oct. 1827, resettled in Petersham 15 Oct. 1834, and is now a professor in Harvard
    university.
NOYES, FRANCIS V. M. D. 22 Sept. 1809, Dart. 1831, is a physician in Newburyport.
NOYES, DANIEL P.   Yale, 1840, is now a tutor in Yale college.
O'BRIEN, JOHN M.   Bowd. 1806, is a lawyer in Boston.
OTIS, REV. GEORGE 14 July, 1797, Harv. 1815, was a tutor and professor, rector of
    Christ church, Cambridge, and died 25 Feb. 1828.
PARISH, MOSES P.   Bowd. 1822.
PARSONS, SAMUEL H. son of Rev. Jonathan P. of Newburyport, b. at Lyme, Conn.
    14 May, 1737, Harv. 1756, was a lawyer in Middletown, Conn. was a major-general
    in the Revolutionary army, was an aid to general Washington, by whom he was
    afterward appointed governor of the Northwestern territory.   He was drowned in Big
    Beaver creek, Ohio, Nov. 12, 1789, aged 52.
PARSONS, MOSES b. 13 May, 1744, at Gloucester, Harv. 1765, practiced law in
    Haverhill, where he died.
PARSONS, THEOPHILUS LL. D. A. A. S. b. 24 Feb. 1750, Harv. 1769.   Chief
    justice sup. jud. court, Mass.
PARSONS, JONATHAN G. 23 July, 1761, Yale 1777, and died
PARSONS, THEODORE b. Aug. 1751, Harv. 1773, went out from Newburyport as
    a surgeon in the Bennington privateer, and was lost in 1779.   A young 'man of emi-
    nent abilities and distinguished virtues.'
PARSONS, THEOPHILUS b. 17 May, 1797, Harv. 1815, and practices law in Boston.
PARSONS, CHARLES C. b. 8 April, 1782, Harv. 1801.
PARSONS, WILLIAM b. 17 Feb. 1800, Harv. 1818.
PEARSON, ELIPHALET LL. D. A. A. S. b. 11 June, 1752, Harv. 1773, and died
    in Greenland, N. H. Sept. 1826, aged 74.   He was prof. lang. Harv. univ. and prof.
    sac. lit. And. theol. sem.
PEARSON, ABIEL M. D. b. 1756, Harv. 1779, was a physician in Andover, where he
    died, May, 1827, aged 71.
PERLEY, JEREMIAH b. 11 March, 1784, Dart. 1803, was a lawyer in Orono, Me.
PERKINS, HENRY C. M. D. b.   Harv. 1824, is a physician in Newbury-
    port.
PETTINGELL, AMOS b. 20 Oct. 1804, Yale, 1821, was tutor three years from 1827,
    and died 30 Nov. 1831, aged 27.
PIDGIN, REV. WILLIAM b. 1 March, 1771, Dart. 1794, ord. in Hampton, N. H. 27
    Jan. 1796, dismissed July, 1807, and resettled in Minot, Me. 11 Feb. and dismissed 14
    Aug. 1819.
PIERCE, NATHANIEL   Bowd. 1844.
PIERCE, DANIEL b.   Harv. 1728.
PIERCE, CHARLES b. 2 Feb. 1720, Harv. 1744, and died 1788.

PIERCE, REV. THOMAS b. 11 Oct. 1737, Harv. 1759, ord. in Scarboro, Me. Sept, 1762, and died 26 Jan. 1775.
PIERCE, EDWIN W. b. 15 May, 1819, Amh. 1838, and died 13 Aug. 1840.
PIKE, REV. JAMES b. 1 March, 1703, Harv. 1725, ord. in Somersworth, N. H. 28 Oct. 1730, and died 19 March, 1792, aged 89.
PIKE, REV. JOHN b. 3 July, 1813, Bowd. 1833, ord. in Rowley 11 Nov. 1841.
PIKE, FRANCIS V. b.   Yale 1833, and died
PIKE, ROBERT G.   Harv. 1843.
PLUMER, THOMAS   Amh. 1838.
PLUMER, DANIEL M. D. b. 4 May, 1819, Dart. 1840, is a physician in Newburyport,
PLUMER, HORACE b. 26 April, 1821, Dart. 1840, is a lawyer.
PLUMER, DAVID M. D.   Brown 1821, is a physician in N. H.
POOR, DANIEL N. M. D. b. 16 July, 1758, Harv. 1777, was a physician in Newbury, where he died 23 Jan. 1837, aged 78.
PRICE, REV. EBENEZER b. 14 Sept. 1771, Dart. 1793, ord. in Belfast, Me. 29 Dec. 1796, left 22 Sept. 1802, and was resettled in Boscawen, N. H. 26 Sept. 1804.
PRINCE, BENJ. L. b. 24 July, 1782, Dart. 1807, and died in Cincinnati 11 Aug. 1815.
RAND. EDWARD S. LL. B. 15 March, 1809, Harv. 1828, is a lawyer in Boston.
RAWSON, REV. EDWARD b.   Harv. 1653.
RAWSON, REV. GRINDAL b. in Boston, Harv. 1678.
ROGERS, JOHN M. D.   Dart. 1816, was a physician in Boscawen, and died 6 Jan. 1830.
ROLFE, REV. BENJAMIN b. 13 Sept. 1662, Harv. 1684, ord. in Haverhill, Jan. 1690, and was killed by the Indians 29 Aug. 1708.
ROLFE. BENJAMIN b. 8 July, 1710, Harv. 1727, was clerk of the county court, and died 21 Oct. 1738.
ROLLINS, JOHN RODMAN   Dart. 1836.
ROLFE, REV. BENJAMIN b. 1734, Harv. 1777, ord. in Parsonsfield, Me. Jan. 1795, dismissed May, 1815, and died 1826, aged 62.
ROBERTS, ROBERT b. 28 Dec. 1754, Harv. 1771, died in one of the W. I. islands.
SAWYER. WILLIAM M. D.   Harv. 1788.
SAWYER, JOSEPH   Williams 1813.
SAWYER, THOMAS   Dart. 1805.
SAWYER, MICAJOH MR. M. D. b. 15 July, 1737, Harv. 1756, was a physician in Newburyport, and died 29 Sept. 1815, aged 78.
*SEWALL, JUDGE SAMUEL b. 28 March, 1652, Harv. 1671, and died in Boston 1 Jan. 1730, ag. 77.
SEWALL, STEPHEN b. 1715, Harv. 1731, taught school for many years in Newbury and Newburyport, and died in 1795, aged 80.
SIMPSON, PAUL M. D. b.   Harv. 1831, is a physician in Boston.
SPRING, PINCKNEY b.   Yale 1819.
SPRING, REV. GARDINER MR. D. D. at Ham. b.   Yale 1805, ord. in N. Y. 8 Aug. 1810.
SPRING, REV. SAMUEL b.   Yale 1811, March 21 ord. in Abington resettled in Hartford, Conn. 6 Dec. 1826.
STEVENS, REV. TIMOTHY b. 23 Sept. 1641, Harv. 1687.
STONE, EBEN F.   Harv. 1843, is studying law.
SMITH. REV. DAVID   Harv. 1790.
STICKNEY, PETER LE BRETON   Dart. 1839, is a physician in Philadelphia.
STICKNEY, JOHN   Harv. 1804. Clerk of the court in Boston, and died 1832.
SWETT. COL. SAMUEL   Harv. 1800, resides in Boston.
SWEETSER, REV. SETH 15 March, 1807, Harv. 1827, was a tutor in Cambridge, ord. in Gardiner, Me. 23 Nov. 1836, dismissed 8 Nov. 1838, and is now settled in Worcester, Mass.
SHORT, REV. MATTHEW b. 14 March, 1688, Harv. 1707, ord. in Attleboro' 12 Nov. 1712. dismissed 31 May, 1715, preached at Saco, Me. resettled in Easton, Mass. and died 15 April, 1731.
SMITH, REV. DANIEL T. b. 17 Sept. 1813, Amh. 1831, was assistant instructor at Andover 1834-6, ord. in Sherburne, Mass. 5 Dec. 1836.
STOREY, CH. W.   Harv. 1835, a lawyer and clerk of h. of rep.
TAPPAN, REV. BENJAMIN b. 28 Feb. 1721, Harv. 1742, ord. in Manchester, Mass. 11 Sept. 1745, and died 6 May, 1790, in his 70th year.
TAPPAN, ENOCH S. M, D. b. 3 March, 1782, Harv. 1801, is a physician in Augusta, Me.
TAPPAN, DAVID b. May, 1784, Harv. 1804.
TAPPAN, REV. BENJAMIN b. Nov. 1788, Harv. 1805, ord. in Augusta, 16 Oct. 1811,

358 APPENDIX.

TAPPAN, REV. DANIEL D. b. 20 Oct. 1798, Bowd. 1822, ord. in Alfred, Me. 23 April. 1828, dismissed 28 Feb. 1832, and settled in N. Marshfield, 23 Jan. 1839.
TOPPAN, REV. CHRISTOPHER b. 15 Dec. 1670, Harv. 1691, ord. in Newbury, 9 Sept. 1696, and died 23 July. 1747.
TOPPAN, EDMUND son of Christopher b. 7 Dec. 1701, Harv. 1720, was a physician in Hampton, and died 28 Nov. 1739, aged 38.
TOPPAN, BEZALEEL brother to Edmund, b. 7 March, 1705, Harv. 1722, settled in Salem, and died 1762, aged 57.
TOPPAN, REV. AMOS b. 7 Feb. 1736, Harv. 1758, ord. in Kingston, 1761, and died 23 June, 1771.
TENNEY, ALBERT G. MR.   Bowd. 1835, resides in Boston.
TENNEY, REV. DAVID b. 1748, Harv. 1768, ord. 18 Sept. 1771, in Barrington, N. H. and died 1778, aged 30.
THOMAS, THOMAS b. 26 Sept. 1773, Harv. 1790.
THURSTON, JOHN MR. M. D. b.   Harv. 1807, died,
TILTON, WARREN   Harv. 1844.
TITCOMB, WILLIAM S. b. 25 Oct. 1781, Harv. 1801, and died 28 June, 1831.
TITCOMB, ISAAC   Amh. 1836.
TOMPSON, SAMUEL b. 1 Sept. 1691, Harv. 1710, ord. in Gloucester, 28 Nov. 1716, and died 9 Dec. 1724.
TRACY, JOHN b. 19 April, 1757, Harv. 1771.
TUCKER, JOHN b. 11 Aug. 1753, Harv. 1774, was clerk of the court in Suffolk, and died
TUCKER, BARNARD b. 2 April, 1760, Harv. 1779, was a physician in Wenham and died 24 Jan. 1832.
TUCKER, REV. ED RICHARD b. 4 Feb. 1816, Dart. 1835.
TUFTS, REV. JOSHUA b. 4 Oct. 1716, Harv. 1736, ord. in Litchfield, Dec. 1741.
TYNG, DUDLEY A. MR. LL. D. b. 3 Sept. 1760, Harv. 1781, and died 1 Aug. 1829, aged 69.
TYNG, REV. STEPHEN H. MR. prof. at Jefferson coll. Harv. 1817, is settled in Philadelphia, in the church of the Epiphany.
TYNG, GEORGE   Harv. 1822.
TYNG, REV. JAMES H. b. in Boston, Bowd. 1827, resides in Philadelphia.
WALSH, JOHN   Harv. 1814, is a lawyer in Kentucky.
WEBBER, D. D. REV. SAMUEL b. 13 Jan. 1760, Harv. 1784, was tutor, professor, and president of Harvard college 1806, and died 11 July, 1810.
WEBBER, REV. JOHN brother to Samuel, b. 11 May, 1762, Dart. 1792, ord. in Sandown, 1796, dismissed in 1800, settled in Campton Feb 1812, dismissed 12 March, 1815, moved to Porter, on the Scioto, and was living in 1829.
WEBSTER, REV. NICHOLAS b. 19 Oct. 1673, Harv. 1695, preached in Manchester in 1700.
WHEELWRIGHT, ISAAC W. b 1801, Bowd. 1821, formerly principal of an Academy in Newburyport, now of one in Quito, in S. America.
WHEELWRIGHT, JOSEPH M. D. b. 29 Dec. 1791, Harv. 1811.
WHEELWRIGHT, WILLIAM W.   Harv. 1824.
WHIPPLE, CHARLES K. b. 17 Nov. 1808, Amh. 1831.
WILBUR, HARVEY M. D.   Amh. 1838, is a physician in Dana, Worcester co. Mass.
WILLIAMS, WILLIAM b. 6 Aug. 1814, Bowd. 1835.
WOART, REV. JONATHAN L.   Harv. 1828, episcop. of Tallahasse, Flor. perished in the Pulaski, June, 1838.
WHITE, HON. PHILLIPS   Harv. 1772, rep. U. S. cong.
WOOD, DAVID   Harv. 1814, a ship master.
WOOD, REV. HORATIO b. 1 Dec. 1807, Harv. 1827, settled in Lowell.
WOOD, BARTHOLOMEW   Dart. 1841.
WOODMAN, REV. JOSEPH b. 1748, Nassau, 1766, ord. in Sanbornton, 13 Nov. 1771, and died 28 Sept. 1807.
*WOODBRIDGE, REV. TIMOTHY b. 1656, Harv. 1674, ord. in Hartford, Conn. 18 Nov. 1685, and died 30 April, 1732.
*WOODBRIDGE, REV. JOHN b.   Harv. 1664, ord. in 1667, in Killingby, Conn. removed to Wethersfield, and was there installed. He died in 1690.
WOODS, LEONARD jun. b. 24 Nov. 1807, U. C. 1827, formerly prof. of sacred literature in the theol. seminary, Bangor, formerly editor of Lit. and Theol. Review, N. Y. appointed president of Bowdoin College, Me. 1839.
WOODBRIDGE, JOHN MR.   Harv. 1710, died in Newbury, 13 Dec. 1731. He taught the public school in Newbury many years.
YOUNG, WILLIAM   Harv. 1810, died at sea.

The preceding catalogue is doubtless far from being complete, notwithstanding the pains that have been taken to make it as full and accurate as possible. Of so large a town as Newbury, from which so many families have emigrated to various parts of the country and the world, and whose history comprehends a period of more than two centuries, there are probably many natives, entitled to a place in this catalogue, whose names thus far have eluded my research. Deficient as it is, it contains the names of more than three hundred persons, which in point of numbers or intelligence, will bear comparison with those of any town in New England or the Union. Among them may be mentioned the late judge Parsons, judge Lowell and his sons John Lowell and Francis C. Lowell, president Webber, professor Pearson, with many others who are also numbered with the dead. Among the living, are three of the professors in Harvard university, the presidents of Bowdoin and Greenville colleges, and others, whom it might be deemed invidious to mention. Nor let any one suppose that the distinguished sons of Newbury are confined to the ranks of those who have received a collegiate education. She has contributed her full proportion of those, who, without the advantages of a liberal education, have, both in civil and military life, done honor to themselves and their country. Nor will her philanthropists, her merchants, her scientific and practical mechanics, be forgotten, so long as Andover seminary and the city of Lowell remain as monuments of the munificence of Messrs. Brown and Bartlet, and the scientific skill of Messrs. Lowell and Moody. To do justice to the characters of such men who have passed from among the living, would require a volume, and even to enumerate the results of the inventive genius of a Perkins, would occupy a larger space in this book than can be spared. A passing notice in its appropriate place, of these and many others, is all that my limits will afford.

CONCLUSION.

—◆—

On reviewing the preceding pages, the intelligent reader will readily discover many omissions and deficiencies, which it is the object of these pages to supply as far as the limited space allotted me will permit. With materials on hand sufficient for another volume, I find no small difficulty in making from them a proper selection. To do this the more correctly, I shall follow the order of time, and of course shall first allude to the Indians, so far as they are connected with the town of Newbury. From history, tradition, and the many specimens of arrow-heads, pestles, gouges, pipes, and hatchets, which have at various times been found in Newbury, it is evident this region was once the habitation and resort of many of them. Says Hubbard, page thirtieth, 'when the English first settled any plantations along the coast since called New England, there were several nations of these Indians, that were in some kinde of confederacy one with another against some other of their po'ent neighbors, that were att enmity, and commonly they agreed to be at peace with those that spake the same language. Those that were seated more eastward about Pemmaquid and Kennebecke, were called Tarratines, betwixt whom and those that lived about Piscataqua, Merrimacke, and Agawam, now called Ipswich, had arisen some deadly feud, upon the accompt of some treachery used by those western Indians against the others; so as every year they were afraid of being surprised by them, which made them upon every occasion to hide themselves among the English, after they were settled in any of those places.' Thus we find in Winthrop, volume first, page twenty-seventh, 'Lord's day [June] thirteenth. In the morning the sagamore of Agawam and one of his men came aboard our ship and stayed all day.' Hubbard, also, page one hundred and thirtieth, says, 'the next morning Masconomo with one of his men came aboard, being the sagamore (which is the land proprietor) of that side of the country towards cape Anne, to bid them welcome.' So few in number was the tribe of this chieftain, that he gladly availed himself of the protection of the English against the Tarrantines, of whom they stood in great fear. Agawam, at that time, comprehended the whole territory from Merrimac river on the north, to Naumkeag river on the south; from Cochichawick, now Andover, on the west, and to the sea-side on the east. Johnson styles it, 'the sagamoreship or earldom of Agawam, now by our English nation called Essex.' From this, and several Indian deeds I have seen, it appears that Agawam included the towns of Bradford, Boxford, Newbury, Rowley, Ipswich, Hamilton, Wenham, and Beverly, and so forth, of which the Indian deed of Bradford calls Masconomo, Masconnomet, Muschanomit, alias Masquanomanit, alias

46

Maschanomet, alias John of Agawam, ' chief sagamore and native proprietor of the whole territory.'

August eighth, 1631, says Winthrop, ' the Tarrantines, to the number of one hundred, came in three canoes and in the night assaulted the wigwam of the sagamore of Agawam, slew seven men, and wounded John Sagamore [Masconomo] and James [of Saugus and some others (whereof some died after) and rifled a wigwam of Mr. Craddock's men, kept to catch sturgeon, and took away their nets and biscuit.'

In December, 1634, the small pox prevailed among the Indians, and removed great numbers. In some places ' the English helped to bury whole families and yet escaped the contagion.'* Thus the remnant of what the pestilence of 1617 had spared, the small pox of 1634 had nearly exterminated before the first white settler had pitched his tent within the limits of Quascacanquen, which was the following spring. The first intimation that we have that any of the aboriginal inhabitants resided at this time in Newbury, has been mentioned, page fortieth, where lot sixty-one is granted to ' John Indian.' That a few Indians resided in Newbury for some years after it was settled by the English, there is sufficient evidence, but the probability is that the number did not at any time exceed a dozen. In 1650, April sixteenth, ' Great Tom, Indian, sold to the selectmen of Newbury all his right, title and interest in all the woods, commons and lands in Newbury together with his th*** † acres of planting land as it is fenced in one entire fence in Newbury *lying neer Indian hill.'* I have as yet seen no other notice, either preceding or subsequent, of ' John Indian or Great Tom.' See page fifty-third. Perhaps John Indian was John Sagamore, alias Masconomo; but it is useless to speculate. In 1638, June twenty-eighth, Masconomo deeds to Mr. John Winthrop, for twenty pounds, ' all the right, property and claim I have or ought to have, unto all the land, lying and being in the bay of Agawam, alias Ipswich, being so called now by the English, as well as such land, as I formerly reserved unto my own use at Chebacco, *as also all other land belonging to me in these parts*, Mr. Dummer's *farm only excepted*,' and so forth. Why Mr. Dummer's farm, which had been granted him by the general court in 1635, and confirmed to him by the town, was excepted, or what arrangement, if any, had been made, concerning the remaining part of Newbury township, I have no means of knowing. The next intimation that I find of any Indians residing and owning land in Newbury, is the following:

' At a generall court held in Boston, May twenty-second, 1661.

' Whereas some Indians as we are informed pretend an interest in some parts of the land of Henry Sewall, which lieth at Newbury falls sometimes Mr. John Spencer's, which lands were purchased of ye said Mr. Spencer and also have been confirmed by the towne. It is therefore ordered by ye court yt if it shall appear to said Sewall yt ye said Indians or any other, have any legal right unto any part of ye said land, that ye said Henry Sewall shall hereby have liberty to purchase ye same of ye said Indians. Vera copia.

' EDWARD RAWSON, *Secretary.*'

The Indians, to whom the preceding court order alluded, must have been the family of ' Old Will,' of whom in 1663, March thirty-first, Richard Dummer bought seven acres for £ 10. Of him and his fami-

* Lewis.   † This should probably be ' three.'

ly I learn nothing further till June eighteenth, 1679, when one ' Andrew Pittimee, attorney for Job, brought an action against Mr. Henry Sewall ' for detaining from the said Job about an 160 acres of land at Newbury falls, that was the land of Old Will the said Job his grandfather.' As usual in such cases, testimony was taken on both sides. On June sixteenth, 1679, Daniel Denison thus writes to Henry Sewall. ' I am desired by Job, (who married Old Will's grandchild, and in her right claims the land at Newbury falls, which he long possessed and now you say you purchased of him,) that you would make out your right and they will be satisfied, or otherwise let him or them have quiet possession, or otherwise let the law decide the title. I can give no advice but believe they will prove Old Will and others long to have possessed land thereabouts and our law confirms their right to what they possessed. I shall trouble you no further, resting your loving friend.' On June twenty-first, Thomas Brown testifies in favor of Mr. Sewall. In favor of Job I copy the following depositions.

'The deposition of Moses Bradstreet and Alice Homes.

' These deponents testifieth and saith that aboute foure yere ago, the spring of the year before the warre begune thaye harde olde Wil ingin of Newbury fales complaining that master Showel ronged him, and that he had got his lande and cept it from him. Moses Bradstreet asked Wil if he had not soulde his lande to Master Showell, he said no, he never had resaved wone farthin of Master Showell for his land.'
' Allis Homes further saith that she lived with Mr. Dummer and knew that Old Will lived and planted at the falls for many yeares till Mr. Sewall's tattle worried him out, and that Mr. Dummer was desirous to buy old Will's land, but old Will sayd he was not willing to sell it from his children.
' June 23, 1679. Sworne to before me
D. DENISON.

' The deposition of John Todd aged about 58 years.

' This deponent saith that several times he heard Old ' Will (so called) Indian complaine that Mr. Showel of Newbury had taken away in his possession a great part of his land at Newbury falls, which complaint was before the late wars with the Indians, at which complaint this deponent saith that he was much troubled and grieved at it That an old Indian should so complaine of such Injury done him by any English. He further saith he knew Old Will lived above Newbury falls above five and thirty years since, and that for the most of that time he lived there.'
' Sworne before me June 23, 1679,
DANIEL DENISON.'

How this case was decided, if decided at all in court, I am not informed, but from two subsequent deeds that I have seen, it appears that the claims of Old Will's heirs were considered valid, as in 1681, May fourteenth, Henry Sewall buys for £20 of ' Job Indian, grandchild, Hagar Indian, and Mary Indian, daughters to Old Will Indian, late of Newbury Falls deceased, the Indian field, containing by estimation one hundred and sixty acres be it more or less together with all their land in Newbury bounds though without ye said lines, and so forth, and that no other Indians can lay any rightful claim thereto.'
From these and other papers it appears that in 1663, there was in Newbury but one Indian family, and that was the family of Old Will, which consisted of himself, wife and three daughters, Hagar, Mary, and Kate, who had probably married out of town. From the Ipswich records it appears that Masconomo the sagamore of Agawam, was living in February, 1656, as they say ' left to the seven men to grant to the sagamore six acres of planting land, where they shall appoint, for

to plant, but not propriety to any one but himself.'   In 1658, June eighteenth, the town ' granted to the sagamore's widow, to enjoy that parcel of land, which her husband had fenced in, during the time of her
widowhood.'   This gives us nearly the time when Masconomo died.
His widow was living in 1676, aged sixty-eight.   From the testimony
of Peckanaminet, alias Ned Acocket, alias Old Ned of Ipswich, who
was sixty-eight in 1676, Old Will was then living, but had deceased
before 1679.   From a report made to the legislature of Massachusetts
in 1676, it appears ' that there were at and about Ipswich eight men
and seventeen women and children, Indians, and Wonolanset's company at Dunstable about sixty persons.'

After the death of Old Will it is probable that his family removed
from the town, as I find no recorded intimation of any native Indians
residing in Newbury subsequent to that period, with the exception of
' Gasper Megonier,' who, on rrecords say, died December eighth, 1707.
There is a tradition that an Indian squaw was living near Indian Hill
for a few years after Mr. Samuel Poor bought land and moved there,
which as near as I can ascertain, was not far from 1705.

I hear nothing further of any Indians in Newbury, or of any claims
set up by any of them for any land in Newbury till the year 1700,
when the grand-children of Masconomo the sagamore of Agawam laid
claim to the whole ' sagamoreship or earldom of Agawam, now by our
English called Essex,' which was lying between Bass and Merimac
rivers, and had not been already sold.   This claim was allowed by the
inhabitants, and deeds were given to the towns of Bradford, Boxford,
Newbury, Manchester, Gloucester, Beverly, and so forth.   Gage's history of Rowley contains the deeds to Bradford and Boxford, both of
which contain the following sentence.   ' Whereas divers Englishmen,
many years since in the life time of the said Masquonomonit alias
Muschonomit, *and by and with his knowledge, and license and good
liking, did enter upon subdue and improve* an English plantation, and so
forth.'   These deeds are very long and are signed by ' Samuel English, Joseph English, and John Umpee, grandchildren, and the next
true, rightful and lawful heirs of Masquonomonit' and so forth.   The
deed to Newbury is as follows.

' To all people to whom these presents shall come Samuel English, grandson and
heir of Maschanomet the Sagamore of Agawam, an Indian in the Province of ye Massachusetts in New England, sendeth greeting; Know ye said Samuel English good
and sufficient reasons moving him thereto, but especially for and in consideration of
ye full and just summe of £10 in Current money of New England truly paid unto me
by Cutting Noyes, John Knight, Richard Dole, John Worth and Joseph Pike. selectmen of ye town of Newbury in ye County of Essex in ye Massachusetts Bay in
New England, in ye behalfe of said town of Newbury, wherewith I ye said Samuel
English doe hereby acknowledge myself fully satisfied and paid and content forever
have given, granted, bargained, sold and confirmed and doe by these presents for my
heirs, executors, administrators and assigns forever give, grant, bargain sell and confirm unto ye abovesaid selectmen in the behalfe and for the use and propriety of said
towne and their heirs forever, a tract of land containing 10000 acres be it more or less
lying within ye towneship of said Newbury and containeth the whole towneship of
said town and is abutted and bounded, East by ye sea North and North West by Merrimac river West by Bradford line and South by Rowley line together with all ye
wood, timber, lands, grounds, soyles, waters, streams, rivers, ponds, huntings, fishings,
stones, mines, minerals, hereditaments and all ye appurtenances belonging to ye same
and to every part thereof within said towneship to have and to hold to them ye said
Cutting Noyes, John Knight, Richard Dole, John Worth and Joseph Pike selectmen in
ye name and behalfe and for ye use, benefit, and behoofe of said town of Newbury and
their heirs, executors, administrators and assigns in peaceable and quiet possession

forever freely and clearly acquitting and discharging all, and from all, manner of claims and demands whatsoever, and further I ye said Samuel English doe hereby covenant, promise and grant to and with ye said selectmen in ye behalfe of said towne that at, and until, ye unsealing and delivery of these presents, I had full power and lawful authority to grant and convey ye abovesaid premises with ye appurtenances and every part thereof as aforesaid, it descending to me from Maschanomet Sagamore as aforesaid and I ye said Samuel English shall and will forever hereafter fully and freely release and relinquish my whole right and title thereunto and every part thereof hereby binding myselfe, heirs, executors and administrators forever to defend ye said selectmen and ye town of said Newbury in their possession of all ye above granted and specified premises and their heirs forever from ye lawful claimes of all persons whatsoever in any manner of wise and I ye said Samuel English have hereto set my hand and seal this tenth day of January 1701 in the 12th year of our Sovereign Lord William ye 3d King over England.

SAMUEL ENGLISH and a seal.

Samuel English ye surviving heir of Maschanomet ye Sagamore of Agawam appeared before us ye subscribers ye 10th day of January in ye 12th year of his Majestie's reign Anno Domini 1701 and acknowledged ye above written instrument to be his act and deed before

DANIEL PIERCE } Just.
THOMAS NOYES } Pacis.

The preceding account embodies all the authentic information concerning the Indians of Newbury that I have been able to find, suitable for publication. There are various traditions concerning them, some of which are probably correct, while others cannot be true. To one of these traditions I shall allude in another place. Of the Indians in New England Hubbard, page thirtieth, thus speaks : ' Betwixt Kennebecke and Connecticut were observed to bee about twenty societies or companeyes of these salvages, when the English first came upon this coast. 1. at Kennebecke. 2. Casco bay. 3. Saco. 4. Piscataqua. 5. Merrimacke. 6. The river of Newberry, att the falls of which was a noted plantation of them, by reason of the plenty of fish that almost at all seasons of the yeere used to be found there, both in winter and summer. 7. Att Agawam, called now Ipswich, was another noted and desirable place, for plenty of several sorts of fish found there in time of yeere, both at the harbor's mouth shell fish of all sorts, and other kinds higher up the stream, and *to which belonged those of Newberry falls,* that lyes in the midway betwixt Merrimack and Agawam.'

These Indians were called Aberginians, and however large the population in this region might once have been, it is certain that from various causes the race had become nearly extinct, when the white population had determined to occupy the territory thus providentially vacated, and it was with ' the knowledge, license and good liking' of the few that remained, that the first settlers of Newbury took possession of this then howling wilderness, now the comfortable abode of civilization and all its countless blessings. The ' goodly heritage' that we now enjoy is the fruit of privations, sufferings and labors almost unexampled, and to those who were the pioneers in the subjugation of this rude and rocky region we owe a debt of gratitude which we can in no other way repay than by transmitting to posterity the precious legacy which we now inherit. Rightly to estimate its value we should know its cost, and be able in some good degree to appreciate the sacrifices made by our forefathers. In order therefore to have a better idea of the difficulties they encountered, let us examine a little more minutely than we have done, their qualifications for the task before them. For the purpose of illustration the first settlers of New-

bury may be conveniently divided into three classes, viz. 1. The
rich and educated gentlemen, who by birth or profession were entitled
to the appellation of Mr. 2. The artizans or mechanics, who had
emigrated from the populous towns in various parts of England, but
principally from Wiltshire, and 3. The yeomen, or farmers, laborers
and servants. Of such men the first settlers of Newbury were composed, and the appearance of the first company as they ascended the
river Quascacunquen, to take possession of their new home, accoutred
as they were in the peculiar costume of that day, could we now witness it, would be indeed a curiosity. To them with a slight variation
the words of the poet would be truly applicable,

> "'T were worth whole years of modern life,
> One glance of their array.'

Before them was an unbroken wilderness, covered with a forest, the
heavy growth of centuries, which, with the exception of the few
patches of corn ground, once cultivated by the Indians, had to be
cleared away before they could raise even the necessaries of life. On
witnessing the sufferings and privations of this band of voluntary ex-
iles, most of whom had been accustomed to the privileges, convenien-
ces, and even luxuries of their father-land, and many of whom had
brought with them their rich dresses, and silver plate, making a striking contrast with their log habitations and their rustic fare, the inquiry
would naturally arise,

> ' What sought they thus afar ?
> Bright jewels of the mine ?
> The wealth of seas? the spoils of war ?
> They sought a pure faith's shrine.'

This was the mainspring of all their movements, the secret of their
indomitable perseverance, the guarantee of their success. Of those
qualities, deemed essential to the establishment and perpetuation of
the rights and privileges of a people determined to be free, our ancestors had their full proportion. With a firmness amounting sometimes
even to obstinacy, and a foresight, for which we should ever feel
grateful, they assisted in laying the foundation of those institutions,
which the lapse of more than two centuries has left without any ma-
terial change. In substance their municipal and ecclesiastical regulations were the same then that they are now, subject only to those
incidental variations and improvements consequent upon the increase
of wealth, knowledge, and refinement. In one respect the church at
Newbury was more liberal than any of the neighboring churches.
Says Lechford in 1642, ' of late some churches are of opinion that
any may be admitted to church fellowship, that are not extremely
ignorant and scandalous, but this they are not very forward to practise
except at Newbury.' The difficulties that occurred between them and
Mr. Parker concerning church government, have already been mentioned, and no careful reader can have failed to notice that during the
whole of their twenty-five years controversy with Mr. Parker, they attended his ministrations with the greatest regularity, added new seats
in the meeting house to accommodate the increasing number of worshipers, and paid his salary without hesitation at the very time they
had suspended him from his office of ruling elder, but had with great

condescension granted him liberty ' as a gifted brother, to preach for the edification of the church if he pleased.' See page eighty-second.

In their mode of public worship, they differed but little from their successors. The psalms were sung in regular order, from the first to the last, four on each sabbath. The precentors sat in the pews near the deacons' seat in front of the pulpit. A contribution was made every sabbath afternoon, one of the deacons saying, ' brethren, now there is time left for contribution, wherefore, as God hath prospered you, so freely offer.'* Says Jocelyn, ' on Sundays P. M. when sermon is ended, the people in the gallery come down and march two and two abreast up one ile and down another, until they come before the desk, for pulpit they have none. Before the desk is a long pue, where the elders and deacons sit, one of them with a money box in his hand, in which the people as they pass put their offerings, some one shilling, some two shillings, or a half crown or five shillings according to their ability, and good will, after this they sing a psalm.' This custom of taking a collection every sabbath was omitted, says Mr. Felt, in 1763. In addition to the care of the contribution box, the deacons had every sabbath the charge of the hour-glass, which was set running at the commencement of the sermon, which was hardly considered satisfactory, if it were not continued till the sands of an hour had ceased running. Sometimes the horologe was again turned, and the thirsty congregation invited ' to take another glass.' To this custom, Mr. Shepard, of Lynn, thus alludes : ' thou art restless till the tiresome glass be run out and the tedious sermon be ended.' In their mode of living, they differed in many respects from us. For nearly a century after Newbury was settled, the inhabitants had never used or seen either tea, coffee, or potatoes. As a substitute, they used bean and pea porridge, broth, hasty pudding and milk, both morning and evening, and turnips in abundance. In the county records of 1657, I find the following : ' Steven Dow did acknowledge to him it was a good while before he could eate his masters food viz. meate and milk or drinke beer, saying he did not know it was good, because he was not used to eat such victuall, but to eate bread and water porridge and to drink water.' Large quantities of barley were raised, and malt was a staple article, and for many years after the first settlement, excellent crops of wheat were raised. The common beverage was beer, till the growth of their orchards enabled them to substitute cider, the consumption of which has of late years been very much diminished. Of fish, they had an abundance, especially sturgeon, cod-fish and bass, of which the two latter were used, not only for food, but to manure their corn-fields, till forbidden by law in 1639. Though living near the ocean, there does not appear to have been among the original settlers, for many years, but two persons, who were at all acquainted with nautical affairs, till Aquila Chase was hired in 1646, to remove from Hampton to this place, for the purposes already mentioned. The inconveniences of their want of foresight in laying out the highway called Water street, in what is now Newburyport, are felt to this day, the road being laid out only two rods in width, while in all other parts of the town, the highways were from four to seven rods wide. From many other considerations, it is also evident that nearly all the first settlers were not a

* Lechford.

maritime people, and therefore did not appreciate their commercial advantages. Of the ninety-one grantees of Newbury, two were clergymen, eight were 'gentlemen,' two or three had been bred as merchants, one maltster, one physician, one schoolmaster, one sea-captain, one mate of a ship, one dyer, one glover, three or four tanners, seven or eight shoemakers, two wheelwrights, two blacksmiths, two 'linnen weavers,' two weavers, one cooper, one saddler, one sawyer, and two or three carpenters. Of the remainder, only a few are styled yeomen.

Such were the men, who commenced and accomplished the task of subduing this part of the American wilderness, here planted the tenth church in Massachusetts, and covered these delightful hills and valleys, once the gloomy abode of savages and wild beasts, with the evidence and result of untiring industry and patient perseverance, with all that is agreeable in civilization, and consoling in christianity. That the first settlers of New England in general, and of Newbury in particular, possessed the fullest confidence in the righteousness of their principles, and that their design to plant the standard of the cross in this heathen land met the approbation of their heavenly Father, who would grant success to their undertaking, there is abundant evidence. The first judge Sewall, whose father was one of the most distinguished pioneers in the settlement of Newbury, thus speaks in his ' New Heaven upon the New Earth,' under date of 1697, in answering the objections of those, who asserted that there was ' an imposibility of subsisting here : '
' It is remarkable that Mr. [Thomas] *Parker*, who was a successfull Schoolmaster at *Newbury* in *Barkshire*, in the happy days of Doctor [William] Twisse; was much about this time [1634] preaching and proving at *Ipswich* in Essex [Mass.] That the passengers came over upon good Grounds, and that God would multiply them as he did the children of Israel. His text was Exodus 1: 7. And the children of Israel were fruitful and increased abundantly, and multiplied, and waxed exceeding mighty ; and the land was filled with them. As Mr. *Nicholas Noyes*, who was an Auditor, and is yet living, lately informed me, Mr. *Parker* was at this time, 1634, principally concerned in beginning *Newbury*, where the learned and Ingenious Mr. *Benjamin Woodbridge, Doctor Twisse's* Successor had part of his Education under his Uncle Parker. *Mary Brown* [now Godfrey] the first-born of Newbury is yet alive: and is become the Mother and Grandmother of many children. And so many have been born after her in the Town, that they make three or four large Assemblies, wherein God is solemnly worshipped every Sabbath. And

' As long as *Plum Island* shall faithfully keep the commanded Post ; Notwithstanding the hectoring words and hard Blows of the proud and boisterous Ocean : As long as any Salmon, or Sturgeon shall swim in the streams of *Merrimack;* or any Perch, or Pickeril in *Crane Pond;* As long as the Sea Fowl shall know the Time of their coming, and not neglect seasonably to visit the Places of their Acquaintance ; As long as any Cattel shall be fed with the Grass growing in the Meadows, which do humbly bow themselves before Turkie-Hill ; As long as any Sheep shall walk upon *Old-Town Hills*, and shall from thence pleas-antly look down upon the River *Parker*, and the fruitful *Marishes* lying beneath ; As long as any free and harmless Doves shall find a White Oak or other Tree within the Township, to perch, or feed, or build a

careless Nest upon; and shall voluntarily present themselves to perform the office of Gleaners after Barley-Harvest; As long as *Nature*
shall not grow Old and dote; but shall constantly remember to give
the rows of Indian Corn their education, by Pairs; So long shall
Christians be born there; and being first made meet, shall from thence
be Translated to be made partakers of the Inheritance of the Saints
in Light. Now, seeing the Inhabitants of *Newbury*, and of *New
England*, upon the due Observance of their Tenure, may expect that
their Rich and gracious LORD will continue and confirm them in the
Possession of these invaluable Privileges: *Let us have grace, whereby
we may serve God acceptably with Reverence and godly Fear, For our
God is a consuming* Fire Hebrews 12: 28, 29.'

The anticipations of the good old man, thus quaintly expressed, have,
I trust, thus far been realized, though sheep no longer walk on 'Old-
town hills,' and 'barley harvest' has ceased to be. The 'three or four
large assemblies,' in 1697, have increased to seventeen, as may be seen
by the following tables, containing the names of the pastors in the
churches in Newbury, Newburyport, and West Newbury.

47

FIRST CHURCH IN NEWBURY.

Names.	Birthplace.	Time.	Graduated.	Settled.	Deceased.	Age.
THOMAS PARKER,	Wilts, Eng.	1595,	Studied at Oxford,	1635,	24 April, 1677,	In 82d year.
JAMES NOYES,	Choulderton,	1608,	do. do.	1635,	22 Oct. 1656,	" 48th "
JOHN WOODBRIDGE,	Stanton,	1613,		1663,	17 Mar. 1695,	" 82d "
JOHN RICHARDSON,	Unknown,	1646,	1666, Harv.	20 Oct. 1675,	27 April, 1696,	" 50th "
CHRISTOPHER TOPPAN, D. D.	Newbury,	25 Dec. 1675,	1691, Harv.	9 Sept. 1696,	23 July, 1747,	" 76th "
JOHN TUCKER, D. D.	Amesbury,	1720,	1741, Harv.	20 Nov. 1745,	22 Mar. 1792,	" 73d "
ABRAHAM MOOR,	Londonderry,	1769,	1789, Dart.	23 Mar. 1796,	24 June, 1801,	" 33d "
JOHN S. POPKIN, D. D.	Boston,		1792, Harv.	9 Sept. 1804,	Resides in Cambridge.	
LEONARD WITHINGTON,	Dorchester,	9 Aug. 1789,	1814, Yale,	31 Oct. 1816,		

SECOND CHURCH IN NEWBURY, NOW FIRST IN WEST NEWBURY.

Names.	Birthplace.	Time.	Graduated.	Settled.	Dismissed.	Deceased.
SAMUEL BELCHER,	Ipswich,	1638,	1659, Harv.	10 Nov. 1698.		10 March, 1715.
JOHN TUFTS,	Medford,		1708, Harv.	30 June, 1714,	2 Mar. 1738,	Aug. 1750.
THO. BARNARD,	Andover,	1716,	1732, Harv.	31 Jan. 1739,	15 Jan. 1751,	5 Aug. 1776.
MOSES HALE,	Newbury,	1715,	1734, Harv.	20 Feb. 1752,		15 Jan. 1779.
TRUE KIMBALL,	Plaistow, N. H.	18 Jan. 1757,	1778, Harv.	20 Nov. 1782,	4 April, 1797.	
SAMUEL TOMB,	Salem, N. Y.	28 Jan. 1766,	1777,	28 Nov. 1798,	Jan. 1808,	D. in Salem, N. Y. 28 Mar. 1832.
EBENEZER HUBBARD,	Marblehead,		1805, Harv.	11 May, 1809,	16 Oct. 1811.	
GILBERT T. WILLIAMS,	Fogs Manor, N. J.	8 Oct. 1761,	1784, Dart.	1 June, 1814,	26 Sept. 1821,	24 Sept. 1824, aged 63.
HENRY C. WRIGHT,	Sharon, Conn.			21 June, 1826,	7 July, 1833.	
BENJAMIN OBER,	Beverly,	4 April, 1805,	Amherst,	1 Jan. 1834,	25 Dec. 1833.	
HENRY AUGUSTUS WOODMAN,	Newburyport,			30 Nov. 1842,		1844.

THIRD CHURCH IN NEWBURY, NOW FIRST IN NEWBURYPORT.

Names.	Birthplace.	Time.	Graduated.	Settled.	Deceased.	Age.
JOHN LOWELL,	Boston,	14 Mar. 1703,	1721, Harv.	19 Jan. 1726,	15 May, 1767,	In 64th year.
THOMAS CARY,	Charlestown,	18 Oct. 1745,	1761, Harv.	11 May, 1768,	24 Nov. 1808,	63.
JOHN ANDREWS,	Hingham,	3 Mar. 1764,	1786, Harv.	10 Dec. 1788,	Resigned May 1, 1830.	
THOMAS B. FOX,	Boston,	20 Aug. 1808,	1828, Harv.	3 Aug. 1831.		

FOURTH CHURCH IN NEWBURY, NOW SECOND IN WEST NEWBURY.

Names.	Birthplace.	Time.	Graduated.	Settled.	Deceased.	Age.
WILLIAM JOHNSON,	Newbury,	31 May, 1706,	1727, Harv.	15 Sept. 1731,	22 Feb. 1772,	In 60th year.
DAVID TOPPAN, D. D.	Manchester,	21 April, 1752,	1771, Harv.	18 April, 1774,	Ap. prof. at Cambridge 1792, and d. 27 Aug. 1803, aged 51.	
LEONARD WOODS, D. D.	Princeton,	19 June, 1774,	1796, Harv.	5 Dec. 1798,	And. Inst. May, 1808.	
JOHN KIRBY,	Middletown, Conn.	30 June, 1783,	1807, Union,	12 June, 1816,	Drowned at Ohrakok bar, N. C. 5 Dec. 1818.	
ELIJAH DEMOND,	Barre,		1816, Dart.	7 Mar. 1821,	22 August, 1826, resigned.	
PAUL COUCH,	Newburyport,	20 June, 1803,	1823, Dart.	21 Mar. 1827,	Resigned 14 August, 1828.	
JOHN Q. A. EDGELL,	Westminster. Vt.	15 Aug. 1802,	1827, Vt. Un.	19 Sept. 1832.		

BYFIELD PARISH CHURCH.

Names.	Birthplace.	Time.	Graduated.	Settled.	Deceased.	Age.
MOSES HALE,	Newbury,	10 July, 1678,	1699, Harv.	17 Nov. 1706,	Jan 1719,	In 66th year.
MOSES PARSONS,	Gloucester,	1715,	1736, Harv.	21 June, 1744,	11 Dec. 1783,	" 68th "
ELIJAH PARISH. D. D.	Lebanon, Conn.	7 Nov. 1762,	1785, Dart.	19 Dec. 1787,	15 Oct. 1825,	" 64th "
ISAAC R. BARBOUR,	Bridport, Vt.	14 Feb. 1794,	1819, Med.	20 Dec. 1827,	Resigned April, 1833.	
HENRY DURANT,	Acton.	18 June, 1802,	1827, Yale.	25 Sept. 1833.		

FIFTH CHURCH IN NEWBURY, AFTERWARD THE FOURTH.

Their first and only minister was the reverend Oliver Noble. He was born in Coventry, Connecticut, in 1736, graduated at Yale, 1757, settled in Newbury 1 Sept. 1762, resigned 7 April, 1784, was afterward resettled in New Castle, N. H., where he died 15 Dec. 1792, aged 56. After the departure of Mr. Noble, nothing effectual was done toward settling another minister, till 1807, when a new society was formed, a new meeting-house was erected in High street, and on the following spring, a new church organized, and a minister settled. It is now called the second church in Newbury.

SECOND CHURCH IN NEWBURY. BELLEVILLE PARISH.

Names.	Birthplace.	Time.	Graduated.	Settled.	Deceased.
JAMES MILTIMORE,	Londonderry, N. H.	4 Jan. 1755,	1774, Harv.	27 Apr. 1808,	25 Mar. 1836, ag. 81.
JOHN C. MARCH,	Newburyport,	9 Oct. 1805,	1825, Yale,	Mar. 1832.	

EPISCOPAL CHURCH, QUEEN ANN'S CHAPEL, NEWBURY.

Names.	Birthplace.	Time,	Settled.	Resigned.	Deceased.
LAMPTON,	England,				
HENRY LUCAS,	England,		1712,	1715,	23 Aug. 1720.
MATTHIAS PLANT,	England,	1691,	Jesus Coll. Camb. 1712, 29 Apr. 1722,	1715,	2 Apr. 1753.

In 1738, St. Paul's church was erected in what is now Newburyport. During the latter part of the reverend Mr. Plant's ministry, and the former part of bishop Bass's, meetings were held in both churches, but in 1766, Queen Ann's chapel was abandoned, as both congregations could more conveniently assemble in St. Paul's church.

ST. PAUL'S CHURCH, NEWBURYPORT.

Names.	Birthplace.	Time.	Graduated.	Settled.	Deceased.
EDWARD BASS, D.D.	Dorchester, Mass.	23 Nov. 1726,	1744, Harv.	1752,	10 Sept. 1803.
JAMES MORSS, D.D.	Newburyport,	25 Oct. 1779,	1800, Harv.	Nov. 1803,	26 April, 1842.
JOHN S. DAVENPORT,	Stamford, Conn.		1833, Yale,	March, 1843,	Resid Nov. 1844.

FIRST PRESBYTERIAN CHURCH IN NEWBURYPORT.

Names.	Birthplace.	Time.	Graduated.	Settled.	Deceased.	Age.
JONATHAN PARSONS,	W. Springfield,	30 Nov. 1705,	1729, Yale,	March, 1746,	19 July, 1776,	71st year.
JOHN MURRAY,	Antrim, Ireland,	22 May, 1742,	Edin. Univ.	4 Jan. 1781,	13 Mar, 1793,	51.
DANIEL DANA, D.D.	Ipswich,	24 July, 1771,	1788, Dart.	19 Nov. 1794,	Resigned 19 Nov. 1820, for pres. of Dart. coll.	
SAMUEL P. WILLIAMS,	Weathersfield,	22 Feb. 1779,	1796, Yale,	8 Feb. 1821.	23 Dec. 1826,	49.
JOHN PROUDFIT, D. D.	Salem, N. Y.	1803,	1821, Union,	4 Oct. 1827.	Resigned Feb. 1833.	
JONATHAN F. STEARNS,	Bedford, Mass.	4 Sept. 1808,	1830, Harv.	16 Sept. 1835.		

TITCOMB STREET CHURCH, THIRD IN NEWBURYPORT.

Names.	Birthplace.	Time.	Graduated.	Settled.	Deceased.	Age.
CHRISTOPHER B. MARSH,	Boston,	11 Oct. 1743,	1761, Harv.	19 Oct. 1768,	3 Dec. 1773,	31st year.
SAMUEL SPRING, D.D.	Uxbridge,	27 Feb. 1746,	1771, Nassau,	6 Aug. 1777,	4 Mar. 1819,	74th "
LUTHER F. DIMMICK,	Shaftesbury, Vt.		1816, Harv.	8 Dec. 1819.		

HARRIS STREET, SECOND PRESBYTERIAN IN NEWBURYPORT.

Names.	Birthplace.	Time.	Graduated.	Settled.	Deceased.	Age.
JOHN BODDILY,	Bristol, England,	12 Apr. 1755,		28 June, 1797,	4 Nov. 1802,	48th year.
JOHN GILES,	Caerlæon, Monmouthshire, Eng.	1758,		20 July, 1803,	28 Sept. 1824,	66th "
WILLIAM FORD,	Scotland,			11 Aug. 1824,	23 Mar. 1826,	Resigned.
DANIEL DANA, D. D.	Ipswich,	24 July, 1771,	1788, Dart.	24 May, 1826,		

TEMPLE STREET CHURCH.

Names.	Birthplace.	Time.	Graduated.	Settled.	Deceased.	Age.
CHARLES W. MILTON,	St. Andrew's Parish, London,	29 Nov. 1767,	Lady Huntingdon's Sem.	20 Mar. 1794,	1 May, 1837.	69.
RANDOLPH CAMPBELL,	Woodbridge, N. J.	31 Dec. 1800,	1809,1829, N. J.	12 Oct. 1837.		

BAPTIST CHURCH, CONGRESS STREET.

This church and society originated in 1804, and the first meeting was held 22 July of that year, when Mr. Joshua Chase officiated. He preached for them till June, 1805, was ordained as evangelist, and went elsewhere. Their first meetings were held in a school-house in Marlborough street. They commenced building their meeting-house in Liberty street, near Newburyport market, April, 1807, which was completed in July, 1808, at an expense of 16,000 dollars. It was destroyed by the great fire in Newburyport, in 1811, and rebuilt in Congress street, in 1812, and enlarged in 1831.

Names.	Birthplace.	Time.	Graduated.	Settled.	Deceased.
JOSHUA CHASE,	Newbury,				
JOHN PEAK,	Walpole, N. H.	26 Sept. 1761,		2 Feb. 1809,	Died in Berwick, 1825.
HOSEA WHEELER,	Dunbarton, N. H.	8 Mar. 1791,		9 Dec. 1818,	Resigned 25 June, 1818.
JOSIAH HOUGHTON,	Waterford, Me.		1811, Dart.	Apr. 1823,	27 Jan. 1823, at Eastport.
NATHANIEL WILLIAMS,	Salem,			2 Nov. 1831,	Dismissed 24 May, 1829.
WILLIAM B. JACOBS,	Pomfret, Conn.		1833, Bro.	27 Oct. 1836,	Dismissed 11 Aug. 1836.
JONATHAN ALDRICH,				21 Apr. 1839,	13 Nov. 1838.
ALBERT N. ARROLD,	Providence,			14 Sept, 1841,	Oct. 1840.
NICHOLAS B. MEDBURY,				29 Jan. 1844.	Dismissed, June 1843.

METHODIST CHURCHES.

There are three methodist churches in ancient Newbury. The first was erected in Adelphi street, Newbury, in 1825. Their first preacher was reverend John Adams, who commenced his labors in 1819. On June twentieth, 1827, a church of fifteen persons was organized in Newburyport by reverend B. Otheman, and their meeting-house dedicated the same day. It stands on the site of the first baptist meeting-house in Liberty street. There is another methodist meeting-house in West Newbury. The preacher in charge at Adelphi street, is the reverend Horace Moulton, from Monson, Mass. The reverend Bradford K. Peirce, a native of Royalton, Vt., a graduate in 1841 from the Wesleyan university, officiates in Liberty street church. In 1834, one hundred and fifty persons were added to the church.

UNIVERSALIST CHURCH, MIDDLE STREET.

The universalist society was incorporated in 1835, their meeting-house in Middle street was built in 1840, and dedicated in October of the same year. Their clergymen have been the reverend Woodbury M. Fernald, from Portsmouth, N. H., reverend Darius Forbes, and the reverend Edwin A. Eaton, from Gloucester, Mass., who is their present pastor.

The preceding notices of the ecclesiastical affairs of Newbury are thus chronologically presented to supply the deficiencies in the former part of the book. A brief sketch of some of the principal actors in the religious and secular concerns of the town with a few incidental remarks, is all that my limits will allow. Prominent among these was the reverend Thomas Parker. He was the only son of the reverend 'renowned Robert Parker, one of the greatest scholars in the English nation.'* He was admitted into Magdalen college, Oxford, but after the exile of his father, he removed unto Dublin, and studied under doctor Usher, thence he went to Holland, 'where doctor Ames favored him.' At the age of twenty-two, seventeen years before he came to America, he wrote and published a treatise on repentance, entitled 'De traductione peccatoris ad vitam,' which was highly celebrated. He also wrote several volumes on the prophecies, of which only one on Daniel was published. After his return to England, he taught 'the free school in Newberry.' 'From thence removing with several devout christians out of *Wiltshire*, into *New England*, he was ordained their *pastor*, at a town, on his and their account called *Newberry*, where he lived many years, by the *holiness*, the *humbleness*, the *charity*, of his life, giving his people a perpetual and most lively commentary on his doctrine.'† 'He was a person of most extensive *charity;* which grain of his temper might contribute unto that largeness in his principles about *church government*, which exposed him unto many *temptations*, amongst his neighbours, who were not so principled.' † Mather thus concludes his notice of him. 'He went unto the *immortals* in the month of April, 1677, about the eighty-second year of his age ; and after he had lived all his days a *single man*, but a great part of his days engaged in *apocalyptical studies*, he went unto the *apocalyptical virgins*, who follow the Lamb whithersoever he goes.' Says his nephew, the reverend Nich-

* Cotton Mather.   † Cotton Mather's Magnalia.

olas Noyes, ' he kept a *school*, as well as preached, at *Newbury*, in *New England*. He ordinarily had about 12 or 14 scholars. He took no pay for his pains, unless any present were freely sent him. Though he was blind, yet such was his memory, that he could in his old age teach *Latin, Greek* and *Hebrew*, very artificially.' Tradition states, ' that some ministers, being dissatisfied with some of his opinions, came to reason with him on those subjects : they addressed him in English, he replied in Latin ; they followed him in Latin, he retired to Greek, and to Hebrew; they pursued ; but in Arabic he stopped them. He then refused to be examined by them.' *

Mr. JAMES NOYES, who was settled as teacher in Newbury with Mr. Parker as pastor, was the son of a minister, who married a sister of Mr. Robert Parker, and was, of course, a nephew of Mr. Thomas Parker. ' They taught in one school [in England ;] came over in *one ship;* were pastor and teacher of *one church;* and Mr. Parker continuing always in celibacy, they lived in *one house,* till death separated them for a time.' †

For a few years after the settlement of the town, their residence was on the west side of the lower green, but, on the removal of the meeting-house, Mr. Noyes built a house in what is now called Parker street. It is still standing, and owned by one of his descendants, Mr. Silas Noyes, and is one of the oldest houses in Newbury. Of Mr. James Noyes, his uncle Parker thus writes :

' Mr. James Noyes, my worthy colleague in the ministry of the gospel, was a man of singular qualifications, in piety excelling, an implacable enemy to all heresie and schism, and a most able warriour against the same. He was of a reaching and ready apprehension, a large invention, a most profound judgment, a rare and tenacious, and comprehensive memory, fixed and unmovable in his grounded conceptions; sure in words and speech without rashness ; gentle and mild in all his expressions, without all passion or provoking language. And as he was a notable disputant, so he never would provoke his adversary, saving by the short knocks and heavy weight of argument. He was of so loving, and compassionate, and humble carriage, that I believe never were any acquainted with him, but did desire the continuance of his society and acquaintance. He was resolute for truth, and in defence thereof, had no respect to any persons. He was a most excellent counsellor in doubts, and could strike at an hair's breadth, like the *Benjamites,* and expedite the entangled out of the briars. He was courageous in dangers, and still was apt to believe the best, and made fair weather in a storm. He was much honored and esteemed in the country, and his death was much bewailed. I think he may be reckoned among the greatest worthies of the age.'†

In reference to the celibacy of Messrs. Parker and his nephew, the reverend Nicholas Noyes, of Salem, some person thus speaks. ' Salem, December thirteenth, 1717. A specimen of New England celibacy.

' Though Rome blaspheme the marriage bed
And vows of single life has bred
Chaste *Parker*, Stoughton, Brinsmade, *Noyes,*
Show us the odds 'twixt force and choice.
These undefiled contracted *here,*
Are gone to heaven and married *there.*'

Next in order comes Mr. JOHN WOODBRIDGE, son of the reverend John Woodbridge who married a daughter of Robert Parker. ' Our

---

* Reverend doctor Popkin.   † Magnalia.

young Woodbridge with the consent of his parents, undertook a voyage to New England in the year 1634 ; and the company and assistance of his worthy uncle Mr. Thomas Parker, was not the least encouragement of his voyage.'* He was then twenty-two years of age, and brought with him a younger brother Benjamin, of whom see page 350. His farm was north of Green street, Newbury, and his house stood on the east side of the pond on the upper green. In 1641 he married Mercy Dudley, a daughter of governor Thomas Dudley. He was ordained September sixteenth, 1644, the first minister of Andover, and was the first teacher ever ordained in this country. In 1647 he returned to England, where all his children but the first two were born, and preached in Andover and other places, till his return to Newbury, July twenty-sixth, 1663, and here preached for a short time. Of his eleven adult children, three, John, Timothy, and Benjamin, were clergymen, and of his descendants, forty-three by the name of Woodbridge have received a liberal education. For his eulogy see Mather's Magnalia. His wife Mercy died July first, 1691, aged seventy. No monuments to the memory of these distinguished men are now to be found in the burying ground where their dust reposes. On the monument erected in memory of the successor of Mr. Parker, is the following inscription.

' A Resurrection to immortality—is here expected—for what was mortal—of the Reverend Mr. JOHN RICHARDSON (once Fellow of Harvard College, afterwards Teacher to the Church of Newbury) putt off Apr. 27 1696 in the fiftieth year of his age.

' When Preachers dy, the Rules the pulpit gave,
To live well are still preached from the grave.
The Faith & Life, which your dead Pastor taught
In one grave with him, Syrs bury not.

' Abi, Viator.
A Mortuo disce vivere moriturus
E Terris disce cogitare de Cœlis.'

Or in English : ' Go, Traveler : From the dead learn to live, as one that must die. From the earth learn to think of the Heavens.'

He married Mary Pierson, of Cambridge, October twenty-eighth, 1673.

On the monument of his successor is the following.

' Here lyes the Body of the Rev. Mr. CHRISTOPHER TOPPAN, Master of Arts, fourth Pastor of the First Church in Newbury; a Gentleman of good Learning, conspicuous Piety and Virtue, shining both by his Doctrine and Life, skilled and greatly improved in the Practice of Physiek and Surgery, who deceased July 23, 1747, in the 76th year of his age and the 51st of his Pastoral Office.'

Dr. Toppan was a man of talents, energy and decision of character, and ' would speak his mind.' A specimen of this latter trait may be seen on page 213. Other instances might be given, but I shall mention only one. A Mr. —— and his wife once presented a child for baptism. Not having confidence in the man's sincerity, he addressed the congregation in these words, while performing the rite, ' I baptize this child wholly on the woman's account.' In the latter part of his life he was at times partially deranged, and on one occasion, as I have been credibly informed, carried a whip into the church under his cloak,

* Mather's Magnalia.

in order, as he said, to scourge out the enthusiasts, or 'schemers,' as he called them, during the period of the excitement at the time of the 'great revival' and its incidental extravagancies. On one occasion he sent the following note of thanks to the officiating clergyman of the parish. It is accurately copied from the original, and was probably written during a period of partial derangement.

'Christopher Toppan desires to return thanks to God for his goodness to him in preserving of him, when the Devil cast a mist before his and his horse's eyes, throwing of him down, being in great danger, butt God in his good providence and his Angels garding of him out of the hand of the Devil, and after this I could not rest night nor day thinking of it what the Cause should be till Fryday morning it was revealed to me that it was because I oposed that great work of the Devil. It seemed that the voyce came to me and said I need not truble myself, it was that Devil did it and Deseaved all the people, and now I hope God will enable me to oppose that great work of the Devil and the Instruments of it more than ever I did.'

The following hitherto unpublished letter, written much earlier, is inserted as a better specimen of the author's style. It was addressed to judge Sewall.

Aug. 11, 1721.

'Hon. Sir.
'Please to pardon my boldness for troubling you to read a few lines more. That expression in my writing. which your Honor intimated, you did not well understand, namely, That the Indians should have convenient Lands allowed ym for themselves and posterity, I meant thus, that in case it be found that the Indians formerly disposed of so much of their Land as that they have not left Lands convenient for themselves, that then so much as may be thought proper, of what was purchased of them should be relinquished to them again. Further to open what I intend I would offer a few things.
'1. That the Indians were the first Proprietors of the Lands in this Country.
'2. That they had in themselves power to dispose of and convey away said Lands.
'3. That what lands they formerly sold and conveyed away they can have no just claim unto. Now I make no doubt but as your Honor says, they have as full and firm a Right to their Lands. as any which men have to theirs, but then I presume your Honor means, Lands they have not sold.
'4. That if through Imprudence and Inadvertency they have conveyed away so much of their Land to the English, as that, if what be conveyed away, be taken up and settled by the English, there be not convenient places left for themselves and posterity, I think it very agreeable to Reason and Religion, that the Government take care that such places as may be thought convenient be allowed them and Recompense made to such Persons (whose Predecessors formerly purchased said Land of the Indians) of Province Lands elsewhere.
'5. That the Government, having offered and done what may reasonably be thought just and fair on this score, that then, if the Indians continue their Insolent Carriages, the English may justly commence a warr against them and expect God's blessing to be with them in their Endeavours to subdue them, and in the mean time, that the English in the Eastern parts may be secure and safe I see no way but for the Government to keep out some hundreds of men, or a sufficient number to keep the Indians in awe till the People are become strong enough to defend themselves, which they would in a few years be, were they compelled to settle regularly, and secured from fear and danger by a sufficient Army kept in a body in those parts well provided with snow-shoes for the Winter and a sufficient number of whale-boats for passage by water in the Summer—but let me not forget to mention here that I can but think it a duty to make a further offer of the Gospel to them and by degrees to Instill into their minds the true Doctrines of Religion. doubtless some of them might be gained, more especially if the Fryers could be fairly removed from among them. I went the last Spring to the Eastward and being at Damariscotta on a Sabbath day, there a Family there and several Persons besides, I preacht to them both forenoon and afternoon, and there being hard by an Indian wigwam, belonging to it a Netop and his squaw, he about seventy, and she near an hundred years of age, not able to stand or goe, both maintained by a Kinsman, a young pretty fellow, who went a hunting and returned once a week or fortnight and brought them provisions to live upon—The old Sannop came of his own accord on the Sabbath day to hear the word preacht and gave diligent attention. The

48

subject I insisted on was that in Romans 10. 13. ' And whosoever shall call on the name of the Lord shall be saved' and in the application I applyed myself to the Indian, shewing that their nation if they call aright on the name of the Lord should be saved as well as the English. The next day I went to his Wigwam. He told me 'very good speak-um yesterday' and desired me to speak to his squaw 'all one I speak yesterday for that very good.' — I went several times to his Wigwam and gave the best advice I could to the poor old Woman. She seemed to understand what I said, but was not seemingly so much affected therewith as her husband. The day I came away he came on board the vessel and prayed me to goe once more to his Wigwam and speak to his old Squaw about Gód and Christ and Heaven, for may be, me never see her any more. So I went again and at my coming away, the old man took me by the hand expressing a great deal of thankfulness for the counsel and advice I had given his Squaw. In my discourse with the old man I used to mention and open the Articles of the Christian Religion, which he always readily assented unto, and I am persuaded that by prudent methods in managing of them sundry of them might be wrought upon, and amongst other methods I have thought — but why should I presume to dictate to any, who know much better than myself what will best serve the Interests of our gracious Lord, in whose service that I may be found faithful, let me have your prayers, as you have his, who is, Sir, your most humble servant,

CHRISTOPHER TOPPAN.'

To the difficulties which attended and followed the settlement of the reverend JOHN TUCKER, the colleague and successor of doctor Toppan, some allusion has been made, pages 215, 16. His published works amount to twenty-two, many of them controversial and defensive. ' These affairs,' says the reverend doctor Popkin, 'he met with firmness and strength of mind, and a portion of native wit, which he appears to have reserved for such occasions. His sermons are very serious, solid and perspicuous.' In the latter part of his ministry 'he enjoyed much quietness, and always the high esteem of his friends in this and other places; and those, who differed from him in sentiment, bare witness to his good life and conversation.' ' His epitaph records his character and the esteem of his friends.'

' Beneath are the remains of the Rev. John Tucker, D. D. Pastor of the first Church and Congregation in this Town; who died March 22d, 1792 Ætat 73 — Blessed with strong mental powers, a liberal education, and an uncommon mildness of Temper; all directed and improved by that faith, which purifies the heart; rendered him dearly beloved in every Relation in which he was placed; and more especially made him conspicuously useful as a Minister of the Gospel. When meeting with peculiar Difficulties, he eminently complied with that direction of his Master to the first Preachers of his Gospel; Be ye wise as serpents, and harmless as doves. As he lived a life of piety, he met death with serenity. — By his doctrine and example he taught 'the humility, and at his death he exhibited the dignity and triumph, of the real Christian.' ' To perpetuate the memory of so excellent a character, and as a testimony of their affectionate regard, the bereaved flock have erected this Sepulchral Stone.'

No monument has as yet been erected to the memory of Mr. MOOR, 'who,' says the reverend doctor Popkin, 'was a man of genius, as well as goodness.' He was the son of deacon Moor, of Londonderry, New Hampshire.

The first settled minister in the second parish, now the first, in West Newbury, was the reverend SAMUEL BELCHER. Of him, much to the supposed discredit of the parish, the story has been often told that when he grew old, and unable to preach, his parishioners cast him off and *carted* him back to Ipswich, his native place. The facts are these. He was settled, as was then the custom, as their pastor for life, with this proviso, that if he remained in town, he should have the use of the parsonage-house and land as long as he lived, but if he chose to leave town, they should revert to the use of the parish.

Preferring, when no longer able to preach, to spend the few remaining days of his pilgrimage in his native place, he relinquished the use of the parsonage, and had his goods and furniture put into an ox-cart for removal. He then said to his friends, 'if you will place the beds in the cart properly, I will ride with the goods, as I can go that way easier than any other.' This was accordingly done, the old gentleman placed on the bed, and, at his own request, he was literally carted out of town. This, in the absence of any thing, in that day, like a chaise, or any other modern vehicle, was undoubtedly the easiest and most comfortable mode, in which he could be conveyed home, and should never be mentioned as a transaction at all discreditable to the persons thus engaged. In the Boston News-Letter of 1715, I find the following:

'*Ipswich, March 12th*, 1714-15.
'This day we buried Rev. Samuel Belcher in a good old age having lived near 76 years. He was for many years a preacher of the gospel at the Isle of Shoals and afterward settled at Newbury. His religion was pure and undefiled. His divinity sound and orthodox, his conversation very cheerful and agreeable, yet grave withal. But that which highly distinguished him in his order was his excellent gift in preaching, nothing being more entertaining than his ordinary sermons. Like a well instructed scribe, as he was, he always brought forth things new and old, profitable and pleasant.
'*Omne tulit punctum, qui miscuit utile dulci.* A few months before his death he removed to Ipswich, the place of his birth.'

Of the successors of Mr. Belcher, I have seen no monuments or epitaphs, as only one of them, the reverend Moses Hale, died in Newbury.

On the monument, erected on 'burying hill,' in Newburyport, to the memory of the reverend JOHN LOWELL, is the following inscription:

'Here lies buried the body of the Rev. John Lowell, M. A. late pastor of the Congregational Society in Newburyport. He was born in Boston March 14, 1703, educated at Harvard in the University of Cambridge, where he took his degree anno 1721, and was settled in the sacred ministry of the gospel Jan. 19, 1726. He was a gentleman well skilled in the learned languages, of great reading and extensive knowledge, and of conspicuous piety and virtue, and of talents peculiarly adapted to the ministerial office. While he lived, he was highly respected and beloved by his people, for whose welfare he had a tender and affectionate concern, and was honored and greatly lamented by them when he died, which was on Friday morning May 15 1767 in the 64th year of his age and 42d of his pastoral office.
'This monument, erected to his memory by the unanimous voice of the people of his charge, testifies to the world their grateful remembrance of his faithful services.'

On the monument to the memory of the reverend THOMAS CARY, is the following:

'Sacred to the memory of the Rev. Thomas Cary, A. M. Senior Pastor of the First Religious Society in Newburyport. He was born in Charlestown, Mass. 18 Oct. 1745, educated at Harvard, 1761, settled 11 May, 1768, and died 24 Nov. 1808. A man of strong comprehensive and improved mind, of active and extended benevolence, engaging manners, fervent piety and inflexible integrity. A preacher, plain, evangelical, earnest and pathetic. Deeply impressed with the importance of his office, he spoke with dignity, force and feeling, enlightening the understandings of his hearers and warming their hearts. A firm believer in the religion he taught, it was his support and consolation, the rule of his life and the ground of his hope. A good and respected citizen, a kind husband, a most affectionate father and a most ardent friend. He was just, candid and sincere, charitable without ostentation, affable without pride, proving his faith by his works, and looking to Jesus for his reward.
'In the 42d year of his age, it pleased God to take him off his labors by a stroke of the palsy.

'Twenty years he languished under the pressure of infirmities, but he was patient and God rewarded him.

'Though his usefulness was diminished, his friends never forgot him. To the last he had their warmest affections, their reverence and their sympathy. He felt this and was happy. His sufferings had prepared him for his departure. The messenger came at midnight and he was ready. God will remember his servant at the last day.'

On the grave-stone erected in West Newbury to the memory of the reverend WILLIAM JOHNSON, is the following inscription :

'Rev. William Johnson was born in Newbury 31 May, 1706, graduated at Harvard 1727, ordained 15 Sept. 1731, and died 22 Feb. 1772 in his 66th year.

'He was a gentleman of good understanding, of uniform piety and virtue, of a very amiable temper, tender and affectionate in his family connections, a benevolent and faithful friend.'

The reverend MOSES HALE, who was settled in Byfield parish in 1706, 'labored in word and doctrine' with the people of his charge from 1702, 'about 41 years, during which term he was an orthodox and lively preacher of the great truths of religion and a soldier of Jesus Christ.' Prince's Christian History, volume first, page 382.

On the tomb erected to the memory of the reverend MOSES PARSONS, is the following inscription :

'To the memory of the Rev. Moses Parsons, late Pastor of the church of Christ in this Parish, who died Dec. 14, 1783 in the 68th of his age and in the 40th year of his ministry.

'Farewell, blest man ! soon may we meet again
In climes celestial, free from toil and pain,
Where joys eternal swell the pious heart,
And worth like thine shall meet its just desert,
Where thou, dear saint, art flown, by Jesus lov'd,
By angels welcom'd and by God approv'd.'

'Erected in memory of Rev. ELIJAH PARISH, who was ordained Pastor of the congregation in this place Dec. 20, 1787 and who died Oct. 15, 1825 aged 63 years. Also in memory of Mrs. Mary Parish, who died May 20th 1831 aged 64 years.
''Saved by grace,' they rest from their labors and their works do follow them.'

In addition to what has already been said concerning MR. PLANT, I make a few extracts from the reverend doctor Morss's century sermons, and from Mr. Plant's private journal, which have not hitherto been published.

'Mr. Plant at the commencement of his duty Nov. 1722 drew up articles to be a standing order, by which the Parishioners shall proceed for the good Regulating and ordering of the Affairs of the Church for future and that nothing should be allowed or added to them without the consent of the Minister.' * This was signed by eighteen persons, who the doctor supposes 'must have enjoyed advantages of early education, and to have been above the common class of free holders, because their names are in their own hand writing, and are all written in a fair and legible hand,' an inference altogether erroneous, and which a more extended acquaintance with the chirography of that period would not have induced him to make.

'Mr. Plant appears to have been a man of strict integrity, of a high

* Dr. Morss's century sermons.

sense of decorum, and of the distinctive rights of the Clergy and Laity. He was exact and methodical; punctual in the discharge of the duties of his station; and anxious that Clergy and Laity should move in their distinct sphere without interference.' *

During the period of the difficulties that had arisen between Mr. Plant and the proprietors of St. Paul's church, some one of them had written to the society in England complaining that his habit was not canonical. To this complaint he makes a reply to doctor Bearcroft, June twenty-fifth, 1742, from which I extract the following:

'You inform me of a complaint made against me that I even officiate in the Church with a coloured handkerchief round my neck instead of a band. Moreover you say it was with some difficulty that you prevented the complaint from being laid before the society. . . . It is a little surprizing that the author of it should stoop so low, or at least be so malicious as to notice my habit without first giving me notice that it was offensive to him. . . . . I never once in my whole time of preaching here, went to Church to officiate without a band, nor do I remember the time when I ever wore a speckled handkerchief, nor any other about my neck in time of divine service, nay I never buried an infant in the most tempestuous weather without a band, though I have rode several miles to perform it.' In another letter to the same person, alluding to other difficulties, he thus writes, 'Mr. Mossom of Marblehead says there are but three old England clergymen in these parts viz. Mr. Harris, myself and you (viz. Mr. Plant) and these fellows † are going home for orders and they will get the best places in the country and take the bread from off our trenchers. There is the new church in Boston. Of right it first belongs to Mr. Harris. If he refuses, to myself, and next to you, but they make no offer of it to any of us, and we that have served the church must serve the church as we have, and take up with their leavings. We now who have stood the brunt of the battle and laid the foundation of the churches in this country are not so much as consulted, who shall be their minister. Mr. Harris is resolved to write to my Lord Bishop to oppose their ordination, and I'll join with him and am come up to acquaint you with it and we would have you join with us for a three-fold cord is not easily broken. I answered him, I do not know whether I may be permitted to say as Moses once said 'I wish to God they were all the Lord's people. but I think we are right, and therefore I'll say that were all church ministers and church people in these conditions, I would cheerfully resign up my salary and dig for my bread. Had Mr. Mossom sent these zealous expressions to the Society I suppose the venerable members would not from thence draw the conclusion that I was willing to resign my £60 a year to Dr. Cutler and take up digging and hoeing 6 days for my bread, and preach on the seventh day for nothing.'

'Notwithstanding all the contempt showed me by the water-side people, and the slight and so forth, I have had honor done me by the leading gentlemen in these parts. His Excellency Gov. Shute did me the honour to come to my church and carry me with him in his coach. His Honour Gov. Wentworth frequently attended the Holy Communion. His Excellency Gov. Burnet the first time I had the honour to wait on him, told me he intended to be at my church at such a day. and said can you any where thereabout lodge me and provide hay for my horses. I told him I did not know of any person near my church that could entertain better than myself. His Excellency Gov. Belcher generously offered me the honour of nominating two persons in my church one for a justice, the other for a coroner. And in the time of his government there was application made by some gentlemen to him for his interest to get an act passed in their behalf. they knowing it would meet with great difficulty, it being thrice attempted and as often rejected, he promised them his interest, but withal recommended it to them to apply to some person, who had a prevailing interest in that government. They asked his Excellency to recommend them to such a person: he replyed, if you can make Mr. Plant your friend, he will get the act passed for you, for Mr. Plant has the best interest of any person I know of in the Government. The General Assembly did me the honour to pass it at my representation. . . . . If I would relate the whole of this affair, I believe, Rev. Sir, you would allow it a great honour done me. . . . . Likewise at all times of performing divine service at Kittery, I had a large audience, and gentlemen of Portsmouth did me the honour to attend there. . . . . The people of Kittery refused to admit Mr. Brown into

---

* Dr. Morss's century sermons.

† This alludes to a consultation which had been held on the subject of sending over candidates for orders, one of whom probably was intended to officiate in St. Paul's church.

their church, before they had took my advice and asked my consent. . . . . . To conclude boasting. the last time I was at Portsmouth, I waited on the Governor and some leading gentlemen about an affair, that is too long to relate. . . . . I took my leave of the Governor, upon which he said to me, Mr. Plant, you will stay and dine with me. I excused myself—but says his Excellency it shall never be said you came to Piscataqua and not dine with me. If these things will not satisfy you that I have both honour and friendship with these gentlemen I must conclude myself to fail. I can't conclude this long letter without adding one remarkable instance of my hearty affection and zeal, shewed in a publick manner for the honour of the church. It happened to be at the house of Gov. Belcher on one of the princesses' birth days. Several gentlemen being present were invited to dine with the Governor. His Excellency says to Capt. Atkins: ' When did you see my mother Partridge ? How does she do?' Capt. A. replyed ' I saw her on Sunday in the afternoon at Mr. Lowell's meeting.' Says the Gov. you call *ours* the *meeting*, and *yours* the *church*, but you should call *ours* the *church* and *yours* the *meeting*. He added when I was in England I waited on Viscount Townsend and talking on the state of the church in New England, said his Lordship, I suppose you call the church people dissenters there, and yours the church, as we here call *ours* the *church*, and *you* the dissenters, so that we are the church and *you* are the *dissenters* says the Governor. Dr. Harwood the assistant at the King's chapel, being my senior, I waited to see what answer he would return to his Excellency's speech (resolving it should not want an answer) every person present being silent. and Mr. Harwood and Esqr. Atkins, the only two persons of the church being seemingly thunderstruck, I thus addressed myself to the Governor. May it please your Excellency, I do not know what my Lord Townsend may say to you in his chamber, nor what his opinion was in his study, but if he expressed himself in these terms to your Excellency, his opinion was in direct opposition to the Lords Justices, who in their letter to Lt. Gov. Dummer ordered their Secretary to inform him that they had no regular establishment of any church in this Province; neither have you said I, to the Governor any other establishment. but what is on the same footing with other sectaries, viz. the act of toleration. I went on very warmly for 2 or 3 minutes, but the Governor put a stop to me, Mr. Plant, I'll not dispute the matter with you, ' nor I with your Excellency.' When Mr. Harwood and myself returned from the Gov's. house, I asked him whether he took notice of the affront he attempted to put upon two Clergymen in their habit. He said 'yes.' I asked him why he did not give the Gov. an answer? He said to me, I do not give myself any trouble about these things; the Gov. is kind to me and I dine with him two or three times a week and when I want a good dinner I always go there. I am always welcome, and you cannot help yourself, if they do say so of you. What signifies it for you to show your resentment. They do not in England mind us that are here. I then said to Mr. Harwood I am sorry you are tyed so fast by the teeth as not to resent such a designed affront as that was. For my own part I will eat bread and cheese so long as I live before I'll sneak to the Gov. for a dinner, and at his table hear myself called a Dissenter, and my Church represented a Conventicle.'

Mr. Plant concludes his letter thus: ' I do most humbly and earnestly entreat the Right Rev. members . . . . to recommend it to these gentlemen . . . to look on me as their minister and treat me as such, that they would come to pay me a visit — that every thing on their part should be buried in oblivion and I should do the same on my part, to be confirmed by the usual compliment of mutually and cordially shaking of hands. If the Right honorable members would be pleased to grant my request in some such form of direction to them, the matter would I think be justly stated on both sides, and there would be no foundation for the gentlemen to say in a domineering way, ' We have got the better of Plant at the Society, the Society have ordered Plant to allow our minister £20 and if we can but get the money (as is a common expression with them) we do not care what becomes of Plant.' Such expressions must be grating to a generous mind. I entreat that what I have written may find favor and not blame with the Society. If they would condescend to answer the request of their missionary in some such sort, it would be satisfactory, but if it cannot be obtained, be pleased to send me their directions and they shall be cheerfully and readily obeyed by Rev. Sirs your most obedient

' MATTHIAS PLANT.'

In another letter dated twenty-third October, 1747, he says ' I was desired to attend a meeting of the church and all the proprietors. — I told them the Society had allotted to me the honour of being the chief minister of the whole parish, and of annually paying an assistant £20 sterling, but that I might be the minister of the whole parish, it would be necessary they should induct me into the church, and desired the church wardens, vestry and proprietors to give me induction. They said there was no occasion for it, and asked me of what service it could be to me. I told them it gave me a right to the desk and pulpit, that none could officiate in the church or parish. This they refused to give. . . . How, says I, can I be the chief minister of the whole parish, if I have no privilege to act in your parish or officiate in your church without asking your leave every time I come. Capt. —— said they would not allow me to be their minister, or to have any thing to do in their parish. They would sometimes give me leave to preach in their new church. . . . . . They said they would neither give me nor any other clergyman, whom they might hereafter have, a power to keep out a minister, whom they should wish to hear. It was their own property, and they would invite whom they pleased to preach. . . . . I am not bound to sacrifice the good discipline of the church, which these gentlemen are endeavouring to wrest from me. . . . This usurpation would soon diffuse itself into an universal precedent in the churches to their told ruin.' During the continuance of this dispute Mr. Plant notices in many places the smallness of the audiences in St. Paul's church. Thus: June twenty-second, 1746, preached at St. Paul's church and had only ten men 'belonging to the church there. July 26 A. M. 9 men, P. M. 10 men. 12 Oct. had 7 men and one woman. 17 Nov. 1745, A. M. 10 men and 2 women. P. M 13 men and 2 women.' He thus speaks of the treatment he received from some of his opponents. 'If they met me in the street, or saw me nigh to them, some of them would turn their backs, or glower with their eyes from under their hats, or give it a little nugg with their hands and sneeringly walk off.'

These extracts from Mr. Plant's journal, which I copied from the original, and of which many more pages might be given, are strikingly characteristic of the state of society at that period, and of the great importance attached to an acquaintance with the rich, the titled, and the great. To shake hands with a 'squire, or to be familiar with a judge, was an honor never to be forgotten, but to dine with a governor, was a distinction confined to a favored few, and worthy of perpetual remembrance. Burns in one of his poems gives us some idea of his feelings of exaltation when

> 'On a ne'er to be forgotten day,
> So far he sprackled up the brae,*
> He dinner'd with a Lord!'

It was not until five years after the date of this letter, which very clearly explains the subject of contest between Mr. Plant and the proprietors, that the difficulties were settled by their acceding to Mr. Plant's demands. On June twenty-fourth, 1751, Mr. Plant became the chief minister of the whole parish, and on December twenty-third, 1751, he made choice of Mr. Edward Bass as his assistant, allowing him twenty pounds per annum. In 1752 Mr. Bass went to England for orders, and took with him a letter signed F. Miller, from which I extract the following.

'REV. SIR.— The bearer, Mr. Bass is a young gentleman, bred at Harvard College, and has preached for some time among the dissenters to good acceptance, but now,

* Clambered up a hill.

upon mature consideration, thinks it his duty to conform to the church of England, and come over for holy orders, and to be appointed to the new church in Newbury. Both Mr. Plant and the people are highly pleased with him, and indeed he is universally spoken of as a man of piety and sense, a good preacher and of an agreeable temper. He brings full testimonials from the college, where he has lived, I think about ten years, which are confirmed by the clergy of Boston &c. A person so qualified and recommended can never want your favor and assistance,' &c.

On the monument erected to the memory of bishop Bass, is a Latin inscription, of which the following is a translation, copied from a note in a sermon, preached by the reverend James Morss in 1811.

' Beneath this stone are interred the remains of the Right Rev. Edward Bass D. D. Bishop of Mass. and R. I. He was born at Dorchester near Boston 23 Nov. 1726, was admitted member of Harvard College, aged 13, received the honors of the University 1744, and was soon after inducted to the pastoral care of St. Paul's Church in this town, of which he was rector 51 years, during which time he always supported an unspotted character and discharged the duties of his office with uncommon fidelity and exactness. He was a man of distinguished virtue, uncommon humility, great modesty and sincere piety and was firmly attached to the cause of religion. He was remarkable for his urbanity and placidness of disposition and for his venerable and dignified manner. He thus became the tender husband, the instructive and agreeable companion, the warm and lasting friend, the true and faithful monitor. He united the character of a sound divine, an erudite scholar, a polished gentleman and devout christian. The tears of an affectionate people bear the best testimony to his superior virtue, and upon their hearts is his memory more durably engraved than upon the hardest marble.
' The just rest from their labors and their works follow them.'

The following inscription is engraved on the monument erected in memory of the reverend JAMES MORSS.

' Erected in memory of the Rev. James Morss D. D., who for 39 years was the beloved rector of St Paul's Church. He was born in Newburyport 25 Oct. 1779, graduated at Harvard College 1800, was chosen rector of this church in 1803 and remained with his attached people until his decease, which took place Apr. 26, 1842.
' Mr. Morss was a sound divine, and to his devotion to the church was added a zeal for her interests, and a moral courage in her defence never excelled. In his deportment were blended the courtesies of the gentleman with the graces of the christian. He was distinguished in all the sweet charities of social life, the tender father, the faithful friend, yet none shone more prominent than his kindly care for the widow and orphan. Their tears embalm his memory, and the prayers of an affectionate people rise as incense to the throne of grace.
' This is his record on high.'

The society, of which the reverend JONATHAN PARSONS was the first pastor, had its origin in the time of the great excitement, produced by the labors of Edwards, Whitefield, and others, one of whom was the reverend Joseph Adams, who preached to the new society, consisting at first of only twelve families, until by the advice and recommendation of Whitefield, Mr. Parsons was called from Lyme, Connecticut, (where he had been settled as a minister, from March, 1731, till October, 1745,) to take charge of the new society. In November of the same year, he came to Newbury, and took the charge of the congregation in March, 1746. In his journal he thus writes: ' I found a number of serious Christians in the congregation, which I came to visit, who appeared to be understanding, solid, and in some measure established in the main points of Christian doctrine. But many others appeared of an Antinomian turn, full of vain confidence, self-conceit, false affections &c., and some that were the greatest Christians in their own esteem, appeared to be worldly and covetous.'

In this church and congregation, which from small beginnings arose to be one of the most numerous on the continent, Mr. Parsons labored with great diligence and success until his death in 1776, when he was buried by the side of his friend Mr. Whitefield, beneath the pulpit which he had for so many years occupied. From Mr. Searl's funeral sermon on the death of Mr. Parsons, I make the following extract.

'He was a faithful and vigilant pastor; applying himself with great care to the wants of his people, both in public and in private. The success attending his ministry was great. During his residence at Lyme, he entertained charitable hopes that near 200 persons were savingly converted; and in Newburyport also, he had the satisfaction of seeing large accessions made to the church through his instrumentality.'

The reverend JOHN MURRAY, the successor of Mr. Parsons, commenced preaching in his native country, Ireland, at the age of eighteen. Before he was twenty years of age, he came to America, was first settled in Philadelphia, then in Boothbay, Me., where he remained eight years. In 1779, he came to Newburyport, where, at a public lecture January fourth, 1781, he was 'recognized by the presbyterian church and congregation to be their minister.' On the monument erected to his memory, is the following inscription :

'This monument is erected to the memory of the reverend John Murray, A. M., late pastor of the Presbyterian Society in this town, who was born in Ireland 22 May, 1742, and died 13 March, 1793.

'Pause reader! and silently muse over the remains of a man, in whom were united the tender husband, the faithful father, the instructive companion, the obliging friend, the animated preacher, and the able defender of the gospel. His death was triumphant.'

The inscription on the monument erected to the memory of Mr. WILLIAMS, is the following :

'The Rev. Samuel P. Williams was born in Wethersfield Conn. 22 Feb. 1779, graduated at Yale College 1796, ordained in Marsfield, Conn. 1 Jan. 1807, removed from Marsfield 7 Sept. 1817, installed 8 Feb. 1821 and died 23 Dec. 1826. His ancestors were the people of God. He was a preacher of the gospel. Let his hearers, if they would honor him, obey that gospel.

'And if in life he tried in vain to save,
O let them hear him preaching from the grave.'

Epitaph in memory of reverend CHRISTOPHER B. MARSH.

'Beneath are the remains of the Rev. Christopher B. Marsh the only son of Deac. Daniel Marsh of Boston and the much beloved and lamented Pastor of the North Church in this town. He exchanged this mortal for an endless life Dec. 3, 1773, aged 30 years and 2 months, having little more than completed the fifth year of his ministry. He was a hard student, a good scholar, a great christian, a deep, yet plain and pungent preacher, a meek, humble and prudent Pastor. His whole life blameless and exemplary, his ministry, tho' short, was important, conveying much instruction and bearing a noble testimony to the great doctrines of God's grace. His grateful flock to shew their respect to his memory, erect this monument.

'The Reverend man, let all things mourn;
Sure he was some atherial mind,
Fated in flesh to be confined,
And ordered to be born,
His soul was of the angelic frame ;
The same ingredients, and the mould the same
When the Creator makes a minister of flame.
He was all formed of heavenly things,
Mortals, believe what my Urania sings,
For she hath seen him rise upon his flamy wings.'

Epitaph in memory of the reverend SAMUEL SPRING, D. D.

' In memory of the Rev. Samuel Spring, born at Uxbridge 27 Feb. 1746, graduated at Nassau 1771, ordained Pastor of the North Church, 6 Aug. 1777, and died 4 March, 1819, in his 74th year. A man of original and vigorous mind, distinguished for a deep sense of human depravity, specially for his own unworthiness, and for exalted views of the character and perfections of God and the Redeemer; of great integrity, firmness, benevolence and urbanity; an able, faithful and assiduous Pastor, an ensample to the flock, over which he was placed, an affectionate husband, a tender father, a sincere friend. He was a Visitor of the Theological Seminary at Andover from its commencement, President of the Mass. Missionary Society Vice Pres. of the American Board of Commissioners for Foreign Missions and in most of the other important offices of the other benevolent societies around him. He lived eminently useful and died universally lamented. In testimony of the grateful estimation with which the memory of their Pastor is cherished, this monument is erected by the bereaved and afflicted church and congregation.

' The righteous shall be held in everlasting remembrance.'

On the monument erected to the memory of the reverend JOHN BODDILY, is the following inscription:

' The Rev. John Boddily was born in England, educated at Lady Huntingdon's College and came to America 1795. This church was founded that year. He was an affectionate evangelical preacher of the gospel. He died 4 Nov. 1802, aged 47 years.'

On that to the memory of the reverend JOHN GILES, is the following:

' Here lies interred the remains of the Rev. John Giles for twenty two years Pastor of the Second Presbyterian church in this town. He died 28 Sept. 1822 aged 66.'

On the marble pyramid erected to the memory of the reverend CHARLES W MILTON, is the following:

' This monument is erected to the memory of the Rev. Charles William Milton, born in London 29 Nov. 1767, educated for the gospel ministry by Lady Huntingdon, he was ordained a missionary in Spa Field's Chapel, London 17 Feb. 1788, commenced the work of the ministry in the British Provinces in America, invited to this town by the Rev. John Murray, he accepted the invitation to become the Pastor of a new church, called the fourth church and religious Society and was installed 20 March, 1791. As a man he was upright, independent and philanthropic; As a friend (though his intimacies were few) warm-hearted and faithful; As a christian, zealous and stable; for personal piety eminent. His religion was in the heart rather than on the lip; As a minister of the New Testament, he was earnest, decided and evangelical; a scribe instructed unto the kingdom of heaven; In his style and manner truly unique. No man was his model. In the fervour and eloquence of public prayer unsurpassed, if not unequalled. Forty three years he preached the gospel of Christ to his people with a fidelity and success preeminently signal and suddenly passed into glory May 1, 1837 aged 70. Many at the last day shall rise up and call him blessed.'

To these epitaphs, which I have inserted by particular request, I shall add only the following inscription, which is on the monument erected in the Federal Street church to the memory of the reverend GEORGE WHITEFIELD, by the munificence of the late William Bartlet, esquire.

' This Cenotaph is erected with affectionate veneration to the memory of the Rev. George Whitefield, born at Gloucestershire Dec. 16, 1714, educated at Oxford University, ordained 1736. In a ministry of 34 years he crossed the Atlantic 13 times, and preached more than 18000 sermons. As a soldier of the cross, humble, devout, ardent, he put on the whole armor of God, preferring the honor of Christ to his own interest, repose, reputation and life.' As a Christian orator, his deep piety, disinterested zeal and vivid imagination gave unexampled energy to his look, utterance and action. Bold, ardent, pungent and popular in his eloquence, no other uninspired man ever preached to so large assemblies, or enforced the simple truths of the gospel by motives, so persuasive and awful, and with an influence so powerful on the hearts of his hearers. He died of Asthma, September 30, 1770, suddenly exchanging his life of unparalleled labors for his eternal rest.'

Having thus disposed of the deceased clergy, I shall now occupy a few pages with brief notices of the laity, in addition to what may be found in the genealogy, which will be given alphabetically.

ROBERT ADAMS resided within a few rods of the spot where his descendants, colonel Daniel Adams and Robert Adams, now live. The posterity of Robert Adams are numerous. On the grave stone erected to his memory in the Byfield burying ground, there is a mistake; one generation having been omitted, thus making Abraham Adams the son of his grandfather Robert, instead of his father Abraham.

JOHN ATKINSON, hatter, resided where captain Stephen Little now resides.

Reverend STEPHEN BACHILER resided for a short time in Newbury. A particular account of him may be found in Lewis's History of Lynn. Suffice it to say that he came to America in 1632, at the age of seventy one, went to Lynn, thence to Ipswich in 1636, thence to Yarmouth in 1637, thence to Newbury in 1638, thence to Hampton in 1639. From 1647 to 1650 he was in Portsmouth. In the latter year he married his third wife Mary. He was then nearly ninety years of age. In the same year, the court, in consequence of a matrimonial difficulty, ordered that 'Mr. Bachiler and his wife shall lyve together as man and wife, as in this Court they have publiquely professed to doe, and if either desert one another, then hereby the Court doth order that ye Marshall shall apprehend both ye said Mr. Bachiler and Mary his wife and bring them forthwith to Boston,' and so forth. In October, 1656, his wife Mary petitioned the Court for a divorce, stating that 'Mr. Bachiler upon some pretended ends of his owne hath transported himselfe unto ould England and betaken himselfe to another wife,' and so forth. At the time of Mr. Bachiler's running away and taking a fourth wife, he was in the ninety-sixth year of his age! Quite a sprightly specimen of clerical gallantry, and certainly unique. He died at Hackney, England, aged about one hundred. Prince says of him, 'he was a man of fame in his day, a gentleman of learning and ingenuity, and wrote a fine and curious hand.' His posterity are very numerous in New Hampshire.

JOHN BAILEY came to New England in a ship called the 'Angel Gabriel,' which was cast away in the terrible storm of August 1635, at Pemaquid. He was so frightened by the dangers he had encountered, that he never again dared to cross the Atlantic. As his wife was equally unwilling to come to New England, they never met. He brought his son John with him. In his will he says, 'son John is to pay his mother £6, provided she come over, son Robert £15 and daughters £10 apiece if they come over, and £5 apiece, if they do not.'

The BARTLET families, three in all, settled on and about the place called Bartlet's cove, in Newbury, opposite Amesbury ferry, where some of his descendants of the same name still remain, and engaged in the same occupation, and perhaps on the same spot that John Bartlet, 'the tanner,' occupied nearly two centuries ago. The name is an ancient one, and may be found in various ancient records. Adam de Barttlot, went to England with William the conqueror, in 1066, and settled at Stapham in Sussex, where the elder branch of the family still resides. In 1280 the name was spelled Bartelot, afterward Bartholot, Bartolot, Bartelet, Bartlett, and Bartlet. In John Fox's Book of Martyrs, printed in 1610, I find Richard, Robert, Sarah and Isabella Bartlet, protestant martyrs, persecuted by John Longland, popish bishop of the diocese of Lincoln in the year 1521.

HENRY BODWELL, who married Bethia Emery, was one of the few survivors of the company under captain Thomas Lathrop, who were slain at the disastrous battle of Muddy Brook, September eighteenth, 1675, now most appropriately styled Bloody Brook. An account of this battle, or rather massacre, should have been given on page 117, but was omitted for want of some information, which, having been since obtained, will be here inserted, compiled from the honorable Edward Everett's elegant address, delivered September thirtieth, 1835, at Bloody Brook, in South Deerfield, in commemoration of the fall of the 'flower of Essex' at that spot in king Philip's war, September eighteenth, 1675, and from Mr. Robert Adams's manuscript history of Newbury, and a document copied from the original on file in the state house, in Boston, and written by the reverend John Russell, of Hadley. Those who are familiar with the history of Philip's war, will recollect that Philip was at this time on Connecticut river. It therefore became necessary for the English to establish a formidable opposing force, in some convenient position. As Hadley was selected, an increased supply of provisions in that place was necessary. 'A considerable quantity of wheat being preserved in stacks at Deerfield, it was deemed expedient to have it threshed and brought down to Hadley. Captain Lathrop and his company volunteered to proceed to Deerfield and protect the convoy. This company consisted of 'the flower of the population of Essex — her hopeful young men — all culled out of the towns belonging to that county.' Of the twenty-three men impressed from Newbury on the fifth, sixth, and twenty-seventh of August to go against the Indian enemy, Henry Bodwell and John Toppan were two, and it is not unlikely that the remaining twenty-one were a part of captain Lathrop's company, which consisted in all of eighty men. The whole company arrived safely at Deerfield, threshed the wheat, placed it in eighteen wagons, and while on their return through South Deerfield, as they were stopping to gather grapes, which hung in clusters in the forest that lined the narrow road, they were surprised by an ambuscade of Indians, outnumbering captain Lathrop's company ten to one, who poured upon them a murderous fire. Hubbard states that not above seven or eight of captain Lathrop's company escaped. This is probably near the truth, as the reverend John Russell states that seventy-one men were slain at Muddy Brook bridge on the eighteenth of September, and gives the names of sixty of them. 'From August fifth to September twenty-seventh, there were impressed,' says Mr. Everett, 'in the single town of Newbury, thirty men and forty-six horses; facts that show the prodigious severity of the military service of the colony at that period, — vastly greater than at any subsequent period in the history of the country.' To which Mr. Everett might have added, that in December of that same year, twenty-four additional men were impressed from Newbury, and, on the second of the next January, thirteen more, making in all, with Richard Kent's man, who was impressed on September twenty-ninth, sixty-eight men and forty-six horses, from August fifth, 1675, to January second, 1676. The ratable polls at this time were only one hundred and fifty-nine. Mr. Samuel Jaques, who died June twenty-fourth, 1824, aged ninety-five years and four months, was well acquainted with three of the soldiers from Newbury, who were in the battle of September eighteenth, or the Petaquamscot fight at Narragansett, December nineteenth; namely, Jonathan Emery, Samuel Hills, and John Toppan. From them Mr. Jaques ascertained the following particulars, which he communicated to Mr. Robert Adams in 1817. Jonathan Emery was wounded, December nineteenth, in the neck by an arrow. At the battle of Bloody Brook, John Toppan, who was wounded in the shoulder, concealed himself in a water course that at that time was almost dry, and hauled grass and weeds over his head, so that, though the Indians sometimes stepped over him, he was not discovered. Henry Bodwell had his left arm broken by a musket ball, but, being a man of great strength and courage, he seized his gun in his right hand, and swung it round his head, and so forced his way through the Indians, by whom he was almost surrounded. 'The catastrophe of the eighteenth of September, was the heaviest, which had befallen the colony.' 'It was a sadder rebuke of Providence,' says doctor Increase Mather, 'than any thing that hitherto had been'—'a black and fatal day wherein there were eight persons made widows, and twenty six children made fatherless, and about sixty persons buried in one fatal grave.' In the course of Philip's war, which was brief, 'six hundred of the inhabitants, the greatest part of whom were the flower of the country, fell in battle, or were murdered. Twelve towns in Massachusetts, Plymouth and Rhode Island were utterly destroyed, and many more greatly injured. Six hundred buildings, mostly dwelling houses, are known to have been burned, and, according to doctor Trumbull's calculation one man in eleven of the arms bearing population was killed, and one house in eleven laid in ashes.'

The following is a copy, sent to the general court by the reverend John Russell, of Hadley. It has never, to my knowledge, been printed, only in part. Those belonging to Newbury who were killed under captain Lathrop, were serjeant Thomas Smith, Samuel Stevens, his brother John Stevens, John Littlehale, at that time of Haverhill. John Plummer was killed August twenty-fifth. There were probably others from Newbury, whose names are not known.

'A list of the men slain in the County of Hampshire (though we cannot gett the names of all, yet as many as we can gett,) are here inserted. Also the time when and place where they were slain.
'1675, Aug. 2. John Eyres, Richard Coy, John and Samuel Pritchard, Henry Young, Zachary Phillips, Sydrach Harkwood, Samuel Smeadley, Edward Coburn, James Hovey, Capt. Edward Hutchinson, 13 were slayn. At the swamp beyond Hatfield ye 25 August were 9 men slayn. Azariah Dickinson, James Lewis, Samuel Mason, Richard Fellows, John Plummer, Mark Pitman, Joseph Pearson, Matthew Scales, William Cluffe.
'At Squakeage ye 4 Sept. 16 men were slayn.
'Capt. Richard Beers, John Chenary, Ephraim Child, Benjamin Crackbone, Robert Pepper, Joseph Dickinson, William Markham, George Lyrass, John Gatchell, James Miller, John Wilson.

'Squakeage ye 2d of Sept. 8 men were slayn.

'Serg. Samuel Wright, Ebenezer and Jonathan Jeans, Ebenezer Parsons, Nathaniel Curtis, Thomas Scott, and John Peck.

'At Deerfield 2 men were slayn. James Eaglestone, Nathaniel Cranberry.

'At Muddy Brook bridge ye 18th Sept. 71 men were slayn.

'Capt. Thomas Lathrop, Ser. Thomas Smith, Samuel Stevens, John Hobbs, Daniel Button, John Harriman, Thomas Bailey, Ezekiel Sawyer, Jacob Kilborn, Thomas Manning, Jacob Wainwright, Benjamin Roper, John Bennet, Thomas Mentor, Caleb Kimball, Thomas Hobbs, Robert Homes, Edward Trask, Richard Lambert, Josiah Dodge, Peter Woodbury, Joseph Balch, Samuel Whittridge, William Duy, Serg. Samuel Stevens, Samuel Crampton, John Plum, Thomas Buckley, George Ropes, Joseph Kirge, Thomas Alexander, Francis Friend, Abel Osyer, John Littlehale, Samuel Hudson, Adam Clarke, Ephraim Farah, Robert Wilson, Steven Welman, Benjamin Farrell, Solomon Alley, John Merritt, Robert, Samuel, Barnabas and John Hinsdall, Joseph Gillett, John Allin, Joshua Carter, John Barnard, James Tufts, Jonathan Plympton, Philip Barsham, Thomas Welles, William Smeade, Zebadiah Williams, Eliakim Marshall, James Mudge and George Cole.

'At Northampton 2 men were slain, Praiseever Turner, and Uzacaby Shackspeer.

'At Springfield Oct. 4, four men and a woman were slain. Lieut. Thomas Cooper, Thomas Miller, Nathaniel Browne, Edmund Primrides.

'At Hatfield Oct. 19 ten men were slain. Serg. Freegrace Norton, Thomas Mekins, Nathaniel Collins, Richard Stone, Samuel Clarke, John Pocock, Thomas Warner, Abraham Quiddington, William Olverton, John Petts.

'At Westfield Oct. 27, were three men slayn, William and John Brooks, and John Dumbleton.

'At Northampton 29 Oct. were 4 slain Joseph Baker sen. Joseph Baker jun. Thomas Salmon, and John Roberts.

'Three men of Capt. Moseley's, when he went to relieve Capt. Lathrop, John Oates, Peter Barron,——

'The whole number is 145 persons. Blow ye a trumpet in Zion, sanctify a fast, call a solemn assembly, gather the people, sanctify the congregation, assemble the elders, gather the children and those that suck the breasts. Let the priests, the ministers of the Lord weep between the porch and the altar, and let them say spare thy people, O Lord, and give not thy heritage to reproach that the heathen should rule over them. Wherefore should they say among the people where is thy God? Then will the Lord be jealous for his land and pity his people.

'Rev. John Russell.'

I am the more inclined to publish the preceding account, as Mr. Everett observes, page twenty-fourth, that ' with the exception of Capt. Lathrop himself I am not aware, that we have positive information as to any that fell, officers or men,' and in a note at the close of the book, page thirty-seventh, he says that the contemporary 'historians are silent as to the names of those, who fell with Lathrop,' but observes that ' since the foregoing pages were printed off, I have been furnished with a list of those, who fell with Capt. Lathrop.' This list agrees in substance with the list in the preceding page, which I copied from the original some fifteen years ago. Each list contains sixty names, but the names of eleven persons, who were killed, are not mentioned.

Thomas Browne, weaver, resided in the vicinity of Turkey-hill. His daughter Mary was the first white child born in Newbury. His son Francis was ancestor of John Brown, whose family were carried off by the Indians in 1695, and ancestor of Mr. Robert Brown, who resides on the land once owned by his first ancestor.

Richard Brown resided on the spot now occupied by captain Daniel Lunt, on the corner of what was once called South street, but now Parker street.

William Chandler resided near the foot of what is now Federal street, then called Chandler's lane.

Doctor JOHN CLARK, the first physician of Newbury, tradition asserts, was the first regularly educated physician, who resided in New England. In Thacher's Medical Biography, it is said that 'he was honored with a diploma for his success in cutting for the stone.' In 1651 he sold a part of his farm, which was originally four hundred acres, near Cart Creek to Matthew Chaffey of Boston, who sold it to Richard Thorlaye of Rowley, for one hundred and fifty-five pounds. From him descended all of the name of Thorla or Thurlow now in Newbury. A likeness of doctor Clark is in possession of the Massachusetts Historical Society, from which the lithograph in this volume is taken.

THOMAS COLMAN, resided in Byfield, on land, which is now owned by one of his descendants, colonel Jeremiah Colman. The family of Colemans in Nantucket are also descended from Thomas Colman's elder children, and those in Newbury are descended from the youngest son Tobias, the son of Margery, the third wife of Thomas, and who was the widow of Thomas Rowell of Andover. The name was originally Coultman, that is, Coltman, or one who had the care and management of horses. So say English writers.

TRISTRAM COFFIN, junior, about 1654 erected the house, in which the compiler of this work now resides, and which is occupied by Tristram's descendants of the seventh generation. Tristram Coffyn, senior, of whom I have said something on pages 298 and 9, is said to have been the first person who ever used a plough in Haverhill, where his name is found as a witness to the Indian deed of that town, March fifteenth, 1642. He always wrote his name ' Coffyn.' He was a royalist, and was, as far as I can ascertain, the only one of the early settlers of Newbury, who came to America in consequence of the success of Oliver Cromwell. From Prince's Worthies of Devonshire, I find that ' the ancient family of this name was settled at Portledge, by the sea-side in the parish of Alwington, five miles from Biddeford, and flourished there from the conquest, and that from the time of King Henry first, unto the age of King Edward second, the space of 200 years, the heir of this family was always called Richard. The present representative of this most ancient family, is the Rev. John Pine Coffin, of Portledge.' One of Tristram Coffin's descendants was admiral sir Isaac Coffin, who was born in Boston June third, 1759, and entered the British navy as midshipman about the year 1770. He was the founder of the Coffin school in Nantucket, which was designed for the benefit of all the descendants of Tristram Coffyn, senior.

Captain JOHN CUTTING, tradition states, was a ship-master, and sailed from Boston and crossed the Atlantic thirteen times. He was a man of a great deal of humor, and many stories are told to this day concerning his peculiarities, which afforded much diversion to himself and others, but which want of room compels me to omit. Winthrop in the year 1637, mentions ' Capt. Cutting's ship and a captive Pequod, whom the government gave him to carry to England.'

RICHARD DOLE resided on the same spot of ground, which his descendants of the same name now occupy. His ancestors went from the town of Dole in Bretagne, in 1066, to England. He probably came from Bristol, as I find his name signed in 1639, to an obligation written by Mr. John Lowle, then in Bristol, and came with the Lowles in the latter part of the same year to Newbury. He was then but fifteen years of age, and was probably their clerk.

RICHARD DUMMER was one of the fathers of Massachusetts, was chosen a magistrate, warmly espoused the cause of sir Henry Vane, was one of the disarmed adherents of Mrs. Hutchinson, and 'no man,' says Eliot, 'more deserved the praise of doing well.' He was very rich and equally benevolent. He contributed greatly to the improvement and growth of that part of Newbury, where he lived. The lands, upon which the academy is built, were his, and were left for the support of this institution. The house in which he lived, stood a few rods southeast of the present mansion house. His son Jeremy Dummer, was a goldsmith, resided in Boston, and there died in 1718. He was the father of the celebrated Jeremy Dummer, and of lieutenant governor William Dummer, who founded Dummer academy. Eliot in his Biographical Dictionary, says he was born in this province, which is correct, but not sufficiently definite. The compiler of the Dummer academy catalogue says he was born in Byfield, but this is not correct. He was undoubtedly born in Boston. This I infer from the will of Jeremy Dummer, senior. In it he mentions sons William, Jeremy, Samuel, and daughter Anna, who married John Powell. Governor Dummer in his will 1761, mentions his sister Anna Powell. 'He was a man,' says Eliot, 'of such correct judgment, and steady habits, such a firm and temperate conduct, when he supposed himself right, that the vessel of state was secure though exposed to the dangers of a tempestuous sea.' Douglas always styles it 'the wise administration of Dummer.' He was in the chair from November, 1722, to July nineteenth, 1728, and again from governor Burnet's death, September seventh, 1729, till April eighth, 1730. He died October tenth, 1761. By his will he gave his valuable farm and stately mansion house, which is still standing, for the endowment of the academy, which was the first incorporated academy in the state.

Mr. NICHOLAS EASTON, another of the early settlers of Newbury, was one of the three disarmed. adherents of Mrs. Hutchinson, and in 1639, removed to Rhode Island, where he was lieutenant governor of the state in 1650, 1672, and 1673. His son John, who was fifteen years of age when he came with his father to Newbury, was afterward chosen to the same office, from 1690 to 1695. Mr. Nicholas Easton's house stood near where Mr. Nathaniel Dole now lives.

JOHN EMERY senior, in the latter part of his life resided on the farm where Mr. Eliphalet Emery now lives.

Captain WILLIAM GERRISH resided near the parsonage land, on the road leading to Trotter's bridge.

LAUNCELOT GRANGER lived for some time on Kent's island, and with his brother-in-law, Jacob Adams, removed to Suffield, Connecticut, and was ancestor of the honorable Gideon Granger of that place.

Captain EDMUND GREENLEAFE, whom Johnson styles an 'ancient

and experienced lieutenant' under captain Gerrish, in 1644, went from Newbury to Boston soon after the removal of the meeting-house from the lower green. In his will, he says : 'next my will is being according to God's will and revealed in his word, that wee must pay what wee owe and live of the rest, unto whose rule the sons of men ought to frame their wills and actions, therefore,' and so forth. He mentions his son Stephen, daughter Elizabeth Browne, daughter Judith Coffin, grandchildren Elizabeth Hilton, Enoch Greenleafe, Sarah Winslow, and James Greenleafe, his eldest son's son,' and concludes with the following queer memoranda. ' When I married my wife I kept her grandchild, as I best remember three years to schooling, Dyet and apparel, and William Hill her son had a bond of £ 6 a year, whereof I received no more than a barrell of pork of £ 3, of that £ 6 a yere he was to pay me, and I sent to her son Ignatius Hill to the Barbadoes in Mackrell, Sider, bread and pease as much as come to £ 20, I never received one penny of it. His aunt gave to the three brothers £ 50 apiece. I know not whether they received it or not. I never received any part of it. Beside when I married my wife she brought me a silver bowl, a silver porringer, a silver spoon ; she lent or gave them to her son James Hill without my consent. Witness my hand. EDMUND GREENLEAFE. Twenty-fifth December, 1668.'

THOMAS HALE resided on the south side of the river Parker. The family of Hale is of considerable antiquity and of high respectability in England. Thomas Hale, of Codicote, in Hertfordshire, married Anne, daughter of Edmund Mitchell, and had three sons, *Richard*, William, and John. *Richard*, the eldest son, purchased the estate of Kings Walden in Hertfordshire, and died in 1620. His son *William* succeeded him, and died in August, 1634, aged sixty-six. He left nine children, Richard, born in 1596, William in 1597, Rowland, his heir, George, born July thirtieth, 1601, Alicia, in 1603, Winefreda, 1604, *Thomas*, 1606, Anne, 1609, and Dionisia, March seventeenth, 1611. The last mentioned Thomas is supposed to be the Thomas Hale who came to Newbury.

In the notice of WILLIAM HILTON, page 305, a mistake should be corrected. It should be thus : 'a William Hilton, probably *not* the same person, died in Charlestown September seventh, 1675, leaving sons Nowell, Edward, and Charles.'

Mr. JOSEPH HILLS, a man of some distinction in the early history of the country, came, as I am informed, from Shrewsbury, in England. His original name was Hill, but to distinguish his family from the large number of families named Hill, he added the letter 's' to his name. Since that time all his descendants have borne the name of Hills. Mr. Joseph Hills was representative from Malden, and speaker of the house, in 1647. He was also a representative from Malden from 1650 to 1656. In 1648 he was appointed by the Court with Mr. Edward Rawson to compare the amendments of the books of laws passed, and make them as one, and one of them to remain in the hands of the Committee, for the speedy committing of them to the press.' In consequence of his labors in compiling and preparing the 'laws,' he was exempted from paying taxes for the last five years of his life.

50

From his will I make the following extracts: ' My will further is that for the good of the inhabitants of the towne of Newbury that there be the sum of forty shillings in money paid into the hands of captain Daniel Pierce (or such other person as the town shall appoint) towards the procuring of a good bell for the meeting house, or such other as shall be built for the better comfort of the inhabitants, provided the said inhabitants shall make it up the sum of thirty pounds within three years after my decease.' ' Also I give my wife my great testament, my book of martyrs and new warming pan.' Three excellent articles, and rather more consistent with each other than ' my great bible, my fowling-piece and negro boy Tom.'

SOLOMON HOLMAN, was one of the early settlers in the west parish of Newbury. He was born in England, served seven years on board of a man of war, ran away in Bermuda, when sent after milk, secreted himself in the barn till the vessel sailed, and lived by milking the cows. He was discovered by the owner of the barn, who befriended him, and gave him employment. He afterward married his employer's daughter Mary, came to Newbury, built him a bark, and then a log house, on land of which he bought thirteen acres for a fat heifer. The land is now owned by Mr. Jonathan Ilsley, from whom I obtained this account. Mr. Holman died May seventh, 1753, in his eighty-second year.

JOHN KELLY, one of the original settlers of Newbury, was of Irish, as well as of English, descent. Shortly after he settled in Newbury, he determined to run the risk of building his house on the north side of Old-town hill. His neighbors remonstrated with him on his rashness, and finally the town passed a vote, that if, in consequence of his temerity, he lost his life, his blood should be on his own head. This I am informed on good authority, though the record is not now to be found. Tradition also states, that one night, hearing a disturbance among his sheep, he went and killed what he supposed to be a dog, but which in the morning proved to be a wolf. His son John built, prior to 1690, the house, still standing, which was formerly owned by Mr. Nicholas Lunt, on the west side of the road north of gravel hill, and now owned by his grandson, Mr. Joseph Lunt. The only descendant of John Kelly, and bearing his name, in Newbury or Newburyport, is doctor Elbridge G. Kelly, though many descendants are found in New Hampshire, and most of the New England and other states. Twenty-six persons of the name are known to have graduated at the different colleges in the union. Tradition states that the father of John Kelly, the first who came to Newbury, emigrated from Ireland to Newbury, England, became attached to a lady of rank, and having on one occasion, by his courage, successfully defended her father's house when attacked by robbers, he obtained his consent to a marriage with his daughter.

Deacon RICHARD KNIGHT and his brother JOHN resided on land now owned by John Knight's descendants of the same name. The deacon left no male heirs. I have a piece of poetry which he left to his children. It contains good advice, but whether original or selected, I am

not able to say.   It is too long for insertion.   The following lines are
a fair specimen.

> ' For other men give not thy word
> No farther than thou canst afford,
> Lest afterwards thou shouldest rue
> To pay the debt when it is due.'

RICHARD KENT, senior, lived near, or in, Kent street. RICHARD KENT,
junior, resided on the island which bears his name.   The present
owners are descendants of James, brother of Richard, junior.   The
island was entailed to the oldest male heir, but in process of time a
difficulty occurred, which the testator had not anticipated.   The wife
of one of his descendants had twin sons, Joseph and Stephen, born
May ninth, 1741.

It has never yet been decided which was the older of the two, although a long and troublesome law-suit was the consequence of the
uncertainty, which was at last settled by an equal division of the
property.

GEORGE LITTLE resided on the land now owned by Messrs. Silas,
Tristram, and Henry Little, and but a few rods from the house now
occupied by Silas Little, esquire.   He was remarkable for his strength
of mind, as well as strength of body, but was not an educated man.
The farms, which he selected contain some of the best land in the
town, and are still owned by his descendants, at Oldtown, and Turkey-
hill, where the houses which he built are in part standing.

The descendants of WILLIAM MOODEY occupy both at Oldtown and
Byfield, the lands once owned by him.   Tradition states that the first
oxen ever shod in Newbury, or perhaps in New England, were shod
by Samuel Moody of Oldtown.   He at first tried the experiment on a
dead hoof, and, believing it would answer the purpose, soon tried it,
successfully, on the living animal.   For want of a more suitable place,
I will here mention, that his wife Mary was a *grand-daughter* of captain
John Cutting.

It has been supposed by many persons, that the name SILOWAY is a
corruption of Musslewhite.   This is not the case.   John Musslewhite
had no descendants, and, in the next place, I have before me an indenture, made the twenty-fifth of May, 1665, between Daniel Mussiloway,
alias Roger Waldron, in which the said Daniel, 'late servant unto Joseph Plummer yeoman, being infected with a very dangerous disease,
for and in consideration of cure out of said disease, do bind myselfe as
an apprentice unto Mr. Henry Greenland, Phisition or Chyrurgion . .
. . until the full end and term of sixe yeares bee compleatly expired,
&c.   And further the said Daniel alias Roger doe promise and engage
himselfe unto the abovesaid Mr. Henry Greenland, that if it please
God that he shall be cured of the disease he is now afflicted with, he
will confirm this his act by owning it before the county court or two
magistrates.' . . . . .   The Indenture is a very long one, and
contains, among other conditions, the following. ' Taverns or alehouses
he shall not haunt, except he bee about his master's business.'   See
page 311.

JOSEPH MUSSEY or MUZZEY, who lived in what was called Muzzey's lane, now Marlborough street, was from Ipswich, and was a son of Robert Muzzey, in whose will, dated 1647, I find the following. ' I give to ye use of ye poore one ewe goate to be disposed of by the overseers of my will to such as are godly; only the first yeare's use, I appoynt to my brother Dane, the ewe, if she brings kidds, or else longer, and when the goat grows old, I will that one of the kidds be reserved for such a use.' ' Goats,' says Josselyn, in 1663, ' were the first small cattle they, [the New England people,] had in the country. He was counted nobody, that had not a trip or flock of goats. Hogs are innumerable.'

The descendants of the reverend JAMES NOYES and NICHOLAS NOYES, reside on the land and in the houses erected by them. The house occupied by Mr. Silas Noyes in Parker street, is one of the oldest buildings in Newbury.

MR. HANANIAH ORDWAY, who was born December second, 1665, was one of the first settlers in the westerly part of Newbury, near Indian hill. He died in June 1758, aged ninety-two and a half years. His house was a garrison house, and, on one occasion, in the early part of his residence in that part of the town, he saw, in the evening, an Indian creep in by the gate that led to the house. He immediately seized his musket, and fired at the spot where he had seen him enter. On examination, he could find no trace of the Indian, who had left his gun, and his powder horn filled with rum, and which had been shot off from the belt by which it had been fastened to his body. Some weeks after, the body of an Indian was found dead in the woods, who Mr. Ordway supposed was the one at whom he fired and wounded. The gun and horn are now in possession of his descendants, from whom I obtained this information. This was perhaps the only Indian ever killed in Newbury by any of the inhabitants, but continual caution was necessary for many years after seventeen hundred, to guard against attack, which the natives might be disposed to make on the white inhabitants.

The land on which MOSES PETTINGELL, esquire, now lives, was purchased by his ancestor, Richard Pettingell, of John Spencer, about 1652.

WILLIAM PILSBURY, originally Pillesburgh, bought of Mr Edward Rawson, the farm which is now in possession of Mr. Joshua Pilsbury, one of his descendants, whose house was built as early as 1700, and is consequently one of the very few old houses, which remain in town. There is another ancient house, about the age of which there has been much inquiry, and some dispute. I allude to the stone house on Pierce's, now Pettingell's farm. My own opinion is, that it was not built till after 1660 or 70, perhaps later. Some suppose it was erected by Mr. John Spencer, to whom the farm was first granted. This is not probable, as Mr. Spencer returned to England, and made his will in 1637. In that will, he gives his farm to his nephew, Mr. John Spencer, who did not deed any part of it away till fifteen or sixteen years after. He then sold a part to Richard Pettingell, and about the same time sold the remainder to Mr. Daniel Pierce, brother of John Spencer, senior. On the files of the court, January, 1679, I find the following, namely :

'The deposition of Anthony Somerby aged 70.

'This deponent saith that about ye yeare 1651 or 52 I was at the farm yt Mr. John Spencer sold to Mr. Daniel Pierce in Newbury, and Mr. Spencer and Mr. Pierce with myselfe and another, I suppose it was Mr. William Thomas, and as we were going through the land of ye said farme, Mr. Pierce said to Mr. Spencer, you promised to give me possession by turfe and twigge. Mr. Spencer said so I will, if you please to cut a turfe and twigge, and Mr. Pierce did cut off a twigge off a tree, and cut up a turfe, and Mr. Spencer tooke the twigge and stuck it into the turfe, and bid us bear witness that he gave Mr. Pierce possession thereby of the house and land and farme that he had bought of him and gave the turfe and twigge to Mr. Pierce and further saith not.'　　　　　　　'Taken upon oath 10 Jan. 1679 before me.

'JOHN WOODBRIDGE, *Commissioner.*'

Now it is not probable that Mr. Pierce, before he had obtained legal possession of the farm, would be at the expense of building a costly stone house. Other information also leads me without hesitation to place the erection of the stone house at least over thirty years after the incorporation of the town. It was at one time used as a safe place to store the town's powder, and on one occasion, tradition informs us, one of Mr. Pierce's slaves placed a lighted candle in a keg of powder, which, after some time, took fire, blew out one side of the house and lodged the poor negro, bed, and all, among the limbs of a large apple-tree, to her very great amazement. The farm, which has had several owners, it was the intention of Mr. Pierce to entail, as in his will, he says, 'it shall never be sold, nor any part divided.'

The descendants of JOHN POOR, who lived and died on the south side of the river Parker, still own the land, once possessed by their New England ancestor.

The descendants of FRANCIS PLUMER still own the land, which was once his, near the river Parker. About the year 1784 or 85, one of them, Mr. Simeon Plumer, found a quantity of gold, of which, since much has been said and more conjectured, some account may be expected. The story, however, has been much exaggerated, and instead of a 'pot,' a small amount only was found, probably not far from three hundred dollars. The first piece was picked up by a child, from some dirt, which had been carried out of the cellar. Shortly, another piece was found, and search being made, the amount above stated was found in various parts of the cellar, but how it came there, and by whom deposited, will probably ever remain a mystery. Five of Francis Plumer's descendants, and bearing his name, have been members of congress. One of them, George, son of Jonathan, was the first white child born in Pennsylvania, west of the Alleghany mountains.

Mr. EDWARD RAWSON, afterward secretary of the colony of Massachusetts, was the first town clerk of Newbury. He was a nephew of the reverend John Wilson, of Boston. Two of his sons, David and John, went to England. William married Anna, daughter of Nathan Glover, July thirty-first, 1673. They settled in Braintree, and had twenty children in twenty-five years. One of the daughters married the reverend Mr. Torrey, of Weymouth, another, Mr. Thomas Broughton, of Boston, and Rebecca married Thomas Rumsey, as appears by the two following papers, now on file in the state house, Boston.

'The testimony of Theodore Atkinson and Mary his wife inhabitants of Boston in New England saith.

'That about the 3d month in ye year 1678 Thomas Rumsey came to me and tendered his service to me for one year to work with me and he told me that he was a Kentish man, and that his father lived near Canterbury, and that he was a yeoman and had an estate of about £400 a year, and also that his father died when he was but young, that his father's estate did fall to him at his mother in law's decease, and also he pretended that he came over to New England upon the account of religion, and further he hired himself with me for a year, for to attend my business and to keep my book of accounts, and for the gathering in of my debts, but when he had been about a month with me, he pretended he was one that had been highly bred, but he would not say further what he was, but about 5 months after he came to me, then he told me his father was a Knight and a Baronet, and that his mother in law was a Lady. So he lived and carried himself, pretending he was highly bred that I the said Atkinson did not set him on work, because he promised me he would satisfy me for what charges and expenses . . . about him, but a little time after he came to me he began to discover himself so as his religion did seem to wear away, and before the year was expired he changed his name and said his name was Hale, and professed he had been a great traveller in ye Streights for about two and twenty months, and that his mother was called the Lady Hale. and paid him his money by bills of exchange from time to time, that she was a Lady that had £300 per annum of her own that she brought with her, and that his father had about £800 a year and a vast estate, which he durst not, nor would not mention least he should be laughed at, and not believed, that all his fathers estate after his mother's decease was his, those and such like unheard of stories as those, in which is not the least shadow of truth (as the deponents are informed) and as the deponents now perceive he made use of as a delusion to put a cheat on Mr. Edward Rawson of Boston aforesaid to accomplish his abominable villainy and deceive of his daughter Mrs. Rebecca Rawson, whom he was married unto by a minister of the gospel on the first day of July 1679 in the presence of near 40 witnesses.'

The sequel of this 'abominable villany' is quite tragical. The other paper states that

'Thomas Rumsey pretended to be Sir Thomas Hale jr. nephew of Lord Chief Justice Hale, made a respectable appearance, appeared to be well acquainted with Lord Hale and being a person of a very handsome address, paid his devoirs to Rebecca Rawson, who was accounted one of the most beautiful, polite, and accomplished young ladies in Boston, and had the vanity to think herself suitable to make the young Lord a wife. Accordingly they were married and handsomely furnished, sailed for England and safely arrived. She went on shore in a dishabille, leaving her trunks on board the vessel and went to lodge with a relation of hers. In the morning early he arose, took the keys and told her he would send the trunks on shore that she might be dressed before dinner. He sent the trunks up and she waited impatiently for the keys till one or two o'clock, but he not coming she broke open the trunks and to her inexpressible surprise she found herself stript of every thing, and her trunks filled with combustible matter, on which her kinsman ordered his carriage, and they went to a place where she stopt with her husband the night before. She enquired for Sir Thomas Hale jr., they said he had not been there for some days. She said she was sure he was there the night before. They said Thomas Rumsey had been there with a young Lady, but was gone to his wife in Canterbury, and she saw him no more. Having learned many curious works, such as painting on glass, she thought herself able to support herself, and on her return to America, she was swallowed up by the earthquake at Port Royal in America.'

Mr. HENRY SEWALL came to Newbury in 1635, in 1646 was married, went to England the same year, was there settled as a clergyman till 1659; in 1661 he sent for his family to come to Newbury, where he resided till his death. He resided in Parker street, (formerly South street,) on the north side, a few rods N. W. from Mr. Silas Noyes's house. Of Mr Sewall, Mr. Savage thus speaks. 'This ancestor of one of the most venerated families, which has given three of its members to preside in the highest court of civil and criminal jurisdiction in Massachusetts, was one of the first settlers at Newbury. The biographies of Eliot and Alden, and especially the copious collection of

American epitaphs, II., 115, have well perpetuated the memory of his descendants.'

A note in the Quarterly Register of February, 1841, to a biography of judge Samuel Sewall, states that 'during the one hundred and forty-eight years that have elapsed since a supreme court, as such, was first established in Massachusetts, a place among its judges has been held eighty-four collectively (more than half of that period) by four descendants of the above mentioned patriarch of Newbury; and the office of chief justice by three of them during the collective term of eighteen years.'

The descendants of HENRY SHORT now occupy the same farm, and live on the same spot, where their first ancestor resided more than two centuries ago. The same may be said of the descendants of THOMAS SMITH, who reside on the spot where he resided, near the 'clay pitts,' as they were called, at the foot of Hill street, alias ' West India lane.' Captain James, son of lieutenant James Smith, born in 1670, and married in 1696, and ensign Enoch Little, son. of Joseph Little, and born in 1685, were the first settlers on Crane-neck hill. When they went up to clear the land, which was about the year 1708, the Indians were very troublesome. On one occasion, ensign Little placed his hat on a post, which an Indian mistaking for his person, pierced it with a ball. When Mr. Little first came to live on the hill, he rode up, bringing his wife, as was the custom of that day, behind him on a pillion. The garrison-house, at his first coming to Crane-neck hill, was on the spot where the late deacon Samuel Tenney's house stands. Another garrison-house was Mr. Hananiah Ordway's, near where Mr. Joshua Ordway now lives. Mr. Ezra Pilsbury, who died in 1797, aged ninety-four, frequently mentioned that he well recollected an Indian wigwam, which he had often seen in Ash swamp.

ANTHONY SOMERBY resided in a house which stood on the spot where the jail now stands. The family derives its name from the village of Somerby, in Lincolnshire, where the family was settled previous to the conquest. The first we have any account of, is Adam de Somerby, mentioned in Doomsday Book as a landholder in Lincolnshire. Little Bytham, is a village in South Heath, eight miles from Stamford, in Lincolnshire.

ABRAHAM TOPPAN resided a few rods north from the house of captain Richard Adams, and between that and the house, now owned by the heirs of the late Mr. Joseph Toppan, one of his descendants. A part of Mr. Abraham Toppan's posterity have conformed the orthography of the word Toppan to the usual pronunciation of the name, and write it Tappan; for instance, the brothers, Messrs. Arthur, Lewis, Charles, and John, and Benjamin, late senator in congress from Ohio, and a few other families.

There are doubtless many others, unknown to the writer, who reside on the soil, which was first occupied by their ancestors, especially in the western part of Newbury, which was settled many years later than the lower part of the town. There were but few families in the upper parish prior to 1700, and the greater part of those resided on or near the main road. South of that road, tradition says, one of the first settlers was Hananiah Ordway, son of James, the next Samuel Poor, son of Samuel, about 1705, near Indian hill; the next were Enoch Little and James Smith, who commenced a settlement on Crane-neck hill about 1707, the year that Mr. Little was married. The next was Stephen Sawyer, who was married in 1719. John Chase, son of Aquila, born in 1655, was the first of that family who settled in any part of the upper parish. The first physician in that part of the town, was Dr. Matthew Adams, who resided on Crane-neck hill, and died November twenty-fourth, 1755, aged sixty-nine and a half years. The first person who ever went to market in Newbury as a butcher, was an Englishman, named Smith, who was sent by John Chase, in the year 1731, with his son David, then a lad of fourteen, whose business was to take care of Smith, and keep him sober. Nearly all these first settlers lived to an advanced age. Hananiah Ordway died in June, 1758, aged ninety-two and a half years. Samuel Poor died July eleven, 1769, in his eighty-sixth year. Ens. Enoch Little died April twenty-eighth, 1766, in his eighty-first year. Captain James Smith died in December, 1757, in his sixty-second year. John Chase died 26 February, 1740, aged eighty-five, and his son David died 17 Dec. 1802, aged 92 years and 2 months. Ezra Pilsbury died in 1797, aged 94. Captain Edmund Little, son of ensign Enoch, died 29 Aug. 1803, in his 88th year. Mr. Samuel Dole built his house on Crane-neck hill in 1730. He died 15 Dec. 1776, in his 75th year. David Dole died 15 Oct. 1839, aged 84. Judith Dole died 17 Aug. 1837, aged 90. Jane died 3 Feb. 1825, aged 81. Amos Dole died 28 March, 1816, aged 83. The first person buried in the grave-yard near the foot of Crane-neck hill, was Micah Dole, who died in his 7th year 22 Dec. 1747. The first person buried in the grave-yard east of Mr. Stephen Thurlow's, was Mary, wife of Thomas Chase, 3d, who died 12 Oct. 1725, aged 21. In the same yard, a granite pyramid is erected in memory of the late doctor Daniel Noyes Poor, and his ancestors, on which, there are, as I apprehend, several mistakes. The inscription, I believe, should stand thus : Samuel Poor was born in 1623, and died 31 Dec. 1683, aged 60. Samuel Poor, his son, was born 14 Oct. 1653, married Rachel Bailey 16 Feb. 1680, and died 29 Nov. 1727, in his 75th year. Samuel Poor, his son, was born 3 June, 1682, married Hannah, daughter of deacon Benjamin Morse, in Sept. 1705, and died 11 July, 1769, aged 85. Benjamin, his son, was born 5 Sept. 1723, and died 18 March, 1817, aged 93 1-2 years. The mistakes are, I think, in the first and second generations. John Poor died 23 Nov. 1684, aged 69, and not 23 Nov. 1694, aged 81, see page 142. Samuel was born in 1653, and not in 1648, and was not a son of John Poor. Where the first Samuel Poor resided, I have never ascertained. His son, Samuel, lived on Water street, near the foot of Moody's lane, and was living there in 1695. See page 163. Prior to 1724, the people in the West Parish buried all their dead in Sawyer's hill, with the exception of those, who used the burying-ground around Queen Ann's chapel. This burial-ground is now called the Belleville cemetery. The earliest record of a burial in that place, which has been found, is that of the reverend Henry Lucas, who died August twenty-third, 1720. The oldest stone is in memory of Mrs. Sarah Bartlet, who died January seventeenth, 1727. From this date, until about 1760, there are many names found here, principally, if not wholly, episcopalians, while all others used the upper yard. The ground, on which the chapel stood, with the yard around it, is said to have been given by a Mr. John Eayr. For many years, it was entirely neglected, but, in 1790, it was enclosed with a stone wall, and somewhat enlarged. In 1820, it was again enlarged, one hundred dollars having been bequeathed for that purpose by Robert Dodge, esquire, on condition that another hundred dollars should be raised. In the fall of 1843, an associate was formed for the purpose of making repairs and enlarging the yard. These things have been done in a substantial and beautiful manner, two new gates and a receiving tomb have been added, and the whole yard enclosed with stone-wall and palings in a neat and durable manner. The total expense has been about four hundred and fifty dollars, and the cemetery now reflects great credit on all concerned in the undertaking. A substantial granite wall was erected in front of the grave-yard in the first parish in 1823, and much enlarged by a bequest of an acre of land by the late doctor Nathan Noyes, but the yard itself, and some of the tombs need repairs, and monuments should be erected to the memory of Messrs. Parker, Noyes, and Moor. The burying-ground, on the hill near Frog pond, was enclosed for that purpose in 1730. The first person buried in it was a miss Swasey. The hill was once called Snelling's hill, probably from doctor William Snelling, the second physician in Newbury. The alterations and embellishments, which have, within a few years, been made round the pond and the vicinity, have greatly added to the beauty of the scenery. These, with the elegant new buildings lately erected on High street, together with the Putnam school-house, which is soon to be erected at the corner of Green street, will, when finished, render that beautiful part of the town still more attractive. The burial-ground in Byfield parish was first used as such in 1702. The two eldest inscriptions on the grave-stones in this place are as follows :

'Mehetable Dater of Mr. Henry and Jane Sewall, wife of Mr. William Moodey, Promoted settling the worship of God here, and then went to her glorified son William, leaueing her son Samuel and four Daters with their Father Augus ye 8th 1702 Ætat 38 was the first interred in this place.'

'HERE LIES YE BODY OF MR.
JOSHUA WOODMAN
WHO DIED MAY YE 30TH
1703, AGED 67 YEARS,
FIRST MAN CHILD BORNE
IN NEWBURY
& SECOND INTURID IN
THIS PLACE.'

The parish, as has been mentioned, was so named, in honor of Nathaniel Byfield, who was son of the reverend Richard Byfield, of Long Dutton, in Sussex, and the youngest of twenty-one children. He came to Boston in 1674, at the age of twenty-one, and on April twenty-fifth, 1676, sent the following petition 'to the governor and council sitting in Boston.'

'The Petition of Nathaniel Byfield,
Humbly sheweth, That your Petitioner is a stranger in the country and lately married and is now Prest to goe out to warre against the Indians And whereas the Law of God is plain in 24 Deut. 5 That when a man hath taken a new wife, he shall not goe out to warre, neither shall he be charged with any business but he shall be free at home one yeare. Your petitioner doth humbly request the favour of yr. Honours to grant him the Priviledge and benefit of the said law and to grant him a discharge from the present service. So shall he pray for your Honours.
'NATHANIEL BYFIELD.'

The portrait of judge Byfield, with his coat of arms, was presented to the parish of Byfield June first, 1835, by George Lyde, esquire, of New York, a descendant of the venerable judge, who died the sixth of June, 1733, in his eightieth year.

From monuments in the grave-yard of the first parish, I copy the following:

' To the memory of TRISTRAM COFFIN, Esq., who having served the first church of Newbury in the office of a Deacon 20 years died Feb. 4, 1703-4 aged 72 years.

> ' On earth he pur-chas-ed a good degree,
> Great boldness in the faith and liberty,
> And now possesses immortality.'

' To the memory of Mrs. JUDITH late uirtuous wife of Deac. Tristram Coffin, Esqr. who having lived to see 177 of her children and children's children to the 3d generation died Dec. 15, 1705 aged 80.

> ' Graue, sober, faithful, fruitfull vine was she,
> A rare example of true piety.
> Widow'd awhile she wayted wisht-for rest
> With her dear husband in her Savior's breast.'

' Here lies in a state of perfect oblivion JOHN ADAMS, who died Sept. 2, 1811 aged 79. Death hath decomposed him, and at the general resurrection Christ will recompose him, when perception and thought shall resume their several functions, and he shall become identically the same person, which Deity composed him, and shall be happy or miserable according to his dispositions.'

' Here is interred Mr. ROBERT ADAMS, who departed this life March ye 5, 1773 in ye 71st year of his age.

> ' For near 12 years
> This man an asthma had,
> Above ten years
> He was not in a bed.
> He to murmur
> Was never heard by won
> But waited patiently
> Till his change did come.'

' Here lys ye body of BENJAMIN PIERCE, Esqr. who died May ye 19th 1711 aged 42 years and three months.

> ' Pillar 'i th' State he was
> Bid fair still
> At greater things,
> To all yt knew him well,
> Pattern of Vertue,
> Kind to all was he,
> Loued by frinds,
> Feard of his enemie.
> Embalmd in tears,
> Enuey itselfe stood dumb,
> Snacht from ye world,
> In times most troublesome.'

' Here Iyes interred what was mortal of ye Honourable DANIEL PIERCE Esqr. who having faithfully served his generation both in church and military station fell asleep April ye 22d 1704 aged 66.
> ' Here lies interred a soul indeed,
> Whom few or none excelled.
> In grace if any him exceed,
> He'll be unparallelled.'

'Here lyes ye body of Mr. DANIEL NOYES, who died March ye 15th 1716 aged 42 years 4 monthes and 16 days.

> 'As you are, so was I,
> God did call and I did dy.
> Now children all,
> Whose name is Noyes,
> Make Jesus Christ
> Your only choice.'

'Here lies ye body of Mr. TIMOTHY NOYES, who died in 1718, aged 63.

> 'Good Timothy in
> His Youthfull days
> He liued much
> Unto Gods prays
> When age came one
> He and his wife
> Thay liud a holy
> & a pious life
> Therefor you children
> Whos nams are noyes
> Make Jesus Christ
> Your only Choyse.'

Other specimens of every variety, some of them exceedingly beautiful, might be given in abundance, but my limits will not permit. They remind us of that stanza in Gray's elegy, in a country churchyard, in which he says,

> 'Their names, their years, spelt by th' unletttered muse,
> The place of fame and elegy supply;
> And many a holy text around she strews,
> That teach the rustic moralist to die.'

There are, in Newbury, several other burial-grounds, both public and private, that have not been noticed, but of which, I shall mention only two; one, near the Rocks bridge, in which Mrs. Ann March, wife of Samuel March, who died June eighteenth, 1724, was the first person buried, the other is the Oak-hill cemetery, a beautiful and romantic spot, bounded on its northern and western sides by High street, and the Newburyport turnpike, and containing four acres.

It was laid out in 1842, and so far completed, as to be used for its appropriate purpose the same year. The whole expense for the purchase of land, making avenues, grading and embellishments, has been two thousand, five hundred dollars, and, when finished according to its original design, will possess still greater attractions as a rural walk, especially for those, who, 'Isaac-like, love to go forth and meditate at even-tide.' This beautiful and appropriate addition to the cemeteries, and burial-places, within the limits of Ould Newberry, owes its origin principally to the exertions of Messrs. John Porter, John Wood, and the reverend Thomas B. Fox, as I have been informed.

Originally, it was my design to furnish a table of mortality, for a specified number of years, of those persons, who died in Newbury above the age of eighty, and of those above ninety years of age, but the list has increased to so large a number, that is impracticable, and is, at the same time, so imperfect, that, were it published, it would not be of much value. A few instances of longevity, in addition to those found in the genealogy, I here insert.

In 1753, June 8, Stephen Sawyer died in his 91st year. He was then ' the oldest man in town.' In June, 1758, Hananiah Ordway died, aged 92 1-2 years. He was, at that time, ' the oldest man in town.' Since then, a large number of much more aged persons have deceased in Newbury. In Feb. 1796, Mrs. Susanna Coombs died, aged 96. The newspaper notice is, that she was the oldest ' female in town.' Abel Huse died 11 March, 1757, in his 94th year. Ebenezer Huse died 31 July, 1792, aged 97. Mrs. Sarah Jackman died Dec. 1794, aged 96. Widow Catharine Poor died 22 July, 1827, aged 95. Widow Sarah, relict of Caleb Morse, died 11 Dec. 1815, aged 100 years and two months. Mr. Caleb Morse died 22 June, 1740, aged 95. Mrs. Lydia Chase, formerly wife of Samuel Sawyer, died Nov. 1815, aged 94. Deborah, widow of Barnes Short, died 16 Sept. 1767, aged 93 years and 8 months. Mrs. Molly Toppan died 9 Jan. 1833, aged 105 years, one month, and 15 days. Widow Elizabeth Moody died 20 Feb. 1827, aged 97 1-2 years. In 1773, Jan. 25, died Joseph Atkins, esq. in his 93d year. He was born in Sandwich, Old England, was ' of the royal navy was in the famous seafight between the English and French in 1692, was at the taking of Gibralter and was a noted captain in the merchants service.' His widow, Mary Atkins, and daughter of gov. Joseph Dudley, died Nov. 19, 1774, in her 84th year. In Nov. 1774, Mrs. Lydia, widow of William Sawyer, died, aged 93. Ann Hoyt, widow of Joseph, died 23 Jan. 1794, aged 96. Deac. Amos Chase, a native of Newbury, died in Saco March 2, 1818, aged 99 years and 11 months. Nathaniel Little died 25 March, 1839, aged 93 1-4 years. Sept. 13, 1843, Nicholas Noyes died, aged 95 years, 7 months, and 10 days. Mary Woodbridge died 15 June, 1817, aged 92. Anna Moody died 15 Feb. 1834, aged 97 years and 7 months. Mrs. Prudence Bailey died 15 May, 1841, aged 93. Mrs. Judith Colby died 18 April, 1843, aged 95. Mrs. Abigail, widow of Nathaniel Emery, died 10 Dec. 1843, aged 97 1-4 years. Mary, widow of Jonathan Rogers, died 7 March, 1824, aged 99. Mr. Timothy Toppan died 2 Sept. 1796, aged 99 years, and months. Mary, relict of capt. William Woodbridge, died 15 June, 1817, aged 92. In 1807, Sept. 12, Lydia Smith, widow of Moses S. died, aged 91 nearly. Nov. 24, 1809, Elizabeth, widow of Henry Rolfe, died in her 92d year. Mr. Abner Greenleaf died 1810, Jan. 10, aged 91. Ezekiel Bailey died 6 Feb. 1813, aged 95 1-2 years. Elizabeth, relict of Moses Moody died 19 Feb. 1817, aged 97 1-2. Alexander Haskell died 11 March, 1817, aged 93. Stephen Greenleaf died 13 Oct. 1743, aged 91 years and 2 months. Mrs. Elizabeth, relict of deac. Cutting Noyes, died 20 Jan. 1746, in her 92d year. Deac. Archelaus Woodman died 17 March, 1766, aged 94. Robert Adams died 3 Feb. 1769, aged 95. Joshua Baynton died Oct. 29, 1770, aged 94. Daniel Sawyer died 22 Oct. 1781, aged almost 93. William Grant died 20 April, 1785, aged 91. A large number of the descendants of Henry Jaques have been remarkable for longevity. Deac. Stephen Jaques died about 1779, aged 93. Samuel Jaques died in June 24, aged 95 1-2 years. His sister, Deborah, widow of capt. Israel Adams, died 20 May, 1837, aged 99 years, and 43 days. Stephen Jaques died 29 March, 1841, aged 92 years and 8 months. John Jaques died in 1802, aged 84. Sarah died 7 June, 1805, aged 88. Thankful and Betty Jaques died in 1831 and 1835, aged each 77. Mr. Parker Jaques is now living in his 92d year, and John Jaques in his 90th year. Eliphalet Jaques died in June, 1804, aged nearly 90.

The average age of twelve children of Samuel and Hannah Plumer, born between 1719 and 1740, was 73 years. Mrs. Sarah Bartlet died Jan. 1815, aged 99. Joshua Noyes died Jan. 23, 1803, aged 96. Elizabeth Thurston died 15 Nov. 1819, in her 97th year. Mr. Abraham Jaques of Wilmington, Mass. had 10 children, whose ages were 88, 77, 80, 86, 85, 84, 86, 70, 90, 80 = 826, average age, 82 3-5 years. Col. Moses Little died 19 Oct. 1780, aged 90. Catherine, relict of Ebenezer Davis, died 4 Feb. 1840, aged 99. Henry Adams died 30 Aug. 1837, aged 94 1-2 years. Eunice Dummer died 28 Feb. 1838, aged 96 3-4 years. Mary Thurlow died in 1803, aged nearly 100. William Bartlet, esq. 8 Feb. 1841, aged 93. Beetfield Sawyer died   aged 97. Mary Jaques died 30 March, 1805, aged 94 years and 5 months. Jonathan and David Whitmore, twin-brothers, born in 1736, were nearly 100 years of age. The former died 29 March, 1832, aged about 97.

It was my intention to devote a few pages to biographical sketches of many of the natives of ' Ould Newberry,' who have, in various ways, distinguished themselves, and had collected copious materials for that purpose, but my limits will not allow of any thing more than a mere mention of the names of a very few, whose memoirs, were justice done them, would fill a volume. Of these, one of the most able, useful, and patriotic citizens of the country, and who rendered great service to the nation, during the French and revolutionary wars, by purse, sword, and pen, was brigadier-general JACOB BAILEY, who died in Newbury, Vermont, March first, 1816. He was born in Newbury, Massachusetts, July second, 1728, settled in Hampstead 1745, raised a company, of which he was captain, at the commencement of the French war in 1756, was at the capture of fort William Henry, and run the gauntlet at the dreadful massacre that occurred by the violation of the plighted faith of the enemy in August, 1757, and was one, who escaped to fort Edward. He was made a colonel by general Amherst, with whom he was at the taking of Ticonderoga and Crown point in 1759. In 1763, he obtained a charter for a township in Vermont, whither he removed in 1764. He was there appointed by New York, brigadier-general, and soon after by general Washington, commissary-general of the northern department, which involved great responsibilities, and subjected him to dangers, difficulties, and sacrifices, of an extraordinary character, and many anecdotes might be related of his exploits, hair-breadth escapes, encounters with the enemy-Indians and tories, the constant vigilance to escape the scouts, sent from Canada to take him, and for whom a reward of five hundred guineas had been offered, dead or alive. He made a treaty with the St. Francis tribe of Indians, by whom, and the friendly Indians, he was looked up to as a father. By means of spies, he acquired important intelligence respecting the movements of the British, and rendered great services with his purse, pen and person at or before the capture of Burgoyne, where he was engaged with two or three of his sons. He sacrified a large estate in the service of his country, for which he never received any compensation, and was equally distinguished for his talents, his patriotism, and his piety. See reverend Grant Powers' historical sketches of Coos, and Exeter News Letter, October third, 1842.

Brigadier general JOHN BOYD was born in Newburyport, Dec. 21, 1764. In 1786, October twentieth, he was appointed an ensign in the second American regiment, and when the army was disbanded by act of congress, he was discharged. On January twenty-eighth, 1787, he was appointed, by John Hancock, lieutenant of a company in Boston. On April nineteenth, 1788, he sailed for India, arrived at the Isle of France January second, 1789, and in July, went to Madras, having procured recommendatory letters to the English consul, residing at the court of his highness the Nizam, and by whom he was presented in form to his highness, who presented him with the command of one thousand infantry. The Nizam was then in alliance with the English, and had taken the field against Tippoo Sultan, with one hundred and fifty thousand infantry, sixty thousand horse, and five hundred elephants. In 1793, he was a prisoner of war at Ougene, and was released August fourth. In 1794, he writes, he was raising two battalions on the partizan principle. In Sepember, 1797, he was in camp Hydrabad, and after many years' service, he sold out to captain Felose, a Neapolitan partizan. He was in Paris in 1808, and, in 1809, was appointed a colonel by Thomas Jefferson, and, in August, 1812, was appointed a brigadier-general by James Madison in the United States' service, commanded the detachment of fifteen hundred men at the battle of Williamsburg, Upper Canada, November eleventh, 1813, distinguished himself by his courage and military skill at fort George, and the celebrated battle at Tippecanoe. He was appointed by general Jackson naval officer of Boston, March fourth, 1830, where he died October fourth, 1830, aged sixty-six. See Weekly Messenger, volume eighth, page seven hundred and seventy-fourth.

Mr. RALPH CROSS was born in Ipswich August fourteenth, 1706, came to Newbury, married Sarah Johnson, and was one of the most useful, patriotic, and pious citizens of the town, was one of the seven persons, who made a present of a house to Mr. Parsons, whom he boarded gratis at his own house for three years, and gave a large share of the expense of building a meeting-house. His two sons, ' Stephen and Ralph Cross, were among the most influential citizens of Newburyport. The former was born in 1731, and the latter in 1738. They were ship-builders. Ralph joined the northern army as lieutenant-colonel of a regiment raised in this quarter,' and on October eighth, was at the taking of Burgoyne. The brothers, with others, built the frigates Hancock, Boston, and Protector, for the state. Stephen, ' at the close of the war, was appointed superintendent of the excise, and afterwards collector of the customs in Newburyport.'

Ralph also filled various honorable offices. From 1790 to 1796, brigadier-general of the brigade to which the corps of Newburyport were attached. He was a commissioner of bankruptcy, and, in 1802, was appointed collector of the customs, where he continued till his death.

Colonel MOSES LITTLE was another of those patriots, whose sterling qualities of mind and heart, the trying scenes of the revolution brought into notice. He was born in Newbury, May eighth, 1724, and died May twenty-seventh, 1798. In April, 1775, he marched to Lexington with a company, was colonel of a regiment, formed his men in Indian file, and marched on to Bunker hill on the morning of that celebrated battle. His black velvet clothes were sprinkled with the blood of the wounded and dying. In August, he returned home to attend the funeral of two of his children, staid two days, and returned. After the troops evacuated Boston, he went to New York, was with his regiment at Trenton and Princeton, and came home in 1777, on account of ill health. In 1779, he was appointed by the commonwealth to take command of the naval armament, which was designed to dislodge the enemy at Penobscot, but declined, on account of his health. By a shock of the palsy, he lost his speech in 1781. For sagacity, strength of mind, and imperturbable self-possession, which, in the most trying emergencies, never failed him, he was unsurpassed.

WILLIAM PLUMER was born in Newburyport June twenty-fifth, 1759, went to Epping, New Hampshire, 1768, elected representative in general court 1785, and continued such several years. In 1791 and 1797, he was speaker of the house, was admitted to the bar 1787. He was senator of New Hampshire in 1810 and 1811, and president of the senate both years. He was also senator of the United States from June seventeenth, 1802, till March third, 1807. He was governor of New Hampshire 1812, 1816, 1817, 1818, and one of the presidential electors in 1820. He is member of Massachusetts Historical society, American Antiquarian society, and first president of Natural History society.

It would be gratifying to notice many other natives of ould Newbury, with others, who resided here, such as major Enoch and general Jonathan Titcomb, Jonathan Jackson, Jonathan Greenleaf, Tristram Dalton, colonel Jacob, and colonel Joseph Gerrish, senior, and Joseph

Gerrish, junior, Nicholas Pike, author of the System of Arithmetic, Moses Brown, William Bartlet, Jacob Perkins, Theophilus Parsons, whose reputation as a lawyer, and whose profound knowledge in almost every department of science, has probably never been surpassed, if equalled, in the United States. But the grateful task must be postponed to some more propitious occasion. During the sanguinary scenes of the revolution, her citizens, both by land and sea, furnished their full proportion of money and men, to carry on the war, with a zeal and unanimity seldom equalled, and if, with their characteristic energy, they entered largely into the business of privateering, and captured many large and valuable prizes, their losses were also unusually great. Twenty-two vessels, with all their crews, from thirty up to one hundred and seventy men each, went to sea and never returned, a loss of life, compared with which, the massacre at Bloody Brook, which sent a thrill of anguish through the whole colony, was a trifle. One of these vessels was the Yankee Hero, carrying twenty guns, with a complement of one hundred and seventy men, commanded by James Tracy. 'Some fifty of her crew were volunteers from the enterprising young men from Newburyport and vicinity.' Some families gave up two. There were two brothers named Brookings, two Bradbury, two Willard, two Stickney, and several others. Twenty-three were sons of widows. The flower of many families, embarked on board of her, found thus together a watery grave, as after leaving Boston she was never seen. The America, captain William Coffin, a twenty gun ship; the Wexford, captain Philip Trash, an eighteen gun brig; a letter of marque, captain Jonathan Jewett; brig Bennington, captain Hart; schooner Civil Usage, carrying eighty men, captain Jeremiah Hibbard; a schooner, commanded by captain Springer; with fifteen other vessels, of various sizes, all shared the same fate. The crews of these twenty-two vessels, all owned in Newburyport, probably amounted to more than one thousand persons. What, then, must have been the loss of life, at sea, to say nothing of property, during the revolutionary war, from the sea-coast of New England alone? We at the present day can have but a faint conception of the enthusiasm, that pervaded the country during that momentous crisis, or of the sufferings and privations, experienced by our fathers, in that fearful struggle. One of the first privateers, fitted out from Newburyport, was called the Game Cock. On leaving the harbor, the captain sent a note to his minister, desiring prayers that God would preserve him in his attempt to scour the coast of our unnatural enemies! The extent of his petition may be inferred from the fact, that his vessel was a sloop of about twenty or thirty tons, and carried four swivels! Another privateer, called the General Ward, commanded by captain William Russell, was still smaller, as it carried one swivel, and thirteen men, each of whom had a musket. In a short time it took two brigs and a schooner. The schooner, which had been given to two of the captors, was retaken, but the brigs arrived in safety. I have had the use of several journals, kept by those who had been engaged in privateering. From one kept by captain John O'Brien, I make a few extracts. On June ninth, 1779, he sailed in the armed schooner Hibernia. On June twenty-first, took an English brig and sent her in. On June twenty-fifth, had an engagement with a ship of sixteen guns, from three till five o'clock, P. M., when the Hibernia left her, having had three men killed, and several wounded, and was then chased by a frigate till twelve o'clock. On July seventh, took a schooner, and sent her to Newburyport. July tenth, in company with captain Leach, of Salem, took a ship carrying thirteen four pounders, and on the same day took a brig, and then a schooner laden with molasses. July eleventh, took an hermaphrodite brig in ballast, and having a number of prisoners on board, gave them the brig, and gave chase to another brig that was in sight, and took her. He concludes by saying, that, ' if captain Leach and he had not parted in the fog, they could have taken the whole fleet.' Captain O'Brien was engaged in many enterprises and battles, but was never taken. I have also two other journals, kept by the late doctor Samuel Nye, of Salisbury, Massachusetts, who went as surgeon on board the Vengeance, carrying twenty six pounders, and one hundred men, commanded by captain Wingate Newman, who sailed sixteenth of August, 1778, and returned to Newburyport, twenty-ninth May, 1779, having taken and sold in Spain, or sent home, September seventeenth, ship Harriet, packet, sixteen guns and forty-five men; September twentieth, Snow Eagle, twelve guns and forty-three men; December third, took brigantine Elizabeth; twenty-seventh December, took brig Francis, having on board two thousand quintals dry fish; on the nineteenth of April, 1779, took letter of marque brigantine Mary, bound from Liverpool to Antigua, with forty-eight men and sixteen four pounders. His second cruise was on board the ship America, John Somes, commander, who sailed eighteenth June, 1780, and returned ninth of August, having taken, with the assistance of the Brutus, on July fifteenth, ship William, brigantines Duke of Burlue, Kitty and Bell, and Snow Beaver; and on July eighteenth, the America took ship Everetta and brigantine Nancy. From a record which appears to have been kept by one of the crew of the brigantine Dalton, I learn that that vessel, commanded by captain Eleazer Johnson, was taken December twenty-fourth, 1776, and carried into Plymouth. Of the crew, one hundred and twenty-four in number, who were put into Mill prison, fifty-four belonged to Newbury and Newburyport. Among them were Anthony Knapp, Daniel, Cutting, Richard and Henry Lunt, Offin Boardman, Samuel Cutler, Paul Noyes, Charles Herbert, Jonathan Whitmore, and so forth. The crews of many other Newburyport vessels were also in Mill prison, Plymouth, and in Portsmouth. In these two prisons there were at one time five hundred and seventy-four American citizens. Forty-seven of the crew of the Warren, together with the captain, Timothy Newman, died on board. Many of the prisoners were detained in prison four years. Of the prisoners taken in the Dalton, two, namely, Henry and Cutting Lunt,* were on board the Bon Homme Richard, commanded by John Paul Jones, and were his lieutenants in the terrible action with the Serapis, September twenty-third, 1779.

Mr. Richard Smith, who went out in a privateer, in the spring of 1778, was taken prisoner, put on board the Jersey prison ship November seventeenth, 1778, and discharged twenty-seventh of April, 1779, dur-

---

* Cooper, in his Life of John Paul Jones, states that his lieutenants Cutting and Lenry Lunt, were from New Hampshire. This is a mistake. Both of them were natives of Newbury. In a letter to his father, dated Nantz, April twentieth, 1779, lieutenant Cutting Lunt thus writes : ' I am happy to inform you of our deliverance from a horrible prison, where we fared very hard. I refer you to brother Richard for particulars. I have shipped myself for another cruise, and hope I shall have better success. I am going in a ship called the Poor Richard, commanded by John Paul Jones, esquire, but our expedition is secret, but I hope to be at home next christmas, if my life is spared.'

ing which time twelve hundred and seventy prisoners died. When discharged, he was obliged to return to Newbury barefoot, and beg his way. This is one specimen of the sufferings occasioned by war. What, then, must have been the aggregate of privation and distress, experienced by the whole country during the revolutionary struggle?

One instance more, and I have done. On December seventeenth, 1776, the selectmen of Newbury sent a petition to the general court, by way of remonstrance, in which they say: 'on the nineteenth of April, 1775, our minute men and others were called upon to march to the assistance of our distressed brethren at Cambridge. On the twentieth of the same month we followed them with provisions necessary for their support. In about two days after they arrived at Cambridge, they informed us that they had received our provision in plenty, but were obliged to eat it uncooked, they being destitute of kettles to cook it in.' In another place they say, that 'blankets being unprocurable of the merchants, we were obliged to get a great part of them in particular families one or two in a place in different parts of the town.' 'The clothing also was collected in small quantities from more than two hundred places in different parts of the town.' 'By an order of court, bearing date December, 1775, we were ordered to send three tons of English hay to head-quarters at the same price allowed to those towns not one fifth of the way distant,' and so forth.

Notwithstanding the difficulties, distresses, and privations, which the people of America were called to encounter, and of which, petitions, like the preceding, give us some faint idea, it is remarkable with what cheerfulness they were encountered, and what unwavering confidence they had in their ultimate success. Thus, in a letter written by Mr. Jeremiah Dole to his wife, dated June eighteenth, 1775, he says: 'through the good providence of God my life* was saved, but we expect to go at it again today very hot.' On June twentieth, 1775, he thus writes: 'I am well, yet I want to come home, but can't yet before we have killed or drove the regulars, and got the day. I keep up my courage yet to fight them, and will till I die.' His last letter was written September third, 1777. He says, 'we have been dragged very bad, and expect to drive on very soon towards the enemy to drive them.' On the 19th of September, the day of Burgoyne's surrender, he was killed. In a letter, dated R. I, Oct. 14, 1778, written to a friend in Newburyport, Mr. Henry Hudson thus writes: 'the night before last our tents all blew down, and we were obliged to get shelter where we could, some in houses, some under stone walls. Our mess found pretty good quarters in an old quaker's house. It would be pretty tolerable, if it was fair weather all the time, but these oznabrig houses are not so clever in rainy weather. Who would not be a soldier? I must now conclude praying I may be preserved through the campaign, till we've drubbed the dogs away.' Here I must cease making any more allusions to the interesting events of the revolution, and return my thanks to Mr. Jonathan Kettell, for his copy of Mr. Samuel Rolfe's journal of a campaign to Louisburg in 1758, and for the reminiscences and facts, furnished him by captain William Noyes, who lost his left hand at the siege of Louisburg. The journal of Mr. Rolfe contains twenty-six pages, but I have no room for an abstract, nor even to give the names of those, who were present at the siege, nor

---

* A ball passed through his hat in the battle of Bunker hill.

the names of the soldiers commanded by captains Jacob Gerrish, William Rogers, Ezra Lunt, and Benjamin Perkins, as intended. On that subject, a volume might easily be written, and another on those eccentric characters, who were born or resided in ' Ould Newberry.' Who, that ever knew, will ever forget Madame Hooper, or Timothy Dexter, or Jonathan Plumer, or Benjamin Uran, or colonel Cotton, and a host of others too numerous to mention, who whilom flourished in this region? Could I roll back the wheels of time, and present to the eyes of my readers a view of Newbury, as it was in 1775, the picture of the actors of that day, arrayed in their antique costume, and surrounded by appropriate scenery, would both startle and amuse them. The huge cocked hat, the full-bottomed wig, the tight breeches with the massive silver knee and shoe buckles, the polished manners of the *gentlemen* of that day, together with those marked distinctions in society, which the revolution and its consequences have almost entirely obliterated, have passed away, and with them have passed the stocks and the whipping-post, those relics of a less refined age, which once stood near the head of Marlborough street. In 1751, I find the following: ' carving the head of the whipping post, eighteen shillings and ten pence.' In 1765, I find the following charge in Newburyport: ' iron works for the town stocks, four shillings and sixpence, and a bowl of toddy, eight pence.' These appendages of civilization stood till about 1793, either in Federal street, near the jail, or in Water street, near where the custom-house now stands. In the plants of Newbury, there is nothing peculiar, with the exception of three species of beach-plum on Plum island, the *prunus littoralis* of Bigelow, and the *arenaria peploides*, or sand-wort, discovered on Plum island by doctor Richard Spofford of Newburyport. There is, also, a kind of grass, now called black grass, which was once called pigeon grass. It made its first appearance, less than a century ago, on the banks of Little river, just below Trotter's bridge, near the place of a ' stand,' where wild pigeons were once caught in great numbers, and thence derived its name. It is now spread over thousands of acres, and is every year gaining ground. Among the minerals of Newbury, are to be found amianthus, asbestos, precious serpentine, limestone, fibrous and granular, dolomite, tremolite, iron pyrites, arsenical iron pyrites, iron ore. Nearly all these are found in what is called the Devil's den, near Mill bridge on Little river, where excavations were first made for limestone in 1697. Among the curiosities in Newbury, may be mentioned this locality, and the floating island in the meeting-house pond, which is in the rear of the burying-yard, near the first parish meeting-house in Newbury. A good description of it may be found in Silliman's Journal for 1827, page 122, by Amos Pettingell, junior. It contains about half an acre of land, which rises and falls with the water, which is sometimes eight feet higher than at other times. There are on it six large trees, which rise and fall with the island, which, in dry seasons, is perceptibly lower than the surrounding land. On this island, for more than a century, there has been, yearly, a pair of those birds called moor hens, which regularly visit it about the tenth of May, and depart in the fall, with a brood of young ones. Whether it is the same pair, or their heirs, who never forget their annual visit, I am unable to say. The veteran elm of Newbury, mentioned on the last page, is worthy of a visit. Another elm tree, still larger, but not so well proportioned, stands in Byfield, near the house of Mr. Benjamin Pearson. Both of them are much larger than the famous elm on Boston common. Of birds and wild fowl, that frequent Newbury at different seasons of the year, there are between one and two hundred species, of which more than half are edible. Wild turkies were abundant in Newbury, as late as 1707. Fish, from the ocean, and the rivers Merrimac and Parker, are caught in abundance, and oysters of a large size once abounded in the latter river, and there is not a day in the year, in which the inmates of the alms-house, situated on its banks, cannot obtain a sufficient supply for their own use. In addition to the agricultural and maritime advanta·ges, possessed by the citizens of ancient Newbury, with the facilities of conveyance and transportation, may be mentioned the impulse given to all kinds of business, by the erection of manufactures.

Since 1836, four cotton factories have been erected, and a fifth incorporated. The Essex mills, 1836, contain six thousand and seven hundred spindles, one hundred and seventy-three looms, which manufacture one million and six hundred thousand yards of No. 20 printing cloths, uses one thousand and one hundred bales of cotton, one thousand tons of coal, and pays to its one hundred and forty-five operatives, about thirty thousand dollars per annum. The Bartlet mills, No. 1 and 2, 1836 and 1840, contain seventeen thousand one hundred and thirty-six spindles, three hundred and sixty-seven looms, and with four hundred operatives, who receive about six thousand dollars per month, manufacture about two million yards of No. 40 sheetings and shirtings, from one thousand and one hundred bales of cotton, with one thousand tons of coal. These two buildings are one hundred and fifty-six by fifty, and two hundred and sixty by fifty feet in length and breadth. The James mills, 1842 and 1844, will, when completed, contain seventeen thousand and one hundred spindles, three hundred and fifty looms, four hundred operatives, who will receive about five thousand dollars per month, manufacture about one million and eight hundred thousand yards of No. 40 and 60 cloth, from one thousand bales of cotton, and use one thousand tons of coal per annum. Its length is three hundred and twelve by fifty feet. The Globe mills now in process of erection, are calculated to contain twelve thousand and five hundred spindles, three hundred and twenty-five looms, and with two hundred and seventy-five operatives, to manufacture seventy thousand yards of No. 14 and 20 cloth per week, use four thousand bales of cotton, and one thousand tons of coal per annum, at an expense for wages of about four thousand dollars per month. The goods manufactured at these mills are of the first quality, and furnish employment in various ways, for several thousand persons.

As much has been asserted, concerning the abduction of a certain bell by certain persons unknown, and much said that is rather apocryphal in its character, I have been requested to state the facts concerning it, which, as near as I can ascertain, are these.

On Monday morning, October fourteenth, 1839, a bell was found on the front door steps of the Belleville church, and, near to it, a sealed letter, of which the following is an exact copy.

' Know all men, to whom these presents shall come.

' I was born in the year ——, in London, England, was soon after transported to this country and presented to queen Anne's chappel in Newbury, state of Massachusetts, (as my label shows,) by the lord bishop of London. After remaining quietly in the belfry of said chappel for many years I was taken by force and secretly burried. After the lapse of a few years I reappeared and was placed in the belfry of a schoolhouse in this vicinity. Soon after I was taken down and placed in the belfry of *this church*, where I called together the congregation for many years — but in the year 1838 I was taken down to make room for a larger personage — in a few moments after reaching the ground I was stolen — by whoom? no one knows — and placed in the belfry of the same schoolhouse now in another street, where I remained until last Saturday evening, when I received a call from some friends, which I gladly accepted, and have treated me well and placed me where you now find me.

' Restore me to my lawful owners or beware ! '

If the writer of the preceding letter intended to tell the truth, he was either extremely ignorant, or extremely unfortunate in the choice of words to convey his ideas, as the following brief narrative of facts will show. Queen Anne's chapel, as has already been shown, was originally built for a congregational meeting-house, but the builders, finding that both town and state refused to allow them to use it for such a purpose in that place, afterward converted it into an Episcopal church, which they called queen Ann's chapel. The bell, which was regularly used from the time of its arrival till 1766, with the exception of a few of the last years, when it was used but once in a month, had on it the following label : 'presented to queen Anne's chapel by the bishop of London.' The discontinuance of public worship in the chapel, three sabbaths out of four, induced those who lived in the vicinity, a greater part of whom had attended the chapel, to form a new parish, build a meeting-house, which was raised June twenty-third, 1761, constitute a new church, and settle a congregational minister. In 1766, public worship ceased entirely in the chapel, which, 'being thus deserted, went to decay.'* 'The christening basin, which is of silver, is in the possession of St. Paul's church.'* The bible was given, by a Mr. Jackman, to the church in Boscawen, New Hampshire, and the communion cloth was worn, as a shawl, by a Mrs. Palmer ; the bell remained for ten years unmolested, and apparently unclaimed by any person or society, in the belfry of the deserted chapel, when the steeple was blown down, about a year before the fall of the house, throwing the bell into the street. Seeing this, Mr. David Whitmore, an innholder in the neighborhood, wheeled it into his barn, where it remained for some time, unconcealed and unclaimed, till, at the request of Mr. Whitmore, colonel Josiah Little removed it to his own house, where it remained, unconcealed, as is well known, till the building of the Belleville school-house, where it was used, both for school-house and meeting-house, ready to be delivered to any person or society legally or equitably entitled to it. Requests were made to Mr. Little to give up, or sell, the bell to St. Paul's church. To all these requests, Mr. Little's uniform answer was, in substance, this. 'The bell is not mine to give or sell. Any person or society, claiming it, can have it by substantiating the claim.' Satisfied that no such claim could be legally made, certain persons, who they were, or for what motive, I pretend not to say or know, determined to obtain possession of the bell, and accordingly, as it would seem, employed, for that purpose, some stupid agent or agents, whose organs of acquisitiveness must have vastly exceeded those of locality, as they did not appear to know the difference between Kent street school-house in Newburyport, and Pilsbury's lane in Newbury. They accordingly made a sad mistake, and instead of taking queen Anne's chapel bell, carried off the Kent street school-house bell, which has the following label : 'Joseph Joyet fecit 1787. Lebeau alia grande ange,' which they, no doubt, supposed meant, being interpreted, 'presented to queen Ann's chapel by the bishop of London.' The selectmen of Newburyport, however, thought differently, and, in the course of the day, reclaimed the bell. Having failed in this attempt to obtain the right bell, the thieves, having studied topography for over two months, and having selected what they doubtless deemed a suitable time for the accomplishment of their design, determined to try again.

* Reverend doctor Morss.

'''T was the eve before Christmas, when all thro' the house,
Not a creature was stirring, not even a mouse,'
Excepting three persons, with their coach and one wheel,
Intending, of course, the right bell to steal;
Who, with footsteps quite noiseless, crept up Pilsbury's lane,
Accomplished their purpose, and crept back again;
And from that day to this, the compiler believes,
The bell has been missing, and so have the thieves.

And now, lest it may be said of the compiler, as of Herne, the antiquary,

'To future ages may thy dulness last,
As thou preserv'st the dulness of the past,'

I close my book with the following beautiful lines of poetry, by miss Hannah Gould, concerning the magnificent elm tree, now standing in Parker street, before the house of Mr. Richard Jaques, which was transplanted and set out by his grandfather, Mr. Richard Jaques, in 1713.

THE OLD ELM OF NEWBURY.

Did it ever come in your way to pass
The silvery pond with its fringe of grass,
And threading the lane hard by to see
The veteran Elm of Newbury?
You saw how its roots had grasped the ground,
As if it had felt the earth went round,
And fastened them down with determined will
To keep it steady, and hold it still.
Its aged trunk, so stately and strong,
Has braved the blasts, as they've rushed along.
Its head has towered and its arms have spread
While more than a hundred years have fled.
Well, that old Elm, that is now so grand,
Was once a twig in the rustic hand
Of a youthful peasant, who went one night
To visit his love by the tender light
Of the modest moon and her twinkling host,
While the star, that lighted his bosom most,
And gave to his lonely feet their speed,
Abode in a cottage beyond the mead.
'T was the peaceful close of a summer's day,
Its glorious orb had passed away.
The toil of the field, till the morn, had ceased
For a season of rest to man and beast.
The mother had silenced the humming wheel
The father returned for the evening meal,
The thanks of one, who had chosen the part
Of the poor in spirit, the rich in heart,
Who having the soul's grand panacea,
Feel all is added that's needful here,
And know this truth of the human breast,
That wanting little is being blest.
The good old man in his chair reclined
At a humble door with a peaceful mind
While the drops of his sun-burnt brow were dried
By the cool sweet air of the eventide.
The son from the yoke had unlocked the bow,
Dismissing the faithful ox to go,
And graze in the close; he had called the kine
For their oblation at day's decline.
He'd gathered and numbered the lambs and sheep
And fastened them up in their nightly keep,
He'd stood by the coop till the hen would bring
Her huddling brood safe under her wing,
And made them secure from the hooting owl
Whose midnight prey was the shrieking fowl.

When all was finished he sped to the well,
Where the old grey bucket hastily fell,
And the clear cold water came up to chase
The dust of the field from his neck and face,
And hands and feet, till the youth began
To look renewed in the outer man,
And soon arrayed in his Sunday's best,
The stiff new suit had done the rest,
And the hale young lover was on his way,
Where through the fen and field it lay,
And over the bramble, the brake and the grass,
As the shortest cut to the house of his lass.
It is not recorded how long he staid
In the cheerful home of the smiling maid,
But, when he came out, it was late and dark
And silent — not even a dog would bark,
To take from his feeling of loneliness,
And make the length of his way seem less.
He thought it was strange that the treacherous moon
Should have given the world the slip so soon,
And whether the eyes of the girl had made
The stars of the sky in his own to fade,
Or not, it certainly seemed to him,
That each grew distant, and small, and dim;
And he shuddered to think that he now was about
To take a long and lonely rout,
For he did not know what fearful sight
Might come to him through the shadows of night.
An elm grew close by the cottage's eaves,
So he plucked him a twig well clothed with leaves,
So sallying forth with the supple arm
To serve as a talisman parrying harm,
He felt that though his heart was big,
'Twas even stouter for having the twig,
For this he thought would answer to switch
The horrors away as he crossed the ditch,
The meadow and copse wherein perchance
Will-o'-the-wisp might wickedly dance,
And wielding it keep him from having a chill
At the menacing sound of Whip-poor-Will,
And his flesh from creeping beside the bog
At the harsh bass voice of the viewless frog.
In short he felt, the switch would be
Guard, play-thing, business and company.
When he got safe home and joyfully found
He still was himself and living and sound,
He planted the tree by his family cot,
To stand as a monument marking the spot
It had helped him to reach, and what was still more,
Because it had grown by his fair one's door,
The twig took root, and as time flew by,
Its boughs spread wide and its head grew high,
While the priest's good service had long been done,
Which made the youth and the maiden one,
And their young scions arose and played
Around the tree in its leafy shade.
But many and many a year has fled
Since they were gathered among the dead,
And now their names with the moss o'ergrown
Are veiled from sight on the church-yard stone,
That bears away in a lingering fall
And owns the power that shall level all.
The works that the hand of man hath wrought
Bring him to dust, and his name to nought,
While near in view, and just beyond
The grassy skirts of the silver pond,
In its green old age stands the noble tree
The veteran Elm of 'Ould Newberry.'

INDEX.

INDEX TO JOSHUA COFFIN'S *A SKETCH OF THE HISTORY OF NEWBURY, NEWBURYPORT AND WEST NEWBURY*

Note: This index does *not* include the names listed alphabetically by family surname in the Genealogical Appendix, pages 293-322.

Index prepared by Mr. and Mrs. James Garvin